THE TRANSPARENT CABAL

I'm pleased to be here at the American Enterprise Institute. I have some long-time friends here, as you know if you've studied the published wiring diagrams that purport to illuminate the anatomy of the neocon cabal.

—Douglas Feith
"Winning Iraq," May 10, 2004

No special offices within OSD or cabals of neoconservatives created the dominant perception of the danger of Iraqi WMD.

—Joseph J. Collins
Choosing War, April 2008

THE
TRANS

Stephen J.
Sniegoski

THE NEOCONSERVATIV

AND THE NATIONAL IN

FOREWORD by *former Congressma*

ARENT CABAL

ENDA, WAR IN THE MIDDLE EAST,

EST OF ISRAEL

ndley ⭐ INTRODUCTION by *Prof. Paul Gottfried, Ph.D.*

Norfolk, Virginia • 2008

Information from mainstream periodicals available through the Internet with relative permanence is referred to in endnotes as "online" (and, where applicable, identified by the web-based source title), in lieu of page numbers or URLs. Digital object identifiers or other online publication reference numbers are provided if available. Readers should be aware that hyphens introduced into URLs for typesetting purposes may or may not be appropriate to include when entering URLs into Web browsers.

DUST JACKET PHOTO: Former Israeli Prime Minister Ariel Sharon (right) is escorted by Col. Thomas Jordan (center), U.S. Army, and former Secretary of Defense Donald H. Rumsfeld (left) as he inspects the honor guard during his arrival at the Pentagon on March 19, 2001. Department of Defense photo by R. D. Ward. (Released)

ISBN-13: 978-1-932528-17-6
ISBN-10: 1-932528-17-2

Library of Congress Cataloging-in-Publication Data

Sniegoski, Stephen J.
    The transparent cabal : the neoconservative agenda, war in the Middle East, and the national interest of Israel / Stephen J. Sniegoski ; foreword by former Congressman Paul Findley ; introduction by Paul Gottfried.
        p. cm.
    Includes bibliographical references and index.
    ISBN-13: 978-1-932528-17-6
    ISBN-10: 1-932528-17-2
    1. United States--Foreign relations--Israel. 2. Israel--Foreign relations--United States. 3. Conservatism--United States. 4. United States--Foreign relations--Middle East. 5. Middle East--Foreign relations--United States. 6. Iraq War, 2003---Causes. 7. United States--Foreign relations--1989- 8. Israel--Foreign relations--Middle East. 9. Middle East--Foreign relations--Israel. I. Title.
    E183.8.I7S635 2008
    327.7305694--dc22

                                                                    2008006124

Printed in the United States of America.

Contents

CONGRESSMAN PAUL FINDLEY

WHEN MY BOOK *They Dare to Speak Out* was first published 25 years ago, I might have hoped, if I had thought about it at the time, that the pervasive and inordinate power of what is known as the "Israel lobby" might have been diminished somewhat in this country by now, for the good of the United States as well as that of Israel. After all, during those years Israel has become a prosperous, self-sustaining nation, and though surrounded by potentially hostile neighbors is far and away the most militarily powerful state in the region. And in reality, with a stockpile of atomic weapons reliably estimated to number in the hundreds, is among the four or five most powerful nations in the world.

Yet in spite of this, the lobby has not seen fit to curtail its influence. In fact, if anything, it has expanded it; and today exerts an even greater influence on both U. S. domestic and foreign policy than ever before. And it is the intertwining of the power of the various factions of the lobby with the predominantly pro-Israel neoconservative forces in our government that helped produce what Professor Richard Norton of Boston University called a "monumentally ill-informed and counterproductive" decision on the part of President Bush to invade and occupy the sovereign nation of Iraq.

But as the American public's disenchantment with the war has grown, the remaining supporters (dwindling though they may be) continue to push for continued involvement in Iraq. For example, a pro-war group called Freedom's Watch sponsored a $15-million ad campaign in the late summer of 2007 targeting Republican congressmen who were beginning to go soft on their support for the war. Now the fact that Ari Fleisher, former Bush White House spokesman, is a member of the board at Freedom's Watch would be of little or no interest here except for this curious detail: As headlined by the *Jewish Telegraphic Agency* (*JTA*), lead wire service for Jewish news, the "Pro-Surge Group [Freedom's Watch] Is Almost All Jewish." In fact, according to *JTA*, four out of five members of the board are Jews, as are half of its donors.

This in no way means to imply that there is anything intrinsically wrong with Freedom's Watch wanting to continue support for the war in Iraq. That's their choice. But in the overall context of this volume, it is the motivation for that support that merits comment. Author Philip Weiss, a self-described "progressive Jew," maintains that "it is no coincidence that the biter-enders [war supporters] draw on heavy Jewish support" (*The American Conservative*, Oct. 8, 2007). These supporters of Israel, according to Weiss, have managed to convince themselves, and the current administration, that the United States is in the same war against terror as Israel is. And it is this same conviction that, in my view, also drives the efforts of the Israel lobby and the neoconservatives – to the potential detriment of the United States.

Details of the role played by the most hard-line component of the Israel lobby in leading us to war are found in this scrupulously researched and referenced book written by Dr. Stephen Sniegoski. *The Transparent Cabal: The Neoconservative Agenda, War in the Middle East and the National Interest of Israel* deals, in its own unique way, with themes also treated by two recent best-selling books. With rarely seen candor, Jimmy Carter's *Palestine Peace or Apartheid* and Mearsheimer and Walt's *The Israel Lobby and U.S. Foreign Policy* also deal in different ways with the results of lobby/neocon influence at home as well as on the ground in Israel. And, as we have sadly come to expect, they came under attack from the usual suspects as being anti-Semitic.

The same fate is likely to befall Dr. Sniegoski and his equally candid book. Which is too bad, because to the objective reader it can no way be seen as either anti-Jewish or anti-Israeli. In fact, Dr. Sniegoski goes out of his way to make it clear that the neocon movement did not single-handedly compel the United States to embark on war with Iraq. Support for that aspect of the neocon agenda from a number of other key groups was both necessary and instrumental for bringing it to fruition. In addition, neither the neoconser-

vative movement nor the Israel lobby are entirely Jewish. Many pro-Israel groups, for example, are found among what the media generally term the "religious right," and these tend to be mainly the Christian Zionists. (The term Christian Zionist, of course, is somewhat of a misnomer; they are more Zionist than Christian.) Moreover, in spite of charges to the contrary, the term "neocon" is not a codeword for "Jew." But the fact is, as author Philip Weiss points out, the neoconservatives originated as a largely Jewish movement in the 1970s "in good part out of concern for Israel's security."

On the other hand, though the Bush Administration hawks that argued for war had a goodly number of Jews among them (many of whom had very close political and financial connections to Israel), one cannot ignore the non-Jewish actors, among whom we might mention Vice President Cheney, former Defense Secretary Rumsfeld, Colin Powell, Condoleeza Rice, William Bennet, and of course, the President himself, in the ill-fated decision to go to war.

At the same time, a fear of being smeared with the "anti-Semite" label should not, and does not, prohibit Dr. Sniegoski from pointing out the fact that people – all people – are affected to a greater or lesser degree in their foreign policy views by ethnic and emotional ties to a foreign country (often the country of their forebears). He maintains, and I agree, that the foreign policy views of various ethnic groups – be they German-American, Irish-American, Polish-American, or whatever – are based at least in part on their ethnic identities and loyalties. Can it not be reasonably posited, then, without charges of bigotry and worse, that within the heavy concentration of Jewish neocons in the White House circle of war planners that their identification with Israel helped shape their views on Middle East policy?

Sadly, for well over a half century, with rare exceptions, Jewish influence in the halls of political and governmental power has been off-limits for rational, reasoned discussion. In my 22 years as a member of the U.S. House of Representatives, I became all too painfully aware that there are many in our government – too many, in my view – who are pre-primed to roar approval for all things Israeli, right or wrong; whether it be perpetual financial aid or going to war on their behalf. It was my opposition to this rubber-stamp approval for Israel that ultimately led to my to downfall. In 1980, my opponent charged me with anti-Semitism. Money poured into his campaign from across the country and two years later I was defeated by a narrow margin. In 1984, Senator Charles Percy, a sometimes critic of Israel, also lost his seat. Leaders of the Israel lobby claimed credit for defeating both Percy and me.

I relate these stories for one reason only. Let it be said that neither I nor any of those with whom I associate would ever engage in or endorse anti-Semitism, namely, hatred or persecution of Jews based on their race or religion. But it is a lamentable fact that all too often the calculated, knowingly false charge of anti-Semitism is used as a means of preventing rational discussion even in matters of life and death importance, or to crush political opposition that might otherwise prevail in a reasoned debate. Nowhere can a greater necessity for free and open debate be found than among the ranks of the neoconservatives in the top echelons of our government – many of whom just happen to be Jewish – who have, in my view, led our nation to the brink of disaster.

I hope that this book will motivate the American people to demand fundamental change in the way in which public policy is formed by our elected officials: That is, without fear of intimidation from any ethnic or ideological group, but with only the best interests of our nation in mind.

TEPHEN SNIEGOSKI'S study *The Transparent Cabal: The Neo-conservative Agenda, War in the Middle East, and the National Interest of Israel* is a meticulously prepared and strenuously argued brief against the neoconservatives' continued influence over American foreign policy. Although Dr. Sniegoski does not investigate all aspects of this pervasive influence on the Bush Two administration, he does focus methodically on the effects of the neoconservatives' rise to power in terms of U.S. relations with the Middle East. What is most impressive about Sniegoski's study is its rigorous demonstration of the persistence with which neoconservative "policy advisers" have pushed particular agendas, driven by their strident Zionism, over long periods of time. Indeed these activists have stayed with their agenda until both historic opportunities and their personal elevation have allowed them to put their ideas into practice.

Sniegoski does not have to reach far to prove his case. As his documentation makes crystal (rather than Kristol!) clear, much of the evidence for his thesis is readily available, or has been at least alluded to, in the national press and in the published works of neoconservative celebrities. As a European historian, I have been struck by the resemblance between this situation and the way certain European statesmen before the First World War, who were eager for a showdown with a particular national enemy, kept climbing back into power in ruling coalitions, until they could carry out their purpose. This was true for both of the sides that went to war in the summer of 1914.

It might be argued that the recent bestseller by John Mearsheimer and Stephen J.Walt, *The Israeli Lobby and U.S. Foreign Policy*, has pre-empted Sniegoski's work, by making a wide readership aware of the machinations of the American Israeli Political Action Committee (AIPAC) and its neo-conservative shock troops. These well-known professors of international relations, whom Sniegoski cites, have recently delved into the ways that the American Zionist lobby has colored and distorted American foreign policy in relation to the Middle East. Mearsheimer and Walt have documented (and this may be the most effective part of their presentation) the war of vilification that has been conducted against any politician who has questioned the U.S.'s "special relation" with Israel. Equally important, Norman Finkelstein, who paid for his investigative zeal with his academic career, has shown the way that AIPAC and its allies have played the double game of being allied to the pro-Zionist Christian right while attacking Christianity as "a major cause of the Holocaust." And my own articles have provided further evidence of how neoconservatives have been particularly adept at playing both of these angles at different times.

Nevertheless, Sniegoski has cut out for himself a less glamorous but historiographically valuable task, which is to detail exactly *how* the neoconservatives moved into a position to realize their purposes and, moreover, how closely their purposes dovetail with the foreign-policy aims put forth by the Israeli right since the 1980s and even earlier. Sniegoski performs these scholarly tasks while avoiding certain oversimplifications; and it might be useful to point out what he expressly does not do, because if the neoconservative press does decide to deal with his work, one can count on its efforts to misrepresent his arguments. Nowhere does Sniegoski suggest that the Israeli government controls its neoconservative fans in the U.S. – or even less that Richard Perle, Douglas Feith, Michael Ledeen, and other neoconservative presidential advisors have been Israeli agents. In fact Sniegoski points to cases in which American neoconservatives have been vocally unhappy with peace initiatives begun by or with military restraint exercised by actual Israeli governments. While neoconservatives have generally opposed the Israeli Labor Party as too soft on Israel's Arab enemies, it has also scolded Likud premiers Ariel Sharon and Ehud Olmert when they have not met neoconservative standards of being tough enough with the Palestinians or with Hezbollah in Lebanon. Probably the ideal Israeli leader, from the neoconservative perspective, is Benjamin Netanyahu, for which one major reason is that this Likudnik hawk has spent considerable time in the U.S. and around the neoconservatives, and he slavishly imitates their rhetoric about Israel as a Middle Eastern advocate of "global democracy."

Another argument that Sniegoski never makes, and which should not be ascribed to him, is to identify the neoconservatives and their beliefs with the pursuit of Israeli interests alone. The author's position is far more sophisticated and goes something like this: The neoconservatives bring with them a distinctive worldview, and in terms of their positions on American internal politics, one can easily fit them into a certain tradition of New Deal-Great Society American progressivism. Nor have the neoconservatives ever tried to hide this identification, or their huge differences with either small-government, isolationist Taft Republicans or with the anti-Communist interventionists grouped around William F. Buckley and *National Review* in the 1950s and 1960s. What has made the neoconservatives seem "conservative" has been primarily their role in foreign policy, as critics of détente with the Soviet Union and as hardliners on Israel. Their anti-Soviet posture helped the neoconservatives relate to the conservative movement that had been there before; nonetheless, once they took over that movement (which is the subject of my latest book), they turned a hardline Likudnik view of Middle Eastern affairs into a litmus test of who is or is not an "American conservative."

Finally, Sniegoski never suggests that the Israeli *government* pushed the U.S. into invading Iraq. What he does argue is that the neoconservatives, who played a decisive role in plunging us into that quagmire, were acting in harmony with what *they* perceived as the interests of the Israeli government and the position of the Sharon government. Nobody coerced President Bush into launching an unwise war; and if he were a more prudent and better-informed statesman, he would not have chosen to listen to Vice President Cheney and his neoconservative hangers-on about invading Iraq. Foreign states and domestic lobbies may agitate to get us to do questionable things internationally, but it is the duty of intelligent leaders to ignore such coaxing and threats. Nor does Sniegoski attach to the Israeli government any special quality of nastiness or deny that internally it is arguably a more civilized state than one might find among many of its Muslim adversaries. Israeli leaders are simply trying to advance the interests of their country, as they perceive them. What Sniegoski is challenging is the management of American foreign policy by extreme Zionists, who can never seem to make the proper distinctions between American and (their vision of) Israeli interests.

Although my views of the plight of the Israelis is probably far more sympathetic than that of Dr. Sniegoski, I am appalled by the evidence he adduces of the activities of neoconservative "policy-advisors" in pushing the U.S. into conflicts they thought were "good for Israel." The dogged, obsessive character of these efforts, some going back to blueprints for change constructed in the late 1960s, gives the lie to any view that the neoconservatives are only trying to help the Israelis on an *ad hoc* basis. Sniegoski's research also illustrates the tremendous gulf between what the neoconservatives want for Israel and intend to have the U.S. government provide and what the Israeli public, when polled, thinks is necessary to achieve peace with the Palestinians.

The neocons invariably seem more extreme, and the paper trail they have left behind about how the U.S. should advance "democratic" interests in the Middle East indicates something far less than even-handedness. The fact that the neoconservative press still denies what few Israelis would hesitate to acknowledge, that Palestinians were subject to ethnic cleansing in 1948, speaks volumes about Sniegoski's subjects. Sniegoski also stresses the divergence between the bellicosity of neoconservative presidential advisors and the general lack of enthusiasm for the Iraq war expressed by American Jews. Whereas the general American population, according to a Gallup Poll conducted in February 2007, opposed the war by a margin of 56 to 42 percent, Jewish opposition to the war policy was as high as 77 percent. One must of course factor in that the vast majority of American Jews, despite their residual Zionism, are on the Democratic left; and since this war was started by a "rightwing" Republican, they are predictably opposed to it. But the question – unanswered, naturally – remains whether or not they would oppose it, if they saw it as being in Israel's interest, or if it were started by Jewish liberal Democrat war-hawk Senator Joe Lieberman. Sniegoski is nonetheless correct to note that in the present circumstances Jewish "public opinion" seems far less war-happy than the policy pursued by the Zionist neoconservatives.

In closing I would observe that this book compares favorably to the recent bestseller by Mearsheimer and Walt, although because of the author's more modest professional position and because of the limited public rela-

tions funds available to Enigma, Sniegoski may never gain as much attention as these other critics for his scholarly efforts. His work covers many of
the same themes as those found in *The Israeli Lobby and U.S. Foreign Policy*,
but he covers them with more voluminous documentation. By the time the
reader gets to the end of this volume, he is pleasantly overwhelmed with
facts and citations that amply support Sniegoski's argument. Moreover,
unlike Mearsheimer and Walt, Sniegoski does not ascribe to this group
"decades" of evil doing, and he also points out that the Zionist lobby is acting in a perfectly "American" way to carry out what it regards as reasonable
goals. He shows how the neoconservatives rose to national prominence,
taking over the American conservative movement while maintaining extensive contacts within the liberal establishment. From this springboard,
members of this group eventually became government advisors in Republican administrations – and more particularly in the Bush II administration;
and this leverage allowed them to carry out particular plans for reconfiguring the Middle East, which some of them had been working on for many
years. The argument is thoroughly convincing, and Dr. Sniegoski, who is a
trained practitioner of the historian's craft, merits high praise for what he
has produced.

The history discussed in this book has not come to an end but belongs
to an ongoing problem. Neoconservatives continue to have direct influence both in the Bush administration and with the leading contenders for
the presidency. Rudolph Giuliani, the first leading Republican candidate,
had his campaign war chest filled up with donations from neoconservative
funding sources, and his roster of advisors looked like a gathering of the
editors and contributors to *Commentary* magazine. And neoconservatives
have now become the major advisors to the Republican presidential nominee John McCain, who explicitly expresses their democratic universalism
and hawkish foreign policy. Nor is the neoconservative influence on presidential politics limited to Republicans. Such prominent neocon spokesmen
as William Kristol and William Bennett initially eyed as a presidential
candidate socially liberal Zionist hawk Joe Lieberman, and they have since
adapted to circumstances by going from speaking of a Rudy-Lieberman
dream team to having the Connecticut Senator on McCain's ticket. Mean-
while, the *New York Times*'s token (neo)"conservative" David Brooks has
heaped praise on Hillary, and a feature article in an issue of *The American
Conservative* from late last year demonstrated that Hillary's advisory staff

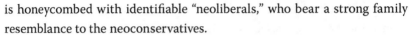

is honeycombed with identifiable "neoliberals," who bear a strong family resemblance to the neoconservatives.

If any one of these neocon-preferred presidential candidates gets into the White House, the story told in this book will be only a prelude to a much greater national disaster. Therefore intelligent and patriotic Americans are urged to purchase, study, and talk about this important work. If Stephen Sniegoski can help to create the public awareness necessary to deal with the problem that he painstakingly examines, we might be able to rejoice that his book pointed to, and warned of, an ultimately avoidable future.

THE TRANSPARENT CABAL

*" . . . a passionate attachment of one nation for another
produces a variety of evils. Sympathy for the favorite
nation, facilitating the illusion of an imaginary common interest in cases where no real common interest
exists, and infusing into one the enmities of the other,
betrays the former into a participation in the quarrels
and wars of the latter without adequate inducement
or justification. It leads also to concessions to the favorite nation of privileges denied to others which is apt
doubly to injure the nation making the concessions; by
unnecessarily parting with what ought to have been
retained, and by exciting jealousy, ill-will, and a disposition to retaliate, in the parties from whom equal
privileges are withheld. And it gives to ambitious, corrupted, or deluded citizens (who devote themselves to
the favorite nation), facility to betray or sacrifice the interests of their own country, without odium, sometimes
even with popularity; gilding, with the appearances of
a virtuous sense of obligation, a commendable deference for public opinion, or a laudable zeal for public
good, the base or foolish compliances of ambition,
corruption, or infatuation."*

—George Washington
Farewell Address
1796

chapter 1

THE TRANSPARENT CABAL

THERE IS A GROWING realization that the U.S. war against Iraq and American Middle East policy in general has been disastrous to American interests. In the words of A. Richard Norton, professor of international relations at Boston University, who served as an adviser to the James Baker-led Iraq Study Group, "Surveying U.S. history, one is hard-pressed to find presidential decisions as monumentally ill-informed and counterproductive as the decision to invade and occupy Iraq; however, a decision to go to war against Iran would arguably surpass the Iraq war as the worst foreign-policy decision ever made by an American president."[1] The unnecessary American war against Iraq has not only killed and wounded thousands of Americans and hundreds of thousands of Iraqis,[2] but has also actually increased the terrorist threat to the United States. An American attack on Iran would compound this damage geometrically, bringing about a major conflagration in the heart of the oil-producing region of the Middle East that would reverberate throughout the entire world. This disaster is highly likely unless the United States completely eschews all elements of the Middle East war policy.

How did the United States come to formulate this colossally erroneous policy? This is not simply a question of significance to those who study history; it is of vital importance to everyone alive today. For it is only by understanding the origins of and motivation behind the current policy that we may establish the proper alternative policy, to extricate the United States from the existing quagmire and bring about the best settlement now possible.

This work examines a controversial and in some respects taboo subject: the close relationship of the American neoconservatives[3] with the Israeli Likudnik right, and their role as the fundamental drivers of the Bush administration's militant American policy in the Middle East – a policy which inspired both the 2003 war in Iraq and the equally militant solutions contemplated since for other Middle East policy problems. It marshals evidence to illustrate that the war in Iraq (a foreign-policy blunder of colossal proportions, considered from the perspective of the American national interest) and the policy that inspired it and continues to inspire our approach to other actors and issues in the Middle East, have their common origin in the orientation of the neoconservative policy towards service of the interests of Israel. This orientation is at the root of the explanation for why our policy does not seem to address or correspond with the genuine security needs of the United States. Such an understanding does not mean that the neoconservatives necessarily or consciously sought to aid Israel *at the expense of* the United States, but rather that they have seen American foreign policy through the lens of Israeli interest. Ideology and personal ties have blinded them to what most others clearly see as the foreign policy reality.

The term "neoconservative" is of popular usage, though like the description of political groups in general, it lacks clear-cut precision. What the term "neoconservative" refers to should become apparent in the following pages. While not focused on the neoconservative movement per se, this book reviews the background of the neoconservatives – their network and agenda – as it relates to the aforementioned foreign-policy theme. And what characterizes neoconservatives is not only their ideology – which basically consists of support for a militarily oriented American global interventionism and a big government, welfare statist form of conservatism – but also their personal interconnectedness in terms of organizations, publications, schooling, and even blood. Of crucial importance, as the work will show, is how the neocons, over the years, identified closely with the interests of Israel, and how their Middle East agenda paralleled that of the Israeli Likudnik right. In fact, much of the neocon approach to the Middle East can be seen to have originated in Likudnik thinking. And the Israeli government of Ariel Sharon worked in tandem with the neocons in supporting both the war on Iraq and later militant policies toward Iran and Syria.

The overarching goal of both the neocons and the Likudniks was to create an improved strategic environment for Israel. To reiterate, this does not necessarily mean that the neocons were deliberately promoting the interest of Israel at the expense of the United States. Instead, they maintained that an identity of interests existed between the two countries – Israel's enemies being ipso facto America's enemies. However, it is apparent that the neoconservatives viewed American foreign policy in the Middle East through the lens of Israeli interest, as Israeli interest was perceived by the Likudniks.

The aim of the neoconservative/Likudnik foreign policy strategy was to weaken and fragment Israel's Middle East adversaries and concomitantly increase Israel's relative strength, both externally and internally. A key objective was to eliminate the demographic threat posed by the Palestinians to the Jewish state, which the destabilization of Israel's external enemies would achieve, since the Palestinian resistance depended upon external support, both moral and material. Without outside support, the Palestinians would be forced to accede to whatever type of peaceful solution Israel offered.

The neoconservative position on the Middle East was the polar opposite of what had been the traditional United States foreign policy, set by what might be called the foreign policy establishment. The goal of the traditional policy was to promote stability in the Middle East in order to maintain the flow of oil. In contrast to the traditional goal of stability, the neocons called for destabilizing existing regimes. Of course, the neocons couched their policy in terms of the eventual *restabilization* of the region on a democratic basis. This work questions the genuineness of the neocons' motives with respect to democracy – at least in light of how democracy is normally understood. Likudnik strategy saw the benefit of regional destabilization for its own sake – creating as it would an environment of weak, disunified states or statelets involved in internal and external conflicts that could be easily dominated by Israel. The great danger from the Likudnik perspective was the possibility of Israel's enemies forming a united front.

The book has been entitled *The Transparent Cabal* because the neoconservatives have sometimes been referred to as a cabal, and, in fact, the term has been taken up by neoconservatives themselves. By implying secret plotting, the aim of such a term is often to make the whole idea of neoconservative influence appear ridiculous. For while the neoconservatives represent a tight group devoted to achieving political goals, they have worked very much in the open to advance their Middle East war agenda. Thus, unlike a true "cabal," characterized by secrecy, the neoconservatives are a "transparent cabal" – oxymoronic as that term might be. The neoconservatives quite openly publicized their war agenda both before and after September 11, 2001. In developing this history, the author has relied heavily on published sources produced by the neoconservatives themselves. In fact, it is the very transparency of the neoconservatives that has allowed this work to exist.

Like a "cabal," the neoconservatives have worked in unison to shape major policy. And though acting largely in the open, they nonetheless have been shrouded in a certain measure of secrecy, especially regarding their connection to Israel, because of the taboo nature of the issue. In short, the mainstream media has not probed this relationship to avoid the lethal charge of "anti-Semitism."

Over the years, the neocons had developed a powerful, interlocking network of think tanks, organizations, and media outlets outside of government with the express purpose of influencing American foreign policy. By the end of the 1990s, the neoconservatives developed a complete blueprint for the remaking of the Middle East by military means, starting with Iraq. The problem they faced was how to transform their agenda into official United States policy. It was only by becoming an influential part of the administration of George W. Bush that they would be in a position to make their Israelocentric agenda actual American policy.

The neocons, however, did not gain the upper hand in formulating the foreign policy of the Bush administration until the terror attacks of September 11, 2001 – which proved to be the pivotal event in the neocon ascendancy. When the administration looked for a plan to deal with terrorism, the neocons had an existing one to offer, and a network, inside and outside of the government, to promote it.

The second President Bush was essentially a convert to the neoconservative policy. Examples of national leaders' falling under the influence of their advisers are commonplace in history. And it would be especially understandable in the case of George W. Bush, who prior to 9/11 never exhibited any strong understanding or interest in Middle East policy, and was therefore in need of guidance, which the neocons could easily provide and present in a simple paradigm that Bush could find attractive.

The neocons did not drag the majority of the American people into war in 2003 against their collective will. In large measure, the neocon militaris-

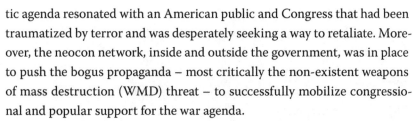

tic agenda resonated with an American public and Congress that had been traumatized by terror and was desperately seeking a way to retaliate. Moreover, the neocon network, inside and outside the government, was in place to push the bogus propaganda – most critically the non-existent weapons of mass destruction (WMD) threat – to successfully mobilize congressional and popular support for the war agenda.

The thesis outlined above is elaborated in the pages that follow. This work does not purport to be an overall history of the war on Iraq or the Bush Middle East policy; rather, evidence has been marshaled concerning the specific thesis of the neoconservative influence on U.S Middle East policy. In demonstrating the thesis, the work addresses various counter-arguments, dealing not only with allegations of the neocons' powerlessness but also with arguments offered by critics of the war, that oil and the quest for global dominance motivated the American war on Iraq and overall Middle East policy. The evidence presented in the work demonstrates that the neoconservative pro-Israel thesis is far more compelling than other explanations for the Bush II Middle East policy.

Lest any reader misinterpret this work, it is necessary to further explain what the book is not. Since it is not an analysis of neoconservatism per se it does not claim that neoconservatism is simply a cover for the support of Israel. Undoubtedly, the overall neoconservative viewpoint does not revolve solely around the security needs of Israel, and the same is true even of the neocons' positions on foreign policy and national-security policy. To state that neoconservatives viewed American foreign policy in the Middle East through the lens of Israeli interest – and that this was the basis of the neocon Middle East war agenda – is not to say that their support for Israel has been the be-all and end-all of their foreign policy ideas, which encompass the entire world.

There is nothing exceptional in this work's interpretation as it has just been outlined. It is hardly controversial to propose that elites, rather than the people as a whole, determine government policies, even in democracies. We see that idea in, for example, Robert Michels's "Iron Rule of Oligarchy" and Pareto's concept of "circulating elites." Even a cursory look at American historiography reveals that the premise of elite domination is widely shared.

Furthermore, there is nothing *outré* in the view that people would be affected in their foreign policy views by ethnic and emotional ties to a foreign country. The fear that such motives would shape American foreign policy loomed large in George Washington's Farewell Address of 1796. American historians, for their part, have often broached the idea that the foreign policy views of various ethnic groups – German-, Polish-, Irish-, and Cuban-Americans – have been based on their ethnic identities and loyalties. This clearly corresponds to the contention that the neocons' predominantly Jewish background and their identification with Israel shaped their view of Middle East policy.

This motivation ascribed to the neocons, however, does not imply that a majority of American Jews held the same view as the neoconservatives on the war in the Middle East. The American Jewish Committee's 2002 Annual Survey of Jewish Opinion – conducted between December 16, 2002, and January 5, 2003 – showed that 59 percent approved of the United States taking military action against Iraq to remove Saddam Hussein from power while 36 percent opposed military action. This finding was comparable to polls of the general American population.[4] Other polls showed less support for the war among American Jews than among the public at large. A compilation of public opinion polls by Pew Research Center in the first quarter of 2003 showed war support among Jews at 52 percent compared to 62 percent among the general public.[5]

As the occupation of Iraq continued, opposition to the war become the majority position among American Jews. The 2003 Annual Survey of American Jewish Opinion, conducted between November 25 and December 11 of that year showed Jews opposing the war by 54 percent to 43 percent.[6] The 2005 Annual Survey of American Jewish Opinion revealed that 70 percent of Jews opposed the war on Iraq, while only 28 continued to support it.[7] A Gallup Poll conducted in February 2007 found that 77 percent of Jews believed that the war on Iraq had been a mistake, while only 21 percent held otherwise. This contrasted with the overall American population in which the war was viewed as a mistake by a 52 percent to 46 percent margin.[8] To be perfectly clear, there was nothing like monolithic Jewish support for the war on Iraq; in fact, Jews tended to be more anti-war than the American public in general. This work, however, does not focus on general American Jewish opinion, but rather on the neoconservatives and Israel.

In short, there is nothing about the overall thesis presented in this book that should cause one to reject it out of hand as somehow implausible. The question is: does the information provided back up the thesis? The following chapters, containing evidence both extensive and detailed, should answer that in the affirmative.

Of course, no work can be definitive, especially one dealing with a contemporary issue that is still unfolding. Obviously, much information is yet to come, especially with the future release of archival collections. Evidence undoubtedly could appear that would alter this work's interpretations. All historical interpretations are only tentative. However, it would seem impossible to find new evidence that would remove the neoconservatives and Israel from the picture concerning the American war on Iraq and the succeeding developments in the wider Middle East. As George Packer, a staff writer for the *New Yorker* magazine, asserts in *The Assassins' Gate*: "The Iraq War will always be linked with the term 'neoconservative.'"[9]

chapter 2

THE "NEOCON-ISRAEL" CLAIM: BITS AND PIECES

THE CONNECTION of neoconservatives and Israel to the American war on Iraq, and on the further developments in the Middle East that sprang from that war, is hardly a novel thesis peculiar to this author nor one confined to fringe elements on the Internet. On the contrary, it has been put forth by numerous commentators dating back to the time of the build-up for war. But while these commentators have been candid about the role neoconservatives played in making and effectively selling the case for war in Iraq, at times even locating the roots of the neoconservative argument in concern for the security of Israel, none have dealt comprehensively with the topic, nor has anyone put together a thorough and systematic evidentiary base to support the intimation. Neither has their assessment, by any means, become mainstream. Indeed, the perspectives offered by many of these individuals have frequently been dismissed as mere assertion, if not outright "anti-Semitic" bigotry. Thus, a brief examination of some of these references will help to set the stage for the more extensive elaboration of the thesis that will be made in the succeeding chapters. It is hoped that this elaboration will ultimately show that their position, despite the dismissal and ridicule these individuals have at times encountered, is defensible, reasonable, and supported by an overwhelming amount of evidence.

Among those significant figures making the connection with the neoconservatives was Howard Dean, who in early August 2003, when he was the Democratic Party's leading candidate for President, said that while President George W. Bush was "an engaging person," he had been "captured by the neoconservatives around him."[1] Senator Joseph Biden, the ranking Democrat on the Senate Foreign Relations Committee, said in several major speeches in 2003 that neoconservatives had been driving U.S. foreign policy into a dangerous direction. As Biden put it: "This is the most ideological administration in U.S. history, led by neoconservatives who believe that the only asset that counts is our military might."[2] Regarding the war in Iraq, anti-war Republican presidential candidate Ron Paul proclaimed in September 2007 that "The American people didn't go in. A few people advising this administration, a small number of people called the neoconservative [sic] hijacked our foreign policy. They're responsible, not the American people."[3]

Former acting ambassador to Iraq and former career foreign service officer, Joseph Wilson, who had been sent on a CIA mission to determine the veracity of the administration's claim that Saddam had attempted to procure yellow cake uranium from Niger, presents in his memoirs the neoconservatives as the major proponents of the war. "This enterprise in Iraq," Wilson writes, "was always about a larger neoconservative agenda of projecting force as the means of imposing solutions. It was about shaking up the Middle East in the hope that democracy might emerge."[4] Craig R. Eisendrath and Melvin A. Goodman in their *Bush League Diplomacy: How the Neoconservatives are Putting the World at Risk* focus on the neoconservative dominance of Bush foreign policy.[5] Expressing a similar view of neoconservative control of Middle East policy during George W. Bush's first term were Stefan Halper and Jonathan Clarke in *America Alone: The Neoconservatives and the Global Order*. The authors consider themselves conservatives, and Halper served in the White House and the State Department during the Nixon, Ford, and Reagan administrations.[6]

When serving as the director of the Nonproliferation Project at the Carnegie Endowment for International Peace, Joseph Cirincione wrote on the organization's web site: "We have assembled on our web site links to the key documents produced since 1992 by this group, usually known as neoconservatives, and analysis of their efforts. They offer a textbook case of how a small, organized group can determine policy in a large nation, even when the majority of officials and experts originally scorned their views."[7]

Joshua Micah Marshall authored an article in the liberal *Washington Monthly* entitled: "Bomb Saddam?: How the obsession of a few neocon hawks became the central goal of U.S. foreign policy."[8] "The neoconservatives ... are largely responsible for getting us into the war against Iraq," observed veteran journalist Elizabeth Drew in her article "The Neocons in Power," appearing in the prestigious *New York Review of Books* in June 2003. Drew maintained that "The neoconservatives are powerful because they are cohesive, determined, ideologically driven, and clever (even if their judgment can be questionable), and some high administration officials, including the vice-president, are sympathetic to them."[9]

"The neocon vision has become the hard core of American foreign policy," declared Michael Hirst in *Newsweek* magazine.[10] Liberal columnist Robert Kuttner titled one of his articles, "Neo-cons have hijacked U.S. foreign policy."[11] News commentator Chris Matthews, of MSNBC's television program "Hardball," saw the move to war on Iraq as an alliance "demanded by neo-conservative policy wonks and backed by oil-patchers George W. Bush and Dick Cheney."[12] Billionaire financier and philanthropist George Soros stated that the "neocons form an influential group within the executive branch and their influence greatly increased after September 11."[13]

Investigative reporter Seymour Hersh went so far as to say that

> the amazing thing is we are been taken over basically by a cult, eight or nine neo-conservatives have somehow grabbed the government. Just how and why and how they did it so efficiently, will have to wait for much later historians and better documentation than we have now, but they managed to overcome the bureaucracy and the Congress, and the press, with the greatest of ease. It does say something about how fragile our Democracy is. You do have to wonder what a Democracy is when it comes down to a few men in the Pentagon and a few men in the White House having their way.[14]

(This present work adds some of that "better documentation," which shows that the neocons represented far more than a small cult of "eight or nine" individuals, but an interlocking network in the United States that often acted in tandem with the government of Israel. In fact, Hersh, through his investigative reporting, actually provided some of the evidence for this interpretation.)

The idea that the neoconservatives are motivated by their support for Israel is somewhat taboo, implying, as it does, external loyalties and Jewish power; nonetheless, it has received public attention. It is popular among rightist opponents of the neoconservative interventionist foreign policy and, in particular, of the Iraq war – that is to say, among paleoconservatives and paleolibertarians.[15] Patrick J. Buchanan, the well-known political commentator, former third-party Presidential candidate and editor of *American Conservative*, consistently pushed this theme; in his often-cited essay "Whose War?," he charged "that a cabal of polemicists and public officials seek to ensnare our country in a series of wars that are not in America's interests . . . . What these neoconservatives seek is to conscript American blood to make the world safe for Israel."[16]

Lambasting the neoconservatives in his thrice-weekly column on the popular Antiwar.com web site, paleolibertarian Justin Raimondo summarized his views in his "The Neocons' War," in which he described the neoconservatives as "Israel's fifth column in America."[17] Among other leading paleoconservative journalists who expressed the neoconservative-war-for-Israel theme were Paul Craig Roberts, a former assistant secretary of the treasury under Ronald Reagan, and Sam Francis, one of the major intellectuals of the movement.[18]

On the left, there was also mention of Israel's relationship to the war on Iraq. Eric Alterman stated that "The war was planned by neoconservatives, many of whom worked directly with their counterparts in the Israeli government, who helped perpetuate the deception."[19] Long before the buildup for the war on Iraq, Jim Lobe was a close follower of the neoconservatives for the *Interpress Service News Agency*; and his writings are referred to many times in this work.[20] In Lobe's view, "neoconservatives put Israel at the absolute center of their worldview."[21] Journalist and radio program producer Jeffrey Blankfort wrote one of the more extensive pieces on the subject, "War for Israel."[22] And *CounterPunch*, one of the most frequently visited leftist websites on the Internet, is very sympathetic to the view that links neocons to Israel. For example, *CounterPunch* frequently publishes pieces by former CIA officials, Bill and Kathleen Christison, which focus on this subject. Bill Christison, for example, maintained that that "the neocons definitely wield real power and influence" and that they were able to direct the Bush administration's policy agenda for the Middle East, which involved the "strengthening of Israeli/U.S. partnership and hegemony throughout the region and, in furtherance thereof, advocacy of war, first against Iraq and then if necessary against Syria, Iran, and possibly other Middle Eastern states."[23] Others on the *CounterPunch* web site who expressed that view included academics James Petras and Gary Leupp, journalists Stephen Green and Kurt Nimmo, and editor Alexander Cockburn.[24] Petras would expand on this theme in his book, *The Power of Israel in the United States*, which was published in 2006.[25]

In the leftist *Nation* magazine, British author and consultant on Middle East affairs Patrick Seale stated that

> The neocons – a powerful group at the heart of the Bush Administration – wanted war against Iraq and pressed for it with great determination, overriding and intimidating all those who expressed doubts, advised caution, urged the need for allies and for UN legitimacy, or recommended sticking with the well-tried cold war instruments of containment and deterrence.

Seale continued:

> Right-wing Jewish neocons – and most prominent neocons are right-wing Jews – tend to be pro-Israel zealots who believe that American and Israeli interests are inseparable (much to the alarm of liberal, pro-peace Jews, whether in America, Europe or Israel itself). Friends of Ariel Sharon's Likud, they tend to loathe Arabs and Muslims. For them, the cause of liberating Iraq had little to do with the well-being of Iraqis . . . . What they wished for was an improvement in Israel's military and strategic environment.[26]

The Israeli connection to the war is not the preserve solely of the antiestablishment left and right; mainstream figures have also mentioned it. In February 2003, a month before the invasion of Iraq, an article entitled "Bush and Sharon Nearly Identical On Mideast Policy" appeared on the front page of the *Washington Post*. The author, reporter Robert Kaiser, quoted a senior U.S. official as saying, "The Likudniks are really in charge now [of U.S. policy]." Pointing out that Sharon often claimed a "deep friendship" and "a special closeness" to the Bush administration, Kaiser asserted that "For the first time a U.S. administration and a Likud government are pursuing nearly identical policies."[27]

Author and political analyst Michael Lind, who has been labeled "our first notable apostate from neoconservatism" by Scott Malcolmson in the *Village Voice*[28] because of his former neoconservative ties, stressed the leading war role of the neoconservatives. Lind held that

> [a]s a result of several bizarre and unforeseeable contingencies, the foreign policy of the world's only global power is being made by a small clique that is unrepresentative of either the U.S. population or the mainstream foreign policy establishment.

Lind continued: "The core group now in charge consists of neoconservative defense intellectuals." And "The neocon defense intellectuals, as well as being in or around the actual Pentagon, are at the center of a metaphorical 'pentagon' of the Israel lobby and the religious right, plus conservative think tanks, foundations and media empires."[29]

Columnist and television commentator Robert Novak referred to the American war on Iraq as "Sharon's war."[30] Maureen Dowd of the *New York Times* stated, in a column entitled "Neocon Coup at the Department d'Etat," that the neo-conservatives seek to make sure that U.S. foreign policy "is good for Ariel Sharon."[31] Arnaud de Borchgrave, who had been a senior editor of *Newsweek* and president and CEO of United Press International, wrote in February 2003: "Washington's 'Likudniks' – Ariel Sharon's powerful backers in the Bush administration – have been in charge of U.S. policy in the Middle East since President Bush was sworn into office."[32] He pursued that theme in a later, postwar article: "So the leitmotif for Operation Iraqi Freedom was not WMDs, but the freedom of Iraq in the larger context of long-range security for Israel."[33] Harvard professor Stanley Hoffman included neocon concern for Israel as one of the motives for the war, writing that

> there is a loose collection of friends of Israel, who believe in the identity of interests between the Jewish state and the United States – two democracies that, they say, are both surrounded by foes and both forced to rely on military power to survive. These analysts look at foreign policy through the lens of one dominant concern: Is it good or bad for Israel? Since that nation's founding in 1948, these thinkers have never been in very good odor at the State Department, but now they are well ensconced in the Pentagon, around such strategists as Paul Wolfowitz, Richard Perle and Douglas Feith.[34]

In *The One-State Solution: A Breakthrough for Peace in the Israeli-Palestinian Deadlock*, academician Virginia Tilley includes a discussion of the role of the neoconservatives in bringing about the war on Iraq. After mentioning the various official justifications for the war on Iraq, Tilley writes: "But sheltered under the U.S. vice president and secretary of defense was a cadre of advisors who had long planned the invasion on a very different agenda: to reconfigure the Middle East in ways favorable to Israeli security."[35]

Jeffrey Record, a prominent national security analyst, who during 2003 was a visiting research professor at the Strategic Studies Institute of the Army War College, writes: "The primary explanation for war against Iraq is the Bush White House's post-9/11 embrace of the neoconservatives' ideology regarding U.S. military primacy, use of force, and the Middle East." Regarding Israel, Record maintains:

The neoconservatives who populated the upper ranks of the Bush administration had been gunning for Saddam Hussein for years before 9/11. They had an articulated, aggressive, values-based foreign policy doctrine and a specific agenda for the Middle East that reflected hostility toward Arab autocracies and support for Israeli security interests as defined by that country's Likud political party.[36]

Some significant United States government figures, mostly retired or about to retire, also commented about the Israeli role in the war. On May 23, 2004, retired Marine General Anthony Zinni, stated on the popular "60 Minutes" television program that the neoconservatives' role in pushing the war for Israel's benefit was

the worst-kept secret in Washington . . . And one article, because I mentioned the neoconservatives who describe themselves as neoconservatives, I was called anti-Semitic. I mean, you know, unbelievable that that's the kind of personal attacks that are run when you criticize a strategy and those who propose it . . . . I know what strategy they promoted. And openly. And for a number of years. And what they have convinced the President and the secretary to do. And I don't believe there is any serious political leader, military leader, diplomat in Washington that doesn't know where it came from.[37]

Zinni had been in charge of all American troops in the Middle East as commander-in-chief of the U.S. Central Command, and had also served President George W. Bush as a special envoy to the Middle East.

Zbigniew Brzezinski, National Security Advisor to former President Jimmy Carter, expressed a mild version of the war-for-Israel scenario, pointing out that "various right-wing, neoconservative, and religiously fundamentalist groups" hold the view "that America's goal should be to reorder the Middle East, using America's power in the name of democracy to subordinate the Arab states to its will, to eliminate Islamic radicalism, and to make the region safe for Israel."[38]

In May 2004, U.S. Senator Ernest "Fritz" Hollings, Democrat of South Carolina, who was in his last term of office, addressed Israel's connection to the war:

With Iraq no threat, why invade a sovereign country? The answer: President Bush's policy to secure Israel.

Led by Wolfowitz, Richard Perle and Charles Krauthammer, for years there has been a domino school of thought that the way to guarantee Israel's security is to spread democracy in the area.[39]

When called upon to retract his claims, which influential American Jews deemed "anti-Semitic," Hollings instead reiterated them on the floor of the U.S. Senate on May 20, 2004. "That is not a conspiracy. That is the policy," he said. "Everybody knows it because we want to secure our friend, Israel."[40]

It was even revealed that a Bush administration figure, Philip Zelikow, who then served on the President's Foreign Intelligence Advisory Board and supported the war, publicly acknowledged that the Iraqi threat was primarily against Israel, not the United States, in a speech at the University of Virginia on September 10, 2002. "Why would Iraq attack America or use nuclear weapons against us? I'll tell you what I think the real threat [is] and actually has been since 1990 – it's the threat against Israel," Zelikow asserted.

> And this is the threat that dare not speak its name, because the Europeans don't care deeply about that threat, I will tell you frankly. And the American government doesn't want to lean too hard on it rhetorically, because it is not a popular sell.[41]

Zelikow later became the executive director of the National Commission on Terrorist Attacks Upon the United States, better known as the 9/11 Commission. In late February 2005, he was appointed a senior adviser on foreign policy issues to Secretary of State Condoleezza Rice.[42]

Perhaps the most prominent proclamation of Israel's connection to the war was made by two leading scholars in the field of international relations, John Mearsheimer and Stephen Walt, who produced an 82-page essay (42 pages of narrative and 40 pages of endnotes), "The Israel Lobby and U.S. Foreign Policy," that became public in March 2006.[43] The paper was not published in the United States but did come out in an abbreviated form in the *London Review of Books*. In the United States, it remained only a "working paper" on a Harvard faculty website. Nonetheless, the work did gain a considerable degree of attention, especially in the intellectual press.[44] The authors transformed this work into a longer book, *The Israel Lobby and U.S. Foreign Policy*, which was published in September 2007.[45]

The Mearsheimer and Walt essay covered the broader "Israel Lobby," of which they see the neoconservatives to be a part. They maintain that the pro-Israel lobby, made up of an extensive network of journalists, think-tankers, lobbyists, and officials of the Bush regime – largely but not solely of Jewish ethnicity – has played a fundamental role in shaping American Middle East policy. The lobby's goal has been to enhance Israeli security, often at the expense of U.S. interests. Regarding the neoconservatives, they hold that "the main driving force behind the Iraq war was a small band of neoconservatives, many with close ties to Israel's Likud Party."[46]

The essay drew a firestorm of criticism to the effect that it was anti-Semitic.[47] This has been the standard reaction to anyone who violates the existing taboo. In fact, the neocons have been quick to claim that criticism of the neoconservatives is really anti-Semitic. In doing so, they acknowledged the Jewish background of neoconservatism. For example, neocon Joshua Muravchik argued: "The neoconservatives, it turns out, are also in large proportion Jewish – and this, to their detractors, constitutes evidence of the ulterior motives that lurk behind the policies they espouse."[48]

Norman Podhoretz, the doyen of neoconservatism, used the very popularity of the claim of the connection of neocons and Israel to the war as reason to reject it as classical "anti-Semitism."

"Before long, this theory was picked up and circulated by just about everyone in the whole world who was intent on discrediting the Bush Doctrine," Podhoretz asserted in *Commentary* magazine in September 2004.

> And understandably so: for what could suit their purposes better than to expose the invasion of Iraq – and by extension the whole of World War IV – as a war started by Jews and being waged solely in the interest of Israel?
>
> To protect themselves against the taint of anti-Semitism, purveyors of this theory sometimes disingenuously continued to pretend that when they said neoconservative they did not mean Jew. Yet the theory inescapably rested on all-too-familiar anti-Semitic canards – principally that Jews were never reliably loyal to the country in which they lived, and that they were always conspiring behind the scenes, often successfully, to manipulate the world for their own nefarious purposes.[49]

Even Jews outside the distinctly neocon orbit became very upset about the criticism of neocons and turned to the "anti-Semitism" defense. In May 2003, Abraham Foxman, national chairman of the Anti-Defamation League, wrote an essay, "Anti-Semitism, Pure and Simple," bemoaning the fact that

> The accusation about Jews and Jewish interests is being aired almost daily, on the airwaves, in the nation's editorial pages and from a range of pundits who want to pin the blame for this war on the Jews. The spread of this new lie is not surprising, because it is really not so new. In times of crisis, in times of

uncertainty, at times nations face danger, Jews continue to be a convenient and tempting option for scapegoating.[50]

A year later, Foxman would demand that Senator Hollings retract his comments about neoconservatives and Israel, charging that "[t]his is reminiscent of age-old, anti-Semitic canards about a Jewish conspiracy to control and manipulate government."[51]

Undercutting the charge of "anti-Semitism" was the fact that more than a few individuals of Jewish heritage shared the view that neocons played a major role in driving the United States to war, including Rabbi Michael Lerner, Michael Lind, Paul Gottfried, Robert Novak, Jim Lobe, Seymour Hersh, Stanley Heller, Philip Weiss, Joshua Micah Marshall, Jeffrey Blankfort, Eric Alterman, and George Soros.[52]

In fact, Rabbi Lerner, editor of the liberal Jewish publication *Tikkun*, went much further than most gentile commentators in branding Jews pro-war:

> The State of Israel seems unequivocally committed to the war, the most prominent advocates of this war inside the administration have been Jews, the major sentiment being expressed inside the Orthodox synagogues is that of support for the war, and the voices of liberals who might normally be counted on to be raising questions are in fact silent. Isn't that enough reason for most people to feel that this is a war supported by the Jewish community, though in fact it is only the organized community and not most Jews who support it?[53]

Paul Gottfried explained what was really meant by those who ascribe a major role in the war to the neoconservatives: "No one who is sane is claiming that all Jews are collaborating with Richard Perle and Bill Kristol. What is being correctly observed is a convergence of interests in which neoconservatives have played a pivotal role."[54]

Obviously, there are those who would label the war as the work of all Jews – an imaginary monolithic World Jewry – but all views can be distorted into fallacious, and even hostile ones. The war on Iraq, of course, spawned anti-Arab and anti-Muslim feelings, just as the World War II spawned anti-Japanese sentiment (and World War I Germanophobia). These developments, by themselves, would not undermine the causes to which they were attached, e.g., World War II.

Joshua Micah Marshall held that use of "blanket criticisms of anti-Semitism" were intended "to stigmatize and ward off any and all criticism" of the Bush administration foreign policy and Ariel Sharon.[55] "But I must tell you that I am growing more than a little weary of the Jewlier than thou comments emanating from some of my co-religionists on the other side of the aisle," Marshall averred. He countercharged that

> those who make these charges are exploiting and trivializing the issue of anti-Semitism by using it as a tool to blunt criticism of their foreign policy views and the foreign policy pursued by this administration. One does not have to agree with the policies of Ariel Sharon's government to be a Jew in good standing or even an Israeli for that matter.[56]

Intertwined with the "anti-Semitic" charge was the implication that the very idea of neoconservatives exercising power or possessing inordinate influence was preposterous. For example, Robert J. Lieber, professor of government and foreign service at prestigious Georgetown University, titled an essay, "The Neoconservative-Conspiracy Theory: Pure Myth," claiming that

> [t]his sinister mythology is worthy of the Iraqi information minister, Muhammed Saeed al-Sahaf, who became notorious for telling Western journalists not to believe their own eyes as American tanks rolled into view just across the Tigris River.[57]

It might be pointed out that Lieber himself was closely connected with the neoconservatives, and could legitimately be considered a neoconservative, being a member of the Committee for the President Danger, which was revived in July 2004 to promote war against Islamic terrorism and was made up of such neocon luminaries as Norman Podhoretz, Midge Decter, Joshua Muravchik, Kenneth Adelman, Laurie Mylroie, Frank Gaffney, and Max Kampelman,[58] Lieber's argument here represents an ironical one pushed by many neocons – to wit, while the neoconservatives form many groups to influence public policy, they often deny that they are in any way successful in doing so.

Sometimes, however, neoconservatives do admit their influence on American war policy. For example, in the course of trying to deny the leading role of neoconservatives in the war on Iraq, neoconservative Max Boot in December 2002 had to admit that the national security strategy of the Bush administration "sounds as if it could have come straight from the pages of *Commentary* magazine, the neocon bible."[59]

And in that very "neocon bible," *Commentary*, Joshua Muravchik went a long way in the direction of acknowledging that America's war on Iraq had reflected neoconservative policy. Ironically, the article, published in September 2003, was entitled "The Neoconservative Cabal," seemingly intended to imply the ridiculousness of the critics' charges, but the piece actually did much to provide confirmation. Muravchik acknowledged that the September 11 terrorist atrocities enabled long-standing neoconservative plans to come to the fore.

> Not only did the neocons have an analysis of what had gone wrong in American policy, they also stood ready with proposals for what to do now: to wage war on the terror groups and to seek to end or transform governments that supported them, especially those possessing the means to furnish terrorists with the wherewithal to kill even more Americans than on September 11. Neocons also offered a long-term strategy for making the Middle East less of a hotbed of terrorism: implanting democracy in the region and thereby helping to foment a less violent approach to politics.

After 9/11, policies espoused by neoconservatives were "embraced by the Bush administration."

Muravchik purported to be agnostic as to whether the neocons themselves caused the adoption of their policies: "Was this because Bush learned them from the likes of Wolfowitz and Perle? Or did he and his top advisers – none of them known as a neocon – reach similar conclusions on their own?" But Muravchik made the neoconservative authorship of American foreign policy more explicit in his final conclusion, where he wrote that if

> the [Bush administration] policies succeed, then the world will have been delivered from an awful scourge, and there will be credit enough to go around – some of it, one trusts, even for the lately much demonized neoconservatives.[60]

In December 2003, the neocon Hudson Institute and the neocon fellow-traveling, pro-Israel *New Republic* magazine sponsored a conference entitled "Is the Neoconservative Moment Over?" Obviously, the title itself implied that neoconservatism had been influential at least for the "moment" of the Iraq war. Moreover, Richard Perle, a leading neocon who was a speaker at the conference, would maintain that "Not only is the neoconservative movement not over, it's just beginning."[61]

Acknowledging neocon influence, of course, is not the same thing as saying that the neocons were motivated by Israeli interests. However, after General Zinni's remarks in May 2004, the Jewish weekly, *Forward*, concluded that that the argument that Israeli security was the motivation for the American war on Iraq had to be confronted by ideas, and could not be simply tossed aside as sheer bigotry. Its editorial stated:

> As recently as a week ago, reasonable people still could dismiss as antisemitic conspiracy mongering the claim that Israel's security was the real motive be-

hind the invasion of Iraq. No longer. The allegation has now moved from the fringes into the mainstream. Its advocates can no longer simply be shushed or dismissed as bigots. Those who disagree must now argue the case on the merits.

What was required, the *Forward* opined, was open debate.

> The line between legitimate debate and scapegoating is a fine one. Friends of Israel will be tempted to guard that line by labeling as antisemites those who threaten to cross it. They already have begun to do so. But it is a mistake. Israel and its allies stand accused of manipulating America's public debate for their own purposes. If they were to succeed in suppressing debate to protect themselves, it only would prove the point. Better to follow the democratic path: If there is bad speech, the best reply is more speech.[62]

The *Forward* has here offered wise counsel. Truth can only be obtained through freedom of inquiry, not by intimidation and suppression, and it is the arrival at a better understanding of the truth to which this work is dedicated. As noted earlier, the thesis here presented is neither novel nor particularly original. What is newly presented, however, is the extensive evidence, from matters of public record, necessary to evaluate the claims made by, e.g., those identified in this chapter, whose assessments have up to now typically been dismissed as lunacy, bigotry, or both. Also new, and hopefully useful, is the tying together of the strands of evidence and argument into a coherent whole, the luxury for which is available in a work of this length, while such hasn't been the case for many of those cited above who have dealt with the issue more briefly and, therefore, less thoroughly. Anyone wishing honestly to determine whether it is myth or reality that the neoconservatives were the driving force behind the Iraq war and the Bush administration's later militant policy in the Middle East, and whether that neoconservative policy was and is designed to benefit Israel, must consider this evidence. The author believes the case made by it to be overwhelmingly persuasive.

chapter 3

WHO ARE THE NEOCONS?

ALTHOUGH THE TERM neoconservative is in common usage, a brief description of the group might be helpful. The term was coined by socialist Michael Harrington as a derisive term for leftists and liberals who were migrating rightward. Many of the first generation neoconservatives were originally liberal Democrats, or even socialists and Marxists, often Trotskyites. Most originated in New York, and most were Jews. They drifted to the right in the 1960s and 1970s as the Democratic Party moved to the anti-war McGovernite left.[1]

The Jewish nature of the neoconservatives was obvious. It should be pointed out that Jews in the United States have traditionally identified with the liberals and the left, and most still do. (Liberals in the American context represent the moderate left.) Liberalism seemed to allow for advancement of Jews in an open, secular society; to many Jews, conservatism, in contrast, represented traditional Christian anti-Semitism. Moreover, as political scientist Benjamin Ginsberg points out in his *The Fatal Embrace: Jews and the State*, Jews were in favor of American liberalism's creation of the welfare state in the period between Franklin Delano Roosevelt's New Deal in the 1930s and Lyndon B. Johnson's Great Society in the 1960s, which brought many Jews into power positions in the federal government apparatus.[2]

But those individuals who became neoconservatives were perceptive enough to see that in the 1960s liberals and the left were identifying with issues that were apt to be harmful to the collective interest of Jewry. As historian Edward S. Shapiro, himself of a Jewish background, points out:

Many of the leading neoconservative intellectuals were Jewish academicians who moved to the right in the 1960s in response to campus unrest, the New Left, the counterculture, the Black Power movement, the excesses of the Great Society, the hostility of the left to Israel, and the left's weakening opposition to Communism and the Soviet Union. They became convinced, Mark Gerson, a perceptive student of the neoconservatives, has written, that the left was "distinctively bad for the Jews."[3]

In response to efforts to deny the neoconservatives' Jewishness, Gal Beckerman wrote in the Jewish newspaper *Forward* in January 2006: "[I]t is a fact that as a political philosophy, neoconservatism was born among the children of Jewish immigrants and is now largely the intellectual domain of those immigrants' grandchildren." In fact, Beckerman went so far as to maintain that "[i]f there is an intellectual movement in America to whose invention Jews can lay sole claim, neoconservatism is it."[4]

Concern for Jews abroad and Israel, in particular, loomed large in the birth of neoconservatism. Proto-neocons adopted a pronounced anti-Soviet policy as the Soviet Union aided Israel's enemies in the Middle East and prohibited Soviet Jews from emigrating. "One major factor that drew them inexorably to the right," writes Benjamin Ginsberg,

> was their attachment to Israel and their growing frustration during the 1960s with a Democratic party that was becoming increasingly opposed to American military preparedness and increasingly enamored of Third World causes [e.g., Palestinian rights]. In the Reaganite right's hard-line anti-communism, commitment to American military strength, and willingness to intervene politically and militarily in the affairs of other nations to promote democratic values (and American interests), neocons found a political movement that would guarantee Israel's security.[5]

Neoconservative Max Boot acknowledged that "support for Israel" had been and remained a "key tenet of neoconservatism."[6]

In the United States, it is sometimes taboo to say that the neoconservatives are primarily Jewish or that they are concerned about Israel, but neocons did not conceal these connections. The original flagship of the neoconservative movement was *Commentary* magazine, which is put out by the American Jewish Committee and has styled itself as "America's premier monthly journal of opinion." The American Jewish Committee pronounces as its mission: "To safeguard the welfare and security of Jews in the United States, in Israel, and throughout the world."[7]

It was Norman Podhoretz, editor-in-chief of *Commentary* for 35 years until his retirement in 1995, who transformed the magazine into a neoconservative publication, offering writing space to many who would be leading figures in the movement. Ironically, when Podhoretz first became editor, he allied himself with New Left radicals, who vociferously opposed the war in Vietnam. Murray Friedman writes in *The Neoconservative Revolution: Jewish Intellectuals and the Shaping of Public Policy* that under Podhoretz's editorship, "Commentary became perhaps the first magazine of any significance to pay serious attention to radical ideology." However, Podhoretz started his move rightward by 1967, and by 1970, "his conversion to neoconservatism was complete."[8]

Friedman points out that Podhoretz, like most who gravitated to neoconservatism, did not dwell on Jewish interests and the fate of Israel until the latter half of the 1960s and the early 1970s, when his "sense of this own Jewishness intensified."[9] Friedman notes that

A central element in Podhoretz's evolving views, which would soon become his and many of the neocons" governing principle was the question, "Is It Good for the Jews," the title of a February 1972 *Commentary* piece.[10]

Exemplifying this greater focus on Jewish interests, Friedman observes that

Commentary articles now came to emphasize threats to Jews and the safety and security of the Jewish state. By the 1980s, nearly half of Podhoretz's writings on international affairs centered on Israel and these dangers.[11]

Benjamin Ginsberg similarly maintains:

A number of Jews ascertained for themselves that Israeli security required a strong American commitment to internationalism and defense. Among the most prominent Jewish spokesmen for this position was Norman Podhoretz, editor of *Commentary* magazine. Podhoretz had been a liberal and a strong opponent of the Vietnam War. But by the early 1970s he came to realize that "continued American support for Israel depended upon continued American involvement in international affairs – from which it followed that American withdrawal into [isolationism] [preceding brackets in original] represented a direct threat to the security of Israel."[12]

Having a married daughter and grandchildren living in Israel, Podhoretz's identification with the Jewish state transcended intellectual conviction. With the beginning of the Gulf War of 1991, Podhoretz actually went to live with his daughter in her home in Jerusalem in order to show his solidarity with Israel, which Saddam had threatened to attack by missiles, and did so to a limited extent.[13]

Podhoretz was a neoconservative of exceptional influence. As neoconservative Arnold Beichman contends, "in the ideological wars of the 1970s and 1980s, Podhoretz had become an intellectual force who by himself and through his magazine contributed mightily to the global victory against communism."[14] Denoting Podhoretz's significance, President George W. Bush awarded him the Presidential Medal of Freedom, the nation's highest civilian honor, on June 23, 2004.[15]

In terms of membership, neoconservatism is not exclusively Jewish. There are gentiles who identify with the neoconservative movement – some because of its ideas but probably also because membership can be career enhancing at a time when it has been difficult for scholars, especially white male scholars, to even break into academia, where supply greatly exceeds demand and where the environment has not been hospitable to individuals of a conservative bent. For one thing, the numerous neoconservative think tanks and media outlets offer numerous jobs. "One thing that the neocons have that both other factions of conservatives and liberals don't have," wrote Scott McConnell, editor of the *American Conservative*, "is they can employ a lot of people."[16] Work in those jobs can provide credentials for important positions outside neocon-controlled domains – government, academia, media, and the literary world. Moreover, the extensive neoconservative network can facilitate personal advancement in all parts of the establishment.

It would appear that Jewish neoconservatives seek to feature their gentile members, and use their existence to deny the Jewish nature of their movement. But the fact of the matter is that the movement has been Jewish inspired, Jewish-oriented, and Jewish-dominated. As historian Paul Gottfried, himself Jewish and a close observer of the neoconservative scene, pointed out in April 2003:

> [T]he term "neoconservative" is now too closely identified with the personal and ethnic concerns of its Jewish celebrities. Despite their frequent attempts to find kept gentiles, the game of speaking through proxies may be showing diminishing results. Everyone with minimal intelligence knows that Bill Bennett, Frank Gaffney, Ed Feulner, Michael Novak, George Weigel, James Nuechterlein, and Cal Thomas front for the neocons. It is increasingly useless to depend on

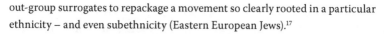

out-group surrogates to repackage a movement so clearly rooted in a particular ethnicity – and even subethnicity (Eastern European Jews).[17]

Similarly, John J. Mearsheimer and Stephen M. Walt in *The Israel Lobby and U.S. Foreign Policy* point out in their reference to the existence of non-Jewish neoconservatives that "Jews nonetheless comprise the core of the neoconservative movement."[18]

Neoconservatives are distinguished by more than just their ideology and ethnicity; they are not simply conservative Jews. They have formed and sustained close personal connections between themselves over a long period of time. As will be discussed later, this network has been perpetuated by becoming institutionalized in a number of influential think tanks and organizations. These close ties help to explain the neocons' great power, which far exceeds their rather limited numbers.[19]

Social anthropologist Janine R. Wedel describes the successful neocon network as a "flex group," which she defines as an informal faction adept at "playing multiple and overlapping roles and conflating state and private interests. These players keep appearing in different incarnations, ensuring continuity even as their operating environments change."

Wedel continues:

> As flex players, the neocons have had myriad roles over time. They quietly promoted one another for influential positions and coordinated their multi-pronged efforts inside and outside government in pursuit of agendas that were always in their own interest, but not necessarily the public's.

The neocon flex players

> always help each other out in furthering their careers, livelihoods and mutual aims. Even when some players are "in power" within an administration, they are flanked by people outside of formal government. Flex groups have a culture of circumventing authorities and creating alternative ones. They operate through semi-closed networks and penetrate key institutions, revamping them to marginalize other potential players and replacing them with initiatives under their control.[20]

But while personal advancement is involved, the flex players pursue much more than this, being "continually working to further the shared agenda of *the group*."[21] What Wedel fails to bring out, however, is that the "shared agenda of the group" involves the advancement of the interests of Israel, as the neocons perceive Israel's interests.

The neocon network is especially solidified by the existence of relationships by blood and marriage. Norman Podhoretz is married to Midge Decter, a neoconservative writer in her own right. Their son, John Podhoretz, was a columnist for the neoconservative *New York Post* and *Weekly Standard* before being announced as the new editor of *Commentary* in October 2007. And their son-in-law is Elliott Abrams, who worked for Senator Robert Henry "Scoop" Jackson (D.-Wash.) and later served in the State Department during the Reagan administration, where he was involved in the Iran/Contra scandal. Abrams was director of Near Eastern Affairs in the National Security Council during George W. Bush's first term and was promoted to Deputy National Security Adviser in the second term.[22]

Irving Kristol, who is regarded as the "godfather" of neoconservatism (though his focus tended more to domestic matters in contrast to Podhoretz's concern for foreign policy), is married to Gertrude Himmelfarb, also a major neoconservative writer. The Kristols' son, William (Bill) Kristol, is currently a leading figure in the neoconservative movement as editor of the *Weekly Standard*, which surpassed *Commentary* to become the major neoconservative publication.[23]

Meyrav and David Wurmser are another neoconservative couple. Israeli-born Meyrav Wurmser was Director of the Center for Middle East Policy at the Hudson Institute. In 2005, she became head of the Hudson Institute's Zionism Project, which involves a two-year study to look at "the identity crisis of Israel and Zionism," and to come up with recommendations "that can aid" in resolving it.[24] She also wrote for the *Jerusalem Post* and was co-founder of the Middle East Media Research Institute. Her husband, David Wurmser, is a leading neoconservative writer who was director of the Middle East program at the American Enterprise Institute prior to entering the Bush II administration, where he held a various positions, becoming in 2003 an adviser on Middle Eastern affairs to Vice President Dick Cheney.

Neoconservatives Richard Perle, R. James Woolsey Jr., and Paul Wolfowitz were all acolytes of the late Albert Wohlstetter, a professor at the University of Chicago and the University of California at Berkeley and a nuclear strategist at the RAND corporation, who now has a conference center named for him at the influential neoconservative American Enterprise Institute (sometimes referred to as "Neocon Central") in Washington, D.C. Gary Dorrien in *Imperial Designs* describes Wohlstetter as the

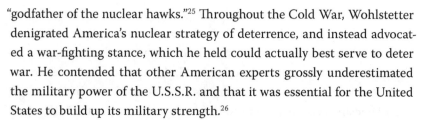

"godfather of the nuclear hawks."[25] Throughout the Cold War, Wohlstetter denigrated America's nuclear strategy of deterrence, and instead advocated a war-fighting stance, which he held could actually best serve to deter war. He contended that other American experts grossly underestimated the military power of the U.S.S.R. and that it was essential for the United States to build up its military strength.[26]

In 1969, Wohlstetter landed Wolfowitz and Perle[27] their first Washington jobs as interns for Senator "Scoop" Jackson. Jackson was a hard-line Cold Warrior, champion of Israel's interests, and neoconservative icon.[28] It was likely through Wohlstetter that Perle met the now-notorious Ahmed Chalabi, who would head the Iraqi exiles and play a significant role in inducing the United States to make war on Iraq in 2003.[29]

While Wolfowitz would stay only briefly with Jackson, Perle would remain for over a decade. During this time, Jackson's office became an incubator for the incipient neoconservatives. Staff would include Elliott Abrams, Douglas Feith, Frank Gaffney, R. James Woolsey, and Michael A. Ledeen.[30]

Many significant neoconservatives were followers of political philosopher Leo Strauss. These included Paul Wolfowitz; William Kristol; Stephen Cambone, under secretary of defense for intelligence in the Bush II administration; and Robert Kagan, who teamed with William Kristol at the *Weekly Standard*. Kagan is the son of leading Yale University Straussian Donald Kagan and brother of Frederick W. Kagan of the American Enterprise Institute.[31]

This list of connections is far from complete (and will be developed more in other chapters) but it helps to reveal an important fact about the neoconservative movement. As political writer Jim Lobe explains it:

> Contrary to appearances, the neocons do not constitute a powerful mass political movement. They are instead a small, tightly-knit clan whose incestuous familial and personal connections, both within and outside the Bush administration, have allowed them to grab control of the future of American foreign policy.[32]

It should also be emphasized that the neoconservatives are far from being an isolated group; to the contrary, they work closely with others, where common interests serve as the attraction. For example, neoconservatives have received broad support from the Christian evangelical right for most of their activities. To attract support on their particular issues, neoconservatives often have created ad hoc citizen groups, such as the Committee for the Liberation of Iraq. Moreover, their advocacy of a strong military attracts defense intellectuals, some mainstream conservatives, and representatives from defense interests. On the other hand, the neocons find allies among various Jewish Americans, who may not support all of their hard-line militaristic positions or their more conservative domestic positions, but agree on the issue of staunchly supporting Israel and its foreign policy objectives. In this latter category are such liberal pro-Zionists as Senator Joseph Lieberman, former Congressman Stephen Solarz, Congressman Tom Lantos, the *New Republic's* Martin Peretz, and representatives from the American Israel Public Affairs Committee (AIPAC). A few more traditional conservative Jews such as columnist William Safire, who pre-existed the neocons on the right, closely identify with the neoconservatives regarding Israel and American policies in the Middle East. As commentator Bill Christison, a former CIA analyst, observes: "It suffices to know . . . that the neocons and the [Israel] lobby together form a very powerful mutual support society, and their relationship is symbiotic in the extreme."[33]

When they first emerged in the early 1970s, the neoconservatives worked primarily through the Democratic party – they sought to combat the leftist orientation that had enabled George McGovern to become the Democratic presidential standard bearer in 1972. "The 1972 campaign proved to be a watershed for the neoconservatives," Gary Dorrien notes, "For them, the McGovern candidacy epitomized the degeneration of American liberalism. McGovern's world view, like his slogan – 'Come Home, America' – was defeatist, isolationist, and guilt-driven."[34]

McGovernites were not simply opposed to American military involvement in Vietnam, they were opposed also to the continuation of the Cold War with its global opposition to Communism and its concomitant massive military spending. The military retrenchment they sought, however, would have had negative repercussions for Israel, dependent as it was on American military assistance, and especially since it was targeted as an ideological enemy by the Communist countries and the world left. As Benjamin Ginsberg writes of that era:

> Many liberal Democrats . . . espoused cutbacks in the development and procurement of weapons systems, a curtailment of American military capabilities and commitments, and what amounted to a semireturn to isolationism. These

policies all appeared to represent a mortal threat to Israel and, hence, were opposed by many Jews who supported Israel.[35]

"Increasingly," Murray Friedman maintains,

> neocons came to believe that the Jewish state's ability to survive – indeed, the Jewish community's will to survive – was dependent on American military strength and its challenge to the Soviet Union, the primary backer of Arab countries in the Middle East.[36]

Neoconservatism's first political manifestation was as the Coalition for a Democratic Majority, which was formed in 1972, when most neoconservatives entertained hopes of reclaiming the Democratic Party and American liberalism. As James Nuechterlein, himself something of a neocon, notes:

> Most of the leading neoconservatives were Jewish . . . and Jews found it extraordinarily difficult to think of themselves as conservatives, much less Republicans. In the American context, to be a Jew – even more a Jewish intellectual – was to be a person of the left.[37]

Murray Friedman similarly writes in *The Neoconservative Revolution* that at that time

> neocons still associated conservatism with golf, country clubs, the Republican Party, big business – a sort of "goyishe" fraternity – and with the ideological posturing of right-wing fanatics. They viewed traditional conservatives as having little empathy for the underdog and the excluded in society. They thought of themselves as dissenting liberals, "children of the depression," as Midge Decter declared, who "retained a measure of loyalty to the spirit of the New Deal."[38]

In the 1970s, the neoconservatives' political standard bearers were Senator "Scoop" Jackson and Daniel Patrick Moynihan. Neoconservatives basically wanted to return to the anti-Communist Cold War position exemplified by President Harry Truman (1945–1953), which had held sway through the administration of Lyndon B. Johnson (1963–1969). Anti-Communist foreign policy, however, had been widely discredited among mainstream liberal Democrats by the Vietnam imbroglio. While neoconservatives were opposed to the McGovern liberals in the Democratic Party, whom they viewed as too sympathetic to Communism and radical left causes, they did not identify with the foreign policy of mainstream Republicans. Rather, neoconservatives opposed Henry Kissinger's policy of détente with the Soviet Union, with its emphasis on peace through negotiations, arms control, and trade, which was being pushed by the Nixon and Ford administrations.

They viewed the détente policy as defeatist and too callous toward human rights violations in Communist countries.

For the neoconservatives, the human rights issue centered on the right of Jews to emigrate from the Soviet Union. That right was embodied in the Jackson-Vanik amendment, which was especially the work of Jackson's staffer Richard Perle. By requiring that American trade favors to the Soviet Union be based on the latter's allowance of freer emigration, this amendment undercut the Nixon-Kissinger policy of détente, which sought to establish better relations with the Soviets through trade. While neoconservatives were only a small minority among Jews, on this issue they were joined by the Jewish mainstream.[39]

The Jackson-Vanik amendment was a major achievement for American Jewry. "Congress had rolled over administration resistance and passed a proactive law that changed the structure of U.S.-Soviet relations," writes J. J. Goldberg. "Whether or not the legislation helped its intended beneficiaries, the Jews of Russia, it sent an unmistakable message around the world that the Jews of America were not to be trifled with."[40]

The neoconservatives remained loyal Democrats in 1976 and looked with hope toward the presidency of Jimmy Carter. But the neoconservatives soon came to realize that Carter did not seem to perceive a dire Soviet expansionist threat. From the neocon viewpoint, the Soviet Union was advancing around the globe while Carter appeared to lack the will to resist. Norman Podhoretz would maintain that under Carter, the United States "continued and even accelerated the strategic retreat begun under the Republicans."[41]

Moreover, Carter pursued policies that went directly against what the neoconservatives considered to be Jewish interests, especially in his failure to provide sufficient support for Israel. The neoconservatives were alarmed by the Carter administration's attempt to pursue what it styled an even-handed approach in the Middle East, fearing that Israel would be pressured to withdraw from the occupied territories, with only minor border modifications, in return for Arab promises of peace. What especially caused neoconservative outrage was the media revelation that UN Ambassador Andrew Young had a secret meeting in New York with the United Nation's Palestinian Liberation Organization observer. Reports surfaced that Israeli intelligence had recorded the diplomats' conversation and leaked it to the American press. Negotiating with the PLO was a violation of American policy. Young was one of the pre-eminent black leaders in the America and blacks made up a key part of Carter's constituency. Faced with strong Jewish protests, Carter replaced Young at the UN. However, his successor, Donald McHenry, supported a Security Council resolution declaring Jerusalem to be occupied territory and charging Israel with extraordinary human rights violations, which led to further Jewish outrage. As a result of these activities, Friedman writes, "Carter ... was seen by neocons as fundamentally hostile to Israel."[42]

By the beginning of 1980, the neoconservatives had given up on the Democratic Party. According to John Ehrman, a historian of neoconservatism:

> In the neoconservatives' view, its foreign policies were firmly in the hands of the left and the party no longer opposed anti-Semitism or totalitarian thinking – indeed, they believed that these tendencies were now in the party's mainstream.[43]

The neoconservatives gravitated to the Republicans where they found kindred spirits among that party's staunchly anti-Communist conservative wing, which was also disenchanted with the détente policy of the Nixon and Ford administrations. It was only among the right-wing Republicans where there still remained firm support for the idea that Soviet Communism was an evil and implacable ideological enemy – an attitude that the conventional wisdom of the times looked upon as outdated and gauche.[44]

Welcomed in as valuable intellectual allies by the conservative Republicans, the neoconservatives had made their momentous shift just as the most successful right-wing Republican of the modern era, Ronald Reagan, won the presidential election of 1980.

Despite being newcomers to the conservative camp, neoconservatives were able to find places in the Reagan administration in national security and foreign policy areas, although at less than Cabinet-level status. "Reagan's triumph in the election," Friedman contends, "provided the neocons with their version of John F. Kennedy's Camelot."[45]

A fundamental reason for their success was that the neoconservatives had the academic and literary standing and public reputations, which traditional conservatives lacked. The neoconservatives had published widely in prestigious establishment intellectual journals. Some had impressive academic backgrounds and influential contacts in political and media circles. This is not to say that neoconservatives necessarily exhibited superior intellectual skills or academic scholarship compared to many traditional conservative intellectuals, but rather that they possessed establishment

credentials and respectability. The fact that they had recently espoused liberal positions bolstered their credibility in the establishment. None had
ever expressed rightist views that might be considered taboo from the liberal perspective. Consequently, they could not be easily ignored, ridiculed
or smeared, as could many marginalized traditional conservatives. Reagan
political strategists believed that neocons could serve as effective public
exponents of administration policy.[46] It should also be added that the more
illustrious neoconservatives tended to bring in other, usually younger, neocons with negligible scholarly or public achievements.[47]

Significant neoconservatives in the Reagan administration included
Richard Perle, assistant secretary of defense for international security policy; Paul Wolfowitz, assistant secretary of state for East Asian and Pacific
affairs and later ambassador to Indonesia; Elliott Abrams, assistant secretary of state for human rights and later as assistant secretary of state for
hemispheric affairs, where he played a central role in aiding the Contras in
the Iran-Contra affair, for which he was indicted; Jeane Kirkpatrick, ambassador to the United Nations (who had on her staff such neocons as Joshua
Muravchik and Carl Gershman);[48] Kenneth Adelman, director of the Arms
Control and Disarmament Agency, 1983–1987; Richard Pipes, member of
the National Security Council on Soviet and East European affairs; and
Max Kampelman, ambassador and head of the United States delegation to
the negotiations with the Soviet Union on nuclear and space arms, 1985–89.
Michael Ledeen was a special advisor to Secretary of State Alexander Haig
in 1981–1982, consultant for the Department of Defense (1982–1986), and a
national security advisor to the president, who was intimately involved in
the Iran-Contra scandal. Frank Gaffney and Douglas Feith served under
Perle in the Defense Department. Feith also served as a member of the National Security Staff under Richard Allen in Reagan's first term.

In the Reagan administration, the neoconservatives allied with the militant right-wing anti-Communists and combated Republican establishment
elements in order to fashion a hard-line anti-Soviet foreign policy. Neoconservatives were in the forefront of pressing for Reagan's military build-up and
de-emphasizing arms control agreements, which had been a foreign policy
centerpiece of previous administrations, both Republican and Democrat.[49]

In contrast to the longstanding American defensive Cold War strategy
of containing Soviet communism, the neoconservatives pushed for destabilizing the Soviet empire and its allies. They did not invent this strate-

gic doctrine, which originated with such seminal conservative thinkers as James Burnham and Robert Strausz-Hupe. The goal behind this offensive strategy was to actually bring about the defeat of the Soviet Union, instead of just achieving stalemate, which would be the best that could be obtained by defensive containment. But while not the originators of an offensive Cold War strategy, the neocons were the first to successfully promote its implementation.[50]

In their effort to implement the offensive Cold War strategy, the neocons especially supported the provision of extensive military aid to the militant Islamic Afghan "freedom fighters" in their resistance struggle against the Soviet occupation. The military aid, which had begun in the Carter administration, had been very limited. Richard Perle played a pivotal role in equipping the "freedom fighters" with the all-important shoulder-borne Stinger missiles, which proved to be lethal to the previously invincible Soviet helicopter gunships.[51] Ironically, the neoconservatives now portray these very same Muslims that they helped to militarize as a deadly terrorist threat to America and the world.

The neocons played a significant role in the success of Reagan's policies. Steven Hayward, an AEI fellow and the author of *The Age of Reagan*, maintains that "Ronald Reagan would not have been elected and would have been able to govern us effectively without some of the prominent neoconservatives who joined the Republican side."[52] Murray Friedman writes, "The neocons reinforced Reagan's hard-line beliefs on international communism and provided much of the administration's ideological energy, giving the Reagan revolution 'its final sophistication.'"[53]

In essence, the neocons did not invent a new strategy for international relations, but lent an air of establishment respectability to doctrines that had been in the repertoire of the American right from the early days of the Cold War. The related elements of sophistication and respectability contributed by the neocons were very important because the hard-line policies implemented by Reagan had traditionally been ridiculed and reviled by the liberal establishment as being completely beyond the pale.[54] The liberal establishment pedigrees of the neocon Reaganites and the power in the media exerted by such neocon instruments as *Commentary* magazine were able to partially deflect the liberal media criticism, preventing Reagan from being successfully caricatured as a zany right-wing warmonger, as had often been the case with previous conservative leaders.[55]

Admirers credit the neoconservatives with playing a major role in bringing about the demise of the Soviet Union.[56] "History has proved the neoconservatives largely right on the Cold War," writes Gal Beckerman in the
Forward.

> Among the many factors that brought an end to the Soviet Union – already a
> dying animal by the 1980s – was the shove given to it by this rhetoric. By chal-
> lenging the Soviet Union head on, rhetorically, in covert action and through an
> expensively renewed arms race, the United States managed to call the Soviet
> bluff. Neoconservatives provided language that depicted the Cold War as an ur-
> gent zero-sum game in which America the Good had to assert itself so that Evil
> Communism could be obliterated. And indeed, the Soviet Union collapsed.[57]

However, critics of the neocons point out that Reagan, during his second
term, moved toward rapprochement with Gorbachev's Soviet Union – a
move that was strongly resisted by the hard-line neoconservatives – and
that it was that softer approach that allowed Gorbachev to enact his reforms, bringing about the unraveling of the Soviet empire. Historian John
Patrick Diggins observes that the difference between the neoconservatives
and Reagan was that

> he believed in negotiation and they in escalation. They wanted to win the cold
> war; he sought to end it. To do so, it was necessary not to strike fear in the
> Soviet Union but to win the confidence of its leaders. Once the Soviet Union
> could count on Mr. Reagan, Mr. Gorbachev not only was free to embark on
> his domestic reforms, to convince his military to go along with budget cuts, to
> reassure his people that they no longer needed to worry about the old bogey of
> "capitalist encirclement," but, most important, he was also ready to announce
> to the Soviet Union's satellite countries that henceforth they were on their own,
> that no longer would tanks of the Red Army be sent to put down uprisings. The
> cold war ended in an act of faith and trust, not fear and trembling.[58]

Even if Reagan's moderation of the neoconservative hard-line anti-Soviet policy ultimately induced the voluntary unraveling of the Soviet empire, nonetheless, it seems reasonable to believe that the hard-line policies
espoused and implemented by neocon Reaganites helped move the Soviet
Union to that position. During the 1970s, expert opinion considered the
Soviet regime quite sturdy, notwithstanding the country's economic difficulties; no one envisioned, at the time, the regime's inevitable collapse
within the decades that followed. And this was the vision that guided
American policy in the Nixon, Ford, and Carter administrations. Nor was
any Soviet leader, Mikhail Gorbachev included, seeking the downfall of

the Soviet system and its military machine. With all this in mind, it would seem to be a mistake to discount or deny the neoconservative contribution to the downfall of the seemingly invulnerable Soviet empire at the end of the 1980s – a downfall that, most incredibly, did not involve a major military confrontation. From the American perspective, it can be seen as a major victory.

The role of the neoconservatives in the Reagan administration is highly relevant to the thesis of this book. For if it is appropriate to perceive the neocons as influential regarding Reagan administration foreign policy, one should be able to connect them to Bush II's war on Iraq and his overall Middle East policy. In fact, as the following pages illustrate, the neocons were far more powerful during the Bush II administration than they had been during Reagan's time, both inside and outside of government. In the Reagan era, they were relative newcomers; by the time of the Bush II era, they had become an established, institutionalized force. Moreover, in the Reagan administration the neocons were basically implementing an anti-Soviet policy, which had long been the staple position of the traditional right and, consequently, they had extensive support from numerous administration figures of a traditional conservative bent and from President Ronald Reagan himself; in the Bush II administration, in contrast, the neocons single-handedly converted the administration to their Middle East war agenda, overcoming significant internal opposition in the process.

A fundamental point about neoconservatives, which is not always noted, is that they did not become traditional conservatives. Instead of adopting traditional American conservative positions, they actually altered the content of conservatism to their liking. Neoconservatives have been anything but the hard right-wingers that their leftist critics sometimes make them out to be. Neoconservatives supported the modern welfare state, in contrast to the traditional conservatives, who emphasized small government, states' rights, and relatively unfettered capitalism. Neoconservatives identified with the liberal policies of Franklin Delano Roosevelt and even Lyndon Johnson, the bête noires of traditional conservatives, though rejecting much of the multiculturalism and group entitlements of more recent liberalism. "The neoconservative impulse," Murray Friedman maintains, "was the spontaneous response of a group of liberal intellectuals, mainly Jewish, who sought to shape a perspective of their own while standing apart from more traditional forms of conservatism."[59] Gary Dorrien in *The Neoconservative Mind* points out that the neoconservatives "did not convert to existing conservatism, but rather created an alternative to it."[60]

What especially characterizes neoconservatives is their focus on foreign policy. This is underscored by the fact that some who have espoused leftist views on domestic matters, such as Carl Gershman and Joshua Muravchik (who have been members of the Social Democrats USA), can be full-fledged members of the neoconservative network by virtue of their identification with neocon foreign policy positions.[61]

Although the American conservatives of the Cold War era were anti-Communist and pro-military, they did not identify with the strong globalist foreign policy, which is the sine qua non of neoconservatism, but actually harbored a strain of isolationism. Conservatives' interventionism was limited to fighting Communism, even rolling back Communism, but not nation-building and the export of democracy, which is the expressed goal of the neocons. Conservatives were perfectly comfortable with regimes that were far from democratic. Nor did traditional conservatives view the United States as the policeman of the world. Most significantly, traditional conservatives had never championed Israel, which had largely been the position of the liberal Democrats.[62]

While traditional conservatives welcomed neoconservatives as allies in their fight against Soviet Communism and domestic liberalism, the neocons in effect acted as a Trojan Horse within conservatism: they managed to secure dominant positions in the conservative political and intellectual movement, and as soon as they gained power they purged those traditional conservatives who opposed their agenda. "The old conservatives of the eighties were being swallowed up by the alliance that they initiated and sustained," notes historian Paul Gottfried.[63]

Neoconservatives were especially active in setting up or co-opting various right-of-center think tanks and corralling the money that funded them. "Neoconservative activists," Gottfried observes, "have largely succeeded in centralizing both the collection and distribution of funding for right-of-center philanthropies."[64]

The neocons would even take over that great intellectual citadel of the conservative movement, the *National Review*, founded by the icon of the

Cold War right, Bill Buckley. As Gary Dorrien writes in *Imperial Designs*, "By the late 1990s even the venerable *National Review* belonged to the neocons, who boasted that they had created or taken over nearly all of the main ideological institutions of the American right."[65]

The ultimate result of the neoconservatives' maneuvering was to effectively transform American conservatism and, to a lesser extent, the Republican Party. Jacob Heilbrunn, senior editor at the liberal *New Republic*, would write in 2004 that neoconservatives "formed, by and large, the intellectual brain trust for the GOP over the past two decades."[66]

Some intellectual conservatives, who eventually took on the name paleoconservatives, tried to resist this takeover from the days of the Reagan administration.[67] "Long before French protesters and liberal bloggers had even heard of the neoconservatives, the paleoconservatives were locked in mortal combat with them," wrote Franklin Foer in the *New York Times*.

> Paleocons fought neocons over whom Ronald Reagan should appoint to head the National Endowment for the Humanities, angrily denouncing them as closet liberals – or worse, crypto-Trotskyists. Even their self-selected name, paleocon, suggests disdain for the neocons and their muscular interventionism.[68]

In essence, the neoconservatives are not like the traditional American conservatives, whom they have effectively supplanted and marginalized. As Paul Gottfried observes, the transformation of American conservatism involved

> personnel no less than value orientation . . . as urban, Jewish, erstwhile Democratic proponents of the welfare state took over a conservative movement that had been largely in the hands of Catholic, pro-[Joe] McCarthy and (more or less) anti-New Deal Republicans. That the older movement collapsed into the newer one is a demonstrable fact.[69]

The neoconservatives have done nearly the same thing in the Republican party, at least in regard to its national security policy; there they have replaced not only the traditional conservative figures, but also the more moderate establishment wing that was identified with the elder George H. W. Bush. The upshot of all this is to say the neocon influence is very substantial. As Murray Friedman writes in his *The Neoconservative Revolution:* "The most enduring legacy of neoconservatism . . . has been the creation of a new generation of highly influential younger conservative Jewish intel-

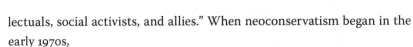

lectuals, social activists, and allies." When neoconservatism began in the early 1970s,

> the movement consisted of perhaps two dozen individuals. Their numbers today [2005] have increased to hundreds of individuals threaded throughout the news media, think tanks, political life, government, and the universities .... Their influence has been felt everywhere.[70]

None of this is to say that neoconservatism is anything like a mass movement. It has, however, ascended to the heights of power. While the grass roots conservatives and Republicans do not know, much less subscribe to, the full neoconservative agenda, the trauma of 9/11 and the "war on terror" made them largely unwitting followers of the neocon leadership. The post-9/11 success of the neoconservatives and their war agenda will be discussed at length in the following chapters.

Neoconservatives have not been unaware of their successful takeover of the conservative movement. Irving Kristol, who has championed "a conservative welfare state," writes that

> one can say that the historical task and political purpose of neoconservatism would seem to be this: to convert the Republican party, and American conservatism in general, against their respective wills, into a new kind of conservative politics suitable to governing a modern democracy.[71]

In his 1996 book, *The Essential Neoconservative Reader,* editor Mark Gerson, a neocon himself who served on the board of directors of the Project for the New American Century, jubilantly observes:

> The neoconservatives have so changed conservatism that what we now identify as conservatism is largely what was once neoconservatism. And in so doing, they have defined the way that vast numbers of Americans view their economy, their polity, and their society.[72]

Friedman, in *The Neoconservative Revolution,* sums up the major impact that neocons have had on conservatism, and, in so doing, is not averse to emphasizing their Jewish orientation: "This book suggests that Jews and non-Jews alike are becoming more conservative, in part because of their neoconservative guides, who have made it more respectable to think in these terms." He suggests that the motivation of the neoconservatives derives from the beneficent impulse inherent in Judaism: "The idea that Jews have been put on earth to make it a better, perhaps even a holy, place continues to shape their worldview and that of many of their co-religionists."[73]

A more negative result of neoconservative takeover has been presented by the rightist evolutionary biologist Kevin MacDonald, who likewise focuses on the issue of Jewishness. MacDonald contends that the

> intellectual and cumulative effect of neoconservatism and its current hegemony over the conservative political movement in the United States (achieved partly by its large influence on the media and among foundations) has been to shift the conservative movement toward the center and, in effect, to define the limits of conservative legitimacy. Clearly, these limits of conservative legitimacy are defined by whether they conflict with specifically Jewish group interests in a minimally restrictive immigration policy, support for Israel, global democracy, opposition to quotas and affirmative action, and so on.

Significantly, MacDonald holds that

> [t]he ethnic agenda of neoconservatism can also be seen in their promotion of the idea that the United States should pursue a highly interventionist foreign policy aimed at global democracy and the interests of Israel rather than aimed at the specific national interests of the United States.[74]

Although neoconservatives of the Reagan era were adamantly pro-Israel, the issue of Israel versus the Arab states of the Middle East did not loom large then. Israel did have a favored place in American foreign policy. Neoconservative Reaganites identified Israel as America's "strategic asset" in the Cold War, and Israel actually helped the United States fight communism in Latin America and elsewhere.[75] J. J. Goldberg maintains that

> the Reagan administration set about making itself into the most pro-Israel administration in history. In the fall of 1981, Israel was permitted for the first time to sign a formal military pact with Washington, becoming a partner, not a stepchild, of American policy. Israel and American embarked on a series of joint adventures, both overt and covert: aiding the Nicaraguan contras, training security forces in Zaire, sending arms secretly to Iran. Cooperation in weapons development, sharing of technology, and information and intelligence reached unprecedented proportions. Israel's annual U. S. aid package, already higher than any other country's, was edged even higher. Loans were made into grants. Supplemental grants were added.[76]

Despite its support for Israel, the United States under Reagan also relied heavily on Arab and Islamic governments to counter Soviet influence, sometimes to the consternation of neoconservatives and other proponents of Israel, as when the Reagan administration successfully pushed for the sale of early warning radar aircraft (AWACS) to Saudi Arabia in 1981.[77] On the whole, however, the issue of Israel versus other Middle Eastern countries would not move to the forefront until the end of the Cold War during the administration of President George H. W. Bush (1989–1993). But before we continue with this history of the American neoconservatives, it is appropriate to examine developments in Israel.

chapter 4

THE ISRAELI ORIGINS OF THE MIDDLE EAST WAR AGENDA

WHILE THE NEOCONSERVATIVES were the driving force for the American invasion of Iraq, and the attendant efforts to bring about regime change throughout the Middle East, the idea for such a war did not originate with American neocon thinkers but rather in Israel. An obvious linkage exists between the war position of the neoconservatives and what has been the long-time strategy of the Israeli right, and to a lesser extent, of the Israeli mainstream.

The idea of a Middle East war had been bandied about in Israel for many years as a means of enhancing Israeli security. War would serve two purposes. It would improve Israel's external security by weakening and splintering Israel's neighbors. Moreover, such a war and the consequent weakening of Israel's external enemies would serve to resolve the internal Palestinian demographic problem, since the Palestinian resistance depends upon material and moral support from Israel's neighboring states.

A brief look at the history of the Zionist movement and its goals will help to provide an understanding of this issue. The Zionist goal of creating an exclusive Jewish state in Palestine was complicated by the fundamental problem that the country was already settled with a non-Jewish population. Despite public rhetoric to the contrary, the idea of expelling the indigenous Palestinian population (euphemistically referred to as a "transfer") was an integral part of the Zionist effort to found a Jewish national state in Palestine. "The idea of transfer had accompanied the Zionist movement from its very beginnings, first appearing in Theodore Herzl's diary," Israeli historian Tom Segev observes.

> In practice, the Zionists began executing a mini-transfer from the time they began purchasing the land and evacuating the Arab tenants . . . . "Disappearing" the Arabs lay at the heart of the Zionist dream, and was also a necessary condition of its existence . . . . With few exceptions, none of the Zionists disputed the desirability of forced transfer – or its morality. However, the Zionist leaders learned not to publicly proclaim their mass expulsion intent because this would cause the Zionists to lose the world's sympathy.[1]

The challenge was to find an opportune time to initiate the mass expulsion process when it would not incur the world's condemnation. In the late 1930s, Ben-Gurion wrote: "What is inconceivable in normal times is possible in revolutionary times; and if at this time the opportunity is missed and what is possible in such great hours is not carried out – a whole world is lost."[2] The "revolutionary times" would come with the first Arab-Israeli war in 1948, when the Zionists were able to expel 750,000 Palestinians (more than 80 percent of the indigenous population), and thus achieve an overwhelmingly Jewish state. Leading Israeli historian Benny Morris has concluded that the expulsion of Palestinians by the Zionist leadership was a deliberate policy. "Of course. Ben-Gurion was a transferist," Morris asserted in a *Ha'aretz* interview with Ari Shavit in January 2004. "He understood that there could be no Jewish state with a large and hostile Arab minority in its midst. There would be no such state. It would not be able to exist."[3]

Many in the Israeli leadership did not think that the original 1948 boundaries of the country included enough territory for a viable country, much less the longed-for entirety of Palestine, or the "Land of Israel." The opportunity to acquire additional land came as a result of the 1967 war; however, the occupation of the additional territory brought the problem of a large Palestinian population. World opinion was now totally opposed to forced population transfers, equating such an activity with the unspeakable horror of Nazism. The landmark Fourth Geneva Convention, ratified in 1949, had "unequivocally prohibited deportation" of civilians under occupation.[4]

Since the 1967 war, the major issue in Israeli politics has been what to do with that conquered territory and its Palestinian population. A fundamental concern has been the significantly higher birth rate of the Palestinians. Demographers have pointed out that by 2020 the Jewish population of

Israel proper and the occupied territories would be a minority. This would threaten the very Jewish identity of Israel, which is the very reason for its existence.[5] "In fact," historian Baruch Kimmerling notes, "the loss of that demographic majority could be a prelude to politicide and the physical elimination of the state."[6]

The concern about a Palestinian demographic threat to the Jewish state was intimately related to the belief in the need for war against Israel's external enemies. Because the Zionist project of creating an exclusive Jewish state was opposed by Israel's neighbors, the idea of weakening and dissolving Israel's Middle East neighbors was not just an idea of the Israeli right but was a central Zionist goal from a much earlier period, having been promoted by David Ben-Gurion himself. As Saleh Abdel-Jawwad, a professor at Birzeit University in Ramallah, Palestine writes:

> Israel has supported secessionist movements in Sudan, Iraq, Egypt and Lebanon and any secessionist movements in the Arab world which Israel considers an enemy. Yet the concern for Iraq and its attempts to weaken or prevent it from developing its strengths has always been a central Zionist objective. At times, Israel succeeded in gaining a foothold in Iraq by forging secret yet strong relationships with leaders from the Kurdish movement.[7]

It was during the Suez crisis in 1956 that Prime Minister Ben-Gurion would present a comprehensive plan, which he himself called "fantastic," to representatives of the British and French governments to reconfigure the Middle East. This took place in secret discussions in Sèvres, France in October 22–4, 1956, where the plot was worked out by officials of the three states to attack Egypt with the goal of taking over the recently-nationalized Suez Canal and ultimately removing Egyptian President Gamal Abdel Nasser, who as the leader of Arab nationalism, was seen as a threat to Western and Israeli interests.[8]

Ben-Gurion's comprehensive plan would have greatly expanded the war objectives. He called for the division of Jordan, with Israel gaining control of the West Bank as a semi-autonomous region. The remainder of Jordan would go to Iraq, then run by a pro-Western monarchy, in return for the latter's promise to resettle Palestinian refugees there and make peace with Israel. Israel would also expand northward to the Litani River in Lebanon, an area inhabited mainly by Muslims, thus serving to turn rump Lebanon into a more compact Christian country. The Straits of Tiran in the Gulf of Aqaba would also come under Israeli control. These changes would take place after the replacement of Nasser's regime with a pro-Western government, which would make peace with Israel. Ben-Gurion's proposal failed to generate support. The French, who were the major force behind the war plot, emphasized the need for immediate action, which precluded the move for more expansive war objectives. Needing French support for the anti-Nasser venture, Ben-Gurion backed away from his broader geostrategic scheme.[9]

Israel's goal has been not simply to weaken external enemies, but, by so doing, also isolate and weaken the position of the Palestinians – the internal demographic threat that poses the greatest danger to the Jewish supremacist state. Kimmerling refers to the Palestinians as Israel's only "existential" enemy because "only the stateless Palestinians could have a moral and historical claim against the entire Jewish entity established in 1948 on the ruins of their society."[10] The neighboring Arab states thus threaten Israel by providing spiritual and material aid to the Palestinian cause. Without outside aid the Palestinians would give up hope and be more apt to acquiesce in whatever solution the Israeli government might offer. Abdel-Jawwad writes:

> Sequential wars with the Arab world have given Israel opportunities to exhaust the Arab world, as well as tipping the demographic and political situation against Palestinians. Even regional wars which Israel has not participated in have benefited Israel and weakened the Palestinian national movement. The first and second Gulf War are a few examples.

Abdel-Jawwad goes on: "Finally, the second Gulf War of 1991 resulted in the expulsion of the Palestinian community from Kuwait, which formed one of the primary arteries of Palestinian income and power in the occupied territories."[11]

In general, however, during the first phase of Israel's existence with the left in power, the idea of using offensive war to bring about regime change and regional reconfiguration tended to be only a small undercurrent in the government's strategic thinking. With the coming to power of the right-wing Likud government in 1977 under Prime Minister Menachem Begin, Israel would pursue a more militant policy where war would be seen as the major means of improving Israel's geostrategic situation. Historian Ilan Peleg in *Begin's Foreign Policy, 1977–1983* refers to this dramatic change as the start of Israel's "second republic."[12] Peleg writes:

> Begin quickly deserted the traditional defensive posture [of the Israeli left], of which he was highly critical in the first three decades of Israel when he was

in the opposition. He adopted an offensive posture characterized by grandiose expansionist goals, extensive and frequent use of Israel's military machine, and political compellence rather than military deterrence as a controlling factor.

Begin

> did not believe that coexistence between Jews and Arabs – in Israel, on the West Bank, or in the region in general – was possible. He was determined to establish Israeli hegemony in the area, a new balance of power in which Israel would be completely dominant.[13]

The right had not governed Israel until 1977, and while there was not a total dichotomy between the left and right regarding internal and external relations with Arabs, the Israeli right had been the most militant in its policies toward the Palestinians and toward Israel's Arab neighbors – beliefs that rested on a strong ideological foundation.

The Israeli right originated in Revisionist Zionism, whose founder and spiritual guide was the gifted writer Ze'ev Jabotinsky. Jabotinsky protested the exclusion of Transjordan from British Mandate Palestine, and in response he established the Revisionist Party in 1925, which was so named because it sought to "revise" the terms of the League of Nations Mandate by the re-inclusion of Transjordan in Mandatory Palestine. Its policies were characterized by the quest for "Eretz Israel" – which, at the minimum, entailed complete Jewish control of all land on both sides of the Jordan River – and also by the primacy of military force in foreign policy matters. Peleg writes: "Jabotinsky's approach to the conflict came to be dominated by popular ideas of 'blood and soil,' a Jewish version of Social Darwinism."[14]

Jabotinsky's most remembered phrase was the "iron wall," the name of an essay he wrote in 1923. Jabotinsky's essay holds that the Arabs would never voluntarily accept a Jewish state and would naturally fight it. To survive, the Jewish state would have to establish an "iron wall" of military force that would crush all opposition and force its Arab enemies into hopelessness. From this position of unassailable strength, the Jewish state could make, or dictate, peace.[15] It was the "iron wall" strategy that would characterize the thinking of the Israeli right, and to a certain extent, as historian Avi Shlaim points out, the Israeli left and the State of Israel itself.[16]

It was inevitable that Israel under the leadership of Menachem Begin would follow the hard-line policy of Jabotinsky. In fact, historical events had made Begin and his followers even more militant than Jabotinsky.[17] The more militant radicalism resulted from Begin's leadership of the terrorist Irgun, which fought the British and Palestinians in the 1940s, and the trauma of World War II and Nazism in Germany. Begin tended to view all criticism of Israel as tantamount to "anti-Semitism" and the militant resistance of the Arabs as comparable to Nazi genocide.[18]

With the beginning of independent Israel in 1948, Begin headed the Herut Party. But it was not until the formation of the Likud bloc of right-wing parties in 1973, of which the Herut constituted the central core, that the right had the chance to win enough votes to govern.

The first Begin government in 1977 had its moderate and restraining elements, and its crowning achievement was the Camp David Accords with Egypt. Defense Minister Ezer Weizman, along with Foreign Minister Moshe Dayan, steered Begin away from his warlike instincts. With the departure of these moderates, the Begin Cabinet became dominated by more militant individuals, the most important of whom was Ariel Sharon, who served as Defense Minister from 1981 to 1983. Sharon, who came from a military background involving counter-terrorism and even terrorism, translated Begin's hard-line attitude into actual policy.[19]

With the Likud's assumption of power, the most far-reaching militant proposals entered mainstream Zionist thinking, involving militant destabilization of Israel's neighbors and Palestinian expulsion. An important article in this genre was by Oded Yinon, entitled "A Strategy for Israel in the 1980s," which appeared in the World Zionist Organization's periodical *Kivunim* (Directions) in February 1982. Yinon had been attached to the Foreign Ministry and his article undoubtedly reflected high-level thinking in the Israeli military and intelligence establishment. According to Peleg,

> The Yinon article was an authentic mirror of the thinking mode of the Israeli right at the height of Begin's rule; it reflected a sense of unlimited and unrestrained power . . . . There can be no question that the hard-core Neo-Revisionist camp as a whole subscribed, at least until the Lebanese fiasco, to ideas similar to those of Yinon.[20]

Yinon called for Israel to bring about the dissolution of many of the Arab states and their fragmentation into a mosaic of ethnic and sectarian groupings. Yinon believed that this would not be a difficult undertaking because nearly all the Arab states were afflicted with internal ethnic and religious divisions. In essence, the end result would be a Middle East of powerless ministates that could in no way confront Israeli power. Lebanon, then facing divisive chaos, was Yinon's model for the entire Middle East. Yinon wrote:

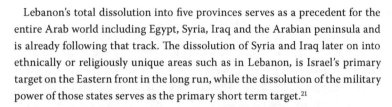

> Lebanon's total dissolution into five provinces serves as a precedent for the entire Arab world including Egypt, Syria, Iraq and the Arabian peninsula and is already following that track. The dissolution of Syria and Iraq later on into ethnically or religiously unique areas such as in Lebanon, is Israel's primary target on the Eastern front in the long run, while the dissolution of the military power of those states serves as the primary short term target.[21]

Note that Yinon sought the dissolution of countries – Egypt and Saudi Arabia – that were allied to the United States.

Yinon looked upon Iraq as a major target for dissolution, and he believed that the then on-going Iran-Iraq war would promote its break-up. It should be pointed out that Yinon's vision for Iraq seems uncannily like what has actually taken place since the U.S. invasion in 2003. Yinon wrote:

> Iraq, rich in oil on the one hand and internally torn on the other, is guaranteed as a candidate for Israel's targets. Its dissolution is even more important for us than that of Syria. Iraq is stronger than Syria. In the short run it is Iraqi power which constitutes the greatest threat to Israel. An Iraqi-Iranian war will tear Iraq apart and cause its downfall at home even before it is able to organize a struggle on a wide front against us. Every kind of inter-Arab confrontation will assist us in the short run and will shorten the way to the more important aim of breaking up Iraq into denominations as in Syria and in Lebanon. In Iraq, a division into provinces along ethnic/religious lines as in Syria during Ottoman times is possible. So, three (or more) states will exist around the three major cities: Basra, Baghdad and Mosul, and Shiite areas in the south will separate from the Sunni and Kurdish north.[22]

Yinon's prediction that war would bring about the religious/ethnic fragmentation of Iraq fits in quite closely with the actual reality of the aftermath of the United States invasion in 2003, with the division among Shiite, Sunni, and Kurds positively fostered by the occupation government in Iraq.[23] Certainly, his forecast in 1982 was far more accurate than the neocons' rosy public prognostications prior to the 2003 invasion about the easy emergence of democracy. But from the Likudnik perspective, the reality of a fragmented Iraq was much to be preferred to the neocon pipe dream.

Significantly, the goal of Israeli hegemony was inextricably tied to the expulsion of the Palestinians. "Whether in war or under conditions of peace," Yinon asserted,

> emigration from the territories and economic demographic freeze in them, are the guarantees for the coming change on both banks of the river, and we ought to be active in order to accelerate this process in the nearest future.

In Yinon's view,

> It should be clear, under any future political situation or military constella-
> tion, that the solution of the problem of the indigenous Arabs will come only
> when they recognize the existence of Israel in secure borders up to the Jordan
> river and beyond it, as our existential need in this difficult epoch, the nucle-
> ar epoch which we shall soon enter. It is no longer possible to live with three
> fourths of the Jewish population on the dense shoreline which is so dangerous
> in a nuclear epoch.[24]

In a foreword to his English translation of Yinon's piece, Israel Shahak,
a noted Jewish Israeli critic of Zionism, made the interesting comparison
between the neoconservative position and actual Likudnik goals.

> The strong connection with Neo-Conservative thought in the USA is very
> prominent, especially in the author's notes. But, while lip service is paid to the
> idea of the "defense of the West" from Soviet power, the real aim of the author,
> and of the present Israeli establishment is clear: To make an Imperial Israel
> into a world power. In other words, the aim of Sharon is to deceive the Ameri-
> cans after he has deceived all the rest.[25]

To reiterate, the Yinon article embodied the general thrust of Likud
strategists of the early 1980s. As Noam Chomsky wrote in *Fateful Triangle*: "much of what Yinon discusses is quite close to mainstream thinking."
Chomsky described the Israeli incursion into Lebanon in 1982 as representing an attempt to implement Yinon's geostrategy.

> The "new order" that Israel is attempting to impose in Lebanon is based on a
> conception not unlike what Yinon expresses, and there is every reason to sup-
> pose that similar ideas with regard to Syria may seem attractive to the political
> leadership.[26]

To bolster his thesis regarding Likudnik war strategy, Chomsky discussed an analytical article by Yoram Peri – former Adviser to Prime Minister Yitzhak Rabin and European representative of the Labor Party, and a
specialist on civil-military relations in Israel – which came out in the Labor
party journal *Davar* in October 1982. Peri described a "true revolution" in
"military-diplomatic conception," which he dated to the coming to power of
the Likudniks. (Chomsky saw the shift as being more gradual and "deeply-
rooted" in the Israeli elite.) Summarizing Peri, Chomsky wrote:

> The earlier conception [during the reign of the leftwing Zionists] was based
> on the search for "coexistence" and maintenance of the status quo. Israel aimed
> at a peaceful settlement in which its position in the region would be recognized

and its security achieved. The new conception is based on the goal of "hegemony," not "coexistence." No longer a status quo power, having achieved military dominance as the world's fourth most powerful military force, and no longer believing in even the possibility of peace or even its desirability except in terms of Israeli hegemony, Israel is now committed to "destabilization" of the region, including Lebanon, Syria, Saudi Arabia and Jordan. In accordance with the new conception, Israel should now use its military dominance to expand its borders and "to create a new reality," a "new order," rather than seek recognition within the status quo.[27]

Destabilization of its surrounding enemies would seem to be a perfectly rational strategy for Israel. Certainly, all countries, if they had enemies, would prefer them to be weak rather than strong. As Chomsky pointed out:

> It is only natural to expect that Israel will seek to destabilize the surrounding states, for essentially the reasons that lead South Africa on a similar course in its region. In fact, given continuing military tensions, that might be seen virtually as a security imperative. A plausible long-term goal might be what some have called an "Ottomanization" of the region, that is, a return to something like the system of the Ottoman empire, with a powerful center (Turkey then, Israel with U.S.-backing now) and much of the region fragmented into ethnic-religious communities, preferably mutually hostile.[28]

Peri, however, thought that this destabilization policy would ultimately harm Israel because it would alienate the United States, upon whom Israel's security ultimately depended. Chomsky summarized Peri's critical stance:

> The reason is that the U.S. is basically a status quo power itself, opposed to destabilization of the sort to which Israel is increasingly committed. The new strategic conception is based on an illusion of power, and may lead to a willingness, already apparent in some of the rhetoric heard in Israel, to undertake military adventures even without U.S. support.[29]

Israel embarked on just such a unilateral adventure in its invasion of Lebanon in 1982. And the disastrous result demonstrated the grave limitations of a unilateral war-oriented strategy for Israel.

When Israel Defense Forces invaded Lebanon on June 6, 1982, "Operation Peace for Galilee" was announced to the public as a limited operation to remove Palestinian bases. The real objectives of the operation were far more ambitious: to destroy the PLO's military and political infrastructure, to strike a serious blow against Syria, and to install a pro-Israeli Christian regime in Lebanon. Israeli troops advanced far into Lebanon, even beyond

Beirut, coming into conflict with Palestinians, Lebanese Muslims, and Syrians. Despite Israeli's deep military penetration, the objectives remained
unachievable. Israel became ensnared in Lebanon's on-going civil war,
from which it was unable to free itself for the next three years.[30]

Israel's invasion of Lebanon, which caused well-publicized civilian casualties, including the massacre of Palestinians at Sabra and Shatila refugee camps outside Beirut, was a public relations disaster for the Begin
government. World opinion turned against Israel. Strong criticism even
arose in Israel, with Israel's first mass peace movement demonstrating on
the streets of Tel Aviv. The Israeli military was angry about the no-win
war. And recriminations even flew back and forth within the Likud Party
that Defense Minister Sharon had not informed Begin of the extent of the
planned invasion.[31]

Significantly, Israel's brutal actions in Lebanon shook support for the
country in the United States, even among American Jews. On August 12,
1982, President Reagan personally demanded of Begin that Israel stop the
bombardment of Beirut. Later that month, Reagan insisted that Israeli
forces withdraw from West Beirut. Israel quickly complied. Given the fact
that Israel was so heavily dependent on American arms, the Begin government realized that it would severely harm Israel's power if it were to alienate its major sponsor.[32]

The war in Lebanon ultimately led to Begin's resignation in 1983. The
invasion of Lebanon turned out to be Israel's least successful and most unpopular conflict in its history. It was Israel's Vietnam.

The failure in Lebanon led to much soul-searching in Israel. Israeli
foreign policy expert Yehoshafat Harkabi critiqued the overall Likudnik
war-orientation strategy – "Israeli intentions to impose a Pax Israelica on
the Middle East, to dominate the Arab countries and treat them harshly"
– in his significant work, *Israel's Fateful Hour*, published in 1988. Harkabi
believed that Israel did not have the power to achieve the goal of Pax Israelica, given the strength of the Arab states, the large Palestinian population involved, and the vehement opposition of world opinion. Harkabi
hoped that "the failed Israeli attempt to impose a new order in the weakest
Arab state – Lebanon – will disabuse people of similar ambitions in other
territories."[33]

Likudniks, however, did not see the Israeli strategy in the Lebanon debacle to be inherently flawed. Some on the Israeli right held that Israel did

not push hard enough to crush its enemies – that it was affected too much by outside criticism. Harkabi maintained, however, that even if Israeli forces had crossed into Syria and occupied Damascus, Israel still would have failed to achieve true victory, but instead would have brought about an interminable guerilla war. Harkabi wrote that

> [t]he Lebanon War revealed an ongoing Israeli limitation: no matter how complete Israeli military triumph, the strategic results will prove to be limited. Ben-Gurion understood this when he said that Israel could not solve its problems once and for all by war. But this view is in stark contradiction to the spirit of the Jabotinsky-Begin ethos. It is no wonder that those who adhere to it cannot accept that the great event is of no avail.[34]

Harkabi was correct about the "spirit of the Jabotinsky-Begin ethos." To many strategically-minded Likudniks, the fiasco of the 1982 invasion of Lebanon had not disproved the idea that destabilization of the region would be beneficial to Israeli security; nor had it disproved that such destabilization was achievable. Instead, the principal lessons many Likudnik-oriented thinkers drew from Israel's failed Lebanon incursion was that no military campaign to destabilize Israel's enemies could achieve success if it antagonized Israeli public opinion and if it lacked extensive backing from Israel's principal sponsor, the United States.

One person who seemed to have learned these lessons was Ariel Sharon, who had implemented the invasion of Lebanon. As historian Baruch Kimmerling writes in *Politicide: Ariel Sharon's War Against the Palestinians*:

> Sharon [in 1982] faced only two major constraints that curbed him in some measure and prevented him from fully implementing his grand design – American pressure and Israeli public opinion, which was clearly influenced not only by the horror of Sabra and Shatila, but also by the heavy casualties and by the sense that the government had violated an unwritten social contract that the military, which was largely staffed by reserve soldiers, could only be used for consensual wars. Sharon learned this lesson well.[35]

What was needed was a military operation that had American support and did not burden the Israeli population.

But the idea that the United States would back Israeli destabilization efforts, much less act as Israel's proxy to fight its enemies, would have seemed impossible in the 1980s. At that time, U.S. Middle Eastern policy, although supportive of Israel, differed significantly from Israel's on the issue of stability. As Yoram Peri recognized, the United States was supportive of the status quo. While Likudnik thinking focused on destabilizing Israel's Middle East enemies, the fundamental goal of U.S. policy was to promote stable governments in the Middle East that would allow the oil to flow to the Western industrial nations. It was not necessary for oil-rich nations to befriend Israel – in fact, they could openly oppose the Jewish state. The United States worked for peace between Israel and the Arab states, but it was a compromise peace that would try to accommodate some demands of the Arab countries – most crucially demands involving the Palestinians.

Peri had argued that if Israel went off on its own in destabilizing the Middle East, the United States would abandon Israel, to Israel's detriment. What was needed for the Israeli destabilization plan to work was a transformation of American Middle East policy. If the United States adopted the same destabilization policy as Israel, then such a policy could succeed. For the United States' influence among its allies and in the United Nations, where it held a veto, would be enough to shelter Israel from the animosity of world public opinion, preventing it from ending up as a pariah state such as the white-ruled Republic of South Africa. Better yet, though perhaps even unimagined in the 1980s, would be to induce the United States to act in Israel's place to destabilize the region.

Such a policy transformation was impossible in the 1980s. However, through the long-term efforts of the American neoconservatives, that transformation would occur in the Bush II administration. The neocon advocacy of dramatically altering the Middle East status quo stood in stark contrast to the traditional American position of maintaining stability in the area – though it did, of course, mesh perfectly with the long-established Israeli goal of destabilizing its enemies. Virginia Tilley observes in *The One-State Solution* that

> this vision of "dissolving" Iraq and Syria is antithetical to U.S. strategic interests, as it would generate entirely new and unpredictable local governments prone to unexpected policy changes. Nevertheless, it was wholly endorsed by a cohort of neoconservative ideologues, who later gained control of U.S. foreign policy in the administration of the second President Bush and fused Israeli policy into U.S. strategy.[36]

To reiterate the central point of this chapter: the vision of "regime change" in the Middle East through external, militant action originated in Israel, and its sole purpose was to advance the security interests of Israel. It had nothing to do with bringing "democracy" to Muslims. It had nothing to do with any terrorist threat to the United States. These latter arguments accreted to the idea of regime change as the primary military actor changed from Israel to the United States. But the Israeli government would continue to be a fundamental supporter of the regional military action, even as the ostensible justifications for the action changed. Israel advocated the American attack on Iraq and preached the necessity of strong action against Iran.

It would appear that for Ariel Sharon during the Bush II administration, the strategic benefits that would accrue to Israel from such a militant restructuring of the Middle East were the same as those that Likudniks sought in the 1980s. But unlike Begin's failed incursion into Lebanon in 1982, the Bush II effort not only relied upon the much greater power of the United States but was also wrapped in a cover of "democracy" and American national interest, effectively masking the objective of Israel hegemony. That helps to explain the much greater success of this intervention, which has come at no cost to Israel – but at a heavy cost to the United States.

chapter 5

STABILITY AND THE GULF WAR OF 1991:
PREFIGUREMENT AND PRELUDE TO THE 2003 IRAQ WAR

THE WATCHWORD for American policy in the Middle East was stability, which was perceived as a fundamental prerequisite for maintaining the vital flow of oil to the West. In its quest for stability in the Middle East, the post-World War II U.S. supported the conservative monarchies of Saudi Arabia and the Gulf sheikdoms, and opposed radical elements that threatened to disturb the status quo.

American security policy was quite different from the position of Israel, especially the Likudnik goal of having Israel surrounded by weak, fragmented statelets. The position of the United States was to defend Israel's existence, but within the broader framework of regional stability. As Virginia Tilley writes in *The One-State Solution*:

> Every president before Bush recognized that although Israel and the United States are fast allies, their interests in the Middle East are very different. Israel is a local contender for regional influence; the United States is a global superpower exerting hegemonic influence over multiple regions and seeking alliances with numerous states. These different roles generate quite different strategic goals for the two states regarding the region as a whole. From the perspective of U.S. pragmatists (e.g., advisors to the Reagan, Bush *père*, and Clinton administrations), the best scenario for the United States in the Middle East is clearly a strong state system, in which friendly Arab regimes can contain domestic dissent and help secure a stable oil supply.[1]

What seemed especially dangerous during the Cold War was the likelihood that the radical Arab elements were tied to Soviet Communism and that their success would enable the Soviet Union to gain significant control over the vital Middle East oil producing region – which could raise havoc with the economies of the West.

Undoubtedly this fear of the Soviet Communist specter in the Middle East went back to the President Eisenhower's Secretary of State John Foster Dulles' anti-Communist foreign policy of the 1950s. But while Dulles viewed radical Arab nationalism, embodied then by Egyptian President Gamal Abdel Nasser, as a danger, this attitude did not make him a proponent of war in the region. For Dulles simultaneously believed that militant measures against Nasser, interpreted by Arabs as western imperialist aggression, would drive the Middle East into the hands of the Soviet Union. Thus, Dulles opposed the Anglo-French-Israeli attack on Suez in 1956 and pressured the aggressors to retreat.[2]

In the aftermath of the Suez War, President Eisenhower declared a major new regional security policy in early 1957, which pledged that the United States would offer economic and military aid and, if necessary, provide military forces to help anti-Communist governments in the Middle East stop the advance of Communism. The policy, which became known as the Eisenhower Doctrine, could be seen as a specific application of America's global policy of containment of Communism. Like the broader containment policy, the Eisenhower Doctrine was conservative in that it was intended to shore up existing regimes. Of course, the more militant thinkers in Israel sought just the opposite – the destabilization of the region.

In the 1970s, Washington feared that Baathist Iraq, under the banner of Arab nationalism and socialism, threatened the conservative Persian Gulf states. In 1972, Iraq formalized its close ties with the Soviet Union, signing a 15-year Treaty of Friendship and Cooperation and becoming a recipient of Soviet armaments. Consequently, during the 1970s, the United States backed the Shah's Iran as the protector of the weak Arab monarchies and guardian of stability in the Gulf. Washington became a major arms provider to the Shah's government, offering it almost anything it could purchase, short of nuclear weapons.[3]

With the overthrow of the Shah in early 1979 and the establishment of the Islamic Republic, American policy was forced to change. Now the United States identified revolutionary Shiite Islamism, directed by the Ayatollah Khomenei, as the foremost threat to the stability of the Middle East. When Saddam launched an attack on Iran in 1980, the American government saw it as a positive move that would serve to rein in the Iranian revolutionary threat.[4]

American policy would soon begin to tilt to supporting Iraq. Iraq was removed from the American list of terrorist states in 1982, and diplomatic relations, which had been severed in 1967, were restored in 1984. Ironically, Donald Rumsfeld, serving as a special envoy, paved the way for the restoration of relations in a December 1983 visit to Iraq.[5]

In fall 1983, a National Security Council study had determined that Iran might defeat Iraq, which would be a major catastrophe for American interests in the Gulf in its threat to the flow of oil. Consequently, the United States would have to provide sufficient assistance to Iraq to prevent that risk from materializing.[6]

Thus, by the mid-1980s, the United States was heavily backing Iraq in its war against Iran, although for a while the United States also had provided more limited aid to Iran (under an arrangement that came to light as the Iran-Contra scandal). American help for Iraq included battlefield intelligence information, military equipment, and agricultural credits. And the United States deployed in the Gulf the largest naval force it had assembled since the Vietnam War, ostensibly for the purpose of protecting oil tankers, but which engaged in serious attacks on Iran's navy.[7]

During this period when the United States was providing aid to Iraq, numerous reports documented Iraq's use of chemical weapons against the Iranians. The United States was opposed, in principle, to the use of poisonous gas, which was banned by the Geneva Protocol of 1925. But the Reagan administration considered this legal and moral issue of secondary importance compared to the pressing need to prevent an Iranian victory.[8]

In fact, U.S. satellite intelligence facilitated Iraqi gas attacks against Iranian troop concentrations. Moreover, Washington allowed Iraq to purchase poisonous chemicals, and even strains of anthrax and bubonic plague from American companies, which were subsequently identified as a key components of the Iraqi biological warfare program by a 1994 investigation conducted by the Senate Banking Committee.[9] The exports of those biological agents continued to at least November 28, 1989.[10]

In late 1987, the Iraqi air force began using chemical agents against Kurdish resistance forces in northern Iraq, which had formed a loose alliance with Iran. The attacks, which were part of a "scorched earth" strategy to eliminate rebel-controlled villages, provoked outrage in Congress, and in 1988 the Senate Foreign Relations Committee called for sanctions to be imposed on Iraq affecting $800 million in guaranteed loans. The State Department did issue a condemnation of the gassing of the Kurds at Halabja in 1988, but overall American relations with Iraq were not impaired, despite Saddam's most gruesome atrocities, accounts of which were being broadcast by numerous international human rights groups.[11]

"The U.S.-Iraqi relationship is . . . important to our long-term political and economic objectives," Assistant Secretary of State Richard W. Murphy wrote in a September 1988 memorandum addressing the chemical weapons question. "We believe that economic sanctions will be useless or counterproductive to influence the Iraqis."[12] In short, the United States was fundamentally concerned about the maintenance of stability in the Gulf region, which took precedence over any humanitarian considerations. The irony of this is that, despite clearly realizing the implications of what it was doing, the United States helped arm Iraq with the very weapons of horror that Bush II administration officials in 2002–3 trumpeted as justification for forcibly removing Saddam from power.

The United States rapprochement with Iraq was very upsetting to Israel which feared the geopolitical ramifications of an Iraqi victory. Israel looked upon Iraq as its most potent military threat, as illustrated by its bombing of the French-built Osirak nuclear reactor in 1981, which Israel claimed was part of an Iraqi secret nuclear weapons program. Thus, while the United States was supporting Iraq, Israel was selling war material to Iran – a significant example of how Israeli policy had differed from that of the United States. Israel's support of Iran reflected the long-held Israeli policy of supporting the periphery of the Middle Eastern world against Israel's closer neighbors. Being farther away, Iran was perceived as a much lesser danger to Israel than Iraq. As long as Iraq was involved in this prolonged conflict, it could not join Syria or Jordan to pose a danger to Israel's eastern border. Moreover, Israel's goal was to facilitate a drawn out war of attrition, in which both of its enemies would exhaust each other.[13]

Israel essentially had supported the Shah and continued to pursue a pro-Iranian policy after the Shah's downfall, despite the Islamic Republic's open ideological hostility to Zionism. There was a belief in leading Israeli foreign policy circles that Iran was a natural ally of Israel against the Arab states and that it would inevitably return to this position after it got over its revolutionary fervor. Israel's sale of arms to Iran was done covertly, but it was a rather open secret. Israel valued Iran not only as a counterweight to Iraq, but also as a market for arms sales, which was Israel's major export commodity.[14]

In addition, Israel had some influence on American policy, which it sought to tilt in favor of Iran. Israelis conspired with officials of the National Security Council to bring about the policy of covert American arms sales to Iran for a period in 1985–6, in what came to be known as the Iran-Contra affair. Israel offered to serve as a bridge to bring about better relations between the United States and Iran.[15]

Neoconservatives loomed large in the covert dealings with Iran, which involved such figures as Michael Ledeen, who served as an agent for National Security Advisor Robert C. McFarlane. Ledeen initially arranged the secret initiative by meeting with then-Israeli Prime Minister Shimon Peres in May 1985.[16] Robert Dreyfuss has noted, in his *Devil's Game: How the United States Helped Unleash Fundamentalist Islam*, that "[w]ithin the Reagan administration, a small clique of conservatives, and neoconservatives, were most intimately involved in the Iran-contra initiative, especially those U.S. officials and consultants who were closest to the Israeli military and intelligence establishment."[17] As Trita Parsi puts it in *Treacherous Alliance: The Secret Dealings of Israel, Iran, and the United States*, "neoconservatives were masterminding a rapprochement with Khomeini's government."[18]

Secretary of State George Shultz expressed concern about the Israeli-orientation of that policy. In a letter to McFarlane, he noted that Israel's position on Iran "is not the same as ours" and that American intelligence collaboration with Israel regarding Iran "could seriously skew our own perception and analysis of the Iranian scene."[19] The latter, as Dreyfuss points out, was the actual aim of the neoconservatives and CIA director William Casey, "who sought to reengage with Iran, in direct opposition to the official U.S. policy of supporting Iraq in its resistance to Iranian expansionism."[20]

The neocons and Israel were unsuccessful in altering American foreign policy away from Iraq and toward Iran. The exposé of the Iran/Contra affair certainly sounded the death knell to this diplomacy. Some neoconservatives, however, continued to seek this change. Michael Ledeen would write in a *New York Times* opinion piece on July 19, 1988, that it was essential for the United States to begin talking with Iran. He wrote that the "The United States, which should have been exploring improved relations with Iran before . . . should now seize the opportunity to do so."[21] (When Israel later perceived Iran to be a crucial threat, Ledeen would become a leading proponent of the view that Iran was the center of world terror and that regime change was the only solution.[22])

After the Iran/Iraq war ended in August 1988 with an inconclusive cease-fire, Iraq's development and use of chemical weapons drew increasing criticism in the United States, especially in Congress. By November 1988 both houses of Congress had passed legislation that would have had the effect of imposing sanctions on Iraq.

Congress's efforts to sanction Iraq, however, were countered by the administration of George H.W. Bush, which came into office in January 1989. The Bush administration essentially continued the Reagan administration's favorable treatment of Iraq, providing it with military hardware, advanced technology, and agricultural credits. Washington apparently looked to Saddam to maintain stability in the Gulf, and believed that trade and credits would have a moderating effect on him.[23]

Israel's view of Iraq was quite different from that of the United States. Israel looked upon the Iraq military build-up as a dire threat to its military supremacy in the Middle East. For it appeared that Iraq was developing the capability to counter, at least to a degree, Israel's superior arsenal of conventional, chemical, and nuclear arms.[24] As noted reporters Dan Raviv and Yossi Melman observed in April 1990: "the Israelis say that, whatever they have, they must ensure it is far more powerful than anything the Arabs may get."[25]

Israel could conceivably destroy the budding Iraqi arsenal by a preemptive strike, but such an attack would have serious drawbacks. "Eliminating the technological capacity of Iraq, as in 1981, is becoming impractical," said Gerald Steinberg, a military expert at the Bal-Ilan University in Tel Aviv. "The potential costs of it have gone up, and the effectiveness is diminished each time it is done."[26] Nonetheless, Israel began making secret preparations to attack Iraq's chemical weapons plants.[27]

In early 1990, tensions in the Middle East began to escalate. On March 15, Iraq hanged a British Iranian-born journalist, Farzad Bazoft, as an alleged spy for Iran and Israel, causing Great Britain to recall its ambassador to Baghdad the following day. On March 22, Gerald Bull, a Canadian ballistics expert who provided engineering assistance to Iraq to develop long-range artillery – especially a so-called "super-gun" that could reach Israel – was murdered in Brussels, and agents of the Israeli Mossad were suspected in that crime. On March 28, the British arrested five men charged with attempting to smuggle American-made nuclear bomb triggers to Iraq. It was also reported that Iraq had deployed six SCUD missile launchers to the western regions of the country, placing Israeli cities within range.[28]

Fearing that Israel may have been planning an air raid similar to the one it launched against Iraq's nuclear reactor at Osirak in 1981, Saddam Hussein in early April 1990 announced that if Israel attacked Iraq, he would drench half of Israel with chemical weapons. The Western media portrayed Saddam's threat as outrageous, often omitting the *defensive* context of his warning. In response to Saddam's speech, Ehud Barak, Israel's chief of staff, asserted that Israel would strike at Iraq any time its forces became a threat to Israel.[29]

Angering Israel and its American supporters further was the Bush administration's effort to rekindle the Middle East peace process. The PLO, which had recognized Israel in 1988, seemed more willing to negotiate than the Israeli government headed by Likud Prime Minister Yitzhak Shamir, which was resistant to giving up control of the occupied territories. On January 14, 1990, Shamir insisted that the influx of Soviet Jews necessitated Israel's retention of the West Bank. On March 1, 1990, Secretary of State James Baker stipulated that American loan guarantees for new housing for the Soviet immigrants in Israel hinged on the cessation of settlements in the occupied territories. And on March 3, President Bush adamantly declared that there should be no more settlements in the West Bank or in East Jerusalem.[30]

But Shamir rejected, forthwith and openly, the Bush administration's entire effort to bring about a solution. And Israel's American supporters, especially of the right, were thoroughly on the side of the Israeli prime minister.[31] *New York Times* pro-Israel columnist William Safire complained that "George Bush is less sympathetic to Israel's concerns than any U.S. President in the four decades since that nation's birth." Safire continued:

> Mr. Bush has long resisted America's special relationship with Israel. His secretary of state, James Baker, delights in sticking it to the Israeli right. His national security adviser, Brent Scowcroft, and chief of staff, John Sununu, abet that mind-set.[32]

Safire was outraged that Bush would threaten to abstain from abetting the Israeli government's colonization of the occupied West Bank. "This is the first Administration to openly threaten to cut aid to Israel," he wrote.

> This is also the first Administration to tie aid directly to Israel's willingness to conform to U.S. policy demands: unless the West Bank is barred to Jews

who want to move there, no loans will be guaranteed to help Soviet Jews start new lives.

Safire claimed that Jewish settlement of the West Bank was essential for Jewish Russian immigrants because a resurgence of anti-Semitic pogroms was allegedly imminent in post-Communist Russia.[33]

The U.S. media, especially the pro-Israel media, was reporting that Iraq was rapidly producing nuclear materials, chemical weapons, and guided missiles. For example, *U.S. News and World Report,* owned by the pro-Israel Mortimer Zuckerman, titled its June 4, 1990 cover story about Saddam, "The World's Most Dangerous Man."[34] The Bush administration, however, firmly resisted efforts to alter its relationship with Iraq.

Reacting to congressional protests of Saddam's threat to use chemical weapons against Israel, Secretary of State Baker correctly noted the defensive context of the threat in testimony before the Senate appropriations subcommittee on April 25, 1990, and even went so far as to insinuate that it was appropriate for Iraq to have such weapons as a defensive deterrent. Baker said that while the Bush administration regarded the use of chemical weapons as "disturbing," Saddam only threatened to use "chemical weapons on the assumption that Iraq would have been attacked by nuclear weapons."[35]

What ultimately led to the Bush administration's break with Iraq, of course, was its aggressive move on the tiny sheikdom of Kuwait. Saddam's desire to control Kuwait was not unique for an Iraqi leader. Iraqis had long regarded Kuwait as a rightful part of their national domain. In 1963, in fact, Iraq's then president had asserted an Iraqi claim to Kuwait, only to back down when the British deployed a detachment of regular troops in the emirate. What especially caused Saddam to look longingly toward Kuwait and its oil was Iraq's dire economic situation. Iraq's victory over Iran had been a Pyrrhic one, leaving the country economically devastated with an enormous debt of tens of billions of dollars – Saddam admitted to $40 billion. Significant portions of the debt were owed to Arab oil producing neighbors – Saudi Arabia and Kuwait. To pay off the debt, Iraq would have to rely on its oil production, but much of Iraq's oil producing capacity in the southern part of the country had been destroyed in the war. Moreover, the price of oil had plummeted.[36]

Kuwait seemed a reasonable scapegoat for Iraq's problems and it simultaneously offered a solution. Kuwait, having felt threatened by Iranian radicalism, had provided Iraq with extensive loans during the war with Iran. With the end of the war, however, the Kuwaiti government demanded full repayment from Iraq, whereas Iraq expected Kuwait to write off its debt as a reward for its having provided the tiny emirate with protection from Iran. Moreover, Kuwait continued to flagrantly exceed its OPEC production quota, overproducing by 40 percent, which helped to depress the oil prices that Iraq desperately needed elevated. Saddam also accused Kuwait of siphoning off oil from the Iraq section of their shared Rumaila oil field through slant drilling and demanded a revision of the territorial boundary to favor Iraq.[37]

In their *War in the Gulf, 1990–91*, historians Majid Khadduri and Edmund Ghareeb, in assessing responsibility for the Gulf War, assign some culpability to Kuwait for its unwillingness to even consider Iraq's proposals, which were not totally unreasonable. "Settlement of the crisis by Arab peaceful means," they maintain, "would have been much less costly to the Arab world than by foreign intervention."[38] In the long run, it would have been less costly for the United States, too.

At the end of May 1990, in an Arab summit meeting in Baghdad, Saddam Hussein threatened to retaliate against Kuwait if it continued to exceed oil production quotas. On July 17, 1990, a belligerent Saddam accused Kuwait and the United Arab Emirates of being "imperialist agents" whose policy of keeping oil prices low was a "poison dagger" in Iraq's back. Shortly thereafter, Saddam began to move his military forces toward the Kuwaiti border.[39]

Saddam's critics expressed outrage. Neoconservative Charles Krauthammer compared Saddam to Hitler. "What makes him truly Hitlerian is his way of dealing with neighboring states," Krauthammer asserted in the *Washington Post* on July 27.

> In a chilling echo of the '30s, Iraq, a regional superpower, accuses a powerless neighbor of a "deliberate policy of aggression against Iraq," precisely the kind of absurd accusation Hitler lodged against helpless Czechoslovakia and Poland as a prelude to their dismemberment.[40]

The Bush administration, however, seemed quite indifferent to the imminent Iraqi threat to Kuwait. In a press conference on July 24, State Department spokesperson Margaret Tutwiler did express moral opposition to "coercion and intimidation in a civilized world," but pointed out that

"We do not have any defense treaties with Kuwait, and there are no special defense or security commitments to Kuwait." On July 25, Saddam Hussein summoned U.S. Ambassador April Glaspie to a meeting that would later gain great publicity and vociferously complained that Kuwait was engaging in acts of war against Iraq by not assisting with Iraq's war debt or agreeing to limit its production of oil. If Iraq attacked Kuwait, Saddam vehemently argued that it would be because Kuwait was already making war on Iraq. To Saddam's overt threat, Glaspie mildly responded that "We have no opinion on your Arab-Arab conflicts." It has been widely argued that Glaspie's response persuaded Saddam that the United States would not militarily oppose his invasion. He had been given the green light to attack.[41]

Then, on July 31, 1990, Assistant Secretary of State for Near Eastern and South Asian Affairs John Kelly, in his testimony before the Subcommittee on Europe and the Middle East of the House Foreign Affairs Committee, pointed out that the United States had no defense treaty relationship with Kuwait or other Persian Gulf countries. The subcommittee chairman, Lee Hamilton (Democrat, Indiana) pressed Kelly for specifics: "If Iraq, for example, charged across the border into Kuwait, for whatever reasons, what would be our position with regard to the use of U.S. forces?" Kelly responded: "That, Mr. Chairman, is a hypothetical [sic] or a contingency, the kind of which I can't go into. Suffice it to say we would be extremely concerned, but I cannot get into the realm of 'what if' answers."

Hamilton pressed further: "In that circumstance, it is correct to say, however, that we do not have a treaty commitment which would obligate us to engage U.S. forces?"

"That is correct." Kelly responded.[42]

On August 1, the eve of the Iraqi invasion of Kuwait, the Bush administration approved the sale of advanced data transmission devices to Iraq, which could be used for missiles. The Bush administration gave no hint that it would oppose an Iraqi invasion of Kuwait militarily.[43]

On August 2, Saddam Hussein's Iraqi army swarmed into Kuwait, meeting minimal Kuwaiti resistance. The ruling Al-Sabah family fled, and Iraqi forces occupied the entire country.

With Iraq's invasion, American policy soon performed an abrupt and complete volte-face. President George H. W. Bush denounced Saddam's move as heinous aggression that could not be allowed to stand. Whereas various allegations and reports of atrocities by Saddam, dating from some years earlier, had been more or less ignored by the administration up to that point, they were now trumpeted to high heaven – even to the point of repeated reference to notorious stories like the alleged killing of babies and theft of incubators by the invading Iraqi forces in Kuwait.[44]

President Bush quickly made preparations to send troops to Saudi Arabia to protect the kingdom from an Iraqi attack that he alleged to be imminent. But King Fahd of Saudi Arabia was hesitant about allowing American "infidels" on Islam's most sacred soil. A U.S. influx of that kind would certainly ignite fierce opposition from many of his strongest religious supporters. Thus, the Saudi monarchy, along with other Arab leaders, especially King Hussein of Jordan, was initially not disposed to the use of force against Saddam's Iraq, preferring instead to rely on compromise to encourage Saddam to remove his forces from Kuwait. If the Saudi ruler rejected the American troops, however, the United States would not be able to fight Saddam.[45]

To win King Fahd's support, therefore, the Bush administration not only relied on diplomatic pressure but even resorted to deception. It exaggerated the threat of an Iraqi armed invasion of Saudi Arabia, through the use of doctored satellite pictures, in order to scare the Saudis into accepting both U.S. troops on their territory and eventual military action against Iraq.[46]

Israel was ecstatic at the reversal in American policy toward Iraq, which vindicated Israel's claim of the threat posed by Saddam. "We are benefiting from every perspective," said Yossi Olmert, the director of the Israeli government press office. "Of course, we can lose big if Saddam decides to attack us next. But at least the rest of the world now sees what we have been saying all along."[47]

Israel wanted strong measures to be taken by the United States and other Western nations against Iraq. Likud officials compared Saddam to Hitler and its invasion of Kuwait to German aggressive acts in the 1930s. The Israeli goal was not simply to drive Iraq from Kuwait but, more important, to remove Saddam Hussein, destroy Iraq's military power, and thus eliminate a regional rival.[48] Israeli President Chaim Herzog even called upon the United States to use nuclear weapons in its attack. But Israel did not fully trust the United States to carry out a military attack, fearing that it might actually opt for a negotiated peace. On December 4, 1990, Israeli foreign minister David Levy reportedly threatened the U.S. ambassador, David Brown, to the effect that if the United States failed to attack Iraq, Israel would do so itself.[49]

The crisis in the Persian Gulf also helped Israel by eliminating the American pressure to make concessions to the Palestinians.[50] As it turned out, however, that would simply be a respite for Israel, as the Bush administration would reapply the pressure in war's aftermath.

Neoconservatives played a leading role in promoting the U.S. war on Iraq, setting up the Committee for Peace and Security in the Gulf, co-chaired by Richard Perle and New York Democratic Congressman Stephen Solarz, chairman of the House Foreign Affairs subcommittee on Asian and Pacific affairs. The new pressure group would focus on mobilizing popular and congressional support for war.[51] War hawks such as Perle, Frank Gaffney, Jr., A. M. Rosenthal, William Safire, and the quasi-neocon organ *The Wall Street Journal* emphasized in the media that America's war objective should not be simply to drive Iraq out of Kuwait but also to destroy Iraq's military potential, especially its capacity to develop nuclear weapons. This broader goal meshed with Israel's fundamental objective. The Bush administration would come to embrace this position.[52]

Support for the war often closely equated with support for Israel. As columnist E. J. Dionne wrote in the *Washington Post:*

> Israel and its supporters would like to see Saddam weakened or destroyed, and many of the strongest Democratic supporters of Bush's policy on the gulf, such as Solarz, are longtime backers of Israel. Similarly, critics of Israel – among conservatives as well as liberals – are also among the leading critics of Bush's gulf policy. "That's embarrassing," said William Schneider, a political analyst at the American Enterprise Institute, "because there seems to be a hidden concern – either pro- or anti-Israel."[53]

Patrick J. Buchanan would make the much-reviled comment that "There are only two groups that are beating the drums for war in the Middle East – the Israeli Defense Ministry and its amen corner in the United States."[54] Even the liberal Jewish columnist Richard Cohen opined in late August that "The problem I have with those who argue for a quick military strike is that they seem to be arguing from an Israeli perspective." In contrast, "the United States is not immediately threatened by Iraq – as Israel was [in 1981] and is." Cohen concluded, "Those who plump for war are a bit premature, attempting to make the Middle East safe for not only oil [the American interest] but for Israel as well."[55]

The goal of eliminating Saddam's military power undercut diplomatic efforts to get Saddam out of Kuwait put forth by numerous parties – the Arab

League, France, the Soviet Union. And Iraq itself made various informal compromise offers. Early on, however, the Bush administration precluded any face saving gesture being offered to Iraq by its assertion that aggression could not be rewarded. The United States offered Saddam only a choice between war and total capitulation. Needless to say, such a hard line had not been applied to numerous other aggressors.

On August 22, Thomas Friedman, the *New York Times'* chief diplomatic correspondent, ascribed the Bush administration's rejection of the "diplomatic track" to its fear that if it became

> involved in negotiations about the terms of an Iraqi withdrawal, America's Arab allies might feel under pressure to give the Iraqi President, Saddam Hussein, a few token gains in Kuwait to roll back his invasion and defuse the crisis.[56]

What explained the complete transformation on the part of the Bush administration policy toward Iraq? Why would the administration not simply opt for a compromise agreement, since that seemed to be an acceptable condition before Saddam's invasion? Explanations run the gamut. One implies a conspiracy – that the Bush administration intended to fight Saddam and deliberately gave Saddam Hussein the impression he could get away with an invasion of Kuwait in order to establish a casus belli. At the same time, the United States urged Kuwait to resist Saddam's demands in order to bring about war.[57]

Steven Hurst offers another explanation in his *The Foreign Policy of the Bush Administration*. He contends that the United States pursued a hard line to accommodate Israel, presumably to make it amenable to granting concessions regarding Palestine. Establishing peace in the all-important Palestinian/Israeli conflict would be impossible, Hurst states, if the U.S. went too far in appeasing Saddam.[58] Given the less than even-handed approach of Israel to the Palestinians and the peace process, it is difficult to see how appeasing the Israelis vis-à-vis Iraq could have reasonably been expected to produce much by way of concessions regarding a question of national survival, which the Israelis, particularly those on the right wing of its politics, take so seriously.[59]

At any rate, it would also seem that President Bush's personality was a significant factor in the policy shift. Bush was only tangentially involved in Iraq policy prior to the Kuwait invasion. Baker and the State Department essentially had directed the policy to placate Saddam, unaffected by cries

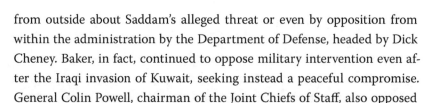

from outside about Saddam's alleged threat or even by opposition from within the administration by the Department of Defense, headed by Dick Cheney. Baker, in fact, continued to oppose military intervention even after the Iraqi invasion of Kuwait, seeking instead a peaceful compromise. General Colin Powell, chairman of the Joint Chiefs of Staff, also opposed military action and supported a reliance on sanctions.[60]

President Bush's intention upon learning of the invasion was actually to follow the pacific policy laid out by Baker. However, the hard-liners toward Iraq were bellowing about American appeasement. Bush was now on center stage, and he was concerned about appearing weak, which was how the critics were already characterizing his policy toward Iraq.

An encounter with British Prime Minister Margaret Thatcher on August 3 in Aspen, Colorado, where Thatcher was attending a conference, drove Bush from uncertainty to avid support for war. Thatcher insisted that the Iraqi occupation of Kuwait could not be allowed. "Don't go wobbly on me, George," Thatcher lectured the president. As one of Thatcher's advisors later quipped: "The prime minister performed a successful backbone transplant."[61]

Bush's biographers Peter and Rochelle Schweizer explain his adoption of a militant war stance:

> George Bush, like so many of the others in his family, was obsessed with the notion of measuring up to the challenge . . . . George had become convinced in the early weeks of August 1990 that his great test would be the struggle against Saddam Hussein. For the first time in his life he made a geopolitical struggle intensely personal. Before, he had always spoken about war and geopolitics in terms of national interest and American security; now he was more direct and personal.[62]

The United States would ultimately unleash Operation Desert Storm, beginning with a massive air bombardment on January 16, 1991, followed, 39 days later, by a four-day ground war that expelled Iraqi forces from Kuwait and induced Saddam to accept a cease-fire on March 3. The war established a peace that would greatly weaken Saddam, including the requirement that Iraq not possess an arsenal of chemical, bacteriological or nuclear weapons. That comported with the position of Israel, which sought to weaken its enemy.

The quick and decisive defeat of Saddam was a stunning and humiliating blow to the Arabs of the Middle East. But for the defeat of Saddam to be advantageous to Israel, Iraq would have to be devastated. During the

American bombing campaign, neocon Bruce Fein wanted to make sure that Iraq was reduced to rubble. Fein was concerned that the United States, in its effort to avoid civilian casualties, was not creating sufficient havoc. Especially upsetting was the "woolly-headed acquittal of the Iraqi people of any responsibility for the arch-villainous actions of their president." It was necessary, he asserted, to punish the Iraqi people.

> Why, therefore, should Mr. Bush instruct the U.S. military scrupulously to avoid civilian targets in Iraq even if a contrary policy would more quickly destroy Iraqi morale and bring it to heel? During World War II, the Allied powers massively bombed Berlin, Dresden and Tokyo for reasons of military and civilian morale. Winston Churchill instructed the Royal Air Force to "make the rubble dance" in German cities. Why is Mr. Bush treating Iraqi civilians more solicitously than the enemy civilians of World War II?

Fein did not just want to kill the Iraqi people during the war; he held that in the postwar period the Iraqi people should be assessed reparations.[63]

Beyond the destruction of Iraq's infrastructure, the neoconservatives hoped that the war would lead to the removal of Saddam Hussein and the consequent American occupation of Iraq. However, despite the urging of Defense Secretary Dick Cheney and Under Secretary of Defense Paul Wolfowitz to adopt a military plan to invade the heartland of Iraq, that approach was never taken, in part, because of the opposition from General Colin Powell, chairman of the Joint Chiefs of Staff, and General Norman Schwarzkopf, the field commander.[64]

Moreover, the U.S. had a UN mandate to liberate Kuwait, not to remove Saddam. To attempt the latter would have caused the warring coalition to fall apart. America's coalition partners in the region, especially Turkey and Saudi Arabia, feared that the elimination of Saddam's government would cause Iraq to fragment into warring ethnic and religious groups. That could have involved a Kurdish rebellion in Iraq, spreading to Turkey's own restive Kurdish population. And the Shiites in Iraq who were of Iranian origin or sympathy, and comprised some fraction of Iraq's total Shiite population, would likely have fallen under the influence of Iran and increased the threat of Islamic radicalism in the vital oil-producing Gulf region, exactly as has happened since the U.S. invasion of 2003 and the subsequent political restructuring that followed it.[65]

In 1998, the first President Bush would explain his reason for not invading Iraq to remove Saddam thus:

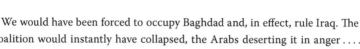

We would have been forced to occupy Baghdad and, in effect, rule Iraq. The coalition would instantly have collapsed, the Arabs deserting it in anger . . . . Had we gone the invasion route, the United States could conceivably still be an occupying power in a bitterly hostile land.[66]

In his 1995 memoirs, Secretary of State James Baker would similarly observe that the administration's "overriding strategic concern in the [first] Gulf war was to avoid what we often referred to as the Lebanonisation of Iraq, which we believed would create a geopolitical nightmare."[67]

George H. W. Bush had essentially realized his major goals: the unconditional withdrawal of all Iraqi forces from Kuwait; the restoration of the legitimate Kuwaiti government; and the protection of the region from any future Iraqi aggression. In short, the foremost concern of the first Bush administration, in line with the traditional American position on the Middle East, was regional stability. As Norman Podhoretz would negatively sum up Bush I's policy thirteen years later:

[W]hen Saddam Hussein upset the balance of power in the Middle East by invading Kuwait in 1991, the elder Bush went to war not to create a new configuration in the region but to restore the status quo ante. And it was precisely out of the same overriding concern for stability that, having achieved this objective by driving Saddam out of Kuwait, Bush then allowed him to remain in power.[68]

Israel and its neocon allies sought just the opposite: a destabilized, fragmented Iraq (indeed a destabilized, fragmented Middle East) that would enhance Israel's relative regional power.

Rejecting an American occupation as too dangerous, the first President Bush sought to remove Saddam by less aggressive means. In May 1991, he signed a presidential finding directing the CIA to create the conditions for Saddam's ouster. As it emerged, the plan consisted largely of supporting propaganda and Iraqi dissidents who came to form the Iraqi National Congress. The hope was that members of the Iraqi military would turn on Saddam and stage a military coup. That was not to happen.

In the process of terminating the war on Iraq, the Bush administration allowed Saddam to brutally suppress uprisings by the Kurds and the Shiites. What made this seem like an especially immoral betrayal was the fact that, during the war, Bush had called for the people of Iraq to rise up against Saddam. Now, as Saddam smashed the rebellions, neoconservatives and other supporters of Israel were outraged. A. M. Rosenthal angrily declared that "by betraying the rebels the U.S. is truly intervening – on the side of the killer Hussein." To the argument that American intervention might break up Iraq, Rosenthal questioned the need for a unified Iraq: "Anyway, were Americans sent into combat against Saddam Hussein so that Washington should now help him keep together the jigsaw country sawed out of the Middle East by the British after World War I?"[69] Here Rosenthal was questioning the entire principle of stability that had traditionally guided American policy in the Middle East.

"Two months after a brilliant military campaign ended in victory, Mr. Bush has achieved the worst of worlds for millions of Iraqi rebels and for American policy in the Mideast," opined Rosenthal in the *New York Times* of April 23, 1991. But the solution he had in mind was more than just providing immediate protection for the Kurds and Shiites. Rosenthal emphasized that "there will be no peace as long as Saddam Hussein rules, and threatens to rise again."[70]

Rosenthal presented what would become the key neoconservative solution for the Middle East – regime change and democracy. And he contrasted the reliance on a democratic approach to the traditional policy of "realism" in the Middle East, which the Bush administration continued to pursue in the aftermath of the Gulf War. "For many years now," Rosenthal asserted,

> the "realists" have dominated American foreign policy, particularly on the Middle East. They constantly search for a "balance of power" that is unattainable because it is based on dictatorships, which by their very nature are the cause of instability. They dismiss the concept of morality in international affairs and believe that democracy is impossible in the Middle East.
>
> Yes, it is impossible – as long as the realists have their way and we appease the Saddam Husseins and Hafez al-Assads of the area, coddle the oil despots and are in a constant twitch of irritation about our support of Israel, the only democracy in the area.
>
> Just see where realpolitik has gotten us in the Mideast: Iran in the hands of religious fanatics, Syria and Libya ruled under terrorist fascism, Saddam Hussein still in power, marauding – and a million Iraqi refugees clawing for food, crying out their hunger and betrayal.[71]

New York Times columnist William Safire, too, wrote of the immorality of the abandonment of the Kurds and Shiites. "Must history remember George Bush as the liberator of Kuwait and the man who saved Iraq for dictatorship?" Safire asked rhetorically. "U.S. troops will return home with a sense of shame at the bloodletting that followed our political sellout."[72]

Krauthammer would blame Bush's failure to intervene to save the Kurds and Shiites to his risk-averse personality, in respect of which his war on Iraq represented an aberration.

> After seven months of brilliant, indeed heroic, presidential leadership, George Bush's behavior after the Persian Gulf War – his weak and vacillating hands-off policy – is a puzzle. The best explanation is this: Bush was like the man who wins the jackpot in a casino and walks right out the front door refusing even to look at another table. There are many reasons Bush decided to cash in his chips even if that meant abandoning the Iraqi rebels to Saddam Hussein's tender mercies – a policy partly reversed when the extent of the Kurdish catastrophe became clear. There was the fear of getting dragged into a civil war, a belief that international law and the wartime coalition would support saving Kuwait's sovereignty but not violating Iraq's, and his susceptibility to pressure from his Saudi friends, who feared both the fracturing and democratization of Iraq. These were all factors, but the overwhelming one was the president's persona: A man of pathological prudence, having just risked everything on one principled roll of the dice, was not about to hang around the gaming room a second longer. It was a question of political capital. After 30 years in politics Bush had finally amassed it. He was not about to spend it in Kurdistan. The willingness to risk political capital is not just a sign of greatness in a leader, it is almost a definition of it.[73]

But the fact of the matter is that while the Bush administration continued the traditional concern of American foreign policy for stability in the Middle East, it was willing to risk political capital by return to the pressuring of Israel to move away from its effort to colonize the West Bank. In defying the powerful domestic Israel lobby, that policy was bound to stir up a hornets' nest for the Bush administration. But the post-Gulf War public opinion polls showed overwhelming support for President Bush. In early March, just as the war ended, Bush's approval rating stood at a stratospheric 90 percent.[74] That seemed to provide enough political cushion against the inevitable damage that Bush and Baker would suffer in pursuing their foreign policy agenda.

Essentially, the Bush/Baker approach sought to fit policy toward Israel within the overall framework of maintaining stability in the region. It saw Israel as the unstable element. If the Jewish state would make concessions to the Palestinians, tensions would subside across the entire Middle East, for it was the Israeli oppression of the Palestinians that created a major Arab grievance exploited by anti-American destabilizing elements in the region.

The Bush administration now was especially desirous of placating the Arab coalition that had supported the war by making American policy in the Middle East more even-handed. In supporting a Western attack on a fellow Muslim and Arab country, the leaders of the Middle Eastern states had risked engendering internal opposition from religious and nationalistic elements, and those rulers expected some reward for their loyalty to the United States.

The Bush administration thus returned with vigor to its pre-war effort of trying to curb Israeli control of its occupied territories. It focused on a demand that Israel stop constructing new settlements in the occupied territories as a condition for receiving $10 billion in U.S. loan guarantees for the resettlement of hundreds of thousands of immigrants from the former Soviet Union. Despite Washington's objections, Israel had launched a building boom in the occupied territories, intended by Prime Minister Yitzhak Shamir's rightist government to ensure permanent Israeli control there. The plan would boost the Jewish settler population by 50 percent in two years. Asked in early April 1991 how Israel would respond to a U.S. request to freeze Jewish settlement activity, Ariel Sharon, then the housing minister, adamantly stated that "Israel has always built, is building and will in future build in Judea, Samaria [biblical names for the West Bank] and the Gaza Strip."[75] In May 1991, Secretary Baker harshly condemned the Jewish settlements in testimony before the Foreign Operations Subcommittee of the House Appropriations Committee, asserting that "I don't think that there is any bigger obstacle to peace."[76]

Shamir's Likud government and Israel's America's supporters strongly resisted the Bush administration's efforts. In his September 12, 1991 news conference, Bush went before the television cameras to ask Congress to delay consideration of the $10 billion in loan guarantees being demanded by Shamir. Bush dared to speak directly of the pro-Israel pressure, saying that

> I'm up against some powerful political forces, but I owe it to the American people to tell them how strongly I feel about the deferral .... I heard today there was something like a thousand lobbyists on the Hill working the other side of the question. We've got one lonely little guy down here doing it.[77]

In performing an end run around the Israel-friendly mainstream media and appealing directly to the American people, however, Bush struck a responsive chord. A public opinion poll only two days later found that 86 percent of the American people supported the president on that issue. But that public support apparently made some members of the administration complacent about the political power of the pro-Zionist lobby. When the danger of alienating Jewish Americans was broached to Secretary of State Baker, he was alleged to have uttered that most taboo-shattering of profanities: "F**k the Jews. They didn't vote for us."[78]

Jewish-Americans had been enraged by Bush's speech. "For a great many Jews, then, Bush's September 12 press conference was like a blinding flash in the night that would not go away," wrote J. J. Goldberg. "Jews of every political stripe began writing letters of protest to their newspapers, to their representatives, and to the White House."[79] Goldberg further wrote that

> the Jews were indisputably a powerful political force. George Bush was not wrong in believing that when he convened his September 12 press conference. Bush's mistake was saying it aloud.[80]

Bush's opposition to Shamir's policy probably contributed to bringing down the Shamir government in January 1992. In the subsequent Israeli national election in June 1992, Shamir lost to the Labor Party led by Yitzhak Rabin, which ran on the popular slogan "Land for Peace." (While Rabin was amenable to pursuing a peace process with the Palestinians – for which he was awarded a Nobel Peace prize in 1994 – the extent to which Jewish settlements on the West Bank would be reduced and the chances for a future viable Palestinian state were always questionable.)

However, while the situation changed in Israel, supporters of Israel in the United States remained intransigent. They were outraged over the Bush administration's public pressuring of Israel. The neoconservatives set up an organization to back the Israeli position on settlements, giving it the Orwellian moniker, Committee on U.S. Interests in the Middle East. Members included such neoconservative stalwarts as Douglas Feith, Frank Gaffney, Richard Perle, and Elliott Abrams.[81]

As the 1992 election approached, the Bush administration, seeing its popularity plummet, would try to mend fences with his pro-Israel critics. In July, Bush announced that the U.S. would provide the loan guarantees after all. His concession won him no pro-Israel support.

The role of Israel's chief lobby, the American Israel Public Affairs Committee (AIPAC), in the loan guarantee episode was starkly revealed in a private conversation in October 1992 between the president of AIPAC, David Steiner, and potential contributor Harry Katz, which the latter had secretly taped. Steiner boasted about AIPAC's political sway, saying he had "cut a deal" with James Baker to give more aid to Israel. He had arranged for "almost a billion dollars in other goodies that people don't even know about."[82]

When Katz brought up the concern that Baker had cursed the Jewish people, Steiner responded: "Of course, do you think I'm ever going to forgive him for that?" He acknowledged that AIPAC was backing Clinton and had supported him from before he received the Democratic nomination. Steiner boasted that AIPAC had numerous supporters in the Clinton campaign and that Clinton would put their people in key positions when he entered office.[83] In fact, the Democratic platform contained a strong pro-Israel plank, and the Clinton campaign attacked the Bush administration for "bullying" Israel.

Like other supporters of Israel, some neoconservatives were tending towards Clinton. Richard Schifter, assistant secretary of state for human rights under Reagan and George H. W. Bush (until March 1992), had become a senior foreign policy adviser for the Clinton campaign. Schifter was also working with AIPAC's David Ifshin to bring fellow neoconservatives back into the Democratic Party.[84] And a number of neoconservatives such as Joshua Muravchik, Penn Kemble, Morris Amitay, Edward Luttwak, and R. James Woolsey, would openly back Bill Clinton. Even long-time conservative commentator William Safire would support Clinton. Many others remained at least cool to Bush's re-election.[85] Moreover, Clinton appealed to neocons by his support of the neoconservative idea that promotion of democracy should be a central feature of American foreign policy.[86] Neocons profess to believe in the promotion of global democracy and such an approach would serve to undermine Israel's enemies in the Middle East, none of which was ruled in a democratic manner.

Many neocons with strong Republican connections were hesitant to completely make the switch to Clinton, but they would at best be lukewarm Bush supporters. Even a defense of Bush by one of these supporters, Daniel Pipes, acknowledged the difficulties in supporting the president. "If there's a lot of agreement on anything this election year," Pipes wrote, "it's that friends of Israel should not vote to re-elect George Bush. The mere mention of his name in Jewish circles evinces strong disappointment, even anger."[87]

Clinton received the highest level of Jewish support of any Democratic presidential candidate since Franklin D. Roosevelt. According to an American Jewish Congress exit poll, 80 percent of American Jews voted for Clinton, compared to 11 percent for Bush. 35 percent of American Jews had backed Bush in 1988.[88] And the George H. W. Bush who emerged from the Gulf War with an astronomical 90 percent approval rating went down to a humiliating election defeat.

What one sees in the Gulf War was a temporary and partial shift from America's traditional policy of working to maintain stability in the Middle East to a policy firmly aligned with that of Israel to militarily defeat Israel's greatest enemy at the time. While the United States had provided arms to Israel before to enable it to defeat its enemies – most conspicuously the military arms airlift during the Yom Kippur War of 1973 – the United States had never before gone to war against a primary enemy of Israel. In fighting an enemy initially identified by Israel and its American supporters, American policy in the Gulf War prefigured the Bush II administration's war on Iraq, which would be on a much grander scale.

Under the Bush I administration, the war and defeat of Saddam still took place within the overall foreign policy framework of maintaining stability – and in its rejection of an American occupation of Iraq, the Bush administration certainly did everything it could to try to restore the status quo, to the great consternation of the friends of Israel who desired regime change and continued destabilization. However, as it happened, the very establishment of the American military presence in the Middle East had a destabilizing effect. It would feed into the popular grievances in the Middle East, exploited by Islamists such as Osama bin Laden. To many radicals, America became a fundamental enemy on par with Israel.

The drastic American military intervention into Middle East affairs had unleashed forces that could not be reversed. The tinder was dry and needed only the neocons of the Bush II administration to light the spark for a new American war and a complete transformation of American policy. To avoid the chances of a future war, the United States would have had to pull out of the region after 1991, and that was an approach alien to all establishment geo-strategic thinkers, wedded as they have been to a policy of global intervention on the part of the U.S. government.

The second, greater war would not have started when it did had the neocons not been able to gain control of foreign policy in the George W. Bush

administration, a seizure of power that resulted from the 911 terrorist disaster. However, the neocons, though empowered, could not have initiated the 2003 war if the earlier war had not taken place. In that sense, the 1991 Gulf War was a prelude to the 2003 war on Iraq, in which the United States government would pursue a policy in complete harmony with the thinking of the neocons and the Israeli Likudniks to precipitate regime change and destabilize the Middle East.

Also of benefit to the neocon Middle East war agenda, the first Bush administration left a document that reflected neoconservative national security strategy and would provide a basis for the national security policy for the George W. Bush administration. This was the draft of the Defense Planning Guidance, which would set a new post-Cold War rationale for American military power. In his *Rise of the Vulcans*, James Mann refers to this document as

> one of the most significant foreign policy documents of the past half century. It set forth a new vision for a world dominated by a lone American superpower, actively working to make sure that no rival or group of rivals would ever emerge.[89]

The draft of the Defense Planning Guidance was prepared under the supervision of Paul Wolfowitz, the Department of Defense's under secretary for policy. I. Lewis Libby, Wolfowitz's top assistant, Richard Perle, and Albert Wohlstetter also had a role in its input. The draft was composed by Zalmay Khalilzad.[90]

In addition to emphasizing the goal of American world supremacy, the document cited the existence of weapons of mass destruction in the hands of hostile countries as the greatest danger to the United States and advocated "pre-emptive" strikes to counter such a danger. The document was for military planning and not intended to be released to the public. However, a draft of the document was leaked to the press and a huge outcry arose around the world over the implication of American militaristic imperialism on a global scale. Embarrassed, the administration called for the language to be softened. Most particularly, the emphasis on unilateral action in the draft was altered to mention collective security. Nonetheless, even in the final softened form, the document provided key ideas for the neoconservatives. It served to justify overwhelming American global power even at a time when, with the demise of the Soviet Union, there was no obvious global threat. Thus, it continued the Cold War alliance between the neoconservatives and both American conservative imperialists and the military industrial complex, even when some conservative anti-Communists, such as Pat Buchanan, were drifting back to the American right's traditional non-interventionist moorings.

Moreover, the focus on a WMD threat to the U.S. could be used to attack Israel's Middle East enemies, since most of those nations would certainly like to possess WMD as a deterrent to Israel's nuclear arsenal. In short, the document, which explicitly focused on maintaining American global supremacy, could simultaneously serve to enhance Israel's regional supremacy in the Middle East.

chapter 6

DURING THE CLINTON YEARS

LTHOUGH SOME neoconservatives supported Bill Clinton, and his administration promised to include them in foreign policy positions, he did not give them a role. "There is no question that they were short-shrifted," complained neocon Ben Wattenberg in early 1993.

> By its appointments and its policy moves so far, the administration is creating a culture that makes moderates and conservatives feel unwelcome. It is as though the old antiwar activists are applying a litmus test to everyone, and when they decide someone is ideologically impure, the administration is unwilling to go to the mat about it.[1]

Unrewarded, the neoconservatives quickly began to criticize Clinton as simply another liberal Democrat, who had disguised himself as a moderate during the 1992 campaign, and who was failing to maintain American military strength.[2]

During the Clinton years, neocons promoted their views from a strong interlocking network of think tanks – such as the American Enterprise Institute (AEI), Middle East Media Research Institute (Memri), Hudson Institute, Washington Institute for Near East Policy, Middle East Forum, Jewish Institute for National Security Affairs (JINSA), Center for Security Policy (CSP), and Project for the New American Century (PNAC) – which had significant influence in the media and became essentially a "shadow defense establishment."[3] These think tanks would eventually provide key staff for the administration of George W. Bush.

It was this interlocking group of organizations, staffed by many of the same individuals, that helped to give the neocons power far transcending their small numbers. As Jim Lobe points out, the neocons have been extremely adept "in creating new institutions and front groups that act as a vast echo chamber for each other and for the media, particularly in media-obsessed Washington."[4]

Some of these organizations were originally set up by mainline conservatives and taken over by neoconservatives;[5] others were established by neoconservatives themselves. Some had a direct Israeli connection. For example, Yigal Carmon, formerly a colonel in Israeli military intelligence, was a co-founder of Memri. And all of the organizations have been closely interconnected, with prominent neoconservatives having multiple affiliations. For example, the other co-founder of Memri, Israeli-born Meyrav Wurmser, was also a member of the Hudson Institute, while her husband, David Wurmser, headed the Middle East studies department of AEI. David Wurmser also was director of institutional grants at the Washington Institute for Near East Policy from 1994 to 1996. Richard Perle was a "resident fellow" at AEI, a member of the advisory board of JINSA, and a trustee of the Hudson Institute.[6] Michael Ledeen was a resident scholar with AEI and a member of the JINSA advisory board. As Jim Lobe writes:

> This proliferation – not to say duplication and redundancy – of committees, projects and coalitions is a tried and true tactic of the neo-cons and their more traditional Republican fellow travelers, at least since the 1970s. The tactic appears largely to persuade public opinion that their hawkish policies are supported by a large section of the population when, in fact, these groups represent very specific interests and its [sic] views are held by a small, highly organized and well-disciplined elite.[7]

The think tank that is usually considered the nerve center for neoconservatism is the American Enterprise Institute. The American Enterprise Institute for Public Policy Research (AEI) was founded in 1943 by anti-New Deal businessmen, long before the existence of neoconservatism, to promote conservative free-market economic views in an intellectual culture then in the thrall of statist liberalism. It remained a quite modest institution until the 1970s, dwarfed by such liberal Washington think tanks as the Brookings Institution. AEI began the 1970s with a budget of $1 million and a staff of only ten; at the decade's end, it had a budget of $8 million and a staff of 125. Its explosive growth took place as neoconservatives, by virtue of their prestige and networking skills, moved into leading positions in conservatism. AEI especially sought a reputation for respectability. This gave the establishment-credentialed neoconservatives an advantage over traditional conservatives, who had been marginalized in mainstream circles. Neoconservatives would fill more and more of the positions in AEI until they came to dominate it, although the bulk of its major financial contributors have been neither Jewish nor particularly devoted to Israel. (The chairman of AEI's board of trustees, however, is Bruce Kovner, a pro-Zionist Jewish billionaire.[8]) AEI would have among its staff such neocon luminaries as Richard Perle, David Wurmser, Michael Ledeen, Joshua Muravchik, and Jean Kirkpatrick. Staff from AEI would emerge as the leading architects of the Bush II administration's foreign policy.[9]

In contrast to AEI, the Jewish Institute for National Security Affairs (JINSA) was set up in 1976 to put "the U.S.-Israel strategic relationship first."[10] In the late 1980s, JINSA widened its focus to U.S. defense and foreign policy in general, without dropping its focus on Israel.[11]

Until the beginning of the Bush II administration, JINSA's advisory board included such notable neocons as John Bolton, Stephen Bryen, Douglas Feith, Max Kampelman, Michael Ledeen, Joshua Muravchik, Richard Perle, Kenneth Timmerman, and R. James Woolsey. Dick Cheney was also a member of the board.[12]

In a seminal article in the September 2002 issue of *The Nation*, Jason Vest discussed the immense power held in the current Bush administration by individuals from two major neoconservative research organizations, JINSA and the Center for Security Policy (CSP). Vest detailed the close links among these organizations, right-wing politicians, arms merchants, military men, Jewish multi-millionaires/billionaires, and Republican administrations.[13]

Vest noted that "dozens" of JINSA and CSP

> members have ascended to powerful government posts, where their advocacy in support of the same agenda continues, abetted by the out-of-government adjuncts from which they came. Industrious and persistent, they've managed to weave a number of issues – support for national missile defense, opposition to arms control treaties, championing of wasteful weapons systems, arms aid to Turkey and American unilateralism in general – into a hard line, with support for the Israeli right at its core.

And Vest continued:

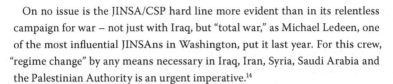

On no issue is the JINSA/CSP hard line more evident than in its relentless campaign for war – not just with Iraq, but "total war," as Michael Ledeen, one of the most influential JINSAns in Washington, put it last year. For this crew, "regime change" by any necessary in Iraq, Iran, Syria, Saudi Arabia and the Palestinian Authority is an urgent imperative.[14]

Both JINSA and CSP, which is headed by Frank Gaffney, a protégé of Perle going back to their days as staffers for Senator Henry Jackson, have been heavily underwritten by Irving Moskowitz, a California business magnate whose money comes from bingo parlors. Moskowitz heavily funds right-wing American Zionist organizations such as the far-right settler group Ateret Cohanim. Ateret Cohanim believes that the acquisition of land in the now Muslim section of Jerusalem's Old City and the concomitant re-building of the Jewish Temple at its former site will hasten the coming of the Messiah. The Temple Mount where the Temple stood, however, is sacred to Muslims and has been occupied for centuries by Muslim holy buildings – the Dome of the Rock and the Al-Aqsa mosque. Moskowitz provided the money that enabled the 1996 reopening of a tunnel under the Temple Mount, which resulted in 70 deaths due to rioting.[15]

A major financier of CSP has been New York real estate investor Lawrence Kadish. Kadish has been one of the Republican Party's leading donors giving some $500,000 during the 2000 presidential election campaign. Kadish served as chairman of the Republican Jewish Coalition, which was closely allied to Israel's Likud government and which supported the construction of the controversial Jewish settlement at Har Homa in East Jerusalem in the late 1990s, over Palestinian objections that the project jeopardized the peace process.[16]

Another major CSP financial backer has been Poju Zabludowicz, heir to a formidable diversified international empire that includes Israeli arms manufacturer Soltam.[17]

During the 1990s, the neoconservatives also greatly expanded into the media, once a preserve of mainstream liberalism. In 1995, the *Weekly Standard* was established, founded and edited by William Kristol, with financing from media mogul Rupert Murdoch, a strong proponent of Israel and conservative causes. The *Weekly Standard* immediately became the leading voice of the neoconservatives, moving ahead of *Commentary* because of its greater frequency of publication. As Jonathan Mark wrote in the *Jewish Week*: "Murdoch's *Weekly Standard* has been at the epicenter of the neocon political movement that has urged a Middle Eastern policy premised on Israel's security."[18]

Despite a relatively small circulation of around 55,000, the *Weekly Standard* has had a major impact. With the Murdoch subsidy, the magazine could achieve a broad newsstand presence and provide thousands of complimentary issues, especially to influential figures.[19] "Reader for reader, it may be the most influential publication in America," wrote Eric Alterman in the *Nation* magazine. "Their circulation may be small but they are not interested in speaking to the great unwashed. The magazine speaks directly to and for power."[20]

While not appealing directly to the general public, the *Weekly Standard* served to credential its writers for roles in the mass media. As Halper and Clarke point out in *America Alone*, the *Weekly Standard*

> has succeeded in a main purpose, namely to provide legitimacy for its staffers in their role as 'experts' on Fox and MSNBC television where *Weekly Standard* contributors have become recognized faces. These platforms have, in turn, allowed neo-conservatives to establish themselves as experts providing an important perspective on the major networks' Sunday talk shows.[21]

Most especially, the editorship of the *Weekly Standard* brought William Kristol into the limelight of the Washington media/political world. In 2000, the *Washington Post's* Howard Kurtz described Kristol as having "become part of Washington's circulatory system, this half-pol, half-pundit, full-throated advocate with the nice-guy image" who is "wired to nearly all the Republican presidential candidates."[22] Kristol was a leading media advocate of war against Iraq. In 1997, the *Weekly Standard* became one of the first publications to publicly call for regime change in Iraq. Referring to Kristol's numerous articles and media appearances in support of the Iraq war, *Washington Post* syndicated columnist Richard Cohen in mid-2002 dubbed it as "Kristol's War."[23]

While the *Weekly Standard* is oriented to the political and intellectual class, neoconservative views reach the more general public through other instruments of Rupert Murdoch's global media empire, with its vast holdings in the United States, Australia, United Kingdom, and China. Murdoch's News Corporation is the largest English language news group in the world. In 2004, it consisted of more than 175 newspapers (40 million papers sold each week) and 35 television stations. That Murdoch's media outlets have been noted for their sensationalism has made them popular with the mass public.[24]

Of Australian birth, Murdoch has been an American citizen since 1985, but he also has strong political and business attachments to Israel and was a close friend of Ariel Sharon. As Murdoch put it:

> I've always had sympathy for Israel, but it certainly intensified when I moved to New York [from Australia] in 1973. I got to know Prime Minister Sharon, way back in the late '70s. Through the years, the support intensified. It was just a matter of thinking about it. I've been [to Israel]. I liked it. I felt a tremendous excitement.[25]

It should also be added that it has been alleged that Murdoch's mother, Elisabeth Joy Greene, was an Orthodox Jew, which would make him Jewish by Jewish standards, although Murdoch does not publicly mention this.[26]

Murdoch enforces a pro-Israel line in his publications. As one reporter, Sam Kiley, who resigned in protest from the Murdoch-owned *Times* of London, exclaimed: "No pro-Israel lobbyist ever dreamed of having such power over a great national newspaper." Pro-Israel groups have honored Murdoch for his support. In 1982, the American Jewish Congress voted Murdoch the "Communications Man of the Year."[27] In 1997, the United Jewish Appeal Federation bestowed upon Murdoch its "Humanitarian of the Year" award.[28] Murdoch's News Corporation was one of three U.S. companies lauded for its support of Israel at the America-Israel Friendship League Partners for Democracy Awards dinner in June 2001. Murdoch himself co-chaired the dinner.[29]

During the build-up to the 2003 invasion of Iraq, all 175 Murdoch-owned newspapers worldwide editorialized in favor of the war.[30] Murdoch's most important outlet for disseminating neoconservative views is Fox News, which has been the most popular cable news network, according to some rating criteria. Although its motto is "fair and balanced," it has relied heavily on neoconservatives for its news experts and is slanted in a neoconservative direction.[31]

Neoconservatives in the media provided the cultural preparation for an American war in the Middle East. While it cannot be said that prior to 2001 their views dominated the media, neocons definitely had an important presence. Most importantly, the neoconservatives were perfectly situated in the media to be able to exploit the post-911 environment and thus manipulate the American public in their desired direction. As Halper and Clarke note in their *America Alone*:

> [N]eo-conservatives had built up a range of media outlets and national fora that enabled them to underpin their policy interpretations to the many constituents of the American public. The cable networks, the conservative talk radio shows, and the conservative print outlets were all in place to carry the abstract war into the governing philosophy of American foreign policy by inundating people with the discursive reality created by neo-conservatives. The neo-conservatives, both in and out of the administration, inserted themselves into this environment before 9/11 and benefited from it afterward. It was the arm with which they represented their views to the larger segments of the American body politic. It was the machinery that synthesized the popular mindset that proved so critical in making war with Saddam Hussein.[32]

The neocons' presence in the mainstream meadia was significantly enhanced because of the existence of their think tanks and their media outlets. In short, the neocon apparatus served to credential them for the mainstream media.[33]

Although there is much talk of a neoconservative "cabal" and a neoconservative "conspiracy," usually in an effort to discredit the idea that neocons could have been a (or the) major force among those whose influence contributed heavily to the initiation of war with Iraq in 2003, secrecy did not envelop the neocons' war strategy. During the 1990s, the neoconservatives were quite open about their goal of war in the Middle East to destabilize Iraq and other enemies of Israel. A clear illustration of the neoconservative thinking on this subject – and the intimate connection with Israeli security – was a 1996 paper entitled "A Clean Break: A New Strategy for Securing the Realm," published by an Israeli think tank, the Institute for Advanced Strategic and Political Studies. Included in the study group that produced the report were figures who would loom large in the Bush II administration's war policy in the Middle East – Richard Perle, Douglas Feith, and David Wurmser. (Wurmser was then actually affiliated with the Institute for Advanced Strategic and Political Studies.) Perle was listed as the head of the study group. Others included in the study group were James Colbert (JINSA), Charles Fairbanks, Jr. (Johns Hopkins University), Robert Loewenberg (President, Institute for Advanced Strategic and Political Studies), Jonathan Torop (Washington Institute for Near East Policy), and Meyrav Wurmser (Johns Hopkins University).[34]

The "realm" that the study group sought to secure was that of Israel. The purpose of the policy paper was to provide a political blueprint for the incoming Israeli Likud government of Benjamin Netanyahu. The paper stated that Netanyahu should "make a clean break" with the Oslo peace process and reassert Israel's claim to the West Bank and Gaza. It presented a plan by which Israel would "shape its strategic environment," beginning with the removal of Saddam Hussein and the installation of a Hashemite monarchy in Baghdad. Significantly, the report did not present Saddam Iraq as the major threat to Israel. Rather, Iraq was more like the weak link among Israel's enemies. By removing Saddam, the study held that Israel would be in a strategic position to get at its more dangerous foes. In short, elimination of Saddam was a first step toward reconfiguring the entire Middle East for the benefit of Israel. "Israel can shape its strategic environment, in cooperation with Turkey and Jordan, by weakening, containing, and even rolling back Syria," the study maintained. "This effort can focus on removing Saddam Hussein from power in Iraq – an important Israeli strategic objective in its own right – as a means of foiling Syria's regional ambitions."[35]

A Hashemite[36] kingdom in Iraq would enable Israel to weaken Syria and Iran, and cut off support for Hezbollah, which threatened Israel from its bases in Lebanon. "The predominantly Shia population of southern Lebanon has been tied for centuries to the Shia leadership in Najf [Najaf], Iraq rather than Iran. Were the Hashemites to control Iraq, they could use their influence over Najf to help Israel wean the south Lebanese Shia away from Hizballah, Iran, and Syria. Shia retain strong ties to the Hashemites: the Shia venerate foremost the Prophet's family, the direct descendants of which – and in whose veins the blood of the Prophet flows – is King Hussein."[37]

It should be emphasized that the same people – Feith, Wurmser, Perle – who advised the Israeli government on issues of national security would later advise the George W. Bush administration to pursue virtually the same policy regarding the Middle East. In 2004, political observer William James Martin would astutely comment about "A Clean Break": "This document is remarkable for its very existence because it constitutes a policy manifesto for the Israeli government penned by members of the current U.S. government."[38] Martin next pointed out that the similarity between that document's recommendation for Israel and the neocon-inspired Bush administration policy, purportedly for the benefit of American interests, was even more remarkable. "It is amazing how much of this program, though written for the Israeli government of Natanyahu of 1996, has already been implemented, not by the government of Israel, but by the Bush administration."[39]

Similarly, Craig Unger wrote in the March 2007 issue of *Vanity Fair*, "Ten years later, 'A Clean Break' looks like nothing less than a playbook for U.S.-Israeli foreign policy during the Bush-Cheney era. Many of the initiatives outlined in the paper have been implemented – removing Saddam from power, setting aside the 'land for peace' formula to resolve the Israeli-Palestinian conflict, attacking Hezbollah in Lebanon – all with disastrous results."[40]

What was dramatically similar between the "Clean Break" scenario and actual Bush II administration Middle East policy was not only the objectives but the sequence of events. It is notable that the "Clean Break" report held that removing Saddam was the key to weakening Israel's other enemies; while the United States would quickly threaten Iran and Syria and talk of restructuring the entire Middle East after removing Saddam in 2003.[41]

The "Clean Break" scenario would combine the attack on Israel's external enemies with efforts to undermine the Palestinians. The study urged Israel to abandon any thought of trading land for peace with the Arabs, which it depicted as a "cultural, economic, political, diplomatic, and military retreat." It implied that there could be little or no compromise on the issue of land. "Our claim to the land – to which we have clung for hope for 2,000 years – is legitimate and noble." It continued: "Only the unconditional acceptance by Arabs of our rights, especially in their territorial dimension, 'peace for peace,' is a solid basis for the future." In short, the fundamental need was for the Palestinians to abandon violent resistance, without Israel offering any territory as a quid pro quo. This approach would entail nurturing alternatives to Arafat. Significantly, this approach to peace was basically implemented after the 9/11 terrorist attack.[42]

Notably, the authors of the study presented it as a policy of "preemption" – analogous to the way the neocons would present the American war in the Middle East, with the United States, of course, replacing Israel as the preemptor. And the strategy presented in the "Clean Break" was openly motivated by the strategic interests of Israel, which, if carried out,

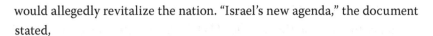

would allegedly revitalize the nation. "Israel's new agenda," the document stated,

> can signal a clean break by abandoning a policy which assumed exhaustion and allowed strategic retreat by reestablishing the principle of preemption, rather than retaliation alone and by ceasing to absorb blows to the nation without response.
>
> Israel's new strategic agenda can shape the regional environment in ways that grant Israel the room to refocus its energies back to where they are most needed: to rejuvenate its national idea, which can only come through replacing Israel's socialist foundations with a more sound footing; and to overcome its "exhaustion," which threatens the survival of the nation.[43]

While neocons present American policy in a very idealistic light, their policy prescriptions for Israel, which involved similar concrete policy objectives, were devoid of such sentiment. Written in terms of Israeli interest, the study made little mention of the benefits to be accrued by Israel's neighboring countries, such as the establishment of democracy. The goal of creating a Hashemite kingdom was certainly a non-democratic approach. Moreover, the study made no mention of fundamentalist Islam or Al Qaeda.

Regarding the United States, the report did discuss tactics as to how Israel could get American sympathy and support for the proposed policy to advance Israel's interests. To prevent the debilitating American criticism of Israeli policy that took place during Israel's invasion of Lebanon in 1982, the "Clean Break" report advised Netanyahu to present Israeli actions "in language familiar to the Americans by tapping into themes of American administrations during the cold war which apply well to Israel." For example, the report stated that

> Mr. Netanyahu can highlight his desire to cooperate more closely with the United States on anti-missile defense in order to remove the threat of blackmail which even a weak and distant army can pose to either state. Not only would such cooperation on missile defense counter a tangible physical threat to Israel's survival, but it would broaden Israel's base of support among many in the United States Congress who may know little about Israel, but care very much about missile defense.[44]

Israel could also gain American support, the report maintained, by appealing to Western ideals. The Netanyahu government should "promote Western values and traditions. Such an approach . . . will be well received in the United States." The appeal to American values loomed large in the reference to Syria and the key role of Lebanon. "An effective approach, and one with which American can sympathize, would be if Israel seized the strategic initiative along its northern borders by engaging Hizballah, Syria, and Iran, as the principal agents of aggression in Lebanon." In short, the report saw the use of moral values in largely utilitarian terms. References to moral values were for American consumption and would serve as a means to obtain American support for a policy whose sole purpose was to advance Israeli national interests.[45]

While the authors of "A Clean Break" saw the vital need to win over American sympathy and support, the purpose of their strategy was simultaneously to free Israel from American pressure and influence. "Such self-reliance," the report explained, "will grant Israel greater freedom of action and remove a significant lever of [United States] pressure used against it in the past." It was highly noteworthy that Americans would advise the Israeli government how to induce the United States to support Israeli interests and how to avoid having to follow the policies of the United States government.[46]

In sum, the "Clean Break" study was an astounding document that has been given insufficient attention by the mainstream American media. Though written to advance the interests of a foreign country, it appears to be a rough blueprint for actual Bush administration policy, with which some of the "Clean Break" authors – Perle, Feith, and Wurmser – were intimately involved. The question that immediately arises concerns the loyalty and motives of the three authors. When formulating and implementing American policy for the Bush II administration, were they acting in the interests of America or of Israel?

Crucial parts of the "Clean Break" study show that Israeli interests trumped American ones. For the "Clean Break" study called for presenting actions to advance Israel interests under the cover of American interests and American morality. Moreover, one of the objectives of the "Clean Break" was to free Israel from American influence. In short, Israeli policy should become independent of American interests.

Finally, all of this leads to the ultimate question: If the "Clean Break" authors discussed ways to mask the purpose of the proposed Israeli policy, did administration neocons use a similar type of deception in publicly justifying the Bush administration's Middle East war policy? Certainly, the alleged "mistakes" regarding WMD and Saddam's ties to Al Qaeda would point in that direction. (The issue of this deception and the neocon role in the matter of war propaganda will be developed in later chapters.)

In its concern about presenting Israeli pre-emptive actions to Americans in ways that would gain their sympathy and support, the "Clean Break" study can be seen as a transitional evolutionary stage from Oded Yinon's thinking in the 1980s to the neocon-directed U.S. policy of the Bush II administration. Yinon thought in terms of Israeli action, with only a little mention of the United States beyond a general reference to couching Israel's actions in terms of the Cold War and Western values. The "Clean Break" provided much greater emphasis on the need to have United States support for what was still Israeli military action, and it also prescribed specific tactics to achieve this support. As a transitional stage, it was a mild uptick compared with what would come about in the post-911 Bush II administration when the United States itself would engage in the military action in the Middle East. (This would parallel evolution in nature, as described by the now-popular punctuated equilibrium version, with its long periods of very small changes interrupted by short, sudden periods of rapid transformation, usually after a catastrophic event.)

It should be emphasized that the proposed strategic actions and military targets for all three evolutionary stages were similar and the fundamental beneficiary was identical – Israel. Again, since neocons assume, or at least publicly proclaim, that Israeli interests are American interests (a claim that will be discussed at length in chapter 11), the American interest presumably would be enhanced in each case. Certainly, Bush policy has been presented to the American people as advancing American interests – though sometimes the alleged reasons later turned out to be bogus.

David Wurmser authored a much longer follow-up document to "A Clean Break" for the same Israeli think tank, the Institute for Advanced Strategic and Political Studies, entitled "Coping with Crumbling States: A Western and Israeli Balance of Power Strategy for the Levant." In this work, Wurmser emphasized the fragile nature of the Middle Eastern states and linked the U.S. and Israel together in dealing with security matters in the region. As in the more general "Clean Break" document, control of Iraq was presented as the strategic key to the entire Middle East region, at least as far as Israeli interests were involved. As the subtitle stated, Israel's fundamental security concern was its close neighbors in the Levant, but Wurmser emphasized that the correlation of power in that area was critically impacted by developments in the broader Middle East region.[47]

It was notable that rather than presenting Iraq as a powerful aggressor, Wurmser characterized the country as weak and breaking apart, with the state ideology of Baathism failing to serve as a unifying force. "The residual unity of the nation is an illusion projected by extreme repression of the state," Wurmser asserted.

> While there is a sense of common destiny among many Iraqis in ousting Saddam, the mechanism for doing so most reliably remains working through clan, family, and tribal connections. Indeed, only the most primordial, almost instinctual ties, manage to survive the watchful eye and heavy hand of Saddam.

Nonetheless, Iraq played a pivotal role in Israeli security. The "battle to dominate and define Iraq," Wurmser wrote, "is, by extension, the battle to dominate the balance of power in the Levant over the long run," and "the United States and Israel" should fight this battle together. Wurmser saw the United States and Israel confronted with a "Saudi-Iraqi-Syrian-Iranian-PLO axis." In Wurmser's view, the Levant consisted of "crumbling states, like Syria, locked in bitter rivalries over a collapsing entity (Iraq)." He opined that

> [g]iven the cross-border alliances of tribes and the fragility of the secular-Arab nationalist states in the Levant, strategic competition over Iraq may well lead to the collapse of some of the engaged regimes. Thus, whoever inherits Iraq dominates the entire Levant strategically.[48]

The danger to Israel arose from the fact that Iraq might fall under the control of Syria. Wurmser pointed out that Syria was trying to topple Saddam and gain dominance over Iraq by working with various Iraqi Shiite groups. Syrian ties to these groups derived from the leverage it had with Hezbollah, a fundamentalist Shiite organization, which operated in Syrian-occupied Lebanon.[49]

If Iraq fell under the sway of Hashemite Jordan, however, Syria would be imperiled. Wurmser maintained that "events in Iraq can shake Syria's position in Lebanon." Wurmser held that Syria's leader, then Hafez al-Assad,

> works primarily through the strong Shiite presence in the South to maintain his pressure on Israel. This pressure is necessary to preempt the Israelis from engaging more deeply in Lebanese affairs and undermining Syria in its Sunni or Christian core.

It is significant to note that Wurmser portrayed the Syrian actions as a largely defensive in order to prevent Israel from going on the offensive in Lebanon and Syria itself.[50]

Moreover, Wurmser pointed out that "one of the most important bolts Assad retains in his arsenal to retain his strong grip on Lebanon is Hizballah," explaining that "[a]s long as Hizballah is the primary force in southern Lebanon, the Lebanese Shia are linked ideologically to Iran." That situation would change radically if the Hashemites gained control of Iraq. "A Hashemite presence in Iraq, especially within the Shia centers in Najaf," Wurmser maintained, "could break Iran's and Syria's grip on the Shiite community of Lebanon." The result would be a major strategic benefit for Israel. "Close cooperation between Israel and Jordan could undermine Syria's pressure on Israel's northern border as the local Shia are weaned from Hizballah's domination. In short, developments in Iraq could potentially unravel Syria's structure in Lebanon by severing the Shia-Syrian-Iranian axis." The power of Israel's enemies would be dissipated while Israeli hegemony would be augmented.[51]

As in the general "Clean Break" study, Wurmser in his "Coping with Crumbling States" presented Iraq as a strategic regional key to controlling the Middle East. The value of attacking of Iraq was set in geostrategic terms, not in terms of any special danger coming from Saddam's power; in fact, Iraq was described as being especially weak, which was one fundamental reason for targeting it.

While this portrayal of Iraq's provocative weakness would carry weight among strategic thinkers concerned about Israel's regional security, such a geostrategic analysis would have little impact with the general American public, whose support would be essential if America itself were to be actively involved in the planned war. To achieve the latter, it would be necessary to show that Saddam was some type of lethal threat to America. And this is what the neocons would proceed to do.

Wurmser himself would turn to emphasizing the danger of Saddam Hussein to the United States. In *Tyranny's Ally: America's Failure to Defeat Saddam Hussein*, published in 1999 by AEI, Wurmser expanded on his "Coping with Crumbling States" thesis with a focus on the need to militarily remove Saddam's regime. Wurmser claimed that Saddam's Iraq was a definite threat to the United States because it was "a totalitarian tyranny. Such tyranny is, by its very nature, violent, aggressive, and rabidly anti-Western."[52]

Wurmser contended that America's failure to bring down Saddam during the Gulf War had allowed for his revival, and the concomitant strengthening of all America's enemies in the Middle East, which would ultimately mean defeat for the United States in the region. "The longer Iraq remains under Saddam's control and the more his power revives," Wurmser stated, "the brighter the prospects and the stronger the resilience of the anti-western alliance."[53]

In calling for an American militant strategy toward the Middle East, Wurmser presented the major enemy as secular, pan-Arabic nationalism, which he described as totalitarian. This differed radically from the post-9/11 emphasis on the danger of Islamism – though Wurmser maintained that the elimination of Saddam's regime would likewise bring about the destruction of the Islamic Republic in Iran.[54] Furthermore, Wurmser held that the destabilization of the existing governments of the Middle East would actually improve the lives of its people because "for much of the Arab world, factionalism constitutes the sole barrier against the absolute power of its tyrants." Wurmser, though an advocate of "American values," proposed not an advance to modern democracy – the dominant neoconservative theme since the build-up of the war on Iraq – but rather a return to the rule of the Hashemites and the powerful traditional families. And he presented Ahmed Chalabi, the notorious Iraqi exile, as representing this viable, positive tradition. "He, his family, and the organization he created represent an older Iraq and a traditional elite that have been battered, oppressed, and enslaved by pan-Arabic nationalist governments for forty years."[55] While Wurmser depicted decentralization as a means of advancing liberty for the Arab people, such a dissolution of centralized states, of course, coincided with the Israeli security goal of surrounding itself with fragmented, powerless statelets.

Significantly, in regard to the role of Israel in his thinking, Wurmser alleged that Saddam was the key to PLO strength. "Saddam views his connection with the PLO and Arafat as a valuable strategic asset," Wurmser asserted. "Any U.S. policy that allocates a higher priority to the Arab-Israeli peace process than to the Iraqi challenge leaves the United States vulnerable to an Iraqi veto or sabotage, as long as the PLO responds to Saddam's direction."[56] In essence, Wurmser was correctly pointing out that without external support the Palestinians would be less able to resist Israeli policy. His assumption, of course, was that Israel should have a free hand to deal

with the Palestinians and that the United States should simply support Israeli policy.

In the book's acknowledgments, Wurmser praised the key neoconservatives who influenced his work, which provides a good illustration of the closeness of the neoconservative network. Wurmser was most lavish with his praise for Richard Perle, who wrote the foreword for the book. Wurmser credited Perle with liberating Eastern Europe from Soviet Communism:

> Richard showed the world how to successfully convert theory into practice in confronting tyranny. It is thus a singular honor for me to have earned his continuing support, suggestions, and encouragement – without which I would neither have arrived at AEI nor been given opportunity to write.

Wurmser also lauded AEI scholar Michael Ledeen, who had "continually reinforced the centrality of promoting freedom and combating tyranny." Wurmser paid tribute to Ahmed Chalabi, "who guided my understanding of the Middle East," and praised Douglas Feith and R. James Woolsey. Wurmser also gave special thanks to Irving Moskowitz, the long-time funder of Israel's settlement movement, whom he described as a "gentle man whose generous support of AEI allows me to be here."[57]

While Wurmser focused on the danger of Saddam, he still did not go so far as to portray him as a diabolical terrorist threat to the American homeland, which would be necessary to rouse the American people to support a war. The key figure who moved to this level was Laurie Mylroie, also of the American Enterprise Institute. She served as the neocons' leading expert on Saddam Hussein. From the time of the World Trade Tower bombing in 1993, Mylroie developed a complex conspiracy theory that identified Saddam as the mastermind behind that action and numerous other terrorist activities directed against the United States, such as the 1995 Oklahoma City bombing and the attack on the USS *Cole* off the coast of Yemen in 2000.[58]

Mylroie presented her thesis in *Study of Revenge: Saddam Hussein's Unfinished War Against America*, which was published by the AEI in 2000. "It is the contention of this book," Mylroie wrote,

> that the rash of terrorist attacks directed at the United States, beginning with the 1993 bombing of the New York World Trade Center, does not represent an amorphous . . . new kind of terrorism. Rather, the United States is involved in a new kind of war – an undercover war of terrorism, waged by Saddam Hussein.

Or, perhaps, the terrorism is best characterized as a phase in a conflict that began in August 1990, when Iraq invaded Kuwait, and that has not ended.[59]

Mylroie's Saddam conspiracy theory was far outside mainstream thinking, and she would have been considered something of an oddball if it were not for her connections to people with power.[60] Peter Bergen in the *Washington Monthly* in 2003 dubbed her "the neocons' favorite conspiracy theorist."[61] The *Study of Revenge* had considerable input from the neocon network. In her acknowledgements, Mylroie credited Paul Wolfowitz for providing "crucial support" and his then-wife Clare Wolfowitz as having "fundamentally shaped the book." Mylroie also thanked three individuals who would become top aides to Vice President Cheney – chief of staff Lewis (Scooter) Libby and foreign-policy advisors John Hannah and David Wurmser – as well as John Bolton, an under secretary of state under and later ambassador to the United Nations under Bush II. She would also credit Michael Ledeen.[62] Once published, other neocons praised the work. Richard Perle described the book as "splendid and wholly convincing." R. James Woolsey, Paul Wolfowitz, and Jeane Kirkpatrick also gave their plaudits.[63]

Mylroie's book was originally published by the AEI, but after September 11, 2001, Regan Books, an imprint of HarperCollins Publishers, released the book in paperback, with the new title, *The War Against America: Saddam Hussein and the World Trade Center Attacks*, and with an introduction by R. James Woolsey. HarperCollins was owned by Rupert Murdoch, whose Fox News, in turn, booked Mylroie as an Iraq expert during the build-up to the war.[64]

Interestingly, there is substantial evidence that in the late 1980s Mylroie had served as a go-between in secret contacts between Israel and Iraq. At that time, elements in the Israeli government were interested in improving relations with Iraq, which ultimately came to naught. Mylroie was then publicly espousing a position favorable to Iraq, which she said had become friendlier toward Israel.[65]

Perhaps the most significant figure in the Bush II administration who argued at length for Saddam's forcible removal by the United States was Paul Wolfowitz, a firm adherent of Mylroie's views. His first direct expression of that view was the article "Overthrow Saddam," co-authored by Zalmay Khalilzad, which appeared in the December 1, 1997 issue of the *Weekly Standard*. In that work, Wolfowitz and Khalilzad held that American military force should focus on creating a liberated zone in southern Iraq that could aid the Iraqi resistance in overthrowing Saddam's regime.[66]

A key neoconservative umbrella group that would be in the forefront of urging war on Iraq was the Project for a New American Century (PNAC), which was founded in 1997 to promote a strategy for American military dominance of the globe. PNAC was initiated by the New Citizenship Project (NCP), which was an affiliate of the Project for the Republican Future, a conservative Republican think tank founded by William Kristol. Kristol was the chairman of PNAC, and Robert Kagan, one of Kristol's close associates as a contributing editor of *The Weekly Standard*, was one of the directors. NCP and PNAC were headquartered at 1150 17th St., NW, Washington, D.C., which was also the headquarters of AEI.[67] Many figures who would become prominent war hawks in the Bush II administration were associated with PNAC: Dick Cheney, Donald Rumsfeld, I. Lewis Libby, Paul Wolfowitz, Richard Perle, Douglas Feith, Elliott Abrams, John Bolton, and Zalmay Khalilzad.[68]

On January 26, 1998, PNAC sent a letter to President Clinton urging him to take unilateral military action against Iraq to overthrow Saddam and offering a plan to achieve that objective. It especially counseled the president to avoid involving the UN Security Council. "American policy cannot continue to be crippled by a misguided insistence on unanimity in the UN Security Council," the letter said. Among the letters' eighteen signatories were Donald Rumsfeld, Paul Wolfowitz, Zalmay Khalilzad, Elliott Abrams, John Bolton, Robert Kagan, William Kristol, R. James Woolsey, and Richard Perle.[69] The letter was privately delivered by Perle and former Democratic Congressman Stephen Solarz to Sandy Berger, Clinton's national security advisor.[70]

After the Clinton administration failed to take action on the suggestions, a second open letter to Clinton, dated February 19, 1998, was made public. It included an expanded list of forty names; among those signers added were Douglas Feith, Michael Ledeen, Joshua Muravchik and David Wurmser. It was sent under the banner of the resurrected Committee for Peace and Security in the Gulf, which had played a major role in promoting the 1991 Gulf War. The letter was more detailed than the one of January 26, proposing "a comprehensive political and military strategy for bringing down Saddam and his regime." It continued: "It will not be easy – and the course of action we favor is not without its problems and perils. But we believe the vital national interests of our country require the United States to [adopt such a strategy]."[71]

Unsatisfied with Clinton's response, PNAC wrote another letter on May 29, 1998, to former House Speaker Newt Gingrich and Senate Republican Majority Leader Trent Lott, with almost the same signatories as its January letter to the President, saying that

> U.S. policy should have as its explicit goal removing Saddam Hussein's regime from power and establishing a peaceful and democratic Iraq in its place. We recognize that this goal will not be achieved easily. But the alternative is to leave the initiative to Saddam, who will continue to strengthen his position at home and in the region. Only the U.S. can lead the way in demonstrating that his rule is not legitimate and that time is not on the side of his regime.[72]

Numerous bills were put forward in Congress to provide aid to the Iraqi opposition to Saddam's regime. Ultimately, President Clinton would only go so far as to sign the Iraq Liberation Act in September 1998, which called for the United States "to support efforts to remove the regime headed by Saddam Hussein," but limited that support to an allocation of $97 million for training and military equipment for the Iraqi opposition. Neoconservatives regarded that response as woefully insufficient. As Richard Perle wrote: "the administration refused to commit itself unequivocally to a new strategy, raising questions as to whether any meaningful shift had occurred in U.S. policy."[73]

The Iraq Liberation Act did not imply a military attack on Iraq. As Ambassador Joseph Wilson noted,

> American administrations have long had regime-change policies in place toward countries whose leaders we did not like – Cuba, Libya, and Sudan, for instance. There had been a number of precedents for effecting regime change without resorting to war, including successful efforts during the Reagan administration in Poland and in the southern Africa countries of Namibia and South Africa.

But Wilson added that, unrealized at the time by most observers, the legislation would serve as a "rallying point for the prowar crowd. It was a preliminary stride toward invasion, not just another small step in the political campaign to undermine Saddam."[74] The Iraq Liberation Act was sometimes even cited by war proponents as a legal justification for the American invasion of Iraq in 2003.[75]

In September 2000, PNAC issued a report, "Rebuilding America's Defenses: Strategy, Forces and Resources for a New Century," which envisioned an expanded global posture for the United States. In regard to the Middle East, the report called for an increased American military presence in the Gulf, whether Saddam was in power or not, maintaining:

> The United States has for decades sought to play a more permanent role in Gulf regional security. While the unresolved conflict with Iraq provides the immediate justification, the need for a substantial American force presence in the Gulf transcends the issue of the regime of Saddam Hussein.

The report struck a prescient note when it observed that "the process of transformation, even if it brings revolutionary change, is likely to be a long one, absent some catastrophic and catalyzing event – like a new Pearl Harbor."[76]

It was apparent that during the Clinton years the neocons had formulated the entire plan for a Middle East war and had established the mechanisms, with their think tanks and media outlets, to disseminate this view to politicians and the public at large.

They had become wedded to the idea, developed earlier by Likudnik thinkers, that it was necessary to bring about a reconfiguration of the Middle East, not only by removing those regimes that opposed Israel but also by fragmenting some of those countries. And they perceived Iraq as the initial target for the overall Middle East effort. Significantly, they saw the need for American involvement – quickly moving from the idea that the United States would be supportive of Israeli military action to the point where the United States would initiate military action itself. To achieve such American involvement it would be necessary to show how the United States itself was directly threatened; thus, by the end of the 1990s the neocons were portraying Saddam as an especially lethal threat to the American homeland. In actuality, however, the removal of Saddam was simply intended to be the beginning phase in the overall restructuring of the Middle East.

The neocons were quite unified in presenting the danger Saddam allegedly posed to the United States, and their think tanks and media outlets could effectively disseminate this view. However, they could not achieve their goal by simply being a "shadow defense department"; what was needed was to gain a prominent role in the foreign-policy and national-security apparatus of the next administration, and then perhaps await a "catastrophic and catalyzing event" (as the PNAC report deemed necessary) to fully implement their program. All of this would soon come to pass.

chapter 7

SERBIAN INTERLUDE AND THE 2000 ELECTION

WHILE NEOCONS were developing their think tanks and expanding in the media, the political climate of the 1990s was not propitious for them. Their domination of the conservative intellectual movement was not translating into success at the presidential level; the neocon goal of setting the national foreign policy agenda from inside the executive branch seemed no closer than ever. If neocons were upset by the Clinton administration, their view of the Republicans was mixed at best. For it seemed that many grass roots Republicans in the aftermath of the Cold War were trending toward non-interventionism (the neocons' dreaded "isolationism"). And they were turning to Patrick Buchanan – the bête noire of Israel and American Zionists, who had opposed the 1991 Gulf War, charging that it had been promoted by supporters of Israel (the "Amen Corner").[1]

In 1992, Buchanan ran against President George H. W. Bush in the Republican primaries and was able to garner a substantial number of votes. In addition to supporting protectionism and various conservative domestic positions, Buchanan ran on a non-interventionist foreign policy platform. All of this Buchanan called his "America First" program, using the name of an American organization that had opposed American intervention into World War II – a stance that was anathema to neoconservatives.[2]

Despite the hostility of the neocons, Buchanan did even better in 1996, winning the first presidential primary election in New Hampshire, and scoring close seconds and thirds in other states. Buchanan especially did substantially better than the candidates or prospective candidates favored by the neo-conservatives – Jack Kemp, Bill Bennett, Dan Quayle, Phil Gramm, Lamar Alexander, and Steve Forbes.

Even though the Republican Party ultimately rejected him, many Republicans adopted much of Buchanan's non-interventionist foreign policy stance. In 1995, a year after Republicans became the majority in the U.S. House of Representatives, 190 of them voted to deny funds for American peacekeeping troops stationed in Bosnia. By the end of the decade, condemnations of "foreign policy as social work" and "nation building" had become standard Republican fare.[3]

The major international concern in the 1990s was the conflict in Yugoslavia – with the focus first on Bosnia and then on Kosovo. After the downfall of Communism, Yugoslavia broke apart, with the secession in 1992 of Croatia, Macedonia, and Slovenia. Bosnia also declared its independence, despite the objections of Bosnian Serbs, who wanted to remain united with Serbia. Civil war broke out between the Bosnian Serbs, supported by Serbia, and the Muslim-dominated Bosnian government. Untold thousands were killed, raped and displaced in what became known as ethnic cleansing. The West generally looked, however unfairly, upon the atrocities, both real and imagined, as being primarily perpetrated by the Serbs.[4]

In 1992, the UN peacekeeping forces intervened for allegedly humanitarian reasons and set up several so-called safe areas for refugees, including the Bosnian capital of Sarajevo. The UN forces were mostly composed of British and French troops, while American ships and airplanes enforced an arms embargo. Respectable liberal opinion saw the Serbs as the perpetrators of terrible atrocities and advocated "humanitarian" military intervention to protect the Muslims. Neocons were on the interventionist bandwagon and blamed Clinton for not taking sufficient action to aid the Bosnian Muslims. Joshua Muravchik, for example, claimed that Clinton's embrace of multilateralism was tantamount to "isolationist internationalism" in that Clinton "welcomed international action but not the exertion of American power."[5]

Finally, in 1999, President Clinton orchestrated the NATO war on Serbia, as a result of the Serbs alleged "ethnic cleansing" of Muslims in their province of Kosovo.[6] While Clinton limited American actions to air strikes, neoconservatives went beyond Clinton in calling for the use of ground troops. Members of the interventionist Balkan Action Committee, which advocated NATO ground troops for Kosovo, included such prominent neoconservative mainstays as Richard Perle, Jeane Kirkpatrick, Max M. Kampelman, Morton Abramowitz, and Paul Wolfowitz. Other announced proponents of a tougher war included Eliot Cohen, Elliott Abrams, John Bolton, William Kristol, William Kagan, and Norman Podhoretz.[7]

Traditional conservatives were the polar opposite of the neoconservatives on the American war on Serbia. "It's a complete reshuffling of the Cold War deck and a fracturing of the old Cold War conservative coalition," said Thomas Moore, international studies director at the conservative Heritage Foundation. "The far left is largely in favor of the bombing. Traditional conservatives are the least supportive. And the neoconservatives feel we should intervene." David Keene, president of the American Conservative Union, concurred. "I think this is crazy," Keene asserted. "Clinton has not made the case that this is in our national interests, and most of the traditional conservatives agree with me."[8] Pat Buchanan condemned Clinton for launching "an illegal, presidential war" against Yugoslavia. He said the United States "has no vital interest in whose flag flies over Kosovo's capital and no right to attack and kill Serb soldiers fighting on their own soil to preserve the territorial integrity of their own country."[9]

With neoconservative interventionism on the downslide in the Republican Party, it was a piece of amazingly good fortune for the neoconservatives that they came to power with the advent of the George W. Bush presidency. Such a neocon ascendancy had not been anticipated, since many observers expected the second Bush to follow in his father's foreign policy footsteps. As discussed earlier in this work, the elder Bush had been far from a friend of Israel's and as a "realist" with a Big Oil background had pursued a policy promoting stability in the Middle East. And George W. Bush, on the rare occasions he spoke on foreign policy, often expressed the non-interventionist attitude that was gaining dominance in the post-Cold War Republican Party, at least on the grass roots level.

Many neocons, Michael Lind wrote,

> feared that the second Bush would be like the first – a wimp who had failed to occupy Baghdad in the first Gulf War and who had pressured Israel into the Oslo peace process – and that his administration, again like his father's, would be dominated by moderate Republican realists such as Powell, James Baker and Brent Scowcroft.[10]

Despite the seemingly inauspicious circumstances, influential neocons Paul Wolfowitz and Richard Perle managed to obtain significant roles in the Bush foreign policy/national security advisory team for the 2000 campaign. Headed by Soviet specialist Condoleezza Rice, the team was referred to as the "Vulcans" – named for the Roman god Vulcan whose statue graced Rice's hometown of Birmingham, Alabama. The name conveyed an image of toughness and power, as intended. Of the eight "Vulcans," there were two other neocons in addition to Wolfowitz and Perle: Stephen Hadley and Dov Zakheim.[11]

The Vulcans would tutor Bush on foreign policy and national security matters. Bush admitted that he had little knowledge of foreign affairs, as clearly illustrated by his gaffes – confusing Slovakia with Slovenia, referring to Greeks as "Grecians" and failing a pop quiz on the names of four foreign leaders.[12] Moreover, it was not evident that he had the interest or ability to learn. Journalist Christopher Hitchens would characterize Bush in 2000 as "unusually incurious, abnormally unintelligent, amazingly inarticulate, fantastically uncultured, extraordinarily uneducated, and apparently quite proud of all these things."[13]

Given his shallowness, if not empty-headedness, in foreign affairs, it was apparent that George W. Bush would need to rely heavily on his advisers. "His foreign policy team," neoconservative Robert Kagan observed during the campaign, "will be critically important to determining what his policies are." Columnist Robert Novak noted: "Since Rice lacks a clear track record on Middle East matters, Wolfowitz and Perle will probably weigh in most on Middle East policy."[14]

Despite these neocon advisers, however, there is no evidence that Bush had adopted distinctively neoconservative foreign policy positions during the 2000 campaign. Halper and Clarke in *America Alone* write:

> Far from reaching out to neoconservatives, the efforts of Bush's advisers were aimed at distinguishing his approach from, on the one hand, Clinton's "dilettantism" and, on the other, nativist Republican isolationism and protectionism. Neo-conservatives such as Richard Perle had to battle for access to Bush and were constantly on the telephone to Austin to reassure themselves that their views were being acted on. "It's almost as though they did not trust Bush," commented one member of the campaign team in Austin.[15]

From his references to foreign policy during the campaign, it appeared that Bush largely wanted to stick with the status quo. Fitting in with all American presidents of the postwar era, he emphasized the importance of alliances. He stressed that he would vehemently defend American interests, implying that Clinton had been something of a pushover in that area; and he stated that America should rely more on military muscle, a definite neoconservative theme. But at the same time, Bush frequently criticized the Clinton administration for nation building, which was an activity dear to the hearts of neoconservatives, but was staunchly opposed by more traditional conservatives. Nation-building was not the proper role of the military, Bush told a crowd on November 7, 2000, one day before the election. "I'm worried about an opponent," he said, "who uses nation building and the military in the same sentence. See, our view of the military is for our military to be properly prepared to fight and win war and, therefore, prevent war from happening in the first place."[16]

The speech was an explicit criticism of the Clinton administration for allegedly stretching the military too thin with peacekeeping missions in Haiti, Somalia and the Balkans. Moreover, Bush argued, it was just improper for the United States to run other countries. As Bush stated in his second presidential debate on October 11: "I just don't think it's the role of the United States to walk into a country and say, we do it this way, so should you." Any attempt to dictate to other countries, Bush maintained, would be counterproductive "If we're an arrogant nation, they'll resent us; if we're a humble nation, but strong, they'll welcome us."[17]

Furthermore, during the campaign Bush never suggested that terrorism was a major problem or blamed Clinton for being lax on this issue. Nor did Bush ever place any emphasis on the danger of Iraq. Nor did he dwell on the reports or allegations of brutality by Saddam towards his people, or lobby, as a consequence, for their liberation from his government. Like Vice-President Al Gore, the Democratic Presidential nominee, and the rest of the Clinton administration, Bush simply said that the United States should continue to contain Iraq through sanctions. Authors Ivo H. Daalder and James M. Lindsay summarize Bush's bland foreign policy statements during the 2000 campaign in their *America Unbound: The Bush Revolution in Foreign Policy*: "What the campaign suggested was that for Bush, as for Bill Clinton in 1992, foreign policy was not a matter of passion. He attempted to do so in ways that maximized his appeal to voters, or at least limited the chances that he would offend."[18] There was no hint of the revolution in foreign policy that was to come.

When Condoleezza Rice became Bush's campaign advisor at the start of the 2000 campaign, she broached the subject of Iraq to him. Bush told her that he disagreed with critics who complained that his father had terminated the 1991 war too soon without invading Iraq and removing Saddam. Bush told Rice that his father and his advisors did "the right thing at the time."[19]

Rice herself expressed some views on Iraq quite contrary to those of the neoconservatives. In an article in the January-February 2000 issue of *Foreign Affairs*, Rice wrote that "rogue nations" such as Iraq and North Korea

> are living on borrowed time, so there need be no sense of panic about them. Rather, the first line of defense should be a clear and classical statement of deterrence – if they do acquire weapons of mass destruction, that weapon will be unusable because any attempt to use them will bring national obliteration.[20]

While some neoconservatives served as Bush's foreign policy advisers, the actual favorite candidate for many leading neoconservatives in 2000 was Senator John McCain, Bush's Republican rival in the primaries, who did express unambiguous neoconservative positions.[21] As Franklin Foer, editor of the liberal *New Republic* put it:

> Jewish neoconservatives have fallen hard for John McCain. It's not just unabashed swooner William Kristol, editor of *The Weekly Standard*. McCain has also won over such leading neocon lights as David Brooks, the entire Podhoretz family, *The Wall Street Journal*'s Dorothy Rabinowitz, and columnist Charles Krauthammer, who declared, in a most un-Semitic flourish, "He suffered for our sins."[22]

Jeane Kirkpatrick also backed McCain. Another significant neoconservative for McCain was Randy Scheunemann, who served as a Defense and Foreign Policy Adviser in the McCain 2000 Presidential Campaign. Among Scheunemann's neocon credentials was membership in the Board of Directors of PNAC and the presidency of the Committee for the Liberation of Iraq.[23] Another self-proclaimed neocon who served as an advisor was Marshall Wittmann.[24]

McCain was especially championed by William Kristol, editor of the *Weekly Standard*, and his associate David Brooks. They held that McCain would promote their idea of "national greatness," as opposed to what they regarded as the standpatness of the conservative Republicans. The "national greatness" program would entail a greater role for the federal government and also more extensive intervention throughout the world to promote American values. Kristol, in fact, pronounced the death of the conservative movement. "Leaderless, rudderless and issueless, the conservative movement, which accomplished great things over the past quarter-century, is finished."[25]

The neocons support for McCain underscored their differences with the traditional conservatives, who backed Bush, since McCain advocated a bigger federal government and was quite critical of the role of religion in public life – and also supported such fashionable liberal causes as campaign finance reform, environmentalism, gun control, homosexual rights, and anti-tobacco legislation. McCain essentially ran as a reformer. While antagonizing many conservatives, McCain garnered support from numerous liberals and the mainstream media.[26]

Neoconservatives admired McCain for his support of the American war on Serbia, toward which many mainstream conservatives were decidedly cool. The attack on Serbia, ostensibly for humanitarian reasons, provided the intellectual groundwork for the attack on Iraq, since it set the precedent of violating international law's prohibition against initiating offensive wars. No longer would the United States have to be attacked, or even threatened, to engage in war. In fact, McCain criticized Clinton for being too soft in his war policy toward Kosovo because of his refusal to send in ground troops. As Kristol and Brooks put it:

> For all his conventional political views, McCain embodies a set of virtues that today are unconventional. The issue that gave the McCain campaign its initial boost was Kosovo. He argued that America as a great champion of democracy and decency could not fail to act. And he supported his commander in chief despite grave doubts about the conduct of the war – while George W. Bush sat out the debate and Republicans on the Hill flailed at Clinton.[27]

What would be far more important for the neoconservatives than the specific issue of Serbia was McCain's advocacy of an overall policy of "rogue state rollback," which pointed directly at the enemies of Israel. McCain had been a member of the neoconservative Committee for the Liberation of Iraq and was a leading senatorial sponsor of the Iraq Liberation Act of 1998, which called upon the United States government to press for Saddam's elimination.[28] Antiwar commentator Justin Raimondo sized up the fundamental reason for the *Weekly Standard's* political infatuation with McCain: "Never mind all this doubletalk about 'sacrificing for a cause bigger than yourself' – what the authors of this piece really mean to say is that this is a candidate who will not hesitate to lead his country into war."[29]

McCain took a very pro-Israel position and had been doing so for some time, unlike Bush's father who had been considered hostile to Israeli interests. As a result McCain was the 1999 recipient of the Defender of Jerusa-

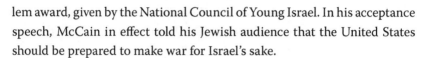

lem award, given by the National Council of Young Israel. In his acceptance speech, McCain in effect told his Jewish audience that the United States should be prepared to make war for Israel's sake.

> Certainly, no one would argue with the proposition that our armed forces exist first and foremost for the defense of the United States and its vital interests abroad . . . . We choose, as a nation, however, to intervene militarily abroad in defense of the moral values that are at the center of our national conscientiousness even when vital national interests are not necessarily at stake. I raise this point because it lies at the heart of this nation's approach to Israel. The survival of Israel is one of this country's most important moral commitments . . . . Like the United States, Israel is more than a nation; it is an ideal . . . . [30]

McCain admitted that the defense of Israel was a significant factor for his support for war against Iraq. In a interview with political commentator Chris Matthews in late 2001, McCain, in justifying a United States attack, stated: "My nightmare – I have several nightmares about Saddam Hussein, but one of them is the that SCUD missile which he has . . . that's in the view of most, aimed at Israel. Aimed at Israel."[31]

For those who blame Bush and Cheney for the war on Iraq, a significant hypothetical question is: How would a President John McCain have responded to the September 11 attacks? Given his willingness to make war on a country (Serbia) that did not threaten America in the least, his advocacy of forcible regime change in Iraq prior to 2001, and his staunch support for the attack on Iraq during the war build-up (and his later hawkishness on Iran),[32] there is no reason to think that a President McCain would have avoided a war on Iraq. In fact, he likely would have pursued a belligerent approach toward Iraq even if a major terrorist attack on the United States had not taken place.

chapter 8

GEORGE W. BUSH ADMINISTRATION: THE BEGINNING

IT WAS THE BUSH II administration that would bring the neo-conservatives into power. Upon taking office, neoconservatives would fill key positions in the administration involving defense and national security policy. On Secretary of Defense Donald Rumsfeld's staff were Deputy Defense Secretary Paul Wolfowitz and Under Secretary for Policy Douglas Feith. On Vice President Cheney's staff, the principal neoconservatives included I. Lewis "Scooter" Libby, Eric Edelman, and John Hannah. David Wurmser would come aboard, replacing Edelman, in 2003. Elliott Abrams was a member of the National Security Council who in December 2002 would be put in charge of Near East policy. Over at the Department of State was John Bolton who became Under Secretary of State for Arms Control.

A few weeks before launching the attack on Iraq, President Bush paid homage to the importance of the neoconservatives when he spoke before the neoconservative American Enterprise Institute. "At the American Enterprise Institute some of the finest minds in our nation are at work in some of the greatest challenges to our nation," Bush exclaimed. "You do such good work that my administration has borrowed twenty such minds."[1]

While Bush might give thanks to the neoconservatives, it was Vice President Dick Cheney, with his long-time neoconservative connections, who played the major role in bringing them into the administration and thus shaping American foreign policy. Cheney had a key role in the Bush's campaign and his selection as vice-president was, as James Mann points out in his *Rise of the Vulcans*, "of surpassing importance for the future direction of foreign policy. It went further than any other single decision Bush made toward determining the nature and the policies of the administration he would head."[2]

Although never identified as a neoconservative, Cheney was closely connected to the neoconservative elite. Halper and Clarke in *America Alone* view Cheney's connection to the neocons in terms of a similarity of ideas. They describe him as an "American nationalist," rather than a full-fledged neoconservative, whose views on American exceptionalism and American power "paralleled" those of the neoconservatives.[3] But Cheney's neocon ties transcended ideas. Prior to becoming vice-president, Cheney had been a member of the board of advisors of the Jewish Institute for National Security Affairs (JINSA), a member of the board of trustees of the American Enterprise Institute (AEI), and a founding member of the neoconservative Project for a New American Century (PNAC). It also should be noted that Cheney's wife, Lynne Cheney, who had chaired the National Endowment for the Humanities under Presidents Reagan and George H. W. Bush, was a prestigious member of AEI.

Whereas George W. Bush had not expressed any interest in eliminating Saddam, Cheney, at a celebration dinner after the 2000 presidential campaign, reportedly told a group of friends that the new administration might have an opportunity to correct the mistake of the previous Bush administration of having left Saddam Hussein in control of Iraq.[4] Cheney would be in a position to facilitate this development.

Cheney was in charge of the new administration's transition team between the election in November 2000 and Bush's inauguration in January 2001, and used that position to staff national security positions with his neoconservative associates, who would promote the Middle East war agenda. "It was Cheney's choices that prevailed in the appointment of both cabinet and sub-cabinet national-security officials, beginning with that of Donald Rumsfeld as defense secretary," columnist Jim Lobe observed.[5] Regarding the fundamental implications of Cheney's leadership of the presidential transition, Michael Lind pointed out that

> Cheney used this opportunity to stack the administration with his hard-line allies. Instead of becoming the de facto president in foreign policy, as many had expected, Secretary of State Powell found himself boxed in by Cheney's right-wing network, including Wolfowitz, Perle, Feith, Bolton and Libby.[6]

Significantly, Cheney created a large national-security staff in his office, constituting a virtual National Security Council in miniature, which had a major effect in shaping American national policy. Glenn Kessler and Peter Slevin, writing in the *Washington Post*, likened Cheney's office to "an agile cruiser, able to maneuver around the lumbering aircraft carriers of the departments of State and Defense to make its mark."[7] Robert Dreyfuss notes in *The American Prospect* that

> [a] the high-water mark of neoconservative power, when coalition forces invaded Iraq in March 2003, the vice president's office was the command center for a web of like-minded officials in the White House, the Pentagon, the State Department, and other agencies, often described by former officials as "Dick Cheney's spies."[8]

Many observers regarded Cheney as being the actual commander-in-chief, which is overblown, but it does appear that Cheney held the reigns of influence in the Bush administration on national security matters. While it would be too much to say that Bush was Cheney's puppet, Cheney's views generally prevailed (during Bush's first term, at least) because of his obvious knowledge, relative to Bush's, and because of his connection to other important figures in the administration.[9] Kessler described Cheney as "arguably the most powerful vice president in U.S. history."[10]

The critical role of Cheney in bringing in the neoconservatives who would shape American foreign policy in the Middle East cannot be overstated. When George W. Bush entered office, a general assumption was that he would depend on his father and his coterie of foreign/national security policy advisors – James Baker, Brent Scowcroft, Lawrence Eagelburgher – who were quintessential realists wedded to the traditional American policy of stability-maintenance in the Middle East, and not noted for any friendship toward Israel.[11] All of those individuals turned out to be cool, if not outright opposed, to George W. Bush's war policy in the Middle East. In all likelihood, had they held the reigns of power there would not have been war.

The crucial importance of Bush's neoconservative advisors in shaping American foreign policy was acknowledged by neocon Richard Perle: "If Bush had staffed his administration with a group of people selected by Brent Scowcroft and Jim Baker, which might well have happened, then it could have been different, because they would not have carried into it the ideas that the people who wound up in important positions brought to it.

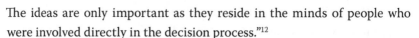

The ideas are only important as they reside in the minds of people who were involved directly in the decision process."[12]

Why did Cheney come to dominate? First, it must be said that he was chosen for his obvious administrative know-how. Someone with insider skills was needed to direct the administration. As Sidney Blumenthal wrote: "Most observers assumed that Cheney would provide balancing experience and maturity, serving in his way as a surrogate father and elder statesman."[13] And to those realists around the elder Bush, the choice of Cheney probably appeared to be a safe move. It could not have been apparent that Cheney would be able to move the Bush II administration Middle East policy in a neocon direction. First, the neocons he appointed were not in the topmost positions, which were in non-neocon hands, with Condoleezza Rice heading the National Security Council and Colin Powell running the State Department. Neocons had been rather numerous in the Bush I administration, too, but were precluded from implementing their position on the Middle East by the overarching power of Secretary of State James Baker.

Even shortly after 9/11, Brent Scowcroft was "dismissive" of the neoconservatives in private conversations with Joseph Wilson. Wilson writes that while he himself was "more alarmed," Scowcroft "reassured me that they did not enjoy senior administration support, even as their rhetoric reached fever pitch."[14]

What the neocons had in the Bush II administration was potential power or stealth power. They had significant numbers whose power was magnified by their notable networking skills. But such potential power could be fully actualized only if it had positive support from the top, otherwise the neocons would remain on the periphery as they had in the Bush I administration. Cheney would serve that supportive function by exerting far more power on behalf of the neocon agenda than James Baker had ever been able to wield in pursuing his realist policy in the Bush I administration.[15]

However, at the start of the Bush II administration, it was not apparent that Cheney would exert such an enormous influence in foreign policy. It was unknown for vice-presidents to be able to act in such a fashion. Moreover, Cheney had connections with oil, and as CEO of Halliburton had lobbied against sanctions of Israel's Middle East enemies. In short, the elder Bush and his realist coterie had no reason to expect that the Bush II Middle East policy would turn out as it did, at least until it became too late to do anything about it. Moreover, they could not have foreseen something comparable to the 9/11 disaster that would enable the neocon war agenda to move to the forefront. It was thus the very unlikelihood of this occurrence that facilitated the neocons' success. Scowcroft would later acknowledge that his initial underestimation of neoconservative power stemmed from his monumental misjudgment of Cheney's outlook. "The real anomaly in the administration is Cheney," Scowcroft forlornly explained. "I consider Cheney a good friend – I've known him for thirty years. But Dick Cheney I don't know anymore."[16]

The most crucial individual connected with Cheney was neoconservative I. Lewis "Scooter" Libby. Because of his closeness to Cheney and his bare-knuckle attitude to enemies of the administration, Libby was referred to as "Cheney's Cheney."[17] Bob Woodward described him as "one of the most important players in the Bush national security apparatus,"[18] and *Newsweek's* Evan Thomas, before the Valerie Plame affair gave Libby notoriety, called him "the most powerful Washington figure that most people have never heard of."[19] Libby had three formal titles. He was chief of staff to Vice President Cheney; national security advisor to the vice president; and an assistant to President Bush.

The title of a front-page article by Glenn Kessler in the *Washington Post*, which came out upon Libby's indictment in the Valerie Plame case in October 2005, was "With Vice President, He Shaped Iraq Policy." Kessler wrote that

> [b]ehind the scenes, working with allies in the Defense Department and other parts of the government, the two [Libby and Cheney] were early advocates of removing Saddam Hussein and highly effective in thwarting any opposition from the State Department and other bureaucratic rivals.[20]

"Libby is a neocon's neocon," wrote John Dickerson in *Slate* magazine.[21] Like many neoconservatives, Libby's early political views were not conservative and he served as vice president of the Yale College Democrats in the early 1970s.[22] His views changed as a result of his classes with Paul Wolfowitz, with the two developing a close friendship. After becoming a practicing lawyer, Libby came to work for Wolfowitz when the latter was assistant secretary of state in the 1980s under Reagan. Later, in the Bush I administration, Libby would serve as principal deputy under-secretary of defense for strategy and resources under Wolfowitz when Cheney was secretary of defense.[23] In 1992, Libby, under the direction of Wolfowitz, helped to write

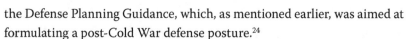

the Defense Planning Guidance, which, as mentioned earlier, was aimed at formulating a post-Cold War defense posture.[24]

Libby was a founding member of the Project for the New American Century and was one of the participants in the PNAC's 2000 report "Rebuilding America's Defenses – Strategy, Forces and Resources for a New Century," along with Paul Wolfowitz, William Kristol, Robert Kagan, and other leading neocons.[25] According to Jonathan Clarke, coauthor of *America Alone*, Libby represented the "pivot" of the neoconservative apparatus in Washington.[26] Libby knew who was who in the neoconservative network. And, as Robert Dreyfuss pointed out, the staff of the Cheney's all-important office would be "hand-picked by Libby." It "was drawn from the ranks of far-right think [neocon] tanks such as the American Enterprise Institute, the Hudson Institute, and WINEP, and from carefully screened Cheney loyalists in law firms around town."[27]

Paul Wolfowitz, the deputy secretary of defense in the younger Bush's first term, who had previously served in the in the Carter, Reagan, and first Bush administrations, became, as an article in the prestigious *Time Magazine* put it, the "godfather of the Iraq war."[28] Similarly, Bob Woodward writes in his *The Plan of Attack*, "The intellectual godfather and fiercest advocate for toppling Saddam was Paul Wolfowitz."[29] Wolfowitz was designated as the "Man of the Year" by the pro-Likud *Jerusalem Post* for the Jewish year 5763, which consisted of the period between October 2002 and October 2003.[30]

Wolfowitz had been one of the founding members of the Project for the New American Century (regarded as its "ideological father") and was one of the signers of the January 26, 1998 PNAC letter sent to President Bill Clinton, advocating the removal of Saddam.[31] Wolfowitz had also been associated with the Jewish Institute of National Security Affairs. In November 2002, JINSA honored Wolfowitz with its 2002 Henry M. "Scoop" Jackson Distinguished Service Award.[32]

Although the major media made clear Wolfowitz's hawkish positions regarding nuclear arms and American interventionism, which he expressed during his government service in the Reagan and Bush I administrations,[33] often ignored were his close ties to Israel. As former CIA analysts Kathleen and Bill Christison point out:

> Even profiles that downplay his attachment to Israel nonetheless always mention the influence the Holocaust, in which several of his family perished, has had on his thinking. One source inside the administration has described him

frankly as "over-the-top crazy when it comes to Israel." Although this probably accurately describes most of the rest of the neo-con coterie, and Wolfowitz is guilty at least by association, he is actually more complex and nuanced than this. A recent *New York Times Magazine* profile by the Times" Bill Keller cites critics who say that "Israel exercises a powerful gravitational pull on the man." Wolfowitz's father Jacob, an emigrant from Poland, who became a college professor in the United States was a committed Zionist all of his life. As a teenager Wolfowitz lived in Israel during his mathematician father's sabbatical semester there. His older sister Laura is married to an Israeli and lives in Israel. Keller even somewhat reluctantly acknowledges the accuracy of one characterization of Wolfowitz as "Israel-centric."[34]

If underplayed by the mainstream media, Wolfowitz's favorable views of Israel and Jewish-orientation were made known by the Jewish press. The *Forward* reported in April 2002 that he was "Known as the most hawkishly pro-Israel voice in the Administration." In November 2002, the *Forward* placed Wolfowitz on the top of a list of fifty leading Jewish figures who "have consciously pursued Jewish activism as they understood it, and all of them have left a mark."[35]

Douglas Feith, as under secretary of defense for policy, was the third most senior executive at the Pentagon, behind Rumsfeld and Wolfowitz. He was closely associated with the right-wing Zionist group, the Zionist Organization of America (ZOA). Living in Poland during the 1930s, Feith's father, Dalck Feith, was active in Betar, the youth wing of the right-wing Revisionist Zionist movement founded by Ze'ev Jabotinsky. In 1997, Douglas Feith and his father were the Guests of Honor at the 100th anniversary dinner of the ZOA in New York City. Dalck Feith received the organization's special Centennial Award at the dinner for his lifetime of service to Israel and the Jewish people. Douglas Feith received the prestigious Louis D. Brandeis Award.[36]

Feith co-founded One Jerusalem, a group whose objective was "saving a united Jerusalem as the undivided capital of Israel."[37] Feith was quite open about the Jewish exclusivism of the Israeli state. In an address he delivered in Jerusalem in 1997, titled "Reflections on Liberalism, Democracy and Zionism," Feith denounced "those Israelis" who "contend that Israel like America should not be an ethnic state – a Jewish state – but rather a 'state of its citizens.'" Feith argued that "there is a place in the world for non-ethnic nations and there is a place for ethnic nations."[38]

Before entering the Bush administration, Feith ran a small Washington-based law firm, Feith and Zell, which had one international office – in Israel. And the majority of the firm's work consisted of representing Israeli interests. Feith's partner, L. Marc Zell, was an American who became an Israeli citizen living in a Jewish settlement on the West Bank.[39]

During the Reagan administration, Feith held a number of positions, including special counsel to Richard Perle, then an assistant secretary of defense. According to investigative journalist Stephen Green, Feith was removed from his position as a Middle East analyst in the Reagan's National Security Council in 1983 because he had been the subject of an FBI investigation into whether he had passed classified material to an Israeli embassy official.[40]

In 1996, Feith coauthored the policy paper "A Clean Break" sent to then-Prime Minister Netanyahu, which called upon Israel to destabilize the Middle East, including an attack on Iraq. Feith was also a member of the advisory board of the Jewish Institute for National Security Affairs (JINSA) before joining the Bush administration.[41]

Colonel Lawrence Wilkerson, who served as Secretary of State Powell's chief of staff, was well aware of Feith's Israeli orientation, stating in regard to him and his neocon associate David Wurmser:

> A lot of these guys, including Wurmser, I looked at as card-carrying members of the Likud party, as I did with Feith. You wouldn't open their wallet and find a card, but I often wondered if their primary allegiance was to their own country or to Israel. That was the thing that troubled me, because there was so much that they said and did that looked like it was more reflective of Israel's interest than our own.[42]

Richard Perle is often described as the most influential foreign policy neoconservative, their *eminence grise*.[43] Perle has been affiliated with almost every major neoconservative think tank and organization: AEI, JINSA, PNAC, Center for Security Policy, Hudson Institute, Committee for the Liberation of Iraq, Committee on the Present Danger, and Foundation for the Defense of Democracies. George Packer in *The Assassins' Gate* describes Perle as the neocons'

> impresario, with one degree of separation from everyone who mattered. More than anyone, he personified the neoconservative insurgent, absolutely certain of himself and his ideas, always drawing new cadres into the cause, staging frequent guerrilla ambushes on the establishment, preparing to seize ultimate power.[44]

Although not technically a member of the Bush II administration, Perle held the unpaid chairmanship of the Defense Policy Board, which afforded him access to classified documents and close contacts with the administration leadership. About the Defense Policy Board, an article in the popular webzine *Salon* opined in September 2002:

> Formerly an obscure civilian board designed to provide the secretary of defense with non-binding advice on a whole range of military issues, the Defense Policy Board, now stacked with unabashed Iraq hawks, has become a quasi-lobbying organization whose primary objective appears to be waging war with Iraq.[45]

As mentioned earlier, Perle was a protégé of Albert Wohlstetter's, which enabled him to benefit from the latter's many Washington connections. During the 1970s, Perle gained notice as a top aide to neocon favorite Senator Henry "Scoop" Jackson. Perle played a major role in pushing through the Jackson-Vanik amendment that made American trade concessions to the Soviet Union dependent on that country's allowance of Jewish emigration.[46]

During the 1980s, Perle served as assistant secretary of defense for international security policy under Reagan, where he was able to exercise extensive influence in shaping American national-security policy. "Mr. Perle's influence in the Reagan Administration far exceeds that normally held by an assistant secretary of defense," observed *New York Times* reporter Jeff Garth. "In the transition, he was able to place associates in important national security positions and, in the Defense Department, he has played a major role in creating policies on arms control and trade with the Soviet Union."[47] Sidney Blumenthal would write in 1987 that Perle had done more to shape the administration's nuclear arms policy than perhaps any individual except Reagan himself.[48]

Murray Friedman in *The Neoconservative Revolution* similarly recognizes Perle's pre-eminence:

> In the shaping of the policies of the Reagan administration, such figures as Kirkpatrick, Rostow, Podhoretz, Pipes, and Perle played a critical role. By the latter part of the 1980s, the very force of Perle's ideas, and the fierce energy he exerted in advancing them, made him perhaps the central figure here, save Reagan himself.[49]

Perle's hardline anti-Soviet positions, especially his opposition to any form of arms control, and what some considered his Machiavellian political tactics, earned him the moniker "Prince of Darkness" from his enemies. His friends, however, considered him, as one put it, "one of the most wonderful people in Washington." That Perle was known as a man of great intellect, a gracious and generous host, a witty companion, and a loyal ally helped to explain his prestige in neoconservative circles.[50] Moreover, his influential connections went beyond the neoconservative orbit to include, as Murray Friedman writes, "a network of allies, friends, and informants throughout the intelligence community, the Capitol, and elsewhere in government"[51]

Perle not only expounded pro-Zionist views, but also had close connections with Israel, being a board member of the *Jerusalem Post* and having worked as a lobbyist for the Israeli weapons manufacturer Soltam.[52] According to author Seymour M. Hersh, while Perle was a congressional aide for Jackson, FBI wiretaps had picked up Perle providing classified information from the National Security Council to the Israeli embassy.[53] In 1983, Perle was the subject of a *New York Times* investigation into a charge that he recommended a weapons purchase from an Israeli company whose owners had paid him a consultancy $50,000 fee two years earlier. In 1987, he was investigated for possible ties to the notorious Israeli espionage case involving Jonathan Pollard. Though not accused of any crime, Perle resigned from the government.[54] Along with Feith and others, Perle coauthored the policy paper "A Clean Break" sent to then-Prime Minister Netanyahu in 1996, which called upon Israel to destabilize the Middle East, including an attack on Iraq.[55]

Given Cheney's power and orientation, it might be asked who would could conceivably check the neoconservative influence. Secretary of State Colin Powell was not a neoconservative, being more of an old-line establishment multilateralist and realist. He frequently opposed the neoconservative war agenda, but his resistance was consistently overwhelmed by the neoconservative network. In the view of veteran foreign affairs commentator, John Newhouse, "not since William Rogers, who served in the first Nixon administration, has a secretary of state been rolled over as often – or as routinely – as Powell." Newhouse continues: "In setting national security policy, the State Department has become a negligible influence on most issues."[56] After ending up on the losing end of policy battles, Powell, instead of continuing resistance or resigning, as did Secretary of State William Jennings Bryan in 1915 in protest against Woodrow Wilson's belligerency toward Germany, would "play the good soldier" and dutifully defend and carry out the policy decisions made by the neoconservatives.[57]

Powell even faced opposition within the State Department itself from neocon John Bolton, undersecretary of state for arms control. Before joining the Bush II administration, Bolton had been Senior Vice President for Public Policy Research at the American Enterprise Institute and a member of the Project for the New American Century and the Jewish Institute for National Security Affairs (JINSA). Bolton also had been a regular contributor to William Kristol's *Weekly Standard*. In December 2005, after becoming U.S. Ambassador to the United Nations, Bolton would be the keynote speaker at the right-wing Zionist Organization of America's Louis Brandeis Award Dinner, where he received the ZOA's Defender of Israel award.[58]

Condoleezza Rice, the National Security Advisor during Bush's first, term was personally close to the president. She had been a protégé of Brent Scowcroft, so she would not be expected to identify with neocon policy. However, she had no detectable impact on shaping policy and after 9/11 would parrot the neocon-inspired war agenda. Perhaps she was simply overmatched. According to journalist Fred Kaplan. "she was outmaneuvered at every turn by the ruthless infighters around her, especially Vice President Cheney and Defense Secretary Donald H. Rumsfeld."[59] David Kay, leader of the CIA's postwar effort to find weapons of mass destruction in Iraq, would refer to her as "probably the worst national security adviser in modern times since the office was created."[60] Or perhaps she realized that Bush accepted the neocon advice and that it would advance her personal interests to go along with the war policy rather than oppose it.[61]

Another crucial figure recognized as being influential with Bush was his top political advisor – Karl Rove. However, Rove, was in the thrall of neoconservative opinion, especially that of one of the most extreme neoconservatives, Michael Ledeen. As an article in the *Washington Post* pointed out: "More than once, Ledeen has seen his ideas, faxed to Rove, become official policy or rhetoric."[62]

The neoconservatives made Iraq a key issue in the Bush administration from the very beginning. According to Richard Clarke, who was a counterterrorism advisor early in the Bush administration, Wolfowitz and other neoconservatives in the administration were fixated on Iraq as the greatest terrorist threat to the United States. When, in April 2001, the White House convened a top-level meeting to discuss terrorism, Wolfowitz expressed the view that Saddam Hussein was a far more important subject than Al Qaeda, which had been Clarke's focus. According to Clarke, Wolfowitz said he could not "understand why we are beginning by talking about this one man bin Laden."[63] The real threat, Wolfowitz insisted, was state-sponsored terrorism orchestrated by Saddam. To bolster his contention, Wolfowitz cited the eccentric views of neocon favorite Laurie Mylroie, who saw the hand of Saddam behind much of the terrorism of the 1990s, including the World Trade Towers attack of 1993.[64]

For Wolfowitz to express Mylroie's unproven Saddam Hussein conspiracy theory was incomprehensible to Clarke, who opined:

> Here was the number two person in the Pentagon saying that he agreed with her and disagreed with CIA, with FBI, disagreed with all the massive evidence that Al Qaeda had attacked the World Trade Center in '93, not Iraq. Why anybody as sophisticated as a Wolfowitz or the others would attach themselves to that sort of stuff, I didn't know.[65]

Of course, if Wolfowitz and other neocons wanted propaganda for a war on Iraq, they would promote such unlikely stories, just as they would later focus on the WMD falsehoods.

In the early months of the Bush administration, Wolfowitz and his neoconservative confreres were spinning plans for an American attack on Iraq. Wolfowitz maintained that the United States military could easily invade southern Iraq and seize the oil fields. This was styled as the "enclave strategy," under which an American foothold in the south would supposedly provide support to the anti-Saddam resistance in the rest of the country to overthrow the dictator. As reported by Bob Woodward, Secretary of State Powell rejected Wolfowitz's proposal as "one of most absurd, strategically unsound proposals he had ever heard." Powell's opposition, however, did not stop Wolfowitz and the neoconservatives from planning an American attack on Iraq. Woodward writes that "Wolfowitz was like a drum that would not stop. He and his group of neoconservatives were rubbing their hands over ideas which were being presented as 'draft plans.'"[66]

While Wolfowitz and the neocons were pushing for war against the allegedly dangerous Iraq, that view found little resonance among the key administration figures charged with formulating American national security policy. Both Secretary of State Powell and National Security Adviser Rice were maintaining that Saddam was no threat to anyone. At a news conference in Cairo, Egypt, on February 24, 2001, Powell said: "He (Saddam Hussein) has not developed any significant capability with respect to weapons of mass destruction. He is unable to project conventional power against his neighbors." On May 15 2001, in testimony before a subcommittee of the Senate Appropriations Committee, Powell stated that Saddam Hussein had not been able to "build his military back up or to develop weapons of mass destruction" for "the last 10 years." America, he added, had been successful in keeping Saddam "in a box." On July 29, 2001, Rice replied to CNN White House correspondent John King by saying, "But in terms of Saddam Hussein being there, let's remember that his country is divided, in effect. He does not control the northern part of his country. We are able to keep arms from him. His military forces have not been rebuilt."[67]

It was apparent that in these early months of the Bush administration, the neoconservatives were not making headway in getting their war agenda accepted. Significantly, there was no real evidence that President Bush was thinking in terms of launching a war.[68] Norman Podhoretz described Bush's mindset during this early period:

> [B]efore 9/11 he was, to all appearances, as deficient in the "vision thing" as his father before him. If he entertained any doubts about the soundness of the "realist" approach, he showed no sign of it. Nothing he said or did gave any indication that he might be dissatisfied with the idea that his main job in foreign affairs was to keep things on an even keel. Nor was there any visible indication that he might be drawn to Ronald Reagan's more "idealistic" ambition to change the world, especially with the "Wilsonian" aim of making it "safe for democracy" by encouraging the spread to as many other countries as possible of the liberties we Americans enjoyed.[69]

It appeared that Bush was largely under the sway of Colin Powell. "In the summer of 2001," writes *Washington Post* reporter Thomas Ricks in *Fiasco: The American Military Misadventure in Iraq*, "it looked like Powell was winning the internal arguments that would shape the foreign policy of the new and inexperienced president."[70] Before the terrorist attacks of September 11, there were no significant changes in Middle East policy; certainly, the administration was not preparing to remove Saddam by military means.

However, while the neocons did not shape administration policy, they were already beginning to run their own separate government. According to journalist Joshua Micah Marshall:

> In the spring of 2001, shortly after the Bush administration had taken office, a delegation of Saudi diplomats attended a meeting at the Pentagon with Deputy

Secretary of Defense Paul D. Wolfowitz. As the meeting was breaking up, one of the attendees, Harold Rhode – a Pentagon employee and Wolfowitz protégé then serving as Wolfowitz's "Islamic affairs advisor" – approached Adel Al-Jubeir, a soft-spoken Saudi diplomat who once served as an assistant to the Saudi ambassador and today is foreign policy advisor to Crown Prince Abdullah.

Rhode told Al-Jubeir that once the new administration got its affairs in order there'd be no more pussyfooting around as there was in the Clinton days, according to a source familiar with the meeting. The United States would take care of Saddam, start calling the shots in the region, and the Saudis would have to fall in line. Al-Jubeir demurred. These were issues the two allies would certainly discuss, Al-Jubeir told the American.

Rhode then shoved his finger in the diminutive Saudi's chest and told him, "You're not going to have any choice!"[71]

From Rhode's language, if reported accurately, it would seem that the neocons had the prescience to know they would be soon directing foreign policy, although it did not seem that their agenda was yet the official Bush administration foreign policy. The Saudi government was outraged by the poking incident, and Rhode was given a strong reprimand by the Bush administration leadership. Rhode, however, still would retain a significant position in the Department of Defense as the Middle East specialist for Douglas Feith, where he would be connected with the collection and dissemination of deceptive and misrepresented intelligence.[72]

Outside the administration the neocons continued to call for Saddam's ouster. In May 2001, the *Weekly Standard* published the article "Liberate Iraq" by Reuel Marc Gerecht, the Director of the Middle East Initiative at PNAC. Gerecht presented a war on Iraq that required as few as 50,000 American troops. "Most Iraqi's would not fight," Gerecht asserted.

> Fear is the principal undergirding of his tyranny. When it vanishes, as it did so explosively throughout the country when Saddam retreated from Kuwait, the Ba'ath police-state overnight becomes a house of cards. Far fewer Iraqis and Americans would die in a U.S.-opposition campaign if the United States engaged as forcefully and as quickly as possible.[73]

But Gerecht recognized that such a policy to remove Saddam would face stiff opposition, even from within the Bush administration. "If he [Bush] answers that Saddam must go, a firestorm of criticism surely awaits him," Gerecht predicted.

> The pummeling that Ronald Reagan took for fielding the contras may well seem like a walk through a spring rain compared with the barrage that will

come at Bush from the timid left and the "realist" right. The State Department, CIA, and Pentagon will likely resist, as they resisted in 1990, doing anything that might upset the status quo, which is to say they will favor doing nothing. Most of our allies overseas will surely scream that the hyper-puissance has run amok.[74]

While the neocons were preparing their war strategy, a quite different foreign policy was being envisioned by those who thought in terms of American global hegemony and the all-important issue of oil.

In the early days of the Bush II administration – as was the case for much of the Clinton presidency – the powerful U.S. oil lobby was intensely lobbying Congress to ease, even to remove, sanctions on Iraq and two other oil producing "rogue" states – Iran and Libya. But an even more influential bloc, the pro-Israel lobby, consistently scuttled the oil lobby's efforts, which would have allowed Washington to re-establish economic relationships with Israel's enemies. A May 2001 piece in *Business Week* by Rose Brady reported that the easing of sanctions on rogue states "pits powerful interests such as the pro-Israeli lobby and the U.S. oil industry against each other. And it is sure to preoccupy the Bush Administration and Congress."[75] Interestingly, Cheney was identified as being in the anti-sanctions camp.

Further, Brady noted that the Bush administration was under mounting pressure from U.S. businesses because the sanctions against these countries allowed foreign firms to profit at the expense of U.S. corporations. "American farmers, workers, and companies have sacrificed without any progress toward U.S. foreign policy objectives," wrote Donald A. Deline, Halliburton's director of government affairs, to Senate Majority Leader Trent Lott (R-Miss.).[76]

Regarding Iraq, the interests of the oil lobby blended in with the view of much of world opinion that the existing sanctions on Iraq were causing a humanitarian disaster. So the campaign to reduce sanctions on Iraq was enveloped by a strong moral aura.[77]

An influential energy task force headed by Vice President Cheney broached the possibility of lifting some economic sanctions against Iran, Libya and Iraq as part of a plan to increase America's oil supply. According to a draft of the task force report, the United States should review the sanctions against the three countries because of the importance of their oil production to meeting domestic and global energy needs.[78]

Regarding U.S. rapprochement with Iran, the motivation involved more than simply the question of oil. It also stemmed from the worsening U.S.

relationship with the Taliban regime in Afghanistan, the country where Osama bin Laden was headquartered. Iran was the only country to actively combat the Taliban regime in Afghanistan, long before much of the American public even became aware that such an anti-Western regime existed. Iran's Shiite Muslim clerical leaders saw their greatest enemy to be across their border in Afghanistan, where the Taliban's Sunni Islamic regime killed thousands of Shiite civilians and even ten Iranian diplomats. Ironically, the Taliban were supported by America's ally Pakistan, while Iran was providing arms to the Northern Alliance, the major internal resistance group.

In mentioning Iran's opposition to the Taliban, it is necessary to go over the fluctuating policy of the United States toward the latter regime. Major oil interests had for some time been eyeing the vast, largely untapped oil and gas resources of the Caspian Basin and Central Asia. However, Central Asia's oil and gas reserves are landlocked, which means that the energy wealth would have to be to be transported through long pipelines to reach global markets. Consequently, the control of Afghanistan was valuable, not because of any oil or gas reserves of its own, but because of its crucial geographic location. Potential transit routes for oil and natural gas exports from Central Asia to the Arabian Sea run through Afghanistan. American oil companies sought to lay such a pipeline across that country, but it was first essential to establish political stability in the turbulent region.

The value of Afghanistan, however, transcended the oil pipeline issue. Elie Krakowski, a former Department of Defense specialist on Afghanistan, pointed out in 2000 that Afghanistan had traditionally been, and remained, a key area in global power politics:

> Why then have so many great nations fought in and over Afghanistan, and why should we be concerned with it now? In short, because Afghanistan is the crossroads between what Halford MacKinder called the world's Heartland and the Indian subcontinent.... With the collapse of the Soviet Union, it has become an important potential opening to the sea for the landlocked new states of Central Asia. The presence of large oil and gas deposits in that area has attracted countries and multinational corporations. Russia and China, not to mention Pakistan and India, are deeply involved in trying to shape the future of what may be the world's most unchangeable people. Because Afghanistan is a major strategic pivot what happens there affects the rest of the world.[79]

American policies reflect certain geopolitical beliefs – connected to the economic interests of particular groups, indeed, but not necessarily related to the immediate financial gain of particular policymakers. The United States, or at least her foreign policy elite, saw a need for the United States to dominate Central Asian energy resources as it had dominated the Persian Gulf oil fields. Obviously, the development of those energy resources would mean financial gain for American investors. But control of the area would also enhance U.S. global power, and such control was thus a critical part of a geostrategic strategy to maintain global primacy.

In higher circles, views differed on how best to achieve the agreed goal of American military and economic penetration of Central Asia. Opinions fell along a continuum between two contrasting foreign-policy models: competitive and cooperative. According to the competitive model, other powers are adversaries in the quest for world power and wealth. It's a zero-sum game – anything that benefits the United States' adversaries automatically harms the United States. America's goal is to achieve world hegemony – any lesser achievement would leave the United States vulnerable to its enemies. To achieve hegemony America must act unilaterally or with its closest allies. In particular, it must monopolize the world's crucial energy sources to keep that wealth out of the hands of potential enemies such as Iran, Russia, and China.

One of the foremost articulators of the competitive position was Zbigniew Brzezinski, national security advisor in the Carter administration. In his 1997 work *The Grand Chessboard: American Primacy and its Geostrategic Imperatives*, Brzezinski portrayed the Eurasian landmass as the linchpin for world power, with Central Asia being the key to the domination of Eurasia.[80] For the United States to maintain the global primacy that Brzezinski equated with American security, the United States must, at the very least, prevent any possible adversary, or coalition of adversaries, from controlling that crucial region. And, of course, the best way for the United States to prevent adversaries from controlling a region would be to control it by itself.[81]

With considerable prescience, Brzezinski remarked that, because of popular resistance to U.S. military expansionism, his ambitious strategy could not be implemented "except in the circumstance of a truly massive and widely perceived direct external threat."[82] When that external threat did materialize, however, the impact on American foreign policy was not as Brzezinski had anticipated. For the neoconservatives would divert American military intervention to Iraq and the Middle East, instead of Central Asia. And Brzezinski would become a major critic of that policy.

The second model envisions global cooperation, rather than competition, in controlling and managing the resources of Central Asia. However, the idea of cooperation with Russia and China in an expanded world state-capitalism, with its concomitant anticipated prosperity, would mean an essential acceptance of the American-dominated status quo. Better transport and communications links in the Central Asian region could transform presently isolated countries into key trading centers at the crossroads of Europe and Asia – reminiscent of the Silk Road of the Middle Ages. U.S. officials have predicted the 21st Century Silk Road running through Central Asia will include railroads, oil and gas pipelines, and fiber-optic cables.[83] Making Central Asia safe for state-managed capitalistic development aimed at enhancing the prosperity of the great powers entails, of course, the suppression of troublesome destabilizing elements, such as Islamic fundamentalism, ethnic nationalism, and tribal divisions.[84]

Whereas U.S. officials would, after the September 11, 2001 attacks, portray the Taliban as the essence of evil, that was not their prevailing view prior to that time. Officially, the United States condemned the Islamic groups that used Afghanistan as their base for terrorism, and demanded the extradition of Osama Bin Laden to face trial for the August 1998 bombings of U.S. embassies in Kenya and Tanzania. (After the 1998 bombings, the Clinton regime even launched missile strikes on Bin Laden's guerrilla camps.) Although the record is convoluted and murky, it seems that, while the United States wanted to apprehend Bin Laden, it also sought to improve relations with the Taliban government, and that the latter goal often took precedence.

American oil companies had cozied up to the Taliban from the time it took over Kabul in 1996. In 1996, the U.S. oil company UNOCAL (Union Oil of California) reached an agreement with the Taliban to build a pipeline, but the continuing Afghan civil war prevented that project from getting started. According to Ahmed Rashid, a Central Asia specialist and author of *Taliban: Militant Islam, Oil, and Fundamentalism in Central Asia,* "Between 1994–96 the U.S. supported the Taliban politically through its allies Pakistan and Saudi Arabia, essentially because Washington viewed the Taliban as anti-Iranian, anti-Shia, and pro-Western." From 1995 to 1997,

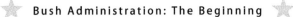

Rashid says, "U.S. support was driven by the UNOCAL oil/gas pipeline project."[85]

As the Taliban consolidated control over Afghanistan, the deposed Prime Minister referred to them as "American puppets." John F. Burns, a foreign correspondent in Afghanistan for the *New York Times* who was a 1997 recipient of the Pulitzer Prize for international reporting, branded this charge as extreme but acknowledged that "there were ties between American officials and the growing movement that were considerably broader than those to any other Western country."

Long before the Taliban had gained control of Afghanistan, Burns maintained that

> American diplomats in Islamabad had made regular visits to Kandahar to see Taliban leaders. In briefings for reporters, these diplomats cited what they saw as positive aspects of the Taliban, which they listed as the movement's capacity to end the war in Afghanistan and its promises to put an end to the use of Afghanistan as a base for narcotics-trafficking and international terrorism.
>
> Unmentioned, but probably most important to Washington, was that the Taliban, who are Sunni Muslims, have a deep hostility for Iran, America's nemesis, where the ruling majority belong to the rival Shiite sect of Islam.
>
> Along the way, Washington developed yet another interest in the Taliban as potential backers for a 1,200-mile gas pipeline that an American energy company, Union Oil of California, has proposed building from Quetta, in Pakistan, to Turkmenistan, a former Soviet republic that sits atop some of the world's largest gas reserves, but has limited means to export them.[86]

After the Taliban had gained virtual control of Afghanistan in May 1997, Burns pronounced that "[t]he Clinton Administration has taken the view that a Taliban victory . . . would act as a counterweight to Iran . . . and would offer the possibility of new trade routes that could weaken Russian and Iranian influence in the region."[87]

A similar view focusing on the economic and geostrategic value of a Taliban victory was expressed in an editorial in the *Wall Street Journal*. It opined that Afghanistan could provide "a prime transshipment route for the export of Central Asia's vast oil, gas, and other natural resources." The editorial emphasized that

> peace in Afghanistan means freedom from dependence on Russia, which currently controls all traditional routes for exports . . . . More significantly, the fighting also has delayed construction of the pipelines and new transit routes by which Central Asian states hope to consolidate their independence.

The *Journal* continued: "Like them or not, the Taliban are the players most capable of achieving peace in Afghanistan at this moment in history."[88]

Military support for the Taliban came from Pakistan's intelligence agency, the Inter Services Intelligence (ISI). Pakistan viewed Afghanistan as a potential client state, and was only one of three countries to give recognition to the Taliban regime.[89] The United States, in turn, supported Pakistan, which meant that, at least indirectly, the United States was backing the Taliban.

Throughout the period when the United States took a favorable stance toward the Taliban, the Taliban was massacring civilians, oppressing women, and, in general, depriving the Afghan people of their basic liberties. It was those very same barbarities that the United States, after September 11, 2001, would cite as justification for its use of military force to overthrow the tyrannical regime and, presumably, liberate the downtrodden populace.

Amnesty International, which was concerned not with gas and oil concessions but rather with the Taliban's violations of human rights, commented negatively about Washington's apparent friendliness toward that regime. A November 1996 report by that organization stated that

> many Afghanistan analysts believe that the United States has had close political links with the Taleban militia. They refer to visits by Taleban representatives to the United States in recent months and several visits by senior U.S. State Department officials to Kandahar.[90]

After the 1998 bombings of the U.S. embassies in Kenya and Tanzania, the U.S. relationship with the Taliban cooled. The Clinton administration publicly moved to a position of opposition to the Taliban, pushing the UN Security Council to adopt UN Resolution 1267, which called on the Taliban to hand over indicted terrorist Osama Bin Laden and to deal with the issue of terrorism. Economic sanctions were imposed to pressure the Taliban to comply. The United States also engaged in some covert operations on Afghanistan's borders and within the country itself, aimed at ultimately removing the regime. The United States even launched missile strikes on Bin Laden's guerrilla camps.[91]

But still Washington seems to have mixed its opposition with covert support. The *International Herald Tribune* reported that in the summer of 1998, "the Clinton administration was talking with the Taliban about potential pipeline routes to carry oil and natural gas out of Turkmenistan to the Indian Ocean by crossing Afghanistan and Pakistan."[92]

In 1999, Congressman Dana Rohrabacher, a Republican who was a senior member of the House International Relations Committee, with oversight responsibility on policy toward Afghanistan, testified before the Senate Foreign Relations Subcommittee on South Asia that "there is and has been a covert policy by this [Clinton] administration to support the Taliban movement's control of Afghanistan." Rohrabacher surmised that U.S. policy was "based on the assumption that the Taliban would bring stability to Afghanistan and permit the building of oil pipelines from Central Asia through Afghanistan to Pakistan."[93]

In testimony on global terrorism before his own committee in July 2000, Rohrabacher pressed his charge that the United States was aiding the Taliban. "We have been supporting the Taliban because all of our aid goes to the Taliban areas," complained Rohrabacher,

> and when people from the outside try to put aid into areas not controlled by the Taliban, they are thwarted by our own State Department. He continued that at a time when the Taliban were vulnerable, the top person in this administration, Mr. [Karl F.] Inderfurth [assistant secretary of state for South Asian affairs], and [Secretary of Energy] Bill Richardson personally went to Afghanistan and convinced the anti-Taliban forces not to go on the offensive. Furthermore, they convinced all of the anti-Taliban forces and their supporters to disarm and to cease their flow of support for the anti-Taliban forces. At that same moment, Pakistan initiated a major resupply effort, which eventually caused the defeat of almost all of the anti-Taliban forces in Afghanistan.[94]

U.S. humanitarian aid to Afghanistan helped to prop up the Taliban regime. The United States provided an estimated $113 million in humanitarian aid to Afghanistan in 2000 and a comparable sum in 2001 prior to September 11.[95]

It appears that in 2001, the incoming Bush administration greatly expanded American efforts to come to terms with the Taliban on the issues of oil and terrorism. From February to August, the Bush regime conducted extensive negotiations with Taliban diplomatic representatives, meeting several times in Washington, Berlin, and Islamabad. A book by French intelligence analysts Jean-Charles Brisard and Guillaume Dasquie, *Bin Laden: The Forbidden Truth*, details that story.[96]

But the Taliban balked at any pipeline deal and refused to eliminate the terrorist camps in their country. Instead of serving as a pliable government that could provide requisite stability for American exploitation of energy resources, the Taliban were exporting their revolutionary Islamic fundamentalism to nearby Central Asian countries, thus destabilizing the entire energy-rich region. According to Brisard and Dasquie, U.S. negotiations with the Taliban broke down in August after a U.S. negotiator threatened military action against the Taliban, telling them to accept the American offer of "a carpet of gold, or you'll get a carpet of bombs."[97]

Months before August 2001, it appears, the United States had been making plans to remove the Taliban. In this connection, it should be noted that it is not unusual for a country to have a multifaced foreign policy, with conflicting if not contradictory contingency plans. In any case, the United States seems to have sought to solve its differences with the Taliban through negotiations, while at the same time making plans to remove the regime, if negotiations failed.

Washington had considered projecting its military power into the Central Asian region for some years. For example, in 1997, U.S. Special Forces took part in the longest-range airborne operation in American history to reach Kazakhstan and Uzbekistan in order to engage in joint military operations with military forces from Russia and the former Soviet Central Asian republics. The *U.S. News and World Report* opined that this demonstration of America's military muscle was primarily aimed at "Iran's Islamic-fundamentalist regime. But it also could be seen as a warning to other potential rivals, including China and the fundamentalist Taliban militia of Afghanistan."[98]

After the September 11 attack, it transpired that the United States and Uzbekistan had been sharing intelligence and conducting joint covert operations against the Taliban for two to three years. That prior secret relationship helped to explain the rapid emergence of the post-September 11 military partnership between the two countries, making Uzbekistan a base for launching attacks on Afghanistan.[99] Furthermore, since 1997 special military units of the CIA had been inside Afghanistan, working with anti-Taliban opposition forces. Not only did the CIA work with the anti-Taliban Northern Alliance, it also helped establish an anti-Taliban network in southern Afghanistan, the area of the Taliban's greatest support.[100]

With the advent of the Bush administration in 2001, evidence indicates that United States policy was considering, if not actually moving toward, military action, in cooperation with other countries, to remove the Taliban regime if negotiations failed. Significantly, some information on those war plans leaked to the public before September 11. A report in the March 15, 2001 Jane's *Intelligence Review*, a noted British publication, contended that the U.S. was working with India, Iran, and Russia "in a concerted front against Afghanistan's Taliban regime." India was supplying the Northern Alliance with military equipment, advisors, and helicopter technicians, the report said, and both India and Russia were using bases in Tajikistan and Uzbekistan for their operations.

"Several recent meetings between the newly instituted Indo-U.S. and Indo-Russian joint working groups on terrorism led to this effort to tactically and logistically counter the Taliban," Jane's related. "Intelligence sources in Delhi said that while India, Russia, and Iran were leading the anti-Taliban campaign on the ground, Washington was giving the Northern Alliance information and logistic support."[101]

According to a June 26, 2001, article in the Indian public-affairs Web magazine Indiareacts.com, the United States, Russia, Pakistan, and India made a pact for war against the Taliban. Iran was considered a covert participant. The plan called for the war to begin in mid October.[102]

A similar story, reported by the BBC on September 18, was provided by Niaz Naik, a former Pakistani foreign secretary. He said he was told by senior U.S. officials in mid July that military action against Afghanistan would go ahead by the middle of October. The broader goal was the removal of the Taliban and the installation of a compliant pro-American regime. According to Naik, he was told that the United States would launch its operation from bases in Tajikistan, where American military advisors were already in place.[103]

Four days later, on September 22, the *Guardian* newspaper confirmed Naik's account and added that Pakistan had passed a warning of the impending attack to the Taliban. The story implied that the warning might have spurred Osama Bin Laden to launch his attacks, stating that "Bin Laden, far from launching the attacks on the World Trade Centre in New York and the Pentagon out of the blue 10 days ago, was launching a preemptive strike in response to what he saw as U.S. threats."[104]

The September 11 terrorist attacks provided the United States with the golden opportunity to intervene militarily in Afghanistan on a major scale and thus go far to achieve its hegemonical goal in Central Asia. To achieve such a goal, however, required more than just removing the Taliban regime but in using American power to establish stability in the region. The

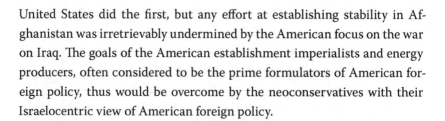

United States did the first, but any effort at establishing stability in Afghanistan was irretrievably undermined by the American focus on the war on Iraq. The goals of the American establishment imperialists and energy producers, often considered to be the prime formulators of American foreign policy, thus would be overcome by the neoconservatives with their Israelocentric view of American foreign policy.

chapter 9

SEPTEMBER 11

S THE BUSH ADMINISTRATION came into office in January 2001, press reports in Israel quoted Israeli government officials and politicians speaking openly of mass expulsion of the Palestinians. The new prime minister, Ariel Sharon (elected in February 2001), had engaged in confrontation with Arabs most of his life in his positions in governmental and military leadership. He commanded special operations "Unit 101" that launched brutal cross-border raids against Israel's enemies in the 1950s, which included the notorious massacre of Palestinian villagers at Qibya in the then Jordanian-controlled West Bank in October 1953. As Begin's Defense Minister, Sharon had masterminded Israel's plunge into Lebanon in 1982 and had been intimately involved in the slaughter of Palestinians by Lebanese Christian militiamen at the Sabra and Shatila refugee camps outside Beirut. In the 1990s, as Minister of Housing, he directed Israel's settlement expansion, earning the sobriquet "bulldozer" by destroying whatever Palestinian possessions stood in the way. And in September 1999, Sharon's highly-publicized, provocative visit to the Jewish Temple Mount compound, near the Dome of the Rock, one of Islam's holiest shrines in Arab East Jerusalem, set off Palestinian riots and lethal Israeli responses, which turned into the Second Intifada.[1]

Sharon, who had helped to found the Likud bloc in 1973, was the embodiment of Jabotinsky's "iron wall" philosophy, though he was not such an ideological purist regarding the Revisionist Zionist idea of "Eretz Israel" as were some on the right, who were unwilling to sacrifice, even temporarily, any part of what they regarded as the "Land of Israel." It was Sharon's

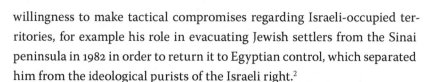

willingness to make tactical compromises regarding Israeli-occupied territories, for example his role in evacuating Jewish settlers from the Sinai peninsula in 1982 in order to return it to Egyptian control, which separated him from the ideological purists of the Israeli right.[2]

While more a pragmatist than an ideologue regarding tactics, Sharon was a staunch supporter of Israeli settlement and control of the West Bank, and the concomitant prevention of the development there of anything approximating a viable Palestinian state. Baruch Kimmerling writes in *Politicide: Ariel Sharon's War Against the Palestinians* that Sharon's ultimate goal was the

> the dissolution of the Palestinian people's existence as a legitimate social, political, and economic entity. This process may also but not necessarily include their partial or complete ethnic cleansing from the territory known as the Land of Israel.[3]

Sharon had said in the past that Jordan should become the Palestinian state where Palestinians removed from Israeli territory would be relocated.[4] In 2001, there was increased public concern in Israel about demographic trends endangering the Jewish nature of the Israeli state. Haifa University professor Arnon Sofer released a study, "Demography of Eretz Israel," which predicted that by 2020 non-Jews would be a majority of 58 percent in Israel and the occupied territories combined.[5] Moreover, it was recognized that the overall increase in population was going beyond that which the land, especially with its limited supply of water, could sustain.[6]

It appeared to some that Sharon intended to achieve expulsion through militant means. As one left-wing analyst put it at the time: "One big war with transfer at its end – this is the plan of the hawks who indeed almost reached the moment of its implementation."[7] In summer 2001, the authoritative Jane's Information Group reported that Israel had completed planning for a massive and bloody invasion of the Occupied Territories, involving "air strikes by F-15 and F-16 fighter bombers, a heavy artillery bombardment, and then an attack by a combined force of 30,000 men . . . tank brigades and infantry." It would seem that such bold strikes aimed at far more than simply removing Arafat and the PLO leadership. But the U.S. opposed the plan and Europe made equally plain its opposition to Sharon's strategy.[8] As one close observer of the Israeli-Palestinian scene noted in August 2001,

[I]t is only in the current political climate that such expulsion plans cannot be put into operation. As hot as the political climate is at the moment, clearly the time is not yet ripe for drastic action. However, if the temperature were raised even higher, actions inconceivable at present might be possible.[9]

And then came the September 11 terror attacks.

The September 11 atrocities created the white-hot climate in which Israel could undertake harsh measures unacceptable under normal conditions. When asked what the terrorist attack would do for U.S.-Israeli relations, former Prime Minister Benjamin Netanyahu blurted out: "It's very good." Then he edited himself: "Well, not very good, but it will generate immediate sympathy." Netanyahu correctly predicted that the attack would "strengthen the bond between our two peoples, because we've experienced terror over so many decades, but the United States has now experienced a massive hemorrhaging of terror." Prime Minister Ariel Sharon depicted Israel as being in the same situation as the United States, referring to the attack as an assault on "our common values" and declaring, "I believe together we can defeat these forces of evil."[10]

In the eyes of Israeli's leaders, the September 11 attack had joined the United States and Israeli together against a common enemy. And that enemy was not in far off Afghanistan, but was geographically close to Israel. Israel's traditional enemies would now become America's as well. Israel now would have a free hand to deal harshly with the Palestinians under the cover of a "war on terrorism." Palestinian resistance to Israeli occupation would simply be portrayed as "terrorism." Conversely, America would make itself the enemy of those who previously had focused on Israel.

It is important to recall that in the period before September 11, Israel had been widely criticized in the U.S. and in the Western world for its brutal suppression of the Palestinians. Israeli soldiers, tanks and helicopter gunships were regularly shown on the television battling with Palestinian youths, who were armed with nothing more than sticks and stones. Israeli tanks bulldozed Palestinian farms and homes. Humanitarian groups complained that captured Palestinians were being tortured and abused in Israeli prison cells. And this negative image was having some effect on Bush. As Damien Cave wrote in *Salon* in November 2001: "Before September 11 Saudi Arabia was reportedly pushing the U.S. to pressure Israel into Palestine peace concessions and, according to a *Newsweek* story, Bush was beginning to comply."[11]

The events of September 11 completely transformed this entire picture. A few months after that horrific day, Israeli commentator Aluf Benn would write:

> The Israeli political-security establishment is coming to the conclusion that the terror attacks on September 11 granted Israel an advantage at a time when Israel was under increasing international pressure because of the ongoing conflict with the Palestinians.
>
> Osama bin Laden's September 11 attacks placed Israel firmly on the right side of the strategic map with the United States. At the same time it put the Arab world at a disadvantage as it now faces its own difficult decisions about its future.[12]

Sharon knew how to take advantage of the situation. "Exploiting the tragedy of September 11, Sharon rushed to declare 'Arafat is Bin Laden,'" writes Baruch Kimmerling.

> Israeli analysts and experts saw this comparison as ridiculous and harmful, but the subsequent adoption of the comparison by both the Bush administration and the American public once again demonstrated Sharon's superior political instincts. This gave him free rein to re-occupy most Palestinian cities and refugee camps and, de facto, to undermine the internal and external legitimacy of the Palestinian authority and to destroy its material and human infrastructure as well.[13]

For the neocons, the terrible tragedy of 9/11 offered the extremely convenient pretext to implement their war agenda for the United States. "Before 9/11," war critic Joseph Wilson writes, "regime change by invasion was still just a fringe part of the debate about how to handle Saddam Hussein."[14] Immediately after the 9/11 attacks, the neoconservatives found the perfect climate to publicly push for a wider war on terrorism that would immediately deal with Israel's enemies, starting with Iraq. "At the beginning of the administration people were talking about Iraq but it wasn't doable. There was no heft," observed neocon Kenneth Adelman. "That changed with September 11 because then people were willing to confront the reality of an international terrorist network, and terrorist states such as Iraq."[15] Perle concurred that "Nine-eleven was the turning point with respect to leaving Saddam unmolested."[16]

In the immediate aftermath of 9/11, there was internal debate within the Bush administration regarding the scope of the "war on terrorism." It was evident from the outset that the magnitude of the harm done, together

with the possibility of future American vulnerability, meant that the United States would initiate war. But the question was: war against whom? And
for what objectives? Al Qaeda, the alleged perpetrator of the attack, was a
globalized network rather than a territorial state. But it was Afghanistan,
under the Taliban regime, that had harbored Osama bin Laden and his Al
Qaeda operation. Consequently, most of the public sought to punish Afghanistan if the Taliban did not freely turn over Osama bin Laden and his
Al Qaeda network. And the anger was so great that the United States made
little effort to negotiate with the Taliban. Neocons were completely in ac-
cord with the war lust, but they sought to direct that war impulse toward
their goal of a war in the Middle East.

According to Bob Woodward in *Bush at War*, as early as the day after the
terrorist attacks, Secretary of Defense Donald Rumsfeld

> raised the question of attacking Iraq. Why shouldn't we go against Iraq, not just
> al Qaeda? he asked. Rumsfeld was speaking not only for himself when he raised
> the question. His deputy, Paul D. Wolfowitz was committed to a policy that
> would make Iraq a principal target of the first round in the war on terrorism.[17]

Woodward continues: "The terrorist attacks of September 11 gave the U.S.
a new window to go after Hussein." On September 15, Wolfowitz put forth
military arguments to justify a U.S. attack on Iraq rather than Afghanistan. Wolfowitz expressed the view that "Attacking Afghanistan would be
uncertain." He voiced the danger that American troops would be "bogged
down in mountain fighting . . . . In contrast, Iraq was a brittle, oppressive
regime that might break easily. It was doable."[18] In fact, Wolfowitz immediately envisioned a wider war that would strike a number of countries
alleged to support terrorism. Wolfowitz held that

> it's not just simply a matter of capturing people and holding them accountable,
> but removing the sanctuaries, removing the support systems, ending states
> who sponsor terrorism. And that's why it has to be a broad and sustained cam-
> paign. It's not going to stop if a few criminals are taken care of.[19]

Though left unnamed, it would appear that the majority of the terrorist
states Wolfowitz sought to "end" were Israel's Middle East enemies.

The neoconservatives, however, were not able to achieve their goal of a
wider war at the outset. The aroused and angry American people wanted
to punish the actual perpetrators of the 9/11 atrocities. And it was Afghanistan, under the Taliban regime, that had harbored Osama bin Laden and

his Al Qaeda operation. Iraq's relationship to the attack, although argued by many neoconservatives, had not become apparent to the mainstream public. It would take more time for the neoconservatives to persuade the American people that Iraq was a dire threat to the United States, and then the primary focus would be on weapons of mass destruction, not a connection to the 9/11 attack.

Secretary of State Colin Powell was most adamantly opposed to attacking Iraq, holding that the war should focus on the actual perpetrators of September 11 because that was what the American people expected. "The American people," he asserted, "want us to do something about al-Qaeda."[20] Moreover, Powell pointed out that an attack on Iraq would lack international support. He held, however, that a U.S. victory in Afghanistan would enhance America's ability to deal militarily with Iraq at a later time, "if we can prove that Iraq had a role" in the September 11 terrorism.[21] Powell publicly repudiated Wolfowitz's call for "ending states" with the retort that

> [w]e're after ending terrorism. And if there are states and regimes, nations, that support terrorism, we hope to persuade them that it is in their interest to stop doing that. But I think "ending terrorism" is where I would leave it and let Mr. Wolfowitz speak for himself.[22]

George Tenet, the director of the CIA, also played a leading role in determining that the initial attack would be on Afghanistan. Tenet had developed a personal relationship with Bush, briefing him every morning.[23] In line with the overall thinking at the CIA, Tenet's focus was on Al Qaeda. The CIA saw no connection between Saddam and Al Qaeda. And of critical importance from the standpoint of selecting the initial theater in the "war on terrorism," the CIA had an existing plan for moving into Afghanistan. As Tyler Drumheller, then the division chief for the Directorate of Operations in the CIA, later described it: "This [CIA] plan was drawn up years before and was in place because of the relationship with the Northern Alliance. Tenet was able to put it on the desk at the White House [four days after 9/11]."[24]

Bush was highly impressed with the CIA's concrete plan to quickly strike at America's enemy, which would provide the American public with the immediate retaliation it sought. Although Bush thought that Saddam had been somehow involved,[25] he was also instinctively oriented to attacking the actual perpetrators of the terrorism, so the Bush administration opted to first target Osama bin Laden in Afghanistan. Thus, the neocon Middle East war agenda was side-tracked for the moment. However, the decision to attack Afghanistan did not preclude Iraq from being a future target. On September 16, 2001, when asked about Iraq on NBC's "Meet the Press," Vice-President Dick Cheney simply replied that Osama bin Laden was the target "at the moment . . . at this stage."[26] Very significantly, however, while the "war on terrorism" would not begin with an attack on Iraq, military plans were being made for just such an endeavor. A Top Secret document outlining the war plan for Afghanistan, which President Bush signed on September 17, 2001, included, as a minor point, instructions to the Pentagon to also make plans for an attack on Iraq, although that attack was not yet a priority.[27]

Neocons with ties to the Bush administration continued to push for war on Iraq. Richard Perle, chairman of the Defense Policy Board, maintained that "[t]here is no question Saddam has been involved in acts of terror. He gives support to terrorists and harbors them . . . . As long as he is around with his desire for vengeance, he will be supporting international terrorism." He held that "we need to take this fight to the countries that harbor terrorists. Chasing individual terrorists is not the way to solve this problem."[28] Obviously, Perle's targets for American military action went far beyond Iraq.

On September 19–20, Perle convened a lengthy, 19-hour meeting of the Defense Policy Board to discuss the ramifications of the September 11 attacks. The board's members agreed on the need to turn to Iraq as soon as the initial phase of the war against Afghanistan was over. That both Rumsfeld and Wolfowitz took part in the meeting illustrated the integral connection of the board to the Defense Department leadership. Moreover, the meeting took place in Rumsfeld's conference room in the Pentagon. (The Pentagon had been hit by a terrorist plane on September 11, but Rumsfeld's conference room was unaffected.) Notably excluded from the meeting were Secretary of State Powell and other members of the State Department, as well as National Security Advisor Condoleezza Rice.[29]

While the group agreed on the goal of ousting Saddam, they presented a range of views, including a discussion of the many political and diplomatic obstacles to military action. "If we don't use this as the moment to replace Saddam after we replace the Taliban, we are setting the stage for disaster," said Newt Gingrich, the former speaker of the House and a member of

the group. Perle held that Saddam's overthrow had "never been a fringe issue.[30]

During the meeting, two of Perle's invited guests, Princeton professor Bernard Lewis, a leading Middle East scholar close to the neocons, who was noted for his negative view of Islam, and Ahmed Chalabi, the president of the Iraqi National Congress, made presentations. Lewis said that the United States should encourage democratic reformers in the Middle East, "such as my friend here, Ahmed Chalabi." Chalabi contended that Iraq was a breeding ground for terrorists and that Saddam's regime possessed weapons of mass destruction.[31]

During another part of the meeting, the attendees prepared a letter for President Bush calling for the removal of Saddam Hussein. Dated September 20, 2001, the letter would be written under the name of the Project for the New American Century. The letter maintained that

> even if evidence does not link Iraq directly to the attack, any strategy aiming at the eradication of terrorism and its sponsors must include a determined effort to remove Saddam Hussein from power in Iraq. Failure to undertake such an effort will constitute an early and perhaps decisive surrender in the war on international terrorism.

Furthermore, the letter opined that if Syria and Iran failed to stop all support for Hezbollah, the United States should also "consider appropriate measures against these known sponsors of terrorism." Also emanating from the letter was the view that Israel was America's crucial ally in the war on terrorism and that therefore its militant actions should not be criticized.

> Israel has been and remains [the letter continued] America's staunchest ally against international terrorism, especially in the Middle East. The United States should fully support its fellow democracy in its fight against terrorism. We should insist that the Palestinian Authority put a stop to terrorism emanating from territories under its control and imprison those planning terrorist attacks against Israel.

Among the letter's signatories were such neoconservative luminaries as William Kristol, Midge Decter, Eliot Cohen, Frank Gaffney, Robert Kagan, Jeane Kirkpatrick, Charles Krauthammer, Richard Perle, and Norman Podhoretz.[32]

Neoconservatives outside the administration beat the war drums for an attack on Iraq. On September 13, the Jewish Institute for National Security

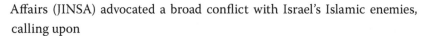

Affairs (JINSA) advocated a broad conflict with Israel's Islamic enemies, calling upon

> the American government and on all world leaders to be decisive in their actions to confront the terrorists and their supporters, who rely on our taking half measures in response.
>
> We must begin by condemning them and their organizations by name; we know who they are. Osama Bin Laden, Hezbollah, Hamas, and Islamic Jihad are only the most prominent. The countries harboring and training them include not just Afghanistan – an easy target for blame – but Iraq, Iran, Pakistan, Syria, Sudan, the Palestinian Authority, Libya, Algeria and even our presumed friends Saudi Arabia and Egypt.[33]

JINSA especially focused on Saddam Hussein, stating that American "actions in the past certainly were not forceful enough, and now we must seize the opportunity to alter this pattern of passivity." Among the anti-Saddam actions recommended by JINSA was the provision of "all necessary support to the Iraq National Congress, including direct American military support, to effect a regime change in Iraq."[34]

It was apparent that JINSA saw the crisis of 9/11 as a means to enhance the security of Israel. JINSA wanted America to engage in belligerent actions toward the Middle East enemies of Israel, who now could be classified as "terrorists" because of their support for the Palestinian resistance. JINSA advocated that the United States

> [b]omb identified terrorist training camps and facilities in any country harboring terrorists. Interdict the supply lines to terrorist organizations, including but not limited to those between Damascus and Beirut that permit Iran to use Lebanon as a terrorist base.[35]

It held that the United States should "Freeze the bank accounts of organizations in the U.S. that have links to terrorism-supporting groups and their political wings." Such belligerency would apply to American allies, too, as JINSA called upon the United States government to "[s]uspend U.S. Military Aid to Egypt while re-evaluating Egypt's support for American policy objectives, and re-evaluate America's security relationship with Saudi Arabia and the Gulf States unless both actually join in our war against terrorism."[36]

For Laurie Mylroie and her neocon backers, the 9/11 attack confirmed her thesis that Saddam was the mastermind of anti-American terrorism.[37] While Mylroie's views were never confirmed by intelligence experts in the

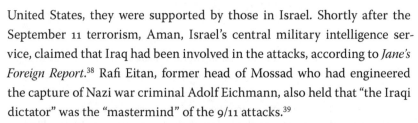

United States, they were supported by those in Israel. Shortly after the September 11 terrorism, Aman, Israel's central military intelligence service, claimed that Iraq had been involved in the attacks, according to *Jane's Foreign Report*.[38] Rafi Eitan, former head of Mossad who had engineered the capture of Nazi war criminal Adolf Eichmann, also held that "the Iraqi dictator" was the "mastermind" of the 9/11 attacks.[39]

Critics of a wider war in the Middle East were quick to notice the neoconservative war propaganda effort. In analyzing the situation in September 2002, journalist Scott McConnell wrote:

> For the neoconservatives . . . bin Laden is but a sideshow . . . . They hope to use September 11 as pretext for opening a wider war in the Middle East. Their prime, but not only, target is Saddam Hussein's Iraq, even if Iraq has nothing to do with the World Trade Center assault.[40]

However, McConnell grossly underestimated the power of the neocons within the Bush administration. "The neo-con wish list," McConnell opined,

> is a recipe for igniting a huge conflagration between the United States and countries throughout the Arab world, with consequences no one could reasonably pretend to calculate. Support for such a war – which could turn quite easily into a global war – is a minority position within the Bush administration (assistant secretary of state [sic] Paul Wolfowitz is its main advocate) and the country.[41]

Expressing a similar view, veteran columnist Georgie Anne Geyer observed:

> The "Get Iraq" campaign . . . started within days of the September bombings . . . . It emerged first and particularly from pro-Israeli hard-liners in the Pentagon such as Deputy Defense Secretary Paul Wolfowitz and adviser Richard Perle, but also from hard-line neoconservatives, and some journalists and congressmen. Soon it became clear that many, although not all, were in the group that is commonly called in diplomatic and political circles the "Israeli-firsters," meaning that they would always put Israeli policy, or even their perception of it, above anything else.

Within the Bush administration, Geyer believed, this line of thinking was being contained by cool heads in the administration, but this could also change at any time.[42] Although the neoconservatives could not realize immediately their goal of a war against the Middle East enemies of Israel, the terrorist events were critical in paving the way for the ultimate adoption of their war agenda. As a result of 9/11, the neocons became the guiding force in American foreign policy.

Former Secretary of State Lawrence Eagleburger in 2004 explained the neocons' success: "The neocons were organized. They had intellectual content. Bush was not totally captured by it but tends in that direction."[43] As time progressed, Bush would follow more and more of their agenda.

While the events of 9/11 did not cause President Bush to immediately adopt all the specifics of the neocon Middle East war program, those traumatic events had a profound impact on Bush's psyche, causing him to embrace the neocons' pre-packaged simple solution of a war of good versus evil. The idea of a war of good versus evil was undoubtedly in line with Bush's purported Christian evangelical beliefs. Furthermore, Bush's adoption of the neocon war agenda provided him with his purpose in life, which he identified as the will of God. As *Washington Post* columnist Dana Milbank wrote:

> Bush has come to view his leadership of post 9/11 America as a matter of fate, or of God's will . . . . With that assumption, it is almost impossible to imagine Bush confining the war on terrorism to al Qaeda. Instead, he quickly embraced the most sweeping foreign policy proposal his most hawkish advisers had developed – a vision of American supremacy and preemption of emerging threats – and that policy leads inexorably to Iraq, and beyond.[44]

This neocon war agenda harmonized not only with Bush's born-again Evangelical Christianity, with its pro-Israel, dispensationalist and millenarian theology,[45] but it also meshed with the vaunted American frontier values of toughness and simplicity, which Bush consciously tried to emulate. Historian Douglas Brinkley, director of the Eisenhower Center at the University of New Orleans, referred to Bush as a "rough and ready" president in the mold of Andrew Jackson, James K. Polk, and Harry S. Truman. "He's absorbed those traditions, this very tough-line attitude," Brinkley contended. "It's a way for him to get intellectual certainty without getting involved in deeper questions. He can cling tenaciously to a belief. When there's a crisis, he resorts to a tough rhetorical line or threat."[46]

Norman Podhoretz presented the September 11 atrocities as a lightning bolt to make President Bush aware of his overarching destiny to rid the world of terrorism. He maintained that Bush, in his "pre-9/11 incarnation," had been something of a "realist" in foreign policy, devoted to maintaining

the status quo.[47] In religious (ironically quasi-Christian) terminology, Podhoretz wrote that after the terrorist attacks

> a transformed – or, more precisely, a transfigured – George W. Bush appeared before us. In an earlier article in these pages, I suggested, perhaps presumptuously, that out of the blackness of smoke and fiery death let loose by September 11, a kind of revelation, blazing with a very different fire of its own, lit up the recesses of Bush's mind and heart and soul. Which is to say that, having previously been unsure as to why he should have been chosen to become President of the United States, George W. Bush now knew that the God to whom, as a born-again Christian, he had earlier committed himself had put him in the Oval Office for a purpose. He had put him there to lead a war against the evil of terrorism.[48]

In essence, the events of September 11 had transformed George Bush's attitude and view of the world. "The duty-bound, born-again, can-do Texan morphed into a man who drew on those qualities and intensity of those early days to focus a searing rage," write Stefan Halper and Jonathan Clarke in *America Alone*.

> He was determined to rally the nation and the civilized world to crush Al Qaeda and the diabolical future it represented. The dynamic forged by the moment distilled the many shades of gray reflecting relations among nations into a black and white Manichean "either you are with us or against us" position. To say that American national security priorities were transformed is an understatement. His declaration of the "war on terror" redefined the strategic landscape. Most significant in terms of the shift was the transition from a "humble" candidate Bush to a president whose administration policy was based on unilateral preemption and millenarian nation building.[49]

According to the United States, the purpose of its attack on Afghanistan was to target Osama bin Laden, suspected of planning and funding the September 11, 2001 terrorist attack, and his terrorist network Al Qaeda, as well as the Taliban government in Afghanistan, which allegedly provided support to Al Qaeda and gave its members safe haven.

A valid argument has been put forth that the United States could have apprehended Osama bin Laden via extradition by the Taliban if it had been willing to pursue a nonviolent, diplomatic solution. The Taliban regime condemned the 9/11 attacks. Its initial response was to demand evidence of bin Laden's culpability in the September 11 attacks and to offer to try him in an Islamic court. Later, as the likelihood of American military action became imminent, it offered to extradite bin Laden to a neutral nation. There was even mention of talks with the United States in order to turn Osama over to the United States. The Bush administration, however, refused to explore any avenues of diplomacy to achieve a peaceful solution.[50]

This peaceful way could have actually led to the apprehension of Osama bin Laden, while the automatic movement to war has yet [January 1, 2008] to bring about his capture. There were a number of reasons for the administration to immediately opt for war, however, including the American public's demand for vengeance. And it also has been persuasively argued that the United States opted to invade Afghanistan for ulterior motives: to acquire the energy resources of the area, and because of its geostrategic location in Central Asia. Most importantly, from the neocon perspective, the success of a peaceful approach might have lessened the public ardor for war on Iraq and the consequent restructuring of the Middle East. The easy apprehension of Osama bin Laden, in essence, would have aborted the opportunity to implement the neocon war agenda.

The September 11 terrorism attack provided the United States the ideal opportunity to militarily intervene in Afghanistan on a major scale. Such a move would have reflected dominant American geopolitical thinking that largely intersected with the aims of American energy producers. Moreover, the war on Afghanistan had relatively strong support from the international community and the American public.

It should be pointed out that an extensive war on Afghanistan posed a significant drawback from the neocons' perspective because Iran, a major enemy of the Taliban, would likely (and did) collaborate with the United States in that endeavor. Since the neocons also planned to eliminate the Islamic regime in Iran, any American-Iranian rapprochement would have caused serious difficulties for the ultimate success of their overall Middle East war agenda.

Whatever the purpose of the United States invasion of Afghanistan, whether it was a sincere effort to apprehend the terrorists said to be responsible for 9/11, or whether it had economic and geostrategic motives, the war effort in Afghanistan would be cut short as the Bush administration's attention quickly shifted to Iraq. Consequently, the Al Qaeda network was able to survive and regroup. As former CIA specialist on Al Qaeda Michael Scheuer would write in *Imperial Hubris* in 2004, "Aside from sporadic, short-term ground operations meant to capture, not kill, al Qaeda and Taleban leaders, and infrequent air strikes . . . al Qaeda and the Taleban have been under almost no military pressure in Afghanistan since March 2002." As a result, Al Qaeda has "retained a strong presence in Afghanistan and seized the initiative."[51] It was due to the genius and power of the neoconservatives that they were able to divert American military attention to Iraq and the Middle East.

The adoption of the neocon agenda with its focus on Iraq and the Middle East would distract the United States from consolidating its control of Afghanistan, which could have been used for the American domination of the Eurasian landmass along the lines of the thinking of Zbigniew Brzezinski. Control of Central Asia had been abandoned, or, at least, put on the back burner, in the move to invade Iraq and thence achieve regime change elsewhere in the Middle East. None of these goals had anything to do with the 9/11 attacks. The morass that the United States would find in Iraq, a quagmire that was easy to predict, would not enhance American global domination. It would, however, bring about the destabilization of the Middle East sought by the neocons and the Israeli Likudniks. In a fundamental sense, American hegemonic interests had been trumped by Zionist ones.

chapter 10

MOVE TO WAR

PRESIDENT BUSH'S public pronouncements and actions would show a rapid evolution in the direction of expanding the war to Iraq. On November 21, 2001, in a speech at Fort Campbell, Kentucky, Bush proclaimed that

> Afghanistan is just the beginning of the war against terror. There are other terrorists who threaten America and our friends, and there are other nations willing to sponsor them. We will not be secure as a nation until all these threats are defeated. Across the world, and across the years, we will fight these evil ones, and we will win.[1]

And it was on November 21, 2001, that Bush ordered Secretary of Defense Rumsfeld to develop, with the military leadership, an updated war plan for an attack on Iraq.[2]

On November 26, in response to a question whether Iraq was one of the terrorist nations he had in mind, the President responded: "Well, my message is, is that if you harbor a terrorist, you're a terrorist. If you feed a terrorist, you're a terrorist. If you develop weapons of mass destruction that you want to terrorize the world, you'll be held accountable."

Note that Bush included possession of weapons of mass destruction (WMD) as an indicator of "terrorism." And none of this "terrorist" activity necessarily related to the September 11 attacks.[3]

The transformation to the wider war was complete with Bush's January 29, 2002 State of the Union speech in which the "war on terrorism" was officially decoupled from the specific events of September 11. Bush did not even mention Osama bin Laden or Al Qaeda. The danger now was

said to come primarily from three countries – Iran, Iraq, and North Korea – which the President dubbed an "axis of evil," which allegedly threatened the world with weapons of mass destruction. "Weapons of mass destruction" had become the new bogeyman. According to Bush, "States like these, and their terrorist allies, constitute an axis of evil, arming to threaten the peace of the world. By seeking weapons of mass destruction, these regimes pose a grave and growing danger. They could provide these arms to terrorists, giving them the means to match their hatred. They could attack our allies or attempt to blackmail the United States. In any of these cases, the price of indifference would be catastrophic."[4]

The phrase "axis of evil" was coined by Bush's neoconservative speechwriter, David Frum, about whom columnist Robert Novak wrote that he

> repeatedly refers to his own Jewishness. It is hard to recall any previous presidential aide so engrossed with his own ethnic roots. Frum is more uncompromising in support of Israel than any other issue, raising the inescapable question of whether this was the real reason he entered the White House.[5]

Novak himself is of a Jewish background, though often critical of Israel.

It was Bush's "axis of evil" speech that made mainstream media commentators aware of the severing of the "war on terrorism" from any connection with 9/11. Journalist Michael Kinsley wrote: "But how did the 'war on terrorism' change focus so quickly from rooting out and punishing the perpetrators of 9/11 – a task that is still incomplete – to something (what?) about nuclear proliferation?"[6] And news commentator Chris Matthews stated that

> [a] month ago, I knew why we were fighting. You knew why we were fighting. We were getting the killers of Sept. 11 before they could get us again . . . . . So what happened to that gutsy war of bringing the World Trade Center and Pentagon killers to justice? Who hijacked that clear-eyed, all-American front of September-to-January and left our leaders mouthing this "axis of evil" line? Who hijacked the firefighters" war of righteous outrage and got us reciting this weird mantra about Iran, Iraq – and North Korea, of all places?[7]

As Robert Novak noted in his comments on the State of the Union speech,

> Bush abandoned seeking some connection between the Sept. 11 terrorist attacks and the next step in the war on terrorism. Indeed, the nexus between the three rogue nations and any kind of terrorism was slender, with the presi-

dent asserting these countries "could provide" weapons of mass destruction "to terrorists."[8]

While the "axis of evil" referred to two states in addition to Iraq, it was Iraq that became the focus of American attention (though after the defeat of Saddam, the neocons would shift that focus to Iran). "The Axis of Evil Speech brought Iraq to center stage and kept it there," notes James Mann in *The Vulcans*. "From January 2002 through the war of 2003," he wrote, "the question of what the Bush administration should do about Saddam Hussein's regime became the dominant issue in U.S. foreign policy and, indeed, in all of American political life."[9]

By April 2002, President Bush was publicly declaring that American policy was "regime change" in Iraq. In June, he stated that the United States would launch pre-emptive strikes on countries that threatened the United States.[10] According to what passed as the conventional wisdom, Iraq now posed such a threat. Moreover, by the spring of 2002, Army General Tommy R. Franks, commander of U. S. Central Command, began giving Bush private briefings every three or four weeks on the planning for war against Iraq.[11]

Neoconservatives promoted the idea that Saddam's alleged weapons of mass destruction (WMD) threatened the United States. The very term "WMD" grouped together weapons of dramatically disparate killing power.[12] This meant that Saddam's use of poison gas on the battlefield more than a decade ago was melded together with strategic nuclear weapons, the ultimate killing weapons, making Saddam appear as a lethal threat to the American population.

Top administration figures would quickly focus on the alleged WMD danger. Vice President Cheney expressed absolute certainty regarding Saddam's possession of WMD. "Simply stated, Saddam Hussein now has weapons of mass destruction," Cheney asserted in a speech before the Veterans of Foreign Wars National Convention on August 26, 2002 in Nashville, Tennessee.

> There is no doubt that he is amassing them to use against our friends, against our allies and against us. There is no doubt that his aggressive regional ambitions will lead him into future confrontations with his neighbors, confrontations that will involve both the weapons he has today and the ones he will continue to develop with his oil wealth.[13]

Cheney was essentially calling for war. "We realize that wars are never won on the defensive. We must take the battle to the enemy."[14]

Thomas E. Ricks points out in *Fiasco: The American Military Adventure in Iraq* that Cheney's speech was crucial in setting the war position of the administration. "After that point," Ricks observes,

> the Bush administration's statements about Iraq were not so much part of a debate about whether to go to war, they were part of a campaign to sell it . . . . In the following weeks, first Condoleezza Rice and then Bush himself would adopt the alarmist tone that Cheney had struck that day in Nashville.[15]

President Bush, in his October 7, 2002 address to the nation (given four days before Congress would vote to give Bush the authority to invade Iraq if it did not turn over its alleged WMD arsenal), claimed that "Saddam Hussein is a homicidal dictator who is addicted to weapons of mass destruction." Bush's allegation was not simply that Saddam would build such weapons, but that his WMD arsenal already existed. "If we know Saddam Hussein has dangerous weapons today, and we do, does it make any sense for the world to wait to confront him as he grows even stronger and develops even more dangerous weapons?"[16]

Furthermore, Bush maintained not only that the U.S. government possessed evidence of an Iraqi WMD arsenal, but also that Saddam could attack neighboring countries, endangering Americans stationed there. "And surveillance photos reveal that the regime is rebuilding facilities that it had used to produce chemical and biological weapons," Bush asserted. "Iraq possesses ballistic missiles with a likely range of hundreds of miles, far enough to strike Saudi Arabia, Israel, Turkey and other nations in a region where more than 135,000 American civilians and service members live and work."[17]

More ominously, Bush declared that Saddam threatened not only Americans living in the Middle East, but the United States itself. One way of striking the United States would be for Saddam to provide WMD to terrorists. "Iraq could decide on any given day to provide a biological or chemical weapon to a terrorist group or individual terrorists," Bush intoned. "Alliances with terrorists could allow the Iraqi regime to attack America without leaving any fingerprints."[18]

More than this, the President avowed that Iraq had the technical capability to strike the United States directly. "We've also discovered through intelligence that Iraq has a growing fleet of manned and unmanned aerial vehicles that could be used to disperse chemical or biological weapons across broad areas," Bush direly warned. "We're concerned that Iraq is exploring ways of using these U.A.V.'s for missions targeting the United States."[19] Secretary of State Colin Powell also made use of the purported UAV threat in his presentation before the United Nations on February 5, 2003. Like all the other alleged dangers concocted by the Bush administration, the UAVs were non-existent.[20]

Nuclear weapons were the most fearsome type of WMD. Some neoconservative proponents for war claimed that Saddam might actually have them. For example, Frank Gaffney, a Perle protégé and head of the neoconservative Center for Security Policy, stated in early 2001 that the "Butcher of Baghdad may also have acquired atomic and perhaps even thermonuclear weapons, as well."[21] While the Bush administration did not explicitly state that Iraq already possessed nuclear weapons, it did claim that Iraq was trying to develop them and would soon have them. "The evidence indicates," Bush declared in his October 7, 2002 speech,

> that Iraq is reconstituting its nuclear weapons program. Saddam Hussein has held numerous meetings with Iraqi nuclear scientists, a group he calls his nuclear mujahedeen, his nuclear holy warriors. Satellite photographs reveal that Iraq is rebuilding facilities at sites that have been part of his nuclear program in the past. Iraq has attempted the purchase [of] high-strength aluminum tubes and other equipment needed for gas centrifuges, which are used to enrich uranium for nuclear weapons.

Bush ominously warned:

> If the Iraqi regime is able to produce, buy or steal an amount of highly enriched uranium a little larger than a single softball, it could have a nuclear weapon in less than a year. And if we allow that to happen, a terrible line would be crossed. Saddam Hussein would be in a position to blackmail anyone who opposes his aggression. He would be in a position to dominate the Middle East. He would be in a position to threaten America and Saddam Hussein would be in a position to pass nuclear technology to terrorists.

Since Saddam allegedly would soon become a nuclear power, the United States would have to take immediate action to forcibly disarm him. "Facing clear evidence of peril, we cannot wait for the final proof, the smoking gun that could come in the form of a mushroom cloud."[22]

That non-neoconservatives such as President Bush and even Secretary of State Colin Powell, most poignantly in his crucial speech to the United

Nations on February 5, 2003, would claim Saddam's possession of WMD stockpiles a certainty was the result of successful efforts by the neoconservatives to distort the intelligence assessment process.

The neoconservatives in the Bush administration worked in unison to advance their war agenda. According to Bob Woodward in his *Plan of Attack*, Powell privately referred to a "separate little government," consisting of "Wolfowitz, Libby, Feith, and Feith's 'Gestapo office.'"[23] Moreover, Powell clearly saw their connection to Israel. According to Powell's biographer, Karen DeYoung, he referred to Rumsfeld's group as the "JINSA crowd."[24]

Powell's reference to a "separate little government," however, was actually an understatement. In reality, the Cheney-Rumsfeld axis had become the actual government in determining American foreign policy, with Powell and the State Department bureaucracy effectively marginalized.

Lawrence Wilkerson, who served as Powell's chief of staff from 2001 to 2005, opined in October 2005 on the correlation of power in Bush administration: "What I saw was a cabal between the vice president of the United States, Richard Cheney, and the secretary of defense, Donald Rumsfeld, on critical issues that made decisions that the bureaucracy did not know were being made."

Wilkerson held that the Cheney-Rumsfeld "cabal" was able to exercise power because President Bush was "not versed in international relations and not too much interested." Regarding the concomitant loss of power by the State Department, Wilkerson remarked: "I'm not sure the State Department even exists anymore."[25]

"There were several remarkable things about the vice president's staff," Wilkerson maintained.

> One was how empowered they were, and one was how in sync they were. In fact, we used to say about both [Rumsfeld's office] and the vice president's office that they were going to win nine out of ten battles, because they are ruthless, because they have a strategy, and because they never, ever deviate from that strategy.... They make a decision, and they make it in secret, and they make [it] in a different way than the rest of the bureaucracy makes it, and then suddenly foist it on the government – and the rest of the government is all confused.[26]

One fundamental activity of the "cabal" was to transmute intelligence assessments into propaganda for war. Journalists John Barry, Michael Isikoff and Mark Hosenball described this modus operandi in *Newsweek*:

Cheney had long distrusted the apparatchiks who sat in offices at the CIA, FBI and Pentagon. He regarded them as dim, timid timeservers who would always choose inaction over action. Instead, the vice president relied on the counsel of a small number of advisers. The group included Defense Secretary Donald Rumsfeld, Deputy Defense Secretary Paul Wolfowitz and two Wolfowitz proteges: I. Lewis (Scooter) Libby, Cheney's chief of staff, and Douglas Feith, Rumsfeld's under secretary for policy. Together, the group largely despised the on-the-one-hand/on-the-other analyses handed up by the intelligence bureaucracy. Instead, they went in search of intel that helped to advance their case for war.[27]

Journalist Robert Dreyfuss concurred in this view:

> The pivotal role of Cheney's staff in promoting war in Iraq has been well documented. Cheney was the war's most vocal advocate, and his staff – especially Libby, Hannah, Ravich, and others – worked hard to "fit" intelligence to inflate Iraq's seeming threat.[28]

The problem for Cheney and the neoconservatives was that the CIA was not interested in Saddam, but saw Osama bin Laden as America's foremost threat. James Risen in *State of War* quotes one top CIA official: "It is hard for people outside the agency to understand how little we were thinking about Iraq." Risen continues: "The CIA's lack of focus on Iraq – and in particular, the agency's failure to see Saddam Hussein as an imminent threat to the United States – infuriated the administration's hard-liners." The latter would effectively exert pressure on the agency to make it conform to their war agenda.[29]

Cheney made repeated visits to the CIA during the build-up for war, going over intelligence assessments with the analysts who produced them. His chief of staff, Lewis "Scooter" Libby, also engaged in the same type of monitoring activities when Cheney was not there. Analysts were being pressured to make their assessments of Iraq's military arsenal advance the Bush administration's case for war.[30] Former CIA analyst Pat Eddington, who remained close to many CIA officials, stated that "in my time there, I never saw anything in the way of the kind of radical pressure that clearly existed in 2001 and 2002 and on into 2003."[31]

It has now been revealed that the U.S. government had considerable intelligence information that undercut any certitude that Saddam possessed WMD. Intelligence experts have claimed that the Bush administration higher-ups manipulated intelligence to mobilize public support for war. As early as the fall of 2002, reporters Warren Strobel and Jonathan Landay found numbers of senior government officials who were irate about the Bush administration's deceptive skewing of intelligence, charging that "administration hawks have exaggerated evidence of the threat of the Iraqi leader Saddam Hussein poses – including distorting his links to the al-Qaida terrorist network." Those senior government officials claimed

> that the administration squelches dissenting views and that intelligence analysts are under intense pressure to produce reports supporting the White House's argument that Saddam poses such an immediate threat to the United States that pre-emptive military action is necessary.[32]

After the March 2003 invasion of Iraq and the concomitant failure to find WMD, various intelligence experts commented on the Bush administration's misuse of intelligence to advance the war agenda. "It's looking like in truth the Iraqi (weapons) program was gray. The Bush administration was trying to say it was black," said former CIA Iraq expert and member of Clinton's National Security Council Kenneth Pollack, who had avidly supported the attack on Iraq.[33] Going even further, Greg Thielmann, who until his retirement in September 2002 was director of the strategic, proliferation and military issues office in the State Department's Bureau of Intelligence and Research, stated that "What disturbs me deeply is what I think are the disingenuous statements made from the very top about what the intelligence did say."[34] Having had access to the classified reports that formed the basis for the U.S. case against Saddam, Thielmann was in a position to make a knowledgeable evaluation of the administration's approach to the intelligence process, which he characterized as "faith-based." He summed up the administration approach thus: "We know the answers, give us the intelligence to support those answers."[35]

While some official studies have claimed that the wrong intelligence was unintentional, such a conclusion seems hardly likely. As John Prados, a senior fellow of the National Security Archive in Washington, DC, pointed out, everyone in the CIA and the other government intelligence agencies knew exactly what type of intelligence information the Bush administration wanted. Bucking this position would definitely not be career-enhancing. Prados wrote:

> This adds up to a classic atmosphere for politicization. And the proof is in the intelligence, not in whether somebody caved. The WMD Commission's report

– and before it, that of the Senate Select Committee on Intelligence – focus on the trees rather than the forest when it condemns the CIA for poor intelligence estimates. Everybody, all the CIA analysts, those at INR, in the Pentagon and elsewhere, knew there was no fresh data on Iraq after 1998. They all knew they were using assumptions rather than data to cast projections. They all knew the Iraqi defectors were an undependable lot, and there were reviews of the defector "take" on the books at the time, that put their reliability in doubt. Those things posed no obstacles to an NIE because those questions were ruled out given the prevailing atmosphere. Politicization.[36]

The fact that the United States was simply tailoring intelligence information to justify a war agenda was known in the highest circles of the British government. On May 1, 2005, the London *Sunday Times* revealed a secret official British government memo, dated July 23, 2002, based on the Prime Minister Tony Blair's meeting of that date with his top security advisers. The meeting consisted of a briefing by Richard Dearlove, then-director of Britain's CIA equivalent, MI-6. Dearlove had just returned from discussions with high CIA officials, including CIA Director George Tenet at CIA headquarters in suburban Washington, and reported on the Bush administration's plans to launch a preemptive war against Iraq.[37]

The memo, which has come to be known as the "Downing Street Memo," read in part:

> C [the head of MI6] reported on his recent talks in Washington [where he talked with CIA counterpart George Tenet]. There was a perceptible shift in attitude. Military action was now seen as inevitable. Bush wanted to remove Saddam, through military action, justified by the conjunction of terrorism and WMD. But the intelligence and facts were being fixed around the policy.[38]

So as the secret British memo indicated, the American intelligence on Saddam's terrorism and WMD was being "fixed" to justify a war agenda. The intelligence did not determine policy, but was rather being selected and manipulated to justify a pre-determined objective. And the neocons were intimately involved in fixing the intelligence.

Going beyond the distortion of information from the existing intelligence agencies, Deputy Secretary of Defense Paul Wolfowitz and Under Secretary of Defense for Policy Douglas Feith set up their own intelligence apparatus in the Defense Department, staffed by loyal neoconservatives, which would specially focus on promoting the war. Initially, the concern seemed to have been regarding Saddam's alleged Al Qaeda ties, but it also would include WMD issue. So far, the Al Qaeda issue has been given attention in government investigations. For example, in releasing the report of the Department of Defense Inspector General on the activities of Feith's office on April 5, 2007, Senator Carl Levin, Chairman of the Senate Armed Services Committee, would observe that

> [t]he Feith office alternative intelligence assessments concluded that Iraq and al Qaeda were cooperating and had a "mature, symbiotic" relationship, a view that was not supported by the available intelligence, and was contrary to the consensus view of the Intelligence Community. These alternative assessments were used by the Administration to support its public arguments in its case for war.[39]

(In order to further dispel any notion of a monolithic Jewry pushing for war, it should be noted that Levin is Jewish.)

George Tenet maintains in his memoir that the evidence presented by "Feith's team" was highly selective. Although the individuals involved

> seemed to like playing the role of analysts, they showed none of the professional skills or discipline required. Feith and company would find little nuggets that supported their beliefs and seize upon them, never understanding that there might be a larger picture they were missing. Isolated data points became so important to them that they would never look at the thousands of other data points that might convey an opposite story.[40]

The exact development of this operation in Feith's office is somewhat murky and there is conflicting information, but the following is an effort to present a consistent account of what has come to light. The operation began with the establishment of a war planning team in Feith's office right at the start of the Bush administration in January 2001, which would be organized by Harold Rhode, a longtime Pentagon official who was a specialist on the Middle East and a protégé of veteran neoconservative Michael Ledeen of the American Enterprise Institute. Rhode also had close ties to Richard Perle. When an assistant secretary of defense under Reagan, Perle had hired him as an advisor, and Rhode would also serve as Hebrew instructor to Perle's son, Jonathan. It was also Rhode, who, it will be recalled, had belligerently informed a Saudi delegation, shortly after Bush entered office, that the United States would take care of Saddam, after which the Saudis would be expected to toe the line. Alan Weisman, the author of the biography of Richard Perle, refers to Rhode as an "ardent Zionist," more pro-Israel than Perle.[41]

Rhode looked to the AEI for crucial staff. Shortly after September 11, he recruited David Wurmser to lead the new intelligence unit, which would be called the Counter-Terrorism Evaluation Group. Wurmser had been the director of Middle East studies for AEI, an author of the "Clean Break" policy paper for Netanyahu, and an articulate advocate of Saddam's forcible removal. Wurmser had been closely connected to Rhode, referring to him as his "mentor."[42] Moreover, Wurmser would be teamed up with another neoconservative, F. Michael Maloof, a former aide to Perle in the Reagan administration. The goal of this group was to find information to confirm the claim that Saddam was connected to Al Qaeda and that he was apt to provide those terrorists with WMD.[43]

As the build up for war against Iraq intensified, Wolfowitz and Feith in August 2002 created a war planning unit within the Pentagon's Near East and South Asia bureau (NESA). NESA was headed by Deputy Under Secretary of Defense William Luti, who came from Vice President Cheney's office. The new planning unit, called the Office of Special Plans (OSP), would incorporate the remnant of the Counter-Terrorism Evaluation Group, though Wurmser and Maloof had departed. The OSP would be headed by Abram N. Shulsky. Both Luti and Shulsky were staunch neoconservatives.[44]

Shulsky had numerous neocon connections. He was Wolfowitz's housemate at Cornell and the University of Chicago. He was a scholarly expert in the works of the political philosopher and neoconservative icon Leo Strauss. He had been an aide to former Senators Henry Jackson and Daniel Patrick Moynihan, and worked in Reagan's Department of Defense, where he became close to Richard Perle. Shulsky also worked for the Rand Institute, where he collaborated with I. Lewis Libby on a study called "From Containment to Global Leadership: America and the World after the Cold War." This study was an early draft of what became an official Pentagon military strategy document.[45]

Robert Dreyfuss and Jason Vest wrote in their seminal article on the OSP, "The Lie Factory," in the January/February 2004 issue of the magazine *Mother Jones*: "Luti and Shulsky not only would oversee war plans but would act aggressively to shape the intelligence product received by the White House."[46] OSP's function was to find intelligence that the Pentagon and vice president could use to press the case for a U.S. invasion of Iraq, which would be disseminated to the president and Congress. Without the

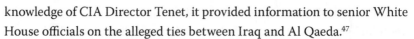

knowledge of CIA Director Tenet, it provided information to senior White House officials on the alleged ties between Iraq and Al Qaeda.[47]

Lt. Colonel Karen Kwiatkowski, an actual eyewitness who had worked for NESA during this period, has provided an extensive account of the Office of Special Plans. Kwiatkowski would seem to be a knowledgeable witness, possessing a Ph.D. in World Politics and having a lengthy background in intelligence, which included a stint for the National Security Agency. When she joined NESA in May 2002, she "didn't know what a neocon was or that they had already swarmed over the Pentagon."[48] She would quickly learn about them, and their identification with Israel, and how they were transforming the Pentagon.

She described the Office of Special Plans as being "organized like a machine. The people working on the neocon agenda had a narrow, well-defined political agenda. They had a sense of mission."[49] Moreover, the people who directed the activities were not Defense Department civilian professionals or military officers, but rather individuals "brought in from the American Enterprise Institute, the Center for Security Policy, and the Washington Institute for Near East Affairs."[50]

Kwiatkowski explained the development of the war propaganda masquerading as intelligence.

> I witnessed neoconservative agenda bearers within OSP usurp measured and carefully considered assessments, and through suppression and distortion of intelligence analysis promulgate what were in fact falsehoods to both Congress and the executive office of the president.[51]

The manipulated intelligence served purposes far different from traditional intelligence information. "This was creatively produced propaganda," Kwiatkowski maintained,

> spread not only through the Pentagon, but across a network of policymakers – the State Department, with John Bolton; the Vice President's Office, the very close relationship the OSP had with that office. That is not normal, that is a bypassing of normal processes. Then there was the National Security Council, with certain people who had neoconservative views; Scooter Libby, the vice president's chief of staff; a network of think tanks who advocated neoconservative views – the American Enterprise Institute, the Center for Security Policy with Frank Gaffney, the columnist Charles Krauthammer – was very reliable. So there was just not a process inside the Pentagon that should have developed good honest policy, but it was instead pushing a particular agenda; this group

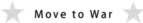

worked in a coordinated manner, across media and parts of the government, with their neoconservative compadres.[52]

Reporter Jim Lobe, referring to the political appointees who worked in NESA/OSP, observed that "[a]long with Feith, all of the political appointees have in common a close identification with the views of the right-wing Likud Party in Israel." Among the NESA/OSP staff he specifically mentioned were Michael Rubin, a Middle East specialist, previously with AEI; David Schenker, previously with the Washington Institute for Near East Policy (WINEP); and Michael Makovsky, "the younger brother of David Makovsky, a senior WINEP fellow and former executive editor of pro-Likud *Jerusalem Post*."[53]

None of the members of OSP had any special technical expertise in intelligence matters. To Greg Thielmann, this indicated the ulterior, propagandistic purpose for the office. "Do they [staffers in the Office of Special Plans] have expertise in Iraqi culture?" he rhetorically asked. "Are they missile experts? Nuclear engineers? There's no logical explanation for the office's creation except that they wanted people to find evidence to support their answers [about war]."[54] [Brackets in the original]

Citing Kwiatkowski, Dreyfuss and Vest point out that "Luti and Shulsky turned cherry-picked pieces of uncorroborated, anti-Iraq intelligence into talking points, on issues like Iraq's WMD and its links to Al Qaeda. Shulsky constantly updated these papers, drawing on the intelligence unit, and circulated them to Pentagon officials, including Rumsfeld, and to Vice President Cheney."[55] In Seymour Hersh's estimation, "the [OSP] operation rivalled both the C.I.A. and the Pentagon's own Defense Intelligence Agency, the D.I.A., as President Bush's main source of intelligence regarding Iraq's possible possession of weapons of mass destruction and connection with Al Qaeda."[56]

In summarizing the OSP's activities, Ray McGovern, a retired CIA intelligence analyst, observed that the office's

de facto chain of command, from division chief to commander-in-chief, was a neocon dream come true: from Abram Shulsky to William Luti to Douglas Feith to Paul Wolfowitz to Donald Rumsfeld to Dick Cheney and George W. Bush. Journalist Seymour Hersh rightly calls this a stovepipe. It is also a self-licking ice cream cone. The lower end of this chain paid for and then stitched together bogus "intelligence" from the now thoroughly discredited Ahmad Chalabi and his Pentagon-financed Iraqi National Congress. Then Shulsky, Luti,

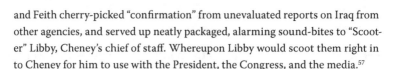
and Feith cherry-picked "confirmation" from unevaluated reports on Iraq from other agencies, and served up neatly packaged, alarming sound-bites to "Scooter" Libby, Cheney's chief of staff. Whereupon Libby would scoot them right in to Cheney for him to use with the President, the Congress, and the media.[57]

In July 2003, due to ever increasing criticism about the role the OSP played in the distorting intelligence, the Pentagon changed the name of the OSP to the Northern Gulf Affairs Office.[58]

The distorted intelligence supplied by the OSP not only served to shape Bush administration policy, but influenced the American public. It was especially fed to the White House Information Group, established in August 2002 by White House Chief of Staff Andrew H. Card for the purpose of selling the invasion of Iraq to the public, which then leaked the information to friendly reporters in the private media. When the stories came out in the private media, Bush administration officials would then make reference to them as proof of the danger of Saddam's regime.[59]

One especially influential reporter who relied heavily on the OSP propaganda for her stories on Iraq was Pulitzer Prize winning columnist Judith Miller of the *New York Times*, who produced a series of reports on WMD in Iraq, and who later would be in the public limelight for her involvement in the Valerie Plame affair. Miller's articles, often placed on the *Times* first page, and having such stunning titles as "U.S. Says Hussein Intensifies Quest for A-Bomb Parts" (September 8, 2002), were very significant in promoting the war among educated and intellectual people, since the *New York Times* is regarded as reliable and politically liberal, unlikely to push the Bush administration propaganda line.[60]

Unbeknownst to almost everyone at the time, however, Miller had significant ties to the neoconservatives. She had been close to Douglas Feith; co-authored a book on Saddam with Laurie Mylroie; was at one time listed as an expert on Islam and the Middle East by the Middle East Forum, a think tank run by Daniel Pipes; and had been represented by the literary agent Eleana Banador, whose clients were almost entirely neocons.[61] Her connection to the Valerie Plame case involved contacts with I. Lewis Libby. Whether Miller identified with the neocon war agenda or not, she had made a career of writing sensational stories (being sometimes cavalier with facts), and her neocon acquaintances could provide her fodder for such stories.[62]

About Miller's writing on Iraq, Franklin Foer noted that it relied heavily on neocon Pentagon sources.

Some of these sources, like Richard Perle and Paul Wolfowitz, would occasionally talk to her on the record. She relied especially heavily on the Office of Special Plans, an intelligence unit established beneath Under Secretary of Defense Douglas Feith. The office was charged with uncovering evidence of Al Qaeda links to Saddam Hussein that the CIA might have missed. In particular, Miller is said to have depended on a controversial neocon in Feith's office named Michael Maloof.... While Miller might not have intended to march in lockstep with these hawks, she was caught up in an almost irresistible cycle. Because she kept printing the neocon party line, the neocons kept coming to her with huge stories and great quotes, constantly expanding her access.[63]

The source for much of Miller's information was the now-notorious Ahmed Chalabi.[64] Miller herself noted, "He [Chalabi] has provided most of the front page exclusives on WMD in our paper."[65] And Miller's fellow reporter at the *New York Times*, Maureen Dowd, wrote:

Judy's stories about W.M.D. fit too perfectly with the White House's case for war. She was close to Ahmad Chalabi, the con man who was conning the neocons to knock out Saddam so he could get his hands on Iraq, and I worried that she was playing a leading role in the dangerous echo chamber that Senator Bob Graham, now retired, dubbed "incestuous amplification." Using Iraqi defectors and exiles, Mr. Chalabi planted bogus stories with Judy and other credulous journalists.[66]

Even Miller's information from the OSP ultimately derived from Chalabi's network of Iraqi exiles.[67]

Ahmed Chalabi had a long history of ties to the neoconservatives. As a youth, Chalabi had fled Iraq with his wealthy family when the monarch was overthrown by a group of army officers in 1958. While studying mathematics at the University of Chicago, he met Albert Wohlstetter, who introduced him to Richard Perle in 1985. Chalabi subsequently became connected with the neocon network.[68] The neocons held Chalabi in high esteem. "He's a rare find," said Max Singer, a trustee and co-founder of the neoconservative Hudson Institute. "He's deep in the Arab world and at the same time he is fundamentally a man of the West."[69] In July 2003, Richard Perle asserted that "the person most likely to give us reliable advice is Ahmed Chalabi."[70]

For the neocons, Chalabi represented the democratic opposition to Saddam, and in the early 1992, he established the Iraqi National Congress (INC). Chalabi sought to be the leader of a future Iraqi government after the removal of Saddam. The Iraqi National Congress was promoted by the

neocons but was opposed by officials in the State Department and the CIA, who viewed Chalabi as a conman.[71]

Chalabi did have something of a checkered past, being a fugitive from Jordan for a 1992 conviction in absentia on 31 charges of embezzlement, theft, misuse of depositor funds and currency speculation. Those charges stemmed from the 1989 collapse of his Petra Bank, the second largest bank in Jordan. Chalabi was sentenced by a Jordanian court to 22 years in jail. After Petra's closure in 1989, the Jordanian government had to put up an estimated $300 million to guarantee the depositors' money – a huge amount for an impoverished country.[72]

It was after his hasty departure from Jordan that Chalabi, with the backing of his neocon allies in Washington, launched the Iraqi National Congress (INC). In November 1993, Chalabi presented the new Clinton administration with a plan for the overthrow of Saddam Hussein. The plan involved an American-supported revolt of a limited number of INC-led Kurds and Shiites, which would supposedly trigger a full-scale national rebellion against Saddam. In March 1995, Chalabi's insurrection was launched, and failed dramatically, which caused the CIA and the State Department to abandon support for his efforts.[73]

The neocons still were promoting Chalabi and his exiles as the liberators of Iraq. Their efforts helped to persuade Congress to pass the Iraq Liberation Act of 1998, which allocated $97 million for training and military equipment for Chalabi's Iraqi opposition. Without strong Clinton Administration support, however, nothing concrete came from this development.[74]

Things would change with the coming of the Bush administration, in which the neocons would be in a prime position to provide Chalabi's organization substantial government aid and to make use of his intelligence information for propaganda purposes.[75] Middle East intelligence experts still regarded his intelligence information as spurious. "The [INC's] intelligence isn't reliable at all," Vincent Cannistraro, a former senior CIA official and counter-terrorism expert, said before the war.

> Much of it is propaganda. Much of it is telling the Defence Department what they want to hear. And much of it is used to support Chalabi's own presidential ambitions. They make no distinction between intelligence and propaganda, using alleged informants and defectors who say what Chalabi wants them to say, [creating] cooked information that goes right into presidential and vice-presidential speeches.[76]

Whitley Bruner, former chief of the CIA's station in Baghdad, bluntly asserted that "Chalabi's primary focus was to drag us into a war."[77] The Senate Intelligence Committee's report on pre-war intelligence on Iraq, released in September 2006, confirmed the correctness of Chalabi's critics, stating that Chalabi's exile group "attempted to influence United States policy on Iraq by providing false information through defectors directed at convincing the United States that Iraq possessed weapons of mass destruction and had links to terrorists."[78]

Why did the neocons accept Chalabi's intelligence information while most experts rejected it? It would seem that the neocons supported Chalabi because their interests converged in removing Saddam. In this symbiotic relationship, the neocons gave him political support while Chalabi provided bogus intelligence that could serve as effective war propaganda.

As Saddam's alleged WMD remained missing long after the start of the United States occupation of Iraq, Ahmed Chalabi in February 2004 candidly told the *London Telegraph* that "we are heroes in error . . . . As far as we're concerned, we've been entirely successful. That tyrant Saddam is gone, and the Americans are in Baghdad. What was said before is not important."[79] The Bush administration neoconservatives could undoubtedly say the same thing. Fallacious as it was, Chalabi's intelligence information advanced the neoconservative war agenda.

Neocons had looked to have Chalabi accede to the position he sought as the ruler of Iraq. And his star was definitely in ascendancy in the immediate post-invasion period. A Pentagon plane flew Chalabi triumphantly into post-war Iraq in March 2003. Chalabi was appointed by the U.S.-led coalition authority to the Iraqi Governing Council, and his power was augmented as relatives and members of his Iraq National Congress were placed in key ministries. He was the second member of the Governing Council to hold its rotating presidency, and was also among a delegation which attended a United Nations Security Council meeting on the future of Iraq in July 2003. His nephew Salem Chalabi was named the lead prosecutor of Saddam Hussein. In January 2004, when President Bush delivered his State of the Union speech to Congress celebrating the success of the war against Iraq, Chalabi sat in a place of honor behind First Lady Laura Bush.[80]

The United States government's honeymoon with Chalabi came crashing to an ignominious end in May 2004 when Iraqi police, backed by American soldiers, raided Chalabi's Baghdad home and the headquarters of the

Iraqi National Congress, where they discovered classified U.S. intelligence material. The raid was in response to United States intelligence agencies' electronic intercepts indicating that Chalabi and his entourage had passed sensitive information on to the Iranians. Chalabi, it seemed, had been something of a double agent. While he was still defended by neocons such as Perle, the State Department and the CIA used the intelligence about his Iranian ties to persuade the president to jettison him once and for all. And the United States government terminated its subsidy for the Iraqi National Congress.[81]

It would be argued that Chalabi had conned the neocons. But, obviously, the neocons did not opt for war because they believed Chalabi. Intelligence experts generally held Chalabi to be a charlatan, so it is hard to believe that the neocons put stock in his stories. Rather, the neocons wanted the U.S. to go to war against Iraq and used Chalabi as their instrument. Chalabi's lies about Saddam's WMD, which the neocons spread in the Bush administration, served to advance their war agenda.[82] Moreover, underscoring the fact that the neocons had not repudiated Chalabi was that after his brief return to power in Iraq as deputy prime minister, he would be invited to speak at the American Enterprise Institute on November 9, 2005.[83]

Returning to the role of the OSP: as a result of a FBI probe of Israeli spying in the United States (ongoing since 1999), which was leaked to the public in the late summer of 2004, it came out that Israeli agents had direct contacts with members of the OSP. In essence, it was not simply that individuals in the OSP were pro-Israel, but that some of them might be conspirators in a clandestine operation launched by Sharon's Likud Party; they were, as Robert Dreyfuss called them, "agents of influence" for a foreign government.[84]

The spotlight shifted to the OSP because the FBI, in its probe of Israeli spying, observed OSP analyst Larry Franklin meeting with an Israeli official in the presence of two officials from the American Israel Public Affairs Committee (AIPAC). In October 2005, Franklin plead guilty to the charge of having turned over highly classified intelligence documents to an Israeli government official and to members of AIPAC, who in turn handed them over to the Israeli Embassy. On January 20, 2006, Franklin was sentenced to over 12 years imprisonment.[85]

However, the FBI investigation implied much more than the spying of Frankin and some AIPAC officials, illustrating the Israeli connection to the

office that had played such a monumental role in providing the propaganda to justify the United States attack on Iraq.[86] For Franklin was intimately involved in secretive activities for the OSP. Without notifying the State Department or the CIA, the OSP had been involved in back channel operations that included a series of secret meetings in Washington, Rome and Paris to discuss regime change in Iraq, Iran, and Syria. These meetings brought together OSP staff and consultants (Franklin, Harold Rhode and Michael Ledeen), expatriate Iranian arms dealer Manichur Ghorbanifar, AIPAC lobbyists, Ahmed Chalabi, and Italian and Israeli intelligence officers.[87] In short, it appears that various neoconservatives connected with the Department of Defense were consciously working with Israel in shaping American Middle East policy.

Israel was also involved in promoting the United States attack on Iraq apart from these covert dealings.[88] Some of the spurious intelligence provided to the United States came directly from Israel, as shown in a study by Shlomo Brom, a senior researcher at one of Israel's leading think tanks, the Jaffee Center for Strategic Studies at Tel Aviv University.[89] A special panel of the Israeli Knesset investigated and confirmed the charge that Israeli intelligence services had greatly exaggerated the Iraqi WMD threat. Yossi Sarid, a member of the Knesset's Foreign Affairs and Defense Committee, charged that Israeli intelligence had deliberately misled the United States.[90]

According to James Risen in *State of War: The Secret History of the CIA and the Bush Administration*, Israeli intelligence officials frequently traveled to Washington to brief top government officials. The CIA was skeptical of the Israeli intelligence and after the Israeli briefings would circulate reports throughout the government discounting the Israeli information. Wolfowitz and other neoconservatives who had met with the Israeli officials, were enraged by the CIA's negative response, with Wolfowitz complaining vehemently to CIA Director Tenet.[91]

It has been alleged that the Office of Special Plans was provided with information by a special unit created in Israeli Prime Minister Ariel Sharon's office.[92] Israel had a history of providing questionable intelligence in regard to Iraq to make that country appear threatening. As pointed out earlier, shortly after the September 11 terrorism, Aman, Isael's military intelligence service, reportedly claimed that Iraq had been involved in the attacks.[93]

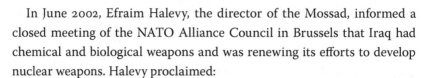

In June 2002, Efraim Halevy, the director of the Mossad, informed a closed meeting of the NATO Alliance Council in Brussels that Iraq had chemical and biological weapons and was renewing its efforts to develop nuclear weapons. Halevy proclaimed:

> As you know, on the eve of the Gulf War, Iraq was on the verge of attaining nuclear capability . . . . Starting from 1998, the year in which the UN monitoring was halted, we must assume that the Iraqis renewed their efforts in this area; we have clear indications that this is what has happened, and it is their great and unshakeable ambition. Together with these efforts, we have reason to believe that the Iraqis have succeeded in preserving parts of their capability in the fields of biological and chemical warfare. We have partial evidence that they have renewed production of VX and perhaps even anthrax germs . . . . They have produced large quantities of nerve gas of the Serin type (GB) and in recent years they are working hard on producing VX nerve gas.[94]

It has been argued that Israel, in its support for war on Iraq, was simply going along with the United States government. Secretary of State Colin Powell's Chief of Staff Lawrence Wilkerson maintains that the Israelis initially wanted the United States to focus on Iran not Iraq, and only shifted to supporting the war on Iraq in early 2002 upon realizing that a war on Iraq had become definite American policy.[95] As mentioned earlier, the report that the IDF's supreme intelligence agency, Aman, at the time of 9/11, promoted the disinformation that Saddam was behind the terrorist attacks militates against the idea that the Israeli government as a unified entity was opposed to the war during this early period.

However, even if there had not been complete Israeli support for a United States attack on Iraq prior to the early spring, the director of the Mossad's public backing of the major WMD justification for the war in June 2002, before an influential NATO audience, would belie any argument that Israel was simply a reluctant follower of United States policy. The fact of the matter is that the Israeli government was pressing the United States to attack Iraq and actively abetting the war propaganda process. "Any postponement of an attack on Iraq at this stage will serve no purpose," Ranaan Gissin, a senior Sharon adviser, told the Associated Press in August 2002. "It will only give Saddam Hussein more of an opportunity to accelerate his programme of weapons of mass destruction."[96]

Gissin said Sharon sent the United States government Israeli intelligence estimates that Saddam had boosted production of chemical and biological

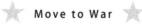

weapons in anticipation of war with the United States. Gissin also claimed that Saddam had recently ordered Iraq's Atomic Energy Commission to speed up work on developing nuclear weapons. "Saddam's going to be able to reach a point where these weapons will be operational," Gissin direly warned.[97]

Former Prime Minister Benjamin Netanyahu was also trumpeting the necessity of war. In September, 2002, the *Wall Street Journal* published a piece by Netanyahu entitled "The Case for Toppling Saddam," in which he held that "This is a dictator who is rapidly expanding his arsenal of biological and chemical weapons, who has used these weapons of mass destruction against his subjects and his neighbors, and who is feverishly trying to acquire nuclear weapons." Netanyahu waved the red flag of Saddam's purported nuclear threat. "Two decades ago it was possible to thwart Saddam's nuclear ambitions by bombing a single installation," Netanyahu exclaimed.

> Today nothing less than dismantling his regime will do. For Saddam's nuclear program has changed. He no longer needs one large reactor to produce the deadly material necessary for atomic bombs. He can produce it in centrifuges the size of washing machines that can be hidden throughout the country – and Iraq is a very big country. Even free and unfettered inspections will not uncover these portable manufacturing sites of mass death.[98]

Netanyahu's focus was Iraq's alleged nuclear threat. "[T]he imperative is to defang the Iraqi regime by preventing its acquisition of atomic weapons," Netanyahu solemnly declared in October 2002. "No inspectors will be able to do that job."[99] In fact, as early as April 2002, Netanyahu was briefing U.S. senators as to the nuclear danger of Saddam Hussein. According to columnist Robert Novak, Netanyahu warned that Saddam "not only is acquiring nuclear weapons but may have the means of delivering them against the United States" via "satchels carried by terrorists."[100]

It is noteworthy that the pro-war position in Israel transcended the Likudnik right, being taken up by Labor leader Shimon Peres, who was serving as Sharon's Foreign Minister. Peres stated in September 2002 that "the campaign against Saddam is a must. Inspections and inspectors are good for decent people, but dishonest people can overcome easily inspections and inspectors."[101] Former Labor Party Prime Minister Ehud Barak also stressed the need for military action.

> Those who prefer to wait and hope for the best should contemplate the following: no one really knows how close Saddam Hussein is to building a crude nuclear device – and it was a crude device that destroyed Hiroshima and Nagasaki. Few will doubt Mr. Hussein's readiness to use a nuclear weapon against American assets or against Israel, if only under extreme circumstances. Once Iraq becomes a nuclear power, the very decision to go to war against it would become a totally different ball game.[102]

In late December 2002, Robert Novak maintained that Prime Minister Sharon was privately urging American lawmakers to support an attack on Iraq for the benefit of Israel.

> In private conversation with [Republican Senator Chuck] Hagel and many other members of Congress, the former general leaves no doubt that the greatest U.S. assistance to Israel would be to overthrow Saddam Hussein's Iraqi regime. That view is widely shared inside the Bush administration, and is a major reason why U.S. forces today are assembling for war.[103]

In February 2003, as the American attack approached, Prime Minister Sharon told a visiting delegation of American congressmen in Israel that the war against Iraq would provide a model for how the United States should also deal with Syria, Libya, and Iran. "These are irresponsible states, which must be disarmed of weapons [of] mass destruction, and a successful American move in Iraq as a model will make that easier to achieve." While Sharon said that Israel would not be directly involved in the attack on Iraq, he emphasized that "the American action is of vital importance."[104] In short, Sharon was advising the United States how it should deal with Israel's enemies.

The pre-war message about Saddam's WMD threat resonated strongly with the American people. Traumatized as they were by the 9/11 terrorist attacks, the American people were ready to believe stories of the most extreme nature. As early as September 2002, when asked in the PIPA/Knowledge Networks poll the question, "Do you think that Saddam Hussein does or does not have the capability to use chemical or biological weapons against targets in the U.S.?," an overwhelming 79 percent of the respondents answered in the affirmative. In the September 2002 CBS/*New York Times* poll, 80 percent believed Iraq had WMD, and 62 percent believed that Iraq would launch a WMD attack on the United States.[105]

Neoconservatives not only shaped the foreign policy for the attack on Iraq, but also played a role in formulating military strategy. Here they were

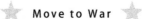

in inhospitable terrain. Top military figures, including members of the Joint Chiefs of Staff, initially expressed opposition to the whole idea of war against Iraq.[106]

Richard Perle and other neoconservatives, however, held that toppling Saddam would require little military effort or risk because of Iraqi opposition to Saddam's rule, which Perle described as a "house of cards." This reflected the line that had been pushed by Ahmed Chalabi. Retired General Wayne Downing, who ran U.S. Special Operations Command during the Gulf War, along with former CIA officer Duane "Dewey" Clarridge became military "consultants" to Chalabi's INC and had updated Chalabi's plan, now dubbed the "Downing Plan." In order to spark a successful overthrow of Saddam, the Downing Plan proposed to use a force of not more than 5,000 INC troops, backed by lightning strikes conducted by U.S. Army Special Forces soldiers along with American air support to destroy Iraqi troop concentrations. Downing served as the Bush II administration's top counter-terrorism official on the National Security Council.[107]

Perle and other neocons insisted that once American forces entered the country, Saddam's army would melt away and the Iraqi people would join the battle for liberation, driving Saddam from power themselves. They claimed that the success of an analogous approach in Afghanistan showed the feasibility of such a strategy in Iraq.[108]

While the neocons were not necessarily wedded to all the specifics of the ultra-low-force-level Downing Plan, they did emphasize the ease of an invasion. In December 2001, Ken Adelman of the Defense Policy Board described an American conquest of Iraq as a "cakewalk," a term picked up by Richard Perle and other neocons.[109] Deputy Secretary of Defense Wolfowitz likened the coming American invasion of Iraq to the liberation of France in 1944: "The Iraqi people understand what their crisis is about. Like the people of France in the 1940s, they view us as their hoped-for liberator."[110]

Within the government, opposition to the small force scenario embodied in the "Downing Plan" abounded, and included the State Department, CIA, and professional military, who maintained that the plan underestimated the loyalty and strength of Saddam's forces and greatly overestimated the strength of the Iraqi opposition. The American military leadership held that it would be necessary to use a much larger number of troops – around 400,000 – which would attack Iraq in a conventional full-scale invasion from its neighboring countries (a la the Gulf War). Such a plan was anathema to the administration neocons. They feared that no neighboring country would provide the necessary bases from which to launch such a massive conventional attack, or that during the lengthy time period needed to assemble a large force, diplomacy might avert war.[111]

Perle angrily responded to the military's demurring by saying that the decision to attack Iraq was "a political judgment that these guys aren't competent to make."[112] Cheney and Rumsfeld went even farther allegedly referring to the generals as "cowards" for being insufficiently gung-ho regarding an Iraq invasion.[113]

Now one might be tempted to attribute the rejection of the military's caution to insane hubris on the part of Perle and the neoconservative crowd – how could those amateurs deign to know more about military strategy than professional military men themselves? Richard Perle may be many things, but stupid is not one of these. Perle undoubtedly thought through the implications of his plan. And it is apparent that the a limited-force option would be a win-win proposition from the neocon perspective. First, it was a plan that could be initiated in the shortest amount of time and with the fewest international entanglements. And if the plan worked – that a few American troops could easily topple Saddam's regime and be welcomed by the Iraqi people – then Perle and the neoconservatives would appear as military geniuses who would then have free reign to prepare a series of additional low-cost wars in the Middle East to deal with the alleged terrorist threat.

On the other hand, if the invasion were a complete fiasco – with American troops killed or captured – then the American people would demand strong military action to avenge the national humiliation. Total war would be unleashed, which would involve heavy bombing of cities. And the American air attacks could easily move from Iraq to the other neighboring Islamic states. This would be the neoconservatives' fondest dream since it would wreck havoc on other alleged terrorist states, who also happened to be the enemies of Israel.

The neoconservatives had a crucial ally in Secretary of Defense Donald Rumsfeld, who placed his faith in a sleek, mobile, high tech military operation and held that an invasion force of 50,000 to 75,000 would be sufficient because of America's vast air superiority and the degraded condition of the Iraqi military.[114] As Bob Woodward writes: "The Iraq war plan was the chess board on which Rumsfeld would test, develop, expand and modify

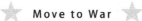

his ideas about military transformation. And the driving concept was 'less is more' – new thinking about a lighter, swifter, smaller force that could do the job better. Rumsfeld's blitzkrieg would vindicate his leadership of the Pentagon."[115] While this was a larger force than the low-key Downing Plan, it would not have the aforementioned drawbacks of the conventional full-scale invasion.

It should be emphasized here that it was this convergence of interests that made Rumsfeld so firmly supportive of the neocon network.[116] The neocon Iraq policy provided him with the type of war to demonstrate the merits of his military thinking. Moreover, Rumsfeld's unconventional military views and management style meant that he had few supporters outside of the neocons, making their support all the more important.[117] In a mutually beneficial symbiotic relationship, the neocons praised and supported Rumsfeld, while Rumsfeld enabled the neocons to play a fundamental role in shaping foreign policy.

In the end, the uniformed military in the Pentagon augmented the magnitude of the Iraq strike force so as to reduce the risk of a defeat. Final force levels basically represented a compromise between the positions of the military brass and Rumsfeld (and the neocons). General Tommy Franks, the theater commander-in-chief, convinced Rumsfeld to send 250,000 troops (augmented by 45,000 British). The military leadership still would have preferred a larger force, for the invasion force was only about one-third the size of the one that liberated Kuwait in 1991.[118] And U.S. commanders were given a far more difficult mission: to travel hundreds of miles to Baghdad; defeat the Iraqi military; overthrow President Saddam Hussein; and then prevent a country the size of the state of California from falling into violence and instability. As it turned out, while this military force was sufficient to defeat Saddam's army, it was too small and ill-equipped (lacking heavy armor) to effectively occupy the country and maintain order. Rather ironically, the difficulties of the occupation caused neocons to argue later that the United States needed a larger occupation force, though not accepting responsibility for having initially championed the small force concept.[119]

Neoconservatives both within and outside of the administration sought a unilateral U.S. attack on Iraq. They viewed the unilateral approach as the easiest and most efficacious way of bringing about an attack on Iraq. It would not be encumbered by the conflicting goals of any coalition partners.

Moreover, the neocons especially did not want any international group inspecting Iraq for WMD that might serve to defuse the crisis and obviate a U.S. rationale for war.[120]

One threat along those lines came from Jose Bustani, the head of global arms-control agency, the Organization for the Prohibition of Chemical Weapons (OPCW). Bustani sought to persuade Saddam Hussein to sign the chemical weapons convention, with the goal of eventually sending chemical weapons inspectors to Iraq. The OPCW had been formed in 1997 to enforce the international Chemical Weapons Convention, which banned chemical weapons.[121]

In his first years, Bustani, who was the founding director-general of the OPCW, appeared to have firm American backing. In May 2000, Bustani had U.S. support for his unanimous re-election as OPCW chief for the 2001–2005 term. Secretary of State Colin Powell praised his leadership qualities in a personal letter in 2001.[122]

Bustani said that he first became aware of Washington's hostility to him at the end of 2001. Bustani viewed the change in the American attitude to the influence of several hawkish officials in the Bush State Department, especially Under Secretary of State for Arms Control and International Security John Bolton.[123] In a March 2002 "white paper," Bolton's office complained that Bustani was seeking an "inappropriate role" in Iraq.[124]

Bolton, a former member of JINSA, flew to Europe in 2002 to confront Bustani and demand his resignation. When Bustani was unwilling to leave voluntarily, Bolton then orchestrated his firing. Bustani was removed by a vote of just one-third of member nations at an unusual special session of the OPCW in April 2002 on the grounds of mismanagement. The U.S. delegation had suggested it would withhold America's dues – 22 percent of the OPCW budget – if Bustani stayed in office, stirring fears of an OPCW collapse. The United Nations' highest administrative tribunal later condemned Bustani's removal as an "unacceptable violation" of principles protecting international civil servants[125]

Former Bustani aide Bob Rigg, a New Zealander, told the Associated Press: "Why did they not want OPCW involved in Iraq? They felt they couldn't rely on OPCW to come up with the findings the U.S. wanted." Top career diplomats in Bolton's arms-control bureau, Ralph Earle and Avis Bohlen, claimed that the idea to remove Bustani did not originate with Bolton, but that he "leaped on it enthusiastically." Bohlen said that "He [Bolton] was very much in charge of the whole campaign," and that Bustani's initiative on Iraq seemed the "coup de grace." Bohlen claimed "It was that that made Bolton decide he had to go."[126]

Another international impediment to a war on Iraq was possible United Nations' involvement. The Downing Street memo illustrated that by the latter part of July 2002, the British government realized that the United States had decided upon war. To the British leadership, the issue of legality was of the utmost importance for Britain's participation in a U.S.-initiated war. Moreover, as the British saw it, an attack on Iraq would only qualify as legal by the standards of international law if it had some type of United Nations authorization. Hence, the British goal was to put Saddam Hussein in a position where he would reject or violate a United Nations ultimatum ordering him to co-operate with UN weapons inspectors. From the British standpoint, UN involvement would serve as a cover for an inevitable war, not as a true effort to allow for a peaceful settlement.[127]

Blair sought to persuade the United States to involve the United Nations in weapons inspections in Iraq, emphasizing that such a veneer of legality was necessary to gain the support of the British public for military participation. Whereas the British government had devised the UN approach as a cover for an inevitable war, not as a means to avoid war, the neocons, not confronted by the need for a substantial legal justification, saw the matter very differently. They were chary of any internationalization of the war endeavor, which they feared would tie American hands and might even disrupt the momentum for war, given the fact that the American military was reluctant to launch an invasion. And the longer the war was delayed, the greater the chance for an American anti-war movement to develop. Other countries might even come up with a peaceful solution, especially since any UN weapons inspectors were not apt to find any WMD.

However, Prime Minister Tony Blair had an ally in Secretary of State Powell. Powell shared Blair's anxiety about the need for international sanction for the war, though Powell was fundamentally concerned about not alienating America's allies, as opposed to the strict legality of the military action or the need to placate domestic opinion. Powell saw the UN as a vehicle to build the necessary international support for a U.S. attack on Iraq.

Unlike the neocons, Powell saw cooperation with America's allies as vital to sustain America's overall global foreign policy.[128]

Powell had lengthy telephone discussions with his British counterpart, Foreign Minister Jack Straw, who is also, incidentally, of Jewish ancestry, on the issue of international cooperation and UN involvement. To Straw, he bemoaned the power of the neocon war party in the administration. In the words of James Naughtie in his *The Accidental American: Tony Blair and the Presidency*:

> Powell was frank about his problems, extraordinarily so. Referring to the Cheney-Rumsfeld-Wolfowitz group in the administration, Powell did not feel it necessary to conceal his irritation and feeling of alienation from their view. He told Straw in one of their conversations that they were "fucking crazies."[129]

On August 5, 2002, Powell made a lengthy presentation to President Bush outlining the grave consequences of an American attack on Iraq – destabilization of friendly Arab regimes, a spike in the price of oil – but offered as a solution the formation of a UN sanctioned coalition to militarily threaten Iraq. Bush found Powell's argument for a UN involvement to be persuasive.[130]

In his *Plan of Attack*, Bob Woodward claims that actually

> Powell had been trying to say more, to sound a warning that too much could go wrong. The Reluctant Warrior was urging restraint, but he had not tossed his heart on the table. He had not said, Don't do it. Taken together the points of his argument could have been mustered to reach that conclusion. Powell half felt that, but he had learned during 35 years in the Army, and elsewhere, that he had to play to the boss and talk about method. It was paramount to talk only within the confines of the preliminary goals set by the boss. Perhaps he had been too timid.[131]

Cheney, however, still tried to derail this move to UN involvement claiming that it was worthless to go the weapons inspection route. On August 26, 2002, the vice president declared in a speech to the Veterans of Foreign Wars convention that a return of United Nations inspectors could provide "no assurance whatsoever" that Iraq did not harbor WMD and could bring only "false comfort."[132]

Bob Woodward writes in *Plan of Attack* that, from Powell's perspective, "The vice-president was beyond hell-bent for action against Saddam. It was as if nothing else existed."[133] Cheney protested that inspectors would likely be fooled by Saddam. Woodward continues: "The end result, Cheney said, would be deliberations or reports that would be inconclusive. So inspections would make getting to a decision to actually take out Saddam much more difficult."[134]

Fearing that Bush might follow Cheney's counsel, Prime Minister Blair flew off to the presidential retreat at Camp David, Maryland, for a talk with Bush on September 7. In a heated discussion, the president gave assurances to Blair that he would take the UN approach when he spoke before that body on September 12.[135]

But things were still not completely settled. Finally, as the speech Bush would deliver on Iraq at the United Nations was drafted, the president decided he would include a line saying the U.S. would work through the UN and seek a new UN resolution on Iraq, despite continuing opposition from Cheney, and to a lesser degree, Rumsfeld.

Two days before the speech, however, the 21st draft did not include language asking the United Nations to enact anything. But the night before the speech, Bush spoke to Powell and Rice to say that he had decided he would ask for a new U.N. resolution in the speech text. But somehow that language was left out of the TelePrompTer version relied upon by Bush when he actually delivered the speech, which focused on Saddam's defiance of previous UN resolutions and his threat to the world. Noticing the phrase's absence, Bush ad-libbed the missing line, saying, "We will work with the U.N. Security Council for the necessary resolutions."[136]

On the surface, this move to the United Nations appeared to be a victory for Powell over the unilateralist approach of the neocons. However, while this decision seemingly slowed the rush to war, and appeared to be a defeat for the neoconservative war juggernaut, it represented only a temporary reprieve. The neocons ultimately were not only able to counter any anti-war effects from the United Nations involvement, but were able to deftly use it to their advantage.

Within a week after Bush's speech, Iraq agreed to allow the return of United Nations weapons inspectors without conditions on the inspectors' work, perhaps as an effort to avert the need for a new, tougher UN resolution. However, the United States expected the Security Council to pass a new resolution that would require Saddam to follow UN orders and would provide for punitive military action if he failed to comply.[137]

On November 8, 2002, the UN Security Council in Resolution 1441 decided that UN inspectors, with sweeping inspection powers, would determine whether Iraq was violating its pledge to destroy all of its weapons of mass destruction. Placing the burden of proof on Iraq to show that it no longer possessed these weapons, Resolution 1441 stated that any false statements or omissions in the Iraqi declaration would constitute a material breach by Iraq of its obligations. This could set in motion discussions by the Security Council to consider the use of military force against Iraq. The resolution, in fact, stated that United Nations inspectors would report to the Security Council "any interference by Iraq with inspection activities, as well as any failure by Iraq to comply with its disarmament obligations." It would then "convene" and "consider the situation and the need for full (Iraqi) compliance."[138]

Although some commentators thought that the UN involvement might serve to avert war,[139] the Bush administration intended to use the new UN resolution as a legal justification for war. As events unfolded, the United States chose to enforce the resolution by means of war without additional UN authorization. British reporter Robert Fisk presciently recognized that strategy in fall 2002. "The United Nations can debate any Iraqi non-compliance with weapons inspectors," Fisk opined "but the United States will decide whether Iraq has breached UN resolutions. In other words, America can declare war without UN permission."[140]

Although critical of Iraq's failure to fully cooperate, the UN inspection team, headed by Hans Blix, never found any weapons or weapons production facilities during the four-months that it was in the country. From the very outset, however, the neoconservatives made a concerted effort to discredit Blix's entire inspection effort. Allegations were made that Blix had been duped by Saddam in the past, and thus would be fooled again, and that America's vital security should not rest on the bemused findings of some foreigners. "The message was clear," Joseph Wilson would write,

> the war party would not be denied its fight by some meddlesome international bureaucrats, even if the WMD threat did not merit war and there were no clear links between Saddam Hussein and Osama bin Laden. They simply would not accept any outcome but war.[141]

The neocons contended that Blix's team's failure to find WMD was meaningless. Perle told British MP's: "I cannot see how Hans Blix can state more than he can know. All he can know is the results of his own investigations. And that does not prove Saddam does not have weapons of mass destruction."[142]

Perle asserted that it was impossible for the inspection team to actually find WMD in Iraq. "But they will never find anything because there are millions of hiding places and just 100 inspectors." Finding weapons was not even Blix's mission, Perle maintained. "The inspections were never intended to find things that have been hidden. They were intended to verify the destruction of things Saddam claims he no longer has."[143] How Saddam was to prove to America's satisfaction the destruction of weapons if those weapons didn't exist was not specified.

In a speech in London in early December 2002, Wolfowitz downplayed the role of the inspectors, saying, "It is not and cannot be [their] responsibility . . . to scour every inch of Iraq. It cannot be their responsibility to search out and find every illegal weapon or program."[144]

Charles Krauthammer argued in January 2003 that the United States could not refrain from war no matter what the UN inspectors reported.

> The president cannot logically turn back. He says repeatedly, and rightly, that inspectors can only verify a voluntary disarmament. They are utterly powerless to force disarmament on a regime that lies, cheats and hides. And having said, again correctly, that the possession of weapons of mass destruction by Hussein is an intolerable threat to the security of the United States, there is no logical way to rationalize walking away from Iraq – even if the president wanted to.[145]

The neocons and the American government made the assumption that Saddam possessed WMD. The onus was placed on Saddam to prove that Iraq had destroyed its WMD. Of course, since Saddam, as it turned out, apparently had not possessed WMD for some time, he was given an impossible task.

Although the U.S. interpretation of the UN resolution would guarantee war, some neocons nonetheless feared that the war could still be derailed. Michael Ledeen lamented that both Bush and Tony Blair "have been boxed in by a combination of so-called friends and allies and by their own advisers who counsel excessive prudence. This antiwar coalition prevented the rapid and decisive action Mr. Bush seemed instinctively inclined to unleash." In this antiwar coalition, Ledeen identified the American "uniformed military," the Saudis, and "the same crowd that produced the end-of-the-Gulf-War debacle, with Scowcroft, Baker, and Powell in the lead, and [Jimmy] Carter, [Thomas] Daschle [Senator, South Dakota], and [Patrick] Leahy [Senator, Vermont] alongside." Ledeen feared a repeat of the failure to remove Saddam after Gulf War of 1991.

The current debacle resembles the final phase of the Gulf War in more ways than the presence of the same failed personalities. In 1991 the Middle East seemed on the verge of an American-led democratic revolution that would have been catalyzed by the liberation of Iraq from Saddam. When Bush the Elder, Scowcroft, and Powell walked away and left Saddam in his many palaces, those who opposed democratic change took heart, concluded the United States really was a paper tiger, and constructed a new terror network to replace the one that had previously depended upon the Soviet Union for support.[146]

But Ledeen's peace fears proved unfounded because the Bush administration, spearheaded by the neocons, was preparing for war. Despite Blix's failure to find any WMD, the United States government nonetheless continued to claim with absolute certitude that such existed. In an effort to sway international opinion to support an armed invasion, Secretary of State Colin Powell would make the Bush administration's case at the UN Security Council on February 5, 2003.

At the end of January, the White House presented Powell with a document, prepared by a team directed by neocons "Scooter" Libby and John Hannah, which was intended as the basis for his UN speech.[147] Skeptical of its evidence and concerned about his own credibility, Powell brought in members of the State Department and the CIA to analyze it. At one point, Powell reportedly threw several pages in the air, saying "I'm not reading this. This is bullshit."[148] Powell subsequently had the most extreme and questionable claims discarded. What he ultimately would allow in his speech had the stamp of approval of CIA director Tenet. The Vice-President's office was unhappy about the deletion of information, and Libby made a last minute effort to have some of it restored, but to no avail.[149]

The revised speech, nonetheless, came down hard in favor of war, alleging proof for Iraqi WMD which Blix's weapons inspectors simply had not found. As an article in *Vanity Fair* magazine would put it: "Powell, for all his carping, delivered a speech that was close to what the White House wanted, describing mobile biological-weapons labs, ties to al-Qaeda, and stockpiles of anthrax. Much of it later proved to be untrue."[150]

Making use of satellite photos and alleged transcripts of intercepted phone conversations of Iraqi military officials, Powell asserted in his February 5 presentation: "Our conservative estimate is that Iraq has a stockpile of between 100 and 500 tons of chemical-weapons agents. That is enough agent to fill 16,000 battlefield rockets."[151]

Powell emphatically claimed concrete proof of Saddam's possession of biological weapons: "There can be no doubt that Saddam Hussein has biological weapons and the capability to rapidly produce more, many more. And he has the ability to dispense these lethal poisons and diseases in ways that can cause massive death and destruction." Among the reasons for his certitude, Powell maintained that "we have first-hand descriptions of biological-weapons factories on wheels and rails. We know that Iraq has at least seven of these mobile, biological-agent factories." Powell gave a detailed account of how Iraq had obtained vast amounts of equipment to produce WMD. And the danger was not simply Saddam's WMD, but the purported "sinister nexus between Iraq and the al-Qaeda terrorist network." Saddam would allegedly provide the terrorists with WMD to use against the West.[152]

After the invasion, no acceptable evidence would be found to substantiate Powell's claims. In a September 2005 television interview for ABC News, Powell acknowledged that the evidence he presented was faulty and a "blot" on his record but laid the blame on lower-level CIA intelligence analysts who knew the information was incorrect but would not speak up.[153]

Having Powell make the case for war was invaluable in gaining the support of undecided Americans, although it failed to gain international support. For Powell had had been a moderate who had resisted the neocon war party. As America's highest placed African-American official, Powell was greatly admired by most Americans. Joseph Wilson writes:

> [I]t was Powell's credibility that finally put public opinion over the top . . . . After his speech and the press analysis of it, Americans were persuaded that the "last resort" of war now was the only course to take. Powell's support for invading Iraq with a pseudo-coalition was essential, and he deserves at least as much of the responsibility for the subsequent situation that we find ourselves in as anybody else in the administration, because, more than anyone else, it was his credibility and standing among the American people that tipped the scales.[154]

Anti-war critic David Corn of the *Nation* magazine similarly held that "With this untrue presentation, the reluctant warrior did more to clear the way for Bush's war than any other administration official."[155] White House aide Dan Bartlett clearly recognized the significance of Powell's action, referring to it as "the Powell buy-in."[156]

Why Powell ultimately abandoned his resistance and made a complete public "buy-in" to the neocon war agenda remains a mystery. The idea that he was persuaded by the evidence of Saddam's alleged threat is difficult to believe considering his apparent realization that the "separate government" was hell-bent for war – and that much of the evidence in his speech was shown to be questionable almost immediately afterwards. That he was a "good soldier" who abided by the decision of his commander-in-chief seems more likely, though this is not thoroughly conclusive. However, war critics' contention of Powell's culpability only means that Powell had the ability to slow-down or even derail the move to war but chose not to do so; in short, he betrayed the hopes of the war critics, and, perhaps, went against his own true judgment of the merits of the case for war. Nonetheless, the entire move to war was a neoconservative operation, as Powell openly recognized. In the end, Powell went along with it, but he did not initiate or drive it.

As war clouds darkened over the Middle Eastern horizon, Blix and the UN pleaded with the Americans and their British allies to hold off for a while to give the weapons inspectors the time to conduct the necessary investigations. Blix argued that Iraq's lack of documentation of having destroyed WMD did not necessarily imply that it possessed such weapons or that it was manufacturing WMD. Had Blix's reasoning prevailed there would have been no war.

Blix's pleading for more time was to no avail. In the end, the United States relied on the bogus WMD threat to American security to justify war. Because of the alleged urgency of the Iraqi WMD threat, President Bush held that he could not rely on UN weapons inspectors to continue their search, but that it was essential to launch an immediate pre-emptive attack, avowing, on March 6, that he could "not leave the American people at the mercy of the Iraqi dictator and his weapons."[157]

As the attack on Iraq began on March 17, Bush once again justified a pre-emptive strike by citing the peril of Iraq's WMD: "Intelligence by this and other governments leaves no doubt that the Iraq regime continues to possess and conceal some of the most lethal weapons ever devised." And Iraq's lethal weapons allegedly threatened the United States itself. "Before the day of horror can come, before it is too late to act, this danger will be removed. The United States of America has the sovereign authority to use force in assuring its own national security. That duty falls to me as commander in chief by the oath I have sworn, by the oath I will keep."[158]

In reality, there did not seem any danger from Iraq during the period of the weapons inspection. "Saddam is in an iron box," declared a study

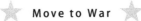

released by the Carnegie Endowment for International Peace in January 2003.

> With tens of thousands of troops around Iraq, an international coalition united in support of the inspection process, and now hundreds of inspectors in the country able to go anywhere at anytime, Saddam is unable to engage in any large-scale development or production of chemical, biological, or nuclear weapons. It would be exceedingly difficult to import significant quantities of proscribed materials or to manufacture longer-range missiles or missile components.[159]

At the beginning of June 2003, Blix delivered his final report to the Security Council, saying that he had no evidence that Iraq had been producing or storing WMD – that

> the Commission has not at any time during the inspections in Iraq found evidence of the continuation or resumption of programmes of weapons of mass destruction or significant quantities of proscribed items – whether from pre-1991 or later.[160]

Although Iraq's old stocks of biological and chemical agents were still not fully accounted for, Blix contended that "It is not justified to jump to the conclusion that something exists just because it is unaccounted for."[161] Blix emphasized that he had not found any evidence of illicit weapons based on information given him by American and British intelligence. As he told the British Broadcasting Corporation: "We went to a great many sites that were given to us by intelligence, and only in three cases did we find anything – and they did not relate to weapons of mass destruction. That shook me a bit, I must say."[162] He added that the United States and Britain had promised him the best intelligence information that they had. "I thought – my God, if this is the best intelligence they have and we find nothing, what about the rest?"[163]

The United States could not persuade the rest of the world to believe in Saddam's dire threat and support its military undertaking. Thus the attack by so-called "coalition of the willing" would neither have UN sanction nor solid support from America's major allies. However, the WMD propaganda barrage was persuasive to the American people. A poll conducted on March 20, a day after the United States began its attack on Iraq, showed that 70 percent of the participants believed that the U.S. "Should have begun action when it did," while only 27 percent said that the U.S. should have waited longer to allow the United Nations inspections to continue.

However, the poll's respondents did expect military venture into Iraq to be a virtual cakewalk – with only 11 percent expecting American deaths and injuries from the "military action" to exceed 1000, with 41 percent believing that the total would be under 100.[164]

It was apparent that the administration propaganda, which was promulgated by the neoconservatives, had taken hold of the American public. The neoconservatives were clearly in the driver's seat and intended to implement their war agenda to reconfigure the Middle East.

chapter 11

WORLD WAR IV

T HOUGH THE THREAT to the United States posed by the alleged Iraqi stockpiles of WMD was sold to the American people as the fundamental reason for attacking Iraq, neoconservatives had, from the outset, a much more ambitious agenda that went far beyond Iraq. They openly advocated the forceful reconfiguration of the entire Middle East to combat an alleged monolithic Islamic terrorist threat to the United States. It must be emphasized that this concept did not emerge after the U.S. occupation of Iraq, in response to post-invasion contingencies. Rather, the neocons expressed this view prior to September 11, and after the American occupation of Iraq they would argue that the so-called insurgency underscored the regional nature of the terrorist danger. In essence, in the neocon depiction of Middle East terrorism, there was nothing singularly dangerous about Iraq. Iraq was never considered to be a stand-alone threat; instead, it was but one part of a larger Middle East menace. And whereas other commentators have generally spoken of the war on Iraq as a war of choice, that conflict was, according to the neocons, a necessary part of a much larger, life-or-death struggle for American survival.

It should be reiterated that the neocons' war agenda for the United States closely paralleled their war agenda for Israel as presented to Netanyahu in 1996, titled "A Clean Break," which was discussed at length in Chapter Six. According to the "Clean Break" scenario, Israel would begin its pre-emptive action to restructure the Middle East for its security needs by removing Saddam.

One of the most illuminating encapsulations of the neocons' far-reaching geostrategy was put forth by veteran neocon Michael A. Ledeen in his *The War Against the Terror Masters*.[1] Ledeen was one of the leading ideological gurus of the neoconservatives.[2] He was a resident scholar with AEI, and a founding member of JINSA and its first CEO. During the Reagan administration he had been a consultant with the State and Defense Departments and the National Security Council. As an undercover agent for Reagan's National Security Director Robert McFarlane, Ledeen became intimately involved in covert dealings with Iran that formed part of the Iran-Contra affair.[3]

Writing early in the war on terror, Ledeen would proclaim that "Our unexpectedly quick and impressive victory in Afghanistan is a prelude to a much broader war, which will in all likelihood transform the Middle East for at least a generation, and reshape the politics of many older countries around the world."[4] Ledeen's central thesis, common among the neoconservatives, was that the Middle East terrorist enemies of the United States were a network comprising various groups, both secular and Islamic: Baathists, radical Wahhabi Sunnis, radical Iranian Shiites, and the PLO. In essence, all these different groups allegedly formed a monolithic threat to America. While many mainstream observers would emphasize the fact that these groups were often enemies of each other, Ledeen argued for their essential unity. "The best way to think of the terror network," Ledeen contended, "is as a collection of mafia families. Sometimes they cooperate, sometimes they argue, sometimes they even kill one another. But they can always put aside their differences whenever there is a common enemy."[5] And they allegedly hated the United States because it was an enemy of the tyranny which they all represented. "The tyrants' hatred of America is not the result of any given American policy," Ledeen firmly asserted. "It is our existence, not our actions, that threaten them, because our existence inspires their people to desire different rulers in a different kind of polity."[6] Such an antithetical relationship made co-existence between the terror network and the United States impossible. "They cannot feel secure so long as we are there, for our very existence – our existence, not out policies – threatens their legitimacy," Ledeen pronounced. "They must attack us in order to survive, just as we must destroy them to advance our historic mission."[7]

Putting the concept of the monolithic nature of the Arab/Islamic enemy in a historical context, Richard Perle and David Frum, in their book *An End to Evil: How to Win the War on Terror*, published in 2003, wrote that

> [g]enerations of extremist leaders in the Middle East – fascists, communists, pan-Arabists, now Islamists – have each in their turn made a bid to lead a uni-fied East against the enemy West. Bin Laden follows where the grand mufti of Jerusalem, Gamal Abdel Nasser, Muammar al-Qaddafi, the Ayatollah Ruhollah Khomeini, and Saddam Hussein have preceded him. Bin Laden offers a new answer, but it is an answer to the same question.[8]

The danger to America, Frum and Perle maintained, was absolutely lethal. America would have to "end this evil before it kills again and on a genocidal scale. There is no middle way for Americans: It is victory or holocaust."[9] Using the term "holocaust" in its modern connotation implied the exter-mination of the American people.

When President Bush presented the war on terrorism as a conflict be-tween good and evil, and referred to those who resist the American oc-cupation of Iraq as simply thugs, he was adopting the neoconservative worldview. The key themes espoused by Bush, which the critical media of-ten portrayed as the simple-minded conceptions of his Evangelical Chris-tian religion or his own limited intelligence, were actually presented in a very similar manner by the neoconservatives. And the neoconservatives were anything but Evangelical Christians or simple-minded, though the aforementioned explanations might reasonably explain why Bush so easily embraced the neocon view. Bush did give this view a messianic religious twist, with the idea that God authorized him to eradicate an unmitigated evil that threatened to destroy all that was good.[10] But even here, neocons said virtually the same thing in a more secular manner. Norman Podho-retz, for example, simply substituted a deified "history" for the Christian God when he wrote that America's security "depends on whether we are ready and willing to accept and act upon the responsibilities of moral and political leadership that history has yet again so squarely placed upon our shoulders."[11]

A major point made by Ledeen, which reflected general neoconservative thinking, was that the "terror network" could not operate without state sponsorship or support, which necessitated the elimination of all the na-tional governments involved in the network. "First and foremost," Ledeen asserted, "we must bring down the terror regimes, beginning with the big three: Iran, Iraq, and Syria. And then we have to come to grips with the Saudis."[12]

Another key premise in the neocons' presentation of the Middle Eastern terror threat was that it did not have to be primarily directed at the United States. Included under the rubric of "terror," which they aimed to eliminate, was militant opposition to the state of Israel in the form of aid provided to the Palestinian resistance and to Hezbollah in Lebanon. As Perle and Frum wrote, "The distinction between Islamic terrorism against Israel, on the one hand, and Islamic terror against the United States and Europe, on the other, cannot be sustained."[13] In short, America would have to combat terrorism directed against Israel. Furthermore, the classification "terrorist" would encompass all the groups that militantly resist Israeli occupation or even Israel intervention in Lebanon. It was necessary, Perle and Frum continued, to "Purge from our own institutional thinking the illusory distinction between the 'political' and 'military' wings of terrorist organizations. These distinctions are a fraud." Moreover, the United States would have to "Cease criticizing Israel for taking actions against Hamas and Hezbollah analogous to those the United States is taking against al-Qaeda."[14] In short, the United States would be providing carte-blanche support, politically and militarily, for all Israeli actions – including those in the occupied territories and in Lebanon. The United States would regard Palestinian resistance to Israeli occupation as illegal. Perle and Frum's outline of such a policy included prohibiting any funding of these anti-Israeli groups in the United States and putting pressure on those foreign countries that allowed such funding, public or private. This prescription for lock-step American solidarity with Israel presumed an identity of interests. Needless to say, this support for all Israeli actions in the occupied territories violated international law and previous American policy.

This identity of interests had to be assumed because the neocons were prescribing for the United States nearly the same strategy that some of the leading neoconservatives, Richard Perle, Douglas Feith and David and Meyrav Wurmser, had advocated for the Israeli government to take in 1996 in their "Clean Break" study.

This assumption of an identity of interests between Israel and the United States loomed especially large in a letter of April 3, 2002 from the Project for the New American Century to President Bush, signed by such neocon luminaries as William Kristol, Ken Adelman, Richard Perle, Midge Decter, Robert Kagan, Joshua Muravchik, Daniel Pipes, Norman Podhoretz, and R. James Woolsey, which urged the president to attack Iraq. Part of the letter went as follows:

> Furthermore, Mr. President, we urge you to accelerate plans for removing Saddam Hussein from power in Iraq .... It is now common knowledge that Saddam, along with Iran, is a funder and supporter of terrorism against Israel .... If we do not move against Saddam Hussein and his regime, the damage our Israeli friends and we have suffered until now may someday appear but a prelude to much greater horrors.[15]

The letter continued with the assertion: "Israel's fight against terrorism is our fight. Israel's victory is an important part of our victory. For reasons both moral and strategic, we need to stand with Israel in its fight against terrorism."[16]

In a review of Ruth Wisse's *Jews and Power*, William Kristol explicitly presented the United States to be the same as the Zionist movement.

> After the attacks of September 11, no one can escape knowledge of the dangers facing the world. And as anti-Judaism, anti-Americanism, and general hostility to the West increasingly merge, the little state of Israel and the entire Jewish people seem once again caught in the crosshairs of history.
>
> But, in a sense, we are all caught in those crosshairs. In *Jews and Power*, Ruth Wisse only hints at how the experience of Zionism has relevance beyond the Jews. But if Zionism is an attempt to marry power and morality – to join religion and liberalism, tradition and modernity, patriotism and principle – then America has a great deal in common with Israel. Indeed, all the people in the world who wish to stand against both death-loving Islamic fanaticism and soulless European postmodernism – what are they, if not Zionists?[17]

Peace between the Israelis and the Palestinians could not come about, neoconservatives maintained, as long as there was external support for the Palestinian resistance, which the neocons defined as terrorism, whether it was directed against Israeli civilians or the Israeli army. As Ledeen wrote, a "fundamental change in the region is required to advance peace."[18] It was impossible to take "meaningful" steps toward establishing peace between Israel and the Palestinians, he argued, until "we have defeated the terror masters in Tehran, Damascus and Riyadh, because the terrorism against Israel gets a lot of support from those evil people."[19] In short, all the governments that supported the Palestinian cause had to be overthrown. Without outside support, the Palestinians would have no choice but to make peace with Israel – on Israel's terms. Obviously, the elimination of Israel's foreign enemies and the consequent total subjugation of the Palestinians would represent the achievement of the Likud's security objectives to the utmost degree.

David Wurmser expressed a comparable view involving the military collaboration of the United States and Israel in an article that came out in January 2001, just as the Bush administration was entering office, and months before September 11. Wurmser recommended that

> Israel and the United States should adopt a coordinated strategy to regain the initiative and reverse their region-wide strategic retreat. They should broaden the conflict to strike fatally, not merely disarm, the centers of radicalism in the region – the regimes of Damascus, Baghdad, Tripoli, Tehran, and Gaza. That would reestablish the recognition that fighting with either the United States or Israel is suicidal. Many in the Middle East will then understand the merits of being an American ally and of making peace with Israel.[20]

The ramifications of the neoconservative belief that American and Israeli interests coincide were monumental for American policy. Wurmser was stating that the United States should guarantee that "fighting with" Israel is "suicidal." In short, the United States should act to destroy all the enemies of Israel. That, of course, would entail a radical change from traditional American policy, under which America was friendly to opponents of Israel, such as Saudi Arabia. And certainly it went much further to justify support for Israel than the moral argument that Israel, as a democracy, deserved to be defended. The neocons were saying that the defense of Israel – in fact, the defense of all the significant military and political policies of Israel, such as the colonization of the West Bank – was based on American self-interest.

The neocon assumption of an identity of interests between Israel and the United States would counter any criticism that the Iraq war and neocon Middle East policy in general were oriented to advance the interests of Israel. Put simply, any aid for Israel ineluctably meant the advancement of American interests. The real question, of course, is whether the interests of Israel and the United States actually do coincide. Certainly, American policymakers had not thought so heretofore, as neoconservatives have acknowledged in their criticism of past U.S. Middle East policy. And those foreign policy experts outside the orbit of neoconservatism would still disagree that the two countries' interests coincide. As has been pointed out in the preceding sections of this work, it would seem apparent that the neoconservatives' ties and loyalties to Israel cause them to view American foreign policy through the lens of Israeli interest. As Kathleen and Bill Christison surmised: the neoconservatives

> are so wrapped up in their concern for the fate of Israel that they honestly do not know whether their own passion about advancing the U.S. imperium is motivated primarily by America-first patriotism or is governed first and foremost by a desire to secure Israel's safety and predominance in the Middle East through the advancement of the U.S. imperium.[21]

Even when the neocons were just beginning to mobilize public support for a war on Iraq, they discussed a broader war in the Middle East. In the October 29, 2001 issue of the *Weekly Standard*, Robert Kagan and William Kristol predicted such a wider war on terrorism, of which the war on Afghanistan was only the beginning step:

> When all is said and done, the conflict in Afghanistan will be to the war on terrorism what the North Africa campaign was to World War II: an essential beginning on the path to victory. But compared with what looms over the horizon – a wide-ranging war in locales from Central Asia to the Middle East and, unfortunately, back again to the United States – Afghanistan will prove but an opening battle . . . . But this war will not end in Afghanistan. It is going to spread and engulf a number of countries in conflicts of varying intensity. It could well require the use of American military power in multiple places simultaneously. It is going to resemble the clash of civilizations that everyone has hoped to avoid.[22]

Despite their professed desire to avoid such a civilizational clash, it seemed that Kagan and Kristol looked forward to that gigantic conflagration.

In a November 20, 2001 article in the *Wall Street Journal*, Eliot A. Cohen would dub the conflict in the Middle East, "World War IV."[23] The term would be quickly picked up by other neoconservatives, as well as their critics. In September 2004, neocons held a conference on the subject in Washington, titled "World War IV: Why We Fight, Whom We Fight, How We Fight," which included among its speakers Cohen, R. James Woolsey, Norman Podhoretz, and Paul Wolfowitz, and was sponsored by the Committee on the Present Danger and The Foundation for the Defense of Democracies.[24]

In describing the conflict as World War IV, Cohen proclaimed that "The enemy in this war is not 'terrorism' . . . but militant Islam."[25] The use of the term "World War IV," with the Cold War being "World War III," was very significant. For the neoconservatives envisioned the war on Iraq as part of the much broader war in the Middle East, which would be comparable to World War II in its massive death and destruction or to the Cold War in its nearly half-century duration. Cohen presented "some key features" that World War IV shared with the Cold War "that it is, in fact, global; that it will involve a mixture of violent and nonviolent efforts; that it will require mobilization of skill, expertise, and resources, if not of vast numbers of soldiers; that it may go on for a long time; and that it has ideological roots."[26]

R. James Woolsey, who had headed the CIA under Clinton, similarly declared that "the United States is engaged in World War IV, and that it could continue for years." Moreover, "This fourth world war, I think, will last considerably longer than either World Wars I or II did for us. Hopefully not the full four-plus decades of the Cold War."[27]

It is necessary here to distinguish between the neoconservatives' goals and the propaganda they used to mobilize public support for the attack on Iraq, since many commentators have tended to confuse the two. Neoconservatives engaged in deception in their claims about WMD, Saddam's ties to al Qaeda, and the ease of the United States controlling Iraq and establishing democracy. Focusing on the merits of these allegations, critics have branded them as naïfs, rigid ideologues, and incompetents.[28] To be sure, the neocons' propagandistic claims have all been proven false, but at the same time, these claims obviously served to effectively mobilize the American people to support the war. On the other hand, the neoconservatives were quite candid in their deeper writings about the vast magnitude of the long-range goal – transforming the entire Middle East by removing existing regimes hostile to Israel – but few mainstream commentators showed an awareness of these writings.

The neocon who most popularized the World War IV theme was Norman Podhoretz, the doyen of neoconservatives. He initially wrote an article entitled "How to Win World War IV," which appeared in *Commentary* in February 2002, and he would continue with that theme in his subsequent writings. Ultimately, in 2007, he would devote an entire book to the subject: *World War IV: The Long Struggle Against Islamofascism.*

Podhoretz identified the overarching threat to America as "militant Islam," which "represents a revival of the expansionism by the sword" of Islam's early years.[29] In a lengthy September 2004 article in *Commentary,* entitled "World War IV: How It Started, What It Means, and Why We Have to Win," Podhoretz presented the threat in an even more ominous light:

> [W]e are up against a truly malignant force in radical Islamism and in the states breeding, sheltering, or financing its terrorist armory. This new enemy has already attacked us on our own soil – a feat neither Nazi Germany nor Soviet Russia ever managed to pull off – and openly announces his intention to hit us again, only this time with weapons of infinitely greater and deadlier power than those used on 9/11. His objective is not merely to murder as many of us as possible and to conquer our land. Like the Nazis and Communists before him, he is dedicated to the destruction of everything good for which America stands.[30]

In short, according to Podhoretz, the radical Islamists not only sought to destroy America and kill Americans, but were engaged in a war against good itself. In essence, Podhoretz portrayed a cataclysmic Manichean conflict of good versus evil in which compromise was impossible. To survive, America would have to utterly destroy its enemy.

In using the World War IV metaphor, Podhoretz, in line with other neoconservatives, imputed immense power to the radical Islamist enemy, holding that it represented a military threat equivalent to that of the Nazis and Communists, who commanded leading industrial countries and fielded modern military forces comparable to that of the United States. This was a most extraordinary view, since the Arab/Islamic Middle East states were essentially militarily weak Third World countries compared to America's superpower status.

To survive resurgent Islam, in Podhoretz's view, the United States could not simply stand on the defensive; it would have to aggressively stamp out militant Islam at its very source in the Middle East. "The regimes that richly deserve to be overthrown and replaced are not confined to the three singled-out members of the axis of evil," Podhoretz emphasized.

> At a minimum, this axis should extend to Syria and Lebanon and Libya, as well as "friends" of America like the Saudi royal family and Egypt's Hosni Mubarak, along with the Palestinian Authority, whether headed by Arafat or one of his henchmen.[31]

Once again, the all-embracing character of America's alleged enemies – including current friends and foes, and secular and Islamist regimes – should be noted. One common denominator for these supposed enemy regimes, however, is apparent: hostility to Israel.

What stood out in the neocons' depiction of a life-and-death struggle with radical Islam was the obvious fact that it was a very much a minority opinion among experts on foreign relations. Certainly, as neocons acknowledged, the dire danger was not recognized by the foreign policy establishment in the United States, nor by Europeans.

Given the fact that the neocon view was such a minority one, it is significant that Israeli officials were disseminating the same message of world war. In June 2002, Efraim Halevy, the director of the Mossad, informed a closed meeting of the NATO Alliance Council in Brussels that the September 11 attacks had been "an official and biting declaration of World War III." Halevy emphasized that there should be no distinction between the various terrorist groups – they should be treated as one. He bemoaned the fact that countries that supported Palestinian terrorists were not being opposed by the world community:

> So, it is possible for Syria, which gives protection to these groups, to receive a seat as a respected member of the security council, and its representative even serves this month as Chairman of the council, and this at the very time when the Palestinian Islamic Jihad sent a suicide attacker to blow up a bus in the north of Israel, and caused the killing of around twenty people.

All Middle East terrorism should be considered the same, and that classification should include those groups that focus solely on Israel. "My appeal to you, here today," Halevy stressed,

> is that the attempts to differentiate and distinguish between colours and targets of Islamic terror are quickly losing their relevancy. Why? First of all because of the extent and the intensity of these terror actions. They are no longer limited to specific areas in the world. Hamburg, Milan, Brussels, London, Miami, Koala Lampur – this is only a random list of large cities in which terrorists are living, and in which they are slowly making their plans and preparing their operations. Secondly, the operation of suicides in New York, Washington, or Jerusalem, is the manifestation of a "modus operandi" that is motivated not only by professional efficacy, but by its being perfectly fitted ideologically and religiously. Therefore the method has attained transcendental, supernatural meaning.[32]

Israeli officials clearly saw the United States attack on Iraq as part of a broader effort to change the Middle East for the interests of Israel. In February 2003, shortly before the American attack on Iraq, Shaul Mofaz, Israel's defense minister, told members of the Conference of Presidents of Major American Jewish Organizations that "We have great interest in shaping the

Middle East the day after" a war. After Iraq, Mofaz stressed that the United States should generate "political, economic, [and] diplomatic pressure" on Iran.[33] Similarly, in the invasion's aftermath in May, Israel's ambassador to the United States, Daniel Ayalon, called for a "regime change" in both Syria and Iran at a conference of the Anti-Defamation League. He argued that, while the American invasion of Iraq and overthrow of Saddam helped create great opportunities for Israel, it was "not enough." "It has to follow through," Ayalon told the audience.

> We still have great threats of that magnitude coming from Syria, coming from Iran . . . . The important thing is to show [international] political unity and this is the key element to pressure the Iranians into a regime change, and the same case is with the Syrians.[34]

A country that the neoconservatives and Israel have especially targeted for attack was Iran, which they insisted, was attempting to develop nuclear weapons that would challenge Israel's nuclear monopoly in the region. Leading the neocon charge on Iran was Michael Ledeen. In an address entitled "Time to Focus on Iran – The Mother of Modern Terrorism," at the Jewish Institute for National Security Affairs (JINSA) policy forum on April 30, 2003, Ledeen declared, "The time for diplomacy is at an end; it is time for a free Iran, free Syria and free Lebanon."[35] Elsewhere Ledeen would write:

> We are now engaged in a regional struggle in the Middle East, and the Iranian tyrants are the keystone of the terror network. Far more than the overthrow of Saddam Hussein, the defeat of the mullahcracy and the triumph of freedom in Tehran would be a truly historic event and an enormous blow to the terrorists.[36]

Ledeen actually argued that the U.S. should first actively press for regime change in Iran, even while the Bush administration was preparing the attack on Iraq. "I have long argued that it would be better to liberate Iran before Iraq," he wrote in November 2002, "and events may soon give us that opportunity."[37]

In early 2002, Ledeen set up the Coalition for Democracy in Iran, an action group focusing on producing regime change in Iran. One of his collaborators in the new organization was Morris Amitay, vice chairman of JINSA and a former executive director of AIPAC. Other members of the group included James Woolsey, Frank Gaffney, and American Enterprise Institute scholars Joshua Muravchik and Danielle Pletka. The coalition

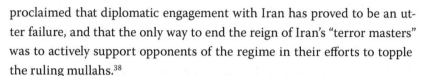

proclaimed that diplomatic engagement with Iran has proved to be an utter failure, and that the only way to end the reign of Iran's "terror masters" was to actively support opponents of the regime in their efforts to topple the ruling mullahs.[38]

The campaign against Iran enlisted broad support among neoconservatives. On May 6, 2003, AEI hosted an all-day conference entitled "The Future of Iran: Mullahcracy, Democracy and the War on Terror," whose speakers included Ledeen, Amitay, and Uri Lubrani from the Israeli Defense Ministry. The convener, Hudson Institute Middle East specialist Meyrav Wurmser set the tone. "Our fight against Iraq was only one battle in a long war," she emphatically stated. "It would be ill-conceived to think that we can deal with Iraq alone . . . . We must move on, and faster."[39]

As Marc Perelman pointed out in the Jewish newspaper *Forward* in May 2003, "A budding coalition of conservative hawks, Jewish organizations and Iranian monarchists is pressing the White House to step up American efforts to bring about regime change in Iran."[40]

Indicating the seriousness of the move to destabilize Iran was the fact that preparations were being made by the Defense Department's Office of Special Plans, which had played such a key role in the United States attack on Iraq. Perelman wrote in May 2003:

> Iran expert Michael Rubin is now working for the Pentagon's "special plans" office, a small unit set up to gather intelligence on Iraq, but apparently also working on Iran. Previously a researcher at the Washington Institute for Near East policy, Rubin has vocally advocated regime change in Tehran.[41]

As mentioned in the previous chapter, Iran was a concern in the Israeli involvement with OSP staff, as revealed in the Larry Franklin/AIPAC affair. Franklin was an expert on Iran.[42]

Despite their reputation as advocates of global democracy, the neoconservatives proposed restoring the monarchy in Iran, in the person of Reza Pahlavi, the exiled son of the former shah. Perelman wrote:

> The emerging coalition is reminiscent of the buildup to the invasion of Iraq, with Pahlavi possibly assuming the role of Iraqi exile opposition leader Ahmed Chalabi, a favorite of neoconservatives. Like Chalabi, Pahlavi had good relations with several Jewish groups. He addressed the board of the hawkish Jewish Institute for National Security Affairs and gave a public speech at the Simon Wiesenthal Center's Museum of Tolerance in Los Angeles, and met with Jewish communal leaders.[43]

There was an apparent strong Israel connection here. According to Perelman, Pahlavi had direct contacts with the Israeli leadership. "During the last two years . . . [Pahlavi] has met privately with Prime Minister Sharon and former prime minister Benjamin Netanyahu, as well as Israel's Iranianborn president, Moshe Katsav."[44]

From Israel's standpoint, Iran represented a serious threat. In July 1996, Benjamin Netanyahu, newly elected as Israel's prime minister, addressed the United States Congress, presenting much of the substance of the justproduced "Clean Break" paper, but adding: "The most dangerous of these regimes is Iran."[45] As David Hirst pointed out in the *Guardian* in February 2002:

> Israel has long portrayed the Islamic republic as its gravest long-term threat, the "rogue state" at its most menacing, combining sponsorship of international terror, nuclear ambition, ideological objection to the existence of the Jewish state and unflagging determination to sabotage the Middle East peace process.[46]

Israel undoubtedly considered Iran a threat because it was believed to be trying to develop nuclear weapons, and thus challenge Israel's regional nuclear monopoly, which has been a major pillar of Israel's security policy.

The danger to Israel did not mean that Iran would launch a nuclear attack on Israel; rather, with nuclear weapons, Iran could deter Israeli attacks and thus place restraints on Israel's military options. By limiting what Israel could do to counter Iranian support of Hezbollah and Hamas, Iran could be emboldened to give greater support to those anti-Israel groups, since Iran itself would no longer be threatened by possible destruction from Israel.

While in New York in early 2002, Israeli Defense Minister Binyamin Ben-Eliezer asserted that Iran would have nuclear a capability as early as 2005.[47] In January 2002, Foreign Minister Shimon Peres, a leading member of the Labor Party and former prime minister, claimed that Iran posed a grave missile threat to Israel: "The ayatollah leadership in Iran is also threatening to destroy Israel . . . inflicting genocide through the use of missiles."[48]

Israeli officials have stressed not only the danger posed by Iran but also the need to counter it. In an interview with the *New York Post* in November 2002, Prime Minister Sharon said that as soon as Iraq had been dealt with, he would "push for Iran to be at the top of the 'to do' list." Sharon called Iran the "center of world terror" and declared that "Iran makes every effort to possess weapons of mass destruction . . . and ballistic missiles . . . . That is a danger to the Middle East, and a danger to Europe."[49]

In a meeting with U.S. Under Secretary of State John Bolton in February 2003, Sharon expressed grave concerns about the security threat posed by Iran and stressed that it was important to deal with Iran even while American attention was focused on Iraq. Bolton responded that the United States would definitely attack Iraq and would then move on to Iran.[50]

In November 2003, the head of the Mossad, Meir Dagan, made a rare appearance before the Knesset's foreign affairs and defense committee to utter dire warnings about Iran's nuclear program, which he said posed "the biggest threat to Israel's existence since its creation." That same month, Israeli Defense Minister Shaul Mofaz visited Washington to warn of the dangers of Iran's nuclear program. "Concentrated efforts are needed to delay, to stop or to prevent the Iranian nuclear program," he said in a speech.[51]

Addressing a conference on national security in December 2003, Avi Dichter, the head of Shin Bet, Israel's internal security agency, said that Iran was sponsoring terrorism and developing unconventional weapons, which posed "a strategic threat to Israel." Dichter declared that "Iran is the No. 1 terror nation in the world."[52] It was reported in the fall of 2003 that Israel also considered a number of ways to unilaterally stop Iran's development of nuclear weapons, including launching a preemptive strike.[53]

After the invasion of Iraq, the neoconservatives made much of Iran's being behind what they called the continuing "insurgency" in that country. As Ledeen wrote:

> The [terrorist] cooperation increased in the run-up to Operation Iraqi Freedom, and was only possible because the regimes who gave the bulk of the operational support to the terrorists – Syria, Iran, Iraq, and Saudi Arabia – worked closely to coordinate the anti-American jihad.[54]

It was support from Iran that maintained the Islamic terrorism in Iraq. "Unlike, say, the Department of State, Iraqi leaders – most definitely including some top Shiites – are quite outspoken about Iran's vigorous actions supporting the terror network inside Iraq."[55]

Ledeen voiced the theme that the American foreign policy establishment was oblivious to the broader threat of the Iran and the transnational linkage of the terrorists. In fact, leading members of the foreign policy establishment, such as Zbigniew Brzezinski, proposed negotiations with Iran in 2004 on the issue of nuclear weapons. Ledeen regarded negotiation as impossible. "This is all very inconvenient for [Richard] Haas, Brzezinski, and the others who keep deluding themselves into believing that we can make a reasonable deal with the mullahcracy in Tehran," Ledeen asserted.

> This is a very dangerous delusion, akin to Neville Chamberlain's conceit that he had achieved peace with Hitler, when, as Churchill put it, given the choice between war and dishonor, Chamberlain chose dishonor and got war. The Council [of Foreign Relations] is making the same humiliating choice.[56]

Ledeen included in his indictment the Bush administration, which he believed was in the thrall of the State Department. He charged that

> after four years in office this administration still has no Iran policy, and the deputy secretary of State, Richard Armitage, has never backed off his claim that Iran is a democracy . . . . I'm afraid we're not going to get serious about Iran without another 9/11.[57]

Significantly, the broader war against militant Islam, which the neoconservatives sought, was to be launched not only against America's enemies in the Middle East, but even against America's friends – most notably Saudi Arabia, whose friendly relationship with the United States served as the lynchpin of American security strategy in the Middle East for more than 50 years. Undoubtedly, Saudi Arabia was clearly a secondary target, with the focus being on Iraq and Iran. Thus, neoconservatives within the administration never fashioned an anti-Saudi policy. A major factor here would be that Israel did not regard Saudi Arabia as an immediate danger. Moreover, because of Saudi Arabia's strong ties with the United States and the Bush family itself, such a policy would be more difficult to achieve. Nonetheless, the 9/11 terrorism led the neoconservatives to devote more negative attention to that country. For example, not long after the 9/11 terror attacks, David Wurmser claimed in his article "The Saudi Connection" in the *Weekly Standard* that the Saudi royal family had actually been behind the atrocity.[58]

Max Singer, co-founder of the neoconservative Hudson Institute and a senior research associate at the Begin-Sadat Center for Strategic Studies in Israel, contended in a May 2002 article that the Saudi brand of Islam, "Wahhabism," constituted the major terror threat in the world. To counter this supposed danger, Singer maintained, it was essential for the United States to attack Saudi Arabia itself – a country which was especially vulnerable because its Eastern Province, the site of the Saudi oil industry, was inhabited by non-Wahhabi Shiites who were discriminated against by the dominant establishment. Singer proposed American-directed dismemberment of the kingdom. "It is well within the power of the U.S. to make it possible for the EP [Eastern Province] to become independent from the Wahhabis, a new Muslim Republic of East Arabia," Singer contended. "The U.S. would neither seek nor gain control of oil policy or any oil profits. Its help to Muslims in the EP, like its help to Muslims in Bosnia and Kosovo, would be a result of U.S. resistance to oppression and pursuit of a safer world."[59]

On June 6, 2002, the Hudson Institute, which included on its Board of Trustees not only Singer, but also such prominent neoconservatives as Richard Perle and Donald Kagan, sponsored a seminar, "Discourses on Democracy: Saudi Arabia, Friend or Foe?," with the strong implication that "foe" was the right answer. Shortly afterwards, on June 19, 2002, the Hudson Institute hosted a discussion of the book *Hatred's Kingdom: How Saudi Arabia Supports the New Global Terrorism* by Dore Gold, who had served the government of Israel as ambassador to the United Nations and had been an advisor to Prime Ministers Netanyahu and Sharon.[60] It is noteworthy that the neoconservative institution would present a former Israeli government official as an objective observer of the Saudi situation. It would be reasonable to conclude that Gold was reflecting the position of the Israeli government on Saudi Arabia and that the neocon Hudson Institute was serving as a conduit for Israel's voice.

Gold depicted Saudi Arabia as the main force behind Islamic terrorism. It was not enough for the United States to win military victories over Afghanistan and Iraq:

> But unless the ideological motivation for terrorism is addressed and, indeed, extinguished, then the war on terror will not be won. Saudi Arabia is the breeding ground for Wahhabi extremism and consequently the source of the hatred that impels international terrorist organizations.[61]

Interestingly enough, Gold regarded the Saudi threat not as military but as ideological in nature: issuing, that is, from ideas that are instilled in the youth of Saudi Arabia – ideas that he alleged lay the groundwork for "hate." Gold admitted that Saudi Arabia's internal practices did not violate international law as currently understood. But that only meant that international standards must expand beyond what they presently were. Gold demanded that international procedures be changed to deal with the alleged Saudi ideological threat. "Diplomats usually deal with international law or the monitoring of armaments, not with incitement and hatred emanating from mosques and featured in textbooks or on national television networks," Gold pointed out. "But this material must be monitored and collected, because such incitement leads to horrible violence."[62] In short, the international community – meaning Israel, the United States and likeminded nations – needed to determine what ideas should be promulgated in Saudi Arabia. The premise that outsiders should determine the views circulating in a sovereign country was definitely novel, and certainly a violation of sovereignty as currently understood. Moreover, the view that outsiders, especially non-Muslim outsiders, should shape the ideas presented in Saudi Arabia in ways counter to traditional religious thinking likely would be seen by the Islamic faithful as a challenge to the word of God.

Neocons within the Bush administration were circumspect about their anti-Saudi program, in recognition of the Bush family's ties to the Saudi regime, but they risked bringing it out in the open on a few occasions. On July 10, 2002, Laurent Murawiec, a senior fellow at the Hudson Institute, briefed the Defense Policy Board, the advisory panel for the Department of Defense, about Saudi Arabia, at the behest of board chairman Richard Perle. Murawiec described the kingdom as the principal supporter of anti-American terrorism – "the kernel of evil, the prime mover, the most dangerous opponent." It was necessary for the United States, he emphasized, to regard Saudi Arabia as an enemy. Murawiec said that the United States should demand that Riyadh stop funding fundamentalist Islamic outlets around the world; that it prohibit all anti-U.S. and anti-Israeli propaganda in the country; and that it "prosecute or isolate those involved in the terror chain, including in the Saudi intelligence services." If the Saudis refused to comply with that ultimatum, Murawiec held that the United States should invade and occupy the country, including the holy sites of Mecca and Medina, seize its oil fields, and confiscate its financial assets.[63]

Murawiec concluded his briefing with a summary of what he called a "Grand Strategy for the Middle East," stating that "Iraq is the tactical pivot. Saudi Arabia the strategic pivot. Egypt the prize."[64] In short, in Murawiec's view, the war on Iraq would achieve the destruction of Israel's other enemies. That certainly was in line with the thinking of Oded Yinon and the authors of "A Clean Break." Of course, these other countries cited by

Murawiec also happened to be the close American allies. And it would be hard to envision a policy better designed to inflame the entire Middle East against the United States.

Predictably, the day after the briefing, the Bush administration disavowed Murawiec's scenario as having nothing to do with actual American foreign policy and pronounced Saudi Arabia to be a loyal ally.[65] However, the White House did nothing to remove or even discipline Perle for holding a discussion of a plan for attacking a close ally, though officials have frequently been removed from administrations for much smaller faux pas. Certainly the Bush administration's inaction failed to assure the Saudis that Murawiec's war plan was beyond the realm of possibility.

It was quite apparent that Perle shared Murawiec's anti-Saudi position. In their *An End to Evil*, Perle and his co-author David Frum, who crafted Bush's Axis-of-Evil speech, wrote that "The Saudis qualify for their own membership in the axis of evil." Frum and Perle explicitly rejected the traditional American policy of friendship with the Saudi rulers: "For thirty years, U.S. Saudi policy has been guided by the dogma that, problematic as the Saudi monarchy is, it is better than any likely alternative. September 11 should have dispelled that illusion forever."[66]

Frum and Perle attributed the cause of America's baneful friendship with Saudi Arabia "not [to] mere error," but rather "because so many of those who make policy have been bought and paid for by the Saudis – or else are looking forward to the day when they *will* be bought and paid for." They continued with the contention that "recent ambassadors to Saudi Arabia have served as shills for Saudi Arabia the instant they returned home."[67] It was highly ironic that Perle would imply that, because of personal connections, American officials could put the interests of a foreign country above those of the United States, considering his own close connections to Israel. But given the neocons' assumption of an identity of interests between the United States and Israel, Perle probably saw his connections to the Israeli government in a completely different light.

Frum and Perle were especially concerned about the Saudis' funding of "terrorism," with "terrorism" interpreted very broadly. Thus it was essential for the United States to "Demand that the Saudis cease the Wahhabi missionary efforts in the United States and elsewhere abroad."[68] Moreover, Frum and Perle stated that the United States should "Warn the Saudis that anything less than their utmost cooperation in the war on terror will have the

severest consequences for the Saudi state." Implied was American support
for the severance of the oil producing Eastern Province from Saudi Arabia.
"Independence for the Eastern Province would obviously be a catastrophic
outcome for the Saudi state," Frum and Perle opined. "But it might be a very
good outcome for the United States. Certainly, it's an outcome to ponder."[69]

In August 2002, Max Singer presented a paper to the Pentagon's Office
of Net Assessment in which he once again urged the dismemberment of
Saudi Arabia. The Eastern Province of Saudi Arabia could, Singer argued,
constitute a new "Muslim Republic of East Arabia," peopled primarily by
Shiite Muslims unsympathetic to the dominant Wahhabi school of Islam
in Saudi Arabia, leaving Mecca and Medina in the hands of the Wahhabis,
while placing the oil fields, concentrated in the east, in the hands of Western oil companies.[70]

Writing in the *Washington Post* on August 2002, Thomas E. Ricks observed that anti-Saudi bellicosity

> represents a point of view that has growing currency within the Bush adminis-
> tration – especially on the staff of Vice President Cheney and in the Pentagon's
> civilian leadership – and among neoconservative writers and thinkers closely
> allied with administration policymakers.[71]

Chas W. Freeman, U.S. ambassador to Saudi Arabia during the 1991 Gulf
War, rightly observed that "What is happening is that neoconservatives
closely aligned with the Likud Party in Israel are on a tear."[72]

Outside the Bush administration, the neocon verbal assault on Saudi
Arabia continued. The July 15, 2002 issue of the *Weekly Standard* featured
an article entitled "The Coming Saudi Showdown," by Simon Henderson of
the Washington Institute for Near East Policy. The July/August 2002 issue
of *Commentary* contained an article titled "Our Enemies, the Saudis"[73] by
Victor Davis Hanson, in which he wrote:

> Saudi Arabia is the placenta of this frightening phenomenon [radical Islam].
> Its money has financed it; its native terrorists promote it; and its own unhappy
> citizenry is either amused by or indifferent to its effects upon the world. Surely
> it has occurred to more than a few Americans that, without a petroleum-rich
> Wahhabism, the support for such international killers and the considerable
> degree of ongoing aid to those who would destroy the West would radically
> diminish.[74]

Hanson went so far as to maintain that the Saudi subversives were already in the process of taking over the United States itself. "Saudi Arabia,"

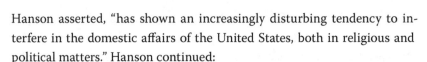

Hanson asserted, "has shown an increasingly disturbing tendency to interfere in the domestic affairs of the United States, both in religious and political matters." Hanson continued:

> Saudi television commercials seeking to influence American public opinion are now nightly fare. Thousands of Saudi students are politically active on American campuses. Local imams reflect the extreme and often anti-American views of senior Muslim clerics who channel the biggest subsidies from the Middle East. Saudi Arabia's cash infusions to Muslim communities in America ensure that Wahhabi fundamentalism takes hold among Arab guests living in the United States.[75]

To deal with the Saudi danger, Hanson advocated a United States policy "to spark disequilibrium, if not outright chaos" in Saudi Arabia. "Even should fundamental changes go wrong in Saudi Arabia, the worst that could happen would not be much worse than what we have now."[76]

The leading neoconservative expert on Saudi Arabia was Stephen Schwartz, author of numerous articles and a book, *The Two Faces of Islam: The House of Sa'ud from Tradition to Terror*, in which he posited a Saudi/Wahhabist conspiracy to take over all of Islam and spread terror throughout the entire world. Schwartz, the son of a Jewish father and gentile mother, has a rather bizarre history, being at one time a member of a left-wing revolutionary Trotskyite revolutionary group and using the name Comrade Sandalio, and then converting to Sufi Islam, taking the name Suleyman Ahmed. In fact, Schwartz remained attached to Trotsky. As he wrote in the conservative *National Review*:

> To my last breath I will defend the Trotsky who alone . . . said no to Soviet coddling of Hitlerism, to the Moscow purges, and to the betrayal of the Spanish Republic, and who had the capacity to admit he had been wrong about the imposition of a single-party state, as well as about the fate of the Jewish people. To my last breath, and without apology.[77]

A former obituary columnist for the *San Francisco Chronicle*, Schwartz endeared himself to neoconservatives not for his apologias to Trotsky, though some neocons once had connections with his movement, but by his bashing of Saudi Arabia. Neocon luminary William Kristol wrote that "No one has done more to expose the radical, Saudi-Wahhabi face of Islam than Stephen Schwartz."[78]

In his *The Two Faces of Islam*, Schwartz argued that there were essentially two fundamentally different types of Islam. Mainstream Islam was basically good and tolerant of other religions. The Wahhabism of Saudi Arabia, on the other hand, allegedly preached hate and violence toward other religious traditions, including other versions of Islam, and was thus not authentic Islam at all. "The real source of our problem," Schwartz wrote in the preface, "is the perversion of Islamic teachings by the fascistic Wahhabi cult that resides at the heart of the Saudi establishment."[79]

Schwartz went so far in his polemical attack on the Saudi government as to claim that Osama bin Laden was not really an enemy of the Saudi regime, but remained "courteous to the Saudi rulers," venturing only weak criticisms such as advocating "drafting of petitions to the king."[80] Indeed, Schwartz presented Osama as nothing more than a member of the Saudi government's worldwide Wahhabi terrorist network. In actuality, Osama, in December 2004, called for the overthrow of the Saudi monarchy in a taped message posted on a website, which was followed by a number of terrorist attacks in the kingdom.[81]

In an apparent flight from reality, Schwartz equated the global threat of Saudi Arabia to that of the totalitarian military mega-powers of Communist Russia and Nazi Germany. "With the collapse of the Soviet state," Schwartz wrote, "Wahhabism effectively replaced the Communist movement as the main sponsor of international ideological aggression against the democratic West."[82] And in the Saudi regime's alleged totalitarian social control, Schwartz saw similarities to Stalinist Russia. "In this respect," Schwartz wrote, "Saudi Arabia resembles the Soviet Union at the height of Stalin's forced collectivizations and famines in the early 1930s; outsiders see only what the regime wants them to see."[83]

But Saudi Arabia's purported similarities with Communist Russia were not enough for Schwartz; he also made a baseless comparison to Nazi Germany. "Wahhabism, Communism, and fascism," Schwartz maintained, "represented the stunted, underdeveloped, and deformed modernism of backward societies attempting, by a forced march, to catch up and surpass the more advanced and prosperous cultures."[84] In Schwartz's delusional view, the

> Wahhabi-Saudi regime . . . . embodies a program for the ruthless conquest of power and a war of extermination against "the other," Islamic as well as Judeo-Christian. The face of Wahhabi Islam is a great deal uglier than that of general Islamism, or Iranian anger at the West, or radical Arab nationalism, or even of

Soviet Communism, and its threat to the peace and security of the whole world is immensely greater.[85]

Schwartz's phantasmagorical idea is mind-boggling – that Saudi Arabia, a sparsely-populated nation that had not attacked any neighboring state and that he acknowledged was "incapable of defending its own territory,"[86] was simultaneously sufficiently powerful to threaten the entire world. Saudi Arabia had to be annihilated, Schwartz insisted, just as had been the case with Nazi Germany. "The war against terrorist Wahhabism is therefore a war to the death, as the second world war was a war to the death against fascism."[87]

Although a, perhaps momentary, neoconservative favorite, Schwartz actually contradicted neoconservatives' negative views of other Islamic and Arab states by making it appear that Saudi Arabia was the ultimate evil. One might especially contrast Schwartz's views with those of Laurie Mylroie, who presented Saddam Hussein as the fount of evil. Moreover, Schwartz described Saudi Arabia as more dangerous than the Islamic Republic of Iran, which became the number primary neocon target after the invasion of Iraq. Schwartz wrote that even the Ayatollah Khomeini had not been much of a threat to his Arab neighbors. Rather, Schwartz charged that Saudi Arabia "fueled" the Iraqi "war of aggression" against Shiite Iran.[88] Moreover, he contended that "Shi'as were a force for progress and social reform, while Wahhabis pursued their usual program of indoctrination in hatred and intolerance."[89] Needless to say, these heterodox views didn't persuade other neoconservatives to diminish their hostility to other alleged Islamic enemies, despite their presentation of Schwartz as an expert on Islam. It would seem that his "expertise" was only to selectively serve as a weapon for bashing Saudi Arabia. However, Schwartz was definitely in line with the basic neocon agenda to advance the interests of Israel. He maintained that the elimination of the Saudi regime would go far to resolve the Arab-Israeli conflict on terms sought by Israel, because the Saudis provided a major source of "support and encouragement for radical rejectionists among the Palestinians."[90]

Because of his virulent anti-Saudi views, Schwartz was dismissed from his short-lived tenure as an editorial writer with the Voice of America at the beginning of July 2002, thus becoming, for the moment, a martyr in neoconservative circles.[91] But as Iran became the primary neocon target for war, Saudi Arabia and its "expert" Stephen Schwartz were relegated to the periphery, even though Schwartz began to equate "political Shiism" as a malevolent danger comparable to Wahhabism.[92]

The neocon advocacy of dramatically altering the Middle East status quo stood in stark contrast to the traditional American position of maintaining stability in the area – though it, of course, meshed perfectly with the long-established Israeli goal of destabilizing its enemies. As Kenneth Adelman observed in the aftermath of the United States invasion of Iraq, "The starting point is that conservatives [referring to neoconservatives] now are for radical change and the progressives – the establishment foreign policy makers – are for the status quo." Adelman emphasized that "Conservatives believe that the status quo in the Middle East is pretty bad, and the old conservative belief that stability is good doesn't apply to the Middle East. The status quo in the Middle East has been breeding terrorists."[93] Similarly, Victor Davis Hanson wrote in the July-August 2002 issue of *Commentary* that "What the United States should strive for in the Middle East is not tired normality – the sclerosis that led to September 11, the Palestinian quagmire, and an Iraq full of weapons of mass destruction." He added, "Only by seeking to spark disequilibrium, if not outright chaos, do we stand a chance of ridding the world of the likes of bin Laden, Arafat, and Saddam Hussein."[94]

In the words of Michael Ledeen: "Creative destruction is our middle name. We do it automatically . . . . It is time once again to export the democratic revolution."[95] In August 2002, Ledeen responded to the fears of former National Security Adviser Brent Scowcroft that an attack on Iraq would turn the whole Middle East into a "cauldron" in the following terms:

> One can only hope that we turn the region into a cauldron, and faster, please. If ever there were a region that richly deserved being cauldronized, it is the Middle East today. If we wage the war effectively, we will bring down the terror regimes in Iraq, Iran, and Syria, and either bring down the Saudi monarchy or force it to abandon its global assembly line to indoctrinate young terrorists.[96]

The neocons' support for destabilizing the Middle East, even partitioning some countries like Saudi Arabia, was right in line with policies put forth by Oded Yinon in 1982 and the "Clean Break" paper of 1996, which had as their purpose the weakening of Israel's external enemies. The difference is that the policies oriented to Israeli interests simply stopped at

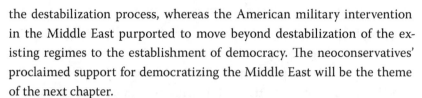

the destabilization process, whereas the American military intervention in the Middle East purported to move beyond destabilization of the existing regimes to the establishment of democracy. The neoconservatives' proclaimed support for democratizing the Middle East will be the theme of the next chapter.

Many critics have portrayed the neocons as being naïve, utopian, or somehow off base in their thinking. For it seemed ridiculous to see a monolithic Islamic threat when, in fact, groups such as Al Qaeda, Saddam's Baathists, the Iranian Shiites, and the Saudi government had quite divergent interests and were mortal enemies of each other. No evidence showed them unified against the United States, except that "evidence" generated by neocons. Moreover, no matter how morally repugnant those religions, ideologies, and regimes might be, this divided congeries of Third World states could hardly be a deadly threat to the United States comparable to that posed by Nazi Germany or the Soviet Union. And it was odd that neocons were virtually alone in recognizing this dire threat. Most other major powers – France, Russia, China – saw no grave Islamic threat to their interests, despite their relative proximity and their own restive Muslim populations.

The fact of the matter is that the lethal Islamic threat, as described by the neocons, did not represent any type of threat actually faced by the United States; but what the neocons did describe roughly approximated the danger faced by Israel, as envisioned by the Likudniks. Moreover, this Likudnik description of the threat to Israel seems to contain much truth. The threat was not mainly from an external attack, since Israel's overwhelming military power could easily dispose of any alliance of Middle East countries. Rather, the threat was an internal demographic one – the ever-growing population of Arabs under Israeli control in the Occupied Territories and Israel proper. And the threat was not to the lives of individual Israeli Jews, but rather to Israel as a collective entity – to the Jewish nature of the Jewish state. For as the Palestinian population became ever larger relative to the Jewish population – owing to a much higher birthrate and the possible emigration of Jews due to deteriorating socio-economic conditions – it threatened to dilute, or even overwhelm, the Jewish majority necessary for a democratic Jewish state. And the Palestinians drew material and moral support from the neighboring Islamic countries. Without such outside support, the Palestinians would be isolated and weakened, and consequently more likely to accede to any solution the Israelis offered.

For the neoconservatives, the interests of Israel and the United States were seen to be identical. Hence any harm to Israel would simultaneously harm the United States. It is not apparent that this identity of interests exists, however, since the Islamic threat is to Israel not to the United States. It appears that neoconservatives have conflated the interests of the United States with those of Israel because of their deep, and well-demonstrated, loyalty to the latter country. This doesn't mean that they deliberately intend to sacrifice American interests for the good of Israel. However, it does appear that the neocons view American foreign policy through the lens of Israeli interest. In short, they have correctly identified a serious Islamic threat – but it is a threat to Israel, not to the United States. Whether they realize it or not, they have subordinated American interests to those of Israel.[97]

chapter 12

DEMOCRACY FOR THE MIDDLE EAST

"**D**EMOCRACY**"** has been the neoconservatives' watchword. During the build-up for the Iraq war, and continuing into the occupation, the neocons' professed object was to transform the Middle Eastern countries into modern Western secular democracies. Democratizing the Middle East was both a moral cause and one that would supposedly provide for America's fundamental security in a very realistic way by eliminating what the neocons claimed was the root cause of terrorism – the lack of democratic freedoms that turned individuals to violence.

Charles Krauthammer spoke openly about the democracy aspect of the impending war in a December 2002 symposium at the Nixon Center in Washington. Krauthammer stated that the necessity of going to war was not simply

> about weapons of mass destruction or American credibility. It's about reforming the Arab world. I think we don't know the answer to the question of whether the Arab-Islamic world is inherently allergic to democracy. The assumption is that it is – but I don't know if anyone can answer that question today. We haven't attempted it so far. The attempt will begin with Iraq. Afterwards, we are going to have empirical evidence; history will tell us whether this assumption was correct or not.[1]

Most neocons did not need such an experiment in order to affirm that democracy would transform the Middle East.

President Bush spoke appropriately to the American Enterprise Institute on February 26, 2003, just before the invasion of Iraq: "The world has a clear interest in the spread of democratic values, because stable and free nations do not breed the ideologies of murder. They encourage the peaceful pursuit of a better life."[2]

Before the invasion, however, democracy was but a secondary reason for war, with the major rationale being Saddam's alleged possession of weapons of mass destruction. As the evidence mounted that Iraq did not possess such weapons, Bush increasingly placed his emphasis on building democracy in Iraq, which he claimed would inspire democratic change across the region. For example, Bush emphasized the significance of promoting democracy to his foreign policy in a speech to the National Endowment for Democracy in November 2003. "Our commitment to democracy," Bush stated, "is also tested in the Middle East, which is my focus today, and must be a focus of American policy for decades to come." In his view, "[t]he establishment of a free Iraq at the heart of the Middle East will be a watershed event in the global democratic revolution."[3]

The administration's full adoption of the democracy theme became apparent in Bush's Second Inaugural Address in January 2005, when he passionately proclaimed that the fundamental goal of American foreign policy was to spread democracy: "It is the policy of the United States to seek and support the growth of democratic movements and institutions in every nation and culture, with the ultimate goal of ending tyranny in our world."[4]

The ideas for Bush's speech derived from *The Case for Democracy: The Power of Freedom to Overcome Tyranny and Terror* by Israeli Natan Sharansky, a work that Bush had recently become infatuated with and that, in all likelihood, had been introduced to him by his neocon advisors. Sharansky was a former Soviet dissident who had been connected with the neoconservatives since the 1970s. And input for the inaugural address came from Elliott Abrams, William Kristol, and Charles Krauthammer.[5]

This call for global democracy contrasted sharply with Bush's explicit rejection of nation building during his 2000 presidential campaign. In fact, the entire occupation of Iraq was an example of a nation-building effort. In essence, Bush had adopted the neoconservative agenda.[6]

Neocons asserted that the existence of democracy in Iraq would be so attractive as to lead other people in the Middle East to desire to adopt it. Now, the possibility that real American-like democracy could flourish in the Middle East was close to nil. International affairs expert General William E. Odom pointed out that the assumption that the United States could create a liberal, constitutional democracy in Iraq defies just about everything known by professional students of the topic. Of the more than 40 democracies created since World War II, fewer than 10 can be considered truly 'constitutional' – meaning that their domestic order is protected by a broadly accepted rule of law, and has survived for at least a generation. None is a country with Arabic and Muslim political cultures. None has deep sectarian and ethnic fissures like those in Iraq.[7]

In the mainstream, the neocons' professed democratic goal generally was considered as a genuine, though largely misguided, motive for the administration's action. As Norman Levine, a professor of international history and executive director of the Institute for International Policy, put it: "The neo-conservative movement is driven by an ethical imperative, the global conversion of the world to democracy."[8] "Realist" critics of America's war policy have focused on the destructive results of relying on democracy as the lodestar for American foreign policy and have branded the neocons as naive idealists, Wilsonians, Jacobin radicals, and Trotskyists.[9]

Despite their lofty rhetoric, however, there is much in the neoconservatives' record that belies the idea that they are really wedded to the democratic ideal. Looking beneath the surface, one sees that the neoconservatives conceived democracy as a system that neither ensures majority rule or freedom of speech. Although critics have charged neoconservatives with being naïve democratic ideologues, when their views are closely examined they are revealed as anything but – with the rhetoric of democracy being closely tied to concrete policy issues.

To be precise, many neoconservative thinkers acknowledged that the United States would not immediately bring about democracy after toppling Saddam. The idea of instant democracy would seem to be simply a propaganda device to mobilize public support for the war. In reality, the neocons generally argued that it was necessary for the United States to "educate" the Iraqis in the principles of democracy during a long period of American occupation. For instance, in September 2002, Norman Podhoretz acknowledged that the people of the Middle East might, if given a free democratic choice, pick anti-American, anti-Israeli leaders and policies. But he proclaimed that "there is a policy that can head it off," provided "that we then have the stomach to impose a new political culture on the defeated parties. This is what we did directly and unapologetically in Germany and Japan after winning World War II."[10]

Similarly, neoconservative columnist Jonah Goldberg wrote just after the fall of Saddam's regime that "elections should be the last on a long list of priorities for Iraq." He feared that if elections were held immediately the "Shiite zealots" would win, "but that would amount to trading one dictatorship for another." In short, U.S. forces would have to "stay in Iraq not only long enough to build up the laws, courts and markets necessary for a successful society, but long enough for the society itself to regenerate."[11]

That is to say, Iraq would be an American colonial puppet state, at least for the near future, until the Iraqis had properly internalized American, or more precisely, neocon-sanctioned views. As neoconservative columnist Bruce Fein put it: "At this time in Iraq's grim history, order and security are more critical than liberty and deliberation; clarity and decisiveness more urgent than nuance and political ballet." He went on: "President Bush should thus state unequivocally that the United States will govern Iraq as a trustee on behalf of its 23 million citizens until the conditions for a stable democracy have taken root." And according to Fein, that U.S. trusteeship would entail detentions without charges; secret trials based on hearsay evidence with no appeals; a mandatory death penalty; and "unforgiving" sentences imposed on those Iraqis who discouraged cooperation with United States.[12]

In *An End to Evil*, David Frum and Richard Perle asserted that establishing democracy must take a back seat when it conflicted with fighting Islamic radicals: "In the Middle East, democratization does not mean calling immediate elections and then living with whatever happens next."[13] Since elections in any Islamic country would always risk the empowering of Islamic radicals, or at least enemies of the United States and Israel, it seems that Perle and Frum would essentially prohibit majority-rule democracy in the Middle East.

Sometimes the neoconservatives went so far in seeing the need for enlightened American rule over foreign lands that they showed nostalgia for imperialism, with the United States emulating the British empire of the "white man's burden" era, exercising an enlightened rule over the "backward" peoples of the world. Thus, Max Boot, in the *Weekly Standard* in October 2001, argued "The Case for Empire." "Afghanistan and other troubled lands today," Boot intoned, "cry out for the sort of enlightened foreign administration once provided by self-confident Englishmen in jodhpurs and pith helmets." While perceiving "nation-building" as perhaps too difficult, Boot held that

> Building a working state administration is a more practical short-term ob-
> jective that has been achieved by countless colonial regimes, including the
> United States in Haiti (1915–1933), the Dominican Republic (1916–1924), Cuba
> (1899–1902, 1906–1909), and the Philippines (1899–1935), to say nothing of the
> achievements of generals Lucius Clay in Germany and Douglas MacArthur in
> Japan.[14]

Needless to say, there was, at best, quite limited democratic self-govern-ment in most of those cases.

The neoconservatives' significant reservations about real democracy in Iraq were not an aberration, but rather accorded with their thinking on the subject elsewhere. Obviously neoconservatives have not shown much interest in democratic majority rule in Palestine, where Israel has sought to elevate individuals who would accede to Israeli demands rather than represent the Palestinian people; nor have neoconservatives cared much about democracy in Israel itself, as shown by their identification with the Israeli right, which promotes an exclusivist Jewish state at the expense of its Arab citizens.

Douglas Feith gave a strong defense of Jewish exclusivism in a speech he delivered in Jerusalem in 1997, titled "Reflections on Liberalism, Democ-racy and Zionism." Feith criticized

> those Israelis who, intent on comparing their country with the United States,
> contend that Israel, like America, should not be an ethnic state – a Jewish state
> – but rather a "state of its citizens." Such Israelis advance a logic that would
> make all states in the world "states of their citizens," a classic, liberal universal-
> ist view, but one that, as we have seen, ignores the reality that human beings
> cherish their ethnic identities and, given free choice, will often prefer to live in
> an ethnic state in which their own people is the majority.

Feith argued that "there is a place in the world for non-ethnic nations and there is a place for ethnic nations."[15] Why Israel could be an "ethnic nation" that discriminated against those of a different ethnicity, while other coun-tries could be condemned for doing the very same thing, was not apparent from Feith's discourse.

In regard to "regime change" in the Middle East, neocons sometimes advocated the restoration of monarchies in Iraq (Hashemite) and Iran (Pahlavi). "Prince Hassan [brother of the late King Hussein of Jordan] is someone who has not been poisoned by the past 40 years of chaos in Iraq and is perhaps the only person who can transcend the ethnic and political complexities," proclaimed Michael Rubin of the American Enterprise Institute in July 2002.[16]

David Wurmser's support for restoring the Hashemites and the traditional ruling families in Iraq as a bulwark against modern totalitarianism, which he discussed at length in his book *Tyranny's Ally: America's Failure to Defeat Saddam Hussein*, hardly meshed with the democracy thesis.[17] The fundamental causes of tyranny in the Middle East, according to Wurmser, were the modern ideological systems of Pan-Arabism and Pan-Islamism, which sought to forge large, collectivistic states. Instead of seeing modern Western democracy as the remedy, he looked back to the past with a call for the Hashemite "idea of a federated Iraqi entity, with maximum autonomy residing in local bases of power, broadly tied to a Jordanian-Iraqi confederation." The proposed "design harks back to the old Ottoman Millet system – decentralized administration along ethnic, sectarian regional, and community lines." Wurmser held that the multiple political divisions inherent in such a system were a positive good for the inhabitants because for

> much of the Arab world, factionalism constitutes the sole barrier against the absolute power of the tyrants. A more stable and safe society can be expected to emerge from the voluntary association of factions around a coordinating but diffuse governmental body. This was the case in the early 1920s, when the Hashemite King Faisal I of Iraq forged his nation by negotiating tribal alliances and unions. Iraq was founded upon, rather than opposed to, these primordial ties that define Arab society.[18]

Obviously Wurmser's proposal did not represent the establishment of modern democracy. Though it must be added that Wurmser did not even claim to be an exponent of democracy. "I'm not a big fan of democracy per se," said Wurmser in an October 2007 interview. "I'm a fan of freedom and one has to remember the difference. Freedom must precede democracy by a long, long time."[19] Whether Wurmser's proposed scenario would expand freedom is uncertain, but what it did represent, however, would be the dissolution of modern centralized states, which coincided with the Israeli security goal of surrounding itself with fragmented, powerless statelets.

As mentioned in the last chapter, Reza Pahlavi, the eldest son of the deposed Shah of Iran and heir to the throne, has had close connections with the neoconservatives and with Israel.[20] Although he publicly spoke of a constitutional monarchy being established by a popular vote,[21] it would seem apparent that the goal of Pahlavi, and his followers, is that the shah would be more than a mere figurehead position.

It should also be noted that when neoconservatives – including Douglas Feith, David Wurmser, and Richard Perle – produced their policy paper "A Clean Break: A New Strategy for Securing the Realm" for Israeli Prime Minister Netanyahu in 1996, they failed to mention spreading democracy but instead dealt simply with altering the political structure of the Middle East to suit the security needs of Israel – the aim being to destabilize countries, not to democratize.[22]

The neoconservatives hardly showed any appreciation for democracy in their buildup for war, either. They expressed nothing but disdain for the European democracies that opposed the war on Iraq. And it was the overwhelming majority of the people in all of those European countries who unequivocally opposed the war in Iraq – poll results showed that support for a war conducted "unilaterally by America and its allies" did not exceed 11 percent in any country – but the United States expected those governments to go against the will of their people.[23]

Those countries that refused to go along with the attack on Iraq were dismissed as "Old Europe," presumably degenerate, cowardly, and resentful.[24] As Frum and Perle wrote: "The United States spent hundreds of billions over half a century doing things for Europe, and, inevitably, many Europeans resent it. They resent America's ability to be generous, and they resent their need for that generosity."[25]

The United States even attempted to bribe the Turkish government to involve the country in the war on Iraq, but that government actually put the decision to the vote of its parliament, which decided in the negative. Paul Wolfowitz was enraged by the Turkish military's failure to sufficiently pressure the government to participate in the war. "I think for whatever reason, they did not play the strong leadership role that we would have expected," Wolfowitz complained. Presumably, Wolfowitz would have preferred a Turkish military coup over the democratic repudiation of American war policy.[26] Later, in 2004, the neoconservatives condemned the new Spanish government for carrying out its election pledge to remove Spanish occupation troops from Iraq.[27]

The neocons indifference to bona fide democracy was revealed in stark colors by events in America's Central Asian ally Uzbekistan, which in May

2005 attracted the media spotlight because of anti-government protests and the concomitant government slaughter of hundreds of the protesters.[28] Long before that time, however, Uzbekistan, run by its dictatorial leader Islam Karimov, was noted for its terrible barbarities. Observers estimated that the Uzbek regime held more than 6,000 political and religious prisoners, many of whom had been sentenced for such non-crimes as wearing an Islamic-style beard or praying at a mosque not sanctioned by the state. In a policy reminiscent of Stalinist Russia, the regime often imprisoned entire families. And those incarcerated in Uzbekistan sometimes underwent the most grisly tortures. International human-rights groups reported that the atrocities committed by Uzbek jailers include applying electrical shocks to genitals, ripping off fingernails and toenails with pliers, stabbing with screwdrivers, and, perhaps the most creative, boiling prisoners to death.[29] Even the U.S. State Department, in pallid understatement, admitted that "the police force and the intelligence service use torture as a routine investigation technique."[30]

Nevertheless, supporters of Israel, including neocons, supported the dictatorial Karimov largely because of his hostility to radical Islam and his support of Israel and the Uzbek Jewish community. As Marc Perelman put it in the May 27, 2005 issue of the *Forward*: "The recent violence in Uzbekistan has cast a spotlight on the cozy relationship between the authoritarian regime of President Islam Karimov and Israel and its American supporters." Perelman continued:

> Observers said that Karimov . . . has used the American Jewish community as a beachhead to cement relations with both Washington and Jerusalem. Israeli and American Jewish communal leaders said that their efforts to cultivate ties with Uzbekistan have been motivated primarily by the regime's positive attitude toward the local Jewish community and Israel as well as its hawkish stand against radical Islam.[31]

Perhaps the greatest American apologist for Uzbekistan's tyrant was Stephen Schwartz, who as previously noted had taken the lead among neocons in lambasting the government and religion of Saudi Arabia. From Schwartz's standpoint, Uzbekistan was the polar opposite of Saudi Arabia. As he wrote in the *Weekly Standard* in 2002, the situation in Uzbekistan was about as good as it could be. Explaining away the grisly record of the Karimov regime, Schwartz asserted that before freedom can be established, the enemies of freedom must be defeated. The fate of democracies that do not defeat the enemies of democracy is illustrated by the histories of Germany and Italy after the First World War. Democracies can grant mercy to their enemies only from a position of unchallengeable strength.[32]

Furthermore, Schwartz held that the United States should not simply tolerate Karimov's repressive actions, but actually abet them. "The United States," Schwartz emphasized, "which has entered into a military alliance with Uzbekistan, must support the Uzbeks in their internal as well as their external combat, and must repudiate the blandishments of the human rights industry."[33] In short, in Schwartz's view, the United States had to be an active partner in Karimov's tyranny.

While the reality of neocon's foreign policy diverged from their professed democratic ideals, the neocons rarely offered the pretense of democracy in their domestic actions. The deceptive means used by the neoconservatives to mobilize domestic support for the war especially belied their identification with the ethos of democracy. The most serious matter for Congress and the President is the decision to go to war. Congress alone has the constitutional authority to declare war. The President has a constitutional responsibility to be truthful with Congress in providing it with the information it needs to properly evaluate the case for war. It is true that since World War II the United States has gone to war without a formal declaration of war. But still Congress is expected to give some type of authorization. And the democratic process depends on Congress' making its decision on the basis of accurate information provided by the executive branch. That did not occur prior to the invasion of Iraq.

What generated support for the war on Iraq were the false statements that Saddam possessed WMD that threatened the United States and that Saddam was tied to the Al Qaeda terrorists. Senator Edward M. Kennedy (Democrat – Massachusetts) succinctly pointed out that it was under these false beliefs that Congress gave the president the power that he used to justify war. "A year ago, the United States went to war in Iraq," Kennedy stated in March of 2004,

> because President Bush and his administration convinced Congress and the country that Saddam Hussein was an urgent threat that required immediate military action . . . . The case for war was based on two key claims: that Hussein was on the verge of acquiring nuclear weapons, and that he had close ties to the

Al Qaeda terrorists responsible for the atrocities of Sept. 11. Both claims proved to be demonstrably false.[34]

The deceptive intelligence information the Bush administration fed Congress and the American people was intended to make them view a U.S. attack on Iraq as a necessary self-defense measure. However, in seeking a congressional authorization that would allow for an attack on Iraq, the Bush administration engaged in additional deception by claiming that such legislation did not mean war. The Bush administration and its congressional supporters presented it as a means to bring about United Nations measures that might force Saddam Hussein to disarm and thereby avoid war.

The October 11, 2002 Joint Resolution to Authorize the Use of United States Armed Forces Against Iraq did not expressly spell out war. As antiwar Congressman Ron Paul (R.-Tex.) argued on October 3, 2002:

> An up or down vote on declaring war against Iraq would not pass the Congress, and the President has no intention of asking for it. This is unfortunate, because if the process were carried out in a constitutional fashion, the American people and the U.S. Congress would vote "No" on assuming responsibility for this war.[35]

On that date, Paul had attempted to test his allegation by submitting to the House International Relations Committee a proposed declaration of war that read, "A state of war is declared to exist between the United States and the government of Iraq." It was rejected.[36]

On October 7, 2002, the eve of the vote in Congress, Bush made a major address to the nation on the Iraqi threat in which he included a denial that the resolution was a mandate for war. He said:

> I have asked Congress to authorize the use of America's military, if it proves necessary, to enforce U.N. Security Council demands. Approving this resolution does not mean that military action is imminent or unavoidable. The resolution will tell the United Nations, and all nations, that America speaks with one voice and is determined to make the demands of the civilized world mean something. Congress will also be sending a message to the dictator in Iraq: that his only chance – his only choice is full compliance, and the time remaining for that choice is limited.[37]

Congress was not aware that the Bush administration had already made the decision to use military force to remove Saddam. And the Bush administration would, in fact, use the resolution as a mandate for war.

This idea that the congressional resolution did not mean war was reflected in speeches by legislators from both parties. Senator John Warner

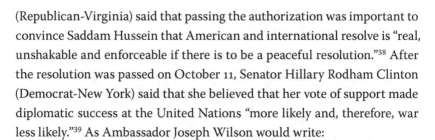

(Republican-Virginia) said that passing the authorization was important to convince Saddam Hussein that American and international resolve is "real, unshakable and enforceable if there is to be a peaceful resolution."[38] After the resolution was passed on October 11, Senator Hillary Rodham Clinton (Democrat-New York) said that she believed that her vote of support made diplomatic success at the United Nations "more likely and, therefore, war less likely."[39] As Ambassador Joseph Wilson would write:

> President Bush argued – disingenuously, as it turned out – that he needed the resolution not to go to war, but to be able to negotiate a strong disarmament resolution at the United Nations. Absent the threat of the U. S. going it alone, the president claimed that the U.N. would never reconstitute an intrusive inspections regime.[40]

While it was not officially presented as a mandate for war, President Bush had pushed for and received the authority to launch a war without further advance notice to Congress. Once Congress passed the resolution, the decision on whether the nation would go to war was left solely to President Bush. Obviously, Congress shirked its constitutional duty by allowing the President to make this decision for war.

Nonetheless, Congress did not give Bush an open-ended choice to go to war at his own will. Rather, it conditioned its grant of authority for war on a formal determination by the President that there continued to exist a threat that could not be dealt with through peaceful diplomacy and that militant actions were consistent with the war against those involved in 9/11. In making the required determination, Bush would give Congress only one purported fact, citing information Colin Powell had provided to the United Nations. Thus, Bush went to war without ever properly complying with the conditions required by Congress. Obviously, Saddam did not have anything to do with September 11 and the weapons inspection by Hans Blix had indicated that Saddam did not pose an immediate threat to the United States.[41] In November 2005, however, in one of his many continuing distortions of history, Bush would claim that Congress actually gave him a mandate for war. "When I made the decision to remove Saddam Hussein from power, Congress approved it with strong bipartisan support."[42]

The Bush administration had given the American people and their representatives a distorted picture of the war issue. The administration had engaged in deception on Saddam's actual threat to the United States and simply used the WMD as a pretext to remove him. It had been deceptive

in requesting a resolution from Congress that it claimed was not a mandate for war after a decision for war had already been made. The American people and their representatives were not given a truthful picture in which to make an educated decision.

The neocons not only showed indifference to the democratic concept of majority rule, but also to civil liberties, which they claimed had to be sacrificed in the name of security. The major legislation enacted here was USA PATRIOT Act,[43] which became law on October 26, 2001, less than two months after the September 11 terror attacks, virtually without debate. It gave the federal government broad powers to conduct surveillance of American citizens and to incarcerate them without charges, without public evidence, and without a trial.[44]

By late December 2005, it was revealed that Bush had gone far beyond the PATRIOT Act in restricting civil liberties, in the area of surveillance. Beginning in 2002, Bush repeatedly authorized the National Security Agency to conduct electronic surveillance without a court warrant, which was a clear violation of the 1978 Foreign Intelligence Surveillance Act (FISA). From the standpoint of national security, such an endeavor would seem completely unnecessary. FISA provided the President with very broad powers to conduct surveillance. It only required the administration to apply to a secret FISA court for warrants, which could be approved in hours, even minutes, if necessary. FISA even contained provisions for warrantless surveillance and the granting of ex post facto warrants.[45]

FISA's purpose was to provide a check on the executive branch's ability to decide who should be subject to such spying in order to make sure that it was really spying on people with connections to terrorism or foreign governments, rather than simply political enemies.[46] Conceivably the reason the administration did not go to the FISA court for warrants was that it had no legitimate reasons for its spying – that it was spying on internal political enemies. As former President Jimmy Carter noted: "Under the Bush administration, there's been a disgraceful and illegal decision – we're not going to the let the judges or the Congress or anyone else know that we're spying on the American people. And no one knows how many innocent Americans have had their privacy violated under this secret act."[47]

More than that, the Bush administration expressed a nearly unlimited view of presidential power, especially as it pertained to war. Bush and his

legal advisors claimed that his virtually unlimited authority on issues related to national security derived from the Constitution's directive that
"the President shall be Commander in Chief of the Army and Navy of the
United States." As is apparent, Bush's alleged commander-in-chief powers far exceeded the Constitution's actual commander-in-chief provision.
Moreover, the administration invoked the theory of the "unitary executive" to justify all-encompassing presidential power. According to its novel
interpretation of the "unitary executive" theory, the president possessed
the authority to overrule and ignore the Congress and the courts, if he
considered their actions to be an unconstitutional encroachment on his
authority. For example, Bush agreed to accept a ban on torture, but he later
quietly reserved the right to ignore this legal ban, even as he signed it into
law. Thus Congress and the Supreme Court become merely advisors, with
no authority over the President.[48]

Bush's position on the powers of the presidency essentially overturns
the basic tenets of the American system of checks and balances stemming
from the constitutional separation of powers. In the *Federalist* Paper No. 47,
James Madison succinctly stated: "The accumulation of all powers, legisla-
tive, executive, and judiciary, in the same hands, whether of one, a few, or
many, and whether hereditary, self-appointed, or elective, may justly be
pronounced the very definition of tyranny."

In looking at the domestic effect of the "war on terror," conservative
war critic Paul Craig Roberts appropriately wrote: "It is paradoxical that
American democracy is the likely casualty of a 'war on terror' that is being
justified in the name of the expansion of democracy."[49]

For the neocons, the concern for national security must supersede individual freedom. Frum and Perle in *An End to Evil* saw nothing threatening
in the PATRIOT Act. "Civil liberties in the United States," they asserted,
"continue robust." Indeed, they implied that even with the PATRIOT Act,
the United States was still allowing too much dissent. "We may be so eager
to protect the right to dissent," they firmly pronounced, "that we lose sight
of the difference between dissent and subversion; so determined to defend
the right of privacy that we refuse to acknowledge even the most blatant
warnings of danger."[50]

Frum and Perle especially insisted that it was necessary for Americans
to monitor fifth-column Islamists in the country. "Although Islamic terrorism originated overseas," they solemnly warned, "it seems to be draw-

ing crucial – and increasing – support from a growing infrastructure of extremism inside this country and in Canada."[51]

Concern for the internal Islamic threat also loomed large in the thinking of Daniel Pipes, a neoconservative scholar of Islamic history, whom Bush appointed to the board of the United States Institute of Peace in 2003. Pipes is the son of noted Harvard historian Richard Pipes, of Polish Jewish background, who escaped from Poland at the start of World War II in 1939. Daniel Pipes was the founder and director of the Middle East Forum, a neocon organization focusing on the Middle East and the alleged danger posed to the United States by Islamic radicalism.[52]

Pipes maintained that the internal security of the United States required racial profiling. "For years," Pipes asserted,

> it has been my position that the threat of radical Islam implies an imperative to focus security measures on Muslims. If searching for rapists, one looks only at the male population. Similarly, if searching for Islamists (adherents of radical Islam), one looks at the Muslim population.

Pipes even went so far as to defend the World War II internment camps for Japanese-Americans and implied that a comparable approach might be needed in the "war on terror." Pipes wrote:

> Although more than 60 years past, these events matter yet deeply today, permitting the victimization lobby, in compensation for the supposed horrors of internment, to condemn in advance any use of ethnicity, nationality, race, or religion in formulating domestic security policy.[53]

The degree to which civil liberties would be curtailed in the name of security would depend on what type of activities were deemed harmful to national security; and neocons had an expansive interpretation of what constitutes terrorism and subversion. Pipes showed a strong concern for the views presented in Middle East Studies programs on American campuses, which he deemed "biased" – i.e., hostile to Israel and the "war on terror." Pipes, along with Martin Kramer, a former director of the Moshe Dayan Center for Middle Eastern and African Studies at Tel Aviv University, helped to establish the "Campus Watch" project in 2002 to monitor those programs. Initially the Campus Watch website published "dossiers" on allegedly biased academics, and it urged students to submit reports on political bias. Pipes and Campus Watch sought to have the U.S. Congress pass legislation mandating that university Middle East departments adhere to "standards" when receiving federal funding, which would have a definite chilling effect on academic criticism of Israel and American war policy in the Middle East.[54]

Frum and Perle looked upon mainstream Islamic groups as dangerous fifth-columnists. "Until the American Muslim Council, the Council on American Islamic Relations, and the Muslim Public Affairs Council purge themselves of their extremists," Frum and Perle asserted, "they should be regarded as fellow travelers of the terrorist enemy and treated with appropriate mistrust and disdain by Congress and the executive branch."[55]

Significantly, the alleged danger posed by these Islamic groups was in the realm of ideas, not actual physical terror in the United States. As Frum and Perle acknowledged: "It remains a very rare event for native-born American Muslims to participate in acts of terror. Militant Islam in the United States expresses itself primarily through lobbying and fund-raising."[56] But they emphasized that

> American society must communicate to its Muslim citizens and residents a clear message about what is expected from them. The flow of funds to terror must stop. The incitement in schools and mosques must stop. The promotion of anti-Semitism must stop. The denial and excuse-making must stop. Community leaders should cooperate wholeheartedly with law enforcement to identify and monitor potentially dangerous people, and Muslim leaders should abjure violence and terror without reservation or purpose of evasion.[57]

Since Perle and Frum acknowledged that American Muslims were not committing acts of terror in the United States, what they focused on was the support for alleged acts of "terror" abroad. Frum and Perle thus conjoined actual violence with ideas and other non-violent actions, which they identified as aiding "terror." And those non-violent actions did not even have to apply to resisting the American military or actual American policy. In short, funding of groups that resisted the Israeli occupation would fall into the proscribed "terrorist" category; in fact, criticism of Israel, or of neoconservatives for that matter, might even be banned as constituting the promotion of "anti-Semitism."

Despite their often-used democratic rhetoric, it is apparent that neocons have not been philosophically wedded to democracy. Neoconservatives have not always even claimed to be exponents of democracy as a policy goal; in fact, it was the rejection of pushing democracy as a foreign policy goal that loomed large in their early years. During the Cold War, the neoconservatives emphasized that it was essential to support dictator-ships, if they were pro-United States, as part of the overall war on Soviet Communism. They were especially critical of President Jimmy Carter's emphasis on human rights in foreign policy, which they held had served to undermine anti-Communist pro-American dictatorships, such as the Shah's Iran and Somoza's Nicaragua, and facilitated their transformation into anti-American dictatorships that might align with the Soviet Union. Journalist Michael Kinsley summed up the neocon worldview of those Cold War days thus:

> The great neocon theme was tough-minded pragmatism in the face of liberal naivete. Liberals were sentimental. They believed that people were basically good or could easily be made so. Domestically, liberal social programs were no match for the intractable underclass or even made the situation worse. In the world, lib-erals were too hung up on democracy and human rights, refusing to recognize that the only important question about other countries is: Friend or foe?[58]

The most celebrated article in this genre was Jean Kirkpatrick's "Dicta-torships and Double Standards," in the November 1979 issue of *Commen-tary*.[59] In it, she unfavorably contrasted totalitarian Communism's com-plete control of society with the authoritarian dictatorships' allowance for some degree of civil society. She argued that pressuring dictatorships to adopt democratic reforms often had the opposite effect of bringing about a more repressive Communist regime. Kirkpatrick emphasized that democ-racy was a gradual process. "Hurried efforts to force complex and unfamil-iar political practice on societies lacking the requisite political culture," she wrote, "not only fail to produce desired outcomes; if they are undertaken at a time when the traditional regime is under attack, they actually facilitate the job of the insurgents."[60]

Kirkpatrick's essay made her an iconic figure in neoconservative circles and consequently gained her strong support among mainstream conserva-tives, especially Ronald Reagan, who named her ambassador to the United Nations.[61] Kirkpatrick's defense of non-Communist dictatorships provided the ideological underpinning for the Reagan administration's support for non-communist dictatorships in Guatemala, the Philippines, and Argenti-na, and the arming of such non-democratic insurgents as the mujahideen in Afghanistan, UNITA in Angola, and the Contras in Nicaragua as a means of ending pro-Soviet Communist rule in those countries. Kirkpatrick thus provided a key ideological weapon in the last stages of the Cold War.

It should be evident that Kirkpatrick's rejection of any attempt to achieve abrupt democratic change, which some observers saw to be in line with the thinking of British conservative Edmund Burke,[62] was the polar opposite of the neoconservative rhetoric in the Bush II era for instant democracy in the Middle East, which commentators have equated with radical Jacobinism.[63]

Of course, Leo Strauss, mentor of many leading neoconservatives (William Kristol, Robert Kagan, Paul Wolfowitz, Adam Shulsky), had little regard for democracy, preaching instead rule by an elite and the necessary deception of the masses. Regarding Strauss' view of democracy, Shadia Drury, author of *Leo Strauss and the American Right,* said: "Strauss was neither a liberal nor a democrat. Perpetual deception of the citizens by those in power is critical [in Strauss's view] because they need to be led, and they need strong rulers to tell them what's good for them"[64]

The conclusion to be drawn is that "democracy" for neoconservatives is quite empty of content. One does not have to look too closely to see that the countries slated to be "democratized" are the enemies of Israel. In essence, "democracy," for the neoconservatives, was a weapon, not a political objective. The neocons were anything but democratic ideologues. "Democracy" was never to be applied when it would hurt the interests of Israel – as on the West Bank or in Israel itself. And democracy was not to be pushed in the United States, either, when it would militate against the Middle East war agenda. The ideology of "democracy" served as a weapon to advance a particular material goal, just as the neocons had made use of Kirkpatrick's quite different philosophy to pursue the Cold War.

chapter 13

NEOCONS' POST-INVASION DIFFICULTIES

THE SUCCESSFUL INVASION in 2003 turned out to be the highpoint for the public support of the Bush Iraq policy. After Bush's triumphal "Mission Accomplished" appearance aboard the aircraft carrier USS Abraham Lincoln on May 1, 2003, however, almost every facet of the neoconservative propaganda arguments for war unraveled. No WMD was found, despite extensive government investigations. Instead of being welcomed in as liberators, the American troops faced stiff resistance causing ever-mounting American casualties. Even though the occupation force was far greater than what the neocons originally had claimed to be necessary, it was insufficient to maintain order in Iraq. And the costs of the occupation were immensely greater than what the neocons had forecasted in their allegation that the oil revenues could cover a substantial portion of the limited costs. In short, the American occupation had turned into a bloody, expensive quagmire.

Although their previous claims had been falsified by events, neoconservatives remained resolutely unapologetic, which underscored the likelihood that they did not really believe their own war propaganda. Their response was merely to create additional propagandistic spin to shore up sagging public support. They spun the WMD story for months after the invasion, concocting innumerable explanations as to why the WMD was not found. They claimed that those illicit weapons had been sent to Syria or that Saddam had destroyed his stockpiles before the war. They maintained that he had produced his WMD in dual use factories that manufactured civilian goods, thus rendering the WMD undetectable. Sometimes the neocons, ever inventive, would come up with some evidence that purported to prove the existence of WMD. And sometimes, even more daringly, they would claim that WMD had not been the public rationale for the war.[1]

Before the actual invasion, the neoconservatives had publicly claimed that there would be little or no resistance to the attack – the cakewalk scenario. As casualties mounted after the invasion, Michael Ledeen would deem them inconsequential. "I think the level of casualties is secondary," Ledeen asserted at an American Enterprise Institute black-coffee breakfast briefing in late March 2003. "I mean, it may sound like an odd thing to say, but all the great scholars who have studied American character have come to the conclusion that we are a warlike people and that we love war . . . . What we hate is not casualties, but losing."[2]

This relative unconcern for American casualties actually fitted into the neocon World War IV concept. If the war on terrorism was somehow comparable to World War II and the Cold War, then the actual casualties in Iraq were relatively light. Norman Podhoretz would write as late as September 2004, when most Americans were deeply troubled by the growing number of American dead and wounded, that "by any historical standard – the more than 6,500 who died on D-Day alone in World War II, to cite only one example – our total losses remained amazingly low."[3] Obviously, the neocons were quite willing to accept many more American casualties given their depiction of the war as a life-and- death struggle for the United States.

After the fall of Baghdad in April 2003, neocons and administration officials held that the continued Iraq resistance to the American occupation represented only the activities of a few extremists – diehard Baathists and Al Qaeda terrorists from outside Iraq – adamantly denying that the growing resistance was drawing significant support from the Iraqi people. On June 2003, Secretary of Defense Donald Rumsfeld dismissed the Iraqi resistance as a few "pockets of dead-enders."[4] As of mid year 2003, Wolfowitz denied that the combatants in Iraq were "insurgents." "An insurgency implies something that rose up afterwards," Wolfowitz staunchly asserted. "This is the same enemy that butchered Iraqis for 35 years."[5]

As Norman Podhoretz would write in September 2004,

> Most supporters of the invasion – myself included – had predicted that we
> would be greeted there with flowers and cheers; yet out troops encountered
> car bombs and hatred. Nevertheless, and contrary to the impression created

by the media, survey after survey demonstrated the vast majority of Iraqis did welcome us, and were happy to be liberated from the murderous tyranny under which they had lived for long under Saddam Hussein. The hatred and the car bombs came from the same breed of jihadists who had attacked us on 9/11, and who, unlike the skeptics in our own country, were afraid that we were actually succeeding in democratizing Iraq.[6]

In actuality, as a May 2004 survey commissioned by the Coalition Provisional Authority leaked to the Associated Press revealed, large numbers of Iraqis were hostile to what 92 percent of them considered to be an "occupying force." Fifty-five percent of Iraqis reported to the pollsters that they would feel safer if U.S. troops immediately left.[7]

But the hostility of the Iraqi populace did not disturb some neocons, it simply demonstrated their ungratefulness after the obvious benefits brought to them by America's liberation. As the *Weekly Standard* complained in January 2004,

> While American soldiers have spent the last eight months getting shot, getting RPG'ed, and getting mortared, many Iraqis, no longer fearful of having relatives disappeared in the night by Saddam's various goon squads, have tripped upon a new national pastime: whining like little girls.[8]

Neocons attempted to transmute negative developments into ammunition for their war agenda. For example, they used the very existence of militant resistance in Iraq to justify the need for widening the war – the World War IV scenario. "The war against us in Iraq and Afghanistan is an existential struggle guided, funded, and armed by tyrannical regimes in Iran, Syria, and Saudi Arabia," Michael Ledeen would write in January 2004, "because they are convinced – rightly enough – that if we succeed, they are doomed to fall in a regional democratic revolution." He continued: "we will remain under attack in Iraq so long as the tyrannical regimes in Damascus, Riyadh, and Tehran are left free to kill us and the embattled Iraqis."[9]

The neoconservatives seized on the revolt of militant Shiite cleric Moqtada al-Sadr to call for an attack on Iran. Having just returned from a stint as a "governance team advisor" for the U.S.-led Coalition Provisional Authority (CPA) in Iraq to his position as a resident fellow at AEI, Michael Rubin wrote in early April 2004 that Iran was providing extensive financial help to the radical clerics in Iraq.[10] The *Wall Street Journal* editorial similarly opined: "If warnings to Tehran from Washington don't impress them

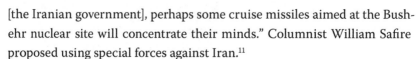

[the Iranian government], perhaps some cruise missiles aimed at the Bushehr nuclear site will concentrate their minds." Columnist William Safire proposed using special forces against Iran.[11]

As the Iraqi resistance intensified, neocons argued that the U.S. military was not acting tough enough. Syndicated columnist Mona Charen asserted in April 2004: "the question of the moment is not whether we've done enough good, but whether we've been tough enough." In her view, "liberating" Iraqis did not entail winning them over but in beating them down so that they would not resist. "But Iraq cannot be truly liberated until it has been transformed," she exclaimed. "And it cannot be transformed if the bad elements are not afraid of American soldiers. Those gleeful faces in Fallujah make the point: They think we are patsies."[12] Even after the revelations of sadistic torture in Abu Ghraib prison and with evidence that the majority of Iraqis opposed the U.S. occupation, neoconservatives persisted in the insufficient military toughness theme. "Crush the Insurgents in Iraq," bellowed an article in the May 23, 2004 issue of the *Washington Post*, co-authored by prominent New York politician-banker Lewis Lehrman and William Kristol. "The immediate task," they proclaimed, "is . . . the destruction of the armies and militias of the insurgency – not taking and holding territory, not winning the hearts and minds of Iraqis, not conciliating opponents and critics, not gaining the approval of other nations."[13]

Journalist Jim Lobe pointed out that the failure of the American military to be sufficiently ruthless "infuriates the neocons who, despite their constant rhetoric about democracy and the importance of the 'war of ideas,' have always considered military force to be the only language their enemies can ever really understand." Lobe observed: "Precisely how Fallujah or other towns and cities are to be 'conquered' without piling up horrendous civilian casualties that alienate people far beyond Iraq's borders is unclear."[14] Of course, inflaming all the Muslim peoples of the Middle East would serve to hasten the neoconservatives' goal of World War IV against Islam.

Nevertheless, despite all the continued neoconservative spin, the general public had turned against the war by the early summer of 2004. A *Washington Post – ABC News* poll, released on June 22, 2004, revealed that fewer than half of those surveyed – 47 percent – believed that the war in Iraq was worth fighting, while 52 percent said it was not.[15] Fifty-four percent of Americans surveyed in a CNN/USA Today/Gallup poll, conducted June 21–3, 2004, held that the United States made a mistake in sending troops to

Iraq.[16] Public opposition to the war came not only from the continuing casualties and the failure to find WMD but from the revelation of American abuse of Iraqi prisoners at Abu Ghraib, which was revealed by the American media in April 2004 and resulted in a substantial political scandal.

Gaining currency in the media was the notion that the unpopularity of the war was boding ill for the neoconservatives and their war agenda. The neocons, it was maintained, were facing renewed opposition from the realists in the administration and the Republican Party. Numerous neocon opponents were being named: the State Department, the military, the CIA, mainstream Republicans. And, of course, the unpopularity of the war increased the possibility of a Democratic victory in the November elections. Norman Podhoretz wrote of the "gloom that afflicted supporters of the Bush Doctrine in the spring of 2004."[17]

In line with the view that the neocons were faltering, the title of a June 10, 2004 editorial in the *Los Angeles Times* put it: "A Tough Time for 'Neocons.'"[18] Also in June, Jim Lobe titled an article "The Rout of the Neocons."[19] Conservative critic Patrick Buchanan wrote:

> The Night of the Long Knives has begun. The military and CIA are stabbing the neocons front, back and center, laying responsibility on them for the mess in Iraq. Meanwhile, the Balkan wars of the American right have re-ignited, with even the normally quiescent Beltway conservatives scrambling to get clear of the neocon encampment before the tomahawking begins.[20]

In the *Christian Science Monitor* issue of July 13, Howard LaFranchi discussed the issue in an article entitled "In foreign-policy battles, are neocons losing their hold?"[21] Columnist Robert Novak forecast that in Bush's second term, "Getting out of Iraq would end the neoconservative dream of building democracy in the Arab world."[22]

Writing in the *Financial Times* in early July 2004, James Mann, author of *Rise of the Vulcans: The History of Bush's War Cabinet,* opined that "in the wake of America's disastrous occupation of Iraq, the administration seems – in intellectual terms at least – a spent force." He discerned that

> [I]nside the Bush administration, the influence and ideas of the neoconservative movement seem to be in decline. The foreign-policy realism fostered by earlier Republican leaders such as Henry Kissinger and Brent Scowcroft is again ascendant.[23]

Foreign Policy editor Moisés Naím expatiated on the neocons' seeming demise in the journal's September/October 2004 issue:

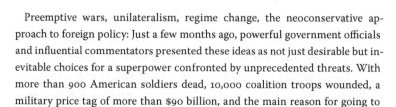

Preemptive wars, unilateralism, regime change, the neoconservative approach to foreign policy: Just a few months ago, powerful government officials and influential commentators presented these ideas as not just desirable but inevitable choices for a superpower confronted by unprecedented threats. With more than 900 American soldiers dead, 10,000 coalition troops wounded, a military price tag of more than $90 billion, and the main reason for going to war dismissed as a "massive intelligence failure," these concepts lie buried in the sands of Iraq.[24]

In August, journalist Martin Sieff commented on the neocons' predicament in *Salon* magazine:

> The neoconservatives who dominate the civilian echelon in the Pentagon and on the National Security Council understandably remain silent. With their every prediction and assurance about Iraq discredited, there is little more they can do but hope for another war, this time with Iran, that will miraculously sweep away all their problems. It is like betting the second mortgage on red when you have already lost your shirt and the roulette wheel is rigged to turn up black.[25]

Besides the developing quagmire in Iraq, other problems beset the neocons. One significant blow was the fall of their leading candidate to rule Iraq, Ahmed Chalabi. Classified U.S. intelligence material was found indicating that Chalabi had passed critical intelligence to Iran. Chalabi had been part of an FBI investigation at least since a raid in May 2004 by Iraqi police and American troops on Chalabi's Baghdad home and the offices of his Iraqi National Congress. Since Chalabi had been a neocon icon, his outing as an apparent Iranian double agent served to discredit them.

Neocons were also consumed by the Valerie Plame investigation. The investigation was triggered by a July 14, 2003, syndicated column by Robert Novak in which he passed on information from a government source which identified Valerie Plame as a CIA operative. Revealing the identity of covert U.S. intelligence agents was illegal.

Plame's husband, former U.S. ambassador Joseph C. Wilson, had been sent by the CIA to Niger in February 2002 to check whether Iraq was trying to get uranium from that country. Wilson, in contrast to the Bush administration's preferred position, maintained that there was no Iraqi connection to the Niger uranium, and he soon would emerge as an opponent of the Iraq war. Novak wrote that two senior administration officials claimed that Wilson's wife, whom they identified as a CIA agent, had proposed him for the trip. Since Plame was working undercover, this exposure ruined her usefulness and her career. An investigation was undertaken to determine whether officials in the administration had sought to undermine Wilson by illegally outing his wife. On December 30, 2003, Patrick Fitzgerald was appointed special counsel to continue the investigation into the Plame affair after then-Attorney General John Ashcroft recused himself from the case because the inquiry would focus on White House personnel, which included such key neocon figures as I. Lewis Libby.[26]

Neoconservatives were also troubled by the investigation of Office of Special Plan's analyst, Larry Franklin, who had passed classified intelligence information to agents of Israel. They were especially upset with the White House's failure to squash the investigation of Franklin, which suggested wrongdoing on the part of a number of pro-Israeli officials at the Defense Department and AIPAC. Anger over the Bush administration's failure to stop this probe was expressed in a memo, alleged to have been written by Michael Rubin, which circulated among neoconservative foreign policy analysts in Washington in early September 2004.[27]

Neocons made a concerted effort to dismiss the importance of the Franklin investigation. In late August, Michael Ledeen belittled the investigation in an article entitled "An Improbable Molehunt" on *National Review* Online.[28] David Frum wrote in *National Review* Online that the entire episode represented the "triumph of media manipulation," and was "a nonstory": whatever transactions occurred between Franklin and the Israelis were just an exchange of "personal opinion," and did not involve classified documents.[29]

Frum maintained that the whole Franklin affair had been orchestrated by enemies of Israel within the government.

> There are figures inside the U.S. government who want to see Israel treated, not as the ally it is by law and treaty (Israel like Japan, Australia, and New Zealand is designated a "major non-NATO ally" for intelligence- and technology-sharing purposes) but as the source of all the trouble in the Middle East and the world. They have injected their own hysterical agenda into the reporting of what would otherwise be a story of an FBI investigation that found nothing much.[30]

It was apparent that the neocons recognized that a significant segment of the establishment opposed their war agenda. And the fact of the matter was that the establishment accusation regarding Franklin was correct, while the neocon effort to dismiss the matter represented a knee-jerk de-

fense of Israel. Franklin would confess to turning over classified documents to Israel in October 2005 and in January 2006 would be sentenced to over 12 year's imprisonment.[31]

One bombshell illustrating establishment opposition to the neocon war agenda from within the federal government was a book entitled *Imperial Hubris: Why the West is Losing the War on Terror*, anonymously authored by Michael Scheuer, a veteran CIA analyst who headed the Agency's bin Laden unit in the late 1990s. While not listed as the author of the book, the author's CIA background made Scheuer's identity transparent. *Imperial Hubris* instantly became a *New York Times* best seller. Scheuer essentially rejected the fundamental positions of America's "war on terrorism," as crafted by the neocons. It was unprecedented that a serving CIA officer was permitted to publish a book that criticized basic American policy. That this was allowed indicated that opposition to the existing neoconservative-directed policy was rife in the high echelons of the CIA.

Scheuer argued that U.S. leaders had failed to recognize that bin Laden and his followers were not evil, apocalyptic terrorists with unlimited global goals, as the Bush administration proclaimed, but rather practical warriors with a specific and limited set of policy goals. Scheuer maintained that they saw themselves as pursuing a "defensive jihad;" they did not hate America because of "what America is," as the Bush administration would have it, but "rather from their plausible perception that the things they most love and value – God, Islam, their brethren, and Muslim lands – are being attacked by America."[32] In short, it was America's policies in the Middle East that the Islamic radicals detested and tried to resist. Among those policies, Scheuer cited the United States' unlimited support for Israel's occupation of Palestine, its propping up of "apostate" Arab puppet governments, its exploitation of Middle East oil resources, and its military occupation of Muslim land. In these views, emphasized Scheuer, Osama bin Ladin and the militant Islamists had the support of most of the Muslim world. And the American war on Iraq had the effect of validating those views among the general Muslim populace. Scheuer was most provocative in dealing with the taboo issue of the Israeli-orientation of American Middle East foreign policy, which he termed a "one-way alliance." Supported by "U.S. citizen-spies," "wealthy Jewish-American organizations," and various other American domestic groups, Scheuer wrote, "The Israelis have succeeded in lacing tight the ropes binding the American Gulliver to the tiny Jewish state and its policies."[33]

David Frum was outraged by Scheuer's work, which he described as an "alarming book, but not in the way its author intended. It delivers an urgent danger signal – not about al-Qaeda, but about intelligence services staffed with analysts who think the way the author of this book thinks."[34] He concluded:

> What distinguishes Scheuer's approach from that of, say, Michael Moore is that Scheuer is not an ignorant activist, but a person charged with informing the nation's leaders about the terrorist threat. It is disturbing, at the least, that a man who had such a large role in defending the nation from Islamic extremism seems to have been mentally captivated by it. I have a strong feeling that Scheuer's 15 minutes of fame have ended already. His book is no longer seen in the shop windows; its ranking on Amazon drops daily. But the spirit of appeasement that produced this book has not, alas, vanished – not from inside the national-security agencies, nor from the larger policy community.[35]

In short, Frum acknowledged and bemoaned the fact that Scheuer did not stand alone; many intelligence professionals, and other members of the American establishment, adamantly opposed the neocon World War IV agenda.

Faced with numerous difficulties, the neoconservatives re-energized their effort to continue and expand the war in the Middle East by reviving the Cold War era Committee on the Present Danger on July 20, 2004 to fight "Islamic terrorism." Chairing the resurrected committee was James Woolsey, the former CIA director. Honorary chairmen were Senators Joe Lieberman (Democrat, Connecticut) and Jon Kyl (Republican, Arizona). Many of the members had neocon connections: Kenneth Adelman, Linda Chavez, Eliot Cohen, Midge Decter, Frank Gaffney (CSP), Max Kampelman, Jeane Kirkpatrick, Joshua Muravchik (AEI), Laurie Mylroie (AEI), Danielle Pletka (AEI), Norman Podhoretz, Michael Rubin (AEI), Randy Scheunemann (Committee for the Liberation of Iraq), Ben Wattenberg, Michael Horowitz (Hudson), Dov S. Zakheim, and Nina Rosenwald (Chairman, Board of Directors, Middle East Media and Research Institute).[36]

James Woolsey said that in its new incarnation the Committee on the Present Danger would combat what he called "a totalitarian movement masquerading as a religion." He continued that the danger that we must address is a danger to the United States but also a danger to democracy and civil society throughout the world, and it is very much our hope to be of support and assistance to those who seek to bring democracy and civil society to the part of the world, the Middle East extended, to which this Islamist terror is now resonant in and generated from.[37]

Despite the all the aforementioned problems, on the presidential campaign trail Bush and Cheney vehemently defended the war and the neocon themes that the administration had adopted. In fact, they often seemed oblivious to the negative developments in the war. In a speech before the National Guard Association in September, 2004, Bush proclaimed that "Our strategy is succeeding . . . . We have led, many have joined, and America and the world are safer."[38] In late October, Cheney referred to the American war in Iraq as "a remarkable success story to date."[39]

Justin Raimondo acidly commented on Bush's roseate depiction of the war:

> Iraq rapidly approaches meltdown, but President Pangloss isn't worried: "Our strategy," boasted George W. Bush to the National Guard last Tuesday, "is succeeding." I keep asking myself what world are he and his advisors living in, momentarily forgetting about the post-9/11 tear in the space-time continuum that catapulted us all into Bizarro World, where up is down, good is bad, and success means abject failure.[40]

Given the sagging public support for the war in Iraq, and the growing opposition by establishment elements, even from within the executive branch, it would have seemed that a change in foreign policy was highly likely. But this was not actually the case, since opposition to the war did not much have much impact on the political realm, especially regarding the election of the president. And it is the president who has the power to determine American foreign policy.

Although it would have seemed that Bush was ripe for defeat, the Democrats did not capitalize on the war issue. Even though the Democratic grassroots were heavily anti-war, the presidential election of 2004 offered little choice regarding Iraq, since John Kerry, the Democratic nominee, advocated virtually the same policy. "Even today," acknowledged pro-neocon Dinesh D'Souza in May 2004,

> there is surprising consensus of opinion regarding Iraq within our national leadership. Even the *New York Times* recently reported that the Iraq policies of Bush and Kerry shared many similarities. They both support the June 30 transi-

tion to civilian power, an increase in U.S. troops if necessary, and no deadline for bringing our troops home.[41]

In essence, the Kerry foreign policy would be neoconservatism without neoconservatives, or at least without the same neoconservatives. As Justin Raimondo put it:

> Kerry, who, in formulating his foreign policy positions, seems as though he might have consulted those volumes of *Commentary* and books on the glories of empire that adorn Feith's shelves. Kerry wants more troops in Iraq, and is apparently conducting a contest with Bush to see who can more slavishly accede to every Israeli demand.[42]

Kerry supported the war on Iraq from the very beginning, and, at times, he had argued for a more extensive military occupation of Iraq than the one pursued by the Bush administration. In a speech to the prestigious Council on Foreign Relations in December 2003, Kerry berated the Bush administration for "considering what is tantamount to a cut and run strategy. Their sudden embrace of accelerated Iraqification and American troop withdrawal without adequate stability is an invitation to failure."[43] Kerry's foreign policy adviser, Rand Beers, said that Kerry "would not rule out the possibility" of sending additional American troops to Iraq to effectively carry out the occupation.[44]

Kerry would seek America's allies, especially NATO, to help with the task of occupying Iraq. "Our goal should be an alliance commitment to deploy a major portion of the peacekeeping force that will be needed in Iraq for a long time to come," he wrote in the *Washington Post* on July 4, 2004.[45] Kerry and his supporters made much of his multilateral approach to Iraq compared to Bush's unilateralism. Originally, this difference possessed considerable validity. Bush, however, by the spring of 2004 was moving in the direction of seeking international support, including the involvement of the United Nations in Iraq.

Kerry underscored his pro-war bona fides by his novel effort to recruit neocon favorite Senator John McCain as his vice-presidential running mate.[46] One area where Kerry was definitely more in line with the neoconservatives than Bush was his hostility toward Saudi Arabia, which neoconservatives had targeted for regime change. Interestingly, Kerry was supported in this view by such key opponents of the Iraq war as Michael Moore, producer of the anti-Bush film, "Fahrenheit 9/11," who suggested that the Saudi government was behind the September 11 attacks. It also should be added that Kerry, whose credibility was undamaged, could conceivably have pursued a neocon-like harder line better than could the Bush administration, whose credibility was much-tarnished.

The crux of the matter was that American policy on the war in Iraq could not be changed by the ballot box. The American people were simply not given a choice on the issue of war in the 2004 election. No leading candidate was mobilizing support against the war. The campaign provided no open debate on the war that could possibly educate the large segment of the public that did not understand the issue, or were still confused by administration propaganda. Only meagerly funded minor candidates such as Ralph Nader opposed the war. Opponents of the war were overwhelmingly backing Kerry as the lesser of two evils.[47] All of this guaranteed that even if the neoconservatives themselves would no longer hold the reins of government power, the policy that they established in the Middle East could largely continue.

chapter 14

BEGINNING OF THE SECOND ADMINISTRATION

AFTER THE 2004 ELECTION, which Bush won by a relatively slender margin, it became apparent that the neocons had managed to weather their difficulties and come out on top. The pre-election conjectures about their impending demise were completely off base. "Far from being headed for the political graveyard," Jacob Heilbrunn of the *Los Angeles Times* observed, "neoconservatives are poised to become even more powerful in a second Bush term, while the 'realists' – those who believe that moral crusading is costly and counterproductive in foreign policy – are sidelined."[1] As Scott McConnell, editor of the *American Conservative*, sardonically commented:

> Among educated Americans, they [the realists] won the foreign-policy debate decisively . . . . But the realists did not win the debate inside Bush's brain – indeed, there is no sign at all that the president was aware that there was a foreign-policy debate going on.[2]

What the neocons would face in the beginning of Bush's second term, however, was not a powerful "realist" opposition from within the administration but the realities of the external situation – both the obvious difficulties in advancing the neocon war agenda and the flagging public support for war.

President Bush proclaimed the public's decision to reelect him as a ratification of his approach toward Iraq and that, consequently, there was no reason to hold any administration officials accountable for mistakes or misjudgments in prewar planning or in managing the violent aftermath. "We had an accountability moment, and that's called the 2004 elections,"

Bush triumphantly declared in an interview with the *Washington Post*. "The American people listened to different assessments made about what was taking place in Iraq, and they looked at the two candidates, and chose me."[3] In reality, of course, the American people didn't have much of a choice in the election, since Democrat John Kerry also supported the continuation of the war.[4]

In the aftermath of the election, a number of moves were made to solidify even further the domination of the neoconservatives and their agenda in the Bush administration, which entailed the purging of dissident elements. "Bush regards the election as a vindication of his Iraq policy. All the naysayers, the doubters, the defeatists have emerged as losers," said Jonathan Clarke of the libertarian Cato Institute, co-author of *America Alone: The Neo-conservatives and the Global Order.* "The neocons are feeling quite confident right now. Things are breaking their way. A group of people who in any rational culture should be looking for other jobs are being promoted."[5] Robert Scheer pointed out that "by successfully discarding those who won't buy into the administration's ideological fantasies of remaking the world in our image, the neoconservatives have consolidated control of the United States' vast military power."[6]

The shake-up of the CIA was launched by Porter Goss, a former Republican congressman from Florida, who became director in September 2004. Numerous problems had been acknowledged in the CIA, highlighted by the failure to detect the plans for the September 11, 2001 terrorist attack. Most knowledgeable observers concurred that the CIA, along with the rest of the U.S. intelligence community, was in serious need of reform. However, the basis for the post-election staff changes seemed to be loyalty to the Bush administration policies. As a *New York Times* editorial stated:

> No one who has read the 9/11 commission's report or the Senate Intelligence Committee's report on the prewar intelligence on Iraq could doubt the need to shake things up in the intelligence apparatus. It's also important to allow the head of a major government agency to make changes without undue second-guessing. But what Mr. Goss is doing at the Central Intelligence Agency is starting to seem less like reform and more like a political purge.[7]

Furthermore, "If accountability for past failures is the issue driving the resignations," former CIA officer Philip Giraldi aptly observed,

> several senior agency officers wonder why no one at any level has been pressured to resign for failing to perform adequately. A CIA Inspector General re-

port that actually names those responsible for the 9/11 intelligence failure is being suppressed by Goss, while a memo circulated to all employees emphasizing that CIA staffers must "support the Administration and its policies" suggests that personnel changes are intended to stamp out opposition and dissent and to establish a litmus test of loyalty to White House policies as a sine qua non for senior-level employment.[8]

The *New York Times* wrote regarding the CIA shake-up:

> Mr. Goss has removed the head of the clandestine operations division and his deputy – both career intelligence officers. The No. 2 C.I.A. official, John McLaughlin, has resigned, along with four other senior people. Others are reported to be thinking about leaving. Many of them feel trampled by Mr. Goss's inner circle of political operatives from the House, where he was chairman of the Intelligence Committee.[9]

Also departing the CIA was Michael Scheuer, the anonymous author of *Imperial Hubris*, who had savaged the war on Iraq. In early November 2004, Scheuer had been defiantly declaring that he would stay on:

> I'm proud to work [at the CIA], and they can say what they want about me, but I have no intention of leaving. They may force me to leave, they may fire me. But it's the best place to work that I know of. I'm proud to be an intelligence officer, and I want to stay one.[10]

Shortly thereafter, however, Scheuer, who had been thoroughly gagged, resigned from the agency with the comment: "I've never experienced this much anxiety and controversy." And he added: "Suddenly political affiliation matters to some degree. The talk is that they're out to clean out Democrats and liberals."[11]

The CIA purge was noted and defended by some neocons as a means of exerting political control over unelected bureaucrats. As neoconservative columnist David Brooks wrote in the *New York Times*:

> It is time to reassert harsh authority so CIA employees know they must defer to the people who win elections, so they do not feel free at meetings to spout off about their contempt of the White House, so they do not go around to their counterparts from other nations and tell them to ignore American policy.[12]

Michael Ledeen had advocated a purge from the very beginning of the Bush administration in March 2001 when he brazenly asserted that "a good old-fashioned purge by the new administration will do wonders for the loyalty of its bureaucrats." Among those he wanted removed were "foreign-policy types on the National Security Council Staff and throughout State,

CIA, and Defense, who are still trying to create Bill Clinton's legacy in the Middle East."[13]

It became apparent that in the CIA dissent from the Bush administration line had become verboten.[14] Shortly after the November election, Goss sent CIA staff a controversial memorandum demanding that they support administration policy: "We support the administration and its policies in our work and as agency employees we do not identify with, support or champion opposition to the administration or its policies." Administration spin-doctors tried to claim that Goss was merely telling his employees to carry out their assignments, but Vincent Cannistraro, a former head of the CIA's counter-terrorist center, accurately observed: "It can only be interpreted one way – there will be no more dissenting opinions."[15]

It was apparent that there had been considerable opposition to the Bush administration war policy in the Middle East by members of the CIA, who leaked information to the media. Investigative reporter Seymour Hersh interpreted the CIA shake-up as an effort to remove any impediments to the neocon war agenda. The task assigned to Goss

> was to get rid of a number of analysts, senior analysts, who work for the intelligence side of the CIA, old-timers who have been skeptical of many of the White House's and Pentagon's operations, and so, as somebody said to me, they really went after the apostates, and they want only true believers in there. That's what the mission has been.[16]

In early January 2005, Haviland Smith, a retired CIA station chief, wrote, "It seems quite possible that the service is being punished for having been right, or at least unsupportive of administration policy." He continued by pointing out that "[t]he agency's statutory responsibility is to speak the truth, whether the truth supports the president's plans or not. It would appear that this concept is not shared by this administration."[17]

While the major shake-up was taking place in the CIA, lesser changes were being made in other parts of the executive branch. Secretary of State Powell, who had provided some resistance, albeit largely ineffectual, to the neoconservative war agenda, would be replaced by Condoleezza Rice. As national security advisor, Rice had served as a mouthpiece for the neoconservatives. Although Rice was not a initially an adherent of neoconservative foreign policy, but rather a protégé of Scowcroft and an exponent of "realism," she consistently toed the neocon war line after September 11,

2001 during Bush's first term. As secretary of state, Rice would follow a more eclectic position, combining neocon elements with "realist" ones.

Moving up into Rice's position as national security advisor was Stephen Hadley, a close associate of the neocons. As Tom Barry, a critic of the neocons, put it:

> The appointment of Hadley as National Security Adviser, following the announced departure of Colin Powell and the nomination of Vulcan team leader Rice, was a clear indication that during his second administration President Bush intends to continue the hard-line global security agenda outlined by the circle of Vulcans. Furthermore, the promotions of Hadley and Rice demonstrated Bush's determination to surround the White House with loyalists that adhere to his view that U.S. national security operations should be unencumbered by facts, dissenting opinions, or international law. All means – including the use of nuclear weapons and first-strike warfare – are justified by the ends of winning what the Vulcans describe as the "global war on terrorism."[18]

Elliott Abrams, who was appointed deputy national security adviser with a focus on promoting global democracy and human rights, would become the brains behind Bush's mission to remake the Middle East. Other changes saw John Bolton becoming Ambassador to the United Nations; neocon Eric Edelman being appointed to replace Douglas Feith as undersecretary of defense for policy; and non-neocon Gordon England being appointed to replace deputy secretary of defense Wolfowitz, who went on to head the World Bank. All in all, the neocon staff was probably no more numerous and probably slightly less influential than it was in Bush's first administration. But within the executive branch, high profile opponents of their agenda had been removed or silenced.

While Bush's reelection allowed a purge of dissidents from the administration, it did nothing to dampen the popular opposition to the war, which was growing as the situation in Iraq seemed to worsen. A December 2004 poll released by ABC News and the *Washington Post* showed 56 percent of those questioned describing the war as not worth fighting.[19] A National Annenberg Election Survey, conducted in mid-January 2005, found 54 percent of those polled responding that the war on Iraq was a mistake, compared to 40 percent who supported the decision.[20]

A *Los Angeles Times* poll conducted in mid-January 2005 revealed that the percentage of Americans who believed that the situation in Iraq was "worth going to war over" had fallen to a new low of 39 percent dropping

5 percentage points since October 2004. The *Times* also reported that 37 percent of the public advocated withdrawing at least some troops immediately; 47 percent of those surveyed said they would like to see most of the troops out within a year. Only 4 percent advocated sending more troops, a position then advocated by much of the establishment media, such as *The New York Times*.[21]

It would seem that reality was inhibiting the further implementation of the neocon war agenda. The conventional view was that the United States could not launch a wider war because it did not have the military wherewithal to do so. Military manpower was simply stretched to the breaking point.[22] As war critic Patrick Buchanan observed in December 2004:

> What appears to be happening is this: While there is no shortage of neocon war plans for a Pax Americana, President Bush is bumping up against reality – a U.S. Army tied down and bleeding in Iraq, the rising costs of war, soaring deficits, a sinking dollar, and an absence of allies willing to fight beside us or even help.[23]

And the difficulties in the occupation of Iraq provided a basis for establishment critics of the war to call for military withdrawal for the good of other global responsibilities. Although the opposition to the neocons within the administration had been largely silenced, there was still opposition from the realists outside, and because of the dire situation in Iraq that opposition was resonating with the public.

In January 2005, members of the foreign policy elite such as Brzezinski and Scowcroft started to call for an exit from Iraq. Brzezinski emphasized the escalating costs of the military enterprise:

> While our ultimate objectives are very ambitious, we will never achieve democracy and stability without being willing to commit 500,000 troops, spend $200 billion a year, probably have a draft, and have some form of war compensation. As a society, we are not prepared to do that.[24]
>
> The Soviet Union could have won the war in Afghanistan too had it been prepared to do its equivalent of what I just mentioned,

Brzezinski continued.

> But even the Soviet Union was not prepared to do that because there comes a point in the life of a nation when such sacrifices are not justified . . . and only time will tell if the United States is facing a moment of wisdom, or is resigned to cultural decay.[25]

In a speech at Rice University, former Secretary of State James Baker advised the Bush administration to consider a phased withdrawal of all U.S.

troops in Iraq. "Any appearance of a permanent occupation of Iraq," Baker asserted, would "both undermine domestic support here in the United States and play directly into the hands of those in the Middle East who – however wrongly – suspect us of imperial design."[26]

James Dobbins of the influential Rand Corporation bluntly asserted that "The beginning of wisdom is to realize that the United States can't win." The United States should

> develop new consultative arrangements to engage all of Iraq's neighbors, as well as its allies across the Atlantic, and secure their active cooperation in stabilizing Iraq, thereby creating the conditions for an early drawdown and, eventually, for a complete withdrawal of U.S. forces.[27]

Leftist war critic Andrew Cockburn assessed the divergent opinions among the elite in mid-January 2005. "The political establishment is split," Cockburn noted.

> James Baker certainly speaks for the oil industry, and most of corporate America thinks America has problems far more pressing than Iraq. The libertarian, and old conservative wing of the Republican Party has never liked this war.
>
> But the Israel lobby, which pitched the war to Bush and got America into it, is still deeply committed and retains considerable power both in the government, the Congress and the para-government of Institutes, Centers and Think-tanks that throttle Washington like kudzu.[28]

But having had their opponents within the Bush administration removed or silenced, the neoconservatives did not intend to abandon their Middle East war agenda because of the difficulties in Iraq, flagging public support, and opposition from the realist elite. Rather, new offensives elsewhere could divert attention from the Iraq morass. The primacy of the neocon agenda in the Bush administration was made manifest in the president's Second Inaugural Address on January 20, 2005. Bush stressed in unqualified terms that the major policy priority of his second term in office would be to "seek and support the growth of democratic movements and institutions in every nation and culture, with the ultimate goal of ending tyranny in our world." The war on terrorism had morphed into a war for freedom and democracy, the purpose of which was not simply to help others but to defend America. "The survival of liberty in our land," Bush pronounced, "increasingly depends on the success of liberty in other lands." He averred that ending tyranny would not be "primarily the task of arms, though we will defend ourselves and our friends by force of arms when necessary."[29]

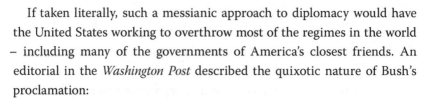

If taken literally, such a messianic approach to diplomacy would have the United States working to overthrow most of the regimes in the world – including many of the governments of America's closest friends. An editorial in the *Washington Post* described the quixotic nature of Bush's proclamation:

> The president is proposing an extraordinary escalation of national aims, but it's not clear what practical action, if any, he has in mind. Inaugural addresses are meant to outline large themes rather than prosaic programs, but Mr. Bush's text seemed exceptional in its untethering from the world.[30]

The ideas for Bush's speech derived from *The Case for Democracy: The Power of Freedom to Overcome Tyranny and Terror* by Israeli Natan Sharansky, a former Soviet dissident who had been connected with the neoconservatives since the 1970s. Bush had become so enamored with this book that he invited Sharansky into the Oval Office in early November 2004 for an hourlong discussion of the book and how it applied to the war on terrorism. (Sharansky would be honored with the Presidential Medal of Freedom in December 2006.) Obviously, since Bush rarely read anything, not even the newspapers, Sharansky's book must have been passed on to him by his neocon advisors. And input for the inaugural address did come from Elliott Abrams, William Kristol, and columnist Charles Krauthammer.[31]

Natan Sharansky was, at that time of Bush's Second Inaugural, the Israeli minister of social and Diaspora affairs in the Sharon government and leader of Yisrael Ba'aliyah, the Russian immigrants' party. Most notably, Sharansky was a very hard-line supporter of Israeli control of the West Bank and the Jewish settlements there. As *Washington Post* reporter Dana Milbank observed, he was "so hawkish that he has accused Ariel Sharon of being soft on the Palestinians."[32]

William Kristol editorialized gleefully in the *Weekly Standard* that Bush's inaugural speech represented the adoption of the neoconservative democracy agenda. Kristol titled his ecstatic article, "On Tyranny," referring to the title of a leading work by the guru of many of the neocons, Leo Strauss. Kristol rhapsodically proclaimed that

> Informed by Strauss and inspired by Paine, appealing to Lincoln and alluding to Truman, beginning with the Constitution and ending with the Declaration, with Biblical phrases echoing throughout – George W. Bush's Second Inaugural was a powerful and subtle speech.

It will also prove to be a historic speech. Less than three and a half years after 9/11, Bush's Second Inaugural moves American foreign policy beyond the war on terror to the larger struggle against tyranny. It grounds Bush's foreign policy – American foreign policy – in American history and American principles. If actions follow words and success greets his efforts, then President Bush will have ushered in a new era in American foreign policy.[33]

The democracy theme of Bush's inaugural address confirmed the intended continuation of the neoconservative agenda as the cynosure of his second administration. As political commentator Andrew Sullivan put it: "The speech was a deep rebuke to conservative foreign policy realists."[34] And Bush had already gotten rid of one of the last vestiges of conservative "realism" from his administration when he unceremoniously removed Brent Scowcroft, his father's closest associate and friend, as chairman of the Foreign Intelligence Advisory Board.[35]

But how would the neoconservative policy be implemented with the U.S. military having its hands full occupying Iraq? It did not take long at all after Bush's re-election, however, for the tensions with Iran and Syria to escalate.

The greatest actual tensions developed with Syria, the weaker of the two countries. A brief summary of U.S.-Syrian relations may be helpful. During the Cold War, the United States was not friendly with Syria, which had been supported by the Soviet Union, but it did not take an aggressive stance toward the country, either. "Washington has long considered Syria, in terms of the region's strategic environment," writes Middle East specialist Flynt Leverett,

as somewhere in between those states well-disposed toward a negotiated peace with Israel and strategic cooperation with the United States (Egypt, Jordan, the states of the Gulf Cooperation Council, and the more moderate North African regimes, along with Turkey on the region's perimeter), on the one hand, and those states opposed or strongly resistant to such developments (the Islamic Republic of Iran and Iraq under Saddam Hussein), on the other.[36]

The United States regarded Syria as a sponsor of terrorism and was concerned about its pursuit of weapons of mass destruction. However, Syria cooperated with the United States in the 1991 Gulf War against Iraq. And the United States largely acquiesced in Syria's presence in Lebanon, although the withdrawal of Syrian troops was a stated American goal.[37]

In the aftermath of the September 11 attacks, Syria began limited cooperation with U.S. in the global war against terrorism. Syria shared intelligence on Al Qaeda and other terrorist groups with the United States. Syria's President Bashar Assad wanted this intelligence connection to expand to broader cooperation in other spheres, and, to demonstrate his bona fides, he indicated that he would be willing to alter his relationship with those terrorist groups with which Syria maintained ties. Neoconservatives in the Bush administration were adamantly opposed to accepting any help from Syria, much less developing any stronger diplomatic engagement, claiming that a positive relationship with a state sponsor of terrorism would undercut the integrity of the United States' war on terrorism. In the end, no rapprochement between the United States and Syria materialized.[38]

Syria was a neoconservative target in the overall design to weaken Israel's enemies. For example, it was named as such in the 1996 "Clean Break" agenda provided to incoming Prime Minister Netanyahu, which noted that Syria's position would be seriously weakened by the removal of Saddam Hussein in Iraq. As David Wurmser had put it in his "Coping with Crumbling States": "events in Iraq can shake Syria's position in Lebanon."[39]

A study titled "Ending Syria's Occupation of Lebanon: The U.S. Role?," produced in 2000 by neoconservative Daniel Pipe's Middle East Forum and Ziad Abdelnour's U.S. Committee for a Free Lebanon, called for the United States to force Syria from Lebanon and to disarm it of its alleged weapons of mass destruction. The study castigated past United States policy for its failure to confront the Assad regime. Among the document's signatories were such neoconservative stalwarts as Elliott Abrams, David Wurmser, Douglas Feith, Richard Perle, Jeane Kirkpatrick, Michael Ledeen, and Frank Gaffney.[40]

Once the United States invaded Iraq in March 2003, the Bush administration began to give greater attention to Syria. In April 2003, citing reports that the Syrian regime was harboring Iraqi leaders and WMD, Wolfowitz asserted that "There's got to be a change in Syria."[41] In early May, Secretary of State Powell visited Syria and told Assad that his government had to consider the "new strategic situation" that existed in the region after Iraq's occupation, implying that Syria would have to accede to American demands for better behavior or face negative consequences.[42]

Some Israeli leaders were seeing Syria as the next target. "Now that Saddam Hussein's regime has collapsed, it's time for a change in Syria, too," said IDF General Amos Gilad on April 10, 2003. Gilad held that Syria was the center for global terrorist organizations. "The collapse of the Iraqi regime removes Syria's strategic base," Gilad emphasized, "and causes Syria to be isolated – especially with the U.S. discovering, to its astonishment, the tight cooperation between Saddam Hussein and Bashar Assad."[43]

On September 16, 2003, Under Secretary of Arms Control and International Security John R. Bolton appeared before the House International Relations Committee to identify Syria among a handful of countries whose alleged pursuit of biological and chemical weapons made them threats to international stability. Moreover, Bolton claimed that Syria not only backed Hezbollah and other terrorist elements in Lebanon, but also allowed foreign terrorists to enter Iraq from Syria.[44]

In December 2003, President Bush signed into law the Syria Accountability and Lebanese Sovereignty Restoration Act of 2003, which provided for the imposition of a series of sanctions against Syria if it failed to terminate its support for Palestinian terrorist groups, end its military presence in Lebanon, cease its development of weapons of mass destruction, and stop any activities that would impede the stabilization of Iraq. In May 2004, the Bush administration determined that Syria had not met these conditions and implemented new sanctions on Syria.[45] On September 2, 2004, the United Nations Security Council, as a result of American pressure, passed Security Council Resolution 1559, mandating a complete Syrian withdrawal from Lebanon and the disarming of Hezbollah, a foe of Israel.

After Bush's reelection in November 2004, neoconservatives focused more attention on Syria. Analysts associated with the Foundation for the Defense of Democracies (FDD), a neoconservative group whose advisors included Richard Perle, William Kristol, Charles Krauthammer, and Frank Gaffney, published an op-ed piece in the *Washington Times* on December 6, 2004, titled "Syria's Murderous Role," which presented a litany of Syrian misdeeds.[46]

Shortly thereafter, a lead editorial in the *Weekly Standard* by William Kristol appeared in which he emphasized that the United States had an urgent and dire "Syria problem." "Of course we also have – the world also has – an Iran problem, and a Saudi problem, and lots of other problems," Kristol explained.

> The Iran and Saudi problems may ultimately be more serious than the Syria problem. But the Syria problem is urgent: It is Bashar Assad's regime that seems to be doing more than any other, right now, to help Baathists and terrorists kill Americans in the central front of the war on terror.

It was thus essential for the United States "to get serious about dealing with Syria as part of winning in Iraq, and in the broader Middle East."[47]

In early February 2005, Secretary of State Rice said that Syria had been "unhelpful in a number of ways," including supporting the insurgency in Iraq and undermining Lebanon's political system by maintaining troops in that country. "It is just not acceptable that Syria would continue to be a place from which terrorists are funded and helped to destroy the very fragile peace process in the Middle East or to change the dynamic of events in Lebanon."[48]

Then came the assassination of the popular former Lebanese Prime Minister Rafik Hariri on February 14, 2005. While riding in a motorcade in a seaside area of Beirut, Hariri was killed in a massive bomb blast. Immediately after Hariri's assassination, the United States placed the blame on Syria and recalled its ambassador from Damascus.

The Syrian government bore the brunt of Lebanese and international outrage at the murder because of its extensive military and intelligence influence in Lebanon, as well as the public rift between Hariri and Damascus that occurred just before his last resignation from office. The obvious effect of the Hariri murder was to put the global spotlight on Syria and its misdeeds. It thus strengthened the neoconservatives, who, from the beginning of the administration had considered using Lebanon as a means of getting at Syria.[49]

Israel was the major beneficiary of Hariri's assassination. Weakening Syria was definitely a key component of Likudnik, if not overall Israeli, geostrategic thinking.[50] Syria had played a major role in trying to prevent Israeli hegemony in the region. In part, Israel opposed Syria because of the latter's crucial support for Hezbollah along with other anti-Israeli armed groups. Hezbollah was the only Arab entity ever to actually defeat Israel, when it forced it to withdraw its military from South Lebanon in 2000. Moreover, Hezbollah had acquired the military capability to deter Israel from invading Lebanon with impunity, as it had often done in the past, and it joined with Syria in its confrontation with Israel over the latter's occupation of the Golan Heights. Hezbollah also blocked Israel's quest for the water of southern Lebanon's Litani River, which Israeli planners have believed to be vital for their nation's growing water needs. Furthermore, the expulsion of Syrian troops from Lebanon could bring about a Lebanese government more pliable to Israeli pressure, especially since Israel could then fill the military vacuum left by Syria.[51]

On March 5, 2005, after intense international pressure, President Bashar Assad made a speech before the Syrian Parliament, in which he announced that Syria would complete a full military withdrawal from Lebanon by May of 2005. Syria pulled out its remaining military forces from Lebanon on April 26, 2005.

The departure of Syrian troops from Lebanon could have a drastic effect on Syria itself. According to Flynt Leverett, the Bush "administration has accepted an assessment of Syrian politics that, by forcing Syria out of Lebanon, this regime is not going to be able to recover from that blow and will start to unravel."[52] Syria, Leverett observed, was a "'fragile mosaic' of ethnic and sectarian communities," held together only by the iron hand of the Assad family.[53]

The findings of the UN investigation into Hariri's assassination, headed by German magistrate Detlev Mehlis, came out in October 2005. Though stopping short of directly accusing Assad or his inner circle, the report blamed Syria for failing to cooperate with the investigation and held that the Hariri assassination plot must have had the blessing of Syrian security officials. Nevertheless, Syrian involvement was far from proven conclusively, and the continued UN probe later moved away from implicating Syrian government officials.[54]

Following the release of the UN report, the United States cut nearly all contact with the Syrian government, as part of its campaign to isolate Assad's regime. Even before the UN report came out, the United States was ratcheting up the pressure on Syria. In September, the U.S. ambassador to Iraq, Zalmay Khalilzad, who had been closely connected with the neocons – his connection included an affiliation with PNAC – directly accused Syria of aiding the insurgents in Iraq and said that America's "patience is running out with Syria."[55]

There were reports of American military cross-border operations in the summer of 2005 aimed at cutting off the alleged flow of insurgents spilling into Iraq. Some of these activities reportedly led to clashes with Syrian forces and the death of Syrian troops.[56]

While Israel wanted to weaken Syria, there was an apparent disagreement as to how far the weakening of Syria should go. Although some Israeli officials advocated regime change, others feared that such a radical move might lead to the rise of a fundamentalist Islamic regime in Damascus, which would be more threatening to Israel.[57]

Israeli legislator Yuval Steinitz, a member of Israel's ruling Likud Party and head of parliament's Defense and Foreign Affairs Committee, called for regime change in Damascus. "As far as I am concerned . . . and here I have a dispute with some of the people in the (Israeli) security establishment, it is not just an American interest but a clear Israeli interest to end the Assad dynasty and replace Bashar Assad."[58]

However, the fact that then-Vice Premier Shimon Peres of the Labor Party leaned toward regime change showed that significant support for the more extreme position transcended party lines. "I think there needs to be change in Syria," Peres told Israel Radio.[59] "If it is true that the (Syrian) government is involved in the murder (of Hariri), this will shake up the rule of the Assads."[60]

While Syria was extremely vulnerable to American power and pressure, it was of secondary concern as an actual danger. The fundamental concern was Iran, a populous nation that was believed to be striving to dominate post-Saddam Iraq and to develop nuclear weapons that would eliminate Israel's nuclear monopoly – the linchpin of the latter's hegemonical position in the Middle East. Just as important, if not more so, Iran was a major supporter of Hezbollah and had become the chief proponent of Palestinian resistance to the Jewish state.

A brief summary of the American position vis-à-vis Iran is called for. Shortly prior to 9/11, while the neoconservatives pushed a strongly hostile position on Iran, a number of elite elements in the United States had advocated improved relations. Oil companies, for example, wanted to end sanctions on Iran.

Following the events of September 11, 2001, American and Iranian interests found much in common in the American war in Afghanistan. Iran had already been the primary sponsor of the Northern Alliance in the effort to bring down the Taliban regime and was quite willing to collaborate with the United States, contributing to America's successes in Afghanistan in 2001. The State Department and the CIA played a major role in seeking collaboration with Iran. Secretary of State Powell, in line with the general thinking within the State Department, wanted this development to be the start of an strategic opening to the Iranian government, not simply a focus on the tactical issues of the war in Afghanistan. However, his proposal to move in this detentist direction was blocked by hard-line neoconservatives in the administration.[61]

This budding improvement in U.S.-Iranian relations was cut short in January 2002. Israel intercepted an Iranian-owned freighter, the Karine A, loaded with arms said to be en route from Iran to Palestinian resistance groups. Whether the Iranian government was involved in this effort was uncertain. The Iranians denied involvement. The Israeli government claimed otherwise. Washington believed the Israelis. No matter what the truth of the matter, it was, as described by Trita Parsi, author of *Treacherous Alliance: The Secret Dealings of Israel, Iran, and the United States*, a "heaven-sent gift for Sharon." Parsi writes that "To the Bush administration, any doubt that may have existed about Iran's continued ties to terrorism was removed. This was a major setback for proponents of dialogue with Iran such as Powell."[62]

Furthermore, the Israelis began warning of Iran's dangerous nuclear weapons ambitions. Consequently, Iran was then named as part of the "Axis of Evil" in Bush's State of the Union Address on January 29, 2002.[63] This rhetorical attack would have a major impact on Iran, undermining its belief in the possibility of rapprochement with the United States. Parsi contends that "Tehran was shocked. Khatami's [Iran's moderate president] policy of détente and the help Iran provided the United States in Afghanistan was for naught."[64] Iranian hard-liners believed that their distrust of America had been confirmed. This was exactly what Israeli and their neocon supporters wanted to happen.

Despite the heightening tensions, Iran still sought rapprochement with the United States in order to end the hostility that had existed since the Iranian revolution of 1979, which overthrew the pro-American Shah. Talks resumed as the United States prepared to attack Iraq. Iran was fearful of the geopolitical implications of such an attack, which would result in Iran's encirclement, but when they saw the attack as inevitable they believed that limited cooperation with the United States was the best approach to take. Cooperation provided by Iran did not reach the levels achieved in the war in Afghanistan in 2001, but Iran especially helped the United States by instructing its Shiite supporters in Iraq to cooperate in the reconstruction of the country rather than engaging in resistance to the occupation.[65]

The easy American defeat of Saddam's forces induced an intense fear in the Iranian leadership and caused the government to offer major concessions to the United States in an effort to appease. On May 4, 2003, a document embodying what became known in diplomatic circles as Iran's "grand bargain" was sent to the U.S. through Switzerland, which represented American interests in Iran. The "grand bargain" entailed broad dialogue on all major issues of contention between Iran and the United States, which included numerous concessions to the United States. The Iranians proposed to sever support for Hamas and the Islamic Jihad, which opposed Israel. They pledged to transform Hezbollah in Lebanon from an armed guerrilla group into a purely political organization. They promised to address U.S. concerns over nuclear weapons, which included allowing more intrusive inspections. Tehran pledged to oppose all terrorist organizations and to coordinate policy with the United States to stabilize Iraq and establish a non-religious government. Finally, the Iranians promised to make peace with Israel and accept a two-state solution to the Palestinian conflict.[66] (Whether Iran could have actually fulfilled those promises, especially with respect to Hezbollah, for instance, is another matter.)

As quid pro quo, Iran expected the United States to lift sanctions; drop threats of a regime change and interference in Iran's internal affairs; recognize Iran's national interests in Iraq and the broader region; and respect Iran's right to have access to nuclear, biological and chemical technology. Moreover, the Iranians wanted to receive the anti-Iranian MEK terrorists in exchange for their turning over Al Qaeda terrorists to the United States. The document laid out a plan for negotiations to achieve a mutually acceptable agreement.[67]

Secretary Powell, reflecting State Department thinking, wanted to make a positive response to the Iranian offer. However, as a result of staunch opposition from the neocon-dominated Pentagon and vice-president's office, the offer was precipitously rejected. In recollecting this event, Lawrence Wilkerson, who at that time was chief of staff to Secretary of State Colin Powell, said that it had been a "very propitious moment" to enter negotiations with Iran. The failure to do so was the result of obstruction by neo-conservatives led by the Vice-President's office. "The secret cabal got what it wanted," Wilkerson wistfully recounted, "no negotiations with Tehran."[68]

This rejection of the Iranian offer, however, did not mean that the administration would adopt the neocon war agenda toward Iran. While neo-conservatives argued for regime change, and Israel ominously implied the need for an armed attack to destroy Iran's nuclear program, the realists in the Bush administration still seemed to have some influence on the Iranian issue.[69] In October 2003, Deputy Secretary of State Richard Armitage told Congress that the administration did not seek "regime change" in Tehran and would consider "limited discussions with the government of Iran about areas of mutual interest."[70] As late as the eve of the 2004 presidential election, according to John Bolton, then undersecretary of state, Powell attempted to shift U.S. policy on Iran by telling key allies he wanted to offer "carrots" to the Islamic Republic to halt its nuclear ambitions. Bolton said, furthermore, that he had to work hard to undercut Powell's plans.[71]

Outside the administration, a major "realist" policy prescription on Iran, produced by a Council of Foreign Relations-sponsored task force, was released in June 2004. The task force was co-chaired by former National Security Adviser Zbigniew Brzezinski and former CIA director Robert M. Gates (who would become secretary of defense in December 2006); among other task force members were Brent Scowcroft, the elder Bush's national security advisor, and Frank Carlucci, who served as national security adviser and defense secretary for President Ronald Reagan.[72]

Titled *Iran: Time for a New Approach*, the report held that the United States should abandon the idea of overthrowing the Islamic Republic of Iran, which it described as "solidly entrenched" and "not on the brink of revolutionary upheaval." On the contrary, it was incumbent for the United States to deal with the current regime. According to the report, the Iranian government was gradually becoming more responsive to its citizenry and more cooperative in international relations, but American threats of regime change tended to impede this natural evolution by inflaming nationalist sentiments.[73]

Although the report viewed as unrealistic a "grand bargain" to settle all outstanding issues between American and Iran, it proposed engagement with Tehran on selected key issues involving regional stability, terrorism, and Iran's nuclear ambitions. The report stressed that the promise of commercial relations with the United States would serve to make Iran more amenable on political and military issues.

But if the American establishment realists wanted a thaw in relations, Israel sought forceful measures toward Iran. In the fall of 2004, there were strong rumors that Israel planned to attack Iran's nuclear installations as it had attacked Iraq's nuclear reactor in 1981. "For Israel it's quite clear, that we're not going to wait for a threat to be realized," said Ephraim Inbar, head of the Jaffee Center for Strategic Studies at Tel Aviv University, in August

2004. "For self-defense we have to act in a preemptive mode."[74] But some Israeli authorities believed that destroying Iran's nuclear capabilities would be far more difficult than the 1981 attack on Iraq's nuclear site. "I don't think there's an option for a preemptive act because we're talking about a different sort of a nuclear program," maintained Shmuel Bar, a fellow at the Institute for Policy and Strategy at the Interdisciplinary Center in Herzliya, Israel. "A hit-and-run preemptive attack can't guarantee much success."[75] In late September 2004, however, it was announced that Israel would purchase 500 "bunker busting" bombs from the United States (paid for by U.S. military aid) which could destroy Iran's underground nuclear stores and laboratories.[76]

In response, Iran threatened all-out retaliation to any Israeli strike on its nuclear installations, which would include long-range missile attacks and terror attacks from its Hezbollah allies in Lebanon. Iran's claim to be able to wreak serious damage on Israel might have been bluster to ward off an attack, but defense experts reported that the latest version of Iran's Shahab-3 medium-range ballistic missile could reach Israel.[77] In an interview with journalist Seymour Hersh, Shahram Chubin, an Iranian scholar who was the director of research at the Geneva Centre for Security Policy, stated,

> You can't be sure after an attack that you'll [Israel and the U.S.] get away with it. The U.S. and Israel would not be certain whether all the sites had been hit, or how quickly they'd be rebuilt. Meanwhile, they'd be waiting for an Iranian counter-attack that could be military or terrorist or diplomatic. Iran has long-range missiles and ties to Hezbollah, which has drones – you can't begin to think of what they'd do in response.[78]

Ironically, by eliminating the hostile regimes bordering Iran – Afghanistan and Iraq – the United States provided Tehran with opportunities to greatly expand its power in the region. At the same time, however, the presence of American forces in those bordering countries put considerable geopolitical pressure on Iran.

In a bombshell article appearing in the *New Yorker* in January 2005, Seymour Hersh claimed that the United States was preparing to make surgical air strikes on the supposed Iranian nuclear and military facilities. An especially stunning revelation made by Hersh was not simply that the United States planned to attack Iran but that U.S. forces were already inside the country. Hersh reported that American special forces teams had been conducting operations inside Iran since summer 2004, selecting suspected weapons sites for possible airstrikes. Hersh said that a government consultant with close ties to the Pentagon told him: "The civilians in the Pentagon want to go into Iran and destroy as much of the military infrastructure as possible."[79] In short, it would seem that while the realists in the State Department and elsewhere were talking about bettering relations with Iran, the neocon Defense Department was ginning up a war, unbeknownst to anyone else.

Significantly, Israel was involved in this war-preparation process. "There has also been close, and largely unacknowledged, cooperation with Israel," Hersh wrote.

> The government consultant with ties to the Pentagon said that the Defense Department civilians, under the leadership of Douglas Feith, have been working with Israeli planners and consultants to develop and refine potential nuclear, chemical-weapons, and missile targets inside Iran.[80]

The results envisioned were sweeping.

> The immediate goals of the attacks would be to destroy, or at least temporarily derail, Iran's ability to go nuclear. But there are other, equally purposeful, motives at work. The government consultant told me that the hawks in the Pentagon, in private discussions, have been urging a limited attack on Iran because they believe it could lead to a toppling of the religious leadership.[81]

There were many reasons to think that the United States was preparing to attack Iran. Israel and the neoconservatives seemed to be pushing for war. In April 2005, Prime Minister Sharon provided Bush photographs of what were supposed to be Iran's nuclear installations and emphasized the danger of relying upon a protracted process of European-directed negotiations to resolve the Iranian issue while the Iranians allegedly were unceasingly advancing their capability to build nuclear weapons.[82]

In May 2005, Richard Perle was the major attraction of AIPAC's annual conference in Washington with his call for an attack on Iran. The danger of Iran also was featured in an AIPAC multimedia show, "Iran's Path to the Bomb." The *Washington Post's* Dana Milbank described the Disneyesqe multimedia show:

> The exhibit, worthy of a theme park, begins with a narrator condemning the International Atomic Energy Agency for being "unwilling to conclude that Iran is developing nuclear weapons" (it had similar reservations about Iraq) and the Security Council because it "has yet to take up the issue." In a succession of rooms, visitors see flashing lights and hear rumbling sounds as Dr. Seuss-like

contraptions make yellowcake uranium, reprocess plutonium, and pop out nuclear warheads like so many gallons of hummus for an AIPAC conference.[83]

The *Jerusalem Post* of June 29, 2005 reported a presentation by the head of the Israel Defense Force (IDF) Intelligence Corps research division that Iran was committed to constructing nuclear weapons in order to help it spread the Islamic revolution across the Middle East.[84] In late June, Israeli Ambassador to the U.S. Daniel Ayalon categorically emphasized the immediacy of the Iranian nuclear threat, warning "The clock is ticking, and time is not on our side."[85]

Israeli officials would continue to urge the United States to take strong action against Iran, and they were becoming disenchanted by its failure to do so. Iran, in turn, would lambaste Israel with extremist rhetoric. In October, Iran's new hard-line president, Mahmoud Ahmadinejad, told Iranian students, as reported in the Western media, that "Israel must be wiped off the map." This immediately drew worldwide condemnation and a later explanation by the Iranian government that his words did not mean genocide as the Western media implied. As a number of commentators pointed out, the Western media actually had mistranslated Ahmadinejad's speech, making it seem that he sought to liquidate the Jewish people in Israel by using nuclear weapons or some other drastic means. But it meant nothing of the kind. Instead of "wiped off the map," a better translation would have been "vanish," and it referred to the Zionist regime, not the Jewish people. Ahmadinejad sought a Palestinian state ruled by the Palestinian people. This could be interpreted as a call for a type of "regime change," but one which would be anathema to the neocons and other pro-Zionists in America.[86] Since Iran supported the Palestinian resistance to Israel, especially Hamas, it would seem reasonable to conclude that Ahmadinejad believed that some degree of violence would be necessary to bring about the downfall of the Zionist regime (i.e., Israel), even if there would be no actual outright attack.

Ahmadinejad would stir up an additional furor when on December 14 he questioned the role played by "the myth of the Holocaust" in modern society: "Today," he said, "they have created a myth in the name of Holocaust and consider it to be above God, religion and the prophets."[87] This statement drew harsh criticism from abroad. It was not apparent that Ahmadinejad had actually denied the existence of the mass murder of Jews during World War II, though he did, at various times, question various

facets of the Holocaust and demanded greater evidential proof. Ahmadinejad's also expressed criticism of the use made by the Holocaust for
politics and international relations, especially in its role in justifying the
dispossession of the Palestinians.[88] Diminishing the severity of the Holocaust, however, even if it would involve less than an outright denial, is a
serious criminal offense in such countries as Germany, France, Poland, and
Israel. Ahmadinejad's inflammatory remarks undoubtedly helped fuel the
campaign by Israel and the neoconservatives to depict Tehran as a dangerous "rogue regime."

But even granting the most inflammatory version of the Iranian President's statements, war critics would still observe that no genuine case for
an American war against Iran could be found in them. "I profoundly disagree with his characterization of Israel, which is a legitimate United Nations member state, and find his Holocaust denial monstrous," Juan Cole
would write the following year.

> But this quite false charge that he is genocidal is being promoted by Right-
> Zionists in and out of Congress as a preparatory step to getting up a U.S. war
> against Iran on false pretenses. I don't want to see my country destroyed by
> being further embroiled in the Middle East for the wrong reasons. If the Israeli
> hardliners and their American amen corner want a war with Iran, let them
> fight it themselves and leave young 18 year old Americans alone.[89]

Notwithstanding the propaganda efforts, the United States did not move
toward war. AIPAC evinced dismay about the lack of a harder line by the
United States towards Iran. In a November 28, 2005 statement, AIPAC
warned that continued negotiation "may facilitate Iran's quest for nuclear
weapons" and consequently "poses a severe danger to the United States
and our allies, and puts America and our interests at risk."[90] On December
1, Sharon said that Israel couldn't accept a nuclear-armed Iran, adding that
Tehran's nuclear program could be stopped by military means.[91]

New neoconservative publications also pushed for stronger measures toward Iran. In *Countdown to Crisis: The Coming Nuclear Showdown With Iran*,
Kenneth Timmerman, a member of JINSA's advisory board and executive
director of the Foundation for Democracy in Iran, claimed that Iran had
collaborated with Al Qaeda in plotting the September 11 terror attacks, and
was currently harboring Osama bin Laden.[92] Timmerman also was one of
the authors of the study "Launch Regional Initiatives," published by AEI
at the end of November. In the section on Iran, the publication portrayed

the Islamic regime as America's irreconcilable enemy with whom détente was impossible. It suggested a number of militant measures for the United States to take in order to bring about regime change:

> The United States must wage total political war against the Islamofascists in Tehran, both inside Iran and from the outside. This war should be designed to keep the Iranian regime off balance (including, where necessary, through the use of covert means), with the ultimate goal of undermining its control.[93]

Most of the proposed American efforts to undermine the existing Iranian regime did not involve a direct American military attack, but the latter was not ruled out to stop Iran's nuclear program: "The stakes are sufficiently high that we must also be prepared to use military force – alone if necessary, with others if practicable – to disrupt Iran's known and suspected nuclear operations."[94]

One way to weaken Iran would be to fragment it into various groups – in line with Oded Yinon's plan for the Middle East. This seems to have been the underlying theme of the October 26, 2005 AEI conference entitled "The Unknown Iran: Another Case for Federalism?," moderated by AEI resident scholar Michael Ledeen. The announcement for the conference stated that

> few realize that Persians likely constitute a minority of the Iranian population. The majority is composed of Azerbaijanis, Kurds, Baluchis, Turkmen, and the Arabs of Khuzistan / al-ahwaz. In the event the current regime falls, these groups will undoubtedly play an important role in their country's future.[95]

The individuals invited to the conference were ethnic separatists.[96]

In late November 2005, Ledeen expressed his concern about the failure of the United States to take action against Iran. "While the president has made many statements about the evils of the mullahcracy in Tehran," Ledeen lamented,

> he has not only failed to carry out any action against the Islamic republic, he has repeatedly authorized unannounced meetings with Iranian representatives, in a futile effort to work out some kind of deal by which Iran would promise to limit its support for terrorism, especially inside Iraq, and we would promise, or hint, or imply, that we wouldn't attempt to support democratic revolution in Iran. These talks have been going on throughout the five years of Bush the Younger, many of them under the auspices of Ambassador Khalilzad, whose conversations with the mullahs have now been publicly acknowledged and formally approved.[97]

A similar jeremiad against the failure to take appropriate action was presented by Charles Krauthammer in his December 16, 2005 column in the

Washington Post titled, "In Iran, Arming for Armageddon." Krauthammer's focus was the Iranian threat to Israeli, not American, security, which Krauthammer saw demonstrated by the pronouncements of Iranian President Mahmoud Ahmadinejad in his denial of the extermination of the European Jews in the Holocaust and his criticism of Israel's existence. Krauthammer equated these words with an imminent Iranian threat to exterminate the Jewish people of Israel. "Holocaust denial and calls for Israel's destruction are commonplace in the Middle East," Krauthammer noted. "But none of these aspiring mass murderers are on the verge of acquiring nuclear weapons that could do in one afternoon what it took Hitler six years to do: destroy an entire Jewish civilization and extinguish 6 million souls." To Krauthammer, it was obvious that once Iran possessed nuclear weapons it would launch them at Israel. "Everyone knows where Iran's nuclear weapons will be aimed. Everyone knows they will be put on Shahab rockets, which have been modified so that they can reach Israel."[98]

More than that, Krauthammer emphasized the dire significance of the Iranian president's alleged belief in an imminent Armageddon. "So a Holocaust-denying, virulently anti-Semitic, aspiring genocidist, on the verge of acquiring weapons of the apocalypse, believes that the end is not only near but nearer than the next American presidential election," Krauthammer maintained. "This kind of man would have, to put it gently, less inhibition about starting Armageddon than a normal person. Indeed, with millennial bliss pending, he would have positive incentive to, as they say in Jewish eschatology, hasten the end."[99]

Krauthammer implied that such a presumed madman as Ahmadinejad could only be stopped by war: "Negotiations to deny this certifiable lunatic genocidal weapons have been going nowhere. Everyone knows they will go nowhere. And no one will do anything about it."[100]

It is necessary to repeat the gist of Krauthammer's message. His explicit concern here was Israel. And his implicit message was that other countries, such as the United States, should launch a preventive war to protect Israel.

While Krauthammer singled out Ahmadinejad as the danger, the fact of the matter was that Israel and the neocons had targeted Iran long before the Islamic hardliner's election. Moreover, it should also be noted that some neocons saw Ahmadinejad's elevation to power as a blessing because he would make more apparent the Iranian threat to the entire world. As Daniel Pipes observed in a *FrontPage* symposium in July 2005, shortly after Ahmadinejad's

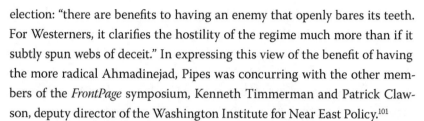

election: "there are benefits to having an enemy that openly bares its teeth. For Westerners, it clarifies the hostility of the regime much more than if it subtly spun webs of deceit." In expressing this view of the benefit of having the more radical Ahmadinejad, Pipes was concurring with the other members of the *FrontPage* symposium, Kenneth Timmerman and Patrick Clawson, deputy director of the Washington Institute for Near East Policy.[101]

Despite the heated rhetoric, however, there would be no expansion of the war into either Iran or Syria at this time. The United States was able to mobilize international pressure against both of those countries – over Syria's role in Lebanon and Iran's nuclear program – and both countries were clearly put on the defensive before the world community. But major military action was not undertaken, nor even overtly brandished by the United States.

The inability to widen the war, as the neoconservatives would have preferred, partly stemmed from the fact that, bogged down in Iraq, the United States lacked the military capability to launch an invasion of Iran. But America still had the power to launch devastating strikes with its awesome airpower. However, militating against any type of expansion of the war was the loss of public support for military adventurism caused by the Iraq quagmire. Except for a slight uptick at the time of the election in Iraq on January 30, 2005, the news was generally bad for the neoconservatives and the Bush administration. The grim reality of Iraq was causing a public loss of faith in the White House with its constant pollyannish portrayal of the situation. According to an AP-Ipsos poll released on June 24, 2005, 53 percent of people surveyed said the United States made a mistake going to war in Iraq[102] In August, support for the war plummeted to 34 percent in a *Newsweek* poll.[103]

By November 2005, the Iraq war had become the dominant issue in Washington, eclipsing everything else. Democrats were becoming vocal in criticizing the war, and the unity of the Republicans behind the Bush administration war policy was fraying.[104]

On November 16, the Republican-controlled Senate managed to reject a resolution from the Democrats demanding that the President set a schedule for withdrawing troops from Iraq; it did pass a weaker resolution embodying the same idea, though without a timetable. It designated 2006 as "a period of significant transition to full sovereignty . . . thereby creating the conditions for the phased redeployment of United States forces from Iraq." Senate Minority Leader Harry Reid (Democrat-Nevada) of Nevada described the vote as tantamount to a declaration of "no confidence" in the Bush administration's direction of the war.[105] While this resolution did not set a timetable for withdrawal, its emphasis was undoubtedly on removing American troops, not winning the war.

While Democrats were willing to criticize the war effort and question the motives for attacking Iraq, they still stopped short of making an all-out effort to remove the troops from Iraq. This reflected the fact that the majority of Democrats, especially the leadership, had all along provided only tepid opposition to Bush war policies, despite overwhelming antiwar opinion among the Democratic Party's rank-and-file.[106]

On November 17, Representative John Murtha (D.-Penn.), a decorated combat veteran with 37 years service in the Marine Corps, with close ties to the military, did call for the withdrawal of the troops "at the earliest predictable date," and his emotional description of the war invigorated antiwar opponents; but his call for a troop pullout was not initially embraced by most congressional Democrats, especially the Democratic leadership. "Mr. Murtha speaks for himself," announced House Minority Leader Nancy Pelosi in response to reporters' questions. Pelosi, however, would soon reverse herself and back Murtha's withdrawal position, as it became apparent that it had overwhelming support among activist Democrats.[107] Yet Hillary Clinton, frequently mentioned as a leading contender for the Democratic presidential nomination in 2008, remained in opposition, asserting that an immediate U.S. withdrawal from Iraq would be "a big mistake" which "would cause more problems for us in America. It will matter to us if Iraq totally collapses into civil war, if it becomes a failed state."[108]

Columnist Harold Meyerson summarized the political situation in late November 2005:

> The president's credibility is reaching Nixonian depths. The Democrats have been pushed to the brink of opposing the war, but there – on the brink – they totter.
>
> And so, on the most urgent question confronting America today, we have reached an absurd and exquisite equipoise. The Republicans cannot credibly defend the war; the Democrats cannot quite bring themselves to call for its end. And the war goes on.[109]

Bush continued to justify the war and say that there would be no pullout during his administration until victory had been achieved. Bush's overall message revolved around the idea that the United States was making progress, and that a withdrawal would signify defeat by the terrorists and lead to a bloodbath.[110] Moreover, Bush, in answering a question about the failure to find Iraqi WMD, the fundamental pretext for the war, still maintained that "knowing what I know today I'd make the same decision again."[111]

And the Bush administration had adopted much of the neocons' World War IV scenario. Vice President Cheney and others spoke of the alleged plan to establish a radical Islamic "caliphate" encompassing much of the Middle East that would pose calamitous consequences for the United States. As Cheney told the American Enterprise Institute:

> The terrorists believe that by controlling an entire country they will be able to target and overthrow other governments in the region, and to establish a radical Islamic empire that encompasses a region from Spain, across North Africa, through the Middle East and South Asia, all the way to Indonesia. They have made clear, as well, their ultimate ambitions: to arm themselves with weapons of mass destruction, to destroy Israel, to intimidate all Western countries and to cause mass death in the United States.[112]

Neoconservative Daniel Pipes had introduced the term "caliphate" in the course of making a pro-war argument in his article, "What Do the Terrorists Want? [A Caliphate]," in the *New York Sun* of July 26, 2005.[113] This idea was echoed in December by neocon Eric Edelman, the undersecretary of defense: "Iraq's future will either embolden terrorists and expand their reach and ability to re-establish a caliphate, or it will deal them a crippling blow."[114]

Nonetheless, despite the president's firm resolve to stay the course on the war, public and political opposition, in conjunction with the dire problems in Iraq, made it difficult to expand the war to other countries in line with the neoconservatives' World War IV scenario. It would seem that a widening of the conflict would first require another serious incident to reignite the public's passion for war.

But a widening of the war was far from being impossible, especially with Israel and its supporters beating the war drums so loudly regarding Iran. Thus journalist Robert Dreyfuss described the condition of the neoconservatives and their war agenda in late November 2005 by saying,

> I never count them out. I think in a way if you look at the broader picture in the Middle East, they knocked down Saddam, and now pressure is building on both Syria and Iran – and that was really part of the original grand design for the region going back to 2001. We're also still in control of Afghanistan, we're

building an empire in Central Asia, and Bush remains committed to this fantasy of democracy in places like Egypt and Saudi Arabia overnight, and so in that sense, I think the neoconservative project for the Middle East is moving forward until it's dead and buried and flowers are growing on its coffin. I don't see that we can relax.[115]

chapter 15

ISRAEL, LEBANON, AND THE 2006 ELECTION

IN THE FIRST HALF OF 2006, it was widely believed that the Bush administration was turning away from the neoconservative formulation of Middle East policy and moving toward the moderate position of the traditional foreign policy establishment, which entailed winding down the war in Iraq and a diplomatic solution regarding Iran. The Bush administration was being led in this direction by the force of circumstances. Public support for the war in Iraq had virtually collapsed. As the situation in Iraq worsened, the appeal of the further implementation of the neoconservative war agenda simultaneously atrophied. Polls showed that the American people, as well as America's allies, sought to pursue a diplomatic approach regarding Iran. Moreover, expert opinion held that war with Iran would have disastrous consequences. Iran was much larger than Iraq, with three times the population, and had a much more effective military, which had been modernized by the country's new oil wealth. War would be apt to wreck havoc with the Persian Gulf oil supply, especially since Iran could disrupt the flow of oil through the narrow Straits of Hormuz simply by sinking two tankers at stragegic positions. Moreover, Iran also had the power to unleash pro-Iranian Shiite fighters in Iraq, which could cause incalculable problems for the United States occupation force.[1]

Congress would play a significant role in trying to move the Bush administration away from the war agenda. The foremost step in this direction was its creation in March of an independent, bipartisan commission, the Iraq Study Group, which would not only provide a solution for Iraq but also deal with the broader Middle East. The commission was the brainchild of Republican Congressman Frank Wolf (Virginia) and had solid Republican congressional backing. The 10-member commission – divided evenly among Republicans and Democrats – would be co-chaired by the elder Bush's close associate and former Secretary of State James A. Baker and by former Democratic Congressman Lee H. Hamilton. After its creation, the group's members consulted with hundreds of high-ranking current and former government officials and other experts to gather information on the situation in Iraq.

Baker was the dominant force in the group, so that it was often referred to as the "Baker Commission." Baker seemed to be the ideal individual to have any influence with President Bush, being a Bush family insider nonpareil. He had run the elder Bush's unsuccessful campaign for president in 1980 and then later served as the latter's Secretary of State. He had acted as chief legal adviser for George W. Bush during the 2000 election campaign and oversaw the Florida vote recount, which assured Bush of the presidency. Speculation arose that Baker's job was to save the legacy of the Bush family by effectively extricating the younger Bush from the Iraq imbroglio. Baker, however, was far from being a family hack, but rather held firm foreign policy views reflecting the thinking of the establishment realists.[2]

It must be recalled from Chapter 5 that, as secretary of state, Baker had been not been supportive of Israel and the neocon agenda in the Middle East. Rather, he sought to placate the Palestinians and maintain stability in the Middle East. Prior to Saddam's invasion of Kuwait in August 1990, Baker had supported good relations with Iraq. And in regard to the Gulf War, he staunchly opposed an invasion of Iraq to remove Saddam. His effort to pressure Israel against building settlements on the West Bank by threatening to deny American loan guarantees brought about a notorious conflict with the Israel lobby.

Baker and Hamilton took the position that the commission would not release its report until after the November elections, claiming the need to avoid politicization. Nevertheless, there were various leaks and even public statements by Baker and Hamilton indicating that the final report would advocate American acceptance of something less than the outright victory pursued by the Bush administration and would propose diplomatic engagement with Iran.[3]

Attuned in part to the changing political climate, the Bush administration itself also seemed to be turning away from the neocon Middle East agenda. This shift was described in an article titled "The End of the Bush Revolution" in the July-August 2006 issue of *Foreign Affairs*, the influential journal of the Council on Foreign Relations, which represented the bastion of the old foreign policy establishment. The author, Philip H. Gold, observed that while the

> rhetoric of the Bush revolution lives on, the revolution itself is over. The question is not whether the president and most of his team still hold to the basic tenets of the Bush doctrine – they do – but whether they can sustain it. They cannot. Although the administration does not like to admit it, U.S. foreign policy is already on a very different trajectory than it was in Bush's first term. The budgetary, political, and diplomatic realities that the first Bush team tried to ignore have begun to set in.[4]

The cover story for the July 17, 2006 edition of *Time Magazine*, one of America's leading news magazines, entitled "The End of Cowboy Diplomacy," also dealt with this change in the Bush administration's foreign policy. (It must be pointed out that the writing of both this article and the aforementioned *Foreign Affiars* piece predated the Israel's attack on Lebanon.) The article in *Time Magazine* referred to a "strategic makeover" of the Bush administration foreign policy. It described Secretary of State Condoleezza Rice as "a foreign policy realist" who was moving away from the "Bush doctrine," which had consisted of a "grand strategy to fight Islamic terrorists and rogue states by spreading democracy around the world and pre-empting gathering threats before they materialize."[5]

While these articles went too far in claiming that the Bush administration had replaced the neocon agenda with that of the traditional foreign policy establishment – for example, it did not seem that Rice had been adopting a position of peaceful compromise with Iran – it was true that the official United States foreign policy as directed by Rice and the State Department was not actively pursuing the neocon war agenda. This failure was clearly noted, and harshly criticized, by the neoconservatives. William Kristol, for example, acerbically observed in May that

> Much of the U.S. government no longer believes in, and is no longer acting to enforce, the Bush Doctrine. "The United States of America understands and believes that Iran is not Iraq." That's a diplomatic way of saying that the United States of America is in retreat.[6]

Comparing Iran's alleged push to gain a nuclear weapon to Adolf Hitler's unopposed 1936 march on the Rhineland, Kristol saw a vital need for "seri-

ous preparation for possible military action – including real and urgent operational planning for bombing strikes and for the consequences of such strikes." He complained that the administration's policy had been "all carrots and no sticks."[7]

Neocon stalwart Richard Perle identified Secretary of State Rice as the culprit for this deleterious policy change. Rice, Perle bemoaned, was "in the midst of – and increasingly represents – a diplomatic establishment that is driven to accommodate its allies even when (or, it seems, especially when) such allies counsel the appeasement of our adversaries."[8]

But the movement away from the neocon Middle East war agenda came to a screeching (though what would turn out to be temporary) halt as a result of Israel's massive attack on Lebanon on July 12. Israel justified the attack as a response to Hezbollah's ambush of Israeli soldiers, capturing two and killing three, in a raid across Israel's border. It was apparent, however, that Israel's onslaught on Lebanon was not simply a response to the attack on its troops. Since Israel withdrew its military forces from southern Lebanon in July 2000, there had been a series of border incidents, with Israel itself engaging in cross border raids that caused the destruction of property and loss of lives. According to the reports of the United Nations observer force, UNIFIL (United Nations Interim Force in Lebanon), Israel had violated the United Nations-monitored "blue line" on a daily basis.[9]

Moreover, there had been, in the past, exchanges of prisoners between Israel and Hezbollah. In short, there was nothing exceptional about Hezbollah's actions of July 12.[10] Rather, the abduction provided Israel with the pretext to launch an attack that had been prepared long in advance. "Of all of Israel's wars since 1948, this was the one for which Israel was most prepared," asserted Gerald Steinberg, a political science professor at Israel's Bar-Ilan University.

> In a sense, the preparation began in May 2000, immediately after the Israeli withdrawal, when it became clear the international community was not going to prevent Hezbollah from stockpiling missiles and attacking Israel. By 2004, the military campaign scheduled to last about three weeks that we're seeing now had already been blocked out and, in the last year or two, it's been simulated and rehearsed across the board.[11]

Maintaining a fragmented Lebanon had long been an Israeli security objective. During the 1950s, David Ben-Gurion sought to weaken Lebanon by creating a separate Christian state.[12] Moreover, Israel leaders historically had viewed the Litani River as a much needed water source for Israel. In 1919, Chaim Weizmann, head of the World Zionist Organization, declared the river "essential to the future of the Jewish national home."[13]

In line with Israeli geostrategic thinking, neoconservatives had discussed the need to reconfigure Lebanon. Such an approach was mentioned in the 1996 "Clean Break" proposal. A key passage read:

> Syria challenges Israel on Lebanese soil. An effective approach, and one with which American [sic] can sympathize, would be if Israel seized the strategic initiative along its northern borders by engaging Hizballah, Syria, and Iran, as the principal agents of aggression in Lebanon.[14]

In May 2000, neocon Daniel Pipes' Middle East Forum published a report by the Lebanon Study Group titled "Ending Syria's Occupation of Lebanon: The U.S. Role." Pipes co-chaired the study, which was signed by such other neocon luminaries as Richard Perle, Elliott Abrams, Douglas Feith, and David Wurmser.[15]

In addition to pointing out moral reasons for removing Syrian influence, the study contended that

> Lebanon occupies an important place in a strategically vital corner of the world. This fact is cause for great alarm when considered with Syria's current domination as Lebanon has unwittingly become a breeding ground for various threats to the stability of the Middle East.

The report ended up with a call for American assertiveness in the area:

> [T]he U.S. has entered a new era of undisputed military supremacy, coupled with an appreciable drop in human losses on the battlefield. But this opportunity will not wait, for as WMD capabilities spread, the risks of such action will rapidly grow. If there is to be decisive action, it will have to be sooner rather than later.[16]

After Israel launched its July 2006 attack on Lebanon, stories surfaced that Israeli officials had earlier discussed the plan for the attack with Vice-President Cheney and other pro-war officials in the Bush Administration. According to one reported scenario, such a discussion of the war plan took place at the June 17 and 18 American Enterprise Institute (AEI) conference in Beaver Creek, Colorado at which former Israeli Prime Minister Benjamin Netanyahu and Knesset member Natan Sharansky met with Cheney. After receiving Cheney's full backing for the invasion, Netanyahu returned to Israel and informed the government of the American position.[17] In another account, Seymour Hersh indicated that Israel's plan on a bombing campaign targeting Lebanon's infrastructure appealed to Cheney as a prelude for a similar U.S. attack on Iran.[18] Mearsheimer and Walt maintain that David Wurmser, Cheney's adviser on Middle East affairs, and Elliott Abrams, the Middle East specialist in the National Security Council, were the key figures in the Bush administration endorsing an Israeli attack on Lebanon.[19]

The most limited Israeli goal was to remove Hezbollah from southern Lebanon. The removal of Hezbollah would not only protect Israel from attack but would eliminate the only force in Lebanon that could deter Israel's domination of the entire country. However, it would seem that the very ferocity and scope of the Israeli air and sea attack indicated more ambitious goals: the massive attack would serve to break the incipient unity of Lebanon and return it the anarchic, sectarian violence of its recent past. The Israeli campaign wrought terrible destruction on the civilian population and infrastructure in Lebanon – bridges, water reservoirs, electric plants, gas stations, mosques, hospitals, milk factories, gas stations, fuel storage depots, airport runways and thousands of homes, including Beirut's main Christian neighborhood – that had little to do with Hezbollah itself.[20] This widespread destruction would seem to be in line with Israel's traditional, more ambitious goal to weaken and fragment Lebanon and perhaps gain hegemonic control of southern Lebanon with its valuable Litani River.[21]

Moreover, Israel linked its attack with the broader "war on terror." Prime Minister Olmert and other leaders in the Israeli government were quick to attribute Hezbollah's seizure of Israeli soldiers to encouragement from Iran.[22] It was apparent that destruction of Hezbollah would mean a stunning defeat for its Iranian patron. If Iran stood aside while Hezbollah, its one real regional client, was crushed, its apparent weakness could induce stronger American demands regarding its nuclear program and its alleged involvement in the violence in Iraq. On the other hand, if Iran became involved openly in the fray to prevent Hezbollah's destruction, the justification would be provided for the United States to take military action against Iran. The argument for protecting Israel would most likely command the support of Congress. In this way, the prospects for furthering the neoconservative war agenda would be greatly enhanced.

In line with neoconservative thinking, President Bush interpreted the conflict in Lebanon as an integral part of the broad war on terror. "But the stakes are larger than just Lebanon," the president told reporters on July 28 after meeting with British Prime Minister Tony Blair. According to Bush, "the root cause of the problem is you've got Hezbollah that is armed and willing to fire rockets into Israel; a Hezbollah, by the way, that I firmly believe is backed by Iran and encouraged by Iran." Bush contended that "Iran would like to exert additional influence in the region. A theocracy would like to spread its influence using surrogates. And so, for the sake of long-term stability, we've got to deal with this issue now."[23]

Bush expressed this war on terror view even as efforts were being made to stop the fighting. "As we work to resolve this current crisis," Bush said in his radio address of July 29, "we must recognize that Lebanon is the latest flashpoint in a broader struggle between freedom and terror that is unfolding across the region." Bush maintained that while the conflict was "painful and tragic," it simultaneously provided

> a moment of opportunity for broader change in the region. Transforming countries that have suffered decades of tyranny and violence is difficult, and it will take time to achieve. But the consequences will be profound – for our country and the world.[24]

In short, the neoconservative agenda to reconfigure the Middle East was back on track, at least in the mind of President Bush.

In reviving the neocon war agenda, the Bush administration stood against America's European and Arab allies who pressed unsuccessfully for an immediate ceasefire.[25] By its refusal to support an early ceasefire, the Bush administration was, in effect, giving a green light to Israel to continue its attack. The Bush administration's apparent goal was to have Israel destroy or severely cripple Hezbollah and in the process strike a blow at Iran, Hezbollah's sponsor.[26]

The Bush administration was more than a passive supporter of Israel's attack. It provided Israel with precision bombs and aviation fuel.[27] U.S. efforts in the United Nations, directed by Ambassador John Bolton, served to block that organization from working for an early ceasefire.[28] Moreover, according to former Bill Clinton adviser Sidney Blumenthal, the National Security Agency was providing intelligence to Israel on whether Syria and Iran were supplying weapons to Hezbollah. According to Blumenthal:

> Inside the administration, neoconservatives on Vice President Dick Cheney's national security staff and Elliott Abrams, the neoconservative senior director for the Near East on the National Security Council, are prime movers behind

sharing NSA intelligence with Israel, and they have discussed Syrian and Iranian supply activities as a potential pretext for Israeli bombing of both countries.

Blumenthal ominously wrote that

[b]y using NSA intelligence to set an invisible tripwire, the Bush administration is laying the condition for regional conflagration with untold consequences – from Pakistan to Afghanistan, from Iraq to Israel. Secretly devising a scheme that might thrust Israel into a ring of fire cannot be construed as a blunder. It is a deliberate, calculated and methodical plot.[29]

Some months after the Israeli incursion, neocon Meyrav Wurmser would affirm that it was neocon influence in the Bush administration that was setting policy on Lebanon, with the aim being a direct Israeli confrontation with Syria. "The neocons are responsible for the fact that Israel got a lot of time and space," Wurmser stated.

They believed that Israel should be allowed to win. A great part of it was the thought that Israel should fight against the real enemy, the one backing Hizbullah. It was obvious that it is impossible to fight directly against Iran, but the thought was that its strategic and important ally should be hit.[30]

Furthermore, "It is difficult for Iran to export its Shiite revolution without joining Syria, which is the last nationalistic Arab country," Wurmser contended. "If Israel had hit Syria, it would have been such a harsh blow for Iran that it would have weakened it and [changed] the strategic map in the Middle East."[31]

Secretary of State Condoleezza Rice's diplomacy tended to veer back and forth between the neocon war agenda and the more moderate position held by the American foreign policy establishment. Her press briefing at the State Department on July 21 represented one of her neocon moments when she described the ongoing attack on Lebanon as representing "the birth pangs of the new Middle East," which should not be aborted by any premature ceasefire that would return "Lebanon and Israel to the status quo ante."[32] Nevertheless, Rice simultaneously made numerous references to the need for Israeli restraint and a ceasefire. As Israel's inability to achieve military success became apparent, she was finally able to persuade Bush to accept a ceasefire.

Neoconservatives from outside the administration gave full support to Israel and saw its attack on Lebanon as providing the perfect opportunity to reinvigorate the war agenda. "All of us in the free world owe Israel an enormous thank-you for defending freedom, democracy, and security against the Iranian cat's-paw wholly-owned terrorist subsidiaries Hezbollah and Hamas," said Larry Kudlow, a neoconservative commentator at the *National Review*.[33]

Richard Perle held that

> Israel must now deal a blow of such magnitude to those who would destroy it as to leave no doubt that its earlier policy of acquiescence is over. This means precise military action against Hezbollah and its infrastructure in Lebanon and Syria, for as long as it takes and without regard to mindless diplomatic blather about proportionality. For what appears to some to be a disproportionate response to small incursions and kidnappings is, in fact, an entirely appropriate response to the existential struggle in which Israel is now engaged.[34]

In David Frum's view, "The war Hezbollah provoked is a war between Israel and Iran, with Hezbollah as Iran's proxy – and the people of Lebanon as Iran's victims."[35]

Michael Ledeen stressed the necessity for the United States to directly enter the fray. "No one should have any lingering doubts about what's going on in the Middle East," Ledeen emphasized.

> It's war, and it now runs from Gaza into Israel, through Lebanon and thence to Iraq via Syria. There are different instruments, ranging from Hamas in Gaza to Hezbollah in Syria and Lebanon and on to the multifaceted "insurgency" in Iraq. But there is a common prime mover, and that is the Iranian mullahcracy, the revolutionary Islamic fascist state that declared war on us 27 years ago and has yet to be held accountable.

In Ledeen's view, much more had to be done to achieve victory over this malevolent power. "The only way we are going to win this war is to bring down those regimes in Tehran and Damascus," Ledeen proclaimed, "and they are not going to fall as a result of fighting between their terrorist proxies in Gaza and Lebanon on the one hand, and Israel on the other. Only the United States can accomplish it."[36]

William Kristol argued the same point in "It's Our War," underscoring the need for direct American involvement in the ongoing conflict. America "might consider countering this act of Iranian aggression with a military strike against Iranian nuclear facilities," Kristol asserted.

> Why wait? Does anyone think a nuclear Iran can be contained? That the current regime will negotiate in good faith? It would be easier to act sooner rather than later. Yes, there would be repercussions – and they would be healthy ones, showing a strong America that has rejected further appeasement.[37]

As the Israeli offensive against Hezbollah bogged down, John Podhoretz, the son of neocon "godfather" Norman Podhoretz, questioned the limits Israel and the United States were placing on the fighting. "Can any war be won when this is the nature of the discussion in the countries fighting the war? Can any war be won when one of the combatants voluntarily limits itself in this manner?" Reflecting the fact that the neocons saw the war against Islam to be comparable to World War II, Podhoretz lamented Israel's unwillingness to engage in more ruthless warfare: "Could World War II have been won by Britain and the United States if the two countries did not have it in them to firebomb Dresden and nuke Hiroshima and Nagasaki?" He implied that a comparable total war approach was needed now.

> Didn't the willingness of their leaders to inflict mass casualties on civilians indicate a cold-eyed singleness of purpose that helped break the will and the back of their enemies? Didn't that singleness of purpose extend down to the populations in those countries in those days, who would have and did support almost any action at any time that would lead to the deaths of Germans and Japanese?[38]

Daniel Pipes, columnist and founder and director of the pro-Israel Middle East Forum, wanted Israel to expand the war. "Rather than travel down the road of predictable failure, something quite different needs to be tried," Pipes wrote in the *New York Sun* on August 1. "My suggestion? Shift attention to Syria from Lebanon, and put Damascus on notice that it is responsible for Hezbollah violence." Pipes proposed warning Damascus that Syrian targets would be bombed each time Israel was hit by a Hezbollah rocket.[39]

Charles Krauthammer, neocon columnist of the *Washington Post*, claimed that Israel was fighting for the interests of the United States. The United States "has counted on Israel's ability to do the job. It has been disappointed. Prime Minister Ehud Olmert has provided unsteady and uncertain leadership."[40]

It would seem that American neocons were demanding more militant action from Israel than the latter country was willing to take.[41] The Israeli government was reluctant to launch a full-scale ground invasion or become involved in a wider war because, unlike the armchair neocons, it would have to face the negative consequences of those decisions. The Israeli public was not willing accept heavy Israeli losses and was becoming disturbed about the level of casualties.[42] And the retaliatory rocket attacks on northern Israel were causing additional public distress. Moreover, the

Israeli government could not be certain that the United States, despite the neocon influence, would come to its aid if it did become embroiled in a wider war with Syria or Iran.

In contrast to the neocons, the American foreign policy establishment vehemently opposed the Israeli attack on Lebanon and sought diplomatic compromise with Syria and Iran. Its members criticized the invasion for destabilizing the region, which was what the neocons sought in their World War IV scenario. "The arrows are all pointing in the wrong direction," maintained Richard N. Haass, who had been President George W. Bush's first-term State Department policy planning director and was now president of the Council of Foreign Relations.

> The biggest danger in the short run is it just increases frustration and alienation from the United States in the Arab world. Not just the Arab world, but in Europe and around the world. People will get a daily drumbeat of suffering in Lebanon and this will just drive up anti-Americanism to new heights.[43]

Edward P. Djerejian, a former ambassador to both Israel and Syria and founding director of Rice University's James A. Baker III Institute for Public Policy, maintained that a lasting solution for the situation in Lebanon necessitated the involvement of all major regional actors. This included getting the "necessary buy-in" from Tehran and Damascus to ensure that Hezbollah would participate.[44]

In a July 30, article in the *Washington Post*, Brent Scowcroft described the problem in Lebanon as requiring a compromise settlement of the entire Israel/Palestine issue. "Hezbollah is not the source of the problem," Scowcroft asserted, "it is a derivative of the cause, which is the tragic conflict over Palestine that began in 1948." The comprehensive settlement Scowcroft outlined would include "A Palestinian state based on the 1967 borders, with minor rectifications agreed upon between Palestine and Israel."[45]

Former President Jimmy Carter similarly advocated a comprehensive peace based on diplomacy and compromise. "Tragically," Carter opined,

> the current conflict is part of the inevitably repetitive cycle of violence that results from the absence of a comprehensive settlement in the Middle East, exacerbated by the almost unprecedented six-year absence of any real effort to achieve such a goal.

Carter delineated a solution hardly palatable to Israel and its supporters.

> There will be no substantive and permanent peace for any peoples in this troubled region as long as Israel is violating key U.N. resolutions, official American

policy and the international "road map" for peace by occupying Arab lands and oppressing the Palestinians. Except for mutually agreeable negotiated modifications, Israel's official pre-1967 borders must be honored. As were all previous administrations since the founding of Israel, U.S. government leaders must be in the forefront of achieving this long-delayed goal.[46]

Carter saw need for much greater diplomatic flexibility on the part of the United States. "A major impediment to progress is Washington's strange policy that dialogue on controversial issues will be extended only as a reward for subservient behavior and will be withheld from those who reject U.S. assertions," Carter emphasized.

> Direct engagement with the Palestine Liberation Organization or the Palestinian Authority and the government in Damascus will be necessary if secure negotiated settlements are to be achieved. Failure to address the issues and leaders involved risks the creation of an arc of even greater instability running from Jerusalem through Beirut, Damascus, Baghdad and Tehran.[47]

Establishment figures viewed the American-backed Israeli invasion as harmful to American geostrategic interests. Zbigniew Brzezinski, for example, held that "These neocon prescriptions, of which Israel has its equivalents, are fatal for America and ultimately for Israel. They will totally turn the overwhelming majority of the Middle East's population against the United States. The lessons of Iraq speak for themselves. Eventually, if neocon policies continue to be pursued, the United States will be expelled from the region and that will be the beginning of the end for Israel as well." He continued by saying that "today it is becoming increasingly difficult to separate the Israeli-Palestinian problem, the Iraq problem and Iran from each other. Neither the United States nor Israel has the capacity to impose a unilateral solution in the Middle East. "[48]

But while the foreign policy establishment was concerned about the negative ramifications of the Israeli attack on Lebanon, America's politicians stood united behind Israel. On July 18, the Senate unanimously approved a nonbinding resolution "condemning Hamas and Hezbollah and their state sponsors and supporting Israel's exercise of its right to self-defense."[49] On July 20, the House of Representatives voted in favor of a comparable bill by the landslide margin of 410-8.[50] The near-unanimity of the vote reflected the immense power wielded by America's pro-Israel lobby, the American Israel Public Affairs Committee (AIPAC). "They [Congress] were given a resolution by AIPAC," noted Brzezinski. "They didn't prepare one."[51]

Even the anti-war left- wing of the Democratic Party, which had become critical of the continued American involvement in Iraq, was fully supportive of the Israeli attack on Lebanon. Many Democrats even wanted to prevent Iraqi Prime Minister Nouri al-Maliki from speaking to a joint session of Congress because he had criticized the Israeli invasion of Lebanon as "aggression."[52]

But despite the support from the United States, an overall advantage in weapons, and the willingness to indiscriminately attack civilian targets, Israel was unable to defeat Hezbollah, and finally after more than a month of war was willing to accept a ceasefire.

Instead of crushing Hezbollah and putting Iran in a corner as the neocons had hoped, just the opposite occurred. Middle East analyst Patrick Seale evaluated results of the conflict thus: "It would appear that the Tehran-Damascus-Hizballah axis has emerged more confident from the Lebanon War, while the United States and Israel look politically weaker, morally tarnished, and acutely vulnerable to guerrilla warfare."[53]

What was the neocon reaction to this defeat? Did it cause them to rethink their war agenda? Not at all! Instead they spun the defeat as providing even greater justification for a wider war. Michael Ledeen, for instance, asserted that the war in Lebanon illustrated that the conflict could not be localized. "Even if the Israelis had conducted a brilliant campaign that killed every single Hezbollah terrorist in Lebanon," Ledeen emphasized, "it would only have bought time. The Syrians and Iranians would have restocked, rearmed and resupplied the Hezbollahis, and prepared for the next battle." It was necessary to attack the sources of the terror. "Israel cannot destroy Hezbollah by fighting in Lebanon alone, just as we cannot provide Iraq and Afghanistan with decent security by fighting only there," Ledeen maintained.

> The destruction of Hezbollah requires regime change in Damascus. Security in Iraq and Afghanistan requires regime change in Damascus and Tehran. Lebanon, Gaza, Iraq, and Afghanistan are not separate conflicts. They are battlefields in a regional war.[54]

Similarly, William Kristol, in the August 21 issue of the *Weekly Standard*, held that events had confirmed the neocon war agenda: "Developments over these extraordinary last few weeks, from Tehran to Baghdad to Lebanon to London, have reminded us of the dangers we face and the implacability of our enemies."[55]

In the September 15 issue of the *Washington Post*, Charles Krauthammer wrote perhaps the strongest call for an American attack on Iran. Krauthammer stated that with diplomacy with Iran reaching an impasse it was necessary to look with "unflinching honesty at the military option." He acknowledged that the "costs will be terrible." An attack on Iran would "send oil prices overnight to $100 or even to $150 a barrel," which would "cause a worldwide recession." Iran would "shock the oil markets by closing the Strait of Hormuz," which the U.S. Navy would be able to reopen eventually but at a "considerable cost." Iran would also unleash its Shiite proxies in Iraq that would do significant damage to the coalition forces and the central government. Anti-American terrorism would increase around the globe. World opinion would be strongly against the United States. The Arab street would be enraged.[56]

Krauthammer, however, painted an even direr picture of a nuclear-armed Iran, which would result from American inaction. Iran then could not be deterred and would "immediately become the hegemonic power in the Arab Middle East." Iran's "nonnuclear Persian Gulf neighbors [would] accommodate to it," which would mean that "jihadist Iran will gain control of the most strategic region on the globe." This geopolitical development, however, would not be the greatest danger to American and the world. The "larger danger" would be the very possession of nuclear weapons by religious fanatics

> seized with an eschatological belief in the imminent apocalypse and in their own divine duty to hasten the End of Days. The mullahs are infinitely more likely to use these weapons than anyone in the history of the nuclear age. Every city in the civilized world will live under the specter of instant annihilation delivered either by missile or by terrorist. This from a country that has an official Death to America Day and has declared since Ayatollah Khomeini's ascension that Israel must be wiped off the map.

The likelihood of a nuclear-armed Iran being deterred by its adversaries, as all other nuclear countries have been, was not seen as a reasonable option. "Against millenarian fanaticism glorying in a cult of death," Krauthammer asserted, "deterrence is a mere wish. Is the West prepared to wager its cities with their millions of inhabitants on that feeble gamble?"[57]

Israel was pressuring the United States to attack Iran. The message to the United States was that Israel would launch a bombing attack if the United States failed to do so. According to Efraim Inbar, professor of political science at Bar-Ilan University and a well-known right-wing Israeli analyst,

Israel can undertake a limited pre-emptive strike. Israel certainly commands the weaponry, the manpower, and the guts to effectively take out key Iranian nuclear facilities .... While less suited to do the job than the United States, the Israeli military is capable of reaching the appropriate targets in Iran. With more to lose than the U.S. if Iran becomes nuclear, Israel has more incentive to strike."[58]

The Bush administration, despite some of its militant rhetoric, continued to consider negotiations with Iran. In October, Michael Ledeen critiqued the Bush administration's contradictory stances on Iran. He praised Secretary of State Rice for her observation that Iran was stirring up anti-American resistance in Iraq, but was dismayed by her continuing support for diplomacy. "If, as I believe, she is entirely right in her view of the malevolent role of Iran in the region, she should be calling for tough action against the Islamic Republic," instead of supporting "negotiations and the United Nations." Ledeen continued, "It's hard to imagine that a serious person can actually believe that, but she insists that the diplomatic option looks better than ever."[59]

The neocons were especially concerned that the United States would turn to Iran to solve the instability in Iraq, which was becoming a grave political problem for the Bush administration as a majority of the population had become fed up with the ongoing, and, in fact increasing, violence there. Such a diplomatic approach had been alluded to by James Baker, whose Iraq Study Group was gaining more attention.

As the November congressional elections approached, the key issue for the American people was the quagmire in Iraq. At least 105 U.S. troops died there in October, the fourth-highest monthly toll of the war.[60] The obvious message to be derived from the situation in Iraq was that things were getting worse rather than better. Political defeat for the Republican Party was in the air. The American people had turned against the Iraq war so strongly that the issue threatened not only to defeat the Republican Party in the 2006 midterm election but in the 2008 presidential election as well.[61]

Bush and Cheney, however, did not adjust their position on Iraq to the political climate but continued to maintain that the fight must continue until total victory. In a speech on September 4, Bush asserted that "we'll accept nothing less than complete victory ... We're on the offensive, and we will not rest, we will not retreat, and we will not withdraw from the fight, until this threat to civilization has been removed."[62]

The Bush administration's call to "stay the course," however, could not overcome the growing consensus among the both the general public and the foreign policy elite that it had become necessary for the United States to find an exit from Iraq. In the October 23 issue of the *Weekly Standard,* Reuel Marc Gerecht bemoaned the emerging disengagement consensus.

> There isn't really much difference between left and right: While Democrats Howard Dean, John Kerry, and John Murtha all wish for a rapid departure, former Republican Secretary of State James Baker will soon release his centrist "alternative," reportedly announcing that victory is impossible and our best bet amounts to "cut, pause, talk to the neighbors, and run." Conservative writers like George Will and William F. Buckley long ago gave up on the idea that the United States could help build a democratic government in Iraq. Fewer and fewer among the nation's political and intellectual elites believe that "staying the course" in Iraq advances the war against terrorism and our national interests in the Middle East.[63]

With the climate of opinion turned so strongly against the war, the neocons were forced to acknowledge that mistakes had been made; however, they did this without abandoning their Middle East war agenda. Despite the costs incurred so far in the war, Norman Podhoretz, for example, contended that the war was worth it. "We've paid an extraordinarily small price by any reasonable historical standard for a huge accomplishment," Podhoretz emphasized. "It's unseemly to be constantly whining."[64]

Much more negative than Podhoretz were a number of leading neocons interviewed by David Rose for an article in *Vanity Fair* magazine, excerpts of which were posted on the Web shortly before the November election. The neocons acknowledged the deepening quagmire in Iraq, but placed the blame on others. Rose summarized: "As Iraq slips further into chaos, the war's neoconservative boosters have turned sharply on the Bush administration, charging that their grand designs have been undermined by White House incompetence."[65]

Focusing on the flawed implementation of a good idea theme, Richard Perle maintained that

> The decisions did not get made that should have been. They didn't get made in a timely fashion, and the differences were argued out endlessly . . . . At the end of the day, you have to hold the president responsible . . . . I don't think he realized the extent of the opposition within his own administration, and the disloyalty.

Perle stated that if he had known how destructive the invasion would turn out, he would not have supported it.

I think if I had been delphic, and had seen where we are today, and people had said, "Should we go into Iraq?," I think now I probably would have said, "No, let's consider other strategies for dealing with the thing that concerns us most, which is Saddam supplying weapons of mass destruction to terrorists." . . . I don't say that because I no longer believe that Saddam had the capability to produce weapons of mass destruction, or that he was not in contact with terrorists. I believe those two premises were both correct. Could we have managed that threat by means other than a direct military intervention? Well, maybe we could have.[66]

David Frum likewise acknowledged failure and similarly faulted the administration's implementation process. Viewing the cause of the Iraq debacle as "failure at the center," Kenneth Adelman said that he had supported the attack because of his presumption of what he

considered to be the most competent national-security team since Truman was indeed going to be competent. They turned out to be among the most incompetent teams in the post-war era. Not only did each of them, individually, have enormous flaws, but together they were deadly, dysfunctional.

Concurring with this view, Eliot Cohen said that "the thing I know now that I did not know then is just how incredibly incompetent we would be."[67]

Continuing the incompetent policy implementation theme, Frank Gaffney held that Bush

doesn't in fact seem to be a man of principle who's steadfastly pursuing what he thinks is the right course. He talks about it, but the policy doesn't track with the rhetoric, and that's what creates the incoherence that causes us problems around the world and at home.

Michael Rubin similarly blamed Bush for failing to match his fine rhetoric with real action, which was similar to his father's actions in the Gulf War of 1991 "when he called the Iraqi people to rise up, and then had second thoughts and didn't do anything once they did."[68]

Rose summarized the neocons' view:

The neocons" position in this debate starts with an unprovable assertion: that when the war began, Iraq was "a doable do," to use a military planner's phrase cited by David Frum. If not for the administration's incompetence, they say, Saddam's tyranny could have been replaced with something not only better but also secure.

Rose was quite charitable with his reference to an "unprovable assertion"[69] since expert opinion before the American invasion predicted negative consequences.

Joshua Muravchik provided a more moderate assessment of the Bush administration's actions. While contending that it was essential to "reflect and rethink," Muravchik held that neocons "ought to do this without back-biting or abandoning Bush. All policies are perfect on paper, none in execution. All politicians are, well, politicians. Bush has embraced so much of what we believe that it would be silly to begrudge his deviations."[70] Muravchik acknowledged that all mistakes should not be attributed to others – the neocons likewise made mistakes.[71]

While acknowledging neocon errors, however, Muravchik's overall assessment was quite positive and represented a defense of the neocon war agenda. "As badly as things have gone in Iraq," he maintained,

> the war has not disproved neoconservative ideas. Iraq is a mess, and the U.S. mission there may fail. If that happens, neocons deserve blame because we were key supporters of the war. But American woes in Iraq may be traced to the conduct of the war rather than the decision to undertake it. In fact, despite the alarming spike of anti-Americanism worldwide, the political space in many Middle Eastern countries – such as Egypt, Lebanon, Morocco and most of the Persian Gulf nations – has widened appreciably in response to Bush's pressure and advocacy.[72]

Whatever the situation in Iraq, Muravchik supported the continuation of the neocon war agenda. "Make no mistake, President Bush will need to bomb Iran's nuclear facilities before leaving office," Muravchik emphasized.

> It is all but inconceivable that Iran will accept any peaceful inducements to abandon its drive for the bomb. Its rulers are religio-ideological fanatics who will not trade what they believe is their birthright to great power status for a mess of pottage. Even if things in Iraq get better, a nuclear-armed Iran will negate any progress there. Nothing will embolden terrorists and jihadists more than a nuclear-armed Iran.[73]

It was apparent that the neocons had not come to regard their Middle East war agenda itself as being faulty. The greatest errors, in their view, were simply in regard to war execution. None held that those errors should rule out the continuation of their war agenda with an attack on Iran. And it should be pointed out that from the standpoint of Israeli interests, Iraq had largely been dealt with – it was fragmentized and weakened as an enemy. Iran was now the target. As Raimondo observed: "The neocons, however, are not really interested in Iraq any longer: that, after all, was yesterday."[74]

The noted public disaffection with the war in Iraq was finally translated into a vote against Bush in the congressional elections of 2006. The election was a veritable disaster for the Republicans, as the Democrats captured enough seats to gain control of both the House of Representatives and the Senate.

Immediately after the election, Bush sacked Secretary of Defense Rumsfeld. Since Rumsfeld was viewed by the public as the symbol of the war on Iraq, it was not apparent, at the time, whether his ouster represented an actual volte-face on Iraq policy or simply a cosmetic gesture. Although he had made many enemies among the military, Rumsfeld had basked in public acclaim when America carried out its successful invasion of Iraq in the Spring of 2003. However, he faced mounting public and congressional opposition thereafter as the occupation turned sour. As early as December 2004, a Washington Post-ABC poll showed that 52 percent of those surveyed wanted Bush to remove him.[75] Rumsfeld had become the fall guy for the war's failures.

Many neocons were quite willing to shift the blame of the war to their erstwhile ally Rumsfeld. Rumsfeld had seen the war on Iraq as a means to demonstrate the value of a small, high tech military. Neocons, of course, had championed this small force approach in the war build-up because it served to facilitate an attack. As the occupation became a quagmire, however, many neocons began to charge that it was the insufficient size of the military that was the cause of the difficulties. In December 2004, William Kristol, for example, complained that Rumsfeld's

> theory about the military is at odds with the President's geopolitical strategy. He [Rumsfeld] wants this light, transformed military, but we've got to win a real war, which involves using a lot of troops and building a nation, and that's at the core of the president's strategy for rebuilding the Middle East.[76]

On January 28, 2005, PNAC released an open letter to the congressional leadership stating that an increase in the size of American ground forces was necessary, which reflected a repudiation of the Rumsfeld doctrine. It was published as the lead editorial in the *Weekly Standard*. "The United States military is too small for the responsibilities we are asking it to assume," the letter read.

> Those responsibilities are real and important. They are not going away. The United States will not and should not become less engaged in the world in the years to come. But our national security, global peace and stability, and the de-

fense and promotion of freedom in the post-9/11 world require a larger military force than we have today. The administration has unfortunately resisted increasing our ground forces to the size needed to meet today's (and tomorrow's) missions and challenges.

Among the letter's signatories were William Kristol, Joshua Muravchik, Randy Scheunemann, Robert Kagan, Max Boot, Eliot Cohen, and Reuel Marc Gerecht.[77] Of course, tossed into the memory hole was the fact that it was the neocons themselves who, prior to the invasion, had argued the sufficiency of a small military force.

In many respects, the focus on Rumsfeld and his ultimate removal served to deflect attention from the neoconservatives, who were the actual architects of the war, whereas Rumsfeld's passion was transforming the military to meet the supposed challenges of the 21st century. Their interests had converged in the move to war on Iraq. Rumsfeld had thought that Iraq offered the ideal venue to demonstrate the advantages of his transformed, high-tech military. The neocons provided him support against the traditionally-inclined military brass. For the neocons, Rumsfeld provided support for their Iraq war and perhaps, equally important, cover. In essence, Rumsfeld's Cabinet position and high-profile activities put him in the media limelight. When public opinion turned against the war, Rumsfeld ineluctably became the magnet for criticism.

Rumsfeld's replacement in December 2006 was Robert Gates, an associate of the elder Bush. In the Bush I administration, Gates served as deputy national security adviser under Brent Scowcroft and then subsequently as director of the CIA. Like Scowcroft, Gates had publicly questioned the war on Iraq. Moreover, he also advocated a more conciliatory approach to Iran, a policy that he advocated in the report he co-authored with Zbigniew Brzezinski for the Council on Foreign Relations in 2004. Gates also had been a member of the Iraq Study Group headed by James Baker.[78] Zbigniew Brzezinski said he hoped the appointment would mean "a major corrective in American policy toward the Middle East."[79]

In his confirmation hearing, Gates made a number of comments that conflicted with the neocons' outlook. He said that even if Iran developed nuclear weapons it was highly unlikely that it would use them to attack Israel, but rather nuclear weapons would serve as deterrence against other nuclear powers in its vicinity, which he included Israel, Russia, Pakistan, and United States. In referring to Israeli nuclear weapons, Gates was breaking a taboo that bothered numerous Israelis. Since the Israeli government had never explicitly acknowledged possession of nuclear weapons, the United States government never officially confirmed Israel's possession of these weapons.[80] Gates further stated that an American attack on Iran would destabilize the region and should be undertaken only as an action of the "last resort."[81]

The apparent repudiation of the Bush war policy by the electorate also led to much greater attention being given to the Iraq Study Group headed by James Baker. According to the prevailing media view, political rejection had forced President Bush to turn to the advisors of his father – the very people who had been rebuffed in his reliance on the neocons. *Washington Post* columnist Jim Hoagland, who heretofore had sympathized with much of the neocon policy, assessed the situation:

> President Bush lost more than a midterm election and a cantankerous defense secretary last week. He also abandoned any lingering chance of remaking U.S. foreign policy into a radical force for democratic change in the Middle East and elsewhere .... History's seemingly unlimited store of irony now makes Bush 43 the evident instrument of the resurgence of the "realist" school of foreign policy so beloved of Bush 41 and so regularly scorned by this president – until he turned to it for salvation in Iraq and elsewhere.[82]

Howard Fineman in *Newsweek* made a similar analysis of the post-election changes. "President George W. Bush's Iraq policy is now in the political equivalent of receivership – a bankrupt project that is about to be placed in the hands of the worldly-wise pragmatists who surrounded the president's own father," Fineman noted. "Think of them as receivers in bankruptcy, looking for ways to salvage America's military and moral assets after a post-September 11 adventure that voters (and most of the rest of the world) concluded was a waste of blood and treasure."[83]

When it was released on December 6, the Iraq Study Group report forthrightly asserted that America could not prevail militarily. However, it rejected a "precipitate withdrawal" of American troops, but rather advocated a gradual exit of all combat units by 2008, with American military personnel remaining to advise Iraqi forces.

The authors eschewed a quick American departure because it

> would almost certainly produce greater sectarian violence and further deterioration of conditions .... The near-term results would be a significant power vacuum, greater human suffering, regional destabilization, and a threat to the

global economy. Al Qaeda would depict our withdrawal as a historic victory. If we leave and Iraq descends into chaos, the long-range consequences could eventually require the United States to return.[84]

The Baker Commission's proposed steps to extricate America from the Iraq imbroglio were constrained by policy parameters determined by what had been considered America's vital interest of stability. Neocon policy had created a condition of fragmentation and instability in Iraq. Such a condition would not be rectified by an American troop withdrawal; rather, it was quite conceivable that without the American occupation more fragmentation and internecine warfare would result. In stipulating that the U.S. must not pull out precipitously, the traditional foreign policy elite inadvertently revealed the genius of neoconservative foreign policy on Iraq. The neoconservatives had driven American policy into a position that their foreign policy adversaries – given their perception of stability as a vital American interest – could not easily abandon, but must now, to some extent, continue. And the longer the United States remained in Iraq increased the possibility that the war would spread to Iran and elsewhere in the Middle East.

The most glaring differences between the Baker Commission and the neocons were not on Iraq, but rather pertained to the issues of Iran and Israel/Palestine. It was on these issues that the Baker Commission offered a radical break with neoconservative policy. On Iran, the Baker Commission pursued rapprochement rather than destabilization and regime change, as sought by the neocons. Iran and Syria were to be made integral partners of an international Iraq Support Group, which would work for the stabilization of that country. Regarding Israel and Palestine, the Baker Commission recognized that stability could not be established in Iraq or elsewhere in the Middle East without first achieving a negotiated solution to the Israeli-Palestinian conflict. This was the polar opposite of the neocon view that a political reconfiguration of the Middle East was the necessary precondition for peace between Israel and the Palestinians.

While the Iraq Study Group's recommendations might not necessarily bring about true peace or satisfy war critics who sought an immediate withdrawal, it did represent a repudiation of the fundamental aspects of the neocon foreign policy. In the *Washington Post*, Glen Kessler and Thomas E. Ricks referred to the report as the "The Realist Manifesto." "Throughout its pages," Kessler and Ricks maintained, "the report reflects the foreign policy establishment's disdain for the 'neoconservative' policies long espoused by

President Bush and his aides."[85] Joe Conason opined in *Salon*: "With the broad establishment acceptance of the Iraq Study Group's new report, the embattled neoconservatives have clearly lost the debate over Iraq. Their belligerent foreign policy has been universally discredited."[86]

War critic Justin Raimondo underscored the critical significance of the report, asserting that

> in spite of its flaws . . . the Baker commission report is a giant leap forward in more ways than one: to begin with, it breaks the long-standing taboo against talking to the Iranians and the Syrians. Secondly, it links the question of Palestine to the broader issue of maintaining peace in the Middle East, and, not only that, it also acknowledges the centrality of the Palestinian problem. Our Israel-centric policy in the region has ruled out dealing with either of these aged sore spots: the great value of the Baker-Hamilton report is that it reasserts the necessity of pursuing American interests, as opposed to purely Israeli interests.[87]

Raimondo continued:

> The significance of this report goes far beyond the issue of how we get out of Iraq: Baker-Hamilton marks the beginning of resistance by some in the elite to our seriously distorted and dysfunctional foreign policy, which puts narrow ideological interests above the national interest.[88]

Neocons, as would be expected, were bitterly hostile to the Baker Commission, and their criticism began before the official release of the report, as the general thrust of the study was being revealed in the media. Michael Rubin, a fellow at the neoconservative American Enterprise Institute (AEI), had resigned from an "expert working group" advising the Iraq Study Group. In October, Rubin accused Baker and his Democratic co-chair, Lee Hamilton, of having "gerrymandered these advisory panels to ratify predetermined recommendations."[89]

Eliot Cohen asserted in *The Wall Street Journal* that

> [t]he creation of the Iraq Study Group reflects the vain hope that well-meaning, senior, former public officials can find ideas that have not already occurred to people inside government; that those new ideas can redeem incompetent execution and insufficient resources; that salvation can come from a Washington establishment whose wisdom was exaggerated in its heyday, and which has in any event succumbed to a kind of political-intellectual entropy since the 1960s; that a public commission can do the work of oversight that Congress has shirked for five years in the misguided belief that it would thus support an administration struggling to do its best in a difficult situation. This is no way to run a war, and most definitely, no way to win it.[90]

The major neocon concern involved the Baker commission's position on Iran and Syria. Charles Krauthammer in his castigation of the "realists," exclaimed that "to suggest that Iran and Syria share our interests in stability is the height of fantasy. In fact, Iran and Syria have an overriding interest in chaos in Iraq – which is precisely why they each have been abetting the insurgency and fanning civil war."[91]

After excoriating the nature of the report, John Podhoretz focused on its reference to Iran and Syria:

> What's even more appalling, if true, is the group's other key recommendation – which is that America should try to find answers to its problems through an international conference that would include Syria and Iran. What do Syria and Iran want more than anything else in the world? To see an American defeat in Iraq . . . . They're going to be a great help. But then, that's Baker for you. Give him a problem and he'll tell you your best hope of solving it can be found in sucking up to an Arab dictator.[92]

Frank Gaffney, head of the neoconservative Center for Security Policy, brought out the anti-Semitic card. "Jim Baker's hostility towards the Jews is a matter of record and has endeared him to Israel's foes in the region," Gaffney asserted.[93] In a later column, "Iraq Surrender Group," Gaffney held that the group's recommendations would "throw free Iraq to the wolves" and "allow the Mideast's only bona fide democracy, the Jewish State, to be snuffed in due course."[94]

When the report was released, Caroline Glick, senior Middle East fellow at the Center for Security Policy and the deputy managing editor of the *Jerusalem Post*, declared:

> When the history of our times is written, this week will be remembered as the week that Washington decided to let the Islamic Republic of Iran go nuclear. Hopefully it will also be remembered as the moment the Jews arose and refused to allow Iran to go nuclear.
>
> With the publication of the recommendations of the Iraq Study Group chaired by former U.S. secretary of state James Baker III and former congressman Lee Hamilton, the debate about the war in Iraq changed. From a war for victory against Islamofascism and for democracy and freedom, the war became reduced to a conflict to be managed by appeasing the U.S.'s sworn enemies in the interests of stability, and at the expense of America's allies.[95]

In successive lead editorials in the *Weekly Standard*, William Kristol and Robert Kagan, strongly attacked the Baker commission and its foreign policy mindset. In their December 4 editorial, they wrote that what passes for "realism" today has very little to do with reality. Indeed, if you look at some of the "realist" proposals on the table, "realism" has come to be a kind of code word for surrendering American interests and American allies, as well as American principles, in the Middle East.

They summarized the realist thinking thus:

> We must retreat from Iraq, and thus abandon all those Iraqis – Shiite, Sunni, Kurd, and others – who have depended on the United States for safety and the promise of a better future. We must abandon our allies in Lebanon and the very idea of an independent Lebanon in order to win Syria's support for our retreat from Iraq. We must abandon our opposition to Iran's nuclear program in order to convince Iran to help us abandon Iraq. And we must pressure our ally, Israel, to accommodate a violent Hamas in order to gain radical Arab support for our retreat from Iraq.[96]

After the report was released they titled their article "A Perfect Failure." Although alleging that the report contained nothing new and that its recommendations would not be accepted by President Bush, they accused the Baker commission of having "deliberately created" the idea that "Jim Baker and not the president was going to call the shots in Iraq from now on."[97]

Ironically, Michael Ledeen believed that what he disparagingly referred to as the "Iraq Surrender Commission Report," had, by its focus on Iran, unintentionally provided the United States the "window of success" to take the necessary militant measures against that country. "At first I, too, thought the Iraq Surrender Commission Report was a total downer," Ledeen opined. "But I'm more and more convinced that it was a great blessing. Not that they intended it to work out this way, but the Wise Men (and the token Lady) have elevated Iran to its rightful place in our national squabble over the war: dead center." The goal of the commission's members was to remove

> American troops out of Iraq, and therefore they advocate appeasing the Syrians and Iranians. But a considerable number of Americans don't want to be humiliated by the clerical fascists in Tehran, and I think it's fair to say the recommendations have largely bombed.

In Ledeen's view, the crux of the situation was that "Iran is waging war against us and our allies throughout the region." As a consequence, "a real debate about Iran," as the Baker commission report proposed, could "force us to face the real (regional) strategic problem." If that were done, America could move on to "a serious war-winning policy, which must have as its basic mission the removal of the regimes in Tehran and Damascus."[98]

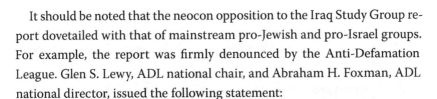

It should be noted that the neocon opposition to the Iraq Study Group report dovetailed with that of mainstream pro-Jewish and pro-Israel groups. For example, the report was firmly denounced by the Anti-Defamation League. Glen S. Lewy, ADL national chair, and Abraham H. Foxman, ADL national director, issued the following statement:

> The Iraq Study Group gets it wrong when it comes to the Arab- Israeli conflict. We reject the suggestion that there is a connection between finding a solution to the war in Iraq and direct involvement of the U.S. in solving the Arab-Israeli conflict based on the recommendations in the report. The goal of resolving the Arab-Israeli conflict should stand on its own and has always been a key objective of U.S. foreign policy. It would be a terrible mistake to confuse the recent disintegration in Iraq with the decades-old Arab-Israeli conflict.[99]

And regarding the Iraq Study Group's recommendation of engagement with Iran, the statement read:

> We are appalled that one of the major principles of planning for the future stability of the region in America's interest does not include the total rejection of a nuclear Iran, because a nuclear Iran would do more to destabilize the region and undermine America's interests than any other single factor. To relegate the issue of a nuclear Iran to the U.N. Security Council for a resolution is unrealistic.[100]

The American Jewish Committee likewise criticized the report. It held that engagement with Iran was inappropriate because "Iran actively supports international terrorism, promotes the annihilation of Israel as state policy, threatens its neighbors, viciously suppresses human rights, and pursues nuclear weapons capability in open defiance of its international obligations."

Regarding the Israel/Palestinian issue, the American Jewish Committee stated that

> there is a quality of either naiveté or ungrounded optimism in the Iraq Study Group's suggestion that Israeli-Palestinian peace will result from internationally convened dialogue between the democratically elected government of Israel and, as the report states, "those (Palestinians) who accept Israel's right to exist."[101]

The Iraq Study Group report clearly brought out the differences between the traditional foreign policy establishment and the neocons. Mike Whitney in *CounterPunch* provided a perceptive analysis of this conflict. "The tension between the Bush administration and the members of the Iraq Study Group," Whitney observed, illustrates the widening chasm between old-guard U.S. imperialists and "Israel-first" neoconservatives. The divisions are setting the stage for a major battle between the two camps. The winner will probably decide U.S. policy in the Middle East for the next decade.

Whitney continued:

> So, the battle lines have been drawn. On one side we have James Baker and his corporate classmates who want to restore order while preserving America's imperial role in the region. And, on the other side, we have the neo-Trotskyites and Israeli-Jacobins who seek a fragmented and chaotic Middle East where Israel is the dominant power. (see "A Clean Break")[102]

As the year 2006 drew to a close, it was apparent that the neoconservative agenda had been discredited. But did this completely rule out its continuation, even without much active effort by neocons within the administration? For, in order to preclude the possibility of war with Iran, it was essential to undertake the difficult endeavor of removing United States forces from the area. Having American forces in nearby Iraq provided the possibility of an incident with Iran that could lead to war. And no matter what the shape of public opinion, or the view of the traditional foreign policy elite, it was President Bush who would have to make the decision to remove the troops and negotiate with regimes that had been targeted for destruction by the neocons. The question was whether President Bush would actually make such a policy volte-face.

chapter 16

2007: ON TO IRAN

WHILE MEDIA COMMENTATORS in the fall of 2006 had expected Bush to reverse course away from the neocon agenda and adopt the establishment foreign policy realism of his father, such a change did not take place. Despite the serious difficulties in Iraq, Bush essentially dismissed the suggestions of the Iraq Study Group and the will of the majority of the American people. He had become personally committed to the war, which had become the defining element of his presidency. On November 28, in Amman, Jordan, Bush emphasized that that he would not withdraw American troops from Iraq until the "job is complete." Bush contended that "This business about graceful exit just simply has no realism to it at all."[1] By the end of December, Bush was considering sending more troops to Iraq for a "surge" to stabilize Baghdad, despite opposition from the Joints Chiefs of Staff.[2]

On January 10, 2007, President Bush presented his new Iraq plan to expand troop numbers in a nationally broadcast address from the White House library. "The most urgent priority for success in Iraq," he explained, "is security, especially in Baghdad." He announced that he was sending more than 20,000 additional troops to Baghdad and Anbar Province.[3]

Like the rest of the Bush administration's policy on Iraq, what was popularly referred to as the "surge" strategy emerged from the neoconservatives. In this case, it was formulated at AEI. Its principal developers were Frederick W. Kagan, a military historian at the American Enterprise Institute, and General Jack Keane, former vice chief of staff of the U.S. Army, and it was presented to Bush in mid-December.[4] "We took the results of our

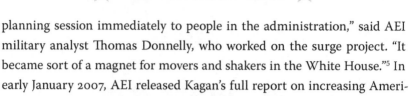

planning session immediately to people in the administration," said AEI military analyst Thomas Donnelly, who worked on the surge project. "It became sort of a magnet for movers and shakers in the White House."[5] In early January 2007, AEI released Kagan's full report on increasing American forces in Iraq, entitled "Choosing Victory: A Plan for Success in Iraq."[6] The policy advocated by Kagan and Keane was not simply a short-time increase of troops but rather represented an escalation of the war.[7]

Once again, President Bush rejected the views of his military advisers. General John Abizaid, head of Central Command, expressed doubts that additional troops would serve any useful purpose. "You have to internationalize the problem, you have to attack it diplomatically, geo-strategically," Abizaid told the *New York Times*. "You just can't apply a microscope on a particular problem in downtown Baghdad . . . and say that somehow or another, if you throw enough military forces at it, you are going to solve the broader issues in the region of extremism."[8] The Joint Chiefs were said to be skeptical of the plan, with Army Chief of Staff General Peter Schoomaker warning Congress in mid-December that the army was already stretched too thin and questioned the value of increasing troop levels in Iraq.[9] Schoomaker would reiterate that view in one of his last testimonies to Congress in February, before retiring from the Army.[10] The view that the military was being stretched too far had also been expressed by Colin Powell in December 2006. "That surge cannot be sustained," Powell maintained. "The current active Army . . . and the Marine Corps is not large enough for the kinds of missions they're being asked to perform."[11]

Bush's plan to increase the number of troops had little support in Congress either. In a letter to Bush released on January 5, the new Democratic congressional leaders, House Speaker Nancy Pelosi and Senate Majority Leader Harry Reid, urged President Bush not to deploy additional U.S. troops in Iraq, referring to the concept as "a strategy that you have already tried and that has already failed."[12] Many Republicans were also cool to the idea of increasing troop levels. As journalist Jim Lobe wrote:

> Indeed, aside from Bush himself, the only forces that appear enthusiastic about what the White House calls a "surge" – and what critics call an escalation – are neoconservatives, who led the drive to invade Iraq, and two of their dwindling number of Congressional supporters, Republican Sen. John McCain and Democratic Sen. Joseph Lieberman.[13]

The general public was also opposed to the surge. An ABC News/Washington Post poll in February 2007 confirmed the public opposition to the surge, finding that two-thirds of the participants to be in opposition to an increase of troops.[14]

As the Bush administration was increasing troop levels in Iraq, a report from the Council on Foreign Relations, the bastion of establishment foreign policy thinking, said that victory in Iraq was impossible and called for withdrawal. "Staying in Iraq can only drive up the price of those gains in blood, treasure and strategic position," wrote Steven Simon, the author of the report, titled "After the Surge: The Case for U.S. Military Disengagement from Iraq."[15]

But it was apparent that Bush was indifferent to both public opinion and establishment thinking on Iraq and that he remained influenced by the neocon agenda. For not only was he unwilling to withdraw American troops from Iraq, but he gave the indication that he actually might widen the war. In his January 10 speech, Bush had strong language for Iran and Syria, maintaining that those countries allowed terrorists "to move in and out of Iraq" and that the Iranians were providing material support for attacks on American troops, which he promised to stop. Illustrating a tougher policy toward Iran, Bush announced the dispatch of an additional aircraft carrier in the Persian Gulf. A few days after the speech, U.S. special forces raided a Iranian liaison office in the Kurdish capital of Arbil and captured five Iranian officials.[16]

These aggressive moves could trigger war with Iran, even if the United States did not deliberately initiate an attack. In fact, the very maintenance of troops in Iraq could engender such a result. "If the United States continues to be bogged down in a protracted bloody involvement in Iraq," Zbigniew Brzezinski testified before the Senate Foreign Relations Committee in February,

> the final destination on this downhill track is likely to be a head-on conflict with Iran and with much of the world of Islam at large. A plausible scenario for a military collision with Iran involves Iraqi failure to meet the benchmarks; followed by accusations of Iranian responsibility for the failure; then by some provocation in Iraq or a terrorist act in the U.S. blamed on Iran; culminating in a "defensive" U.S. military action against Iran that plunges a lonely America into a spreading and deepening quagmire eventually ranging across Iraq, Iran, Afghanistan, and Pakistan.[17]

The possibility of such an incident became apparent with the Iranian arrest of 15 British sailors at the mouth of the Shatt al-Arab waterway for purportedly entering Iranian territory, water boundaries of which are unclear.[18]

American bellicosity would continue. In late May, a U.S. Navy force, including carrier strike groups and an amphibious assault ship contingent, arrived in the Persian Gulf to conduct war games on Iran's virtual doorstep.[19] A few weeks earlier, Vice-President Cheney had made it quite clear that America's military build-up in the region was directed at Iran. Speaking from the deck of an American aircraft carrier 150 miles off Iran's coast, Cheney warned Tehran that the United States would use its naval power to prevent it from interfering with oil shipments or "gaining nuclear weapons and dominating this region."[20]

It should be pointed out that the Bush administration was not alone in taking an aggressive posture toward Iran. In response to a question about military action against Iran, John McCain, who was campaigning in South Carolina for the 2008 Republican nomination, jokingly responded by singing the chorus of the surf-rocker classic song "Barbara Ann" with the altered words: "Bomb bomb bomb, bomb bomb Iran." McCain proclaimed that "Iran is dedicated to the destruction of Israel. That alone should concern us but now they are trying for nuclear capabilities. I totally support the President when he says we will not allow Iran to destroy Israel."[21]

War on Iran was also supported by various liberal congressional champions of Israel. On June 10 on CBS TV's "Face the Nation" program, Senator Joe Lieberman called for the United States to take "aggressive military action" against Iran in response to its supposed attacks on U.S. troops inside Iraq. Lieberman said that on a recent trip to Iraq he learned that "as many as 200 American soldiers" had been killed by Iranians and Iranian-trained forces. "I think we've got to be prepared to take aggressive military action against the Iranians to stop them from killing Americans in Iraq," Lieberman maintained. He stressed that he was not advocating a "massive ground invasion of Iran," but rather a strike at a base near the Iraq border where "they are training these people coming back into Iraq to kill our soldiers."[22] Such a strike, of course, could easily lead to a major conflagration.

In late May, House Foreign Affairs Committee Chair, Tom Lantos (Democratic, California), an outspoken proponent of Israel, introduced the "Iran Counter-Proliferation Act of 2007," designed to establish a virtual economic stranglehold on Iran by expanding sanctions on Iranian imports to include all goods. Significantly, it explicitly called for the expansion of sanctioning to foreign subsidiaries of U.S. companies so that U.S. companies would be penalized for their foreign subsidiaries dealings with Iran. Lantos stated that

"The corporate barons running giant oil companies – who have cravenly turned a blind eye to Iran's development of nuclear weapons – have come to assume that the Iran Sanctions Act will never be implemented. This charade now will come to a long overdue end."[23]

These belligerent measures, however, were insufficient for the neoconservatives. Now outside the Bush administration, John Bolton complained about the Bush administration's supposed reliance on diplomacy toward Iran. ""The current approach of the Europeans and the Americans is not just doomed to failure, but dangerous," he lamented. "Dealing with [the Iranians] just gives them what they want, which is more time." Bolton emphasized that the United States had to pursue a policy of "overthrowing the regime and getting in a new one that won't pursue nuclear weapons," which might necessitate "a last-resort use of force."[24]

Norman Podhoretz was more explicit in advocating war in his article, "The Case for Bombing Iran," in the June 2007 issue of *Commentary*. Fitting Iran into the context of the World War IV scenario, Podhoretz emphasized that "Iran too is a front in World War IV. Moreover, its effort to build a nuclear arsenal makes it the potentially most dangerous one of all."[25] Podhoretz's devoted extensive attention to the allegedly diabolical President Ahmadinejad, the new Hitleresque villain, though he simultaneously portrayed the major enemy as "Islamofascism" – a purportedly virulent ideology transcending an individual or even one country.[26]

Podhoretz outlined the grave danger to Israel, writing that the Iranians' "first priority, as repeatedly and unequivocally announced by their president, Mahmoud Ahmadinejad, is to 'wipe Israel off the map' – a feat that could not be accomplished by conventional weapons alone." However, Podhoretz stressed that Ahmadinejad's ambitions were far more extensive, encompassing the domination of the "greater Middle East" so as "to control the oilfields of the region and the flow of oil out of it through the Persian Gulf." Podhoretz held that if Iran possessed nuclear weapons it could attain this imperial goal by "intimidation and blackmail" alone.[27] (Viewed against the backdrop of Israel's nuclear arsenal, this claim is something less than convincing.)

Podhoretz went on to claim, rather outrageously, that Ahmadinejad's territorial ambitions stretched beyond the Middle East to the encompass the entire globe. In this case, too, hegemony would be the result of nuclear intimidation rather than war. Even America would be so intimidated because "confronted by Islamofascists armed by Iran with nuclear weapons, we would become more and more hesitant to risk resisting the emergence of a world shaped by their will and tailored to their wishes."[28]

Podhoretz equated negotiation with Iran with the West's unsuccessful attempts to appease Hitler prior to World War II. "Like Hitler," Podhoretz opined, "he [Ahmadinejad] is a revolutionary whose objective is to overturn the going international system and to replace it in the fullness of time with a new order dominated by Iran and ruled by the religio-political culture of Islamofascism."[29]

Economic sanctions or any other short-of-war measures, Podhoretz emphasized, were insufficient to deal with such a rapacious enemy.

> In short, the plain and brutal truth is that if Iran is to be prevented from developing a nuclear arsenal, there is no alternative to the actual use of military force – any more than there was an alternative to force if Hitler was to be stopped in 1938.[30]

Ruling out a land invasion of Iran, Podhoretz held that only airstrikes should be undertaken. And he went so far as to acknowledge that various worst-case scenarios could result from such an attack.

> To wit: Iran would retaliate by increasing the trouble it is already making for us in Iraq. It would attack Israel with missiles armed with non-nuclear warheads but possibly containing biological and/or chemical weapons. There would be a vast increase in the price of oil, with catastrophic consequences for every economy in the world, very much including our own. The worldwide outcry against the inevitable civilian casualties would make the anti-Americanism of today look like a love-fest.[31]

Podhoretz, nonetheless, held that such disastrous consequences did not militate against the need for an attack.

Podhoretz addressed the failure of the Bush administration to strike Iran despite President Bush's perception of the grave danger posed by that country. He interpreted Bush's reliance on diplomacy as a way to clearly illustrate that strategy's futility, and thus generate greater public support for the military option, although granting that Bush might see a diplomatic solution as a highly improbable long shot. Podhoretz claimed that he expected Bush to ultimately launch an attack, saying that "my guess is that he intends, within the next 21 months, to order air strikes against the Iranian nuclear facilities from the three U.S. aircraft carriers already sitting nearby."[32] However, Podhoretz seemed far from certain of this outcome, seeing a willing Bush being restrained by external contingencies. "It now remains to be seen," Podhoretz concluded,

> whether this President, battered more mercilessly and with less justification than any other in living memory, and weakened politically by the enemies of his policy in the Middle East in general and Iraq in particular, will find it possible to take the only action that can stop Iran from following through on its evil intentions both toward us and toward Israel. As an American and as a Jew, I pray with all my heart that he will.[33]

It was revealing that Podhoretz's penultimate paragraph emphasized that an attack on Iran was essential to protect Israel and the Jewish people. "Much of the world has greeted Ahmadinejad's promise to wipe Israel off the map with something close to insouciance," Podhoretz bemoaned.

> In fact, it could almost be said of the Europeans that they have been more upset by Ahmadinejad's denial that a Holocaust took place 60 years ago than by his determination to set off one of his own as soon as he acquires the means to do so. In a number of European countries, Holocaust denial is a crime, and the European Union only recently endorsed that position. Yet for all their retrospective remorse over the wholesale slaughter of Jews back then, the Europeans seem no readier to lift a finger to prevent a second Holocaust than they were the first time around.[34]

It can be wondered why Podhoretz would assume that Israel, possessed of something like 200 to 400 nuclear weapons, would have to depend on other states to prevent the extermination of its citizenry. Perhaps, Podhoretz did not really believe that the military threat to Israel's Jewish population was really of this magnitude, but that such frightening scenarios were necessary to engender support for policies to advance Israel's long-term security.

Despite the constant drumbeat for war on Iran, no such war seemed to be getting closer. Any military move on Iran was being held in abeyance by the public's dissatisfaction with war in Iraq, especially the failure of the surge to curb the violence there. Bush, however, was still able to determine policy in Iraq. And despite half-hearted and ineffective Democratic efforts in Congress to include troop-withdrawal timetables and benchmarks in

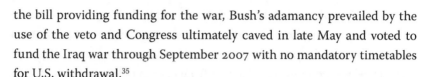

the bill providing funding for the war, Bush's adamancy prevailed by the use of the veto and Congress ultimately caved in late May and voted to fund the Iraq war through September 2007 with no mandatory timetables for U.S. withdrawal.[35]

To William Kristol and Frederick W. Kagan the defeat of domestic, anti-war efforts to restrict the Bush's actions in Iraq would give the United States a chance to succeed in Iraq. "Congressional battles calling into doubt our commitment to winning in Iraq," they wrote,

> have been the major threat to progress since the president began pursuing the right strategy in January. The president, supported by congressional Republicans, has beaten back that threat. Now he needs to deal with his own administration, which has not made up its collective mind to support the president's strategy wholeheartedly. Mixed messages from Bush's advisers and cabinet undermine the efforts of our commanders in the field . . . . This is no time to hedge or hesitate. Now is the time to put everything behind making the president's strategy – which looks to be a winning strategy – succeed.[36]

To Kristol and Kagan, victory in the war was a matter of proper strategy and will. With the surge, the strategy was in place, now the need was to simply implement it.

Despite Bush's ability to achieve a political victory, evidence clearly showed in the first half of 2006 that the situation in Iraq was not improving. An American internal military assessment in late May found that the surge was falling short of its goal, with American and Iraqi government forces having secured less than a third of Baghdad's neighborhoods.[37] Similarly, a Pentagon report to Congress, released in June 15, 2007, observed that levels of violence in Iraq had not declined since the start of the surge.[38] Moreover, 127 American troops lost their lives in Iraq in May, the third worst total for American forces since the March 2003 invasion.[39] Public opinion continued in its anti-war trajectory a CNN/Opinion Research Poll of June 22–4 showing that only 30% of Americans still supported the war.[40]

The mounting opposition to continuing the war in Iraq had the effect of muting any support for launching an attack on Iran, which meant that Secretary of State Condoleezza Rice was able to push what was described as a diplomatic approach to Iran. However, it was a very half-hearted diplomacy.[41] And Rice did not eschew the possible use of more forceful action. "The president has made clear that we are on a course that is a diplomatic course," Rice stated in early June, "but it is a diplomatic course backed up by disincentives for Iran to continue its activities." By early July, her language became even stronger. In a television interview with CNBC, Rice described Iran as a "very dangerous state with very dangerous policies" and that America's "relationship" with Iran was "increasingly difficult."[42] She offered a litany of American grievances regarding Iran: support of Hezbollah and Hamas; "supporting and arming" of militias in Iraq that threaten American forces; "pursuit of the technologies that would lead to a nuclear weapon;" a "crackdown on their own population" and arrests of people with dual Iranian-American citizenship." Rice expressed her support for the existing United States military pressure on Iran and in regard to a possible American military strike in the future, Rice said that "the President's never going to take his options off the table and frankly, no one should want the American President to take his options off the table."[43]

America's diplomatic position was completely one-sided. It should be noted that the United States' complaints against Iran as expressed by Rice involved activities that did not actually affect the United States – support for Israel's enemies and internal repression. Moreover, the United States did not seem to recognize the need for any quid pro quo – the process was simply geared to having Iran make concessions, with no reciprocation made by the United States. In fact, instead of offering to bargain, the United States was seeking to pressure Iran to make concessions. In its stance toward Iran, the United States had not adopted the full-fledged give-and-take diplomacy recommended by the Baker-Hamilton Iraq Study Group and the Council of Foreign Relations 2004 report, *Iran: Time for a New Approach,* directed by Zbigniew Brzezinski and Robert Gates.

With America's forceful actions and threats, concrete results from the very limited Bush administration diplomatic approach to Iran were almost non-existent, as Rice acknowledged when in July 2007 she said the relationship was becoming more difficult. Perhaps the major accomplishment was the first formal meeting between Iranian and United States officials since the 1979 Iranian revolution when the United States ambassador to Iraq, Ryan Crocker, and his Iranian counterpart met for four hours on May 28 in Baghdad. Hosted by Iraqi Prime Minister Nouri al-Maliki the discussion focused on Iraq. Both sides agreed that there was a need for stability, but the United States accused Iran of fomenting violence in Iraq by arming Shiite militia groups while the Iranians claimed that the United States forces in Iraq were the cause of the violence.[44]

As things seemed to reach their nadir for the Bush administration in Iraq, a turn-around would take place. The improvement was especially boosted by the presentation before Congress in September of General David Petraeus, the new commanding general of coalition forces in Iraq, in which he calmly provided facts that showed that the surge was having a positive effect.[45] Undoubtedly, Petraeus' brilliant performance contributed to the aura that the surge was working, but it would become apparent that the surge was really working, at least, in terms of reducing the violence and in diminishing the power and popular support of the Al Qaeda insurgents. In the last months of 2007, U.S. casualties and Iraqi deaths dropped markedly to the lowest points in two years. And the surge clearly worked in terms of Washington politics. By reducing violence it put the antiwar Democrats in disarray and gave Bush a free hand to continue the occupation of Iraq, although a majority of the people still did not support the war.[46]

However, the rationale for the surge was that improved security would provide the opportunity for the central government in Iraq to work for national reconciliation and gain greater popular support. This clearly did not take place. The surge, in fact, militated against national unity because a fundamental United States tactic was to strengthen local Sunni tribal leaders to fight the Al Qaeda insurgents. The tribal leaders effectively fought Al Qaeda but, in the process, set up there own little fiefdoms independent of central government control. In his testimony to the Committee on Iraq of the Senate Foreign Relations Committee in April 2008, retired General William Odom testified that "the decline in violence reflects a dispersion of power to dozens of local strong men who distrust the government and occasionally fight among themselves. Thus the basic military situation is far worse because of the proliferation of armed groups under local military chiefs who follow a proliferating number of political bosses."[47] Marc Lynch, a Middle East specialist at George Washington University, observed that this approach was leading to a "warlord state" in Iraq with "power devolved to local militias, gangs, tribes and power-brokers, with a purely nominal central state."[48] As a report of the United States Institute of Peace released in December 2007 emphasized: "A competent national government in Baghdad is essential to the long-term stability of Iraq. A weak government will be unable to ensure the internal and external security of the country or manage revenues."[49] And a 2008 report by the Carnegie Endowment for International Peace likewise observed that "Despite the presence of over

160,000 U.S. troops in Iraq at the end of 2007 and an improvement in the security situation, Iraq remains an unstable, violent, and deeply divided country, indeed a failed state." The Carnegie report pointed out that the surge did little to improve the chaotic political conditions in Iraq.

> The U.S. invasion unleashed a power struggle that will take years to play out and that effectively prevents the state from functioning. The signs of state failure are obvious: Iraq is unable to contain violence on its own. It was unable to do so until mid-2007, despite the presence of 140,000 U.S. troops. The surge that increased the number of U.S. troops by 30,000 has succeeded in reducing violence, although levels are still extremely high. But Iraq is still unable to discharge the administrative functions of the state. Budgets remain largely unspent, reconstruction is lagging, and services are not being delivered. Different towns and cities are controlled by different groups with little if any allegiance to the central government – competing Shi'i militias, Sunni tribal militias, Sunni-based "concerned citizens' organizations," and Sunni Awakening militias control towns, villages, and neighborhoods, sometimes in cooperation with U.S. and Iraqi security forces, sometimes in opposition to them, or simply on their own. The official governmental institutions compete with unofficial structures that have developed in the vacuum of authority. These are all typical symptoms of state collapse.[50]

This fragmentation of Iraq would be in line with the geostrategic thinking of Likudnik Oded Yinon. None of this is to imply that the surge's empowering of local tribal chiefs represented an intentional effort by the United States to break-up the country. It was simply a pragmatic effort to reduce the violence – and especially cut back on the attacks on American troops. The disintegration of Iraq was ineluctably set into motion with the overthrow of Saddam's regime, as Yinon realized would occur. David Wurmser also had discussed this fragmentation phenomenon at length in his "Coping with Crumbling States: A Western and Israeli Balance of Power Strategy for the Levant."[51] And in *Tyranny's Ally*, Wurmser presented the fragmentation of states in the Middle East and the return to power of local elites as a means of advancing individual liberty.[52] No matter what the impact on individual freedom, such a dissolution of a centralized state coincided with the Israeli security goal of surrounding itself with fragmented, powerless statelets.

The seeming success of the surge in Iraq, and the diminution of congressional calls to withdraw from Iraq, gave renewed vigor for a hard-line with Iran, with the neocons especially beating the drums for war. In September, Reuel Marc Gerecht, director of PNAC's Middle East Initiative, implicated Iran in the killing of American soldiers in Iran. "The brutal Mahdi Army of Moqtada al-Sadr is probably now responsible for about half of all U.S. combat deaths," Gerecht maintained. And he emphasized that Sadr "visits Iran regularly, [and] has developed close ties to the mullahs." The "Iranian Revolutionary Guards have started training his henchmen inside Iraq." Gerecht emphasized that Iran was unlikely to abandon its war against the United States as a result of Washington's

> exercise [of] soft power – through sanctions, resolutions, diplomatic isolation and rougher rhetoric . . . . Instead, they seem set to continue killing Americans in Iraq, waiting to see if and when the United States gives up and run for the exits.[53]

Kimberly Kagan, wife of Frederick Kagan, the principal author of the surge,[54] had been writing periodic reports on the progress of the surge sponsored by the *Weekly Standard* and the Institute for the Study of War since the beginning in March. In her sixth report released in late August, she stressed the role of Iran in destabilizing Iraq: "Iran, and its Lebanese proxy Hezbollah, have been actively involved in supporting Shia militias and encouraging sectarian violence in Iraq since the invasion of 2003 – and Iranian planning and preparation for that effort began as early as 2002." While acknowledging that the "precise purpose" of Iran's involvement was unclear, she emphasized that

> one thing is very clear: Iran has consistently supplied weapons, its own advisors, and Lebanese Hezbollah advisors to multiple resistance groups in Iraq, both Sunni and Shia, and has supported these groups as they have targeted Sunni Arabs, Coalition forces, Iraqi Security Forces, and the Iraqi Government itself. Their influence runs from Kurdistan to Basrah [sic], and Coalition sources report that by August 2007, Iranian-backed insurgents accounted for roughly half the attacks on Coalition forces, a dramatic change from previous periods that had seen the overwhelming majority of attacks coming from the Sunni Arab insurgency and al Qaeda.[55]

Michael Ledeen debuted his new book, *The Iranian Time Bomb, The Mullah Zealots' Quest for Destruction*, on September 10, 2007. In this work, Ledeen maintained that Iran had been the center for terrorism since the establishment of the Islamic regime in 1979, going so far as to argue that Iran had supported Al Qaeda and was involved in 911. He held further that Iran was behind much of the military insurgency in Iraq, supporting both the Shiite and Sunni resistance, and also in Afghanistan. Iran's ultimate goal, he claimed, was the destruction of the United States.

In Ledeen's view, the mullahs in Tehran were global revolutionaries, indifferent even to self-preservation. No diplomatic move by the United States could induce them to change from their revolutionary course. However, the United States government, he held, had been characterized by a "remarkable refusal to fight back against an enemy that never hid its intention to destroy or dominate us, and impose a clerical fascism that is the antithesis of freedom."[56]

Ledeen's focus on Iran as the center for terrorism was quite reminiscent of the neocons' charges against Iraq before the United States's attack. It especially corresponded with the arguments of Laurie Mylroie, Ledeen's colleague at the American Enterprise Institute, that Saddam Hussein was the mastermind behind global terrorism. Interestingly, Mylroie credited Ledeen for his assistance in her work.[57]

As pointed out earlier, Ledeen had not always held such a negative view of Iran, and, in fact, advocated the détente policies with Iran that he now decried. During the Reagan administration Ledeen's support for improved relations with Iran included his involvement in the Israeli-inspired policy of covert American arms sales to Iran in 1985–6.[58] Ledeen wrote in a *New York Times* Op Ed on July 19, 1988 that it was essential for the United States to begin talking with Iran, stating that the "The United States, which should have been exploring improved relations with Iran before . . . should now seize the opportunity to do so."[59] Ledeen expressed the same pro-Iranian theme in February 1991 in a *Wall Street* Journal Op-Ed, "Iran – Back in the Game," as the U.S. waged war against Iraq.[60]

Ledeen's reversal on American policy toward Iran paralleled the shift in the security position of Israel. While Israel was seeking a benign relationship with Iran, so was Ledeen; as Israel came to depict Iran as a relentless enemy, Ledeen did so as well.

Shortly after resigning as Cheney's Middle East advisor, David Wurmser, in an interview with the *London Telegraph* in early October, provided a full outline of the continued goals of the neocon war agenda. Wurmser held that the way to undermine the Islamic regime in Iran was by bringing regime change in Syria, which was Iran's surrogate. "We need to do everything possible to destabilise the Syrian regime and exploit every single moment they strategically overstep," said David Wurmser. Although he sought to begin the destabilization of Syria by non-military activities, he did not rule out an attack, "if necessary." By showing its inability to protect the Assad regime in Syria, Iran would either see its prestige destroyed or would be provoked to respond, which could provide the United States with a casus belli to use military means to destroy the regime. And Wurmser sought to go beyond merely limited airstrikes on Iran. "If we start shooting, we must be prepared to fire the last shot. Don't shoot a bear if you're not going to kill it."[61]

Autumn saw the neocons publicize the need to counter the alleged danger from Iran. For example, David Horowitz and various pro-neocon organization held "Islamo-Fascism Awareness Week" on October 22–6 to publicize the putative Iranian threat along with other alleged Islamic dangers. College campuses were the primary focus on this event.[62]

In the meantime, the neocons' influence remained strong as ever with leading Republican candidates for the presidency. Many neocons were flocking around former New York mayor Rudy Giuliani, who had emerged in the fall of 2007 as the leading Republican contender for president and was a strong hawk for war on Iran. Among his neocon advisors were Norman Podhoretz, Daniel Pipes, Martin Kramer, David Frum, Michael Rubin, and Stephen Rosen.[63] As Jennifer Siegel wrote in the *Forward*, "Rudolph Giuliani is taking steps to claim his place as the field's leading hawk."[64] Correspondent Jim Lobe would quip in late October that Giuliani's foreign policy team "increasingly resembles the cheer-leading squad for the U.S. section of the international Bibi Netanyahu fan club."[65]

It should be added that numerous neocons were also supporting Republican candidate John McCain, as they also had in his 2000 campaign. These included: William Kristol, R. James Woolsey, Gary Schmidt, Randy Scheunemann, Robert Kagan, and Max Boot.[66]

While not implementing the neocon policy against Iran, George Bush began to escalate his belligerent rhetoric, which seemed to be a precursor for some harder action. In an August 28 speech to the American Legion, Bush accused Tehran of putting the Middle East "under the shadow of a nuclear holocaust." He warned that the U.S. and its allies would need to confront Iran "before it is too late."[67] In a press conference on October 17, Bush said he had "told people that if you're interested in avoiding World War III, it seems like you ought to be interested in preventing them from having the knowledge necessary to make a nuclear weapon."[68] Close observers noted that Bush greatly expanded the American goal from preventing Iran from actually having a nuclear weapon to preventing Iran from possessing the knowledge necessary to make a nuclear weapon. Of course, scientists throughout the world possess the knowledge to develop nuclear weapons, so by this revised standard, the United States could attack Iran, or almost any other country in the world.[69]

In an October 21 speech in Washington, Vice President Cheney echoed the President's threat, stating that "The Iranian regime needs to know that if it stays on its present course, the international community is prepared to impose serious consequences." Cheney added: "The United States joins other nations in sending a clear message: We will not allow Iran to have a nuclear weapon."[70]

On October 25, the United States announced new harsh sanctions targeting 28 Iranian companies, most particularly three major state-owned Iranian banks and companies controlled by the Iranian Revolutionary Guard, which were accused by the United States as being primary financial backers of international terrorism and a covert Iranian nuclear arms program. The new sanctions were the harshest imposed by the United States on Iran since the Iranian revolution of 1979. The measure called for the freezing of the named organizations' assets found in the United States and prohibited Americans from doing business with those Iranian entities. The sanctions had an extraterritorial feature, with foreign businesses facing penalties for doing business with the designated Iranian groups.

While the Bush administration portrayed these measures as simply part of its diplomatic strategy, numerous observers saw them as a precursor to war. Such hostile moves obviously served to heighten tensions in the area and discourage any negotiation on the part of Iran.[71]

The increasingly hostile anti-Iranian rhetoric induced a significant increase in the willingness of the American people to resort to war. A Zogby poll conducted October 24 through October 27 found fifty-two percent of likely American voters supported a U.S. military strike to prevent Iran from building a nuclear weapon, and 53 percent expected such a strike before the next presidential election. Only 29 percent said that the United States should not attack Iran.[72]

In short, by the fall of 2007 the Bush administration was moving in the neocon direction. And it might be added the Congress had also moved in that direction. Despite warnings about the disastrous consequences of any attack on the Middle East, the neocons definitely had made their (and Israel's) concern about Iran a mainstream position.

While the Bush administration was seemingly ginning up for war, Mohamed ElBaradei, director general of the International Atomic Energy Agency, repeatedly stated that the there was no evidence that the Iranians were about to produce a nuclear bomb and warned against the escalating rhetoric and actions coming from Washington. In early September, he expressed the concern that "war drums . . . are basically saying that the solution is to bomb Iran. It makes me shudder because some of the rhetoric is a reminder" of the build-up for the Iraq war.[73]

In an interview with CNN on October 28 ElBaradei categorically stated that he had "not received any information that there is a concrete, active nuclear weapon program going on right now." He acknowledged that the agency received information that Iran might be studying such weaponization, and it was making the effort to "clarify these concerns." But it was essential to focus on investigations and peaceful negotiations. "My fear," ElBaradei emphasized, "is that if we continue to escalate from both sides we will end up in a precipice, we will end up into an abyss. The Middle East is a total mess, to say the least. And we cannot add fuel to the fire."[74]

Obviously the march to war would not be stopped by a foreigner any more than foreign opposition, even by weapons experts, could stop the United States attack on Iraq in 2003. What did put a damper on any move to war came from within the United States government in the form of a new National Intelligence Estimate (NIE) representing the consensus view of all 16 of the nation's intelligence agencies, which was released on December 3. Titled "Iran: Nuclear Intentions and Capabilities," the new NIE declared "with high confidence" that Iran had stopped its nuclear weapons program in 2003 and with "moderate confidence" that, as of mid-2007, Iran had not restarted its program. And even if Iran were now restarting its program, the NIE held that it could not produce enough highly enriched uranium for a weapon before 2015. The report also expressed doubt about whether Iran "currently intends to develop nuclear weapons." All of this was a reversal of previous intelligence reports that Iran was actively working to develop nuclear weapons.[75] And it contradicted the bellicose warnings of Bush and Cheney, as well as the neocons, regarding Iran's alleged nuclear activities.[76]

It was widely held in the media that the new NIE revelation undercut any American move to attack Iran. "If there was ever a possibility that President George W. Bush would drop bombs on Iran, the chances have now shrunk to nearly zero," wrote Fred Kaplan in *Slate*. Kaplan saw the release of the new report as representing a victory for the government opponents of the Middle East war policy, who had been unsuccessful regarding Iraq.

> This time, on Iran, the leaders of the State Department, the Defense Department, the military command, and now the intelligence community are on public record as downplaying the wisdom of war – and, with today's NIE, disputing the rationale for even considering war.
>
> Skeptics of war have rarely been so legitimized. Vice President Cheney has never been so isolated. If Bush were to order an attack under these circumstances, he would risk a major eruption in the chain of command, even a constitutional crisis, among many other crises. It seems extremely unlikely that even he would do that.[77]

The intelligence reversal was widely portrayed as a deliberate counter-offensive by the traditional foreign policy establishment against the neo-con war agenda. "It's a fundamental reversal of civil-military relations, and intelligence and political relationships, that were obvious in 2002," maintained Ray Takeyh, a Middle East specialist at the Council on Foreign Relations. Takeyh held that the new NIE was "part of a larger narrative, namely how the formal institutions of government are now determined to resist the White House, which wasn't the case in 2002."[78] Justin Raimondo asserted that "What we are witnessing is a serious rebellion within key military, diplomatic, and intelligence circles against our Israel-centric policy in the Middle East."[79]

Alexander Cockburn, in an article appropriately titled "The Coup Against Bush and Cheney," held that the position reversal was not due to new information, but rather to a change in the correlation of forces in Washington.

> In practice this means that in the late summer senior intelligence officials figured the consensus in Washington and Wall Street against an attack on Iran was powerful enough for them to lower the boom on the neo-cons. The latter have now retreated in disarray to their bunkers at the Weekly Standard and the National Review for a last stand, bellowing that it's a filthy plot by peaceniks in the State Department.[80]

While the report represented a consensus, it was said to have been largely written by Thomas Fingar, a former member of the State Department, who like most officials there, had been opposed to the neocons. And his work was praised by the critics of the neocons.[81] Jon Ward in the pro-neocon *Washington Times* concurred that the principal people involved in the new assessment came from the anti-neocon State Department. "The argument

THE TRANSPARENT CABAL

this week over how to confront Iran," Ward maintained, "is a continuation, carried out by many of the same players, of the battles during Mr. Bush's first term between Secretary of State Colin L. Powell and Under Secretary of State for Arms Control John R. Bolton."[82]

Ward held that

> [t]he three former State officials primarily responsible for the National Intelligence Estimate clashed regularly from 2001 to 2004 with a team of hard-line conservatives led by Mr. Bolton, who later served as U.S. ambassador to the United Nations . . . . All three are now at the Office of the Director of National Intelligence: C. Thomas Fingar, deputy director of national intelligence for analysis; Vann H. Van Diepen, national intelligence officer for weapons of mass destruction and proliferation; and Kenneth C. Brill, director of the national counterproliferation center.[83]

From the neocon perspective, the intelligence community was deliberately trying to undermine the president's policies. "One has to look at the agendas of the primary movers of this report, to judge how much it can really be banked on," said David Wurmser.[84] "Too much of the intelligence community is engaging in policy formulation rather than 'intelligence' analysis, and too many in Congress and the media are happy about it," complained John Bolton.[85]

Bolton maintained that

> many involved in drafting and approving the NIE were not intelligence professionals but refugees from the State Department, brought into the new central bureaucracy of the director of national intelligence. These officials had relatively benign views of Iran's nuclear intentions five and six years ago; now they are writing those views as if they were received wisdom from on high. In fact, these are precisely the policy biases they had before, recycled as "intelligence judgments."[86]

Michael Ledeen titled his piece on the new NIE, "The Great Intelligence Scam." Instead of presenting unvarnished intelligence, Ledeen held that "those 'intelligence professionals' were very happy to take off their analytical caps and gowns and put on their policy wigs." Although maintaining that the "document will not stand up to serious criticism," Ledeen acknowledged that "it will undoubtedly have a significant political impact, since it will be taken as confirmation of the view that we should not do anything mean to the mullahs. We should talk to them instead."[87]

Norman Podhoretz harbored the "darker suspicion" that the NIE represented a conspiracy by the intelligence community against the administration's Middle East policy. He maintained that "the intelligence community, which has for some years now been leaking material calculated to undermine George W. Bush, is doing it again. This time the purpose is to head off the possibility that the President may order air strikes on the Iranian nuclear installations."[88]

Although top Israeli government leaders had been briefed in advance of the NIE's content, its release stunned many. And like the neocons, the Israeli government officials strongly disputed the findings, claiming "clear and solid intelligence" that Iran is continuing to develop nuclear weapons to threaten Israel and Europe.[89] Defense Minister Ehud Barak contended that although Iran's nuclear program was halted in 2003, "as far as we know it has probably since revived it." And some officials hinted that Israel might have to launch its own strike on Iranian nuclear facilities.[90]

Despite their vehement criticism, neocons realized that the NIE had made an American attack on Iran, or even the imposition of harsher sanctions, politically untenable for the near future. But as Jim Lobe pointed out, neocons differed on how to deal with this situation. He distinguished between the harder-line neocons such as Podhoretz who simply resorted to fuming and condemning the "conspiracy," and moderate neocons who saw the tactical need to switch to a softer approach. He depicted Robert Kagan and William Kristol to be in this moderate camp, with Kagan taking the softest line.[91]

"Regardless of what one thinks about the National Intelligence Estimate's conclusion that Iran stopped its nuclear weapons program in 2003," Kagan wrote in the *Washington Post,*

> . . . its practical effects are indisputable. The Bush administration cannot take military action against Iran during its remaining time in office, or credibly threaten to do so, unless it is in response to an extremely provocative Iranian action. A military strike against suspected Iranian nuclear facilities was always fraught with risk. For the Bush administration, that option is gone.
>
> Neither, however, will the administration make further progress in winning international support for tighter sanctions on Iran. Fear of American military action was always the primary reason Europeans pressured Tehran. Fear of an imminent Iranian bomb was secondary. Bringing Europeans together in support of serious sanctions was difficult before the NIE. Now it is impossible.[92]

Despite the changed political environment, Kagan still saw the need for action, recommending that the United States take the initiative and offer to enter into discussions with Iran. Now was an opportune time to do so, he believed, because the United States could operate from a position of strength, with its improved position in Iraq. However, in Kagan's scenario, the benefits to be offered to Iran were very limited and the demands were beyond any likelihood of Iran meeting them. Kagan wrote:

> If Tehran complies with its nuclear obligations; ceases its support for terrorist violence; and treats its people with justice, humanity and liberalism, it will be welcomed into the international community, with all the enormous economic, political and security benefits this brings.

Essentially, Kagan was not calling for negotiations but demanding that Iran peaceably submit to the position of the Bush administration and Israel. Iran would have to cease its backing of the Palestinian resistance and of Hezbollah without Israel having to offer anything to the Palestinians or any guarantees to respect the sovereignty of Lebanon. Iran would have to abandon any effort to develop a nuclear capability, probably even the enrichment of uranium; Israel could presumably expand its existing nuclear arsenal at will. (There was no mention of even moving to a nuclear free Middle East.) Iran would have to treat its people according to American standards of justice and humanity; Israel could continue to violate the human rights of the Palestinians.

If Iran refused to accede to the U.S/Israel position, Kagan emphasized that such intransigence could be used to justify a more aggressive American policy. "If the Iranians stonewall or refuse to talk," Kagan wrote

> they will establish a record of intransigence that can be used against them now and in the critical years to come. It's possible the American offer itself could open fissures in Iran. In any case, it is hard to see what other policy options are available. This is the hand that has been dealt. The Bush administration needs to be smart and creative enough to play it well.[93]

In essence, Kagan was not moderating the overall neocon Middle East strategy, but only adjusting the tactics to fit current realities, with the ultimate goal still being the elimination of Iran as an enemy of Israel's.

It would appear that the new NIE may have temporarily stopped the move to war, but it had not eliminated neocon power. In the analysis of investigative journalist Robert Parry:

> [t]hough Bush and the neocons again find themselves on the defensive, the political battle is far from over. The neocons retain extraordinary strength within

the U.S. news media as well as in the leading Washington think tanks and inside many of the presidential campaigns.[94]

Moreover, as Parry pointed out, the leading Republican candidates for president were "enthusiastic backers of the neocon agenda of an imperial United States with an all-powerful Executive who will subordinate America's constitutional rights to the waging of an indefinite 'war on terror'" and Hillary Clinton, then the leading Democratic candidate, "often votes with neocon hawks." In essence, Parry emphasized, it was likely that "the neocons could find themselves in the enviable position next fall [2008] of having a super-neocon Republican versus a neocon-lite Democrat. Then, whoever wins, the neocons can expect their policies in the Mideast to continue."[95]

The fact of the matter is that while the expansion of the neocon war agenda to Iran was once again placed on hold, there was no effort to actually move away from the war agenda. The tensions that made war with Iran a possibility, and even a likelihood, remained. To obviate that dire possibility, it would be necessary to take positive action to diffuse those tensions.

The way to get out of this war situation would be for the United States to cease its military threats toward Iran, show a willingness to engage in genuine diplomatic bargaining, inform Israel that it would not support it in any way in an attack on Iran, and remove its forces from Iraq and its vicinity. The need for the latter reflects the fact that any occupation incident involving Iran, or said to involve Iran, could be exploited by prowar elements to return the United States to the war track.

On January 6, 2008, an incident took place in the Straits of Hormuz, with American warships allegedly on the verge of opening fire on small speedboats of the Iranian Revolutionary Guard, which were approaching them. What actually went on there is a matter for considerable dispute.[96] However, whether it was a genuine incident or not, the event provided a vivid illustration of the tinderbox nature of the region. To avert in any substantial way the possibility of war with Iran would therefore seem to require a radical change in the Middle East policy of the Bush administration. And, as of the start of 2008, there seemed little likelihood of this taking place. Thus, the neocon war agenda, although currently stymied, could be instantly resuscitated.

chapter 17

THE SUPPORTING CAST FOR WAR

IN DESCRIBING THE ROLE of the neocons as the fundamental factor in bringing about the war on Iraq, it is necessary to mention what this thesis does not mean. It is a caricature to represent the thesis as implying that a few neoconservatives single-handedly hijacked American foreign policy and drove the country to war against the will of the American people. Obviously, this was not the case. While neoconservatives spearheaded the war on Iraq, and without the neoconservatives there would have been no war, they needed propitious circumstances – viz, the 911 attack – which enabled them to enlist a number of auxiliaries, who provided sufficient political support to allow their war agenda to become a reality. A majority of Americans became willing supporters of the war on Iraq, and remained so until mid-year 2004, when the lack of WMD and the mounting difficulties and American death toll dullened the war's attraction, though even then most Americans still preferred remaining in Iraq to an instant departure – and both major presidential contestants, Kerry as well as Bush – supported the continuation of the Iraq occupation. It was not until 2005 that a majority would support some form of withdrawal. Since this book is not an analysis of those who supported the war, but rather those who formulated and directed policy, these auxiliary groups (and individuals) will be dealt with only briefly

Obviously, all wars must have a significant level of popular support. Hitler and Stalin obviously had support for their conquests. But the people of Nazi Germany and the people of the Soviet Union obviously did not determine the policies of their rulers. Now none of this is to say that the

American people were mobilized through propaganda and force to support government policies to the same degree as were the populations of those totalitarian countries; however, government propaganda did make a significant contribution to the mobilization of support for the war on Iraq. But this propaganda needed a favorable environment to be effective. Moreover, there were important predispositions, attitudes, and in a few cases, interests, that tended to make the American people, or at least a significant body of the American people, conducive to war. But a crucial point that must be reiterated is that these groups now to be discussed were supporters, not the planners or instigators of the war policy. Without the intensive neocon leadership, the United States would not have launched a war on Iraq. But without the support of these other groups, the neocon policy would not have materialized into action.

The most crucial supporter of the war, of course, was President George W. Bush. Obviously, if Bush had rejected the war agenda, the United States would not have engaged in war. If George W. Bush firmly held certain types of foreign policy positions and had certain character traits – e.g., the quasi-pacifistic internationalism of Jimmy Carter or the cautious realism of his father, George H.W. Bush – it is unlikely that he would have bought the neocon program, or at least that he would not have accepted it to the extent that he did.[1] As pointed out earlier in this work, Bush never evinced any strong desire for a Middle East war or regime change prior to becoming president. But holding no strong views on foreign affairs, and knowing little about the subject – being a veritable empty vessel – Bush could be easily converted to the neocon program. Just as neocon propaganda could persuade the average American, it could also be persuasive to Bush, who admittedly relied on his advisors, did little outside reading, and was intellectually quite shallow.

Regarding the false propaganda put forth by the administration, it is unclear as to whether Bush was engaged in lying. He may have believed it to have been true, for it was provided to him by his advisors. Bush could have been, as columnist Richard Cohen postulated, a "useful idiot."[2]

Significantly, the simplistic war against evil as portrayed by the neoconservatives harmonized perfectly with Bush's Christian millenarian outlook – the perception of the world in black-and-white, good-versus-evil terms. This outlook was intensified by the trauma of 911 which seemed to call for some type of tough response.

Furthermore, the war provided Bush with a personal mission and pur-pose in life. "I am here for a reason," Bush told Karl Rove shortly after 9/11, "and this is going to be how we're going to be judged."[3] Robert Jervis, profes-sor of international affairs at Columbia University, described Bush's trans-formation. "Bush's response to September 11," Jervis maintained,

> may parallel his earlier religious conversion and owe something to his religious beliefs, especially in his propensity to see the struggle as one between good and evil. There is reason to believe that just as his coming to Christ gave meaning to his previously aimless and dissolute personal life, so the war on terrorism has become, not only the defining characteristic of his foreign policy, but also his sacred mission.[4]

Bush's belief in a divine mission enabled him to pursue in an unwaver-ing fashion the neocon agenda he had adopted despite the serious diffi-culties that would be encountered. "This is why he dispenses with people who confront him with inconvenient facts," as conservative commentator Bruce Bartlett put it. "He truly believes he's on a mission from God. Abso-lute faith like that overwhelms a need for analysis. The whole thing about faith is to believe things for which there is no empirical evidence."[5] This would explain why Bush could be untroubled by the total inconsistency of his preaching democracy and freedom and the reality of the situation in the Middle East, where most of the population disliked the United States. It enabled him to be indifferent to the fact that his fundamental justification for the war – the WMD threat – was not true. Military and intelligence experts could report a debacle in Iraq, but Bush acted as if everything was proceeding swimmingly. Bush prided himself in being resolute and firm in his mission, which often seemed to mean a disregard for reality.

Moreover, Bush would disregard the fact that he was sinking in the opin-ion polls after the occupation of Iraq; a president less devoted to the cause would have undoubtedly been more willing to make course changes. There were numerous times that a more opportunistically-inclined president, one not firmly believing in the cause, could have accepted various propos-als to drop the war agenda in which other people – the Democrats, the Iraq Study Group – would have suffered the blame for any problems that might ensue.

What Bush did not do was to follow the advice of his father and his fa-ther's advisors, such as his father's National Security Advisor Brent Scow-croft and former Secretary of State James Baker. Scowcroft was especially outspoken against the war. The Bush family's sympathetic biographers Peter and Rochelle Schweizer, quote the younger Bush as responding: "Scowcroft has become a pain in the ass in his old age." And the authors' add: "Although he never went public with them, the president's own father shared many of Scowcroft's concerns."[6] James Baker, as co-chair of the Iraq Study Group, had offered Bush a way of abandoning the war agenda in 2006, but Bush completely rejected it.

President Bush gave implicit acknowledgement to his father's opposition to the war when Bob Woodward asked him in an interview as to whether he consulted his father on his decision to go to war. "He is the wrong father to appeal to for advice. The wrong father to go to, to appeal to in terms of strength," Bush responded. "There's a higher Father that I appeal to."[7]

Psychoanalyst Justin Frank in *Bush on the Couch: Inside the Mind of the President George W. Bush* has pointed out that George W. Bush exhibited something like a love-hate relationship with his father. In certain ways his life paralleled that of his father – college, oil business – but he had always, prior to the presidency, fallen far short of his father's accomplishments. This had caused a degree of anger and a desire for self independence in order to achieve something significant on his own. Such an attitude would help to explain why he did not follow his father's advice on Iraq.[8]

In addition to having support on the top, it was necessary for the neo-conservatives to also have support from the grass roots, for pro-war public opinion was necessary to gain congressional support for the war. One cohort of strong backers are loosely referred to as Christian fundamentalists, Christian evangelicals, or the Christian right. Undoubtedly, these names are not completely interchangeable, but they are often used this way, and this conflation does not unduly distort the truth regarding their support for the war. Like Bush, their religious outlook harmonized well with the good versus evil portrayal of the war. Moreover, many have been very strong supporters of Zionism. They identify the Jews of today with those of the Old Testament and believe that the God had given them the land of Israel in an everlasting covenant (something not believed by most Christian denominations and above all by the Catholic Church). For a substantial number of this group, the establishment of Israel as a Jewish state was tied in with Biblical eschatology. The way these Christians looked at it, the "ingathering of the Jews" in Jerusalem is a necessary prelude to the second coming of Christ. These Christians believe that they and others "who accept Christ

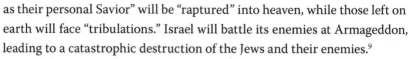

as their personal Savior" will be "raptured" into heaven, while those left on earth will face "tribulations." Israel will battle its enemies at Armageddon, leading to a catastrophic destruction of the Jews and their enemies.[9]

Among the more prominent Christian rightists were Jerry Falwell, Pat Robertson, Gary Bauer, John Hagee, James Dobson, Tim and Beverly La-Haye, Ralph Reed, and Franklin Graham. Estimates from the number of Christian evangelicals in the United States, many of whom were Christian Zionists, range from 40 to 80 million.[10] In his summary of Christian Zionism, David Lutz presents the significance of the movement regarding the war on Iraq, observing that that while the neoconservatives "planned the war" that they could not have been successful in its implementation "without support from tens of millions of Christian Zionist votes."[11] This latter point needs to be emphasized. While these religious Christians provided the popular support for the war on Iraq, and continued to provide support for the Middle East war agenda, they were not involved in designing the war agenda, nor were they among the significant Bush administration officials who pushed for war.

It should also be emphasized that for the Christian right, support for the war also melded with their support for George W. Bush the person. They saw him as one of their own, as Bush had become, in fact, the leader of the religious right. For secular sophisticates and even many regular people, it might seem impossible to view Bush as a charismatic leader, but for the Christian right, such would be the case. As *Washington Post* columnist Dana Milbank wrote a few months after 911:

> For the first time since religious conservatism became a modern political movement, the president of the United States has become the movement's de facto leader—a status even Ronald Reagan, though admired by religious conservatives, never earned. Christian publications, radio and television shower Bush with praise, while preachers from the pulpit treat his leadership as an act of providence. A procession of religious leaders who have met with him testify to his faith, while Web sites encourage people to fast and pray for the president.[12]

Small in number but nonetheless significant, war profiteers and former professional Cold Warriors also supported the war on Iraq. Profit and fraud have accompanied all wars. Wars by their very nature breed war profiteers. And the war on Iraq has many private contractors working at tasks traditionally performed by the military.[13] The Halliburton company certainly comes to mind here, but it is not alone, and it must be acknowledged that despite or because of Dick Cheney's past connections with the firm, it made considerable money during the Clinton administration.[14]

For their part, many old Cold Warriors supported the war because they were emotionally tied up with war and combating enemies in general, and needed a substitute for the Cold War. War-strategizing and war-fighting is their livelihood. The same income and excitement and sense of purpose cannot be had during peacetime. But it should be emphasized that neither the war profiteers nor Cold Warriors necessitated a war in the Middle East; any war or conflict situation would have served their purposes. Certainly, a greater focus on Afghanistan would have been profitable. China, Russia, and South America also were crisis targets for these groups.

For as long as supporting war seemed a winning political strategy, Republican partisans pushed the war; and even when popular support eroded in 2004, Republican party loyalty kept them behind their president. It is interesting to note that whereas most conservative Republican politicians rejected Bill Clinton's talk of nation-building as utopian, only a few of them criticized President Bush over this issue. Karl Rove, the president's political advisor, made it clear early on that the war on terrorism could be used politically and said that Republican politicos should emphasize the war theme. At a Republican National Committee meeting on Jan. 19, 2002, after the successful campaign in Afghanistan, Rove said, "We can go to the country on this issue, because they trust the Republican Party to do a better job of protecting and strengthening America's military might and thereby protecting America."[15] And while support for the war on Iraq dipped under 50 percent, the Bush campaign in 2004 still promoted the war issue – linking it to the concept of American patriotism – and did win the election.

Most importantly, neoconservative policies initially received support from the general American public, especially people of a more conservative, patriotic bent, who were especially numerous in the heartland of America, outside of the urbanized Northeast and the Pacific Coast. This area is frequently referred to as Red State America[16] or Middle America.

The 911 attacks made these average American people angry and fearful. The idea that the United States could be attacked on its own soil was far outside the American people's ordinary thinking. The attacks had shaken the American people's sense of well-being to its very core. They had created what Zbigniew Brzezinski called a "culture of fear." As Brzezinski pointed out:

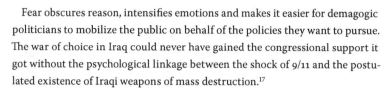

> Fear obscures reason, intensifies emotions and makes it easier for demagogic politicians to mobilize the public on behalf of the policies they want to pursue. The war of choice in Iraq could never have gained the congressional support it got without the psychological linkage between the shock of 9/11 and the postulated existence of Iraqi weapons of mass destruction.[17]

In such an uneasy situation, Americans wanted action to be taken. They wanted the United States to strike back at the terrorist enemy, even though they were not exactly sure who that enemy was. Many could not distinguish between Saddam and Osama bin Laden. Moreover, they were fearful of more attacks and were susceptible to the Administration propaganda that the United States had to strike Iraq before Iraq would somehow attack the United States. In short, the neocons' propaganda found fertile soil in America, though it got virtually nowhere in the rest of the world.

It wasn't that difficult to channel American fear and anger into war against Iraq. Polls and much anecdotal evidence showed a majority of the American people in favor of the war. A poll conducted on March 20, 2003, a day after the United States began its attack on Iraq, showed that 70 percent of the participants said that the U.S. "Should have begun action when it did," while only 27 percent said that the U.S. should have waited longer to allow the United Nations inspections to continue.[18] There was nothing odd about this. Wars generally have engendered popular support when tied to the idea that the homeland was endangered.

While sometimes war has attracted the intellectual class, the war on Iraq appealed the most to the working and lower middle classes, though primarily to the white people of this segment of the population.[19] (Blacks generally opposed the war.) Southern whites seem to have been most supportive of the war. And the fact of the matter is that Southerners have been the most supportive group for most of America's wars.[20]

After the September 11 terrorism, average Americans – policemen, firemen, soldiers – became heroes. Average people who often felt slighted and ridiculed by the intellectual and media elites saw people like themselves gaining status – lifted above the monotony and humdrum of their everyday lives. The new heroism had the effect of boosting the self-esteem of average, ordinary white Americans. It once again became fashionable, if not actually de rigueur, to identify with American patriotism that had long been denigrated by the American intellectual and media elites.[21]

Although the official Bush administration position was that the United States was liberating and democratizing the Arabs, many average Americans actually evinced hatred of the Arabs and the Muslims – instead of their liberation, they sought their destruction. For many white Americans, it could have been a pent up hatred – an anger against Blacks, immigrants, homosexuals, non-Christians, who many believed were getting special favors in the United States and changing the traditional culture. Such negative expressions are an undercurrent in the United States and cannot be expressed publicly. Hatred of Arabs and Muslims thus served as a displacement. As Anatol Lieven put it: "the suppression of feelings at home may have only increased the force with which they are directed at foreigners, who remain a legitimate and publicly accepted target of hatred."[22]

Writing on the war as a displacement of domestic anger, conservative war critic Paul Craig Roberts wrote:

> The Iraqi War is serving as a great catharsis for multiple conservative frustrations: job loss, drugs, crime, homosexuals, pornography, female promiscuity, abortion, restrictions on prayer in public places, Darwinism, and attacks on religion. Liberals are the cause. Liberals are against America. Anyone against the war is against America and is a liberal.[23]

Libertarian political commentator Llewellyn H. Rockwell would observe that

> [i]f you follow hate-filled [web] sites such as Free Republic, you know that the populist right in this country has been advocating nuclear holocaust and mass bloodshed for more than a year now. The militarism and nationalism dwarfs anything I saw at any point during the Cold War. It celebrates the shedding of blood, and exhibits a maniacal love of the state. The new ideology of the red-state bourgeoisie seems to actually believe that the U.S. is God marching on earth – not just godlike, but really serving as a proxy for God himself.[24]

While the grass roots right was overwhelmingly in support of the war on Iraq – and the political left generally opposed the war as a capitalist, imperialist, racist endeavor – liberals (the moderate left) were split on the issue. But notably, members of the liberal elite tended to be more pro-war than grass roots liberals.

That liberal support for the war was most prominent among the political elites rather than among the grass roots had significant ramifications. Illustrating this phenomenon was that fact that 2004 Democratic presidential nominee John Kerry would be pro-war, although as a *Boston Globe* poll

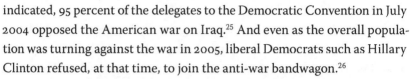

indicated, 95 percent of the delegates to the Democratic Convention in July 2004 opposed the American war on Iraq.²⁵ And even as the overall population was turning against the war in 2005, liberal Democrats such as Hillary Clinton refused, at that time, to join the anti-war bandwagon.²⁶

Establishment liberal support for the war against Iraq was crucial because of power of the liberal elite media – especially the *New York Times* and the *Washington Post*. As historian Robert Blecher writes: "given the lukewarm popular support for the war in Iraq, the march to war could not have succeeded without the assistance of Establishment academics and journalists such as Fouad Ajami and Thomas Friedman, whose mainstream credentials legitimized the administration's agenda among those who otherwise might have been opposed."²⁷

The war liberals supported the Iraqi adventure with certain reservations. Primarily, they were concerned about the lack of international support and implied that the war would have had the support of world opinion if the Bush administration had handled the matter in a less heavy-handed fashion. Moreover, they were generally critical of various aspects of the Bush administration's prosecution of the war: the spurious propaganda, the use of torture, and violations of civil liberties and international law.

Liberal support for the war in Congress was also important for the political success of the war policy. For, by and large, liberal politicians supported the move to war, with few offering stiff opposition, which could have provided greater credibility to the antiwar movement. "Without the support of the liberals," noted Tom Barry, "President George W. Bush's plan to invade and occupy Iraq may have foundered in Congress."²⁸

Why did liberals support the war on Iraq? As Anatol Lieven wrote: "The liberal hawks firmly believed that the Iraq war was both a humanitarian intervention and an important front in the 'war on terrorism,' even if they made no secret of their distrust of the Administration waging it."²⁹ Many war liberals accepted humanitarian idealism as a rationale for the war – the battle for democracy, women's rights, and so forth. Tom Friedman, the noted *New York Times* columnist, proclaimed in November 2003 that "this war is the most important liberal, revolutionary U.S. democracy-building project since the Marshall Plan. The primary focus of U.S. forces in Iraq today is erecting a decent, legitimate, tolerant, pluralistic representative government from the ground up." While acknowledging the great difficulty of this endeavor, he proclaimed that "it is one of the noblest things this

country has ever attempted abroad and it is a moral and strategic imperative that we give it our best shot."[30]

The war liberal thinking reflected, what Lieven called, "muscular liberal democracy."[31] There was nothing new about liberal bellicosity. American liberals had a history of oscillating between near pacifism and support for militant interventionism. Notably, they championed America's major twentieth-century wars – World War I, World War II – viewing them as vehicles for humanitarian ends, including progressive global reform.[32] They were, perhaps, only less supportive of the Cold War because Soviet Communism professed to hold many of their same humanitarian goals.

It should be obvious that the neocons' depiction of the war on Iraq as a war for democracy and freedom against tyranny fitted in liberal thinking. The war liberals and the neocons became ideological soul mates. As Tom Barry wrote: "Apart from their militarist friends in the Pentagon and defense industries, the neocons are finding that their closest ideological allies are the internationalists in the liberal camp."[33]

Another major factor in the liberal support for war is Israel. More than a few of the liberal hawks had strong ties to Israel, such as Senator Joseph Lieberman and Stephen Solarz, who were members of the Committee for the Liberation of Iraq. Richard Cohen, who after the American invasion turned against the war, included Israel as a part of the reason for his support of the attack on Iraq: "Saddam Hussein was a beast who had twice invaded his neighbors, had killed his own people with abandon and posed a threat – and not just a theoretical one – to Israel."[34]

The existence of pro-Israeli ties was also evident in the pro-war Democratic Leadership Council (DLC), which is an important cog in the Democratic Party, and its affiliated think tank, the Progressive Policy Institute (PPI).[35] One of the leading founders of PPI was Michael Steinhardt, a wealthy Jewish philanthropist involved in numerous Zionist causes, such as helping to establish Birthright Israel, a program that sends young Jews to Israel.[36] The vice-chairman of the DLC was David Steiner, a former president of the American Israel Public Affairs Committee (AIPAC), who was forced to resign that position when he was secretly tape-recorded bragging about how he had manipulated U.S. presidential politics on behalf of Israel in the aftermath of the First Gulf War in 1991.[37] Barry Rubin, a featured speaker of PPI, was deputy director of the Begin-Sadat Center for Strategic Studies at Bar-Ilan University in Israel. Rubin also wrote Middle East/Israel briefings for the American Jewish Committee, which sponsors *Commentary*.[38] Marshall Wittmann, a pro-Israel neocon who had been with the Hudson Institute and served as Director of Communications for war hawk John McCain during his 2000 presidential campaign, worked for both the PPI and the DLC and supported Kerry for president in 2004.[39]

The fact of the matter is that pro-Zionists seemed to be top heavy among the elite in the Democratic Party. As Stephen Green and Wendy Campbell wrote: "[Pro-Israel]Jewish donors and activists (not to mention party bosses and a disproportionate number of candidates) basically comprise the new Democratic establishment."[40]

John J. Mearsheimer and Stephen Walt brought out the role of the Israel Lobby in shaping American foreign policy to the interests of Israel.[41] Critics have claimed that the two authors presented the Israel lobby as too much of a monolith.[42] However, the broad Israel Lobby is significant in providing support for the neocon war agenda even its members were not as militant as the neocons, who represent the lobby's cutting edge. It is true that many supporters of Israel did not initially identify with the neocons in promoting the war on Iraq; and it is quite conceivable that if they had been in charge of American foreign policy, the United States would not have gone to war. However, many supporters of Israel backed the war with various reservations once it became government policy and continued to provide significant qualified support to the overall neocon agenda in the Middle East, especially in regard to Iran. As brought out in the previous chapters, Israel and its American lobby have been much more out in front regarding Iran than had been the case with Iraq.[43]

And even those who might not have been active partisans for the war on Iraq, such as Alan Dershowitz, were quite willing to vilify those who would identify the role of Israel and the neocons as bringing about the war.[44] The effect of such efforts, even unintentional, is to shield the neocons from criticism thus protecting the neocon agenda. If critics were free from intimidation to point out that the neocons are supporters of Israel and that the entire neocon Middle East agenda originated in Israel as a means of advancing Israel's geostrategic interests, then the likelihood of success of that policy would precipitously decline.

To summarize, the neocons were the driving force for war, but they could not have achieved success if their agenda did not in some way or other resonate with a significant number of Americans. And, of course, it was the trauma of September 11 that caused a sizeable number of Americans to view war as an attractive option. Without the support of numerous non-neoconservatives, there would have been no war on Iraq. Americans, at least most Americans, willingly went to war. Yet the role of these Americans was supportive and secondary; the original plan, promotion, and initiation of the war on Iraq was mainly the work of the neoconservatives. And it was the neoconservatives who planned to expand the war beyond the borders of Iraq – an agenda that was probably not recognized by most war supporters prior to the March 2003 invasion.

chapter 18

OIL AND OTHER ARGUMENTS FOR THE WAR

TO COMPLETE OUR ANALYSIS, we must examine competing explanations for the American war on Iraq advanced by other critics. The most popular argument proposes that the United States went to war for oil – in short, that the war had nothing to do with combating terrorism. Writing in the *Christian Science Monitor* before the war, Brendan O'Neill reported that "For many in the antiwar movement, the idea that the 'Bushies' plan to invade the Gulf to get their greasy hands on more oil has become an article of faith, an unquestionable truth repeated like a mantra."[1] As America's preeminent left-wing anti-war critic Noam Chomsky put it:

> Of course it was Iraq's energy resources. It's not even a question. Iraq's one of the major oil producers in the world. It has the second largest reserves and it's right in the heart of the Gulf's oil producing region, which U.S. intelligence predicts is going to be two thirds of world resources in coming years.[2]

Although the neoconservative/Israel theory is not without its adherents, a number of factors explain the much greater popularity of the war-for-oil idea among critics of the war. For war critics of the left, the war-for-oil idea fits their notion of rapacious capitalism. Perhaps more importantly, their emphasis on the monetary motives of oil companies placed the war in a simple, good-bad framework. "The well-rehearsed oil argument," O'Neill observed, "attempts to make war a simple issue of good versus evil, with oil-greedy imperialists on one side and defenseless civilians on the other."[3] In other words, the idea that the war was fought to profit the oil companies, complete with the propagandistically effective "No blood for oil" sound-bite, provided a perfect counterpoise to the Bush administration's presentation of an apocalyptic conflict of good versus evil. Even the neoconservative supporters of the war lent some credence to the oil argument with their talk about privatizing Iraqi oil. Of course, that some oil companies might derive benefit from the U.S. takeover of Iraq did not mean they were the war's driving force. The neoconservatives certainly sought allies for their war agenda, and the promise of oil riches was one way of possibly drawing support from the oil companies.

An additional reason for the popularity of the war-for-oil argument is that any reference to Israel and the neoconservatives moves into the taboo area of Jewish power and invites the lethal charge of anti-Semitism. It is far safer to demonize the oil industry, a popular political whipping boy, than to make anything approaching a critical comment regarding predominantly Jewish groups or apparent Jewish interests, even if it is not a criticism of Jews as a whole.

What precisely does the war-for-oil thesis entail? Two motives for such a war suggest themselves, and they are fundamentally different from each other: one is to benefit the American oil industry; the other, to enhance the hegemonic power of the United States by giving it control of the oil spigot of the world.

Let's begin by distinguishing between the oil argument and the current war profiteering. Undoubtedly, the reconstruction of Iraq is a veritable gold mine for some American firms, especially those with close connections to the Bush administration.[4] Some of these firms, such as Halliburton, are in the oil equipment business, and since a significant part of the rebuilding process naturally involves the oil infrastructure, these firms are in a position to derive great profits. But the oil equipment business is not the same thing as what is implied by "the oil industry" – i.e., those firms that actually profit by extracting and selling oil. Halliburton would benefit financially if all the pipelines and oil wells were blown up so that it could rebuild them. Such a scenario would hardly profit oil producers or the United States government. It obviously wouldn't increase the overall oil supply. Nor would rebuilding the Iraq oil industry profit the United States as a whole, since American taxpayers would be funding it. While there are war profiteers in every war, this parasitical group had no reason to press specifically for a war on Iraq.

Moreover, it can be assumed that some oil companies would want concessions in Iraq once it became apparent that Iraq would be invaded; however, this is not the same thing as pushing for an attack on Iraq. They simply sought some possible benefits from a changed situation not of their making.

Second, it should be acknowledged that the United States would have preferred to have gained control of the Iraqi oil. The first locations that the forces of the United States and the United Kingdom secured during the war were the oilfields of southern Iraq, with the aim of preventing Saddam from destroying them. Clearly, any occupier would prefer to exploit rather than destroy a country's assets. Keeping the Iraqi oil industry functioning would certainly alleviate the financial burden of American occupation and help fund Iraq's postwar reconstruction. The United States also sought to prevent Saddam from setting fire to the oil wells and causing an environmental catastrophe, as he had done in Kuwait during the first Gulf War. Environmental considerations aside, such fires could have slowed American troop movements northward to Baghdad.[5] But while the United States would have naturally preferred oil over no oil, the American military's concern for the security of the Iraqi oil wells did not in any way demonstrate that seizing oil resources was the motivation for America to launch its invasion.

It is undisputed that Iraq is an oil-rich country. And we may grant that the war party sought to gain support from the oil industry by promising benefits to be derived from that support. War partisans did the same thing when they tried to get international support by implying that countries that did not support the war would be shut out of the Iraqi oil business.

However, instead of speculating on benefits to be derived by American oil companies from U.S. control of Iraq, it is much more reasonable to actually look at Big Oil's position on attacking Iraq. Did oil companies actually push for war? On the contrary, the representatives of the U.S. oil industry actually sought less hostile relations with Iraq. They had been solid in opposing the embargo on Iraq, which had kept them out of that country. After George W. Bush assumed the presidency in 2000, they lobbied hard for a repeal of the Iran-Libya Sanctions Act and other embargoes that curbed their expansion of holdings in the Middle East. That put the oil industry at loggerheads with the neoconservatives, who for years had been calling for regime change in Iraq.

In a May 2001 *Business Week* article, Rose Brady reported that the easing of sanctions on rogue states "pits powerful interests such as the pro-Israeli lobby and the U.S. oil industry against each other. And it is sure to preoccupy the Bush Administration and Congress."[6] Fareed Mohamedi of PFC Energy, a consulting firm based in Washington, D.C. that advised petroleum firms, asserted that the large oil companies had sought a more peaceful approach to securing their interests in the Gulf region and the Arab world.

> Big oil told the Cheney Task Force on Energy Policy in 2001 that they wanted the U.S. sanctions lifted on Libya and Iran so they could gain access to their oil supplies. As far back as 1990, they were even arguing that the United States should cut a deal with Saddam because he had given signals he was willing to let U.S. oil companies into Iraq.[7]

The upshot of the matter is that while oil companies were obviously concerned about oil, it was that very concern that made them oppose war and seek some peaceful approach to advance their economic interests.

Oil industry representatives did not even move toward a pro-war position in the post-September 11 period. Damien Cave wrote in *Salon* in November 2001 that "there is no clear evidence, right now, of oil company desires affecting current U.S. foreign policy. If anything, the terrorist attacks have reduced the energy industry's influence."[8] According to oil analyst Anthony Sampson in December 2002, "oil companies have had little influence on U.S. policy-making. Most big American companies, including oil companies, do not see a war as good for business, as falling share prices indicate." Sampson contrasted the oil companies' view to that of the neocons: "Many neo-conservatives in Washington are indicating they want the U.S. intervention to go beyond Iraq; and to redraw the diplomatic map of the Middle East." On the other hand, he noted that "[o]il companies dread having supplies interrupted by burning oilfields, saboteurs and chaotic conditions. And any attempt to redraw the frontiers could increase the dangers in both Iran and Iraq, as rivals seek to regain territory."[9]

For years, what oil companies sought in the Middle East was stability, which had been the reigning American policy in the area. They feared that war would bring on a destructive regional conflagration. "War in the Persian Gulf might produce a major upheaval in petroleum markets, either because of physical damage or because political events lead oil producers to restrict production after the war," economist William D. Nordhaus, a member of the President Jimmy Carter's Council of Economic Advisers, wrote in late 2002.

> A particularly worrisome outcome would be a wholesale destruction of oil facilities in Iraq, and possibly in Kuwait, Iran, and Saudi Arabia. In the first Persian Gulf War, Iraq destroyed much of Kuwait's oil wells and other petroleum infrastructure as it withdrew. The sabotage shut down Kuwaiti oil production for close to a year, and prewar levels of oil production were not reached until 1993 – nearly two years after the end of the war in February 1991.[10]

There was never a realistic possibility that Iraqi oil would somehow pay for the costs of the war and benefit the United States economy, though that notion was sometimes bandied about in the media. Paul Wolfowitz, for example, told the House Appropriations Committee on March 27, 2003, "We're dealing with a country that can really finance its own reconstruction, and relatively soon."[11] Obviously, far from providing cheap oil for the United States, the war and occupation of Iraq have proved a serious economic drain on the United States. And the difficulties with the occupation were anticipated before the war started. A number of studies by different U.S. government agencies accurately predicted the problems that would occur. But the Bush administration ignored their warnings.[12]

A year-long pre-war State Department study, called the "Future of Iraq Project," which began in April 2002, foresaw the chaotic conditions that would exist during an American occupation of Iraq. The State Department project brought together a diverse group of Iraqi exiles and American experts from its Middle East Bureau to begin planning for a post-Saddam Iraq, covering a host of topics: democracy-building, oil, health, education, the economy. The study warned that many Iraqis might oppose an American occupation and it predicted extensive looting and lawlessness. However, in January 2003, postwar planning was taken away from the State Department and turned over to the Pentagon, which ignored the State Department findings.[13]

The CIA also warned the Bush administration of extensive post-war resistance. In January 2003, Paul Pillar, the national intelligence officer in charge of the coordinating intelligence on Iraq, completed a high-level report analyzing the problems confronting the United States in post-Saddam Iraq. The report emphasized that establishing a stable democracy in Iraq would be very difficult. There would likely be violent ethnic and religious conflicts, which could explode if the United States did not provide a substantial occupying force. Moreover, the occupation would be costly for the United States, especially since Iraq would be unable to finance its reconstruction through oil revenues.[14]

In February 2003, the Army War College's Strategic Studies Institute published the report, *Reconstructing Iraq: Insights, Challenges and Missions for Military Forces in a Post-Conflict Scenario*, which emphasized the likelihood of strong resistance to the American occupation and the difficulty of establishing any type of political stability. The report held that

> [I]f this nation and its coalition partners decide to undertake the mission to remove Saddam Hussein, they will also have to be prepared to dedicate considerable time, manpower, and money to the effort to reconstruct Iraq after the fighting is over. Otherwise, the success of military operations will be ephemeral, and the problems they were designed to eliminate could return or be replaced by new and more virulent difficulties.[15]

Regarding oil alone, a report conducted in the fall of 2002 by the U. S. Defense Department's Energy Infrastructure Planning Group, which drew on the expertise of government specialists, including the Central Intelligence Agency, and retired senior energy executives, concluded that an oil bonanza would not materialize because of the dilapidated condition of the Iraqi oil infrastructure. After years of decay, that infrastructure would require years of repair work and billions of dollars in investment before it could provide plentiful oil.[16]

In short, pre-invasion government reports made it clear that Iraq, despite its large oil reserves, would not provide an attractive environment for oil investment and production. "As a business decision," remarked Charles A. Kohlhaas, a former Professor of Petroleum Engineering at the Colorado School of Mines and a long-time oil man,

> invading Iraq "for the oil" is a loser, a big loser. Anyone who would propose, in a corporate boardroom, invading Iraq for the oil would probably find his career rather short. No, the slogan "no war for oil" is a blatant misrepresentation propagated for political reasons.[17]

Had the United States been motivated by a desire for oil profits (and the elimination of any Iraqi WMD, as well) an approach other than war could have been pursued. For Iraq, through back channel diplomatic efforts, sought to placate the United States and thus avert an invasion by offering it a share of Iraq's oil wealth and proof of Iraq's WMD disarmament. This effort began in December 2002 when a representative from General Tahir

Jalil Habbush al Tikriti, Saddam Hussein's intelligence chief, made contact with former CIA counter-intelligence head Vincent Cannistraro to talk of negotiations. Cannistraro conveyed this information to senior members of the State Department.[18]

Early in 2003 a rather murky affair concerning Iraq peace offers revolved around a Lebanese-American businessman, Imad Hage, who had a friendly relationship with Defense Department consultant Michael Maloof and had been involved as a go-between for the Syrian government. Hage maintained that he had been involved in secret meetings in Beirut and Baghdad with Tahir Jalil Habbush and Hassan al-Obeidi, chief of foreign operations for the Iraqi intelligence service. The Iraqis insisted that Baghdad had no weapons of mass destruction and offered to allow an on-site investigation by American weapons inspectors to verify their claim. Furthermore, the officials offered the promise of lucrative oil concessions to the U.S. companies. Maloof arranged appointments for Hage with Richard Perle and Jaymie Durnan, the special assistant to Paul Wolfowitz to whom Hage conveyed this information.[19].

One doesn't know where these offers may have led, since they were rejected by the U.S. The Bush administration allegedly demanded Saddam's abdication and departure, first to a U.S. military base for interrogation and then into supervised exile; the surrender of Iraqi troops; and the admission by Iraq of having weapons of mass destruction. Since these demands were tantamount to unconditional surrender, there was little incentive for Saddam to accept them.[20]

If this information were true, and had the United States been willing to accept Iraq's offer, it could have had the benefits of the Iraqi oil wealth and a guarantee of Iraq's WMD disarmament without the difficulties and costs involved in the war and occupation. Saddam's police and military could have maintained the security of his area from Islamic terrorists, as he had been doing very successfully. One would think that this offer would have been especially attractive considering the negative consequences of war foretold by various government studies. It was obvious that those pushing for war sought something other than oil profits.

The other argument citing oil as the motive for war relates not so much to economic gain for the United States or to the interests of Big Oil, but rather to increased power for the United States in world affairs. As one commentator wrote: "Oil appears in Washington's calculations about Iraq as a strategic rather than an economic resource: the war against Saddam is about guaranteeing American hegemony rather than about increasing the profits of Exxon."[21] It has been argued that American control of Iraq's oil would give the United States great leverage over Saudi Arabia and other oil-producing nations in the Middle East in setting production levels. Leveraging the oil supplies of Iraq and the Middle East would enable the U.S. to exercise global domination, since the industrial nations depend on oil for survival. "Controlling Iraq is about oil as power, rather than oil as fuel," averred Michael Klare, author of *Resource Wars*. "Control over the Persian Gulf translates into control over Europe, Japan, and China. It's having our hand on the spigot."[22]

Control of Iraqi oil for American global strategic interests would be a long-term operation and would presuppose a permanent American occupation, making the American-controlled Iraq resemble the World War II-era Japanese puppet state of Manchukuo or Soviet-controlled Eastern Europe. But even those examples may not sufficiently describe the case. In terms of the model of 1940s France, Washington would need not a Vichy Iraq but an Occupied Iraq; not a Marshal Pétain as a client ruler, but a General Stülpnagel as a proconsul. No lesser control would suffice, since there could be no guarantee that even a friendly semi-independent Iraqi government would pursue an oil policy that would sacrifice its own economic well-being for American global strategy. Such an extended occupation would require extensive planning and involve colossal expense. There is no evidence that the Bush administration ever considered the requisite long-term occupation, much less planned for it.

The fact of the matter is that there was no real plan for any type of occupation, much less for a long term one. As the official historian of the Iraq campaign, Major Isaiah Wilson III, pointed out, the U.S. military invaded Iraq without a formal plan for occupying and stabilizing the country. "There was no Phase IV plan" for occupying Iraq after the major combat operations ended, Wilson emphasized. "While there may have been 'plans' at the national level, and even within various agencies within the war zone, none of these 'plans' operationalized the problem beyond regime collapse." In essence: "There was no adequate operational plan for stability operations and support operations."[23]

Marine Colonel Nicholas Reynolds, an official Marine Corps historian, also pointed out that there was no significant planning for the aftermath

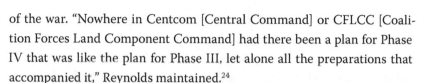

of the war. "Nowhere in Centcom [Central Command] or CFLCC [Coalition Forces Land Component Command] had there been a plan for Phase IV that was like the plan for Phase III, let alone all the preparations that accompanied it," Reynolds maintained.[24]

A briefing paper prepared for British Prime Minister Tony Blair and his top advisers written for a July 23, 2002 Downing Street meeting on Iraq concluded that the U.S. military was not preparing adequately for what the British memo predicted would be a "protracted and costly" postwar occupation of that country. In its introduction, the memo, "Iraq: Conditions for Military Action," noted that U.S. "military planning for action against Iraq is proceeding apace," but contended that "little thought" had been given to "the aftermath and how to shape it."[25]

In his account of his CIA tenure, George Tenet emphasizes that the high-level administration meetings on the war never engaged in any extensive discussion of what would happen after the military defeat of Saddam. Tenet writes that

> there was precious little consideration, that I'm aware of, about the big picture that would come next. While some policy makers were eager to say that we would be greeted as liberators, what they failed to mention is that the intelligence community told them that such a greeting would last for only a limited period. Unless we quickly provided a secure and stable environment on the ground, the situation could rapidly deteriorate.[26]

The warnings were simply ignored at higher levels. It was the civilian Pentagon leadership, namely the neocons, who seemed indifferent to the difficulties that might be faced in the aftermath of an invasion. Michael Isikoff and David Corn conclude in *Hubris: The Inside Story of Spin, Scandal, and the Selling of the Iraq War,*

> The work of government experts and analysts was discarded by senior Bush administration policy makers when it conflicted with or undermined their own hardened ideas about what to expect in Iraq. They were confident – or wanted to believe – that war would go smoothly. They didn't need other views, notions, or plans – not from the State Department, the CIA, or the military. It was their war, and they would run it as they saw fit.[27]

Similarly, George Packer writes in *The Assassin's Gate,* "If there was never a coherent postwar plan, it was because the people in Washington who mattered never intended to stay in Iraq." Packer quotes an unnamed Defense Department official: "Rummy and Wolfowitz and Feith did not believe the U.S. would need to run postconflict Iraq. Their plan was to turn it over to these exiles very quickly and let them deal with the messes that came up."[28]

But did the neocons in the administration really believe that everything would go smoothly in Iraq, despite the extensive expert evidence to the contrary? After serious problems arose during the occupation, General Anthony Zinni made a quite reasonable assessment of the neoconservative motives. "I think . . . that the neocons didn't really give a shit what happened in Iraq and the aftermath," he said.

> I don't think they thought it would be this bad. But they said: Look, if it works out, let's say we get Chalabi in, he's our boy, great. We don't and maybe there's some half-ass government in there, maybe some strongman emerges, it fractures, and there's basically a loose federation and there's really a Kurdish state. Who cares? There's some bloodshed, and it's messy. Who cares? I mean, we've taken out Saddam. We've asserted our strength in the Middle East. We're changing the dynamic. We're now off the peace process as the centerpiece and we're not putting any pressure on Israel.[29]

In summary, the neocons had not made the effort to develop an Iraq that could serve as a completely controlled satellite state, which would slavishly sacrifice itself for American interests. Undoubtedly, the neocons would have preferred a pro-American government run by Chalabi, or someone like him. However, the chances of such an American-controlled satellite ever emerging would be highly unlikely without an extensive American military occupation. The destabilization of Iraq, however, was quite in line with the thinking of the Israeli geostrategists such as Oded Yinon. And it fitted in with David Wurmser's conception of the fragile unity of Middle East states.

Certainly, the type of an army needed for an occupation of Iraq was the polar opposite of Secretary of Defense Donald Rumsfeld's model of a sleek, high-tech military, which would easily smash Saddam's forces in open battle, but would not be well-suited to control the country. In fact, the costly occupation would impact negatively on Rumsfeld's vision of the future high-tech American military. Military analyst Loren Thompson recognized early on that the great cost of keeping U.S. troops in Iraq and Afghanistan would almost certainly damage other Pentagon initiatives. "If the current level of expenditure in Iraq continues," he said in 2003, "Donald Rumsfeld is going to have to kiss much of the technology part of his transformation plan goodbye."[30] And in the period after the 2004 election, the White House pressed the Pentagon to cut tens of billions of dollars from its proposed budgets. The budget cuts would not affect spending on the war in Iraq and operations in Afghanistan, which were paid through separate emergency allocations, but would hit hard on new weapons acquisitions.[31]

The claim that the purpose of the United States invasion of Iraq was to advance American global power was also undercut by the very paucity of foreign policy experts outside the neoconservative orbit who subscribed to that view. Significantly, those cool to the pre-emptive strike on Iraq included the doyens of the Republican foreign policy establishment such as Brent Scowcroft, who served as national security adviser under Presidents Ford and George H. W. Bush; Lawrence Eagleburger, who served as deputy secretary of state and secretary of state under the first Bush; and James Baker, who served as secretary of state in that administration.[32]

In an op-ed piece in the August 15, 2002 issue of *Wall Street Journal*, entitled "Don't Attack Iraq," Scowcroft contended that Saddam was not connected with terrorists and that his weapons posed no threat to the United States. Scowcroft acknowledged that "Given Saddam's aggressive regional ambitions, as well as his ruthlessness and unpredictability, it may at some point be wise to remove him from power." However, "An attack on Iraq at this time would seriously jeopardize, if not destroy, the global counterterrorist campaign we have undertaken."[33]

As noted the previous chapter, the elder Bush himself expressed his opposition to the war in private.[34] Joseph Wilson, an open critic of the impending war in 2002, wrote that he received a "warm note" from the former president, in which the elder Bush stated that he "agreed with almost everything" Wilson had written.[35]

From the neocon perspective, Jeffrey Bell in the *Weekly Standard* noted how the elder Bush's position radically differed from that of his son, and that the adherents of his position staunchly opposed the neocon Middle East war agenda. "There is an alternative Bush I view that is now engaged in a death struggle with Bush II," Bell wrote.

> It has a micro, not a macro, interpretation of what happened on 9/11. It sees Osama and Islamism as limited and aberrational. It mildly supported the invasion of Afghanistan, but would favor no other significant military actions, backing mainly police actions geared toward catching Osama and other al Qaeda figures. It believes many of our problems in the Islamic world relate to our

support for Israel. Bush I does not like Yasser Arafat, but believes the United States and Israel have no choice but to try to strike a deal with him.

In the Islamic world, Bush I favors economic development through trade and internal, top-down reforms. While it does not oppose attempts to achieve democratic reforms in Islamic countries, it has little hope that this will be much of a factor in the immediate decades ahead.[36]

It should be added that this opposition from the elder Bush's close associates and apparently from the elder Bush himself would seem to belie the argument that George W. Bush went to war to avenge Saddam's alleged assassination attempt against his father. There is no evidence that George W. Bush launched the war in the interest, much less advice, of his father.

Also expressing strong opposition to the war on Iraq, and the overall neocon war agenda in the Middle East, was Zbigniew Brzezinski, the National Security Advisor in the Carter administration, who sometimes has been wrongly identified by many hard-line war critics as the central figure in the war cabal.[37] However, as an article from the World Socialist Web Site more perceptively put it: "Brzezinski has emerged as one of the most trenchant establishment critics of Bush foreign policy, arguing from the standpoint of U.S. imperialism's longer-term interests."[38]

To be sure, Brzezinski explicitly advocated American global dominance in his *Grand Chessboard: American Primacy and its Geostrategic Imperatives*. However, during the build up for war, he expressed the concern that a unilateral attack on Iraq would serve to undermine America's global interests. What especially troubled him was the havoc America's unilateral march to war was wreaking on America's alliance with Western Europe, which he considered the central element of American global policy, terming it the "anchor point of America's engagement in world." Brzezinski feared that the "cross-Atlantic vitriol" over the America's plan to attack Iraq despite European opposition had left "NATO's unity in real jeopardy." Moreover, the Bush administration's fixation on Iraq interfered with America's ability to engage in other global hotspots, with Brzezinski observing that "there is justifiable concern that the preoccupation with Iraq – which does not pose an imminent threat to global security – obscures the need to deal with the more serious and genuinely imminent threat posed by North Korea." Brzezinski granted that

force may have to be used to enforce the goal of disarmament. But how and when that force is applied should be part of a larger strategy, sensitive to the

risk that the termination of Saddam Hussein's regime may be purchased at too high a cost to America's global leadership.[39]

Also intriguing was the fact that the war was opposed by international relations academicians of the "realist" school, which consisted of those who emphasize power and national interest in world affairs, as opposed to emphasizing morality and ideals such as freedom and democracy. One would think that they might be apt to support such an endeavor if it actually promised to augment American power. Leading anti-Iraq war realists in academe included John Mearsheimer, Kenneth Waltz, Alexander George, Robert Jervis, Thomas Schelling, and Stephen Walt. They were among 33 academicians who took out an ad in the September 26, 2002 *New York Times* entitled "War With Iraq is Not in America's National Interest." Many signatories to that letter would form the Coalition for a Realistic Foreign Policy in 2003.[40] In fact, the entire foreign policy establishment tended to be cool toward the war policy, as shown by opposition from within the elite Council on Foreign Relations. As columnist Robert Kuttner wrote in September 2003, "it's still a well-kept secret that the vast foreign policy mainstream – Republican and Democratic ex-public officials, former ambassadors, military and intelligence people, academic experts – consider Bush's whole approach a disaster."[41]

In describing the opponents of the war on Iraq and the overall goal of reconfiguring the Middle East, Norman Podhoretz included the liberal internationalists and the realists, both of whom, he acknowledged, had been part of the old foreign policy establishment. The liberal internationalists, he observed,

> were comfortably housed in the political science departments of the universities and in bodies like the Council on Foreign Relations, the Brookings Institution, and the Carnegie Endowment; they were also the dominant force with the populous community of nongovernmental organizations (NGOs).

Their rejection of the Bush administration's approach to Iraq derived from their "virtually religious commitment to negotiations as the best, or indeed the only, way to resolve conflicts; an unshakable faith in the UN; and a corresponding squeamishness about military force."[42]

Podhoretz described the realists as "even more centrally located in the precincts of the old foreign policy establishment than their liberal internationalist neighbors." Podhoretz continued that "Until 9/11, the realists undoubtedly represented the dominant school of thought in the world of foreign policy." For the "realists," "the great desideratum was stability." Although they were not averse to the use of force, it was to be used only "in repelling another state's aggressive effort to upset a previously stable balance of power, while to make war in order to institute 'regime change' was almost always both wrong and foolish."[43] In his advocacy of spreading democracy in the Middle East, and the use of force to achieve this change, Bush "was declaring here a revolutionary change in the rules of the international game."[44] In short, Podhoretz emphasized the fact that the Bush II administration had made a radical break with past United States policy in the Middle East, and that representatives of the old foreign policy elite have resisted such a change.

As pointed out in the previous chapters, the dramatic differences between the neoconservatives and the old foreign policy establishment loomed large before and after the invasion of Iraq, and were ultimately symbolized by the report of the James Baker's Iraq Study Group in late 2006 and its rejection by President Bush. Howard Fineman summarized this situation in November 2006:

> In a sense, the whole story of the internal conflict leading up to the war in Iraq, and a good bit of the backbiting since, has been about a subterranean and never-ending war between the Old Boys of the CIA and the State Department (the pragmatists for want of a better term) and the White House and Defense Department "Vulcans." The pragmatists believe in commerce above all, and in an America that survives through the cold-eyed view that our country has no permanent enemies and no permanent friends – only permanent interests.[45]

Many American military leaders also opposed the U.S. attack on Iraq. Even members of the Joint Chiefs of Staff initially expressed their opposition to initiating war.[46] Remarkably, opposition also came from three retired chiefs of the U.S. Central Command that covers the Gulf region: Marine General Anthony Zinni, General H. Norman Schwarzkopf, and Marine General Joseph P. Hoar.[47] Other prominent retired military figures who opposed the war included: Colonel Mike Turner, a former policy planner for the Joint Chiefs on the Mideast and East Africa; Marine Colonel Larry Williams; former Navy secretary James Webb; and the most decorated soldier of the Vietnam war era, Colonel David Hackworth. All opposed the Iraq war on the grounds that an American occupation of Iraq would be a disaster.[48] Retired generals retain considerable influence in the American military establishment.[49] Schwarzkopf was especially influential because he had led American forces in the first Gulf War of 1991. Moreover, he maintained close connections with the Bush family and even campaigned for George W. Bush in the 2000 presidential election.[50]

As America moved toward war in late 2002, publications from military professionals were filled with articles emphasizing the need for caution. Regarding elite military opinion, Thomas E. Ricks concluded that "This was not a military straining to go to war."[51]

Even a report issued by the Army War College in January 2004 criticized the decision to make war on Iraq. The report, authored by Jeffrey Record, held that war on Iraq "was a war-of-choice distraction from the war of necessity against al Qaeda." It maintained that

> [i]n conflating Saddam Hussein's Iraq and Osama bin Laden's al-Qaeda, the administration unnecessarily expanded the GWOT [Global War on Terrorism] by launching a preventive war against a state that was not at war with the United States and that posed no direct or imminent threat to the United States at the expense of continued attention and effort to protect the United States from a terrorist organization with which the United States was at war.[52]

That such a report should come out under the auspices of the Army War College signaled deep disenchantment in the military with the war on Iraq.[53]

The national security/intelligence bureaucracy was also skeptical of the war on Iraq, a fact that became confirmed with the purging of significant segments of it, such as anti-war critic Michael Scheuer, almost immediately after Bush's reelection in November 2004, which was discussed in Chapter 14. Other high-level CIA officials who voiced opposition to the war included Paul Pillar, the CIA's expert on counterterrorism and Tyler Drumheller, the division chief for the CIA's Directorate of Operations.

As pointed out earlier in the work, George Tenet had wanted to focus on Afghanistan, not Iraq. In his memoir he claims that after 9/11 he was "singularly obsessed with the war on terrorism. My many sleepless nights back then didn't center on Saddam Hussein. Al-Qa'ida occupied my nightmares – not if but how they would strike again."[54] While Tenet went along with the move toward war on Iraq, he certainly did not initiate it.

The neocons recognized the CIA as an enemy of their agenda. As an article in the *Weekly Standard* in late 2005 put it:

> The CIA's war against the Bush administration is one of the great untold stories of the past three years. It is, perhaps, the agency's most successful covert

action of recent times. The CIA has used its budget to fund criticism of the administration by former Democratic officeholders. The agency allowed an employee, Michael Scheuer, to publish and promote a book containing classified information, as long as, in Scheuer's words, "the book was being used to bash the president." However, the agency's preferred weapon has been the leak. In one leak after another, generally to the *New York Times* or the *Washington Post*, CIA officials have sought to undermine America's foreign policy. Usually this is done by leaking reports or memos critical of administration policies or skeptical of their prospects.[55]

The State Department too was not energetic about the war. Although he finally went along with the war, Secretary of State Powell definitely seemed to be retarding the move to war by the neocons and would later claim in July 2007 that he tried to talk Bush out of going to war.[56] Powell's Chief of Staff Lawrence Wilkerson described American foreign policy as being run by a "cabal between the vice president of the United States, Richard Cheney, and the secretary of defense, Donald Rumsfeld" with the State Department ignored to the extent that "I'm not sure the State Department even exists anymore."[57]

Given the opposition from establishment figures and institutions, both inside and outside of the Bush administration, it was obvious that the war on Iraq was a significant break with what had been the normal thrust of American foreign policy. Even Noam Chomsky, who views American foreign policy as a reflection of America's dominant corporate interests, has at times recognized the establishment's opposition to the war on Iraq:

> Their [the neoconservatives] war in Iraq, for example, was strongly opposed by leading sectors of the foreign policy elite, and perhaps even more strikingly, the corporate world. But the same sectors will continue to support the Bush circles, strongly. It is using state power to lavish huge gifts on them, and they basically share the underlying premises even if they are concerned about the practice and the irrationality of the actors, and the dangers they pose.[58]

Chomsky's effort to show corporate support for the Bush administration is extraneous to issue of whether large corporations pushed for the war on Iraq. In short, it would seem that for oil and other corporate interests, the Bush administration's support for their other economic interests outweighed their opposition to the Bush war policy in the Middle East. Obviously, the Bush administration was very supportive of business interests in many crucial respects: taxation, regulation, drilling rights for oil. That corporate interests did not break with the Bush administration because of

the war in the Middle East, however, does not show that they pushed for such a war – a fact which Chomsky acknowledged.

In conclusion, various converging pieces of evidence militate against the arguments that the United States went to war to achieve economic profit for oil interests or to enhance global power. Since oil interests did not push for the war, nor were any great oil profits realistically expected, it is hard to make a claim that the war was for the benefit of the oil companies. Next, the allegation that the United States went to war to control Iraq and its resources is undercut by the failure of the United States to prepare for an effective, long-term occupation that would be essential to attain this goal. Finally, the argument that the purpose of the war was to enhance American global power is refuted by the failure of leading segments of foreign policy/national security elite to support the venture. Why, then, would the neoconservatives see the advantages to be gained for an American war on Iraq and an overall Middle East war agenda that were invisible to most of the foreign policy/national security elite? As this work has illustrated, the peculiarity of the neocon view was shaped by an identification with Israel and the Likudnik view of how to advance that country's interests.

The results of the war have served to fortify this interpretation. There has been no great oil bonanza nor expansion of U.S. global power. On the contrary, with America bogged down in Iraq, it is more much more difficult for Washington to pursue other global goals. In contrast, the neoconservative/Likudnik goal of enhancing Israeli security has been advanced quite well. As Virginia Tilley summarizes in *The One-State Solution,*

> None of these U.S. moves seemed to reflect a realist or even hawkish understanding of U. S. interests and therefore baffled many foreign-policy analysts. The Bush administration's grandiose claims of intent to "democratize" the Arab world actually imperiled U.S. leverage in the region and, in the view of many specialists, damaged U.S. security rather than enhanced it. But as knowledge of *A Clean Break* filtered among the international community and as a spy scandal involving AIPAC and Perle's [sic] Pentagon Office Special Plans began to bloom in the mainstream media in the fall of 2004, the reasoning behind the Iraq effort became clear. U.S. policy did reflect Israel's interests.[59]

As presented in previous chapters, it is also apparent that the traditional foreign policy elite also opposed an extension of the war to Iran. Military leaders were especially averse to launching an invasion.[60] The issue of Iran and the 2006 Israeli invasion of Lebanon should make clear the division between the neocons and the traditional foreign policy elite to anyone who reads the mainstream press.[61] Given the fact that the general public could fall for the neocon propaganda, the political weakness of the anti-war movement, and that even after the bulk of the public turned against the war in Iraq, many politicians, including Democrats, did not eschew militant action against Iran, it could easily be argued that instead of pushing America to war in the Middle East, the traditional foreign policy establishment has played a significant role in restraining such a development. The significance of the traditional foreign policy elites stems from the fact that they continue to exist and exert influence within the Bush administration, Congress, and other power sectors of the United States. In contrast, the popular anti-war movement has virtually no influence over the levers of power. Had the traditional foreign-policy establishment supported the neocon war agenda, there would have much less opposition initially to the Iraq war, and the United States would have likely marched on to complete the neocon agenda with wars against Iran, Syria, and other enemies of Israel.

chapter 19

CONCLUSION

THIS BOOK HAS MAINTAINED that the origins of the American war on Iraq revolve around the United States' adoption of a war agenda whose basic format was conceived in Israel to advance Israeli interests and was ardently pushed by the influential pro-Israeli American neoconservatives, both inside and outside the Bush administration. Voluminous evidence, much of it derived from a lengthy neoconservative paper trail, has been marshaled to substantiate these contentions.

Some have questioned how such a small group as the neocons could wield so much power in influencing U.S. foreign policy. History, however, has shown that small numbers never have precluded success in the political realm, with minorities frequently dominating governments. Moreover, the neoconservatives were perfectly organized to be an influential minority. They were more than a congeries of individuals; rather, they represented people from an extensive, interlocking network of organizations whose very raison d'être was to shape American policy. It was this network that enabled them not only to influence the heights of government power – gaining important positions in the Bush II administration – but also to shape educated and mass opinion. The neocons essentially sold their war agenda to Congress and the American public. It is apparent that the neocons essentially did far more than simply get the president to accept significant parts of their war agenda; they played the major role in having their war policy implemented. Without that effort, it is unlikely that the Bush administration would have had the necessary political support to attack Iraq, even if Bush had personally converted to the neocon cause.

The influence of the neoconservatives was especially manifested by the fact that their war agenda was radically different from the traditional American policy in the Middle East, which had focused on maintaining regional stability. Consequently, neocon policy provoked opposition from members of the traditional foreign policy/national security elite. As this work has illustrated, the neocons faced significant opposition from within the Bush administration – the military, State Department, CIA. To deny the influence of the neoconservatives – to claim that President Bush pursued a war policy almost identical to that long advocated by the neoconservatives but was unaffected by them, and that he would somehow have gotten this war policy implemented without the neocons' ardent efforts – would be an assertion so improbable as to move into the realm of the absurd.

None of this is to ascribe some infinite power to the neoconservatives. In fact, the neoconservatives would not have been able to implement their war agenda had it not been for the trauma of the 911 terrorist attacks, which filled the American people with fear and anger, making them, and their political representatives, highly susceptible to the neoconservatives' war message. As the psychological effects of 911 on the populace subsided, the neocons' ability to widen the war declined.

A fundamental, and rather taboo, part of this work's theme has been Israel's integral connection to the neoconservatives' war agenda. The major outlines of the Middle East war agenda to advance Israeli security by destabilizing Israel's neighbors loomed large in Likudnik thinking in the 1980s. Leading neocons – Richard Perle, David Wurmser, Douglas Feith – proposed a comparable plan to Israeli Prime Minister Netanyahu in 1996. After that time, the neoconservatives' revised war program would have the United States replace Israel as the aggressive party. The Israeli connection, however, continued during America's move toward war on Iraq, as Sharon's government urged the attack and promoted the idea of Saddam's imminent WMD threat. Israel would later play a similar role in urging a hard-line on Iran.

As brought out in this work, the neoconservatives had close ties to Israel and had even, on a number of occasions, cited Israeli security as a goal of their Middle East war agenda. But they insisted that American and Israeli interests coincided and that the fundamental purpose of their policy prescriptions was to enhance American security. To determine the veracity of this neocon claim, it is instructive to assess the fruits of their policy. Namely, to what extent has an enhancement of American security actually materialized as a result of their war policy?

The negative effects of the Iraq war for America are rather obvious. By the end of March 2008, over 4000 American lives had been lost, those wounded exceeded 29,000, and close to $490 billion had been expended on the war.[1] The full economic cost of the war, which would include not only direct war expenditures but the war's overall impact on the economy, was far higher. Joseph Stiglitz, a former chairman of the National Council of Economic Advisors and Nobel-prize winning Columbia University economist, and Linda Bilmes, a Harvard budget expert, calculated in their book, *The Three Trillion Dollar War: The True Cost of the Iraq Conflict,* published in early 2008, that the total cost of the Iraq war would be $3 trillion. (This estimate is based on the assumption that the United States would withdraw all combat troops by 2012.) The war costs have already exceeded those of the twelve-year war in Vietnam. The authors point out that the only war in American history that cost more was World War II. These staggering costs have already been a significant factor in the American economy's downturn.[2]

These immense costs are nothing like the rosy scenario painted by the Bush administration and its supporters to generate support for the war. It is highly unlikely that the American public and Congress would have backed the war had they known its real costs, since only a very small percentage of Americans expected over one thousand American casualties.[3] Had this knowledge been combined with the realization that there was no Iraqi WMD threat, the chances of war would had been virtually non-existent.

And what had the United States achieved in Iraq? Instead of the publicly promised democracy, Iraq became plagued by terrorism and sectarian violence that verged on becoming an actual civil war between the Sunnis and Shiites. The Bush administration claimed that if the American military withdrew political and social order would collapse and the terrorists would win.

Furthermore, the Iraq war has not made America safer from terrorists. A mid-year 2007 report by the U.S. government's National Counterterrorism Center, "Al-Qaida Better Positioned to Strike the West," acknowledged the increased danger from that terrorist group.[4] Americans became less safe, in part, because prosecution of the war in Iraq required the United States' government to divert resources and attention away from hunting down known terrorists and protecting the homeland from terrorist attacks.[5] Moreover, the war on Iraq antagonized many Muslims, bringing more adherents to the anti-American terrorist cause. Before the American invasion, Iraq was not a haven for terrorists, but it became so afterward. The United States occupation created a breeding ground for terrorists. In fact, America antagonized the entire Muslim world by its occupation of Iraq, especially with its well-publicized brutality and torture, real and imagined.[6]

A 2007 study by terrorism specialists Peter Bergen and Paul Cruickshank, using government and Rand Corporation data, showed that the "Iraq conflict has greatly increased the spread of the Al Qaeda ideological virus, as shown by a rising number of terrorist attacks in the past three years from London to Kabul, and from Madrid to the Red Sea."[7] In American terrorism expert Bruce Hoffman's assessment: "Al-Qaida is more dangerous than it was on 9/11."[8] Bruce Reidel, a retired CIA official and a member of the Brookings Institution, wrote in the May/June 2007 issue of *Foreign Affairs* that

> The U.S. invasion of Iraq took the pressure off al Qaeda in the Pakistani badlands and opened new doors for the group in the Middle East. It also played directly into the hands of al Qaeda leaders by seemingly confirming their claim that the United States was an imperialist force, which helped them reinforce various local alliances.[9]

After the release of a new National Intelligence Estimate in July 2007 stressing an increased global Al Qaeda terrorist threat to the United States, Paul Pillar, a former CIA analyst, commented that "We're creating terrorists in Iraq, we are creating terrorists outside of Iraq who are inspired by what's going on in Iraq . . . . The longer we stay, the more terrorists we create."[10]

Not only did the war on Iraq worsen the terrorism situation, but it also weakened America's global power. First of all, the American position in the Middle East had been severely undermined.[11] Richard Haas, President of the Council on Foreign Relations, maintained in his essay, "The End of an Era," in *Foreign Policy*, published in late 2006, that the American war on Iraq had brought about the end of "American primacy" in the Middle East.

> What has brought this era to an end after less than two decades is a number of factors, some structural, some self-created. The most significant has been

the Bush administration's decision to attack Iraq in 2003 and its conduct of the operation and resulting occupation. One casualty of the war has been a Sunni-dominated Iraq, which was strong enough and motivated enough to balance Shiite Iran. Sunni-Shiite tensions, dormant for a while, have come to the surface in Iraq and throughout the region. Terrorists have gained a base in Iraq and developed there a new set of techniques to export. Throughout much of the region, democracy has become associated with the loss of public order and the end of Sunni primacy. Anti-American sentiment, already considerable, has been reinforced. And by tying down a huge portion of the U.S. military, the war has reduced U.S. leverage worldwide. It is one of history's ironies that the first war in Iraq, a war of necessity, marked the beginning of the American era in the Middle East and the second Iraq war, a war of choice, has precipitated its end.[12]

The Iraq imbroglio's adverse impact on overall American global power was highly significant. The view that the American military has been virtually exhausted in Iraq has been expressed by numerous American military leaders.[13] Even Colin Powell declared in December 2006 that the "active Army is about broken."[14] A report released in January 2006 by a study group headed by former Secretary of Defense William Perry stated that America's military forces were stretched so thin that potential enemies might be tempted to challenge the United States elsewhere on the globe.[15] The negative effect on America's power and international standing was apt to be similar to the effect on the Soviet Union of its occupation of Afghanistan.[16]

In its attempt to restructure the Middle East, the United States has inevitably engendered a backlash from other countries of the world. This would seem to be almost an iron law of international relations – the balance of power politics that goes back to at least the time of the Peloponnesian War. Even during the 1990s, other leading powers – Russia, China, France – repeatedly called attention to the dangers of American "hyperpower" and sought the creation of counterweights to U.S. hegemony. The American occupation of Iraq has galvanized other countries' fears that a too-powerful United States will act in ways detrimental to their interests. Moreover, as the United States focused on the Middle East, anti-American leftist forces gained power political power democratically throughout much of Latin America.[17]

American military action in the Middle East has also served to harm the entire global system by increasing the likelihood of strife between nation-states. This derives from America's violation of international law by launching an unprovoked attack on Iraq. America's brazen violation of international law induces other countries to also flout international legality and to be on a war footing to protect themselves from aggressors. This includes the move to develop nuclear weapons by those who do not possess them and the improvement of nuclear arsenals by the existing nuclear powers. Moreover, it leads to the flouting of international economic agreements which American leaders have believed have been valuable for American prosperity.

In short, America's war policy undercut the very international standards for maintaining a stable, peaceful world that American leaders have viewed as beneficial to American interests. America is a wealthy, powerful nation. It has a vested interest in maintaining and even solidifying the status quo. There would seem no reason for risking wars that threaten global stability and lead to the outside chance of nuclear Armageddon.

As pointed out earlier in this work, the negative repercussions of the American attack on Iraq were foreseen by expert opinion. "That the entire plan would very poorly serve U.S. interests was predictable," Virginia Tilley writes in *The One State Solution.*

> The occupation quickly spun into Iraqi nationalist reaction against the U.S. occupation and greatly damaged U.S. credibility in the Arab world. Rather than behaving like a regional hegemon with multilateral interests, the United States was now an occupying power in brash, nineteenth-century "civilizing" mode, exponentially inflating every postcolonial sensitivity and fear in the Arab world.[18]

Zbigniew Brzezinski summed up the negative impacts of the Iraq war in his testimony to the Senate Foreign Relations Committee on February 1, 2007. The attack on Iraq, Brzezinski proclaimed, was a "historic, strategic and moral calamity." Brzezinski held that the war was "undermining America's global legitimacy. Its collateral civilian casualties as well as some abuses are tarnishing America's moral credentials. Driven by Manichean principles and imperial hubris, it is intensifying regional instability."[19]

But what was an unnecessary, deleterious war from the standpoint of the United States, did advance many Israeli interests, as those interests were envisioned by the Israeli right. America came to identify more closely with the position of Israel toward the Palestinians as it began to equate resistance to Israeli occupation with "terrorism." Virginia Tilley writes in *The One-State Solution* that

[a]s all local terrorist groups were now conflated into a single amorphous global foe called "terrorism," Israel's own war on Palestinian terrorists had been redefined as a common cause rather than a causal factor. In other words, Israel was now positioned as an indispensable ally in a "war" against Islamic militancy heavily inspired by outrage at Israel's own policies.[20]

Israel took advantage of the new American "anti-terrorist" position. The "security wall" built by the Sharon government on Palestinian land isolated the Palestinians and made their existence on the West Bank less viable than ever. For the first time, an American president put the United States on record as supporting Israel's eventual annexation of parts of the West Bank.

Obviously, Israel benefited for the very reason that the United States had become the belligerent enemy of Israel's enemies. As such, America seriously weakened Israel's foes at no cost to Israel. The war and occupation basically eliminated Iraq as a potential power. Instead of having a unified democratic government, as the Bush administration had predicted, Iraq was fragmenting into warring sectarian groups, in line with the original Likudnik goal outlined by Oded Yinon.[21]

Middle East reporter Jonathan Cook observed in late 2006:

> Neocons talk a great deal about changing maps in the Middle East. Like Israel's dismemberment of the occupied territories into ever-smaller ghettos, Iraq is being severed into feuding mini-states. Civil war, it is hoped, will redirect Iraqis" energies away from resistance to the U.S. occupation and into more negative outcomes.
>
> Similar fates appear to be awaiting Iran and Syria, at least if the neocons, despite their waning influence, manage to realise their vision in Bush's last two years.
>
> The reason is that a chaotic and feuding Middle East, although it would be a disaster in the view of most informed observers, appears to be greatly desired by Israel and its neocon allies. They believe that the whole Middle East can be run successfully the way Israel has run its Palestinian populations inside the occupied territories, where religious and secular divisions have been accentuated, and inside Israel itself, where for many decades Arab citizens were "de-Palestinianised" and turned into identity-starved and quiescent Muslims, Christians, Druze, and Bedouin.[22]

Although the neocon vision was far from being realized, the benefits to Israel already transcended the elimination of Saddam. America pressured Syria to pull its military out of Lebanon and was openly calling for regime change there. Israeli journalist Aluf Benn summed up Israel's improved geostrategic condition in November 2005:

> Israel is also enjoying an enviable strategic situation, with relative freedom of action, mainly as a result of Bush's aggressive policy in the Middle East. Its rivals, Iran and Syria, are facing international pressure to change their behavior . . . . Iraq is under American occupation, and Saudi Arabia and Egypt have been called to reform and liberalize their regimes. The Palestinians are still devastated by the death of their longtime leader Yasser Arafat last year. Their cause lost some of its global prominence and attention, as Mahmoud Abbas (Abu Mazen), the new P.A. leader, lacks his former mentor's charisma.[23]

One alleged drawback from the standpoint of Israel's security was the seeming improvement of the regional status of Iran as the result of the elimination of Saddam's regime, which had served as a counterweight to Iran, and its replacement by either chaos or by a pro-Iranian Shiite regime. However, it must be emphasized that neocons looked upon the invasion of Iraq as only the initial phase of the of their World War IV scenario, with a regime-change in Iran coming later. Planned strategy, of course, does not always work out in reality – as failed conquerors throughout history have learned to their peril. However, even if the neocons and Israel never succeed in their effort to induce the United States to destabilize Iran, this would have no bearing on the fact that both had pushed for war on Iraq to benefit Israel's interests.

But even here, the overall situation regarding Iran is not necessarily negative from the Likudnik perspective. Israel itself had made connections with the Kurds in their autonomous region of northern Iraq and could rely upon them to oppose a pro-Iranian Iraqi central government and to destabilize the Kurdish areas of Iran, which Kurds would like to control in a united Kurdistan.[24] Moreover, with Iran now surrounded by United States forces in Iraq and Afghanistan, it was certainly in a vulnerable position. Even if the United States refrained from launching a direct attack on Iran, it still was poised to destabilize the country by making use of the Azeris or other ethnic minority groups. In fact, the United States was already supporting minority ethnic separatist groups in Iran to engage in terrorist activities against the Iranian government to foment internal instability.[25]

Furthermore, as a result of American and Israeli charges and threats about Iran's alleged nuclear weapons program, international pressure was being put on Iran to prevent it from developing nuclear weapons. U.N.

and U.S. sanctions have caused significant harm to the Iranian economy. It is important to recognize that the U.S. and even the European effort to prevent Iran from developing nuclear weapons, without any concern about Israel's existing nuclear arsenal, demonstrated de facto international enforcement of Israel's nuclear monopoly in the Middle East, which has been a key factor in Israel's dominance of the region. It is not apparent that these measures would have been taken against Iran's nuclear program had the United States not invaded Iraq and then put pressure on Iran. Prior to the invasion of Iraq, the international spotlight did not shine so brightly on Iran's nuclear program, and had regional peace continued, Iran might have been able to continue its nuclear program with little notice or interference.

Moreover, it is possible that Israel's interest would be advanced by the sectarian conflict in Iraq even if Iran were not attacked. The replacement of Saddam's secular pro-Sunni regime by a religious, pro-Shiite government opened a veritable Pandora's box of sectarian hatred throughout the entire Middle East. Many of the Sunni-dominated countries in the Middle East had significant minority Shiite populations. Most critically for American interests, this included Saudi Arabia where Shiites were concentrated in the oil-producing Eastern Province.[26] "The growing Sunni-Shiite divide is roiling an Arab world as unsettled as at any time in a generation," wrote Anthony Shadid in the February 12, 2007 issue of the *Washington Post*.

> Fought in speeches, newspaper columns, rumors swirling through cafes and the Internet, and occasional bursts of strife, the conflict is predominantly shaped by politics: a disintegrating Iraq, an ascendant Iran, a sense of Arab powerlessness and a persistent suspicion of American intentions. But the division has begun to seep into the region's social fabric, too. The sectarian fault line has long existed and sometimes ruptured, but never, perhaps, has it been revealed in such a stark, disruptive fashion.[27]

The sectarian fighting in Iraq could escalate into to an all-out regional Sunni-Shiite war with the Saudis and other Sunni governments providing the military and arms to combat the Shiite forces backed by Iran. It is not apparent that Iran and the Shiites would easily emerge victorious. Rather, such intra-Muslim fighting on a large scale would sap the strength of all sides, which would have the effect of weakening their capability to cause problems for Israel. Claude Salhani, foreign editor with United Press International, described such a possible internecine conflict that "would tie down fundamentalist forces on both sides for years to come." In regard to Iran, which was seen as the greatest danger to Israel, Salhani held that

> a weakened Iran would be less inclined – and certainly less financially inclined – to pursue its nuclear program or to foment revolts beyond its borders. Or even be too preoccupied by what is going on its own front yard to continue its active support for Lebanon's Hezbollah Party.[28]

Interestingly, allegations existed that the United States had begun to aid Sunni forces to achieve destabilization.[29] In early 2007, Seymour Hersh wrote:

> To undermine Iran, which is predominantly Shiite, the Bush Administration has decided, in effect, to reconfigure its priorities in the Middle East. In Lebanon, the Administration has coöperated with Saudi Arabia's government, which is Sunni, in clandestine operations that are intended to weaken Hezbollah, the Shiite organization that is backed by Iran. The U.S. has also taken part in clandestine operations aimed at Iran and its ally Syria. A by-product of these activities has been the bolstering of Sunni extremist groups that espouse a militant vision of Islam and are hostile to America and sympathetic to Al Qaeda.

Hersh noted that the key players in the "redirection" strategy included Cheney and Deputy National Security Adviser Elliott Abrams.[30]

And the effects of the "surge" which did reduce overt violence also served to fragment Iraq and exacerbate future sectarian conflicts. As pointed out in Chapter 16, by strengthening local Sunni tribal leaders to fight the Al Qaeda insurgents, those tribal leaders set up there own little fiefdoms independent of central government control. Should the Shiite dominated central government attempt to exercise control in these areas, fighting would almost inevitably result. That the United States was arming all sides meant that the exacerbated the destructiveness of such a conflict. [31]

Obviously, such regional instability and fragmentation was anathema to the U.S. foreign policy establishment, whose fundamental foreign policy goal was to prevent such an outcome. Regional instability was something that the Baker Commission sought to forestall by bringing about a conference of all parties in the region, including Iran, to try to peacefully settle area-wide problems. However, such a Sunni/Shiite regional conflagration fitted in with the Likudnik aim of destabilizing Israel's enemies, thus making it more difficult for them to confront Israel.

But even if Israel's external enemies had been weakened, how would this development help Israel in regard to the Palestinian demographic threat? It was widely argued that Israel, instead of engaging in territorial aggrandizement, had made concessions toward the Palestinians regarding the Occupied Territories. These purported concessions initiated by Prime Minister Sharon included his reference to a Palestinian "state" and the evacuation of the Jewish settlements from Gaza. As a result of these actions, Sharon was sharply criticized by some members of the Likud and he ultimately decided to leave that party to establish his own – Kadima – siphoning off a good portion of the leading Likudniks.

However, Sharon's effort to unilaterally establish final borders reflected his goal of solidifying Israel as a Jewish state with a "massive Jewish majority."[32] Moreover, if looked at clearly, Sharon was strengthening the Jewish state at the expense of the Palestinians. Palestinian-American journalist Ramzy Baroud pointed out that in his policy, Sharon

> wished to "secure" Israel, by unilaterally claiming whichever territories he found strategic – based on military logic, access to water aquifers and fertile lands – and ditching smaller pockets of land that were a demographic liability and were strategically irrelevant.[33]

Israel would be forever free of the Palestinian demographic threat and the land and resources left for the Palestinians would be insufficient for the creation of a viable state. Sharon's plan had overwhelming support in Israel, and after his severe stroke in early January 2006, was strongly pursued by his successor as prime minister, Ehud Olmert.

As stated earlier, Sharon had always been more of a pragmatist than an ideologue of the right. The withdrawal from Gaza in 2005 simply reflected the abandonment of a costly and untenable position: the IDF had been required to protect a mere 8,000 Jewish settlers living among 1.3 million Palestinians on a land area comprising only around five percent of the of the overall Occupied Territories.[34] Moreover, the Israeli withdrawal did not mean that Israel had given up effective control of Gaza. Rather, Israel still maintained full control of the water, communications, airspace, and all border entry and exit points. Israel also retained the right to intervene militarily inside Gaza at any time, which it would continue to do.

The pullout from Gaza, which was portrayed to the world as a monumental Israeli concession, was more of a smoke screen to generate international support for Israel's grand plan to destroy any prospect for a viable Palestinian state. For while Sharon pulled out the few Jewish settlers from Gaza and planned to abandon a few isolated Jewish settlements on the West Bank, he had declared his intention to hold on to Israel's major settlement blocs in the West Bank, where intensive new housing construction for Jewish settlers was ongoing. The effect of this was to cut the West Bank in half, thus allowing Israel to control Palestinian movement from one part of their territory to another, while concomitantly isolating Arab East Jerusalem from the rest of Palestine. Since a substantial part of the Palestinian economy was centered on Jerusalem and its tourism, Sharon's plan effectively eliminated the potential productive capability of the envisioned Palestinian "state," rendering it an economically non-viable set of non-contiguous Bantustans surrounded by the "security" wall.

Moreover, Sharon's disengagement effort, continued by his successor Ehud Olmert, still left the control of such vital elements as water, airspace, communications, and borders in the hands of Israel. Water, a scarce commodity in the arid Middle East, which is obviously fundamental for survival, is a key factor in the Israeli-Palestinian controversy rarely mentioned by American commentators. Under its disengagement plan, Israel intended to keep the two main Palestinian West Bank aquifers, which have been essential for its water supply. Israel used far more water per capita than the Palestinians, which not only provided for intensive agriculture but also for the amenities of a Western lifestyle – regular bathing, swimming pools, green lawns. Without those amenities it might be difficult for Israel to attract and retain a Westernized Jewish population. However, the fact that the "state" of Palestine would likely have to depend on Israel for the water its people needed to survive would nullify even the tiniest trace of sovereign statehood.[35]

Furthermore, the Palestinian bantustans would be completely encircled by Israeli territory since Israel planned to annex a strip of land in the eastern West Bank along the Jordan River, separating Palestinian areas from Jordan.[36] To summarize, for the Palestinian people, their economically non-viable "state" would resemble more a large prison than a real independent country.

Former CIA analyst Kathleen Christison concluded in April 2005 that the implicit goal of Sharon's disengagement plan was the gradual removal of the Palestinian population:

> Sharon's actual long-term intent is to make life so miserable for the Palestinians that those left in the small remnants of their territory will simply gradually filter out. This process may take a while, but Sharon is pragmatic and therefore

patient – he and his countrymen have already been waiting 2,000 years to take this land – and it is already beginning to happen in any case. The wall has already turned some of the West Bank cities that it most affects into virtual ghost towns as residents move into the interior where some kind of livelihood might be possible. Sharon and his right wing can wait before he needs to squeeze them further.[37]

In short, despite his much-touted "concessions," Sharon never strayed from his basic goal, which as Baruch Kimmerling points out in *Politicide: Ariel Sharon's War Against the Palestinians*, was "designed to lower Palestinian expectations, crush their resistance, isolate them, make them submit to any arrangement suggested by the Israelis, and eventually cause their 'voluntary' mass emigration from the land."[38] Sharon's "concessions," by serving as cover, helped to generate American and European support for his ultimate goal. Palestinians who resisted the unilateral Israeli offers were negatively portrayed in the Western media as implacable, terroristic foes of the Jewish people.

The refusal of Sharon to make real concessions to the Palestinians, which would allow for a viable Palestinian state, facilitated the Hamas victory by a wide margin in the January 2006 Palestinian democratic election.[39] Hamas was considered by the U.S. government to be a terrorist organization in the "War against Terror." The Hamas victory was widely viewed in the West as serving to justify a harsh policy by Israel toward the Palestinians, which included Israel's refusal to turn over the customs duties it collected on behalf of the Palestinian Authority that provided about one-half of the Palestinian government's operating expenses. The United States coordinated an international funding freeze that stopped all aid to the Hamas-led Palestinian Authority. In essence, the Palestinians' political resistance to policies intended to bring about their demise was equated by the United States with terrorism.

The Israeli attack on Lebanon in July 2006, allegedly in retaliation to Hezbollah's attacks on Israeli soldiers, further underscored the idea that Israel had made gains from the war on terror. In July 2006, Justin Raimondo summarized the situation:

> Examined in light of Israel's postwar actions – the unilateral "withdrawal" from Gaza, the absorption of more territory and the building of more settlements on the West Bank, the war against Hamas, and now the re-invasion of Lebanon – the chief (and only) beneficiary of the new regional balance of power

is clear enough. The American invasion and occupation of the Mesopotamian heartland has empowered the Israelis as never before – and now they are on the offensive, carving out a greatly expanded sphere of influence extending into Kurdistan as well as Lebanon, bringing closer to fulfillment the old Zionist vision of an empire stretching "from the Nile to the Euphrates."[40]

Obviously, Israel did not gain what it sought in its attack on Lebanon. Nonetheless, the international community was now actively working to restrain Hezbollah (something which had not been done before), which was Israel's major enemy in Lebanon.[41]

But by mid-year 2007 both Lebanon and Palestine were in chaos as Hezbollah battled the government forces in Lebanon and as Hamas and al-Fatah fought each other in Palestine. As Robin Wright wrote in the June 17, 2007 issue of the *Washington Post:*

> The broad danger is a breakdown of the traditional states and conflicts that have defined Middle East politics since the 1970s, said Paul Salem of the Carnegie Endowment for International Peace's Beirut office. An increasing number of places – Iraq, Lebanon and the Palestinian territories – now have rival claimants to power, backed by their own militaries.
>
> Also, once divided by the Arab-Israeli conflict, the region is now the battleground for three other rivalries: the United States and its allies pitted against an Iran-Syria alliance in a proxy war regionwide, secular governments confronted by rising al-Qaeda extremism, and autocratic governments reverting to draconian tactics to quash grass-roots movements vying for democratic change.[42]

To reiterate: this regional instability and fragmentation was completely in line with Likudnik Oded Yinon's goal, (which in Israel Shahak's translation was titled *The Zionist Plan for the Middle East*)[43] and had been echoed in the neocons' *Clean Break* study. With Israel's enemies divided and fighting among each other, the more difficult it would be to confront Israel.

Although regional instability had occurred, the neocon Middle East war agenda had not been fully implemented by the spring of 2008, due to opposition within the United States.

Certainly, the neocons and the Israeli right would not be satisfied until Iran was eliminated as a threat to Israel – a threat not simply in terms of its possible development of a nuclear bomb but the threat that it posed by virtue of its support to Hezbollah and the Palestinian resistance. Nevertheless, it was apparent that many Likudnik objectives had been at least partially achieved.

Do the results of the war on Iraq then imply that the neocons were simply agents of Likudnik Israel, hijacking American foreign policy for the interest of that country? Are neoconservatives consciously putting the security interests of Israel above those of the United States? Are they deliberately sacrificing American interests for the good of Israel? Justin Raimondo sometimes writes, perhaps hyperbolically, that this is the case: "Strip away the ideological pretenses, the sexed-up 'intelligence,' and the 'patriotic' window-dressing, and what you see is the naked reality of Israel's fifth column in America."[44]

Raimondo goes so far as to imply that the chaos in the Middle East was the intended consequence of American military involvement – that would help Israel at the expense of the United States.

As he wrote in late May 2007:

> This [the regional chaos] is largely seen as an unintended consequence of the American invasion – but what if it was intended?
>
> It would, after all, make perfect Bizarro "sense." If, instead of trying to build a stable, democratic Iraq, you're trying to wreak as much destruction as possible and turn Arab against Arab, Muslim against Muslim, and the Kurds against everyone else, then the invasion and occupation of Iraq was the right thing to do.[45]

Raimondo continued:

> [Y]ou might wonder if Bush and his neocon advisors lose any sleep at night over what everyone else has deemed their huge "failure" in Iraq. The answer is: certainly not. They sleep deeply, and with a satisfied smile on their faces, because, as far as they're concerned, their mission has been accomplished.[46]

Being unable to look into the neoconservatives' minds, one is not compelled to endorse this radical judgment. Suffice it to say that the neoconservatives viewed American foreign policy through the lens of Israel's interests, as Likudniks have perceived Israel's interest. Quite likely they truly viewed Israel's interests to be America's interests, rather than seeing themselves as sacrificing the interests of the United States for the sake of Israel. Self-deception is not uncommon in ideologically driven individuals.[47]

However, to say that the neoconservatives sought to advance Israeli interests is not to maintain that the neoconservatives carried out the orders of the government of Israel. There is no evidence that they were being so instructed. The positions of the neocons and the Israeli government did dovetail on many crucial issues: war on Iraq, the need to eliminate Iranian power, defense of the Jewish state against Palestinians. In fact, the neoconservatives position on Iran, favorable in the 1980s, hostile in recent years, completely followed that of Israel. However, it would seem that some important elements in Israel voiced more moderate opinions and did not identify with the entire neocon war agenda. That is quite understandable. Even before 2001 it was apparent that the neocons were on the hard-line flank of Israeli opinion, as made evident by their 1996 "A Clean Break" paper, which was called upon the Netanyahu's Likudnik government to break with Labor's "peace process" and take a much more aggressive stance. Even the hard-liner Netanyahu refrained from implementing their hard-line war agenda. Similarly, the Olmert government did not follow the neocon agenda in his invasion of Lebanon in 2006. Obviously, the fractious Israeli domestic political scene places constraints on a political leader's scope of action, so that the implementation of a political program becomes very difficult.

Nonetheless, there has been a definite relationship between the neocons and Israeli politicians that transcends simply ideas. Neocons have been close not only to Netanyahu but also to Sharansky, Dore Gold, and to a lesser extent Sharon. Most significantly, as has been emphasized throughout this book, the neocons' Middle East war agenda did not originate in the minds of the neocons but reflected hard-line Likudnik thinking. Their fundamental ideas on restructuring the Middle East were essentially conceived in Israel to advance Israeli interests.

Despite the connection with Israeli politicians, it would seem that neocons advocated what they thought would be best for Israel, not what they were instructed to hold. It was not abnormal for American Jews (or other American pro-Zionists) to take more militant positions than the bulk of Israeli Jews, especially since Israeli Jews would bear the consequences of any aggressive activities. In short, neocons viewed America through lens of Israeli interests – sometimes their positions conformed with those of the Israeli government, but sometimes Israeli's governing officials were more cautious and moderate than the neocons' harder-line Likudnik views. There is not much evidence available now as to how Israeli government leaders have viewed the neocons. Perhaps, such information will come out in the future. To what degree did Israeli officials regard the neocons as allies? As history has shown, it is not essential that allies hold identical positions.

That some Americans might be motivated by an attachment to a foreign country and that they could be influential in determining American foreign policy is not such an outlandish, unheard-of idea. Historians and other commentators have frequently proposed that German-Americans, Cuban-Americans, Polish-Americans, and other ethnic groups have been influenced in their foreign policy views by an attachment to their ancestral homelands. Historians have claimed that Woodrow Wilson's support for England in World War I was, in part, due to a pro-English bias. It seems commonplace to believe that many Arab-Americans tend to have a view of Middle East foreign policy contrary to that pursued by the United States government. Going back to the beginning of the Republic, Alexander Hamilton tended to be pro-British; Thomas Jefferson pro-French. That a "passionate attachment" to a foreign state could cause some Americans to support a foreign policy detrimental to the interests of the United States was a cardinal warning in George Washington's famous "Farewell Address" of 1796.[48]

It is, nonetheless, quite likely that most people who have identified with a foreign country believed that a policy to support such a country would also strengthen the United States. In the World Wars, American Anglophiles believed that aiding Britain would help the United States. Those Americans who backed revolutionary France during the 1790s, flocking to the banner of Citizen Genet, really believed that it would help the American cause to fight England on the side of France. Undoubtedly anti-Communist Americans Eastern Europeans saw their opposition to the Soviet Union as being for the good of the United States as well as facilitating the liberation of their ancestral homelands. Likewise, the so-called "China Lobby" perceived support for Chiang Kai-Shek to be vital in America's fight against world Communism. On the other hand, Soviet sympathizers and "fellow-travelers" believed that American friendship toward the Soviet Union would serve to benefit the United States. One could go on to say that American agents of the Soviet Union believed they were helping to build a better world, which certainly included the toiling American masses, by aiding Moscow. And undoubtedly Arab-Americans today believe that it would serve America's interest if its foreign policy were not so blatantly biased in favor of Israel.

Commentators on the neocons who want to downplay the Israel connection, taboo subject that it is, make too much of this likelihood that the neoconservatives probably do not see their pro-Israel policies as actually harming the United States. Gary Dorrien, for example, in *Imperial Designs: Neoconservatism and the New Pax Americana,* writes that

> The neocons were American nationalists who believed it was always in America's interest to help Israel succeed over its enemies. They never claimed that the United States needed to sacrifice some interest of its own for the sake of Israel's well-being. To them, the assertion of closely related interests and identical values was an article of faith that secured Israel's protection and provided the United States with its only democratic ally in the Middle East.[49]

To Dorrien, neocons were fundamentally "nationalists" and "unipolarists" – individuals who seek American military global dominance – and he castigates those critics of the neocons who focus on their connection to Israel. It is true that many of the neocons' foreign policy prescriptions can be fitted into Dorrien's classification, for the very fact that neocon foreign policy encompasses far more than just the Middle East. However, the belief that "it was always in America's interest to help Israel succeed over its enemies" does not ineluctably flow from the descriptions "nationalist" and "unipolarist." One could as easily, if not more easily, argue that supporting the Islamic world against Israel would best advance American power in the world. For by pursuing such an alternative policy, the United States would have the support of the major oil-producing region of the world. And if the over one billion Muslims were friendly to the United States, they could be used to undermine America's greatest military adversaries – Russian and China – since both have restive Muslim populations. In short, what specially characterizes the neocons is not their "nationalist" and "unipolarist" inclination but instead their fundamental belief that "it was always in America's interest to help Israel succeed over its enemies," as Dorrien aptly puts it, which implies that American security is contingent on Israeli interests.

Dorrien's position on the neoconservative view of American interest and Israel is similar to the one expressed in this work, and is correct as far as it goes. Dorrien's description of the neocon position allows one to interpret the primary purpose of the neocon war agenda as being the weakening of Israel's enemies in order "to help Israel to succeed over its enemies." But while Dorrien's depiction of neoconservatism and Israel is correct as far as it goes, it is incomplete and insufficient. Dorrien simply stops with an idea, failing to take into account what motives might underlie that idea and the concrete fact that Israel has been inextricably connected to the neocons' Middle East war policy.

That the neocons assumed Israeli security, as perceived by Likudniks, to be a fundamental goal of American foreign policy would seem to reflect a bias for Israel, rather than a detached and objective assessment of American national interest. Dorrien thinks that the issue is solved by attributing it to a neoconservative "article of faith." But how was this "article of faith" arrived at? Was there any underlying motive to explain the adoption of this particular "article of faith?" It would seem reasonable to conclude that the "article of faith" reflected prior attachment to Israel – an attachment that becomes rather obvious in looking at the background of neoconservatism and neoconservatives. Identifying with Israel's interests, the neoconservatives projected the interests of that country onto the United States. That there was a life-and-death struggle with the Arab/Islamic world might very well be true for Israel, but it certainly was not the case for the United States.

It might be added that without promoting policies that advance Israel the neoconservatives would not have earned key institutional and financial support from such pro-Israel groups and figures as the American Jewish Committee, Jewish Institute of National Security Affairs, Rupert Murdoch, and Irving Moskowitz. Such support was crucial for neoconservatism's very existence, which makes it clear that hard-line Zionism is an integral part of neoconservatism.

The neoconservative support for and ties to Israel have been obvious. If a comparable relationship existed involving other peoples, there would be nothing extraordinary about pointing that out. Analysis of the role of ethnic groups in American politics is commonplace in political science and history and it is not considered evidence of hostility toward the groups being analyzed. For instance, political commentators do not hesitate to link Cuban-Americans' goal of making the elimination of Castro a central element of American foreign policy with the fact that they are Cuban émigrés.

However, since Jews and Israel are involved here, the subject approaches the realm of the taboo. One writes "approaches the realm of taboo" because the role of the neoconservatives, and to a lesser extent, Israel, has been noted by the mainstream media, as this work has indicated. But it must be added that while the role of Israel has been noted, it has never received much emphasis in the mainstream media. It is not the subject of the evening news or major news programs. As a result, the Israel/neocon connection is perceived only by that small minority of Americans who are highly attentive to the news. Moreover, media references tend to be brief and lacking substantial development. The "connecting of the dots," as has been done in this work, is still looked upon as either anti-Semitic, foolishly dangerous, or, among a small segment of the population, courageous.

One study which threatened the taboo was the earlier mentioned study "The Israel Lobby and U.S. Foreign Policy" by leading scholars in the field of international relations, John Mearsheimer and Stephen Walt.[50] The work was discussed in numerous media circles, though given greatest attention in the intellectual press. While it received some degree of partial support, it also drew a heavy barrage of vituperation, smears, character assassination, misrepresentation, and other inflammatory rhetoric condemning the essay as anti-Semitic.[51] Initially the full study was not published in the United States but only came out in an abbreviated form in the *London Review of Books*. In the United States it remained as only a "working paper" on a Harvard faculty web site.[52] While more intellectual individuals highly attentive to Middle East policy would have become aware of this controversial work, average Americans who rely on the mainstream media for information remained largely unaware of the study's existence.

"I do not believe that we could have gotten it published in the United States," Mearsheimer told the *Forward*. He said that their paper was originally commissioned in the fall of 2002 by a major American magazine, "but the publishers told us that it was virtually impossible to get the piece published in the United States." Mearsheimer opined that individuals involved in scholarship, media, and politics know that "the whole subject of the Israel lobby and American foreign policy is a third-rail issue." And "Publishers understand that if they publish a piece like ours it would cause them all sorts of problems."[53] After much commotion, a longer version of the work was published as a book in September 2007, titled *The Israel Lobby and U.S. Foreign Policy*.[54]

As former CIA analysts Bill and Kathleen Christison correctly observed:

> Inside the U.S . . . the pressure of the neocons for war on Israel's behalf, or any hint that Bush himself participates in that pressure, is hardly ever mentioned. This taboo on discussing the Israeli link to the war in Iraq, enforced

by the threat of being labeled anti-Semitic, introduces major distortions into practically every effort to examine and change policies that are causing massive hatred of the U.S. around the world.[55]

Since one is dealing with a topic of utmost sensitivity, it should be reiterated that the reference to Israel and the neoconservatives doesn't imply that all or even most American Jews supported the war on Iraq and the overall neocon war agenda. The American Jewish Committee's 2002 Annual Survey of Jewish Opinion conducted between December 16, 2002 and January 5, 2003, showed that 59 percent approved of the United States taking military action against Iraq to remove Saddam Hussein from power while thirty-six percent opposed military action. That finding was comparable to polls of the general American population.[56] Jewish support for the war would drop considerably after the occupation. The 2005 Annual Survey of American Jewish Opinion, taken in December 2005, revealed that 70 percent of Jews opposed the war on Iraq, while only 28 supported it. In the same poll, only a small plurality of 49 percent to 46 percent supported the use of American military force to prevent Iran from getting nuclear weapons.[57] A Gallup Poll conducted in February 2007 found that 77 percent of Jews believed that the war on Iraq had been a mistake, while only 21 percent held otherwise. This contrasted with the overall American population in which the war was viewed as a mistake by a 52 percent to 46 percent margin.[58] It also should be pointed out that some of the most influential opponents of the neocons, such as Senator Carl Levin and George Soros, were Jewish.

It should be pointed out that the move for war on Iran especially was cautioned by some leading Jews who recognized the role of Israel and pro-Israel forces in this effort. In the April 22, 2006 issue, the *Forward* gave this warning:

> Over the past three years, since the invasion of Iraq, it has become de rigueur in the finest circles. It's claimed with growing frequency, from leading magazines to the floor of the Senate to Harvard University, that the war was foisted on America by Jewish and Israeli pressure.
>
> Given this war's disastrous consequences, its growing unpopularity even among Republicans and the hopelessness of any decent exit, anger is building. The anger is misdirected, of course. The very notion that this war was fought for Israel's benefit is a delusion. [The current work, of course, has shown otherwise.] But it is a popular notion.
>
> The looming war against Iran is a different story. This time, Jerusalem's role is not fantasy. Israel's sense of alarm has been at the center of the story from

the get-go. Both *The Washington Post* and *The New Yorker* reported this week that Israeli strategists and intelligence experts were playing a serious role in building support for war. President Bush himself said in Cleveland last month that Israel's safety was a central concern, if not the main one, in assessing the Iranian threat.

What will they say when the Iran war turns sour – multiplied by 25, by 30?[59]

The "anti-Semitic" charge is often an effort, and usually a very effective effort, to silence public discourse on issues displeasing to some influential Jews. But it is necessary to move away from the question as to whether the argument (in fact, any argument) is "anti-Semitic," to the question of whether it is true. This requires free inquiry unimpeded by prohibitions and taboos. As pointed out in Chapter 2, the Jewish newspaper *Forward* acknowledged the need for open discussion when it wrote:

> Israel and its allies stand accused of manipulating America's public debate for their own purposes. If they were to succeed in suppressing debate to protect themselves, it only would prove the point. Better to follow the democratic path: If there is bad speech, the best reply is more speech.[60]

Naturally such an approach is the only way to arrive at truth, be it in science, history, or any field whatsoever. The political realm should be no exception, especially since knowing, and acting upon, the truth here can serve to save thousands of lives.

Evidence for the neoconservative and Israeli connection to the United States war in the Middle East is overwhelming and publicly available. There was no dark, hidden "conspiracy," a term of derision often used by detractors of the idea of a neocon connection to the war. But in the realm of politics, as George Orwell observed, "To see what is in front of one's nose needs a constant struggle."[61] It should be hoped that in the self-proclaimed "Land of the Free," Americans should not fear to honestly discuss the background and motivation for the war on Iraq and the overall United States policy in the Middle East. Only by understanding the truth can the United States possibly take the proper corrective action in the Middle East; without such an understanding, catastrophe looms.

Obviously, in order to shape a Middle East foreign policy in the interest of the United States and its people, it is essential to have a clear view of the situation. Individuals who have been as consistently wrong in their analysis, as have been the neoconservatives in their public pronouncements, should not have a hand in such policymaking. Moreover, in determining such policy, the focus should be on the interests of the United States without the interference of interests of other countries. Individuals with close ties to foreign states should not be shaping American policy in areas dealing with those foreign states' interests. This is a clear conflict of interest. None of this is intended to mean that the United States should not be concerned about international morality – with identical standards applied to all countries – but the United States cannot be expected to pursue policies which might increase the security of particular foreign states at the expense of the interests of the United States. Such an approach should apply to Israel and to all other countries as well. When it appears that the interests of the United States are being sacrificed for those of a foreign country, Americans should not be intimidated from pointing it out. The very survival of the United States and its people might rest on it.

postscript

THE FIRST PART OF 2008 saw the resurgence of the neo-conservatives, as one of their picks, John McCain, won enough delegates in the Republican primaries to guarantee his selection as the party's nominee for the presidency. In the Democratic primaries, Senators Hillary Clinton and Barak Obama were running almost neck-and-neck in their race for the nomination. As Hillary Clinton and Obama continued to battle, relying heavily on negative campaigning, McCain forged slightly ahead in the polls.[1] It was ironic that although the war in Iraq had become very unpopular, and the American economy had taken a severe downturn, it began to look as though McCain could be the victor in the November election.

McCain is a long-time hero of the neocons and was the favored presidential candidate for many of them in 2000. As William Kristol wrote in the *New York Times*:

> McCain can feature an amazing story of personal courage, a record of independence and accomplishment as a senator, and courage and foresight with respect to the most important foreign policy decision of the last couple of years – the surge in Iraq. If any Republican can defend conservative principles and policies, at once acknowledging Bush's failures while pivoting to present his own biography and agenda to the voters, McCain can.[2]

McCain, who has been an ardent and unwavering advocate of the war and has continued to defend it, once cavalierly remarked on the campaign trail that he would not mind the United States staying in Iraq for 100 years, if American casualties were low.[3] His only criticism has been regarding the war's execution. McCain strongly supported the surge, and in the spring of

2008 cautioned against the withdrawal of troops. In fact, McCain advocated more troops for Iraq long before it became Bush administration policy.[4] On March 26, 2008, in his first speech on foreign policy since winning enough delegates to become the presumptive Republican standard-bearer, McCain stated that achieving democracy in Iraq was essential for world peace. "Those who argue that our goals in Iraq are unachievable are wrong, just as they were wrong a year ago when they declared the war already lost in Iraq," McCain said. "Those who claim we should withdraw from Iraq in order to fight al-Qaeda more effectively elsewhere are making a dangerous mistake."[5]

Similarly, McCain has taken a hard line on Iran. He continued to see Iran's nuclear program as highly dangerous and claimed that Iran was supporting the insurgency in Iraq.[6] He firmly backed Israel in its attack on Lebanon in July/August 2006. And he maintained a very favorable, neocon-like view of Israel. In March 2008, McCain visited Israel and had nothing but praise for Israel's military activities against the Palestinians. He described Israel's fight as a "struggle . . . between radical extremist Islamic forces throughout the world, particularly in the Middle East, and West[ern] values and standards and beliefs and everything that we stand for." Israel's war, McCain maintained, "is all part of this struggle that we're in."[7]

McCain was the recipient of JINSA's Henry M. "Scoop" Jackson Distinguished Service Award in 2006.[8] Mark Broxmeyer, a former head of JINSA, was one of McCain's leading advisers.[9] Broxmeyer stated that McCain "has long been a friend of the Jewish community and a defender of the State of Israel."[10] According to Robert Dreyfuss, those neocons who have "have now clustered around the McCain campaign . . . see his effort to become president as a way for them—that is, for the neoconservatives—to return to the position of power they had in the first Bush administration from 2001 to 2005."[11] Neocons supporting and advising McCain included R. James Woolsey, McCain's national security adviser; Randy Scheunemann, McCain's director of foreign policy; and Robert Kagan, Max Boot, Gary Schmitt, John Bolton, and William Kristol.[12]

It must be acknowledged, however, that McCain also has various non-neocon, establishment advisers, such as Colin Powell and Brent Scowcroft. While some McCain backers from the traditional foreign policy establishment expressed wariness about his neoconservative advisers, they also publicly denied that he would pursue neocon policies.[13] "John is a traditional national-security guy," claimed retired Admiral Bobby Ray Inman, a former high-level intelligence official who supports McCain. Inman held that if McCain did become president, "there's going to be a lot of disappointment on the neoconservative side."[14] According to Dmitri Simes, president of the Nixon Center, a citadel of the foreign-policy realists, McCain had privately confided to his leading supporters in the traditional foreign policy camp that "his more exuberant statements don't necessarily reflect his real views." [15] After McCain was assured of the nomination, James Baker endorsed him, saying "John is what I think I am, a principled pragmatist."[16]

Despite what the Republican realists said about McCain, there was little reason to believe that he did not hold the hard, pro-war positions he has publicly expressed; after all, there would seem to be no political benefit in his mentioning them. With most Americans opposed to the war, it would be politically advantageous for McCain to triangulate between the Bush war position and the moderately anti-war positions expressed by the Democratic candidates, Clinton and Obama.

Why then did Republican realists support McCain? A fundamental reason would seem to be that they have no other place to go. Undoubtedly, if they were to have any influence in the Republican Party whatsoever they would have had to back the party's standard-bearer. The best they could hope for was to try to restrain McCain from implementing the entire neoconservative agenda. They would not have any influence on McCain's policy if they did not support him.

McCain's only departure from neoconservative foreign policy was his support for collective action as opposed to the unilateralism espoused by the neocons. He presented his overall foreign policy philosophy in an address to the Los Angeles World Affairs Council on March 26, 2008, much of the speech being written by Robert Kagan.[17] Various mainstream commentators made much of the alleged move away from unilateralism.[18] But while McCain appeared to seek more American cooperation with the rest of the world on such issues as global warming, he offered no indication that input from foreign countries would affect America's militant policy in the Middle East.[19] In fact, on that question McCain revealed himself to be more in harmony with the neocons than was the Bush administration when he stated that the United States could no longer maintain the "strategy of relying on autocrats to provide order and stability" in the Middle East. Among those "autocrats" he named the government of Saudi Arabia, which was left largely

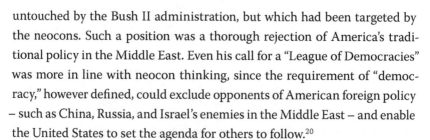

untouched by the Bush II administration, but which had been targeted by the neocons. Such a position was a thorough rejection of America's traditional policy in the Middle East. Even his call for a "League of Democracies" was more in line with neocon thinking, since the requirement of "democracy," however defined, could exclude opponents of American foreign policy – such as China, Russia, and Israel's enemies in the Middle East – and enable the United States to set the agenda for others to follow.[20]

The violence that had subsided in Iraq shot upward in March 2008, with overall attacks more than doubling over those in February.[21] The violence was especially intense in southern Iraq, as the Maliki government tried to launch a full-scale offensive, with American air support, to destroy the independent power of the Shiite militias, especially the Mahdi Army of Shiite cleric Moqtada al-Sadr. Although the Iraqi government's military offensive was focused on the predominantly Shiite areas of southern Iraq, especially the port city of Basra, it inflamed Shiite anti-government violence throughout the country, including Baghdad. Bush praised Maliki's decision to initiate this military action against his fellow Shiites as the "defining moment" for his leadership. Although Sadr would tell his forces to observe a ceasefire beginning March 31, government security forces had been unable to defeat the independent Shiite militias and they remained armed. This illustrated the weakness of the central government. Peace was restored not because of its power but because of Sadr's willingness to stop and the role of Iran in brokering a ceasefire. However, the militias could restart the violence at any time. The fighting portended more intra-Shiite bloodletting that would undo any improvement in security achieved during the surge period. And the question was whether U.S. forces would find themselves in the middle of this conflict.[22]

Neocons blamed the violence on Iran. Kimberly Kagan held that

> the U.S. must recognize that Iran is engaged in a full-up proxy war against it in Iraq. Iranian agents and military forces are actively attacking U.S. forces and the government of Iraq. Every rocket that lands in the Green Zone should remind us that Iran's aims are evidently not benign – they are at best destabilizing and at worst hegemonic. The U.S. must defeat al Qaeda in Iraq, and protect Iraq from the direct military intervention of Iran. Failure to do so will invite Iranian domination of an Arab state that now seeks to be our ally.[23]

Michael Ledeen, who for some time had been arguing the centrality of Iran's destabilizing role in Iraq, believed that the violence absolutely con-

firmed Iran's involvement. In fact, he claimed that Iran was not simply supporting the anti-government violence but directing it. According to Ledeen,
Sadr was totally powerless. "The Iranians had fired him," Ledeen claimed,
"and they restructured the Mahdi Army into smaller, more autonomous
groups. The recent violence came from the new units, headed by Iranian
officers, agents, and recruits." In sum, Ledeen contended that

> Iran, then, is the common denominator of recent events in Iraq: the mullahs
> organized the rocket attacks in Baghdad, they have supported al Qaeda in Iraq
> from the beginning, and they have a major role in the activities of the Shi'ite
> militias. It is going to be very difficult, indeed virtually impossible, to achieve
> durable security in Iraq without forcing an end to Iran's many murderous ac-
> tivities there.[24]

Certainly the blame leveled on Iran for the violence in Iraq indicated that
the United States would have to deal with the source of the trouble. And
there were signs that the Bush administration, in its waning days, might
be preparing for such a war. The Bush administration never accepted the
NIE report that Iran was not building a nuclear bomb. In March 2008,
during his trip to the Middle East, Vice President Cheney stated that Iran
was "heavily involved in trying to develop nuclear weapons enrichment,
the enrichment of uranium to weapons-grade levels," even though neither
international inspectors nor American intelligence experts had found evidence of such an effort.[25] On March 31, the director of the CIA, Michael V.
Hayden, when asked whether he thought that Iran was building a nuclear
weapon, responded in the positive, though adding that his assessment was
not predicated on "court-of-law stuff."[26]

U.S. News and World Report in early March listed six signs portending a
U.S. attack on Iran.[27] Among the signs was the resignation of Admiral William Fallon as commander-in-chief of the U.S. Central Command; Fallon
would have directed any attack on Iran, but he was seen to be opposed to
the pro-war element in the administration headed by Cheney. His opposition to a military attack was highlighted in a much-publicized article in
the March issue of *Esquire*. Fallon's resignation was widely perceived as an
indication that his opposition to war was not in line with U.S. policy and
his departure removed an obstacle to an attack.[28]

Cheney's trip to the Middle East in March, supposedly to help advance
Israeli-Palestinian peace talks, was also interpreted as preparation for war.
It included a stop in Oman, which was a key U.S. ally and would be a logis-

tics base for military operations in the Persian Gulf against Iran. Cheney also traveled to Saudi Arabia, whose support in terms of oil production would be essential for the industrial West in case the oil from Iran were cut off.[29] On March 22, the day following Cheney's visit with the kingdom's rulers, the Saudi newspaper *Okaz* reported that the Saudi Shura Council was preparing "national plans to deal with any sudden nuclear and radioactive hazards that may affect the kingdom following experts' warnings of possible attacks on Iran's Bushehr nuclear reactors."[30]

There was also an increasing build-up of American forces in the Persian Gulf. These included nuclear weapons, missiles, hundreds of aircraft, and invasion forces.[31]

Speculation that there might yet be a U.S. attack on Iran before the end of Bush's term increased with the testimony to Congress on April 8 and April 9 by General David Petraeus, commander of the coalition forces in Iraq, and Ryan C. Crocker, ambassador to Iraq.[32] Petraeus, who was the central figure at the hearings, claimed that although the surge had brought about a lessening of the violence, serious dangers still remained in Iraq, and any significant reduction in American troop strength could lead to greater violence. Hence, he recommended that the United States not reduce troop levels.[33] Most importantly, Petraeus claimed that the primary danger to the American and Iraqi government forces came from Iran, rather than Al Qaeda. The Iranian Revolutionary Guards' Quds Force was supposedly arming and directing so-called special groups – Shiite militia units allegedly associated with the Mahdi Army. "Iran has fueled the violence in a particularly damaging way through its lethal support to the special groups," Petraeus testified. He stated that "[u]nchecked, the special groups pose the greatest long-term threat to the viability of a democratic Iraq."[34] Significantly, Petraeus and Crocker maintained that Iran was providing weaponry that was killing Americans, even providing the rockets that were used to attack the Green Zone in Baghdad, where American and Iraqi officials live and work.[35]

Embracing Petraeus' recommendation, Bush ordered an indefinite halt in U.S. troop withdrawals from Iraq after July 2008, which meant that the number of troops would be near their current level when he would leave office in January 2009.[36] And he emphasized the alleged Iranian promotion of the insurgency inside Iraq, and warned the Iranian government of serious consequences if it continued to support such anti-government violence. "The regime in Tehran has a choice to make," Bush said. It could establish friendly ties with Iraq or it could continue "to arm and train and fund illegal militant groups, which are terrorizing the Iraqi people and turning them against Iran." He warned that "[if]f Iran makes the wrong choice, America will act to protect our interests and our troops and our Iraqi partners."[37]

Other administration figures echoed the mantra of the Iranian government's being behind the insurgency in Iraq. "Iran is very active in the southern part of Iraq," said National Security Adviser Stephen Hadley. "They are training Iraqis in Iran who come into Iraq and attack our forces, Iraqi forces, Iraqi civilians."[38] Secretary of Defense Robert Gates referred to the "malign impact of Iran's activities inside Iraq."[39] However, Gates downplayed the possibility of such activities leading to war with the United States. "I think the chances of us stumbling into a confrontation with Iran are very low," he maintained. "We are concerned about their activities in the south. But I think that the process that's under way is ... headed in the right direction."[40]

If Gates downplayed the possibility of war, Cheney talked quite differently. In a radio interview on April 10, he depicted Iranian President Mahmoud Ahmadinejad as a war-oriented fanatic who sought not only his own death but also the annihilation of his country in a holy war:

> Ahmadinejad is I think a very dangerous man. On the one hand, he has repeatedly stated that he wants to destroy Israel. He also has – is a man who believes in the return of the 12th Imam; and that the highest honor that can befall a man is that he should die a martyr in facilitating the return of the 12th Imam.
>
> It's a radical, radical point of view. Bernard Lewis once said mutual assured destruction in the Soviet-U.S. relationship in the Cold War meant deterrence, but mutual assured destruction with Ahmadinejad is an incentive.[41]

News commentator Pat Buchanan thought that the increasing focus on Iranian activities in Iraq might presage war, which he believed could serve a political purpose, enhancing McCain's election's chances. "This is Bush's last chance to strike," Buchanan maintained,

> and, when Iran responds, to effect its nuclear castration. Are Bush and Cheney likely to pass up this last chance to destroy Iran's nuclear facilities and effect the election of John McCain? For any attack on Iran's "terrorist bases" would rally the GOP and drive a wedge between Obama and Hillary.
>
> Indeed, Sen. Clinton, who voted to declare Iran's Revolutionary Guard a terrorist organization, could hardly denounce Bush for ordering air strikes on the Revolutionary Guards' Quds Force, when Petraeus testified, in her presence, that it is behind the serial murder of U.S. soldiers.[42]

The focus on Iran as America's major enemy in the "war on terrorism" in the early spring of 2008 underscores the durability of the neocon Middle East war agenda. It is apparent that five years after the United States' invasion of Iraq, the neoconservative Middle East war agenda remained alive and well, despite all the difficulties in Iraq and the numerous times it seemed that the approach was being abandoned. In interpreting the violence in Iraq, leading administration figures had adopted neocon thinking on the Middle East. In short, they tied Iran and Iraq together. Everything wrong in Iraq was attributable to the machinations of Iran. To end the insurgency in Iraq, it would be necessary to do something about Iran. Precisely what that would be was not spelled out, but the use of military force against Iran was certainly a high possibility, especially if Iran's alleged interference in Iraq continued.

The idea that success in Iraq necessitated militant action toward Iran demonstrated the success and sheer brilliance of the neocons. It made apparent the crucial importance of attacking Iraq to achieve the entire Middle East agenda. For should the United States attack Iran there would be no reason not to deal likewise with the lesser powers of Syria and Hezbollah in Lebanon, especially in tandem with Israel.

Nothing guarantees the actual implementation of a war on Iran and the additional aspects of the neocon war agenda. However, given the rhetoric expressed in the spring of 2008, such a war certainly seemed a distinct possibility in the waning months of the Bush administration. Given McCain's hard-line positions and closeness to the neocons, the likelihood of a war against Iran would seem even greater if he were elected. And such involvement could not be ruled out under Obama or Clinton, despite their criticisms of the war in Iraq. One thing that definitely can be said is that while there is a long history behind neocons' Middle East policy, that policy — and the neocons themselves – are far from becoming history.

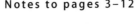
notes

Chapter 1

1. Quoted in Ken Silverstein, "War with Iran?," *Harpers.org*, Posted February 13, 2007, online.

2. Neil King Jr., "Iraqi Death Toll Exceeds 600,000, Study Estimates," *Wall Street Journal*, October 11, 2006, online. See also Gilbert Burnham, Riyadh Lafta, Shannon Doocy, and Les Roberts, "Mortality after the 2003 invasion of Iraq: a cross-sectional cluster sample survey," *www.thelancet.com*, October 11, 2006, online (DOI:10.1016/S0140-6736(06)69491-9).

3. This work will also use the common shortened version of their name, "neocon."

4. American Jewish Committee, "2002 Annual Survey of American Jewish Opinion: Strong Support for War Against Iraq," January 24, 2003, http://www.ajc.org/site/apps/nl/content2.asp?c=ijITI2PHKoG&b=837277&ct=871913, accessed November 24, 2007.

5. Samuel G. Freedman, "Don't blame Jews for this war," *USA Today*, posted April 2, 2003, online.

6. American Jewish Committee, "2003 Annual Survey of American Jewish Opinion," http://www.ajc.org/site/apps/nl/content2.asp?c=ijITI2PHKoG&b=838459&ct=1051549, accessed November 24, 2007.

7. American Jewish Committee, "2005 Annual Survey of American Jewish Opinion, December 20, 2005," http://www.ajc.org/site/apps/nl/content3.asp?c=ijITI2PHKoG&b=846741&ct=1740355, accessed November 24, 2007. This percentage was higher prior to the war, but it is apparent that the majority of American Jews have not adopted the neocon war position in the Middle East.

8. Leonard Fein, "Leaders to the Right, Followers to the Left," *Forward*, March 23, 2007, online.

9. George Packer, *The Assassins' Gate: America in Iraq* (New York: Farrar, Straus and Giroux, 2005), p. 15.

Chapter 2

1. Howard Dean, interviewed by Roger Simon, "College, Vietnam, and The Clintons," *U.S. News & World Report*, August 11, 2003, online.

2. John Shaw, "Many Analysts Say Neoconservatives Driving U.S. Foreign Policy Agenda," *Washington Diplomat*, February 2004, online; Remarks by Sen. Joseph Biden at the Release of "Progressive Internationalism," October 30, 2003, *Democratic Leadership Council Web Site*, http://www.ndol.org/ndol_ci.cfm?kaid=106&subid=122&contentid=252157, accessed November 16, 2007.

3. *New York Times*, "Transcript: Huckabee's Fox Debate Attack on Ron Paul Over the Iraq War," *NewsandPolicy.com*, September 5, 2007, online.

4. Joseph Wilson, *The Politics of Truth: Inside the Lies that Led to War and Betrayed My Wife's CIA Identity* (New York: Carroll & Graf Publishers, 2004), p. 425. Wilson determined that the uranium claim was of no merit. It is believed that members of the Bush administration leaked the identity of his wife, Valerie Plame, as a covert CIA agent because of his criticism of the war on Iraq. See Jeffrey Steinberg, "Far, Far Worse Than Watergate: The "Outing of Valerie Plame," in *NeoCONNED! Again* eds. D. L. O'Huallachain and J. Forrest Sharpe (Vienna, Va.: Light in the Darkness Publications, 2005), 491–504.

5. Craig R. Eisendrath and Melvin A. Goodman, *Bush League Diplomacy: How the Neoconservatives Are Putting the World at Risk* (Amherst, N.Y.: Prometheus Books, 2004).

6. Stefan Halper and Jonathan Clarke, *America Alone: The Neo-conservatives and the Global Order* (Cambridge, U.K.: Cambridge University Press, 2004).

7. Joseph Cirincione, "Origins of Regime Change in Iraq," Carnegie Endowment for International Peace *Proliferation Brief* 6.5 (March 19, 2003), http://www.carnegieendowment.org/publications/index.cfm?fa=print&id=1214, accessed

November 16, 2007.

8. Joshua Micah Marshall, "Bomb Saddam?: How the obsession of a few neocon hawks became the central goal of U.S. foreign policy," *Washington Monthly*, June 2002, online.

9. Elizabeth Drew," "The Neocons in Power," *New York Review of Books*, June 12, 2003, online.

10. Michael Hirsh, "The Mideast: Neocons on the Line," *Newsweek*, June 23,2003, online.

11. Robert Kuttner, "Neo-cons have hijacked U.S. foreign policy," *Boston Globe*, September 10, 2003, online.

12. Christopher Matthews, "The Road to Baghdad," *San Francisco Chronicle*, March 24, 2002, online.

13. George Soros, *The Bubble of American Supremacy: The Costs of Bush's War in Iraq* (New York: Public Affairs, 2004), p. 4.

14. Seymour Hersh, "We've Been Taken Over By a Cult," *CounterPunch.org*, January 27, 2005, online.

15. Many of these individuals identify with the pre-Cold War non-interventionist ("isolationist") right, who opposed American entry into World War II. Their major publications include *American Conservative* and *Chronicles*.

16. Patrick J. Buchanan, "Whose War?," *American Conservative*, March 24, 2003, online.

17. Justin Raimondo, "The Neocons' War," *Antiwar.com*, June 2, 2004, online.

18. Sam Francis, "An Anti-War Column: Bush Likudniks seek to start 'World War IV'", *VDare.com*, March 20, 2003, online; Paul Craig Roberts, "Neo-Jacobins Push For World War IV," *LewRockwell.com*, September 20, 2003, online; see also: Scott McConnell, "The Struggle Over War Aims: Bush Versus the Neo-Cons," *Antiwar.com*, September 25, 2002, online.

19. Eric Alterman, "Neocons for Anti-Semitism," *Altercation* weblog, *MSNBC.com*, September 9, 2004, http://msnbc.msn.com/id/5887234/?#040909, accessed November 18, 2007.

20. See for example: Jim Lobe, " Neoconservatives Consolidate Control over U.S. Mideast Policy," *Foreign Policy in Focus*, December 6, 2002, online.

21. Quoted in Philip Weiss, "Ferment Over 'The Israel Lobby'," *Nation*, posted April 27, 2006 (May 15, 2006 issue), online.

22. Jeffrey Blankfort, "A War for Israel," *Left Curve*, No. 28, online.

23. Bill Christison, "Faltering Neo-Cons Still Dangerous: How They Might Influence the Election," *CounterPunch.org*, March 5, 2004, online; for another example, see Bill and Kathleen Christison, "Israel as Sideshow," *CounterPunch.org*, October 12, 2004, online.

24. For example, see James Petras, "Israel and the Neocons: The Libby Affair and the Internal War," *CounterPunch.org*, November 3, 2005, online; Gary Leupp, "Philosopher Kings: Leo Strauss and the Neocons," *CounterPunch.org*, May 24, 2003, online; Gary Leupp, "The Two-Line Struggle at the Top. Phase Two: Syria and Iran," *CounterPunch.org*, May 5, 2003, online; Stephen Green, "Serving Two Flags: The Bush Neo-Cons and Israel," *CounterPunch.org*, September 3, 2004, online; Kurt Nimmo, "Shock Therapy and the Israeli Scenario," *CounterPunch.org*, October 18/19, 2003, online; Alexander Cockburn, "Will Bush Quit Iraq?," *CounterPunch.org*, January 19, 2005, online.

25. James Petras, *The Power of Israel in the United States* (Atlanta: Clarity Press, 2006).

26. Patrick Seale, "A Costly Friendship," *Nation*, July 21, 2003, online.

27. Robert G. Kaiser, "Bush and Sharon Nearly Identical On Mideast Policy," *Washington Post*, February 9, 2003, p. A-1.

28. Quoted by Thaddeus Russell, "The Limitations of a Neo-Nationalist," *New Politics*, vol. 6, no. 3 (new series), whole no. 23, Summer 1997, online.

29. Michael Lind, "How Neoconservatives Conquered Washington – and Launched a War," *Antiwar.com*, April 10, 2003, online; Michael Lind, "The Weird Men Behind George W. Bush's War," *New Statesman*, April 7, 2003, online. Lind has been an editor or staff writer for *New Yorker*, *Harper's Magazine*, and the *New Republic*.

30. Robert D. Novak, "Sharon's War?," *Townhall.com*, December 26, 2002, online.

31. Maureen Dowd, "Neocon Coup at the Department d'Etat," *New York Times*, August 6, 2003, p. A-17.

32. Arnaud de Borchgrave, "A Bush-Sharon Doctrine?," *Newsmax.com*, February 17, 2003, online.

33. Arnaud de Borchgrave, "Iraq and the Gulf of Tonkin," *Washington Times*, February 10, 2004, online.

34. Stanley Hoffmann, "The High and the Mighty," *American Prospect*, January 13, 2003, online.

35. Virginia Tilley, *The One-State Solution: A Breakthrough for Peace in the Israeli-Palestinian Deadlock* (Ann Arbor, Mich.: University of Michigan Press, 2005), pp. 105–6.

36. Jeffrey Record, "Dark Victory," *Salon.com*, April 29, 2004, online; Jeffrey Record, *Dark Victory: America's Second War Against Iraq* (Annapolis, Md.: Naval Institute Press, 2004), pp. 17–29.

37. "Gen. Zinni: 'They've Screwed Up,'" *CBSNews.com*, May 21, 2004, online.

38. Zbigniew Brzezinski, *The Choice: Global Domination or Global Leadership* (New York: Basic Books, 2004), p. 35.

39. Senator Ernest F. Hollings, "Bush's failed

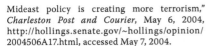

Mideast policy is creating more terrorism," *Charleston Post and Courier*, May 6, 2004, http://hollings.senate.gov/~hollings/opinion/2004506A17.html, accessed May 7, 2004.

40. Matthew E. Berger, "Not so gentle rhetoric from the gentleman from South Carolina," *JTA*, May 23, 2004, online.

41. Emad Mekay, "Iraq was invaded 'to protect Israel' – U.S. official," *Asia Times*, March 31, 2004, online.

42. Kate Andrews. "Philip Zelikow Takes State Department Post", *Daily Progress* (Charlottesville, Va.), February 26, 2005. p. A6.

43. At the time, Mearsheimer was the Wendell Harrison Professor of Political Science and co-director of the Program on International Security Policy at the University of Chicago, and Walt was the Robert and Renee Belfer Professor of International Affairs and the academic dean of Harvard University's John F. Kennedy School of Government.

44. John Mearsheimer and Stephen Walt, "The Israel Lobby," *London Review of Books*, March 23, 2006, online.; Mearsheimer and Walt, "The Israel Lobby and U.S. Foreign Policy," Faculty Research Working Papers Series, Harvard University, John F. Kennedy School of Government, March 2006, http://ksgnotes1.harvard.edu/Research/wpaper.nsf/rwp/RWP06-011/$File/rwp_06_011_walt.pdf, accessed November 16, 2007.

45. John J. Mearsheimer and Stephen M. Walt, *The Israel Lobby and U.S. Foreign Policy* (New York: Farrar, Straus and Giroux, 2007).

46. Mearsheimer and Walt, Harvard University Faculty Research Paper, p. 31. My use of the term "driving force" to describe the neoconservatives' role in bringing about the United States war on Iraq predates the release of the Mearsheimer and Walt essay.

47. Lowell Ponte, "Harvard's New Protocols of the Learned Elders of Zion," *FrontPageMagazine.com*, March 23, 2006, online; Ruth R. Wisse, "Harvard attack on 'Israel lobby' is actually a targeting of American public," *Jewish World Review*, March 23, 2006, online; Eliot A. Cohen, "Yes, It's Anti-Semitic," *Washington Post*, April 5, 2006, p. A-23; Alan Dershowitz, "Debunking the Newest – and Oldest – Jewish Conspiracy: A Reply to the Mearsheimer-Walt 'Working Paper," April 2006, Faculty Research Working Papers Series, Harvard University, John F. Kennedy School of Government, http://www.ksg.harvard.edu/research/working_papers/dershowitzreply.pdf, accessed November 16, 2007.

48. Joshua Muravchik, "The Neoconservative Cabal," *Commentary*, September 2003, online.

49. Norman Podhoretz, "World War IV: How It Started, What It Means, and Why We Have to Win," *Commentary*, September 2004, online; Norman Podhoretz, *World War IV: The Long Struggle Against Islamofascism*, (New York: Doubleday, 2007), p. 63.

50. Abraham H. Foxman, "Anti-Semitism, Pure and Simple," *Jerusalem Report*, May 5, 2003, http://www.adl.org/ADL_Opinions/Anti-Semitism_Domestic/plain_anti_semitism_op_05052003.htm, accessed July 11, 2006.

51. "ADL Urges Senator Hollings to Disavow Statements on Jews and the Iraq War," Anti-Defamation League Press Release, May 14, 2004, http://www.adl.org/PresRele/ASU.S._12/4496_12.htm, accessed November 16, 2007.

52. The writings of these individuals have been mentioned already. For Stanley Heller, see "It's Not Just the Oil," *Antiwar.com*, February 20, 2003, online; for Philip Weiss, see Philip Weiss, "Ferment Over 'The Israel Lobby,'" *Nation*, May 15, 2006, online; Philip Weiss, "Why I'm Right About Liberal Jews and the Antiwar Movement," *New York Observer*, January 21, 2007, online.

53. James D. Besser, "Jews Increasingly Blamed For War: Backlash evident before first shot fired in Iraq; fury over Rep. Moran's comments," *Jewish Week*, March 14, 2003, online.

54. Paul Gottfried, "Goldberg Is Not the Worst," *LewRockwell.com*, March 20, 2003, online..

55. Joshua Micah Marshall, *Talking Points Memo*, January 6, 2004, http://talkingpointsmemo.com/archives/week_2004_01_04.php, accessed November 16, 2007.

56. Joshua Micah Marshall, *Talking Points Memo*, October 22, 2003, http://www.talkingpointsmemo.com/archives/week_2003_10_19.php, accessed November 16, 2007.

57. Robert J. Lieber, "The Neoconservative-Conspiracy Theory: Pure Myth," *Chronicle of Higher Education*, May 2, 2003, online

58. Committee on the Present Danger, "Members," http://www.committeeonthepresentdanger.org/OurMembers/tabid/364/Default.aspx, accessed December 1, 2007.

59. Max Boot, "What the Heck Is a 'Neocon'?" *Wall Street Journal*, December 30, 2002, online.

60. Joshua Muravchik, "The Neoconservative Cabal," *Commentary*, September 2003, online; four years later Muravchik would provide a more qualified version of this theme, maintaining that "However fantastical the conspiracy theories, and however polluted their origins, what is undeniable is that Bush's declaration of war against terrorism did bear the earmarks of neoconservatism .... It is possible that Bush and Cheney turned to neoconservative sources for guidance on these matters; it is also possible, and more likely, that they reached similar conclusions on their own. In either case, the war against terrorism put neoconservative ideas to the test." Joshua Muravchik, "The Past, Present, and Future of Neoconservatism," *Commentary*, October 2007, online.

61. Michelle Goldberg, "Is this the neocon century?," *Salon*, December 17, 2003, online.

62. "The Ground Shifts," *Forward*, May 28, 2004, online.

Chapter 3

1. Gary Dorrien, *The Neoconservative Mind: Politics, Culture, and the War of Ideology* (Philadelphia: Temple University Press, 1993), pp. 1–18; Murray Friedman, *The Neoconservative Revolution: Jewish Intellectuals and the Shaping of Public Policy* (Cambridge, UK: Cambridge University Press, 2005), pp. 127–31.

2. Benjamin Ginsberg, *The Fatal Embrace: Jews and the State* (Chicago: University of Chicago Press, 1993).

3. Edward S. Shapiro, "Jews and the Conservative Rift," *American Jewish History* 87.2–3 (1999), p. 197.

4. Gal Beckerman, "The Neoconservative Persuasion," *Forward,* January 6, 2006, online.

5. Ginsberg, *Fatal Embrace,* p. 231.

6. Max Boot, "What the Heck Is a Neocon?," *Wall Street Journal.* December 30, 2002, online.

7. "Our Mission," American Jewish Committee, http://www.ajc.org/WhoWeAre/MissionAndHistory.asp, accessed June 2, 2004.

8. Friedman, *Neoconservative Revolution,* p. 122.

9. *Ibid.,* p. 148.

10. *Ibid.,* p. 147.

11. *Ibid.,* p. 148. The lodestar of Podhoretz's political thinking was Jewish interests, of which protecting Israel was a primary element. Gary Dorrien points out that Podhoretz "declared that the formative question for his politics would heretofore be, 'Is it good for the Jews?'" (*Neoconservative Mind,* p. 166).

12. Ginsberg, *Fatal Embrace,* p. 204.

13. Norman Podhoretz, "Bush, Sharon, My Daughter, and Me," *Commentary,* April 2005, online; Ralph Z. Hallow, "American Jews Flock to Israel," *Washington Times,* January 16, 1991, p. A-1.

14. Arnold Beichman, "Jolly Ex-Friends for Evermore," *Policy Review,* April/May 1999, online.

15. Presidential Medal of Freedom Recipient Norman Podhoretz, Medal of Freedom, http://www.medaloffreedom.com/NormanPodhoretz.htm, accessed November 16, 2007.

16. Paul Gottfried, *Conservatism in America: Making Sense of the American Right* (New York: Palgrave MacMillan, 2007), p. 59.

17. Paul Gottfried, "What's In A Name? The Curious Case of 'Neoconservative,'" *VDare.com,* April 30, 2003, online.

18. Mearsheimer and Walt, *The Israel Lobby and U.S. Foreign Policy,* p. 132.

19. Mearsheimer and Walt note: "Many neoconservative are connected to an overlapping set of Washington-based think tanks, committees, and publications whose agenda includes promoting the special relationship between the United States and Israel" (*The Israel Lobby and U.S. Foreign Policy,* p. 130).

20. Janine R. Wedel, "Neocon 'Flex Players' Await Bush's Second Term," *Pacific News Service,* November 3, 2004, online.

21. Janine R. Wedel, "Flex Power," *Washington Post,* December 12, 2004, p. B-4.

22. Patricia Cohen, "New Commentary Editor Denies Neo-Nepotism," *New York Times,* October 24, 2007, online; "Elliott Abrams," *RightWeb,* http://rightweb.irc-online.org/ind/abrams/abrams.php, accessed November 16, 2007; Michael Dobbs, "Back in Political Forefront: Iran-Contra Figure Plays Key Role on Mideast," *Washington Post,* May 27, 2003, p. A-1; Friedman, *Neoconservative Revolution,* pp. 168–72.

23. Wilfred McClay, "Godfather," review of *Neoconservatism: Autobiography of an Idea* by Irving Kristol, *Commentary Magazine,* February 1996, pp. 62–4.

24. Shmuel Rosner, "They call it Project Zionism," *Ha'aretz,* August 21, 2005, online.

25. Gary Dorrien, *Imperial Designs: Neoconservatism and the New Pax Americana* (New York: Routledge, 2004), p. 45.

26. For a discussion of Wohlstetter and his relation to Perle and Wolfowitz, see Dorrien, *Imperial Designs,* pp. 43–50.

27. Wohlstetter's daughter Joan was a classmate of Perle's at Hollywood High School. Perle first met Albert Wohlstetter when Joan invited him for a swim at her home's pool. Wohlstetter struck up a conversation about nuclear arms' strategy and gave Perle a copy of his paper, "Delicate Balance of Terror," which Perle perused while sitting on the deck of the pool. Richard Perle interview with Ben Wattenberg, "Richard Perle: The Making of a Neoconservative," *Think Tank with Ben Wattenberg,* 2003, http://www.pbs.org/thinktank/transcript1017.html, accessed November 16, 2007.

28. Alan Weisman, *Prince of Darkness: Richard Perle: The Kingdom, The Power & the End of Empire in America* (New York: Union Square Press, 2007), p. 30.

29. Weisman, *Prince of Darkness,* p. 155; Elizabeth Drew, "The Neocons in Power," *New York Review of Books,* June 12, 2003, online.

30. Weisman, *Prince of Darkness,* p. 34.

31. Jim Lobe, "Neocons dance a Strauss waltz," *Asia Times,* May 9, 2003, online.

32. Jim Lobe, "All in the Neocon Family," *AlterNet.org,* March 27, 2003, online.

33. Bill Christison, "Faltering Neo-Cons Still Dangerous," *CounerPunch,* March 5, 2004, online.

34. Dorrien, *Neoconservative Mind,* p. 166.

35. Ginsberg, *Fatal Embrace,* p. 203.

36. Friedman, *Neoconservative Revolution,* p. 148.

37. James Nuechterlein, "Neoconservative

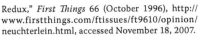
Redux," *First Things* 66 (October 1996), http://www.firstthings.com/ftissues/ft9610/opinion/neuchterlein.html, accessed November 18, 2007.

38. Friedman, *Neoconservative Revolution*, p. 127.

39. Gary Dorrien, *Imperial Designs*, pp. 48–50; Yuri Slezkine, *The Jewish Century* (Princeton, N.J.: University of Princeton Press, 2004), p. 357; Alan Weisman, *Prince of Darkness*, pp. 35–44.

40. J. J. Goldberg, *Jewish Power: Inside the Jewish Establishment* (Reading, Mass.: Addison Wesley Publishing Company, Inc., 1996), p. 175.

41. Norman Podhoretz, "The Present Danger," *Commentary* 69:3 (March 1980), p. 33, quoted in Gary Dorrien, *Neoconservative Mind*, p. 167.

42. Friedman, *Neoconservative Revolution* pp. 149–50.

43. John Ehrman, *Rise of Neoconservatism: Intellectuals and Foreign Affairs, 1945–1994* (New Haven: Yale University Press, 1995), p. 136.

44. For a discussion of the neoconservatives during the Carter and Reagan administrations, see John Ehrman, *Rise of Neoconservatism*, pp. 97–172.

45. Friedman, *Neoconservative Revolution*, p. 152.

46. Regarding their value to the right, Samuel Francis, a conservative critic of the neoconservatives, wrote, "For the right, the main service neoconservatives performed was to lend it a certain respectability that the right generally lacked – not only through academic and literary credentials but in the general tone they adopted . . . . Of course, it never dawned on the conservatives who welcomed them as allies, and soon as leaders, that the 'respectability' the neocons brought them was one defined and conferred by the dominant left and therefore made it impossible for the right to challenge the left at all." Samuel Francis, "The Real Cabal," *Chronicles*, September 2003, online.

47. Paul Gottfried, *Conservatism in America*, p. 65.

48. It is significant that in a Reagan's right-wing administration, there would be rather left-wing individuals such as Muravchik and Gershman. Muravchik has been a prominent member of the Social Democrats USA. This did not preclude Muravchik from being a neocon in good standing with his membership in the American Enterprise Institute and the Jewish Institute of National Security Affairs.

49. Reaganite Paul Craig Roberts (under secretary of the treasury in the Reagan administration), who became a staunch conservative critic of the neocons, writes: "In Reagan's time we did not recognize that neoconservatives had a Jacobin frame of mind. Perhaps we were not paying close enough attention. We saw neoconservatives as former left-wingers who had realized that the Soviet Union might be a threat after all. We

regarded them as allies against Henry Kissinger's inclination to reach an unfavorable accommodation with the Soviet Union." Paul Craig Roberts, "My Epiphany," *CounterPunch.org*, February 6, 2006, online.

50. Emphasis on the war-winning strategy is provided by Jay Winik, *On the Brink: The Dramatic, Behind The-Scenes Saga of the Reagan Era & the Men & Women Who Won the Cold War* (New York: Simon & Schuster, 1996). When this view had been expressed earlier by James Burnham on the pages of the conservative *National Review*, it was simply ignored by the establishment. When the war-winning theme was enunciated by the conservative 1964 Republican presidential nominee Barry Goldwater in his book *Why Not Victory?: A Fresh Look At American Foreign Policy* (New York: McGraw Hill, 1962), he was denounced by the establishment as near-insane advocate of global nuclear destruction. When neocons adopted this very same foreign policy strategy, however, it took on the air of near-respectability. In short, neocons did not invent the positions they advocated; by and large, they were not creative thinkers. Rather, because of their backgrounds in the liberal establishment, they gave an air of intellectual and political respectability to positions on the right that previously had been outside the bounds of discussion.

51. Richard A. Clarke, *Against All Enemies: Inside America's War on Terror* (New York: Free Press, 2004), p. 49.

52. Peter Robinson, "The Fight on the Right," Transcript, Filmed on May 16, 2003, Uncommon Knowledge, Hoover Institution, http://www.hoover.org/multimedia/uk/2939711.html, accessed November 18, 2007.

53. Friedman, *Neoconservative Revolution*, p. 154.

54. Gary Dorrien reflects the establishment view of the evil nature of traditional conservatism: "Neoconservatives opposed feminism, affirmative action, multiculturalism, and modern liberalism without the baggage of a racist and nativist past" (*Neoconservative Mind*, p. 392).

55. Neoconservative support was probably a factor that prevented the liberal establishment from caricaturing Reagan as it had conservative Republican presidential candidate Barry Goldwater in 1964. On the establishment's virulent hostility toward Goldwater, see Lionel Lokos, *Hysteria 1964: The Fear Campaign Against Barry Goldwater* (New Rochelle, New York: Arlington House, 1967).

56. Jay Winik, On the Brink; Friedman, *Neoconservative Revolution*, pp. 158–60, 175–6.

57. Gal Beckerman, "The Neoconservative Persuasion," *Forward*, January 6, 2006, online.

58. John Patrick Diggins, "How Reagan Beat the Neocons," *New York Times*, June 11, 2004, online.

59. Friedman, *Neoconservative Revolution*, p.

128; he writes sympathetically that "The most fundamental ingredient marking neoconservatism has been its realistic and pragmatic approach to problems. The neocons found themselves at odds with that form of conservative libertarianism that seeks individual freedom, unrestrained by government. While increasingly doubtful of governmental solutions to problems, neocons were not hostile to government itself, particularly programs like Social Security. They saw no road to serfdom, as Hayek predicted, in the welfare state that they themselves had played no small role in creating." Friedman, *Neoconservative Revolution*, p. 121.

60. Dorrien, *Neoconservative Mind*, p. 369.

61. The Social Democrats, USA (SD/USA) had its roots in the Socialist Party. The group's philosophical forefather was the intellectual Trotskyite, Max Shachtman. In the 1970s, under the leadership of Carl Gershman, SD/USA supported Senator Henry Jackson, the icon of neoconservatives. It was ironic that in the administration of conservative Ronald Reagan, members of the SD/USA gained positions of power and influence in government. In 1984, Gershman took over the helm of the National Endowment for Democracy, a private but congressionally-funded organization created to support groups around the world that promote democracy. SD/USA member Joshua Muravchik was affiliated with the American Enterprise Institute and the Jewish Institute of National Security Affairs. Other neocons who have been members of SD/USA include Max Kampelman, Penn Kemble, Jeane Kirkpatrick ("Social Democrats, USA," *Right Web*, http://rightweb.irc-online.org/groupwatch/sd-usa.php, accessed November 16, 2007.

62. James Burnham, a major intellectual leader of the conservatism of the 1950s and 1960s observed that neoconservatives also differed attitudinally from traditional conservatives. He pointed out in an essay in *National Review* in 1972 that while the intellectuals who espoused neoconservatism might have broken formally with "liberal doctrine," they nevertheless retained in their thinking "what might be called the emotional gestalt of liberalism, the liberal sensitivity and temperament." In other words, even though neoconservatives no longer consciously believed in certain liberal ideas, they still showed the habits of thought and emotional reactions that those ideas had instilled. James Burnham, "Selective, Yes. Humanism, Maybe," *National Review*, May 12, 1972, p. 516.

63. Paul Gottfried, *The Conservative Movement*, revised edition (New York: Twayne Publishers, 1993), p. 90, pp. 87–96; see also John Ehrman, *Rise of Neoconservatism*, pp. 186–87.

64. Gottfried, *Conservative Movement*, p. 129; see also Gottfried, *Conservatism in America*, pp. 59–61.

65. Dorrien, *Imperial Designs*, p. 195.

66. Jacob Heilbrunn, "The Neoconservative Journey," in Peter Berkowitz, *Varieties of Conservatism in America* (Stanford, Calif.: Hoover Institution, 2004), p. 108.

67. Dorrien, *Neoconservative Mind*, pp. 341–9.

68. Franklin Foer, "Once Again America First," *New York Times*, October 10, 2004, Section 7, p. 22.

69. Gottfried, *Conservatism in America*, p. 32.

70. Friedman, *Neoconservative Revolution*, pp. 226–7.

71. Irving Kristol, "The Neoconservative Persuasion," *Weekly Standard*, August 25, 2003, online.

72. Mark Gerson, "Introduction," in Gerson, ed., *The Essential Neoconservative Reader* (Reading, Mass.: Addison-Wesley Publishing Company, Inc., 1996), p. xvi.

73. Friedman, *Neoconservative Revolution*, p. 242.

74. Kevin MacDonald, *The Culture of Critique: An Evolutionary Analysis of Jewish Involvement in Twentieth-Century Intellectual and Political Movements* (Westport, Conn.: Praeger, 1998), pp. 312–3.

75. Ginsberg, *Fatal Embrace*, pp. 208–9.

76. Goldberg, *Jewish Power*, p. 214.

77. Gary Dorrien, *Neoconservative Mind*, p. 174.

Chapter 4

1. Tom Segev, *One Palestine, Complete: Jews and Arabs Under the British Mandate* (New York: Metropolitan Books, 2000), pp. 404–5; For a history of the Zionist ideas on expulsion, see Nur Masalha, *Expulsion of the Palestinians: The Concept of "Transfer" in Zionist Political Thought, 1882–1948* (Washington: Institute of Palestine Studies, 1992).

2. Norman Finkelstein, "Part I – An introduction to the Israel-Palestine conflict," September 2002, From Occupied Palestine, http://www.fromoccupiedpalestine.org/node.php?id=734, accessed November 16, 2007.

3. Ari Shavit, "Survival of the fittest," *Ha'aretz*, January 8, 2004. Morris agreed with Ben-Gurion's position: "Ben-Gurion was right. If he had not done what he did, a state would not have come into being. That has to be clear. It is impossible to evade it. Without the uprooting of the Palestinians, a Jewish state would not have arisen here." Republished as Ari Shavit, "Survival of the Fittest?: An Interview with Benny Morris," *CounterPunch.org*, January 16, 2004, online; For other comparable views expressed by Morris, see Jonathan Cook, *Blood and Religion: The Unmasking of the Jewish and Democratic State* (London: Pluto Press, 2006), pp. 106–8.

4. Norman Finkelstein, "Part I – An introduction to the Israel-Palestine conflict," September 2002, From Occupied Palestine, http://www.fromoccupiedpalestine.org/node.php?id=734, accessed November 16, 2007.

5. Nur Masalha, *Imperial Israel and the Palestinians: The Politics of Expansion* (London: Pluto Press, 2000), pp. 200–7; Tikva Honig-Parnass, "Israel's Recent Conviction: Apartheid In Palestine Can Only be Preserved Through Force," Between the Lines, September 2001, http://www.between-lines.org/archives/2001/sep/Tikva_Honig-Parnass.htm, accessed February 12, 2003; Phil Brennan, "Israel's Population Bomb in Reverse," *NewsMax.com*, Oct. 19, 2002, online; Ed Hollants, "Israel: Democracy or Demographic Jewish State?," Dissident Voice, February 12, 2004, http://www.dissidentvoice.org/Feb04/Hollants0212.htm, accessed November 16, 2007.

6. Baruch Kimmerling, "The Pied Piper of Hamelin, or Sharon's Enigma," Dissident Voice, January 12, 2006, http://www.dissidentvoice.org/Jan06/Kimmerling12.htm, accessed November 16, 2007.

7. Saleh Abdel-Jawwad, "Israel: the ultimate winner," *Al-Ahram Weekly Online*, (Issue No. 634), April 17- 23, 2003, http://weekly.ahram.org.eg/2003/634/op2.htm, accessed November 16, 2007.

8. Avi Shlaim, *The Iron Wall: Israel and the Arab World* (New York: W. W. Norton & Company, 2001), pp. 172–8.

9. *Ibid.*, pp. 172–8.

10. Baruch Kimmerling, *Politicide: Ariel Sharon's War Against the Palestinians* (London: Verso, 2003), p. 81.

11. Saleh Abdel-Jawwad, "Israel: the ultimate winner," *Al-Ahram Weekly Online*, (Issue No. 634), April 17–23, 2003, http://weekly.ahram.org.eg/2003/634/op2.htm, accessed November 16, 2007.

12. Ilan Peleg, *Begin's Foreign Policy, 1977–1983* (New York: Greenwood Press, 1987), p. 47.

13. *Ibid.*, p. 181.

14. *Ibid.*, p. 5.

15. Vladimir Jabotinsky, "The Iron Wall," (originally published as "O Zheleznoi Stene," *Razsviet* [Paris], November 4, 1923; published in English in *The Jewish Herald* [South Africa], November 26, 1937, see *MidEastWeb.org* at http://www.mideastweb.org/ironwall.htm), http://www.jabotinsky.org/multimedia/upl_doc/doc_191207_49117.pdf, and "The Ethics of the Iron Wall" (originally published as a continuation of "The Iron Wall," *Razsviet* [Paris], November 11, 1923; published in English in *The Jewish Standard* (London), May 9, 1941, see *MidEastWeb.org*, URL noted), http://www.jabotinsky.org/multimedia/upl_doc/doc_191207_181762.pdf.

16. Shlaim, *Iron Wall*; Meron Rapoport, "Avi Shlaim: No peaceful solution," *Ha'aretz*, August 13, 2005, online.

17. Avi Shlaim writes: "Jabotinsky's prescription was to build the Zionist enterprise behind an iron wall that the local Arab population would not be able to break. Yet Jabotinsky was not opposed to talking to the Palestinians at a later stage. On the contrary, he believed that after knocking their heads in vain against the wall, the Palestinians would eventually recognize that they were in a position of permanent weakness, and that would be the time to enter into negotiations with them about their status and national rights in Palestine . . . . The real danger posed by the strategy of the iron wall was that Israeli leaders, less sophisticated than Jabotinsky, would fall in love with a particular phase of it and refuse to negotiate even when there was someone to talk to on the other side. Paradoxically, the politicians of the right, the heirs of Jabotinsky, were particularly prone to fall in love with the iron wall and adopt it as a permanent way of life" (*Iron Wall*, p. 598–9).

18. Peleg, *Begin's Foreign Policy*, pp. 51–93; Shlaim, *Iron Wall*, pp. 352–4.

19. Peleg, *Begin's Foreign Policy*, pp. 95–142; Yoram Peri, "Coexistence or Hegemony? Shifts in the Israeli Security Concept," in *The Roots of Begin's Success*, eds. Dan Caspi, Abraham Diskin, and Emmanuel Gutmann (London, U.K.: Croom Helm Ltd., 1984), p. 204.

20. Peleg, *Begin's Foreign Policy*, p. 184; see also Masalha, *Imperial Israel and the Palestinians*, pp. 94–5; Tilley, *One-State Solution*, pp. 107–8.

21. Israel Shahak, trans. & ed., *The Zionist Plan For the Middle East*, a translation of Oded Yinon, "A Strategy for Israel in the Nineteen Eighties," (Belmont, Mass.: Association of Arab American University Graduates, 1982), http://www.geocities.com/alabasters_archive/zionist_plan.html, accessed November 16, 2007.

22. *Ibid.*

23. As Nir Rosen, a Fellow at the Center on Law and Security at NYU's School of Law, wrote for the Washington Post, "[The] obsession with sects informed the U.S. approach to Iraq from day one of the occupation, but it was not how Iraqis saw themselves – at least, not until very recently. Iraqis were not primarily Sunnis or Shiites; they were Iraqis first, and their sectarian identities did not become politicized until the Americans occupied their country, treating Sunnis as the bad guys and Shiites as the good guys . . . . [T]he Americans imposed ethnic and sectarian identities onto Iraq's regions" ("What Bremer Got Wrong in Iraq," WashingtonPost.com, May 16, 2007, online). Rosen also recently testified before the Senate Foreign Relations Committee, where he pointed out that "Iraq has no history of serious sectarian violence or civil war between the two groups, and most Iraqis viewed themselves as Iraqis first, then Muslims, with their sects having only personal importance. Intermarriage was widespread and indeed most Iraqi tribes were divided between Sunnis and Shiites. The Baath party which ruled Iraq for four decades had a majority Shiite membership. And the Iraqi Army, though a non-sectarian institution that predated the coming of the Baathists, was also majority Shiite, even in its officer corps" ("Prepared Tes-

timony of Nir Rosen Before the Senate Committee on Foreign Relations," Iraq After the Surge: Political Prospects, April 2, 2008, http://foreign.senate.gov/testimony/2008/RosenTestimony080402p.pdf, accessed April 24, 2008). See also Mark Gery, "The Politics of Electoral Illusion," in D. L. O'Huallachain and J. Forrest Sharpe, eds., NeoCONNED! Again (Norfolk, Va.: Light in the Darkness Publications, 2007), pp. 761–95..

24. *Ibid.*

25. *Ibid.*

26. Noam Chomsky, *Fateful Triangle: The United States, Israel and the Palestinians*, Updated Edition, (Cambridge, MA: South End Press, 1999), p. 457.

27. *Ibid.*, p. 462, referring to Yoram Peri, "From Coexistence to Hegemony," *Davar*, October 1, 1982.

28. *Ibid.*, p. 455.

29. *Ibid.*, p. 463, referring to Peri, "From Coexistence to Hegemony."

30. Peri, "Coexistence or Hegemony?" pp. 210–1.

31. Peleg, *Begin's Foreign Policy*, pp. 143–78.

32. Peri, "Coexistence or Hegemony?" p. 211.

33. Yehoshafat Harkabi, *Israel's Fateful Hour* (New York: Harper & Row, 1988), pp. 57–8.

34. Harkabi, *Israel's Fateful Hour*, p. 97.

35. Kimmerling, *Politicide*, p. 99.

36. Tilley, *One-State Solution*, p. 108.

Chapter 5

1. Tilley, *One-State Solution*, p. 106.

2. Peter L. Hahn, "The Suez Crisis: A Crisis That Changed the Balance of Power in the Middle East," *eJournal USA*, April 2006, http://usinfo.state.gov/journals/itps/0406/ijpe/hahn.htm, accessed November 16, 2007.

3. Dilip Hiro, *The Longest War: The Iran-Iraq Military Conflict* (New York: Routledge, 1991), pp. 14–5.

4. See Nita M. Renfrew, "Who Started the War?," *Foreign Policy* 66, Spring 1987, pp. 98–108; Jude Wanniski, "The (Bogus) Case Against Saddam," in D. L. O'Huallachain and J. Forrest Sharpe, eds., *Neo-CONNED!* (Norfolk, Va.: Light in the Darkness Publications, 2007), pp. 56–7.

5. Michael Dobbs, "U.S. Had Key Role in Iraq Buildup," *Washington Post*, December 30, 2002, p. A-1; Malcolm Byrne, Introduction, "Saddam Hussein: More Secret History," December 18, 2003, National Security Archives, George Washington University, http://www.gwu.edu/~nsarchiv/NSAEBB/NSAEBB107/index.htm, accessed November 18, 2007.

6. Hiro, *Longest War*, p. 119.

7. Michael Dobbs, "U.S. Had Key Role in Iraq Buildup," *Washington Post*, December 30, 2002, p. A-1.

8. Dobbs, *ibid*. Documents revealing administration efforts to downplay Iraq's use of chemical weapons are presented at Malcolm Byrne, "Introduction," *Saddam Hussein: More Secret History*, December 18, 2003, National Security Archives, George Washington University, http://www.gwu.edu/~nsarchiv/NSAEBB/NSAEBB107/index.htm, accessed November 18, 2007.

9. Stephen R. Shalom, "The United States and the Iran-Iraq War," *Z Magazine*, February 1990, online; Jeremy Scahill, "The Saddam in Rumsfeld's Closet," *Znet.org*, August 2, 2002, online; Chris Bury, " U.S.-Iraq Relations, Part 1: Lesser Evil," *Nightline* (ABC), September 18, 2002, online; Michael Dobbs, "U.S. Had Key Role in Iraq Buildup," *Washington Post*, December 30, 2002, p. A-1.

10. William Blum, "Anthrax for Export," *Progressive*, April 1998, online.

11. Dobbs, "U.S. Had Key Role in Iraq Buildup," p. A-1.

12. *Ibid.*

13. Hiro, *The Longest War*, pp. 83, 117–8; Robert Dreyfuss, *Devil's Game: How the United States Helped Unleash Fundamentalist Islam* (New York: Henry Holt and Company, 2005), pp. 294–5; Avi Shlaim, *Iron Wall*, pp. 440–1; Trita Parsi, *Treacherous Alliance: The Secret Dealings of Israel, Iran, and the United States* (New Haven, Conn.: Yale University Press, 2007), pp. 104–5, 112.

14. Stephen Green, *Living by the Sword: America and Israel in the Middle East 1968–87* (Brattleboro, Vermont: Amana Books, 1988), pp. 193–212.

15. Shlaim, *Iron Wall*, pp. 440–1; Parsi, *Treacherous Alliance*, pp. 110–26. The U.S. diverted the proceeds from the secret weapons sale to fund the Contras – anti-Communist guerrillas engaged in an insurgency against the socialistic, pro-Soviet Sandinista government of Nicaragua. Funding of the Contras had been prohibited by Congress, so it was necessary to take this secret indirect approach. The policy was presented as being in the American interest – or at least in line with the Cold War position of the Reagan administration – because it would serve to free Western hostages taken by Hezbollah, counter Soviet influence with Iran, and aid the anti-Soviet Contras.

16. Green, *Living by the Sword*, pp. 193–6, 212–8; Parsi, *Treacherous Alliance*, p. 117.

17. Dreyfuss, *Devil's Game*, p. 297.

18. Parsi, *Treacherous Alliance*, p. 110.

19. U.S. Senate Select Committee on Intelligence, "Preliminary Inquiry Into the Sale of Arms to Iran and Possible Diversion of Funds to the Nicaraguan Resistance," February 2, 1987, No. 100–7, pp. 3–4, quoted in Green, *Living by the Sword*, p. 195.

20. Dreyfuss, *Devil's Game*, p. 298. The U.S. move to help Iran was not presented as a way to

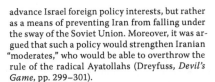

advance Israel foreign policy interests, but rather as a means of preventing Iran from falling under the sway of the Soviet Union. Moreover, it was argued that such a policy would strengthen Iranian "moderates," who would be able to overthrow the rule of the radical Ayatollahs (Dreyfuss, *Devil's Game*, pp. 299–301).

21. Michael Ledeen, "Let's Talk with Iran Now," *New York Times*, July 19, 1988, quoted in Parsi, *Treacherous Alliance*, p. 242.

22. Michael Ledeen, *The Iranian Time Bomb: The Mullah Zealots' Quest for Destruction*, (New York: St. Martin's Press, 2007). See also Chapters 12 and 16.

23. Steven Hurst, *The Foreign Policy of the Bush Administration: In Search of a New World Order* (London: Cassell, 1999), p. 86.

24. Jackson Diehl, "New Arab Arsenals Challenge Israel's Long Regional Dominance," *Washington Post*, April 3, 1990, p. A-35.

25. Dan Raviv and Yossi Melman, "Iraq's Arsenal of Horrors: Baghdad's Growing Menace Alters Israeli Strategy," *Washington Post*, April 8, 1990, p. B-1.

26. Jackson Diehl, "New Arab Arsenals Challenge Israel's Long Regional Dominance," *Washington Post*, April 3, 1990, p. A-35.

27. Andrew and Leslie Cockburn, Andrew and Leslie Cockburn, *Dangerous Liaison: The Inside Story of the U.S.-Israeli Covert Relationship* (New York: Harper Perennial, 1991), pp. 351–2.

28. Majid Khadduri and Edmund Ghareeb, *War in the Gulf, 1990–1991: The Iraq-Kuwait Conflict and Its Implications* (New York: Oxford University Press, 1997), pp. 99–100.

29. Khadduri and Ghareeb, *War in the Gulf*, pp. 100.

30. Hurst, *Foreign Policy of the Bush Administration*, pp. 29–34, 72–6.

31. *Ibid.*, pp. 29–34, 72–6.

32. William Safire, "Bush Versus Israel," *New York Times*, March 26, 1990, p. A-17.

33. *Ibid.*

34. "The Gulf Wars, 1990–1991," *History of the Middle East Database*, http://www.nmhschool.org/tthornton/mehistorydatabase/gulf_war.htm, accessed November 16, 2007; Sam Husseini and Jim Naureckas, "Zuckerman Unbound," *FAIR*, January/February 1993, http://www.fair.org/extra/9301/zuckerman.html, accessed November 16, 2007.

35. Murray Waas, "Who lost Kuwait?," *San Francisco Bay Guardian*, January 30, 1991, online.

36. Dilip Hiro, *Iraq in the Eye of the Storm* (New York: Thunder's Mouth Press, 2002), pp. 32–4; Khadduri and Ghareeb, *War in the Gulf*, pp. 105–8.

37. Hiro, *Iraq in the Eye of the Storm*, pp. 32–4; Khadduri and Ghareeb, *War in the Gulf*, pp. 105–8.

38. Khadduri and Ghareeb, *War in the Gulf*, pp. 234–36.

39. Hurst, *Foreign Policy of the Bush Administration*, p. 88.

40. Charles Krauthammer, "Nightmare From the '30s," *Washington Post*, July 27, 1990, p. A27.

41. Hurst, *Foreign Policy of the Bush Administration*, p. 90; H. Rahman, *Making of the Gulf War: Origins of Kuwait's Long-Standing Territorial Dispute with Iraq* (Reading, U.K.: Ithaca Press, 1997), pp. 298–99.

42. John Edward Wilz, "The Making of Mr. Bush's War: A Failure to Learn from History? " *Presidential Studies Quarterly*, Summer 1996, http://www.mtholyoke.edu/acad/intrel/wilz.htm, accessed November 16, 2007.

43. *Ibid.*

44. Mitchel Cohen, "How the War Party Sold the 1991 Bombing of Iraq to U.S.," *Antiwar.com*, December 30, 2002, online. Wanniski, "The (Bogus) Case Against Saddam," pp. 30–34; Sheldon Rampton and John Stauber, "The Mother of All Clients," in D. L. O'Huallachain and J. Forrest Sharpe, eds., *Neo-CONNED! Again* (Norfolk, Va.: Light in the Darkness Publications, 2007), pp. 831–39; and Fairness and Accuracy in Reporting, "Gulf War Stories the Media Loved – Except They Aren't True," *Extra!* Special Gulf War Issue 1991, http://www.fair.org/index.php?page=1515, accessed April 18, 2008.

45. William Thomas, *Bringing The War Home* (Anchorage, AK : Earthpulse Press, 1998), http://www.earthpulse.com/src/subcategory.asp?catid=2&subcatid=3, accessed November 16, 2007.

46. Scott Peterson, "In war, some facts less factual," *Christian Science Monitor*, September 6, 2002, online; Jon Basil Utley, "Questions About the Supposed Iraqi Threat to Saudi Arabia in 1990 – Aerial Photos Were Never Released!!," Americans Against Bombing, http://www.againstbombing.com/bush.htm, accessed November 16, 2007. Neo-CONNED!

47. Jackson Diehl "Gulf Crisis Boosts Israeli Confidence Over Relations With U.S.," *Washington Post*, August 5, 1990, p. A-13.

48. Shlaim, *Iron Wall*, pp. 473–74, 483–84.

49. Andrew and Leslie Cockburn, *Dangerous Liaison*, pp. 353, 356.

50. Diehl, "Gulf Crisis Boosts Israeli Confidence Over Relations With U.S.," p. A-13.

51. *Washington Post*, "Solarz Forms Group Backing Gulf Policies," *Washington Post*, December 9, 1990, p. A-36.

52. Christopher Layne, "Why the Gulf War was Not in the National Interest," *Atlantic*, July 1991, http://www.mtholyoke.edu/acad/intrel/layne.htm, accessed November 18, 2007.

53. E. J. Dionne Jr., "Gulf Crisis Rekindles Democrats' Old Debate but with New Focus," *Washington Post*, January 3, 1991, p. A-16.

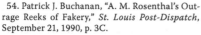

54. Patrick J. Buchanan, "A. M. Rosenthal's Outrage Reeks of Fakery," *St. Louis Post-Dispatch*, September 21, 1990, p. 3C.

55. Richard Cohen, "Those Calls for War," *Washington Post*, August 28, 1990, p. A-17.

56. Thomas L. Friedman, "Confrontation in the Gulf: Behind Bush's Hard Line," *New York Times*, August 22, 1990, p. A-1.

57. Sami Yosif, "The Iraqi-U.S. War: a Conspiracy Theory," in *The Gulf War and the New World Order*, eds. Haim Bresheeth and Nira Yuval-Davis (London: Zed Books, Ltd., 1991), pp. 51–59, and Wanniski, "The (Bogus) Case Against Saddam," pp. 16–24.

58. Hurst, *Foreign Policy of the Bush Administration*, pp. 95–96.

59. As Henry Siegman pointed out recently, "[T]he expectation that uncritical Western support of Israel would lead to greater Israeli moderation and greater willingness to take risks for peace is blatantly contradicted by the [Israeli-Palestinian] conflict's history" ("Tough Love for Israel," *The Nation*, May 5, 2008 [posted April 17, 2008], online).

60. Peter Schweizer and Rochelle Schweizer, *The Bushes: Portrait of a Dynasty* (New York: Doubleday, 2004), p. 394.

61. *Ibid.*, p. 393.

62. *Ibid.*, pp. 393–94.

63. Bruce Fein, "No quarrel with the people of Iraq?," *Washington Times*, February 20, 1991, p. G-4. Fein was a long-time proponent of neoconservative positions although he became strongly critical of the Bush II administration's diminution of civil liberties and expansion of presidential power (phone interview with Paul Gottfried, historian of modern American conservatism, November 2, 2007).

64. Arnold Beichman, "How the divide over Iraq strategies began," *Washington Times*, November 27, 2002, p. A-18.

65. Middle East Media Research Institute (MEMRI), "Senior Shiite Iraqi Ayatollah Residing in Iran: 'Iranian Clerics Are Running Riot in Iraq,'" Special Dispatch Series – No. 1902, April 18, 2008, http://www.memri.org/bin/latestnews.cgi?ID=SD190208, accessed April 25, 2008; Borzou Daragahi, "Iraq conflict is a battle for identity," *Los Angeles Times*, April 16, 2007, online; Renfrew, "Who Started the War?," pp. 100–1; and Wanniski, "The (Bogus) Case Against Saddam," p. 57. See also Mark Gery, "The Politics of Electoral Illusion," *Neo-CONNED! Again*, pp. 761–95.

66. George Bush and Brent Scowcroft, *A World Transformed* (New York: Alfred A. Knopf, 1998), p. 489.

67. James A. Baker III, with Thomas M. DeFrank, *The Politics of Diplomacy: Revolution, War, and Peace, 1989–1992* (New York: G. P. Putnam's Sons, 1995), p. 435.

68. Podhoretz, "World War IV."

69. A. M. Rosenthal, "Why the Betrayal?," *New York Times*, April 2, 1991, p. A-19.

70. A. M. Rosenthal, "The Way Out," *New York Times*, April 23, 1991, p. A-21.

71. A. M. Rosenthal, "The Fear of Morality," *New York Times*, April 16, 1991, p. A-23.

72. William Safire, "Bush's Moral Crisis," *New York Times*, April 1, 1991, p. A-17; see also William Safire, "Follow the Kurds to Save Iraq," *New York Times*, March 28, 1991, p. A-25, and William Safire, "Bush's Bay of Pigs," *New York Times*, April 4, 1991, p. A-23.

73. Charles Krauthammer, "After Winning Big, Bush Ran Away Fast," *St. Louis Post-Dispatch*, May 5, 1991, p. 3-B.

74. Peter Schweizer and Rochelle Schweizer, *Bushes*, p. 399.

75. Tom Diaz, "Israelis aren't making Baker's job any easier," *Washington Times*, April 8,1991, p. A-9.

76. Warren Strobel, "Baker condemns Israeli settlement policy," *Washington Times*, May 23, 1991, p. A-8.

77. George H. W. Bush, "The President's News Conference, September 12, 1991," *Public Papers of George Bush: 1989–1993*, The American Presidency Project, http://www.presidency.ucsb.edu/ws/index.php?pid=19969&st=&st1=, accessed November 16, 2007; Warren Strobel, "Bush won't back loan to Jewish state," *Washington Times*, March 18, 1992, p. A-7; Ginsberg, *Fatal Embrace*, pp. 218–23.

78. Warren Strobel, "Bush won't back loan to Jewish state," *Washington Times*, March 18, 1992, p. A-7; Michael Hedge, "Israeli lobby president resigns over promises," *Washington Times*, November 4, 1992, p. A-3; "Loan Guarantees for Israel," *Washington Times*, September 11, 1992, p. F-2; Frank Gaffney, Jr., "Neocon job that begs for answers," *Washington Times*, October 13, 1992, p. F-1; Andrew Borowiec, "Group counters Bush on Israel," *Washington Times*, February 27, 1992, p. A-1; Ginsberg, *Fatal Embrace*, pp. 218–23; Baker quoted in Ehrman, *Rise of Neoconservatism*, p. 197; Goldberg, *Jewish Power*, p. xxii. An interesting side note, Goldberg in *Jewish Power*, observes (p. 234) that "In 1991, at the height of the Bush administration's confrontation with Israel, no fewer than seven of the nineteen assistant secretaries in the State Department were Jews."

79. Goldberg, *Jewish Power*, pp. xxii.

80. *Ibid.*, p. xxvi.

81. "Committee on U.S. Interests in the Middle East," SourceWatch, http://www.sourcewatch.org/index.php?title=Committee_on_U.S._Interests_in_the_Middle_East, accessed November 22, 2007; "New Committee Explains Israel as U.S. Asset, April 1, 1992 in Security Affairs Archive: U.S.-Israel Strategic and Defense Cooperation – Security Affairs Archive, Jewish Institute for National Security Affairs, http://www.jinsa.

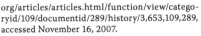

org/articles/articles.html/function/view/categoryid/109/documentid/289/history/3,653,109,289, accessed November 16, 2007.

82. "The Complete Unexpurgated AIPAC Tape," *Washington Report on Middle East Affairs*, December/January 1992/93, online (pp. 13–6).

83. *Ibid*.

84. Robert I. Friedman, "The Wobbly Israel Lobby," *Washington Post*, November 1, 1992, p. C-1; Cathryn Donohoe, "Defection of the Neocons," *Washington Times*, October 27, 1992, p. E-1.

85. Fred Barnes, "Neocons for Clinton: They're Back!" *New Republic*, March 7, 1992, pp. 12–14; Stephen S. Rosenfeld, "Return of the Neocons," *Washington Post*, August 28, 1992, p. A-23.

86. Charles Krauthammer, "Name Neocon to Post at State Dept.," *Chicago Sun-Times*, January 19, 1993, p. 27; "America and Israel: For love of Zion," *The Economist*, November 14, 1992, p. 27.

87. Daniel Pipes, "Bush, Clinton, and the Jews: A Debate," *Commentary* October 1992, online.

88. "Jewish Vote In Presidential Elections," *Jewish Virtual Library*, http://www.jewishvirtuallibrary.org/jsource/U.S.-Israel/jewvote.html, accessed November 16, 2007.

89. James Mann, *Rise of the Vulcans: The History of Bush's War Cabinet* (New York: Viking, 2004), p. 199.

90. For a discussion of the Defense Planning Guidance issue, see Dorrien, *Imperial Designs*, pp. 38–43.

Chapter 6

1. John M. Goshko, "Neoconservative Democrats Complain of Big Chill: Clinton Allies Decry Appointments Tally," *Washington Post*, March 15, 1993, p. A-17; see also, "Foreign Policy Previewed;

Christopher Favors Promotion of Democracy," *Washington Post*, January 9, 1993, p. A-9.

2. Ehrman, *Rise of Neoconservatism*, pp. 203–206.

3. Halper and Clarke, *America Alone*, p. 109.

4. Jim Lobe, "The Neocon Web," *LewRockwell.com*, December 23, 2003, http://www.lewrockwell.com/ips/lobe40.html, accessed November 16, 2007.

5. The neoconservative takeover of the mainstream conservative intellectual movement is presented by Paul Gottfried in *Conservative Movement*.

6. Brian Whitaker, "U.S. thinktanks give lessons in foreign policy," *Guardian*, August 19, 2002, online.

7. Jim Lobe, "The War Party Gets Organized," *AlterNet.org*, November 14, 2002, http://www.alternet.org/story/14547/, accessed November 16, 2007.

8. Gottfried, *Conservatism in America*, pp. 59–

60; See, also: Philip Weiss, "George Soros's Right-Wing Twin," *New York Magazine*, http://nymag.com/nymetro/news/people/features/12353/, accessed November 22, 2007.

9. Gottfried, *Conservative Movement*, p. 92; American Enterprise Institute, "AEI's Diamond Jubilee, 1943–2003," *American Enterprise Institute 2003Annual Report*, http://www.aei.org/about/contentID.20031212154735838/default.asp, accessed November 16, 2007; Halper and Clarke, *America Alone*, pp. 47–48, 107–108, 195.

10. "Jewish Institute for National Security Affairs," *Right Web*, http://rightweb.irc-online.org/org/jinsa.php, accessed November 16, 2007.

11. Bulent Yusuf, "Battle-tanks in the war of ideas," *Observer*, September 1, 2002, http://observer.guardian.co.uk/international/story/0,6903,781387,00.html, accessed November 16, 2007; Center for Media and Democracy, "Jewish Institute for National Security Affairs," *SourceWatch*, http://www.sourcewatch.org/index.php?title=JINSA, accessed November 16, 2007

12. Jason Vest, "The Men From JINSA and CSP," *Nation*, September 2, 2002, online.

13. *Ibid*.

14. *Ibid*.

15. Coalition for Justice in Hawaiian Gardens and Jerusalem, "Gambling on Extremism: How Irving Moskowitz took over a small California town to bankroll Israel's anti-peace settlers," December 15, 2003, http://www.stopmoskowitz.org/gamble.pdf, accessed November 19, 2007; Margot Patterson, "Bingo tycoon subsidizes extremism in Israel," *National Catholic Reporter*, October 18, 2002, online; Vest, "The Men From JINSA and CSP."

16. Interhemispheric Resource Center, "Lawrence Kadish," *Right Web*, http://rightweb.irc-online.org/profile/1237, accessed November 16, 2007.

17. Vest, "The Men From JINSA."

18. Jonathan Mark, "Murdoch's News: Fighting 'Fair' For Israel," *Jewish Week*, November 26, 2004, online.

19. Scott McConnell, "The Weekly Standard's War," *American Conservative*, November 21, 2005, online.

20. Quoted in David Carr, "When this weekly speaks, White House listens," *New York Times*, March 11, 2003, p. E-1.

21. Halper and Clarke, *America Alone*, p. 188.

22. Howard Kurtz, "Right Face, Right Time," *Washington Post*, February 1, 2000, p. C-1.

23. Scott Sherman, "Kristol's War," *Nation*, August 30, 2004, online.

24. Jonathan Mark, "Murdoch's News: Fighting 'Fair' For Israel," *Jewish Week*, November 26, 2004, online.

25. Mark, "Murdoch's News."

26. Richard H. Curtiss, "Rupert Murdoch and William Kristol: Using the Press to Advance Israel's Interests," *Washington Report on the Middle East*, June 2003, pp. 24–26, online.

27. Curtiss, "Rupert Murdoch and William Kristol."

28. Norman Solomon, "Kissing the Boots of the Media Goliath," *AlterNet.org*, Posted April 26, 2000, http://www.alternet.org/columnists/story/5842/, accessed November 19, 2007; James Surowiecki, "Murdoch Knows Best," *Salon*, June 19, 1997, online.

29. Israel Update, June 27, 2001, http://www.israelemb.org/chicago/Israel%20Update/2001/06/IU%2006-27-01.htm, accessed November 16, 2007.

30. Roy Greenslade, "Their master's voice," *Guardian*, February 17, 2003, online.

31. Rogel Alper, "Foxa Americana," *Ha'aretz*, April 10, 2003, online.

32. Halper and Clarke, *America Alone*, pp. 199–200.

33. Grant F. Smith, *Deadly Dogma: How the Neoconservatives Broke the Law to Deceive America* (Washington, DC: Institute for research: Middle Eastern Policy, 2006), pp. 82–85.

34. Study Group on a New Israeli Strategy Toward 2000 at The Institute for Advanced Strategic and Political Studies (IASPS), "A Clean Break: A New Strategy for Securing the Realm," 1996, http://www.iasps.org/strat1.htm, accessed November 16, 2007.

35. *Ibid.*; Institute for Research: Middle Eastern Policy, Inc., "Clean Break or Dirty War? Israel's Foreign Policy Directive to the United States," Middle East Foreign Policy Policy Brief, March 27, 2003, http://www.irmep.org/Policy_Briefs/3_27_2003_Clean_Break_or_Dirty_War.html, accessed November 16, 2007.

36. The Hashemites are believed to be direct descendants of the Prophet Muhammad. Members of the family currently rule the kingdom of Jordan and they were installed as the rulers of the state of Iraq, created after World War I, and continued to rule until their overthrow in 1958. See "The Hashemites," http://www.kinghussein.gov.jo/hashemites.html, accessed April 6, 2008, Charles Tripp, *A History of Iraq* (Cambridge, U.K.: Cambridge University Press, 2007), and "Hashemite," *Encarta*, http://encarta.msn.com/encyclopedia_761562432/hashemite.html, accessed April 5, 2007.

37. The Institute for Advanced Strategic and Political Studies' "Study Group on a New Israeli Strategy Toward 2000," "A Clean Break: A New Strategy for Securing the Realm," 1996 http://www.israeleconomy.org/strat1.htm, accessed November 16, 2007; Institute for Research, "Clean Break or Dirty War?"

38. William James Martin, "Clean Break with the Road Map," *CounterPunch.org*, February

14/15, 2004, online.

39. *Ibid.*

40. Craig Unger, "From the Wonderful Folks Who Brought You Iraq," *Vanity Fair*, March 2007, online.

41. IASPS, "A Clean Break"; Institute for Research, "Clean Break or Dirty War?"

42. *Ibid.*

43. *Ibid.*

44. *Ibid.*

45. *Ibid.*

46. *Ibid.*

47. David Wurmser, "Coping with Crumbling States: A Western and Israeli Balance of Power Strategy for the Levant," Institute for Advanced Strategic and Political Studies, 1996, http://www.israeleconomy.org/strat2.htm, accessed November 16, 2007.

48. *Ibid.*

49. *Ibid.*

50. *Ibid.*

51. *Ibid.*

52. David Wurmser, *Tyranny's Ally: America's Failure to Defeat Saddam Hussein* (Washington, D.C.: AEI Press, 1999), p. 42.

53. *Ibid.*, p. 118.

54. *Ibid.*, pp. 70–71.

55. *Ibid.*, pp. 87, 93, 128.

56. *Ibid.*, p. 98.

57. *Ibid.*, pp. xxi-xxii.

58. Isikoff and Corn, *Hubris: The Inside Story of Spin, Scandal, and the Selling of the Iraq War* (New York: Crown Publishers, 2006), pp. 71–76.

59. Laurie Mylroie, *Study of Revenge: Saddam Hussein's Unfinished War against America* (Washington: AEI Press, 2000), p. 251.

60. Isikoff and Corn, *Hubris*, pp. 71–76.

61. Peter Bergen, "Armchair Provocateur: Laurie Mylroie: The Neocons' favorite conspiracy theorist," *Washington Monthly*, December 2003, online.

62. Mylroie, *Study of Revenge*, pp. ix-xi.

63. *Ibid.*, cover; Isikoff and Corn, *Hubris*, pp. 75–76.

64. David Plotz, "Osama, Saddam, and the Bombs," *Slate*, September 28, 2001, online.

65. Isikoff and Corn, *Hubris*, pp. 67–70; Andrew and Leslie Cockburn, *Dangerous Liaison*, p. 350.

66. Mann, *Rise of the Vulcans*, pp. 235–37: Packer, *Assassins' Gate*, p. 28.

67. Center for Media and Democracy, "New Citizen's Project," *SourceWatch*, http://www.sourcewatch.org/index.php?title=New_Citizenship_Project, accessed November 19, 2007; American Enterprise Institute, "AEI's Organization and Purposes," http://www.aei.org/about/filter.all/default.asp, accessed November 19, 2007.

68. PNAC describes itself as follows: "Established in the spring of 1997, the Project for the New American Century is a non-profit, educational organization whose goal is to promote American global leadership. The Project is an initiative of the New Citizenship Project (501c3); the New Citizenship Project's chairman is William Kristol and its president is Gary Schmitt." Project for the New American Century, "About PNAC," http://www.newamericancentury.org/aboutpnac.htm, accessed November 16, 2007.

69. PNAC Letter to President William J. Clinton, January 26, 1998, PNAC, http://www.newamericancentury.org/iraqclintonletter.htm, accessed November 16, 2007.

70. Richard Perle, "Foreword," Wurmser, *Tyranny's Ally*, p. xi.

71. Committee for Peace and Security in the Gulf, "Open Letter to the President," February 19, 1998, Center for Security Policy Decision Brief, February 24, 1998, http://www.centerforsecuritypolicy.org/Modules/NewsManager/ShowSectionNews.aspx?CategoryID=140&SubCategoryID=141&NewsID=1461, accessed Februery 8, 2008.

72. PNAC Letter to Gingrich and Lott, May 29, 1998, PNAC, http://www.newamericancentury.org/iraqletter1998.htm, accessed November 16, 2007.

73. Richard Perle, "Foreword" in Wurmser, *Tyranny's Ally*, p. xii.

74. Wilson, *Politics of Truth*, p. 289.

75. *Ibid.*, p. 290; Seymour Hersh, "The Iraq Hawks," *New Yorker*, December 20, 2001, online.

76. Neil Mackay, "Bush planned Iraq 'regime change' before becoming President," *Scottish Sunday Herald*, September 15, 2002, online; Project for the New American Century, "Rebuilding America's Defenses: Strategy, Forces and Resources for a New Century," September 2000, http://www.newamericancentury.org/RebuildingAmericasDefenses.pdf, accessed February 8, 2008, pp. 14, 51.

Chapter 7

1. Patrick J. Buchanan, "A. M. Rosenthal's Outrage Reeks of Fakery," *St. Louis Post-Dispatch*, September 21, 1990, p. 3C.

2. The America First Committee was the major anti-war group during the Roosevelt administration's preparations for American entrance into World War II. The America First Committee was smeared by the Roosevelt administration and the interventionist media as a subversive "Nazi-transmission belt." That negative image persists today among the liberal and neoconservative punditry. However, this has not been the case in the scholarly literature, especially in the works of the preeminent historian of the American "isolationists," Wayne S. Cole, who evaluates America First as patriotic and principled: "The committee's leaders rejected rioting and violence. They barred Nazis, Fascists, and anti-Semites from

membership, and tried to enforce those bans. The committee used orderly democratic methods in desperate efforts to keep the United States out of the wars raging abroad. The committee's positions on foreign affairs were consistent with traditions extending back to the beginnings of America's independent history and before. When war burst on America with the Japanese attack on Pearl Harbor, the committee ceased its non-interventionist activities, pledged support to the war effort, and dismantled its organization. Most of its members loyally supported the war against the Axis, and many, including some of its prominent leaders, served in America's armed forces. The America First Committee was a patriotic and honorable exercise of democracy in action at a critical time in American history." Wayne S. Cole, *Determinism and American Foreign Relations during the Franklin D. Roosevelt Era* (Lanham, Md.: University Press of America, 1995), p. 40.

3. Franklin Foer, "Once Again America First," *New York Times*, October 10, 2004, Section 7, p. 22.

4. See, e.g., Michael Parenti, "Yugoslav Sojourn: Notes from the Other Side," *MichaelParenti.org*, January 2000, http://www.michaelparenti.org/YugoslavSojourn.html, accessed April 24, 2008, and "The Rational Destruction of Yugoslavia," *MichaelParenti.org*, November 1999, http://www.michaelparenti.org/yugoslavia.html, accessed April 24, 2008; Daniel Pearl and Robert Block, "Despite Tales, the War in Kosovo Was Savage, but Wasn't Genocide," *Wall Street Journal*, December 31, 1999, online; United Nations Mission in Kosovo, "UNMIK Disputes Belgrade Report on Mass Graves," Press Release, January 23, 2004, http://www.unmikonline.org/justice/pressr/pr1109.pdf, accessed January 31, 2008; and Julia Gorin, "A Jewish Albatross: The Serbs," *FrontPageMagazine.com*, March 16, 2005, online.

5. Joshua Muravchik, "When, Where & How to Use Force: Beyond Self- Defense," *Commentary*, December 1993, p. 21.

6. At the time there were all types of stories of Serb mass killings of Kosovar Albanians, with figures up to 50,000 civilians being slaughtered. Physical evidence for these claims has not been found, and Slobodan Milosevic had not even been charged with crimes of such great magnitude at his trial before the International Criminal Tribunal for the former Yugoslavia (ICTY). According to German government documents no "ethnic cleansing" of Kosovar Albanians was actually taking place until after the NATO bombing. "Internal Documents from Germany's Foreign Office Regarding Pre-Bombardment Genocide in Kosovo," ZNet, http://www.zmag.org/crisescurevts/germandocs.htm, accessed November 18, 2007.

7. Balkan Action Council, Press Release, "Balkan Action Council Urges NATO Intervention, Ground Forces in Kosovo," January 25, 1999,

http://www.southeasteurope.org/documents/pr199.pdf, accessed November 18, 2007; Donald Lambro, "Domestic opinion divided on U.S. role in Balkan fight," *Washington Times*, April 2, 1999, p. A-12; Project for the New American Century, "Letter to Bill Clinton," September 11, 1998, http://www.newamericancentury.org/kosovomilosevicsep98.htm, accessed November 18, 2007.

8. Donald Lambro, "Domestic opinion divided on U.S. role in Balkan fight," *Washington Times*, April 2, 1999, p. A-12.

9. *Ibid.*

10. Michael Lind, "How Neoconservatives Conquered Washington – and Launched a War," *Antiwar.com*, April 10, 2003, online; Michael Lind, "The Weird Men Behind George W. Bush's War," *New Statesman*, April 7, 2003, http://www.mindfully.org/Reform/2003/Bush-Weird-Men7apr03.htm, accessed November 18, 2007.

11. Mann, *Rise of the Vulcans*, p. x, pp. 250–52. Some lay people have suggested that the moniker "Vulcans" must have been intended to imply exceptional intelligence and unemotional rationality as exemplified by the fictional Vulcans in the Star Trek movie/television series. Mann claims otherwise.

12. "Bush fumbles reporter's pop quiz," *USA Today*, November 5, 1999, online.

13. Jake Tapper, "Dumb chic," *Salon*, November 2, 2000, online; John Dean, former counsel to President Richard Nixon during the Watergate scandal, writes about Bush: "No question he is mentally shallow, intellectually lazy, and incurious. He reads little more than his speeches, since his staff briefs him orally on the news, and he demands very short memos and as little homework as possible. Yet he has an abundance of natural intelligence, which he is willing to employ when interested in a subject . . . . But seldom does he want to dig or focus or work hard. He has succeeded in life without doing much mental heavy lifting, and only on rare occasions has he done so as president." John W. Dean, *Worse Than Watergate*, pp. 8–9.

14. Ian Urbina, "Rogues' Gallery, Who Advises Bush and Gore on the Middle East?," *Middle East Report* 216, Fall 2000, http://www.merip.org/mer/mer216/216_urbina.html, accessed November 18, 2007.

15. Halper and Clarke, *America Alone*, pp. 112–13.

16. Terry M. Neal, "Bush Backs Into Nation Building," *Washington Post*, February 26, 2003, online.

17. Online News Hour, Presidential Debate, PBS, October 12, 2000, online.

18. Ivo H. Daalder and James M. Lindsay, *America Unbound: The Bush Revolution in Foreign Policy* (Washington, DC: Brookings Institution Press, 2003), p. 49.

19. Bob Woodward, *Bush at War* (New York: Simon & Schuster, 2002), pp. 328–29.

20. Condoleezza Rice, "Promoting the National Interest," *Foreign Affairs*, January/February 2000, LexisNexis Academic.

21. Mann, *Rise of the Vulcans*, p. 259. The fact that many neocons did back Bush was more for pragmatic reasons. Gary Dorrien writes: "Although most of the [neocon] passion was on the McCain side, some of the neocons judged that Bush was more educable than McCain and had a better chance of winning the presidency" (*Imperial Designs*, p. 72).

22. Francis Foer, "The neocons wake up: Arguing the GOP," *New Republic*, March 20, 2000, p. 13. See also Charles Krauthammer, "A Winner? Yes," *Washington Post*, February 11, 2000, p. A-41; James Nuechterlein, "Conservative Confusions," *First Things*, 103 (May 2000), pp. 7–8, http://www.leaderu.com/ftissues/ft0005/opinion/thistime.html, accessed November 18, 2007.

23. "Randy Scheunemann," *Right Web*, Interhemispheric Resource Center, http://rightweb.irc-online.org/ind/scheunemann/scheunrmann.php, accessed November 18, 2007.

24. James D. Besser, "McCain's Jews Battle The Establishment," *Jewish Week*, January 28, 2000; Marshall Wittmann would explain the fundamental role of Israel in his move to neoconservatism: "Gradually, though, I became disillusioned with liberalism. Like many former Jewish lefties who were becoming neo-conservatives, I thought it was a contradiction to believe in a strong Israel and a weak United States" ("Just a Party Pooper? No, Just Independent," *Washington Post*, September 15, 2002, p. B-2). On Wittmann's neoconservative credentials, see also Peter Carlson, "Quote Cuisine," *Washington Post*, January 4, 2006, p. C-1.

25. William Kristol, "The New Hampshire Upheaval," *Washington Post*, February 2, 2000, p. A-21; see also William Kristol, "The Rebellion Has Just Begun," *Washington Post*, February 21, 2000, p. A-27.

26. Tom Bethell, "Raising McCain," *American Spectator*, February 2000, p. 18.

27. William Kristol and David Brooks, "The McCain Insurrection," *Weekly Standard*, February 14, 2000, online.

28. "Committee for the Liberation of Iraq," *Nationmaster*, http://www.nationmaster.com/encyclopedia/Committee-for-the-Liberation-of-Iraq, accessed November 18, 2007; Laurie Mylroie, "'Iraq Liberation Act' introduced into Congress," *Iraq News*, September 29, 1998, http://www.fas.org/news/iraq/1998/09/980929-in2.htm, accessed November 18, 2007.

29. Justin Raimondo, "John McCain and the War Party," *Antiwar.com*, February 14, 2000, online.

30. "Remarks of Senator John McCain to the National Council of Young Israel in New York City," Press Release, March 14, 1999, quoted by Joseph Sobran, "The Patriot Game," *Wanderer*, February 24, 2000, p. 6.

31. Quoted in Scott McConnell, "Questions About 'Phase II,'" *Antiwar.com*, December 11, 2001, online.

32. Brian Knowlton, "Legislators demand more action on Iran," *International Herald Tribune*, January 22, 2006, online.

Chapter 8

1. George W. Bush, "Freedom and the Future," Speech at the American Enterprise Institute's Annual Dinner, February 26, 2003, *National Review* Online, http://www.nationalreview.com/document/document022703.asp, accessed April 26, 2008.

2. Mann, *Rise of the Vulcans*, pp. 252–53.

3. Halper and Clarke, *America Alone*, p. 14.

4. Carla Anne Robbins, Jean Cummings, "How Bush Decided That Hussein Must Be Ousted from Atop Iraq," *Wall Street Journal*, June 14, 2002, online; At the start of the 2000 campaign, as mentioned earlier, George W. Bush had expressed the opposite view to Condoleezza Rice. Bush said that he disagreed with critics who complained that his father had terminated the 1991 war too soon without invading Iraq and removing Saddam. Bush told Rice that his father and his advisors did "the right thing at the time" (Bob Woodward, *Bush at War* [New York: Simon & Schuster, 2002], pp. 328–29).

5. Jim Lobe, "Dick Cheney, Commander in Chief," *AlterNet.org*, October 27, 2003, http://www.alternet.org/story.html?StoryID=17051, accessed November 18, 2007.

6. Michael Lind, "How Neoconservatives Conquered Washington – and Launched a War," *Antiwar.com*, April 10, 2003, online.

7. Glenn Kessler and Peter Slevin, "Cheney Is Fulcrum of Foreign Policy: In Interagency Fights, His Views Often Prevail," *Washington Post*, October 13, 2002, p. A-1; Michael Lind, "How Neoconservatives Conquered Washington – and Launched a War," *Antiwar.com*, April 10, 2003, online; John Newhouse, *Imperial America: The Bush Assault on World Order*, (New York: Random House, 2004), p. 22.

8. Robert Dreyfuss, "Vice Squad," *American Prospect*, May 2006 (posted April 17, 2006), http://www.prospect.org/web/printfriendly-view.ww?id=11423, accessed May 22, 2006.

9. Jim Lobe, "Dick Cheney, Commander in Chief," *AlterNet.org*, October 27, 2003, http://www.alternet.org/story.html?StoryID=17051, accessed November 18, 2007; Glenn Kessler and Peter Slevin, "Cheney Is Fulcrum of Foreign Policy: In Interagency Fights, His Views Often Prevail," *Washington Post*, October 13, 2002, p. A-1.

10. Glenn Kessler, "With Vice President, He Shaped Iraq Policy," *Washington Post*, October 29, 2005, p. A-1; see also Sidney Blumenthal, "The long march of Dick Cheney," *Salon*, November 24, 2005, online.

11. Lawrence F. Kaplan and Sarah Wildman, "Reorient – Would W.'s Israel policy be as bad as his father's?," *New Republic*, November 6, 2000, p. 24.

12. Packer, *Assassins' Gate*, p. 41.

13. Sidney Blumenthal, "The long march of Dick Cheney," *Salon*, November 24, 2005, online.

14. Wilson, *Politics of Truth*, p. 290.

15. A major documentary on Cheney shown on PBS's *Frontline*, entitled "The Dark Side," describes Cheney as "the chief architect of the war on terror" and the "the most powerful vice president in the nation's history" (June 20, 2006, online.)

16. James Risen, *State of War: The Secret History of the CIA and the Bush Administration* (New York: Free Press, 2006), p. 222.

17. James Gordon Meek, Thomas M. DeFrank, and Kenneth R. Bazinet, "Cheney may be target of probe," *New York Daily News*, October 18, 2005, online.

18. Bob Woodward, *Plan of Attack* (New York: Simon & Schuster, 2004), p. 48.

19. Eisendrath and Goodman, *Bush League Diplomacy*, p. 179.

20. Glenn Kessler, "With Vice President, He Shaped Iraq Policy," *Washington Post*, October 29, 2005, p. A-1.

21. John Dickerson, "Who Is Scooter Libby?," *Slate*, October 21, 2005, online.

22. Jack Mirkinson, "Libby '72 leaned left before serving as Cheney's chief of staff," *Yale Daily News*, November 5, 2005, http://www.yaledailynews.com/article.asp?AID=30668, accessed November 18, 2007.

23. Mann, *Rise of the Vulcans*, p. 112.

24. For a discussion of the Defense Planning Guidance issue, see Dorrien, *Imperial Designs*, pp. 38–43.

25. Project for the New American Century, "Rebuilding America's Defenses."

26. Bryan Bender, "Indictments put focus on neoconservatives," *Boston Globe*, October 29, 2005, online.

27. Dreyfuss, "Vice Squad."

28. Mark Thompson, "The godfather of the Iraq war," *Time*, December 29, 2003, online.

29. Woodward, *Plan of Attack*, p. 21.

30. Bret Stephens, "Man of the Year," *Jerusalem Post*, October 2, 2003, online.

31. "Paul Wolfowitz," Wikipedia, http://en.wikipedia.org/wiki/Paul_Wolfowitz, accessed November 18, 2007.

32. "Defending the 'Ancient Dream of Freedom,'" JINSA Online, November 21, 2002, http://www.jinsa.org/articles/print.html/documentid/1839, accessed November 18, 2007.

33. During his years in government, Wolfowitz, an Albert Wohlstetter protégé, had been a noted

hardline anti-Communist, strong opponent of nuclear arms limitation agreements, and a global interventionist. For a discussion of his views on these issues, see Dorrien, *Imperial Designs*, pp. 27–49.

34. Kathleen and Bill Christison, "A Rose By Another Other Name," *CounterPunch.org*, December 13, 2002, online; Bill Keller, "The Sunshine Warrior," *New York Times*, September 22, 2002, Section 6, p. 48.

35. Rally Unites Anguished Factions under Flag of 'Stand with Israel'," *Forward*, April 19, 2002, online; "Forward 50," *Forward*, November 15, 2002, online.

36. "Douglas Feith," Palestine: Information with Provenance, http://student.cs.ucc.ie/cs1064/jabowen/IPSC/php/authors.php?auid=1005, accessed January 10, 2003; Zionist Organization of America, News Release, "Dalck Feith and Douglas Feith Will Be the Guests of Honor," October 13, 1997, http://www.zoa.org/pressrel/19971013a.htm, accessed January 10, 2003.

37. Tom Barry, "Is Iran Next?," *In These Times*, September 28, 2004, http://www.inthesetimes.com/site/main/article/1114/, accessed November 18, 2007; "About Us," *One Jerusalem*, http://www.onejerusalem.org/blog/about.asp, accessed November 30, 2004.

38. Michael Lind, "A Tragedy of Errors," *Nation*, February 23, 2004, online.

39. Brian Whitaker, "Zionist Settler Joins Iraqi to Promote Trade," World Crisis Web, October 7, 2003, http://www.world-crisis.com/analysis_more/30_0_15_0_C/, accessed November 18, 2007.

40. Stephen Green, "Serving Two Flags: Neocons, Israel and the Bush Administration," *Washington Report on Middle East Affairs*, May 2004, online.

41. Eisendrath and Goodman, *Bush League Diplomacy*, p. 183; James Zogby, "A Dangerous Appointment," April 16, 2001, Arab American Institute, http://www.aaiusa.org/washingtonwatch/1552/page/s/prescampaign, accessed November 18, 2007.

42. Dreyfuss, "Vice Squad."

43. Joshua Micah Marshall, "Bomb Saddam?: How the obsession of a few neocon hawks became the central goal of U.S. foreign policy," *Washington Monthly*, June 2002, online.

44. Packer, *Assassins' Gate*, p. 29.

45. Eric Boehlert, "The Armchair General," *Salon*, September 5, 2002, online.

46. Goldberg, *Jewish Power*, pp. 167–69.

47. Jeff Garth, "Aide Urged Pentagon to Consider Weapons Made by Former Client," *New York Times*, April 17, 1983, p. 1–1.

48. Sidney Blumenthal, "Richard Perle, Disarmed but Undeterred," *Washington Post*, November 23, 1987, p. B-1.

49. Friedman, *Neoconservative Revolution*, p. 160; Similarly, Gary Dorrien notes Perle's inordinate influence: "His extraordinary influence for a third-tier appointee owed much to his considerable skills and even more to the total trust and responsibility that his boss, Defense Secretary Caspar Weinberger, vested in him. Working with Weinberger, Perle turned Reagan's concoction of sentiments about nuclear weapons into a policy" (Dorrien, *Imperial Designs*, p. 60).

50. Eric Boehlert, "The Armchair General," *Salon*, September 5, 2002, online; Sidney Blumenthal, "Richard Perle, Disarmed but Undeterred," *Washington Post*, November 23, 1987, p. B-1.

51. Friedman, *Neoconservative Revolution*, p. 157.

52. Stephen Green, "Serving Two Flags: Neocons, Israel and the Bush Administration," *Washington Report on Middle East Affairs*, May 2004, online.

53. Holger Jensen, "Pre-Emption, Disarmament Or Regime Change? Part III," *Antiwar.com*, October 7, 2002; Jason Vest, "The Men From JINSA and CSP," *Nation*, September 2, 2002, online; Seymour M. Hersh, "Kissinger and Nixon in the White House," *Atlantic Monthly*, May 1982, online.

54. Dilip Hiro, *Secrets and Lies: Operation "Iraqi Freedom" and After* (New York: Nation Books, 2004), p. 18.

55. IASPS, "A Clean Break." Alan Weisman maintains that Perle is not as pro-Zionist as some of his close associates such as Harold Rhode, David Wurmser, Michael Ledeen, and Douglas Feith. Even if this is true, it doesn't equate to a lack of support support for Israel or its policies (*Prince of Darkness*, pp. 135–54).

56. Newhouse, *Imperial America*, pp. 24, 26.

57. *Ibid.*, p. 24.

58. Gary Shapiro, "Bolton 'Maps' A Change for U.N. Culture," *New York Sun*, December 13, 2005, online.

59. Fred Kaplan, "Why Her Dreams Crashed," *Washington Post*, November 4, 2007, p. B-1.

60. Bob Woodward, *State of Denial* (New York: Simon & Schuster, 2006), p. 330.

61. Packer, *Assassins' Gate*, pp. 112–13.

62. Thomas B. Edsall and Dana Milbank, "White House's Roving Eye for Politics: President's Most Powerful Adviser May Also Be the Most Connected," *Washington Post*, March 10, 2003, p. A-1; Jim Lobe, "Veteran neo-con advisor moves on Iran," *Asia Times*, June 26, 2003, online.

63. Richard A. Clarke, *Against All Enemies*, p. 231.

64. *Ibid.*; Isikoff and Corn, *Hubris*, pp. 71–75.

65. Richard Clarke, Interview, "The Dark Side," *Frontline* (PBS), June 2006, online.

66. Woodward, *Plan of Attack*, pp. 21–22.

67. Secretary Colin L. Powell, "Press Remarks

with Foreign Minister of Egypt Amre Moussa," Press Remarks with Foreign Minister of Egypt Amre Moussa, Cairo, Egypt, (Ittihadiya Palace), February 24, 2001, http://www.state.gov/secretary/former/powell/remarks/2001/933.htm, accessed November 18, 2007; John Pilger, "Colin Powell said Iraq was no threat," *Daily Mirror*, September 22, 2003, http://www.coldtype.net/Assets/Pilger/JP.26.%20Sept%2022.pdf, accessed November 18, 2007; James Ridgeway, "Tripping Down Memory Lane," *Village Voice*, October 15–23, 2001, online.

68. Record, *Dark Victory*, p. 26.

69. Podhoretz, "World War IV."

70. Thomas E. Ricks, *Fiasco: The American Military Adventure in Iraq* (New York: Penguin Press, 2006), p. 28.

71. Joshua Micah Marshall, "The Pentagon's internal war," *Salon*, August 9, 2002, online.

72. Joshua Micah Marshall, *Talking Points Memo*, August 9, 2003, http://talkingpointsmemo.com/archives/147369.php, accessed November 18, 2007.

73. Reuel Marc Gerecht, "Liberate Iraq," *Weekly Standard*, May 14, 2001, online.

74. Ibid.

75. Rose Brady, ed., ""Rogue States: Why Washington May Ease Sanctions," *Business Week*, May 7, 2001, online.

76. Ibid.

77. Joy Gordon, "Cool War: Economic sanctions as a weapon of mass destruction," *Harper's Magazine*, November 2002, online; John Pilger, "Squeezed to death," *Guardian*, March 4, 2000, online.

78. Peter Behr and Alan Sipress, "Cheney Panel Seeks Review Of Sanctions: Iraq, Iran and Libya Loom Large in Boosting Oil Supply," *Washington Post*, April 19, 2001, online.

79. Elie Krakowski, "The Afghan Vortex," IASPS Research Papers in Strategy, Institute for Advanced Strategic and Political Studies, April 2000, No. 9, http://www.iasps.org/strategic9/strat9.htm, accessed November 18, 2007.

80. Zbigniew Brzezinski, *The Grand Chessboard: American Primacy and its Geostrategic Imperatives* (New York: Basic Books, 1997). A similar argument that the control of vital resources is the key to global power and global warfare is presented by Michael T. Klare, *Resource Wars: The New Landscape of Global Conflict* (New York: Henry Holt, 2001).

81. Brzezinski echoes the geopolitical theory of 19th-century British geostrategist Halford Mackinder. See Christopher J. Fettweis, "Sir Halford Mackinder, Geopolitics, and Policymaking in the 21st Century," *Parameters*, Summer 2000, pp. 58–71, http://carlisle-www.army.mil/usawc/Parameters/00summer/fettweis.htm, accessed November 18, 2007.

82. Brzezinski, *Grand Chessboard*, p. 211.

83. Stuart Parrott, "Azerbaijan: International Conference Convened to Revive Silk Road," *Radio Free Europe/Radio Liberty*, March 2, 1998, http://www.rferl.org/features/1998/03/f.ru.980302143024.asp, accessed November 18, 2007.

84. Anne Applebaum, "Russia, Oil, and Conspiracy Theories," *Slate*, November 27, 2001, online.

85. Quoted by Nafeez Mosaddeq Ahmed, "Afghanistan, the Taliban, and the United States: The Role of Human Rights in Western Foreign Policy," Institute for Policy Research & Development, January 2001, http://www.institute-for-afghan-studies.org/AFGHAN%20CONFLICT/TALIBAN/afghanistan%20taliban%20and%20us.htm, accessed November 18, 2007.

86. John F. Burns, "How Afghan's Stern Rulers Took Hold," *New York Times*, December 31, 1996, online.

87. John F. Burns, "In Afghanistan. A Triumph of Fundamentalism," *New York Times*, May 26, 1997, online.

88. "Great game endgame?," *Wall Street Journal*, May 23, 1997, p. A-18.

89. "CIA worked in tandem with Pak to create Taliban," *Times of India*, March 7, 2001, http://www.1worldcommunication.org/ciaworkedintandem.htm, accessed November 18, 2007; B. Raman, "Pakistan's Inter-Services Intelligence (ISI)," South Asia Analysis Group, Paper 287, January 8, 2001, http://www.saag.org/papers3/paper287.html, accessed November 18, 2007.

90. Amnesty International, "Afghanistan: Grave abuses in the name of religion," November 1996, http://web.amnesty.org/library/Index/engASA110121996?OpenDocument&of=COUNTRIES%5CAFGHANISTAN, accessed November 18, 2007.

91. Thomas E. Ricks and Susan B. Glasser, "U.S. Operated Secret Alliance With Uzbekistan," *Washington Post*, October 14, 2001, p. A-1.; Bob Woodward, "Secret CIA Units Playing a Central Combat Role," *Washington Post*, November 18, 2001, p. A-1; and Barton Gellman, "Broad Effort Launched After '98 Attacks," *Washington Post*, December 19, 2001, p. A-1.

92. Quoted by Nafeez Mosaddeq Ahmed, "Afghanistan, the Taliban and the United States: The Role of Human Rights in Western Foreign Policy," Institute for Policy Research & Development, January 2001, http://www.institute-for-afghan-studies.org/AFGHAN%20CONFLICT/TALIBAN/afghanistan%20taliban%20and%20us.htm, accessed November 18, 2007.

93. Statement of Congressman Dana Rohrabacher, "U.S. Policy toward Afghanistan," Hearings before the Senate Foreign Relations Subcommittee on South Asia, April 14, 1999, http://www.wapha.org/dana.html, accessed November 18, 2007; Kevin Foley and Julie Moffett, "Afghanistan: U.S. Denies It Secretly Supports Taliban," Radio Free

Europe/Radio Liberty, April 15, 1999, http://www.rferl.org/features/1999/04/f.ru.990415123406.asp, accessed November 18, 2007.

94. Testimony of Congressman Dana Rohrabacher, "Global Terrorism: South Asia – The New Locus," Hearing before the Committee on International Relations, House of Representatives, 106th Congress, 2nd Session, July 12, 2000, 106–173, p. 22, https://www.gpoaccess.gov/congress/house/intrelations/106ch.html, accessed December 30, 2007.

95. U.S. Department of State, "Fact Sheet: Humanitarian Aid to the Afghan People," October, 15, 2001, http://usinfo.state.gov/is/Archive_Index/Humanitarian_Aid_to_the_Afghan_People-4072c45bad525.html, accessed November 19, 2007; Brett Schaefer, "Afghanistan's Worst Enemy," Heritage Foundation, http://www.heritage.org/Press/Commentary/ed110601.cfm, accessed November 19, 2007.

96. Julio Godoy, "U.S. policy on Taliban influenced by oil," *Asia Times* Online, November 20, 2001, online; "Three reviews of *Bin Laden: The Forbidden Truth* by Jean-Charles Brisard and Guillaume Dasquie," http://www.serendipity.li/wot/bl_tft.htm, accessed November 19, 2007.

97. Godoy, "U.S. policy on Taliban."

98. "Asia's big oil rush: count us in," *U.S. News & World Report*, Sept 29, 1997, p. 42; R. Jeffrey Smith, "U.S., Russian Paratroops Join in Central Asian Jump; Exercise Shows Airborne Units' Long Reach," *Washington Post*, Sept 16, 1997, p. A-12.

99. Thomas E. Ricks and Susan B. Glasser, "U.S. Operated Secret Alliance with Uzbekistan," *Washington Post*, October 14, 2001, p. A-1.

100. Bob Woodward, "Secret CIA Units Playing a Central Combat Role," *Washington Post*, November 18, 2001, p. A-1.

101. Rahul Bedi, "India joins anti-Taliban coalition," *Jane's Intelligence Review*, March 15, 2001, http://www.janes.com/security/international_security/news/jir/jir010315_1_n.shtml, accessed November 19, 2007.

102. "India in anti-Taliban military plan," Indiareacts.com, June 26, 2001, http://www.indiareacts.com/archivefeatures/nat2.asp?recno=10∓ctg=policy, accessed November 19, 2007.

103. George Arney, "U.S. 'planned attack on Taleban,'" *BBC News*, September 18, 2001, online.

104. Jonathan Steele, Ewen MacAskill, Richard Norton-Taylor and Ed Harriman, "Threat of U.S. strikes passed to Taliban weeks before NY attack," *Guardian*, September 22, 2001, online.

Chapter 9

1. David Plotz, "Ariel Sharon: The Bulldozer rolls on," *Slate*, October 5, 2000, http://www.slate.com/id/90930/, accessed November 19, 2007.

2. Kimmerling, *Politicide*, pp. 79–80.

3. *Ibid.*, pp. 3–4.

4. *Ibid.*, p. 76; Ronald Bleier, "Sharon Routs Bush: Palestinians now vulnerable to expulsion," Demographic, Environmental and Security Issues Project, August 2001, http://desip.igc.org/SharonRoutsBush.html, accessed November 19, 2007; Ronald Bleier, "The Next Expulsion of the Palestinians," *Middle East Policy*, 8:1 (March 2001), Demographic, Environmental and Security Issues Project, http://desip.igc.org/TheNext-Expulsion.html, accessed November 19, 2007.

5. Tikva Honig-Parnass, "Israel's Recent Conviction: Apartheid In Palestine Can Only be Preserved Through Force," *Between the Lines*, September 2001, http://www.between-lines.org/archives/2001/sep/Tikva_Honig-Parnass.htm, accessed February 12, 2003.

6. Ronald Bleier, "Sharon Gears Up for Expulsion," Demographic, Environmental and Security Issues Project, January 2002, http://desip.igc.org/SharonGearsUp.html, accessed November 19, 2007.

7. Tikva Honig-Parnass, "Louder Voices of War: Manufacturing Consent at its Peak," *Between the Lines*, 1:8 (July 2001) quoted in Ronald Bleier, "Sharon Routs Bush: Palestinians now vulnerable to expulsion," Demographic, Environmental and Security Issues Project, August 2001, http://desip.igc.org/SharonRoutsBush.html, accessed November 19, 2007.

8. Associated Press, "Israeli war plan revealed," July 12, 2001, online; *AFP*, "Israelis Generals' Plan to 'Smash' Palestinians," July 12, 2001, http://www.intellnet.org/news/2001/07/13/5814-1.html, accessed February 8, 2008; Tanya Reinhart, "The Second Half of 1948," *Mid-East Realities*, June 20, 2001, http://www.middleeast.org/premium/read.cgi?category=Magazine&num=251&month=6&year=2001&function=text, accessed November 19, 2007.

9. Bleier, "Sharon Routs Bush."

10. James Bennet, "Spilled Blood Is Seen as Bond That Draws 2 Nations Closer," *New York Times*, September 12, 2001, p. A-22; "World shock at U.S. attacks," BBC News, September 12, 2001, http://news.bbc.co.uk/1/hi/world/americas/1537800.stm, accessed November 19, 2007.

11. Damien Cave, "The United States of Oil," *Salon*, November 19, 2001, online.

12. Aluf Benn, "Israel strives to import America's war on terror," *Ha'aretz*, December 18, 2001, online.

13. Kimmerling, *Politicide*, p. 204.

14. Wilson, *Politics of Truth*, p. 289.

15. Elizabeth Drew, "The Neocons in Power," *New York Review of Books*, June 12, 2003, online.

16. Packer, *Assassins' Gate*, pp. 41, 43.

17. Woodward, *Bush at War*, p. 49; see also George Tenet, *At the Center of the Storm: My Years at the CIA* (New York: Harper Collins, 2007), pp. 306–307.

18. Woodward, *Bush at War*, p. 83; Ron Suskind, *The Price of Loyalty: George W. Bush, the White House, and the Education of Paul O'Neil* (New York: Simon and Schuster, 2004), p. 188.

19. DoD News Briefing – Deputy Secretary Wolfowitz, September 13, 2001, http://www.defenselink.mil/transcripts/transcript.aspx?transcriptid=1622, accessed November 19, 2007.

20. Woodward, *Bush at War*, p. 49.

21. *Ibid.*, p. 84; Also see, Karen DeYoung, *Soldier: The Life of Colin Powell* (New York: Alfred A. Knopf, 2006), pp. 348–50.

22. Patrick E. Tyler and Elaine Sciolino, "Bush's Advisers Split on Scope Of Retaliation," *New York Times*, September 20, 2002, online; Julian Borger, "Washington's hawk trains sights on Iraq," *Guardian*, October 15, 2001, online.

23. Gary Schroen, Interview, "The Dark Side," *Frontline* (PBS), June 2006, online.

24. Tyler Drumheller, Interview, "The Dark Side," *Frontline* (PBS), June 2006, online; see also Tenet, *Center of the Storm*, pp. 306–307.

25. Packer, *Assassins' Gate*, p. 40–41.

26. "Vice-President Appears on Meet the Press with Tim Russert," White House, September 16, 2001, http://www.whitehouse.gov/vicepresident/news-speeches/speeches/vp20010916.html, accessed November 19, 2007.

27. Glenn Kessler, "U.S. Decision on Iraq Has Puzzling Past," *Washington Post*, January 12, 2002, p. A-1; Woodward, *Plan of Attack*, p. 26.

28. "Richard Pearle [sic] Discusses U.S. Defense," (Transcript), CNN, Evans, Novak, Hunt & Shields,, Aired September 16, 2001, http://edition.cnn.com/TRANSCRIPTS/0109/16/en.00.html, accessed November 19, 2007.

29. Elaine Sciolino and Patrick Tyler, "Some Pentagon officials and advisors seek to oust Iraq's leader in war's next phase." *New York Times*. October 12, 2001, online.

30. Bryan Burrough, Evgenia Peretz, David Rose, and David Wise, "The Path to War: Special Report; The Rush to Invade Iraq; The Ultimate Inside Account," *Vanity Fair*, May 2004, online.

31. *Ibid.*

32. William Kristol et al, "Toward a Comprehensive Strategy: A letter to the president," September 20, 2001, *National Review* Online, online; "Project for the New American Century," http://www.newamericancentury.org/Bushletter.htm, accessed November 19, 2007.

33. Jewish Institute for National Security Affairs, "This Goes Beyond Bin Laden," Press Release, *JINSA.org*, September 13, 2001, http://www.jinsa.org/articles/articles.html/function/view/categoryid/963/documentid/1262/history/3,1262, accessed February 8, 2008.

34. *Ibid.*

35. *Ibid.*

36. *Ibid.*

37. Peter Bergen, "Armchair Provocateur: Laurie Mylroie: The Neocons' favorite conspiracy theorist," *Washington Monthly*, December 2003, online.

38. James Bamford, *A Pretext for War: 9/11, Iraq, and the Abuse of America's Intelligence Agencies* (New York: Doubleday, 2004), p. 311; *Jane's Foreign Report*, September 19, 2001, http://www.janes.com/security/international_security/news/fr/fr010919_1_n.shtml, accessed November 19, 2007.

39. Dennis Eisenberg, "Ex-Mossad Chief, Iraq was Behind the Attacks," *Herald Sun* (Melbourne, Australia), September 23, 2001, http://archives.his.com/intelforum/2001-September/msg00129.html, accessed December 8, 2005.

40. Scott McConnell, "The Struggle Over War Aims: Bush Versus the Neo-Cons," *Antiwar.com*, September 25, 2002, online.

41. *Ibid.* Wolfowitz was then deputy secretary of defense.

42. Georgie Anne Geyer, "Pro-Israeli, Anti-Arab Campaigns Could Isolate America," *Uexpress.com*, October 25, 2001, http://www.uexpress.com/georgieannegeyer/?uc_full_date=20011025, accessed November 19, 2007.

43. Thomas Omestad, "Fixin' for a fight: In the GOP, the long knives are out for the neoconservatives," *U.S. News and World Report*, October 25, 2004, online.

44. Dana Milbank, "For Bush, War Defines Presidency," *Washington Post*, March 9. 2003, p. A-1.

45. See David W. Lutz, "*Un*just-War Theory: Christian Zionism and the Road to Jerusalem," in *Neo-CONNED! Again*, pp. 127–69.

46. Quoted in Dana Milbank, "For Bush, War Defines Presidency," *Washington Post*, March 9. 2003, p. A-1.

47. Podhoretz, *World War IV*, p. 132–33.

48. Norman Podhoretz, "In Praise of the Bush Doctrine," *Commentary*, September 2002, online.

49. Halper and Clarke, *America Alone*, pp. 137–38.

50. "U.S. invasion of Afghanistan," *Wikipedia*, http://en.wikipedia.org/wiki/2001_U.S._Attack_on_Afghanistan, accessed November 19, 2007; Noam Chomsky, *Hegemony or Survival: America's Quest for Global Dominance* (New York: Henry Holt, 2004), p. 199.

51. Anonymous [Michael Scheuer], *Imperial Hubris: Why the West Is Losing the War on Terror* (Washington: Brassey's Inc., 2004), p. 66; see also Schroen, "The Dark Side."

Chapter 10

1. "Bush Promises Military All It Needs to Win Long Battle Ahead, President addressed the

troops at Fort Campbell, KY," November 21, 2002, U.S. Department of State, http://usinfo.state.gov/topical/pol/terror/01112113.htm, accessed February 10, 2003.

2. Woodward, *Plan of Attack*, pp. 1–5.

3. "Bush Meets with Aid Workers Rescued from Afghanistan," November 26, 2002, http://usinfo.state.gov/topical/pol/terror/01112607.htm, accessed February 10, 2003.

4. "President Delivers State of the Union Address," January 29, 2002, http://www.whitehouse.gov/news/releases/2002/01/20020129-11.html, accessed November 19, 2007.

5. Matthew Engel, "Proud wife turns 'axis of evil' speech into a resignation letter," *Guardian*, February 27, 2002, http://www.guardian.co.uk/bush/story/0,7369,658724,00.html, accessed November 19, 2007; Robert D. Novak, "The Axis of Ego," *American Conservative*, March 24, 2003, online.

6. Michael Kinsley, "The War Keeps Growing," *Washington Post*, February 8, 2002, p. A-31 (parenthesis in original).

7. Chris Matthews, "Who hijacked our war?," *San Francisco Chronicle*, February 17, 2002, online.

8. Robert Novak, "The war President," *Townhall.com*, January 31, 2002, online.

9. Mann, *Rise of the Vulcans*, p. 332.

10. Woodward, *Bush at War*, p. 330.

11. Glenn Kessler, "U.S. Decision on Iraq Has Puzzling Past," *Washington Post*, January 12, 2003, p. A-20.

12. "Robin Cook: Britain must not be suckered a second time by the White House," *Independent*, May 30, 2003, http://comment.independent.co.uk/commentators/article107068.ece, accessed November 19, 2007.

13. Linda D. Kozaryn, "Cheney Says Grave Threats Require Pre-emptive Action," American Forces Press Service. Aug. 26, 2002, http://www.dod.gov/news/Aug2002/n08262002_200208264.html, accessed November 19, 2007.

14. *Ibid.*; Ricks, *Fiasco*, p. 49.

15. Ricks, *Fiasco*, p. 51.

16. "President Bush's Speech on the Use of Force Against Iraq," *New York Times*, October 8, 2002, online.

17. *Ibid.*

18. *Ibid.*

19. *Ibid.*

20. Bamford, *Pretext for War*, p. 330.

21. Frank J. Gaffney, Jr., "Truth and consequences for Saddam," *Jewish World Review*, February 27, 2001, online.

22. "President Bush's Speech on the Use of Force Against Iraq," *New York Times*, October 8, 2002, online.

23. Woodward, *Plan of Attack*, p. 292.

24. Karen DeYoung, *Soldier*, p. 356.

25. Dana Milbank, "Colonel Finally Saw Whites of Their Eyes," *Washington Post*, October 20, 2005, p. A-4; Jim Lobe, "Powell Aide Blasts Rice, Cheney-Rumsfeld 'Cabal,'" October 20, 2005, *Antiwar.com*, online.

26. Dreyfuss, "Vice Squad."

27. John Barry, Michael Isikoff and Mark Hosenball, "Prelude to a Leak," *Newsweek*, October 31, 2005, online.

28. Dreyfuss, "Vice Squad."

29. Risen, *State of War*, pp. 71–72.

30. Joseph Cirincione, Jessica T. Mathews, George Perkovich with Alexis Orton, "WMD in Iraq: evidence and implications," Carnegie Endowment for International Peace, January 2004, http://www.carnegieendowment.org/files/Iraq3FullText.pdf, pp. 50–1; Bamford, *Pretext for War*, pp. 333–38; "Cheney's CIA visits pressured us: analysts," *Sydney Morning Herald*, June 6, 2003, http://www.smh.com.au/articles/2003/06/05/1054700335400.html, November 19, 2007; Julian Borger, "The spies who pushed for war," *Guardian*, July 17, 2003, online; John Aloysius Farrell, "Cheney's Intelligence Role Scrutinized," *Denver Post*, July 23, 2003, p. A-1; John B. Judis and Spencer Ackerman, "The Operator," *New Republic*, September 22, 2003, online; Walter Pincus and Dana Priest, "Some Iraq Analysts Felt Pressure from Cheney Visits," *Washington Post*, June 5, 2003, p. A-1; John Prados, "Phase II: Loaded For Bear," *TomPaine.com*, November 10, 2005, online.

31. John B. Judis and Spencer Ackerman, "The Operator," *New Republic*, September 22, 2003, online.

32. Warren P. Strobel and Jonathan S. Landay, "Some administration officials expressing misgivings on Iraq," Knight-Ridder Newspapers, October 8, 2002, quoted in Bamford, *Pretext for War*, pp. 327–28.

33. Warren P. Strobel, "Data didn't back Bush's weapons claims, officials say," *Mercury News* (San Jose, Calif.), June 6, 2003, online.

34. John J. Lumpkin, "Ex-Official: Evidence Distorted for War," *Mercury News* (San Jose, Calif.), June 7, 2003, online.

35. *AFP*, "Bush had 'faith-based' intelligence on Iraq: arms expert," July 11, 2003, http://www.spacewar.com/2003/030711162517.v43k5waj.html, accessed February 8, 2008; Julian Borger, "White House 'Lied About Saddam Threat,'" *Guardian*, July 10, 2003, online; see also "Truth, War & Consequences," (Documentary), Interview: Greg Thielmann, PBS, *Frontline*, October 9, 2003, online.

36. John Prados, "Boltonized Intelligence," *TomPaine.com*, April 21, 2005, http://www.tompaine.com/articles/boltonized_intelligence.php?dateid=20050425, accessed November 19, 2007.

37. Risen, *State of War*, pp. 113–15.

38. *The Sunday Times* (London), May 1, 2005, http://www.timesonline.co.uk/article/0,,2087-1593607,00.html, accessed November 19, 2007.

39. "Levin Releases Newly Declassified Pentagon Inspector General Report on Intelligence Assessment Activities of the Office of Under Secretary of Defense Doug Feith," April 5, 2007, Senator Carl Levin Website, http://levin.senate.gov/newsroom/release.cfm?id=271875, accessed November 19, 2007; see also Tenet, *Center of the Storm*, pp. 346–48; Weisman, *Prince of Darkness*, pp. 168–69.

40. Tenet, *Center of the Storm*, p. 347.

41. Robert Dreyfuss and Jason Vest, "The Lie Factory," *Mother Jones*, January/February 2004, online; Joshua Micah Marshall, "The Pentagon's internal war," *Salon*, August 9, 2002, online; Weisman, *Prince of Darkness*, p. 146; The earlier incident involving Rhode is described in Chapter 8.

42. Wurmser wrote in the acknowledgements in *Tyranny's Ally: America's Failure to Defeat Saddam Hussein* (Washington: The AEI Press, 1999): "And special thanks go to Harold Rhode, who has throughout my career in Washington been a mentor, encouraging me, pushing me forward, acting as my chief advocate around town, and opening the window through which I see the Islamic world" (p. xxiii).

43. Dreyfuss and Vest, "The Lie Factory"; Packer, *Assassins' Gate*, pp. 106–107.

44. Packer, *Assassins' Gate*, p. 107.

45. Robert Dreyfuss, "The Pentagon Muzzles the CIA," *American Prospect*, December 16, 2002, online; Seymour M. Hersh, "Selective Intelligence," *New Yorker*, May 6, 2003, online.

46. Dreyfuss and Vest, "The Lie Factory."

47. Greg Miller, "Tenet Bypassed on Iraq-Al Qaeda Briefings," *Los Angeles Times*, March 9, 2004, online.

48. Karen Kwiatkowski, "In Rumsfeld's Shop," *American Conservative*, December 1, 2003, online.

49. Quoted in Dreyfuss and Vest, "The Lie Factory."

50. Karen Kwiatkowski, "Open Door Policy," *American Conservative*, July 19, 2004, online.

51. Karen Kwiatkowski, "The New Pentagon Papers," *Salon*, May 10, 2004, online.

52. Marc Cooper, "Soldier for the Truth: Exposing Bush's talking-points war," *LA Weekly*, February 19, 2004, http://www.laweekly.com/news/news/soldier-for-the-truth/1977/, accessed November 19, 2007.

53. Jim Lobe, "Pentagon Office Home to Neo-Con Network," Inter Press Service, August 7, 2003, http://www.CommonDreams.org/headlines03/0807-02.htm, accessed November 19, 2007.

54. Eric Boehlert, "Rumsfeld's personal spy ring," *Salon*, July 16, 2003, online.

55. Dreyfuss and Vest, "The Lie Factory."

56. Seymour M. Hersh, "Selective Intelligence," *New Yorker*, May 12, 2003, online. |

57. Ray McGovern, "Sham Dunk: Cooking Intelligence for the President," in *Neo-CONNED! Again*, p. 283.

58. Center for Media & Democracy, "Office of Special Plans," *SourceWatch*, http://www.sourcewatch.org/wiki.phtml?title=Office_of_Special_Plans, accessed November 19, 2007.

59. Bamford, *Pretext for War*, pp. 318, 325.

60. Ricks, *Fiasco*, pp. 55–57; Arianna Huffington, "Who is Judy Miller kidding?," *Los Angeles Times*, October 1, 2005, online.

61. Franklin Foer, "The Source of the Trouble," *New York Magazine*, June 7, 2004, http://nymag.com/nymetro/news/media/features/9226/, accessed November 20, 2007.

62. Isikoff and Corn, *Hubris*, p. 57.

63. Foer, "The Source of the Trouble."

64. Isikoff and Corn, *Hubris*, pp. 58–59.

65. Howard Kurtz, "Intra-Times Battle Over Iraqi Weapons," *Washington Post*, May 26, 2003, p. C-1.

66. Maureen Dowd, "Woman of Mass Destruction," *New York Times*, October 22, 2005, online.

67. Seymour M. Hersh, "Selective Intelligence," *New Yorker*, May 12, 2003, online.

68. Halper and Clarke, *America Alone*, pp. 220–21.

69. Quoted in Robert Dreyfuss, "Tinker, Banker, NeoCon, Spy," *American Prospect*, November 18, 2002, online.

70. Quoted in Ricks, *Fiasco*, p. 57.

71. Bamford, *Pretext for War*, p. 294; Risen, *State of War*, pp. 73–76.

72. Dreyfuss, "Tinker, Banker, NeoCon, Spy"; John Dizard, "The Implosion of Chalabi's Petra Bank," *Salon*, May 4, 2004, online.

73. W. Patrick Lang, "Drinking the Kool-Aid," *Middle East Policy*, 11.2 (Summer 2004), http://www.mepc.org/journal_vol11/0406_lang.asp, accessed November 20, 2007; Seymour Hersh, "The Iraq Hawks," *New Yorker*, December 20, 2001, http://www.globalpolicy.org/wtc/targets/1220hawks.htm, accessed November 20, 2007; Isikoff and Corn, *Hubris*, pp. 50–51. For an extensive history of the activities of the INC, see Congress, Senate, Select Committee on Intelligence, "The Use by the Intelligence Community of Information Provided by the Iraqi National Congress," 109th Cong., 2nd sess., September 8, 2006, http://www.fas.org/irp/congress/2006_rpt/srpt109-330.pdf, accessed November 20, 2007.

74. Lang, "Drinking the Kool-Aid"; Weisman, *Prince of Darkness*, pp. 162–63.

75. Isikoff and Corn, *Hubris*, p. 52.

76. Andrew Buncombe, "U.S. Paid $1m for 'Useless Intelligence' from Chalabi," *Independent*, September 30, 2003, http://www.CommonDreams.org/headlines03/0930-06.htm, accessed November 20, 2007.

77. Mark Hosenball and Michael Hirsh, "Chalabi: A Questionable Use of U.S. Funding," *Newsweek*, April 5, 2004, online.

78. Mark Mazzetti, "Senate Panel Releases Report on Iraq Intelligence," *New York Times*, September 8, 2006, online; Walter Pincus, "Report Details Errors Before War," *Washington Post*, September 9, 2006, p. A-12.

79. Jack Fairweather, "Chalabi stands by faulty intelligence that toppled Saddam's regime," *Telegraph*, February 19, 2004, http://www.telegraph.co.uk/news/main.jhtml?xml=/news/2004/02/19/wirq19.xml&, accessed November 20, 2007.

80. Arnaud de Borchgrave, "Chalabi poised to lead Iraq," March 31, 2004, *Washington Times*, online; Robert Scheer, "One more Chalabi black eye," August 10, 2004, *Los Angeles Times*, online.

81. Justin Raimondo, "Chalabi-gate: None Dare Call It Treason," May 28, 2004, *Antiwar.com*, online; Knut Royce, "Iranian spy fears prompt Chalabi raid," *The Age*, May 22, 2004, http://www.theage.com.au/articles/2004/05/21/1085120118034.html?from=top5&oneclick=true, accessed November 20. 2007; Scott Wilson, "Chalabi Aides Suspected of Spying for Iran," *Washington Post*, May 22, 2004, p. A-20.

82. Julian Borger, "U.S. intelligence fears Iran duped hawks into Iraq war," *Guardian*, May 25, 2004, online.

83. David Corn, "Ahmad Chalabi, WMDs, the CIA, No Regrets, and Page 108," *Capital Games* (weblog at *Nation* online), November 9, 2005, http://www.thenation.com/blogs/capitalgames?pid=35322, accessed February 8, 2008; Robert Dreyfuss, "Chalabi and AEI: The Sequel," *TomPaine.com*, November 10, 2005, http://www.tompaine.com/articles/20051110/chalabi_and_aei_the_sequel.php, accessed November 20. 2007; Juan Cole, "Chalabi's curtain call," *Salon*, November 10, 2005, online.

84. Robert Dreyfuss, "Agents of Influence," *Nation*, October 4, 2004, online.

85. Richard Sale, "FBI steps up AIPAC probe," United Press International, *Washington Times*, December 10, 2004, online.

86. Robert Dreyfuss, "Bigger than AIPAC," *TomPaine.com*, August 9, 2005, http://www.tompaine.com/articles/20050809/bigger_than_aipac.php, accessed November 20. 2007

87. Tom Berry, "Is Iran Next?," *In These Times*, September 28, 2004, http://www.inthesetimes.com/site/main/article/1114/, accessed November 20. 2007; Robert Dreyfuss, "Agents of Influence," *Nation*, October 4, 2004, online; Joshua Micah Marshall, Laura Rozen, and Paul Glastris, "Iran-Contra II?," *Washington Monthly*, September 2004, online; Weisman, *Prince of Darkness*, pp.

147–49.

88. Israel has attempted to deny any involvement in the U.S. attack on Iraq. In December 2006, Deputy Prime Minister Shimon Peres said: "American intervention in Iraq was done without agreement with Israel, the Americans have stayed in Iraq without agreement with Israel, which proves that the Iraqi question is not linked to Israel" (Jean-Luc Renaudie, "Israel seeks to downplay policy shifts in U.S. panel report," *AFP*, December 7, 2006, online).

89. *AP*, "General: Israelis Exaggerated Iraq Threat," *USA Today*, December 4, 2003, online; Laura King, "Ex-General Says Israel Inflated Iraqi Threat," *Los Angeles Times*, December 5, 2003, online; Molly Moore, "Israel Shares Blame on Iraq Intelligence, Report Says," *Washington Post*, December 5, 2003, p. A-18.

90. Bamford, *Pretext for War*, p. 310.

91. Risen, *State of War*, pp. 72–73.

92. Seymour M. Hersh, "Selective Intelligence," *New Yorker*, May 6, 2003, online; Richard Cummings, "War, Lies, and WMDs," *LewRockwell.com*, May 22, 2003, http://www.lewrockwell.com/cummings/cummings22.html, accessed November 20, 2007; Robert Dreyfuss, "More Missing Intelligence," *Nation*, July 7, 2003 [posted June 19, 2003], online; Jason Leopold, "Wolfowitz Committee Told White House to Hype Dubious Uranium Claims," *Antiwar.com*, July 17, 2003, online.

93. Bamford, *Pretext for War*, p. 311; *Jane's Foreign Report*, September 19, 2001, http://www.janes.com/security/international_security/news/fr/fr010919_1_n.shtml, accessed November 20, 2007.

94. Bamford, *ibid,*, p. 311; *Jane's Foreign Report, ibid.*; "Document: The Complete Address Of Mossad Head Efraim Halevy, in a rare appearance at the NATO Council In Brussels- 'On September 11 World War III Started,'" *Yediot Ahronot*, June 28, 2002, http://www.aijac.org.au/updates/Jul-02/080702.html, accessed November 20, 2007.

95. Molly Moore, "Israel Shares Blame on Iraq Intelligence, Report Says," *Washington Post*, December 5, 2003, p. A-18; Parsi, *Treacherous Alliance*, pp. 239–40.

96. Jonathan Steele, "Israel puts pressure on U.S. to strike Iraq," *Guardian*, August 17, 2002, online; Jason Keyser, "Israel Urges U.S. to Attack Iraq," Associated Press, August 16, 2002, http://www.firstcoastnews.com/news/2002-08-16/usw_israeliraq.asp, accessed December 8, 2002.

97. Richard Sisk, "Attack Iraq soon, Sharon aide says," *New York Daily News*, August 16, 2002, online; CBS, "Israel To U.S.: Don't Delay Iraq Attack," *CBS News*, August 16, 2002, online.

98. Benjamin Netanyahu, "The Case for Toppling Saddam," *Wall Street Journal*, September 20, 2002, online.

99. Jay Bushinsky, "Netanyahu says Israel expects war," *Washington Times*, October 23, 2002, p. A-14.

100. Robert Novak, "Inside Report: Bebe's Nuclear warning," *Townhall.com*, April 13, 2002, online.

101. Marc Perelman, "Iraqi Move Puts Israel In Lonely U.S. Corner," *Forward*, September 20, 2002, online.

102. Ehud Barak, "Taking Apart Iraq's Nuclear Threat," *New York Times*, September 4, 2002, online.

103. Robert Novak, "Sharon's war?," CNN.com, December 26, 2002, online.

104. Aluf Benn, "Sharon says U.S. should also disarm Iran, Libya and Syria," *Ha`aretz*, February 20, 2003, online.

105. Americans & the World, "Conflict with Iraq," *The Digest Conflict with Iraq*, October 23, 2002, http://americans-world.org/digest/regional_issues/Conflict_Iraq/summary_Iraq.cfm, accessed February 7, 2008.

106. Thomas E. Ricks, "Some Top Military Brass Favor Status Quo in Iraq," *Washington Post*, July 28, 2002, p. A-1; Thomas E. Ricks, *Fiasco*, p. 40.

107. Lang, "Drinking the Kool-Aid."

108. Michael Dobbs, "Old Strategy on Iraq Sparks New Debate," *Washington Post*, December 27, 2001, online.

109. Robert Novak, "No cakewalk," *Townhall.com*, March 27, 2003, online; Dana Milbank, "Upbeat Tone Ended With War," *Washington Post*, March 29, 2003, p. A-1.

110. Quoted in Susan Page, "Prewar predictions coming back to bite," *USA Today*, April 1, 2003, online.

111. Keith Andrew Bettinger, "When the wheels fall off," *Asia Times*, February 13, 2004, online; Jeffrey Record, *Dark Victory*, pp. 97–103.

112. Richard Norton-Taylor, "British military chiefs uneasy about attack plans," *The Age*, July 31, 2002, http://www.theage.com.au/articles/2002/07/30/1027926884871.html, accessed November 20, 2007.

113. Justin Raimondo, "Attack of the Chicken-Hawks," *Antiwar.com*, August 2, 2002, online; Doug Thompson, "Suddenly, the hawks are doves and the doves are hawks," Capitol Hill Blue, April 1, 2002, http://www.capitolhillblue.com/cgi-bin/artman/exec/view.cgi?archive=8&num=165, accessed November 20, 2007.

114. Keith Andrew Bettinger, "When the wheels fall off," *Asia Times*, February 13, 2004, online; Jeffrey Record, *Dark Victory*, pp. 97–103.

115. Woodward, *State of Denial*, p. 82.

116. It must be added that Rumsfeld did have connections with the neocons, being a founding member PNAC. Project for the New American Century, "Statement of Principles," http://www.newamericancentury.org/statementofprinciples.

htm, accessed November 22, 2007.

117. Ricks, *Fiasco*, pp. 68–71, 73–76.

118. Julian Borger, "Pentagon build-up reaches unstoppable momentum," *Guardian*, December 31, 2002, online; Ricks, *Fiasco*, pp. 42–43.

119. Tom Donnelly and Vance Serchuk, "A Bigger, Badder, Better Army: The military needed for the Bush Doctrine," *Weekly Standard*, November 29, 2004, online.

120. *AP*, "Bolton Said to Orchestrate Unlawful Firing," *USA Today*, June 4, 2005, online.

121. *Ibid.*

122. *Ibid.*

123. Hannah M. Wallace, "A Coup in The Hague," *Mother Jones*, June 28, 2002, online.

124. Hanley, "Bolton Said to Orchestrate Unlawful Firing."

125. *Ibid.*

126. *Ibid.*

127. Michael Smith, "Ministers were told of need for Gulf war 'excuse,'" *Sunday Times* (London), June 12, 2005, http://www.timesonline.co.uk/article/0,,2087-1650822,00.html, accessed November 20, 2007; James Naughtie, *The Accidental American: Tony Blair and the Presidency* (New York: Public Affairs, 2004), pp. 119–48.

128. Naughtie, *Accidental American*, pp. 120–21.

129. *Ibid.*, p. 121.

130. Woodward, *Plan of Attack*, p. 150–51.

131. *Ibid.*, p. 151.

132. *Ibid.*, p. 164; Naughtie, *Accidental American*, pp. 123–24.

133. Woodward, *Plan of Attack*, p. 175.

134. *Ibid.*, p. 176.

135. *Ibid.*, pp. 177–78.

136. *Ibid.*, pp. 183–184; George W. Bush, "President's Remarks at the United Nations General Assembly," September 12, 2002, http://www.whitehouse.gov/news/releases/2002/09/20020912-1.html, accessed November 22, 2007.

137. *CBC News*, "Iraq agrees to admit UN weapons inspectors," *CBC News*, September 17, 2002, online.

138. United Nations Security Council, Resolution 1441 (2002), Adopted by the Security Council at its 4644th meeting, on 8 November 2002, http://daccessdds.un.org/doc/UNDOC/GEN/N02/682/26/PDF/N0268226.pdf?OpenElement, accessed November 22, 2007.

139. Justin Raimondo, "War Party Stalled," *Antiwar.com*, November 20, 2002, online.

140. Robert Fisk, "George Bush Crosses Rubicon – But What Lies Beyond?," *The Independent*, November 9, 2002, online.

141. Wilson, *Politics of Truth*, pp. 301–302.

142. Paul Gilfeather, "War, Whatever," *Daily Mirror* (London), November 22, 2002, http://

www.mirror.co.uk/news/allnews/page.cfm?obje ctid=12377231&method=full&siteid=50143, accessed December 8, 2002.

143. Richard Perle, "Why Blix Has Got It All Wrong," January 26, 2003, American Enterprise Institute, http://www.aei.org/news/newsID.15827/news_detail.asp, accessed November 20, 2007.

144. Richard Norton-Taylor, "Bush Has Little Intention of Playing by the Book," *Guardian*, December 9, 2002, online.

145. Charles Krauthammer, "No Turning Back Now," *Washington Post*, January 24, 2003, online.

146. Michael A. Ledeen, "How We Could Lose," *National Review* Online, January 9, 2003, online.

147. Bryan Burrough, Evgenia Peretz, David Rose, and David Wise, "Special Report: The Rush to Invade Iraq; The Ultimate Inside Account," *Vanity Fair*, May 2004, online.

148. Bruce B. Auster, Mark Mazzetti and Edward T. Pound, "Truth and Consequences: New questions about U.S. intelligence regarding Iraq's weapons of mass terror," *U.S. News and World Report*, June 9, 2003, online; Bryan Burrough, Evgenia Peretz, David Rose, and David Wise, "Special Report: The Rush to Invade Iraq; The Ultimate Inside Account," *Vanity Fair*, May 2004, online.

149. Bryan Burrough, Evgenia Peretz, David Rose, and David Wise, "Special Report: The Rush to Invade Iraq; The Ultimate Inside Account," *Vanity Fair*, May 2004, online.

150. *Ibid.*

151. "Transcript: Powell Draws Picture of Iraqi Deception, Links to al-Qaida,"(Secretary's address to Security Council on Iraqi violations of Res. 1441), February 5, 2003, United States Embassy in Israel, http://www.usembassy-israel.org.il/publish/press/2003/february/020601.html, accessed November 20, 2007.

152. *Ibid.*

153. "Colin Powell on Iraq, Race, and Hurricane Relief," ABC News, September 8, 2005, online.

154. Wilson, *Politics of Truth*, pp. 317–18.

155. David Corn, "The Grownup in the Room," *LA Weekly*, November 19–25, 2004 (posted November 18, 2004), http://www.laweekly.com/ink/04/52/news-corn.php, accessed November 20, 2007.

156. Woodward, *Plan of Attack*, p. 312.

157. "Transcript: Powell Draws Picture of Iraqi Deception, Links to al-Qaida,"(Secretary's address to Security Council on Iraqi violations of Res. 1441), February 5, 2003, United States Embassy in Israel, http://www.usembassy-israel.org.il/publish/press/2003/february/020601.html, accessed November 20, 2007.

158. "President Bush Addresses the Nation," *Online NewsHour* (PBS), March 17, 2003, online.

159. Joseph Cirincione, Jessica T. Mathews, and George Perkovich, "Iraq: What Next," Carnegie Endowment for International Peace, January 2003, http://www.carnegieendowment.org/files/iraq_report_final.pdf, p. 12,.

160. Hans Blix, "Notes for the briefing of the Security Council on the thirteenth quarterly report of UNMOVIC," June 5, 2003, http://www.un.org/apps/news/infocusnewsiraq.asp?NewsID=529&sID=6, accessed November 20, 2007.

161. Nicholas Watt, John Hooper and Richard Norton-Taylor, "Blix attacks Blair warnings over Iraqi weapons," *Guardian*, June 6, 2003, online.

"The riddle of the sands," *Sydney Morning Herald*, June 7, 2003, http://www.smh.com.au/articles/2003/06/06/1054700385988.html, accessed November 20, 2007.

162. Ewen MacAskill, Richard Norton-Taylor, and Suzanne Goldenberg, "I was shocked by poor weapons intelligence – Blix," *Guardian*, June 7, 2003, online.

163. "Blix criticises coalition over Iraq weapons," BBC News, June 6, 2003, online.

164. "USA Today/CNN/Gallup poll results," *USA Today*, March 20, 2003, online.

Chapter 11

1. Michael A. Ledeen, *The War Against the Terror Masters* (New York: St. Martin's Press, 2002).

2. As William O. Beeman, a frequent commentator on U.S. Middle East policy, noted shortly after the U.S. invasion of Iraq, "Ledeen's ideas are repeated daily by such figures as Richard Cheney, Donald Rumsfeld and Paul Wolfowitz. His views virtually define the stark departure from American foreign policy philosophy that existed before the tragedy of Sept. 11, 2001. He basically believes that violence in the service of the spread of democracy is America's manifest destiny. Consequently, he has become the philosophical legitimator of the American occupation of Iraq" ("Who is Michael Ledeen?," *AlterNet.org*, May 8, 2003, http://www.alternet.org/story.html?StoryID=15860, accessed November 20, 2007).

3. Unlike many neoconservatives, Ledeen did not have a leftist background, but rather saw the revolutionary aspects of the right, and even had a flirtation with fascism. Ledeen authored *Universal Fascism: The Theory and Practice of the Fascist International, 1928–1936* (New York, H. Fertig, 1972), published in 1972. In the book, Ledeen analyzed European fascism, particularly Italian fascism. Ledeen differentiated between an ideal, revolutionary "fascist movement," which he viewed favorably, and the actual reactionary, authoritarian "fascist regime" of Mussolini. Ledeen claimed that there were few similarities between fascism and Nazism. See John Laughland, "Flirting with Fascism," *American Conservative*, June 30, 2003, online.

4. Ledeen, *War Against the Terror Masters*, p. xxi.

5. *Ibid.*, p. 47.

6. *Ibid.*, p. 153.

7. *Ibid.*, p. 213.

8. David Frum and Richard Perle, *An End to Evil: How to Win the War on Terror* (New York: Random House, 2003), pp. 59.

9. Frum and Perle, *End to Evil*, pp. 8–9.

10. Georgie Anne Geyer, "War as Religion," March 6, 2003, http://www.uexpress.com/georgieannegeyer/?uc_full_date=20030306, accessed November 20, 2007.

11. Norman Podhoretz, "World War IV."

12. Ledeen, *War Against the Terror Masters*, p. 159.

13. Frum and Perle, *End to Evil*, p. 124.

14. *Ibid.*, p. 128.

15. William Kristol, et al., Project for a New American Century, Letter to President George W. Bush, April 3, 2002, http://www.newamericancentury.org/Bushletter-040302.htm, accessed November 20, 2007.

16. *Ibid.*

17. William Kristol, "Defending Zion," *First Things*, November 2007, http://www.firstthings.com/article.php3?id_article=6071, accessed January 4, 2007.

18. Ledeen, *War Against the Terror Masters*, p. 224.

19. Jamie Glazov, "*FrontPage* Interview: Michael Ledeen," *FrontPage Magazine*, December 30, 2003, online.

20. David Wurmser, "Middle East 'War': How Did It Come to This?," AEI Online, January 1, 2001,,http://www.aei.org/publications/pubID.12266/pub_detail.asp, accessed November 20, 2007.

21. Kathleen and Bill Christison, "The Bush Administration's Dual Loyalties," in *The Politics of Anti-Semitism*, eds. Alexander Cockburn and Jeffrey St. Clair (Petrolia/Oakland, CA, CounterPunch and AK Press, 2003), p. 128.

22. Robert Kagan and William Kristol, "The Gathering Storm," *The Weekly Standard*, October 29, 2001, online.

23. Eliot A. Cohen, "World War IV," *Wall Street Journal*, November 20, 2001, online.

24. "World War IV: Why We Fight, Whom We Fight, How We Fight," Symposium sponsored by the Committee on the Present Danger and The Foundation for the Defense of Democracies, September 29, 2004, http://www.defenddemocracy.org/research_topics/research_topics_show.htm?doc_id=240063, accessed November 20, 2007.

25. Cohen, "World War IV."

26. *Ibid.*

27. Charles Feldman and Stan Wilson, "Ex-CIA director: U.S. faces 'World War IV'," CNN, April 3, 2003, online.

28. Murray Polner, "The Neocons Earn an 'F'," *Antiwar.com*, June 25, 2004, online.

29. Norman Podhoretz, "How to Win World War IV," *Commentary*, February 2002, p. 27.

30. Podhoretz, "World War IV."

31. Norman Podhoretz, "In Praise of the Bush Doctrine," *Commentary*, September 2002, online.

32. "Document: The Complete Address Of Mossad Head Efraim Halevy, in a rare appearance at the NATO Council In Brussels, On September 11 World War III Started," *Yediot Ahronot*, June 28, 2002, http://www.aijac.org.au/updates/Jul-02/080702.html, accessed November 20, 2007.

33. James Bennet, "Israel Sees War in Iraq as Path to Mideast Peace," *New York Times*, February 24, 2003, online.

34. Jonathan Wright, "Israeli Ambassador to U.S. Calls for 'Regime Change' in Iran, Syria," Reuters, April 28, 2003, *CommonDreams.org*, http://www.CommonDreams.org/headlines03/0428-07.ht, accessed November 24, 2007.

35. William O. Beeman, "Military Might: The man behind 'total war' in the Mideast," *San Francisco Chronicle*, May 14, 2003, online.

36. Michael Ledeen, "Iran: Back the freedom fighters," *Jewish World Review*, June 24, 2003, online.

37. Michael Ledeen, "The Temperature Rises," *National Review Online*, November 12, 2002, online.

38. "Coalition for Democracy in Iran," *Right Web*, http://rightweb.irc-online.org/profile/1457, accessed November 20, 2007; "To Strike or Not to Strike," National American Iranian Council, May 6, 2003, http://www.niacouncil.org/pressreleases/press083.asp, accessed September 18, 2004.

39. Jim Lobe, "Neo-cons move quickly on Iran," *Asia Times*, May 28, 2003, online.

40. Marc Perelman, "New Front Sets Sights On Toppling Iran Regime," *Forward*, May 16, 2003, online.

41. *Ibid.*

42. Tom Barry, "Is Iran Next?," *In These Times*, October 25, 2004 (posted September 28, 2004), online; Robert Dreyfuss, "Agents of Influence," *Nation*, October 4, 2004, online; Joshua Micah Marshall, Laura Rozen, and Paul Glastris, "Iran-Contra II?," *Washington Monthly*, September 2004, online; James Bamford, "Back to Iran: The Next War," *Rollingstone*.com, posted July 24, 2006, online.

43. Marc Perelman, "New Front Sets Sights On Toppling Iran Regime," *Forward*, May 16, 2003, online.

44. *Ibid.*

45. Benjamin Netanyahu, Address to a Joint Session of the U.S. Congress, July 10, 1996, http://www.netanyahu.org/joinsesofusc.html, accessed November 20, 2007; Craig Unger, "From the Wonderful Folks Who Brought You Iraq," *Vanity Fair*, March 2007, online.

46. David Hirst, "Israel thrusts Iran in line of U.S. fire," *Guardian*, February 2, 2002, online.

47. Michael Donovan, "Iran, Israel and Nuclear Weapons in the Middle East," Center for Defense Information, February 14, 2002, http://www.cdi.org/terrorism/menukes.cfm, accessed November 20, 2007.

48. "FM Peres' Remarks to the Knesset on U.S. Withdrawal from the ABM Treaty," January 30, 2002, http://www.embassyofisrael.org/articles/2002/January/2002013100.html, accessed November 20, 2007.

49. "Sharon: Iran Next on War List," *NewsMax.com*, November, 8, 2002, online; Eric Margolis, "After Iraq, Bush Will Attack His Real Target," *Toronto Sun*, November 10, 2002, http://www.CommonDreams.org/views02/1110-07.htm, accessed November 20, 2007.

50. Aluf Benn, "Sharon says U.S. should also disarm Iran, Libya and Syria," *Ha'aretz*, February 20, 2003, online.

51. "Iran's nuclear program 'threatens existence of Israel': Mossad chief," November 17, 2003, SpaceWar, http://www.spacewar.com/2003/031117155608.6720u0sh.html, accessed November 20, 2007.

52. Gavin Rabinowitz, "Israel: Iran is No. 1 sponsor of terror," Associated Press, December 16, 2003, http://www.independent-media.tv/item.cfm?fmedia_id=4449&fcategory_desc=Iran, accessed September 15, 2004.

53. Nicole Gaouette, "Israel: Iran is now danger No. 1," *Christian Science Monitor*, November 28, 2003, online; "Israeli plans for Iran attack," Aljazeera. Net, October 12, 2003, http://english.aljazeera.net/English/archive/archive?ArchiveId=40549, accessed November 20, 2007.

54. Michael A. Ledeen, The Terror Masters Revisited," *National Review* Online, August 16, 2004, online.

55. Michael A. Ledeen, "The Iraqis and the Neocons: Arab democracy is a work in progress," *National Review* Online, June 28, 2004, online.

56. Michael A. Ledeen, "The Discovery of Iran: Are you sitting down? Iran is a terrorist state," *National Review* Online, July 19, 2004, online.

57. *Ibid.*

58. David Wurmser, "The Saudi Connection: Osama bin Laden's a Lot Closer to the Saudi Royal Family Than You Think," *Weekly Standard*, October 29, 2001, online, accessed November 20, 2007.

59. Max Singer, "Free the Eastern Province of Saudi Arabia," *American Outlook Today*, May 16,

2002, http://www.hudson.org/index.cfm?fuseaction=publication_details&id=1659, accessed November 20, 2007.

60. "Ambassador Dore Gold," Jerusalem Center for Public Affairs, http://www.jcpa.org/dgold.htm, accessed November 20, 2007; Gary Leupp, "On Terrorism, Methodism, Saudi 'Wahhabism' and the Censored 9–11 Report," *CounterPunch.org*, August 8, 2003, online.

61. Dore Gold, *Hatred's Kingdom: How Saudi Arabia Supports the New Global Terrorism* (Washington: Regnery Publishing, Inc., 2003), p. 245.

62. Gold, *Hatred's Kingdom*, p. 247.

63. Thomas E. Ricks, "Briefing Depicted Saudis as Enemies," *Washington Post*, August 6, 2002, p. A-1; Jack Shafer, "The PowerPoint That Rocked the Pentagon; The LaRouchie defector who's advising the defense establishment on Saudi Arabia," *Slate*, August 7, 2002, online; Alan Weisman, *Prince of Darkness*, pp. 175–78.

64. Ricks, *ibid.*; Shafer, *ibid.*; Weisman, *ibid.*

65. Ricks, *ibid.*; Shafer, *ibid.*

66. Frum and Perle, *End to Evil*, p. 138; see also Weisman, *Prince of Darkness*, p. 178.

67. Frum and Perle, *End to Evil*, pp. 141–42.

68. *Ibid.*, p. 139.

69. *Ibid.*

70. Gary Leupp, "On Terrorism, Methodism, Saudi 'Wahhabism' and the Censored 9–11 Report," *CounterPunch.org*, August 8, 2003, online; Sasha Lilly, "A New Age of Empire in the Middle East, Courtesy of the U.S. and UK," *CommonDreams.org*, November 10, 2002, http://www.CommonDreams.org/views02/1110-03.htm, accessed November 23, 2007.

71. Ricks, "Briefing Depicted Saudis as Enemies," p. A-1.

72. Barbara Slavin, "Anti-Saudi arguments get heard," *USA Today*, August 8, 2002, http://www.usatoday.com/news/world/2002-08-08-saudi_x.htm, accessed November 20, 2007.

73. Simon Henderson, "The Coming Saudi Showdown," *Weekly Standard*, July 15, 2002, online; Victor Davis Hanson, "Our Enemies, the Saudis," *Commentary*, July/August 2002, online; see also: Simon Henderson, "The Saudi Way," *Wall Street Journal*, August 12, 2002, online; Claudia Rosett, "Free Arabia," *Wall Street Journal*, August 14, 2002, online.

74. Victor Davis Hanson, "Our Enemies, the Saudis," *Commentary*, July-August 2002, online.

75. *Ibid,*

76. *Ibid,*

77. Stephen Schwartz, "Trotskycons?," *National Review* Online, June 11, 2003, online.

78. William Kristol, Quoted on promotional page at Amazon.com, http://www.amazon.com/Two-Faces-Islam-Tradition-Terror/dp/product-

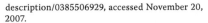

description/0385506929, accessed November 20, 2007.

79. Stephen Schwartz, *The Two Faces of Islam: The House of Sa'ud from Tradition to Terror*, (New York: Doubleday, 2002), p. xiii.

80. Schwartz, *The Two Faces of Islam: The House of Sa'ud from Tradition to Terror*, pp. 117–18.

81. "Osama Tape Rails Against Saudis," December 16, 2004, *CBS News*, online.

82. Schwartz, *Two Faces of Islam*, pp. 175–76.

83. *Ibid.*, p. 260.

84. *Ibid.*, p. 177.

85. *Ibid.*, p. 179–80.

86. *Ibid.*, p. 181.

87. *Ibid.*, p. 180.

88. *Ibid.*, p. 149.

89. *Ibid.*, p. 167.

90. *Ibid.*, p. 282.

91. Ronald Radosh, "State Department Outrage: The Firing of Stephen Schwartz," *FrontPageMagazine.com*, July 2, 2002, online; Stephen Schwartz, "Defeating Wahhabism," *FrontPageMagazine.com*, October 25, 2002, online; William Safire, "State Out of Step," *New York Times*, July 1, 2002, p. A-15.

92. Stephen Schwartz, "What Is 'Islamofascism'?," *TCS Daily*, August 16, 2006, http://www.tcsdaily.com/article.aspx?id=081606C, accessed November 20, 2007.

93. Elizabeth Drew, "The Neocons in Power," *New York Review of Books*, June 12, 2003, online.

94. Hanson, "Our Enemies, the Saudis."

95. Michael Ledeen, "Creative Destruction," *National Review* Online, September 20, 2001, online.

96. Michael Ledeen, "Scowcroft Strikes Out," *National Review* Online, August 6, 2002, online.

97. This point is emphasized in Mearsheimer and Walt, "The Israel Lobby," *London Review of Books*. As noted, an extended version of this article was published as a Faculty Research Working Paper at Harvard University's John F. Kennedy School of Government, in which they write: ""More importantly, saying that Israel and the United States are united by a shared terrorist threat has the causal relationship backwards: rather, the United States has a terrorism problem in good part because it is so closely allied with Israel, not the other way around. U.S. support for Israel is not the only source of anti-American terrorism, but it is an important one, and it makes winning the war on terror more difficult" (p. 5).

Chapter 12

1. Quoted in Wilson, *Politics of Truth*, p. 311.

2. *FOX News*, "Bush Discusses Post-Hussein Iraq," *FOXNews.com*, February 27, 2003, online.

3. The White House, "President Bush Discusses Freedom in Iraq and Middle East," Press Release, November 6, 2003, http://www.whitehouse.gov/news/releases/2003/11/20031106-2.html, accessed April 6, 2008.

4. The White House, "President Sworn-In to Second Term," January 20, 2005, Press Release, http://www.whitehouse.gov/news/releases/2005/01/20050120-1.html, accessed November 20, 2007.

5. Tom Barry, "Elliott Abrams: the Neocon's Neocon," *CounterPunch.org*, February 9, 2005, online; Tom Barry, "Natan Sharansky and U.S. Israel Policy," *Antiwar.com*, February 8, 2005, online; Dan Balz and Jim VandeHei, "Bush Speech Not a Sign of Policy Shift, Officials Say," *Washington Post*, January 22, 2005, p. A-1.

6. Terry M. Neal, "Bush Backs Into Nation Building," *Washington Post*, February 26, 2003, online.

7. William E. Odom, "Victory Is Not an Option," *Washington Post*, February 11, 2007, p. B-1.

8. Norman Levine, "Neocon cabal's dilemmas," UPI, November 4, 2005, Monsters and Critics.com, online.

9. Murray Polner, "The Neocons Earn an 'F'," *Antiwar.com*, June 25, 2004, online.

10. Norman Podhoretz, "In Praise of the Bush Doctrine," *Commentary*, September 2002, online.

11. Jonah Goldberg, "Delay democracy in Iraq," *Jewish World Review*, May 2, 2003, online.

12. Bruce Fein, "Post-Saddam Iraq," *Washington Times*, April 1, 2003, online; Fein was a longtime proponent of neoconservative positions, although he became strongly critical of the Bush II administration's diminution of civil liberties and expansion of presidential power. Phone interview with Paul Gottfried, historian of modern American conservatism, November 12, 2007.

13. Frum and Perle, *End to Evil*, p. 162.

14. Max Boot, "The Case for American Empire," *Weekly Standard*, October 15, 2001, online.

15. Douglas Feith, "Reflections on Liberalism, Democracy and Zionism," Digital Media Tree, http://www.digitalmediatree.com/onelap/warofwords/?21702, accessed November 20, 2007.

16. Brian Whitaker, "Jordan prince touted to succeed Saddam," *Guardian*, July 19, 2002, online.

17. David Wurmser, *Tyranny's Ally: America's Failure to Defeat Saddam Hussein* (Washington: AEI Press, 1999), pp. 80–93.

18. David Wurmser, *Tyranny's Ally*, pp. 87–88.

19. Tony Harnden, "David Wurmser: a neocon unbowed," *Tony Harnden Blog*, October 4, 2007, http://blogs.telegraph.co.uk/foreign/tobyharnden/oct07/david-wurmser.htm, accessed January 6, 2008.

20. Marc Perelman, "New Front Sets Sights On Toppling Iran Regime," *Forward*, May 16, 2003,

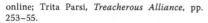

online; Trita Parsi, *Treacherous Alliance*, pp. 253–55.

21. "Shah of Iran's Heir Plans Overthrow of Regime," HumanEvents.com, May 1, 2006, http://www.humanevents.com/article.php?print=yes&id=14424, accessed November 20, 2007.

22. The Institute for Advanced Strategic and Political Studies' "Study Group on a New Israeli Strategy Toward 2000," "A Clean Break: A New Strategy for Securing the Realm," 1996 http://www.israeleconomy.org/strat1.htm, accessed November 20, 2007.

23. Noam Chomsky, "The Iraq War and Contempt for Democracy," *CounterPunch.org*, November 14/23, 2003, online; Noam Chomsky, *Hegemony or Survival*, p. 131.

24. Noam Chomsky, *Hegemony or Survival*, p. 131.

25. Frum and Perle, *End to Evil*, p. 245.

26. H. D. S. Greenway, "The neoconservative style of democracy," *Daily Times* (Pakistan), http://www.dailytimes.com.pk/default.asp?page=story_18-5-2003_pg4_15, accessed November 20, 2007.

27. Christopher Deliso, "Valiant Neocons, Spanish Appeasers: Manipulating Madrid's Tragedy," *Antiwar.com*, March 18, 2004, online.

28. Stephen Khan, Francis Elliott, and Peter Boehm, "Massacre in Uzbekistan," *The Independent*, May 15, 2005, http://news.independent.co.uk/world/asia/article221555.ece, accessed November 20, 2007.

29. Don Van Natta Jr., "U.S. relying on regime notorious for torture?," *Seattle Times*, May 1, 2005, http://seattletimes.nwsource.com/html/nationworld/2002259115_rend01.html, accessed November 20, 2007.

30. U.S. Department of State, Bureau of European and Eurasian Affairs, "Background Note: Uzbekistan," February 2005, http://www.state.gov/r/pa/ei/bgn/2924.htm, accessed November 20, 2007.

31. Marc Perelman, "Uzbek Unrest Shines Light on Leader's Ties to Jewry," *Forward*, May 27, 2005, online.

32. Stephen Schwartz, "How Shall Freedom be Defended?," *Weekly Standard*, July 17, 2003, online.

33. *Ibid.*

34. Edward M. Kennedy, "Bush's Distortions Misled Congress in Its War Vote," *Los Angeles Times*, March 19, 2004, online.

35. Ron Paul, "Is Congress Relevant with Regards to War?," October 3, 2002, http://www.house.gov/paul/congrec/congrec2002/cr100302.htm, accessed November 20, 2007.

36. Office of U.S. Representative Ron Paul, "Paul Calls for Congressional Declaration of War with Iraq," Press Release, http://www.house.gov/paul/

press/press2002/pr100402.htm, accessed November 20, 2007.

37. "President Bush Outlines Iraqi Threat," Remarks by the President on Iraq, Cincinnati Museum Center – Cincinnati Union Terminal, Cincinnati, Ohio, October 7, 2002, http://www.whitehouse.gov/news/releases/2002/10/20021007-8.html, accessed November 20, 2007.

38. John W. Warner, "The War Debate," *Los Angeles Times*, October 9, 2002, online.

39. Alison Mitchell and Carl Hulse, "Congress Authorizes Bush to Use Force against Iraq, Creating a Broad Mandate," *New York Times*, October 11, 2002, p. A-1; "Floor Speech of Senator Hillary Rodham Clinton on S.J. Res. 45, A Resolution to Authorize the Use of United States Armed Forces Against Iraq," October 10, 2002, http://clinton.senate.gov/speeches/iraq_101002.html, accessed November 20, 2007.

40. Wilson, *Politics of Truth*, p. 300.

41. Dean, *Worse Than Watergate*, pp. 146–56.

42. Dana Milbank and Walter Pincus, "Asterisks Dot White House's Iraq Argument," *Washington Post*, November 12, 2005, p. A-1.

43. The act's full name is "The Uniting and Strengthening America by Providing Appropriate Tools Required to Intercept and Obstruct Terrorism (USA PATRIOT ACT) Act of 2001."

44. Charles Doyle, "The USA PATRIOT Act: A Sketch," CRS Report for Congress, April 18, 2002, http://www.fas.org/irp/crs/RS21203.pdf, accessed April 6, 2008; "Return of the Patriot Act," editorial, *New York Times*, November 18, 2005, p. A-28; "An Unpatriotic Act," editorial, *New York Times*, August 25, 2003, p. A-14.

45. Jonathan Alter, "Bush's Snoopgate," *Newsweek*, (Web exclusive) December 19, 2005, online.

46. Editorial, "Unauthorized Snooping," *Washington Post*, December 20, 2005, p. A-30.

47. Kathleen Hennessey, "Ex-President Carter: Eavesdropping illegal," *Associated Press*, February 6, 2006, http://www.breitbart.com/article.php?id=D8FJUP882&show_article=1, accessed February 9, 2008.

48. James Bovard, "Bush's Signing Statement Dictatorship," *LewRockwell.com*, October 11, 2006, http://www.lewrockwell.com/bovard/bovard35.html, accessed December 13, 2007; Jennifer Van Bergen, "The Unitary Executive: The Doctrine Behind the Bush Presidency Consistent with a Democratic State?," FindLaw Writ, January 9, 2006, http://writ.news.findlaw.com/commentary/20060109_bergen.html, accessed December 14, 2007.

49. Paul Craig Roberts, "Bush Has Crossed the Rubicon," *Antiwar.com*, January 16, 2006, online.

50. Frum and Perle, *End to Evil*, p. 74.

51. *Ibid.*, p. 82.

52. Jamie Glazov, "Frontpage Interview: Richard Pipes," *FrontPageMagazine.com*, January 19, 2004, online; Fatima Sayyed, "Bush Nominates Daniel Pipes to Board of US Institute of Peace," *Pakistan Today*, April 15, 2003, http://www.danielpipes.org/article/1061, accessed February 9, 2008; Michael Scherer, "Daniel Pipes, Peacemaker?," *Mother Jones*, May 26, 2003, online; "Fueling a Culture Clash," editorial, *Washington Post*, April 19, 2003, p. A12; Zachary Lockman, "Critique from the Right: The Neo-conservative Assault on Middle East Studies," *CR: The New Centennial Review*, 5.1 (Spring 2005), pp. 63-110. It should be noted that Pipes was a staunch defender of Israel and opponent of any Palestinian state. He wrote in *Commentary* in April 1990: "There can be either an Israel or a Palestine, but not both. To think that two states can stably and peacefully coexist in the small territory between the Jordan River and the Mediterranean Sea is to be either naïve or duplicitous. If the last seventy years teach anything, it is that there can be only one state west of the Jordan River. Therefore, to those who ask why the Palestinians must be deprived of a state, the answer is simple: grant them one and you set in motion a chain of events that will lead either to its extinction or the extinction of Israel"("Can the Palestinians Make Peace?," *Commentary*, April 1990, http://www.danielpipes.org/article/194, accessed February 9, 2008). According to the Middle East Forum website: "The Middle East Forum, a think tank, seeks to define and promote American interests in the Middle East. It defines U.S. interests to include fighting radical Islam, whether terroristic or lawful; working for Palestinian acceptance of Israel; improving the management of U.S. democracy efforts; reducing energy dependence on the Middle East; more robustly asserting U.S. interests vis-à-vis Saudi Arabia; and countering the Iranian threat. The Forum also works to improve Middle East studies in North America" ("About the Middle East Forum," *Middle East Forum*, http://www.meforum.org/about.php, accessed February 9, 2008).

53. Daniel Pipes, "Why the Japanese Internment Still Matters," *New York Sun*, December 28, 2004, www.danielpipes.org/article/2309, accessed November 21, 2007.

54. Joel Beinin, "The New American McCarthyism: policing thought about the Middle East," *Race & Class*, 46:1, (2004), pp. 101–15, http://www-personal.umich.edu/~hfc/mideast/newmccarthy.pdf, accessed November 21, 2007.

55. Frum and Perle, *End to Evil*, pp. 91–92.

56. *Ibid.*, p. 89.

57. *Ibid.*, pp. 93–94.

58. Michael Kinsley, "The Neocons' Unabashed Reversal," *Washington Post*, April 17, 2005, p. B-7.

59. Ehrman, *Rise of Neoconservatism*, p. 119.

60. Jean J. Kirkpatrick, "Dictatorships and Dou-
ble Standards," *Commentary*, November 1979, pp. 37–38, quoted by John Ehrman, *Rise of Neoconservatism*, p. 120.

61. Michael Kinsley, "The Neocons' Unabashed Reversal," *Washington Post*, April 17, 2005, p. B-7.

62. See note 46 in Ehrman, *Rise of Neoconservatism*, p. 222, which refers to historian J. David Hoeveler, Jr.'s analysis of Kirkpatrick's thinking.

63. Paul Craig Roberts, "Neo-Jacobins Push For World War IV," *LewRockwell.com*, September 20, 2003, http://www.lewrockwell.com/roberts/roberts8.html, accessed November 21, 2007; Claes G. Ryn, *America the Virtuous: The Crisis of Democracy and the Quest for Empire* (New Brunswick, NJ: Transaction Publishers, 2003).

64. Regarding Leo Strauss' view of democracy, Shadia Drury, the author of *Leo Strauss and the American Right* (New York: St. Martin's Press, 1997), said: "Strauss was neither a liberal nor a democrat. Perpetual deception of the citizens by those in power is critical [in Strauss's view] because they need to be led, and they need strong rulers to tell them what's good for them" (quoted in Jim Lobe, "Neocons dance a Strauss waltz," *Asia Times*, May 9, 2003, online).

Chapter 13

1. For the various arguments used to explain the missing WMD see Stephen J. Sniegoski, "The WMD Lies," *The Last Ditch*, August 4, 2003, http://www.thornwalker.com/ditch/snieg_wmd_main.htm, accessed November 23, 2007.

2. Courtland Milloy, "War Hawks Blinded by Hardened Hearts," *Washington Post*, March 31, 2003, p. B-1.

3. Podhoretz, "World War IV"

4. Department of Defense, "Secretary Rumsfeld Media Availability with Jay Garner," News Transcript, June 18, 2003, http://www.defenselink.mil/transcripts/2003/tr20030618-secdef0282.html, accessed November 20, 2007.

5. Department of Defense, "Deputy Secretary Wolfowitz on MSNBC *Hardball*," News Transcript, June 23, 2004, http://www.defenselink.mil/transcripts/transcript.aspx?transcriptid=3350, accessed February 9, 2008.

6. Podhoretz, "World War IV."

7. John Solomon, "U.S. poll of Iraqis finds widespread anger at prison abuse, worry about safety," *AP*, June 15, 2004, *Factiva* document A PRS000020040615e06f00now (content partially reprinted at http://www.newsbull.com/forum/more.asp?TOPIC_ID=15695, accessed February 9, 2008).

8. Editorial, "The South Park Division," *Weekly Standard*, January 12, 2004, online.

9. Michael Ledeen, "The Jihad on Iraq: Bad analysis and bad policy," *National Review* Online, January 26, 2004, online.

10. Michael Rubin, "Iraqi Democrats Feeling Sidelined," *Los Angeles Times*, April 4, 2004, online.

11. "Crunch Time in Baghdad," *Wall Street Journal*, April 6, 2004, p. A. 16 ; "Jim Lobe, "Neocons See Iran Behind Shiite Uprising," *Antiwar.com*, April 10, 2004, online; Rowan Scarborough, "U.S. sees Syria 'facilitating' insurgents," *Washington Times*, April 21, 2004, online.

12. Mona Charen, "Are we tough enough?," *Townhall.com*, April 9, 2004, online.

13. William Kristol and Lewis E. Lehrman, "Crush the Insurgents in Iraq," *Washington Post*, May 23, 2004, p. B-7.

14. Jim Lobe, "Neocons Go Macho on Iraq," *Antiwar.com*, May 25, 2004, online.

15. Richard Morin and Dan Balz, "Bush Loses Advantage in War on Terrorism: Nation Evenly Divided on President, Kerry," *Washington Post*, June 22, 2004, p. A1.

16. "Poll: Sending troops to Iraq a mistake," CNN.com, June 25, 2004, online.

17. Norman Podhoretz, "World War IV."

18. Paul Richter, "A Tough Time for 'Neocons,'" *Los Angeles Times*, June 10, 2004, online.

19. Jim Lobe, "The Rout of the Neo-cons," *Asia Times*, June 3, 2004, online.

20. Patrick J. Buchanan, "The dog days of the War Party," *WorldNetDaily.com*, June 7, 2004, online; see also: Tom Engelhardt, "Tomgram: The way we were," TomDispatch.com, July 6, 2004, http://www.tomdispatch.com/index.mhtml?pid=1528, accessed November 21, 2007.

21. Howard LaFranchi, "In foreign-policy battles, are neocons losing their hold?," *Christian Science Monitor*, July 13, 2004, online.

22. Robert Novak, "The military will tell the election winner there are insufficient U.S. forces in Iraq to wage effective war," *Chicago Sun-Times*, September 20, 2004, online.

23. James Mann, "Bush's Team Has Only a Spent Vision," *Financial Times*, July 7, 2004, online.

24. Moisés Naím, "Casualties of War," *Foreign Policy*, September/October 2004, online.

25. Martin Sieff, "Neocon vs. Neocon," *Salon*, August 30, 2004, online.

26. Libby would be indicted October 28, 2005 and would face trial in a federal court. On March 6, 2007, Libby was found guilty of two counts of perjury, one count of making false statements, and one count of obstruction of justice. Carol D. Leonnig and Amy Goldstein, "Libby Found Guilty in CIA Leak Case," *Washington Post*, March 7, 2007, p. A-1.

27. Marc Perelman, "Neocons Blast Bush's Inaction On 'Spy' Affair," *Forward*, September 10, 2004, online.

28. Michael Ledeen, "An Improbable Molehunt," *National Review* Online, August 31, 2004, online.

29. David Frum, "Jewish Conspiracies in the Pentagon," *National Review* Online, August 30, 2004, online.

30. *Ibid.*

31. Richard Sale, "FBI steps up AIPAC probe," United Press International, *Washington Times*, December 10, 2004, online.

32. Scheuer, *Imperial Hubris*, p. 9.

33. *Ibid.*, p. 227.

34. David Frum, "Uncertain Trumpet," *National Review* Online, September 27, 2004, online.

35. *Ibid.*

36. Tom Regan, "Neocons revive Committee on the Present Danger," *Christian Science Monitor*, July 23, 2004, online; Committee on the Present Danger, "Members," http://www.committeeonthepresentdanger.org/OurMembers/tabid/364/Default.aspx, accessed February 9, 2008.

37. Regan, *ibid.*

38. George W. Bush, "President's Remarks to the General Conference of the National Guard Association of the United States," September 14, 2004, http://www.whitehouse.gov/news/releases/2004/09/20040914-23.html, accessed November 22, 2007.

39. Richard and Lynne Cheney, "Vice President and Mrs. Cheney's Remarks in Wilmington, Ohio," October 25, 2004, http://www.whitehouse.gov/news/releases/2004/10/20041026-7.html, accessed November 22, 2007.

40. Justin Raimondo, "Indict the War Party For Treason," *Antiwar.com*, September 20, 2004, online.

41. Quoted in Thomas E. Woods, Jr., "The Progressive Peacenik Myth," *American Conservative*, August 2, 2004, online.

42. Justin Raimondo, "The Neoconservative Moment," *Antiwar.com*, June 18, 2004, online.

43. John Kerry, "Making America Secure Again: Setting the Right Course for Foreign Policy,"
An Address to the Council on Foreign Relations, December 3, 2003, http://www.cfr.org/pub6576/john_f_kerry/making_america_secure_again_setting_the_right_course_for_foreign_policy.php, accessed November 22, 2007.

44. Tom Curry, "Kerry warns of 'cut and run in Iraq,'" *MSNBC.com*, December 3, 2003, online.

45. John F. Kerry, "A Realistic Path in Iraq," *Washington Post*, July 4, 2004, p. B-7.

46. Dan Balz and Jim VandeHei, "McCain's Resistance Doesn't Stop Talk of Kerry Dream Ticket," *Washington Post*, June 12, 2004, p. A-1.

47. Although the neoconservatives and their "theology" are also deeply ensconced in the Democratic party, notwithstanding the feelings of the rank-and-file members, as Paul Gottfried's remarks concluding his introduction to this book – and the actual Democratic policies noted in this chapter – serve to illustrate.

Chapter 14

1. Jacob Heilbrunn, "The Neocons Last Gasp? Not So Fast," *Los Angeles Times*, November 17, 2003, online.

2. Scott McConnell, "Realists Rebuffed," *American Conservative*, December 20, 2004, online.

3. Jim VandeHei and Michael A. Fletcher, "Bush Says Election Ratified Iraq Policy; No U.S. Troop Withdrawal Date Is Set," *Washington Post*, January 16, 2005, p. A-1.

4. As Robert Scheer pointed out: "Actually, the election provided no such moment of accountability because both major-party candidates had supported the war. John Kerry had voted to authorize the use of force against Iraq – and then inexplicably said on the campaign trail that he would have voted the same way even after learning that Congress and the American public had been deceived on the war's justification. The Democratic Party nominee even endorsed larger troop commitments to occupy a country where every Western soldier on the ground fuels nationalist and religious rage" ("Pomp and Improper Circumstance," *Nation*, (posted) January 18, 2005, online).

5. Alan Elsner, "Neoconservatives Gain Strength in New Bush Team," Reuters, November 17, 2004, http://in.news.yahoo.com/041117/137/2hxep.html, accessed November 22, 2007.

6. Robert Scheer, "The Peter Principle and the Neocon Coup," *Los Angeles Times*, November 17, 2004, online; see also: Paul Craig Roberts, "There Is No One Left to Stop Them," *Antiwar.com*, November 19, 2004, online.

7. Editorial, "Politics and the C.I.A.," *New York Times*, November 18, 2004, online.

8. Philip Giraldi, "Deep Background," *American Conservative*, December 20, 2004, p. 23.

9. Editorial, "Politics and the C.I.A.," *New York Times*, November 18, 2004, online.

10. Josh Meyers, "CIA Official Challenges Agency on Terrorism," *Los Angeles Times*, November 9. 2004, online.

11. Julian Borger, "CIA Memo Urging Spies To Support Bush Provokes Furor," *Guardian*, November 18, 2004, online.

12. David Brooks, "The C.I.A. Versus Bush," *New York Times*, November 13, 2004, online.

13. Michael Ledeen, "Time For a Good, Old-Fashioned Purge," *National Review* Online, March 7, 2001, online.

14. Warren P. Strobel and Jonathan S. Landay, "Post-election purge, reform appears likely within CIA," Knight Ridder Newspapers, October 22, 2004, online; Paul Craig Roberts, "There Is No One Left to Stop Them," *Antiwar.com*, November 19, 2004, online.

15. Julian Borger, "CIA Memo Urging Spies To Support Bush Provokes Furore," *Guardian*, November 18, 2004, online.

16. Amy Goodman, "Iran: The Next Strategic Target," (Interview with Seymour Hersh), Democracy Now, January 19, 2005, http://www.alternet.org/waroniraq/21021/, accessed November 22, 2007.

17. Haviland Smith, "Dubious Purge at the CIA," *Washington Post*, January 4, 2005, p. A-15.

18. Tom Barry, "The Vulcans Consolidate Power," *CounterPunch.org*, November 20/21, 2004, online.

19. John F. Harris and Christopher Muste, "56 Percent in Survey Say Iraq War Was a Mistake," *Washington Post*, December 21, 2004, p. A-4.

20. National Annenberg Election Survey, January 17, 2005, http://www.annenbergpublicpolicycenter.org/Downloads/Political_Communication/naes/2005_03_inauguration_01-17_pr.pdf, accessed December 31, 2007.

21. Doyle McManus, "Support for War in Iraq Hits New Low," *Los Angeles Times*, January 19, 2005, online.

22. Tim Dickinson, "The Return of the Draft," *Rollingstone*, posted Jan 27, 2005, online.

23. Patrick J. Buchanan, "The Neocons Haven't Won Yet," *Antiwar.com*, December 15, 2004, online.

24. Brent Scowcroft, Zbigniew Brzezinski, and Steve Clemons, "Charting a U.S. Foreign Policy Road Map for 2005 and Beyond" (transcript), New Solarium Project on U.S. Foreign Policy, New America Foundation, January 6, 2005, http://www.thewashingtonnote.com/archives/Brzezinski-Scowcroft%20Transcript.doc, accessed February 9, 2008.

25. *Ibid.*

26. Barry Schweid, Associated Press, "Baker advises administration to consider a phased withdrawal of troops," *San Francisco Chronicle*, January 13, 2005, online; Matthew B. Stannard, "Aide to Bush's father urges pullout," *San Francisco Chronicle*, January 14, 2005, online.

27. James Dobbins, "Iraq: Winning the Unwinnable War," *Foreign Affairs*, January/February 2005, online.

28. Alexander Cockburn, "Will Bush Quit Iraq?," *CounterPunch.org*, January 19, 2005, online.

29. George W. Bush, "There Is No Justice Without Freedom," Second Inaugural Address, *Washington Post*, January 21, 2005, p. A-24.

30. Editorial, "The Rhetoric of Freedom," *Washington Post*, January 21, 2005, p. A-16.

31. Tom Barry, "Elliott Abrams: the Neocon's Neocon," *CounterPunch.org*, February 9, 2005, online; Tom Barry, "Natan Sharansky and U.S. Israel Policy," *Antiwar.com*, February 8, 2005, online; Dan Balz and Jim VandeHei, "Bush Speech Not a Sign of Policy Shift, Officials Say," *Washington Post*, January 22, 2005, p. A-1.

32. Dana Milbank, "An Israeli Hawk Accepts the President's Invitation," *Washington Post*, November 23, 2004, p. A-27.

33. William Kristol, "On Tyranny," *Weekly Standard*, January 31, 2005, online.

34. Andrew Sullivan, "The Daily Dish," January 20, 2005, http://www.andrewsullivan.com/, accessed November 22, 2007.

35. Sidney Blumenthal, "A state of chaos," *Guardian*, December 30, 2004, online.

36. Flynt Leverett, *Inheriting Syria: Bashar's Trial By Fire* (Washington: Brookings Institution Press, 2005), p. 8.

37. Leverett, *Inheriting Syria*, pp. 10–15.

38. Flynt Leverett, *Inheriting Syria*, pp. 142–44.

39. David Wurmser, Institute for Advanced Strategic and Political Studies, "Coping with Crumbling States: A Western and Israeli Balance of Power Strategy for the Levant," 1996, http://www.israeleconomy.org/strat2a.htm, accessed November 22, 2007.

40. Daniel Pipes and Ziad Abdelnour, "Ending Syria's Occupation of Lebanon: The U.S. Role," Report of the Lebanon Study Group, May 2000, http://www.meforum.org/research/lsg.php, accessed November 22, 2007.

41. Quoted in Leverett, *Inheriting Syria*, p. 152.

42. "Powell Calls on Syria to Adapt to 'New Strategic Situation,'" May 4,2003, American Embassy in Tel Aviv, http://www.usembassy-israel.org.il/publish/press/2003/may/050403.html, accessed November 22, 2007.

43. "Syria's Next," Arutz Sheva – IsraelNationalNews.com, April 10, 2003, http://www.arutzsheva.org/print.php3?what=news&id=41867, accessed April 4, 2005.

44. John R. Bolton, "Syria's Weapons of Mass Destruction and Missile Development Programs," Testimony Before the House International Relations Committee, Subcommittee on the Middle East and Central Asia, September 16, 2003, http://www.state.gov/t/us/rm/24135.htm, accessed November 22, 2007.

45. Leverett, *Inheriting Syria*, p. 144.

46. Richard Carlson, Barbara Newman and William Cowan, "Syria's murderous role," *Washington Times*, December 6, 2004, online.

47. William Kristol, "Getting Serious About Syria," *Weekly Standard*, December 20, 2004, online.

48. "U.S. Slams Syria for Exporting Middle East Terror," Reuters, February 8, 2005, http://www.unitedjerusalem.org/index2.asp?id=552548&Date=2/11/2005, accessed November 22, 2007.

49. Jim Lobe," "Hariri Killing Sure to Bolster U.S. Hawks," *Antiwar.com*, February 16, 2005, online; Robin Wright and Peter Baker, "U.S. Tensions With Syria Escalate," *Washington Post*, February 17, 2005, p. A-1; Flynt Leverett, *Inheriting Syria*, p. 144.

50. Israel Shahak, *Open Secrets: Israeli Nuclear and Foreign Policies* (London ; Chicago, Ill. : Pluto Press, 1997), pp. 47–53.

51. Bill Van Auken, "The assassination of Rafiq Hariri: who benefited?," *World Socialist Web Site*, February 17, 2005, http://www.wsws.org/articles/2005/feb2005/hari-f17.shtml, accessed November 22, 2007.

52. Quoted by Patrick Seale, "A new struggle for Syria is in the making," *Daily Star* (Lebanon), May 16, 2005, online.

53. Leverett, *Inheriting Syria*, p. 1.

54. Associated Press, "UN: Hariri killed by criminal network," *Jerusalem Post*, March 28, 2008, online; Edith M. Lederer, "Investigator: Hariri Killed by Criminals," *ABC News*, March 28, 2008, online; "Bellemare's first report on Hariri assassination," Tenth report of the International Independent Investigation Commission based on UN resolutions 1595 (2005), 1636 (2005), 1644 (2005), 1686 (2006) and 1748 (2007), *Ya Libnan*, March 29, 2008, http://yalibnan.com/site/archives/2008/03/bellemares_firs.php, accessed April 28, 2008. Considering the assassination from the standpoint of who had something to gain from it – and who stood to loose – opens up a much wider range of possible perpetrators. Patrick Seale pointed out that if the assassination had been in fact carried out by Syria, "it must be judged an act of political suicide" ("Who killed Rafik Hariri?," *Guardian*, February 23, 2005,online). From Naseer H. Aruri's point of view, "the important questions are, what the crime will lead to in geo-political terms, and who the greatest beneficiaries are?" ("The Politics of Hariri's Assassination," *Counterpunch.org*, February 22, 2005, online). His conclusion is illuminating: "Hariri's death [as we have noted], no matter who arranged it, is the perfect opportunity to implement the Israeli/US strategy, and revisit Israel's frustrated plans of 1982." Robert Fisk confirmed this indirectly when he wrote that "Lebanon is built on institutions that enshrine sectarianism as a creed.... Anyone setting out to murder Hariri would know how this could re-open all the fissures of the civil war from 1975 to 1990" ("The killing of 'Mr Lebanon': Rafik Hariri assassinated in Beirut bomb blast," *Independent*, February 15, 2005, online).

55. James Risen and David E. Sanger, "G.I.'s and Syrians in Tense Clashes on Iraqi Border," *New York Times*, October 15, 2005, online; Ferry Biedermann, "Syria: A New Iraq in the Making," *Antiwar.com*, September 17, 2005, online.

56. James Risen and David E. Sanger, "G.I.'s and Syrians in Tense Clashes on Iraqi Border," *New York Times*, October 15, 2005, online.

57. Paul Richter, "Despite Warnings, U.S. Leans on Syria," *Los Angeles Times*, October 31, 2005, online.

58. "Israeli leaders call for regime change in Syria after assassination report," Associated Press, October 21, 2005, Israel Insider, http://web.israelinsider.com/Articles/Diplomacy/6879.htm, accessed November 22, 2007.

59. *Ibid.*

60. *Ibid.*

61. Parsi, *Treacherous Alliance*, pp. 225–27; Michael Donovan, "Iran, Israel and Nuclear Weapons in the Middle East," Center for Defense Information, February 14, 2002, http://www.cdi.org/terrorism/menukes-pr.cfm, accessed November 22, 2007; Gareth Porter, "Burnt Offering," *American Prospect, May 21*, 2006, online; John Newhouse and Thomas R. Pickering, "Getting Iran Right," *Washington Post*, December 28, 2001, p. A-23.

62. Parsi, *Treacherous Alliance*, pp. 233–34. Regarding the truth of the Karine A episode, Parsi mentions other possibilities. He allows that it might have been staged by either Israel or Iranian hardliners to prevent rapprochement between the United States and Iran.

63. Michael Donovan, "Iran, Israel and Nuclear Weapons in the Middle East," Center for Defense Information, February 14, 2002, http://www.cdi.org/terrorism/menukes-pr.cfm, accessed November 23, 2007.

64. Parsi, *Treacherous Alliance*, p. 235.

65. *Ibid.*, p. 240–43.

66. Andrew I. Killgore, "Neocons Battle Against U.S. Rapprochement With Iran," *Washington Report on Middle East Affairs*, May 2004, p. 35, online; Glenn Kessler, "In 2003, U.S. Spurned Iran's Offer of Dialogue: Some Officials Lament Lost Opportunity," *Washington Post*, June 18, 2006, p. A-16; Glenn Kessler, "Rice Denies Seeing Iranian Proposal in '03," *Washington Post*, February 8, 2007, p. A-18; Trita Parsi, *Treacherous Alliance*, p. 243–45.

67. Killgore, *ibid.*; Kessler, "In 2003," *ibid.*; Kessler, "Rice Denies Seeing Iranian Proposal," *ibid.*; Parsi, *ibid.*

68. Gareth Porter, "Neo-con cabal blocked 2003 nuclear talks," *Asia Times*, March 30, 2006, online; "Washington 'snubbed Iran offer,'" BBC News, January 18, 2007, online; Andrew I. Killgore, "Neocons Battle Against U.S. Rapprochement With Iran," *Washington Report on Middle East Affairs*, May 2004, p. 35, online; Glenn Kessler, "In 2003, U.S. Spurned Iran's Offer of Dialogue: Some Officials Lament Lost Opportunity," *Washington Post*, June 18, 2006, p. A-16; Trita Parsi, *Treacherous Alliance*, pp. 248–49. Parsi points out that the offer through Switzerland was not an isolated event. Iranian diplomats made a number of other comparable offers, which the United States also ignored (pp. 250–51).

69. Jim Lobe, "Hopes for U.S.-Iranian Rapprochement Fade," *Eurasianet.org*, February 9, 2004, online.

70. "U.S. eyes limited talks with Iran," *BBC News*, October 29, 2003, online.

http://news.bbc.co.uk/2/hi/middle_east/3222649.stm, accessed November 23, 2007.

71. John Bolton, *Surrender Is Not an Option: Defending America at the United Nations and Abroad* (New York: Threshold Editions, 2007), pp. 158–64; Glenn Kessler, "Bolton Book Cites Effort to Halt Powell's Iran Initiative," *Washington Post*, October 22, 2007, p. A-7.

72. Council on Foreign Relations, "Lack of Engagement with Iran Threatens U.S. National Interests in Critical Region of the World, Concludes Council-Sponsored Task Force," News Release, July 19, 2004, http://www.cfr.org/publication.html?id=7195, accessed February 9, 2008.

73. *Ibid.*

74. Joshua Mitnick, "Would Israel Strike First at Iran?," *Christian Science Monitor*, August 18, 2004, online.

75. *Ibid.*

76. Anton La Guardia, "Israel challenges Iran's nuclear ambitions," *Telegraph*, September 22, 2004, online.

77. Ali Akbar Dareini, "Iran Tests New Missile," *AP*, August 11, 2004, http://www.cbsnews.com/stories/2004/08/17/world/main636553.shtml, accessed February 9, 2008.

78. Seymour M. Hersh, "The Coming Wars," *New Yorker*, January 24/31, 2005 (Posted January 17, 2005), online.

79. *Ibid.*

80. *Ibid.*

81. *Ibid.*

82. Matthew Clark, "Israel, Iran, and nuclear weapons programs," *Christian Science Monitor*, posted April 13, 2005, online; Jerome Corsi, "Sharon warns Iranian nuke danger imminent . . . do something now!," *WorldNetDaily.com*, April 13, 2005, online.

83. Dana Milbank, "AIPAC's Big, Bigger, Biggest Moment," *Washington Post*, May 24, 2005, p. A-13.

84. Haviv Rettig, "Kupperwasser: Iran wants bomb to spread Islamic revolution," *Jerusalem Post*, June 29, 2005, online.

85. Barry Schweid, "Israel: U.N. Must Halt Iran Nuke Ambitions," *AP*, June 27, 2005, *Factiva* document APRS000020050627e16r001ob, available at http://www.political-news.org/breaking/12597/israel-un-must-halt-iral-nuke-ambitons.html, accessed November 23, 2007.

86. *The New York Times*, "Iran Backs Off from Direct Threat to Israel," *New York Times*, October 30, 2005, online. Juan Cole, "Informed Consent," April 23 and May 3, 2006, http://www.juancole.com/2006/05/hitchens-hacker-and-hitchens.html, accessed November 23, 2007; Trita Parsi, Treacherous Alliance, endnote 1, p. 285; "Iranian President at Tehran Conference: 'Very Soon, This Stain of Disgrace [i.e. Israel] Will Be Purged From the Center of the Islamic World – and This is Attainable,'" Special Dispatch Series--No. 1013, October 28, 2005, http://memri.org/bin/articles.

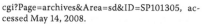

cgi?Page=archives&Area=sd&ID=SP101305, accessed May 14, 2008.

87. AP, "Iran President: Holocaust A Myth," *CBS News*, December 14, 2005, online.

88. "President Ahmadinejad Delivers Remarks at Columbia University," WashingtonPost.com, September 24, 2007, http://www.washington-post.com/wp-dyn/content/article/2007/09/24/AR2007092401042.html, accessed April 26, 2008.

89. Juan Cole, "Ahmadinejad: 'I am not anti-Semitic'; Palestinians should Decide on Two-State Solution," *Informed Comment*, June 26, 2007, http://www.juancole.com/2007/06/ahmadinejad-i-am-not-anti-semitic.html, accessed April 26, 2008.

90. Ori Nir, "Israeli Aides Warn U.S. Not To Drop Ball on Iran," *Forward*, December 9, 2005, online.

91. Joshua Brilliant, "Sharon: Iran nukes may require military response," UPI, December 1, 2005, online; Uzi Mahnaimi and Sarah Baxter, "Israel readies forces for strike on nuclear Iran," *Sunday Times*, December 11, 2005, http://www.timesonline.co.uk/article/0,,2089-1920074,00.html, accessed November 23, 2007.

92. "Books add to rightwing campaign to demonise Iran," *Financial Times*, July 8, 2005, online.

93. Michael Rubin, et al., "Launch Regional Initiatives," chapter 9 of *War Footing: 10 Steps America Must Take in the War for the Free World*, ed. Frank J. Gaffney (Annapolis, Md.: Naval Institute Press, 2005), American Enterprise Institute, November 30, 2005, http://www.aei.org/publications/filter.all,pubID.23499/pub_detail.asp, accessed February 9, 2008.

94. *Ibid.*

95. Ardeshir Ommani, "Iran And U.S. Foreign Policy Designs," Swans Commentary, December 5, 2005, http://www.swans.com/library/art11/ommani02.html, http://www.aei.org/publications/filter.all,pubID.23499/pub_detail.asp; "The Unknown Iran: Another Case for Federalism?," Announcement for AEI conference, October 26, 2005, American Enterprise Institute, http://www.aei.org/events/type.upcoming,eventID.1166,filter.all/event_detail.asp, accessed November 23, 2007.

96. Setare Kaviyan and Ruzbeh Hosseini, "Separatists Discuss Future of Iran," Iranians for a Secular Republic, October 26, 2005, http://www.marzeporgohar.org/index.php?l=1&cat=21&scat=&artid=680, accessed November 23, 2007.

97. Michael Ledeen, "Preemptive Surrender," *National Review* Online, November 30, 2005, online.

98. Charles Krauthammer, "In Iran, Arming for Armageddon," *Washington Post*, December 16, 2005, p. A-35.

99. *Ibid.*

100. *Ibid.*

101. Jamie Glazov, "Symposium: The Showdown [with Iran]," *FrontPageMagazine.com*, July 29, 2005, online. A similar view was expressed by Reuel Marc Gerecht: "LET US STATE THE OBVIOUS: The new president of the Islamic Republic of Iran, Mahmoud Ahmadinejad, is a godsend. The Americans, the Europeans, and even the Russians are now treating clerical Iran's 20-year quest to develop nuclear weapons more seriously. Ahmadinejad's inflamed rhetoric against America, Israel, and the Jews, which is in keeping with the style and substance of the president's former comrades in the praetorian Revolutionary Guard Corps, combined with the clerical regime's decision to restart uranium enrichment, has returned some sense of urgency to efforts to thwart Tehran" ("Coming Soon: Nuclear Theocrats? How to head off the imam bomb," *Weekly Standard*, January 30, 2006, online).

102. "Most Oppose Return To Draft, Wouldn't Encourage Children To Enlist," AP-IPSOS Poll, *Ipsos News Center*, June 24, 2005, online.

103. Frank Rich, "Someone Tell the President the War Is Over," *New York Times*, August 14, 2005, online.

104. Jonathan Weisman and Charles Babington, "Iraq War Debate Eclipses All Other Issues," *Washington Post*, November 20, 2005, p. A-1.

105. Liz Sidoti, "Senate Urges Bush to Outline Iraq Plan," Associated Press, *Washington Post*, November 16, 2005, online.

106. Dave Lindorff, "What Opposition Party?," *CounterPunch.org*, September 29, 2005, online.

107. John Byrne, "Biden seeks to articulate Iraq strategy; Senate Democrats resist pullout," Raw Story, November 21, 2005, http://rawstory.com/admin/dbscripts/printstory.php?story=1494, accessed November 22, 2007; Joshua Frank, "Democratic Hawks: The Avian Flu of the Antiwar Movement," CounterBias.com, November 21, 2005, http://www.counterbias.com/470.html, accessed November 23, 2007; Jude Wanniski, "Iraq and the Cardboard Democrats," Anti-war.com, August 27, 2005, online; Joe Conason, "The only way out," *Salon*, December 3, 2005, online.

108. Alexander Cockburn, "How the Democrats Undercut John Murtha," *CounterPunch.org*, November 26/27, 2005, online; Justin Raimondo, "Democrats Take on Murtha," *Antiwar.com*, November 23, 2005, online; Jimmy Breslin, "Where's Hillary on Iraq?," *Newsday*, November 30, 2005, http://www.CommonDreams.org/views05/1130-35.htm, accessed November 23, 2007.

109. Harold Meyerson, "Exit Strategy in Search of a Party," *Washington Post*, November 23, 2005, p. A-19.

110. Caren Bohan, "Bush says U.S. 'will not run' from Iraq," Reuters, *Boston Globe*, October 15, 2005, online; *CNN*, "Bush: We will stay in Iraq fight," *CNN*, November 19, 2005, online; Mike Allen and Sam Coates, "Bush Says U.S. Will Stay and Finish Task," *Washington Post*, August 23, 2005, p. A-10.

111. *UPI*, "Bush would go into Iraq again," *UPI*, December 12, 2005, online.

112. Elisabeth Bumiller, "Cheney Sees 'Shameless' Revisionism on War," *New York Times*, November 22, 2005, online.

113. Daniel Pipes, "What Do the Terrorists Want? [A Caliphate]," *New York Sun*, July 26, 2005, www.danielpipes.org/article/2798, accessed November 23, 2007; chapter 11, on the neoconservatives' World IV idea, reviews their concept of a monolithic Islamic threat to America, which would be comparable to a "caliphate."

114. Elisabeth Bumiller, "21st-Century Warnings of a Threat Rooted in the 7th," *New York Times*, December 12, 2005, online.

115. Quoted in James Norton, "A history of violence," *Salon*, November 28, 2005, online.

Chapter 15

1. "Iran war 'could triple oil price,'" *BBC News*, June 21, 2006, online; F. William Engdahl, "Calculating the Risk of War in Iran," *Financial Sense*, January 29, 2006, online; Youssef Ibrahamim, "Imagining A War With Iran," *New York Sun*, February 2, 2007, online. See also Gery, "Politics of Electoral Illusion."

2. Michael Abramowitz and Thomas E. Ricks, "Panel May Have Few Good Options to OfferBipartisan Group's Plan Expected in Dec.," *Washington Post*, November 12, 2006, p. A-1, Ryan Lizza, "Baker's Choice," *New Republic*, November 13, 2006 (posted November 2, 2006), online; Robert Dreyfuss, "A Higher Power," *Washington Monthly*, September 2006, online.

3. Gary Kamiya, "Fun, fun, fun till Daddy took the Iraq war away," *Salon*, October 17, 2006, online.

4. Philip H. Gordon, "The End of the Bush Revolution," *Foreign Affairs*, July/August 2006, online.

5. Mike Allen and Romesh Ratnesar, "The End of Cowboy Diplomacy," *Time Magazine*, July 17, 2006 (Posted July 9, 2006), online.

6. William Kristol, "Iran Is Not Iraq," *Weekly Standard*, May 8, 2006, online.

7. William Kristol, "Unacceptable?: Is the America of 2006 more willing to thwart the unacceptable than the France of 1936?," *Weekly Standard*, April 4, 2006, online.

8. Richard Perle, "Why Did Bush Blink on Iran? (Ask Condi)," *Washington Post*, June 25, 2006, p. B-1.

9. Anders Strindberg, "Hizbullah's attacks stem from Israeli incursions into Lebanon," *Christian Science Monitor*, August 1, 2006, online.

10. Tanya Reinhart, "Israel's 'New Middle East,'" *Counterpunch.org*, July 27, 2006, online; Amos Harel, Aluf Benn and Gideon Alon, "Gov't okays massive strikes on Lebanon," *Ha'aretz*, July 13,

2006, online.

11. Matthew Kalman, "Israel set war plan more than a year ago," *San Francisco Chronicle*, July 21, 2006, online.

12. Livia Rokach, *Israel's Sacred Terrorism* (Belmont, Mass.: Association of Arab-American University Graduates, Inc., 1980), pp. 24–30; Shlaim, *Iron Wall*, pp. 172–73.

13. Kaveh L. Afrasiabi, "It's about annexation, stupid!" *Asia Times*, August 5, 2006, online.

14. IASPS, "A Clean Break."

15. Daniel Pipes and Ziad Abdelnour, Co-Chairs, "Ending Syria's Occupation of Lebanon: The U.S. Role Report of the Lebanon Study Group," Middle East Forum, May 2000, http://www.meforum.org/research/lsg.php#signatories, accessed November 23, 2007,

16. *Ibid.*

17. Wayne Madsen, "The Israeli invasion of Lebanon was planned between top Israeli officials and members of the Bush administration," *Wayne Madsen Report*, July 22/23, 2006, http://www.waynemadsenreport.com/articles/20070423_96, accessed November 23, 2007; Thierry Meyssan, "Lebanon as a new target – The Neocons Policy of 'Constructive Chaos,'" *Current Concerns*, August 2006, http://www.currentconcerns.ch/filadmin/docs/CC-Express_01-2006.pdf, accessed November 23, 2007.

18. Seymour M. Hersh, "Watching Lebanon: Washington's interests in Israel's war," *New Yorker*, August 21, 2006 (Posted August 14, 2006), online.

19. Mearsheimer and Walt, *Israel Lobby and U.S. Foreign Policy*, pp. 309–310.

20. "Fighting Rages On," *Kuwait Times*, Jul 26, 2006, http://news.google.com/news?hl=en&lr=&q=arbid%20lebanon%20&btnG=Search&sa=N&tab=wn. accessed August 1, 2006.

21. Tanya Reinhart, "Israel's 'New Middle East,'" *Palestine Chronicle*, July 30, 2006, http://www.globalresearch.ca/index.php?context=viewArticle&code=REI20060730&articleId=2861, accessed November 23, 2007.

22. "Olmert: Iran's diversion plan worked," *Jerusalem Post*, July 18, 2006, online; CNN, "Israel lists conditions needed for peace," *CNN*, July 31, 2006, online.

23. "President Bush and Prime Minister Blair of the United Kingdom Participate in Press Availability," July 28, 2006, http://www.whitehouse.gov/news/releases/2006/07/print/20060728-1.html, accessed November 23, 2007

24. President's Radio Address, July 29, 2006, http://www.whitehouse.gov/news/releases/2006/07/20060729.html, accessed November 23, 2007.

25. Mearsheimer and Walt write: "What makes America's overwhelming support for Israel so remarkable is that the United States was the only

country that enthusiastically supported Israel's actions in Lebanon. Almost every other country in the world, as well as the UN leadership, criticized Israel's reaction as well as Washington's unyielding support for it. These circumstances raise the obvious question: why was the United States so out of step with the rest of the world?" Mearsheimer and Walt, *Israel Lobby and U.S. Foreign Policy*, p. 313.

26. Robin Wright, "Returning to Old Approach, U.S. Faces Risky Path Ahead," *Washington Post*, July 30, 2006, p. A-18; Justin Raimondo, "The Return of the Neocons,"*Antiwar.com*, July 31, 2006, online; Robert Dreyfuss, "Neocons Rise From Mideast Ashes," July 17, 2006, http://www.tompaine.com/articles/2006/07/17/neocons_rise_from_mideast_ashes.php, accessed November 23, 2007.

27. David S. Cloud and Helen Cooper, "U.S. Speeds Up Bomb Delivery for the Israelis," *New York Times*, July 22, 2006, p. A-1; Patrick Seale, "Doomed diplomacy," *Gulf News*, July 28, 2006, http://archive.gulfnews.com/articles/06/07/28/10055499.html, accessed November 23, 2007.

28. Mearsheimer and Walt, *Israel Lobby and U.S. Foreign Policy*, p. 310–11.

29. Sidney Blumenthal, "The neocons' next war," *Salon*, August 3, 2006, online.

30. Quoted in Yitzhak Benhorin, "Neocon: U.S. expected Israel to attack Syria and is angry it didn't," *Israel Insider*, December 18, 2006, http://web.israelinsider.com/Articles/Diplomacy/10092.htm, accessed November 23, 2007.

31. *Ibid.*

32. Condoleezza Rice, "Special Briefing on Travel to the Middle East and Europe," U.S. Department of State July 21, 2006, http://www.state.gov/secretary/rm/2006/69331.htm, accessed November 23, 2007.

33. Larry Kudlow, "Israel's Moment: The Free World's Gain," *National Review* Online, July 17, 2006, online.

34. Richard Perle, "An Appropriate Response," Op-Ed, *New York Times*, July 22, 2006, online.

35. David Frum, "Iran's Showdown with the West," *National Post* (Canada), July 25, 2006, http://www.aei.org/publications/pubID.24709,filter.all/pub_detail.asp, accessed November 23, 2007.

36. Michael Ledeen, "The Same War: Hezbollah, natch," *National Review* Online, July 13, 2006, online.

37. William Kristol, "It's Our War," *Weekly Standard*, July 24, 2006, online.

38. John Podhoretz, "Too Nice to Win? Israel's Dilemma," *New York Post*, July 25, 2006, online.

39. Daniel Pipes, "This Cease-Fire Won't Hold," *New York Sun*, August 1, 2006, online.

40. Charles Krauthammer, "Israel's Lost Mo-

ment," *Washington Post*, August 4, 2006, p. A-17.

41. Tom Regan, "U.S. neocons hoped Israel would attack Syria," *Christian Science Monitor*, posted August 9, 2006, online; Jim Lobe, "Hard-Line Neocons Assail Israel for Timidity," *Antiwar.com*, August 12, 2006, online; Justin Raimondo, "Bush vs. Condi," *Antiwar.com*, August 11, 2006, online.

42. Jonathan Finer and Molly Moore, "'It's Hard to Have the Same Confidence As Casualties Mount," *Washington Post*, August 11, 2006. p. A-10.

43. Peter Baker, "Crisis Could Undercut Bush's Long-Term Goals," *Washington Post*, July 31, 2006, p. A-1.

44. Robin Wright, "Returning to Old Approach, U.S. Faces Risky Path Ahead," *Washington Post*, July 30, 2006, p. A-18.

45. Brent Scowcroft, "Beyond Lebanon: This Is the Time for a U.S.-Led Comprehensive Settlement," *Washington Post*, July 30, 2006, p. B-7.

46. Jimmy Carter, "Stop the Band-Aid Treatment," *Washington Post*, August 1, 2006, A-17.

47. *Ibid.*

48. Zbigniew Brzezinski, "Neocon Policies Ultimately Fatal for U.S., Israel," July 31, 2006, *New Perspectives Quarterly*, Spring 2006, http://www.digitalnpq.org/articles/global/104/07-31-2006/zbigniew_brzezinski, accessed November 24, 2007.

49. U. S. Senate, "Condemning Hezbollah and Hamas and their state sponsors and supporting Israel's right to exercise of its right to self-defense," 109th Cong., 2nd Session, 2006, S. R. 534, July 18, 2006, http://thomas.loc.gov/cgi-bin/query/z?c109:S.RES.534, accessed November 24, 2007.

50. U. S. House of Representatives, "Condemning the recent attacks against the State of Israel, holding terrorists and their state-sponsors accountable for such attacks, supporting Israel's right to defend itself, and for other purposes," 109th Cong., 2nd Session, 2006, H. R. 921, July 20, 2006, http://clerk.house.gov/evs/2006/roll391.xml, accessed November 24, 2007.

51. Ari Berman, "AIPAC's Hold," *Nation*, August 14, 2006 (posted August 4, 2006), online.

52. Peter Beinart, "Pander and Run," *Washington Post*, July 28, 2006, p. A-25.

53. Patrick Seale, "Geopolitical Consequences of the Lebanon War," *Dar Al-Hayat*, August 18, 2006, http://english.daralhayat.com/opinion/contributors/08-2006/Article-20060818-20974ca5-c0a8-10ed-019d-d97b20eb28c2/story.html, accessed November 24, 2007.

54. Michael Ledeen, "The Real War . . . . one more time," *National Review* Online, August 14, 2006, online.

55. William Kristol, "The Bugs Bunny Democrats," *Weekly Standard*, August 21, 2006, online.

56. Charles Krauthammer, "The Tehran Calculus," *Washington Post*, September 15, 2006, p. A-19.

57. *Ibid.*

58. Quoted in Patrick Seale, "Pressures Mount on Bush to Bomb Iran," Agence Global, September 16, 2006, http://www.pej.org/html/modules.php?op=modload&name=News&file=article&sid=5585&mode=thread&order=0&thold=0, accessed November 24, 2007.

59. Michael Ledeen, "Cognitive Dissonance: The Bush administration on Iran," *National Review* Online, October 2, 2006, online.

60. "October U.S. Deaths In Iraq Top 10," CBS News, October 30, 2006, online; "Insurgent Group Claims Thousands Willing to Die," Associated Press, *Washington Post*, November 11, 2006, p. A-18.

61. Gary Kamiya, "Fun, fun, fun till Daddy took the Iraq war away," *Salon*, October 17, 2006, online.

62. *Ibid.*

63. Reuel Marc Gerecht, "Running from Iraq," *Weekly Standard*, October 23, 2006, online.

64. Joseph Rago, "Unrepentant Neocon," *Wall Street Journal*, August 12, 2006, online.

65. David Rose, "Neo Culpa," *Vanity Fair.com*, Posted November 3, 2006, online.

66. *Ibid.*

67. *Ibid.*

68. *Ibid.*

69. *Ibid.*

70. Joshua Muravchik, "Operation Comeback," *Foreign Policy*, November 1, 2006, online.

71. *Ibid.*

72. Joshua Muravchik, "Can the Neocons Get Their Groove Back?," *Washington Post*, November 19, 2006, p. B-3; Joshua Muravchik, "Operation Comeback," *Foreign Policy*, November 1, 2006, online.

73. Muravchik, "Operation Comeback."

74. Justin Raimondo, "The Neocons, Undaunted," *Antiwar.com*, November 3, 2006, online.

75. John F. Harris and Christopher Muste, "56 Percent in Survey Say Iraq War Was a Mistake," *Washington Post*, December 21, 2004, p. A-4.

76. Todd S. Purdum, "Grumbling Swells on Rumsfeld's Right Flank," *New York Times*, December 16, 2004, p. A-26; Robert Novak, "Neocons pin Iraq on Rumsfeld," *Chicago Sun-Times*, December 23, 2004, online.

77. Project for a New American Century, "Letter to Congress on Increasing U.S. Ground Forces," January 28, 2005, http://www.newamericancentury.org/defense-20050128.htm, accessed November 24, 2007.

78. Scott Shane, "Robert Gates, a Cautious Player From a Past Bush Team," *New York Times*, November 9, 2006, online; David E. Sanger, "After Rumsfeld: Bid to Reshape the Brain Trust," *New York Times*, November 10, 2006, online.

79. Scott Shane, "Robert Gates, a Cautious Player From a Past Bush Team," *New York Times*, November 9, 2006, online.

80. Dan Williams, "Israelis piqued by Gates nuclear 'confirmation,'" Reuters, December 7, 2006, http://www.alertnet.org/thenews/newsdesk/L07258813.htm, accessed November 30, 2007.

81. David E. Sanger, "After Rumsfeld: Bid to Reshape the Brain Trust," *New York Times*, November 10, 2006, online.

82. Jim Hoagland, "Right Vision, Wrong Policy – and a Mideast Price to Pay," *Washington Post*, November 12, 2006, p. B-7.

83. Howard Fineman, "The Boys Are Back in Town," *Newsweek*, November 8, 2006, online; see also Georgie Anne Geyer, "Baker on Cleanup Crew after 'Sonny's' Big Adventure," uExpress.com, November 13, 2006, http://www.uexpress.com/georgieannegeyer/?uc_full_date=20061113, accessed November 30, 2007.

84. James A. Baker, III and Lee H. Hamilton, et al., *The Iraq Study Group Report* (New York: Vantage Books, 2006), p. 37, http://www.antiwar.com/ISG.pdf, accessed November 25, 2007.

85. Glenn Kessler and Thomas E. Ricks, "The Realists' Repudiation Of Policies for a War, Region," *Washington Post*, December 8, 2006, p. A-1.

86. Joe Conason, "The last neocon," *Salon*, December 8, 2006, online.

87. Justin Raimondo, "We Can't Wait for 2008," *Antiwar.com*, December 8, 2006, online.

88. *Ibid.*; see also Antony T. Sullivan, "The ISG: Illusions Surrendered Group," *National Interest* Online, December 8, 2006, online; Sullivan wrote: "the ISG report in fact constitutes a massive repudiation of the policy of the Bush Administration. Most importantly, it draws red lines on acceptable policy, greatly diminishing the likelihood of any new, spectacular American military adventures in the Middle East. For example, a U.S. bombing campaign against Iran's nuclear development program, with all the predictably disastrous, region-wide consequences that any such attack would provoke, is now probably off the table. American-initiated regime change in either Iran or Syria is now also likely a dead letter."

89. Michael Rubin, "The stacked Baker-Hamilton Commission," *Weekly Standard*, October 30, 2006, online.

90. Eliot Cohen, "No Way to Win a War," *Wall Street Journal*, December 7, 2006, online.

91. Charles Krauthammer, "This Is Realism?: Iran and Syria Won't Be Riding to Our Rescue," *Washington Post*, December 1, 2006, p. A-29.

92. John Podhoretz, "Witless 'Wisdom,'" *New York Post* Online, December 1, 2006, online.

93. Frank J. Gaffney, Jr., "The new groupthink," *Washington Times*, November 28, 2006, online.

94. Frank J. Gaffney, Jr., "The 'Iraq Surrender Group,'" *Washington Times*, December 5, 2006, online.

95. Caroline Glick, "Column One: Jews Wake Up!," *Jerusalem Post*, December 8, 2006, online.

96. Robert Kagan and William Kristol, "Surrender as 'Realism,'" *Weekly Standard*, December 4, 2006, online.

97. Robert Kagan and William Kristol, "A Perfect Failure: The Iraq Study Group has reached a consensus," *Weekly Standard*, December 11, 2006, online.

98. Michael A. Ledeen, "Into Every Blue Ribbon Commission a Beam of Light Must Shine," *National Review* Online, December 11, 2006, online.

99. Anti-Defamation League, "Iraq Study Group 'Gets It Wrong' on Arab-Israeli Peace Process," December 6, 2006, http://antidefamationleague.us/iraq_study_group.pdf, accessed November 30, 2007.

100. *Ibid.*

101. Jason Isaacson and Aaron Jacob, "American Jewish Committee Statement on Iraq Study Group Report," December 6, 2006, http://www.ajc.org/site/apps/nl/content2.asp?c=ijITI2PHKoG&b=1323269&ct=3283695, accessed November 25, 2007.

102. Mike Whitney, "James Baker Versus the Lobby," *CounterPunch.org*, December 9/10, 2006, online.

Chapter 16

1. Michael Abramowitz and Sudarsan Raghavan "Bush Rejects Troop Reductions, Endorses Maliki," *Washington Post*, December 1, 2006, p. A-24; Bill Nichols and Barbara Slavin, "Don't start planning 'graceful exit,' Bush says," *USA Today*, November 30, 2006, online.

2. Justin Raimondo, "Napoleon in the White House," *Antiwar.com*, December 20, 2006, online; David Ignatius, "Bush's New Look on Iraq: Weary," *Washington Post*, December 27, 2006, p. A-19.

3. George W. Bush, "President's Address to the Nation," January 10, 2007, http://www.whitehouse.gov/news/releases/2007/01/20070110-7.html, accessed January 19, 2008.

4. Jim Lobe, "The Urge to Surge," *Antiwar.com*, December 21, 2006, online. http://www.antiwar.com; Rowan Scarborough, "Armchair generals help shape surge in Iraq," *Washington Examiner*, July 25, 2007, p. 15.

5. Rowan Scarborough, "Armchair generals help shape surge in Iraq," *Washington Examiner*, July 25, 2007, p. 15.

6. Frederick W. Kagan, "Choosing Victory: A Plan for Success in Iraq: Phase I Report,", AEI Papers and Studies, January 5, 2007, http://www.aei.org/publications/pubID.25396/pub_detail.asp, accessed January 19, 2008.

7. Mark Benjamin, "The real Iraq Study Group," *Salon*, January 6, 2007, online.

8. Thom Shanker, "General Opposes Adding to U.S. Forces in Iraq, Emphasizing International Solutions for Region," *New York Times*, December 20, 2006, online.

9. Ann Scott Tyson, "General Says Army Will Need To Grow," *Washington Post*, December 15, 2006, p. A-1.

10. Ann Scott Tyson, "Iraq Troop Boost Erodes Readiness, General Says," *Washington Post*, February 16, 2007, p. A-13.

11. Barbara Slavin, "Powell says troops stretched too thin," *USA Today*, December 17, 2006, http://www.usatoday.com/news/washington/2006-12-17-iraq-troop-surge_x.htm

12. *CNN*, "Democrats to Bush: No more troops to Iraq," *CNN*, January 6, 2007, online.

13. Jim Lobe, "Bush's Surge Strategy Faces Heavy Opposition," *Antiwar.com*, January 6, 2007, online.

14. Gary Langer, "Disapproval on Iraq Hits Record," ABC News, February 26, 2007, online.

15. Lionel Beehner, "Plans for a Post-'Surge' Iraq," February 12, 2007, Council on Foreign Relations, http://www.cfr.org/publication/12576/plans_for_a_postsurge_iraq.html, accessed January 19, 2008.

16. Peter W. Galbraith, "The Surge," *New York Review of Books*, March 15, 2007, online; Patrick J. Buchanan, "Bush's ace up his sleeve," *WorldNetDaily.com*, January 12, 2007, http://www.worldnetdaily.com/news/article.asp?ARTICLE_ID=53736, accessed January 19, 2008; Helene Cooper and Mark Mazzetti, "To Counter Iran's Role in Iraq, Bush Moves Beyond Diplomacy," *New York Times*, January 11, 2007, online; Paul Craig Roberts, "Surge and Mirrors: What Bush Really Said," *CounterPunch.org*, January 12–14, 2007, online; Trita Parsi, "Bush's Iraq Plan; Goading Iran into War," *Inter Press Service News Agency*, January 12, 2007, online; Craig Unger, "From the Wonderful Folks Who Brought You Iraq," *Vanity Fair*, March 2007, online.

17. Zbigniew Brzezinski, Senate Foreign Relations Committee Testimony, February 1, 2007, http://www.senate.gov/~foreign/testimony/2007/BrzezinskiTestimony070201.pdf, accessed January 19, 2008.

18. Mary Jordan and Robin Wright, "Iran Seizes 15 British Seamen," *Washington Post*, March 24, 2007, p. A-11.

19. Adam Zagorin, "Talking to Iran – or Talking War?," *Time Magazine*, May. 25, 2007, online; Mohammed Abbas, "U.S. navy begins war games on Iran's doorstep," Reuters, May 24, 2007, online; Barbara Surk, "U.S. Navy launches show of force off Iran's coast," Associated Press, May 23, 2007, online.

20. David E. Sanger, "On Carrier in Gulf, Cheney Warns Iran," *New York Times*, May 11, 2007, online.

21. *AP*, "McCain Jokes: 'Bomb, Bomb, Bomb' Iran," *Newsmax.com*, April 19, 2007, online; Scott Harper, "McCain visits Murrells Inlet," *Georgetown (S.C.) Times*, April 19, 2007, http://www.zwire.com/site/news.cfm?newsid=18230309&BRD=2081&PAG=461&dept_id=385210&rfi=6, accessed January 19, 2008.

22. Eric Pfeiffer, "Lieberman suggests strikes over Iran ; Says U.S. must 'be prepared,'" *Washington Times*, June 11, 2007, p. A04.

23. Tom Lantos, "Counter-Proliferation Act Steps Up Pressure on Iran," June 26, 2007, Hill's *Congress Blog*, http://blog.thehill.com/2007/06/26/counter-proliferation-act-steps-up-pressure-on-iran-rep-tom-lantos/, accessed January 19, 2008.

24. David Horovitz, "Bolton: I'm 'very worried' for Israel," *Jerusalem Post*, June 27, 2007, online.

25. Norman Podhoretz, "The Case for Bombing Iran," *Commentary*, June 2007, online.

26. Daniel Larison wrote that "The word 'Islamofascism' never had any meaning except as a catch-all for whatever regimes and groups the word's users wished to make targets for military action" ("Term Limits," *American Conservative*, November 19, 2007, p. 15).

27. Norman Podhoretz, "The Case for Bombing Iran," *Commentary*, June 2007, online.

28. *Ibid.*

29. *Ibid.*

30. *Ibid.*

31. *Ibid.*

32. *Ibid.*

33. *Ibid.*

34. *Ibid.*

35. "House, Senate pass war funding bill," CNN, May 25, 2007, online.

36. William Kristol and Frederick W. Kagan, "Congress Gives In On War Funding; Now can we fight the enemy?," *Weekly Standard*, June 4, 2007, online.

37. David S. Cloud and Damien Cave, "Commanders Say Push in Baghdad Is Short of Goal," *New York Times*, June 4, 2007, online; Ann Scott Tyson, "Military Reports Slow Progress in Securing Baghdad," *Washington Post*, June 5, 2007, p. A-11.

38. Ann Scott Tyson, "No Drop in Iraq Violence Seen Since Troop Buildup," *Washington Post*, June 14, 2007, p. A-1.

39. Paul Tait, "U.S. forces face bloody start to June in Iraq," Reuters, June 3, 2007, online.

40. CNN/Opinion Research Corporation Poll, June 22–24, 2007, p. 4, http://i.a.cnn.net/cnn/2007/images/06/26/rel7c.pdf, accessed February 7, 2008.

41. Ken Silverstein, "Six Questions for Laura Rozen on Iran," *Harper's Magazine*, May 4, 2007, online; Adam Zagorin, "Talking to Iran – or Talking War?," *Time Magazine*, online; Helene Cooper and David E. Sanger, "Iran Strategy Stirs Debate at White House," *New York Times*, June 16, 2007, online.

42. "Interview With Maria Bartiromo on CNBC's Closing Bell," Secretary Condoleezza Rice, Washington, DC, July 6, 2007, U.S. Department of State, http://www.state.gov/secretary/rm/2007/87826.htm, accessed January 19, 2008.

43. Glenn Kessler, "Cheney Backs Diplomacy on Iran Program, Rice Affirms," *Washington Post*, June 2, 2007, p. A-8.

44. "U.S., Iran Hold Meeting On Iraq Security," CBS News, May 28, 2007, online; Anne Garrels, "Stability in Iraq on the Table in U.S.-Iran Meeting," National Public Radio, May 28, 2007, online.

45. Winslow T. Wheeler, "Posturing at the Petraeus Hearings," *CounterPunch.org*, October 3, 2007, online.

46. Jonathan Steele, "The surge is a sideshow. Only total U.S. pullout can succeed," *Guardian*, December 7, 2007, online. Other factors besides the surge contributed to the reduction of violence. The violence between Iraqis lessened because extensive sectarian cleansing had already taken place. Ivo Daalder, foreign policy expert at the Brookings Institution, pointed out that "the sectarian violence had to a large extent succeeded in forcing Sunnis from Shiite areas and Shiites from Sunni areas . . . . The violence caused a large-scale movement of people – one in six Iraqis has either left the country entirely or has been internally displaced. A lot of this movement has made sections of the country ethnically more homogeneous, thus stemming a major source of violence" ("Iraq After the Surge," *Brookings*, December 8, 2007, http://www.brookings.edu/opinions/2007/1208_iraq_daalder.aspx, accessed January 5, 2008).

47. William E. Odom, Testimony Before the U.S. Senate Foreign Relations Committee, "Iraq after the Surge: Military Prospects," April 2, 2008, http://www.senate.gov/~foreign/testimony/2008/OdomTestimony080402a.pdf, accessed April 12, 2008.

48. Jim Lobe, "Fears grow of post-'surge' woes," *Asia Times*, November 22, 2007, online.

49. Rend Al-Rahim Francke, "Political Progress in Iraq During the Surge," Special Report No. 196, United States Institute of Peace, December 2007, http://www.usip.org/pubs/specialreports/sr196.html, accessed January 4, 2008.

50. Marina Ottaway, Nathan J. Brown, Amr Hamzawy, Karim Sadjadpour, and Paul Salem, *The New Middle East* (Washington: Carnegie Endowment for International Peace, 2008), pp. 1, 5, online; See also: Jonathan Cook, *Israel and the Clash of Civilisations: Iraq, Iran and the Plan*

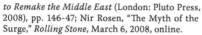
to *Remake the Middle East* (London: Pluto Press, 2008), pp. 146-47; Nir Rosen, "The Myth of the Surge," *Rolling Stone*, March 6, 2008, online.

51. David Wurmser, "Coping with Crumbling States: A Western and Israeli Balance of Power Strategy for the Levant," Research Paper in Policy, IASPS, December 1996, http://www.iasps.org/strat2.htm, accessed November 16, 2007. Wurmser's work was discussed in chapter 6.

52. David Wurmser, *Tyranny's Ally*, pp. 87, 93, 128. See Chapter 12 for a discussion of Wurmser's views on local freedom.

53. Reuel Marc Gerecht, "Deadly Persian Provocations," *Newsweek* International Edition, September 3, 2007, online.

54. Kimberly Kagan was a member of her husband's team that developed the surge. Andrew Sullivan, "Mrs Kagan Reviews Her Own Idea (And Her Husband's)," *The Daily Dish*, March 4, 2007, http://andrewsullivan.theatlantic.com/the_daily_dish/2007/03/mrs_kagan_revie.html, accessed January 20, 2008; and Jim Lobe "Outsourcing the Case for War With Iran," *Lobelog.com*, August 29, 2007, http://www.ips.org/blog/jimlobe/?p=60, accessed January 20, 2008. Given Kimberly Kagan's personal involvement in this strategy, the objectivity of her reporting would seem highly questionable.

55. Kimberly Kagan, "Iran's Proxy War Against the United States and the Iraqi Government," Iraq Report #6, Institute for the Study of War, with *Weekly Standard*, http://www.understandingwar.org/files/reports/IraqReport06.pdf, p. 3, accessed January 20, 2008; Kimberly Kagan, "The Iran Dossier – Iraq Report VI: Iran's proxy war against the U.S. in Iraq,", *Weekly Standard.com*, August 29, 2007,

http://www.weeklystandard.com/Content/Public/Articles/000/000/014/030aryoy.asp, accessed January 20, 2008,

56. Ledeen, *Iranian Time Bomb*, p. 1.

57. Mylroie, *Study of Revenge*, p. ix-xi.

58. Shlaim, *Iron Wall*, pp. 440–41.

59. Michael Ledeen, "Let's Talk with Iran Now," *New York Times*, July 19, 1988, quoted in Trita Parsi, *Treacherous Alliance*, p. 242.

60. Ledeen held that the failure of the United States to have relations with Iran added difficulties in the fight against Iraq. "For there is no country in the world that American diplomats have shunned so totally, indeed avoided so compulsively, as Iran," he bemoaned. "We have done so primarily for political reasons; ever since the Iran-Contra affair, no American leader has wished to be caught talking to an Iranian, even though many recognized the many sound geopolitical reasons for dealing with Iran." But the war with Iraq was forcing the United States to take a more reasonable approach with Iran. "It would have been wiser to have dealt with the Iranians earlier," Ledeen emphasized, "but we now have little choice in the matter. Our contacts will

surely increase, and President Rafsanjani and company will likely sit at the postwar negotiating table, thereby producing the great historical irony that Saddam Hussein, the conqueror of Persia, will have forced us to resume sensible relations with a reemerging Iran" ("Iran – Back in the Game," *Wall Street Journal*, February 1, 1991, online).

61. Toby Harnden, "U.S. hawk David Wurmser 'plotted Iran war,'" Telegraph, October 5, 2007, online; see also Tony Harnden, "David Wurmser: a neocon unbowed," *Tony Harnden Blog*, October 4, 2007, http://blogs.telegraph.co.uk/foreign/tobyharnden/oct07/david-wurmser.htm, accessed January 6, 2008.

62. "Are You Ready for 'Islamo-Fascism Week'?," Inside Higher ED, October 9, 2007, online.

63. *UPI*, "Clinton, Giuliani leading in U.S. race," *UPI*, October 17, 2007, online; Richard Cohen, "Giuliani's War," *Washington Post*, October 23, 2007, P. A-19; Paul Gottfried, "The Giuliani-Driven Christians," *American Conservative*, June 4, 2007, online; Michael Hirsh, "Neocons Converge Around Giuliani Campaign," *MSNBC*, October 15, 2007, online; Alexander Cockburn, "Giuliani and the Dogs of War," *CounterPunch.org*, July 21–22, 2007, online; "Rudy Giuliani Announces Additional Foreign Policy Advisors," Press Release, *JoinRudy2008.com*, October 11, 2007,

http://www.joinrudy2008.com/article/pr/890, accessed January 20, 2008. Stephen Rosen was a signatory of Project for the New American Century's controversial report "Rebuilding America's Defenses: Strategies, Forces and Resources for a New Century" in 2000.

64. Jennifer Siegel, "Giuliani Stacks Campaign Staff With a Who's Who Of Mideast Hawks," *Forward*, July 18, 2007, online;

65. Jim Lobe, "More Neo-Cons for Giuliani," Lobelog.com, October 12, 2007, http://www.ips.org/blog/jimlobe/?p=70#more-70, accessed January 20, 2008.

66. *Washingtonpost.com*, "The War Over the Wonks," *Washington Post*, October 2, 2007, online.

67. Michael Abramowitz, "As Iraq Situation Varies, Bush Sticks With Encouraging Words," Washington Post, August 29, 2007, p. A-4.

68. Sheryl Gay Stolberg, "Nuclear-Armed Iran Risks World War, Bush Says," *New York Times*, Octobe18, 2007, online.

69. Matthew Yglesias, "Defining World Wars Down," *Matther Yglesias* (blog at *TheAtlantic.com*), October 17, 2007, http://matthewyglesias.theatlantic.com/archives/2007/10/defining_world_wars_down.php, accessed January 20, 2008; Patrick Martin, "Bush invokes threat of 'World War III,'" October 19, 2007, *World Socialist Web Site*, http://www.wsws.org/articles/2007/oct2007/bush-o19_prn.shtml, accessed January 20, 2008; Gordon Prather, "WWIII – Bring It On," *Antiwar.com*, October 20, 2007, online.

70. "Vice President's Remarks to the Washington Institute for Near East Policy," White House, October 21, 2007, http://www.whitehouse.gov/news/releases/2007/10/20071021.html, accessed January 20, 2008.

71. Kaveh L. Afrasiabi, "The cost of American bellicosity toward Iran," *Christian Science Monitor*, October 30, 2007, online; *FOX News*, "Iran Sanctions, Bush Administration Rhetoric Worries Lawmakers," *FOXNews.com*, October 29, 2007, online; *AP*, "Bush Administration Announces New Sanctions Against Iran,", *FOXNews.com*, October 25, 2007, online.

72. "Zogby: Majority Favor Strikes on Iran," October 29, 2007, *Newsmax.com*, online; "Survey Methodology [Zogby America Likely Voters] 10/24/07 thru 10/27/07," Zogby International, October 29, 2007, http://www.zogby.com/methodology/readmeth.dbm?ID=1226, accessed January 20, 2008.

73. David R. Sands, "Nuke watchdog defends Iran deal," *Washington Times*, September 8, 2007, online.

74. "IAEA lacks evidence against Iran," Associated Press, *Washington Times*, October 29, 2007, p. A4; Jitendra Joshi, "No evidence Iran is making nuclear weapons: ElBaradei," *AFPs*, October 28, 2007, online.

75. Dafna Linzer and Joby Warrick, "U.S. Finds That Iran Halted Nuclear Arms Bid in 2003," *Washington Post*, December 4, 2007, online; see also Mark Mazzetti, "U.S. Finds Iran Halted Its Nuclear Arms Effort in 2003," *New York Times*, December 4, 2007, online.

76. Ray McGovern, "A Miracle: Honest Intel on Iran Nukes," *ConsortiumNews.com*, December 3, 2007, online; see also Gareth Porter, "Iran NIE Validates 2003 European Diplomacy," *Antiwar.com*, December 5, 2007, online.

77. Fred Kaplan, "Nuclear Meltdown," *Slate*, December 3, 2007, online; see also Steve Clemons, "Iran's Nuclear Weapons Program," *Washington Note*, December 4, 2007, http://www.thewashingtonnote.com/archives/2007_12.php, accessed January 4, 2008; Steve Clemons, "More on Why Bush Won't Bomb Iran," December 3, 2007, *Washington Note*, December 3, 2007, http://www.thewashingtonnote.com/archives/2007_12.php, accessed January 4, 2008.

78. *AFP*, "U.S. reversal on Iran intel reflects breaking of the ranks: analysts," *AFP*, December 7, 2007, online.

79. Justin Raimondo, "Iran: Why Won't We Take Yes For An Answer?," December 7, 2007, *Antiwar.com*, online.

80. Alexander Cockburn, "The Coup Against Bush and Cheney," *CounterPunch.org*, December 8/9, 2007, online.

81. As Ewen MacAskill wrote: "Fingar's findings were met in many Washington offices occupied by foreign policy and intelligence professionals not only with relief but with rejoicing. They had lost out in the run-up to the war in Iraq in 2003, but they are winning this one" ("Intelligence expert who rewrote book on Iran," *Guardian*, December 8, 2007, online).

82. Jon Ward, "NIE authors accused of partisan politics," *Washington Times*, December 7, 2007, online.

83. *Ibid.*

84. *Ibid.*

85. John R. Bolton, "The Flaws In the Iran Report," *Washington Post*, December 6, 2007, p. A-29.

86. *Ibid.*

87. Michael Ledeen, "The Great Intelligence Scam," *Faster, Please!*, December 3, 2007, http://pajamasmedia.com/xpress/michaelledeen/2007/12/03/the_great_intelligence_scam.php, accessed January 20, 2008.

88. Norman Podhoretz, "Dark Suspicions about the NIE," *Contentions*, (a blog at *Commentary*), December 3, 2007, http://www.commentarymagazine.com/blogs/index.php/podhoretz/1474, accessed January 20, 2008.

89. Joshua Mitnik, "Israel challenges report on nukes," *Washington Times*, December 5, 2007, online; *Israel Insider*, "Israeli officials and experts stunned by U.S. estimate on Iranian nukes," *Israel Insider*, December 4, 2007, online, accessed January 4, 2008.

90. Rory McCarthy, "Israel considering strike on Iran despite U.S. intelligence report," Guardian Unlimited, December 7, 2007, online.

91. Jim Lobe, "Key Neocons Giving Up on Iran Attack?," *Antiwar.blog* (a blog at *Antiwar.com*), December 12, 2007, http://www.antiwar.com/blog/2007/12/12/4114/, accessed January 3, 2008.

92. Robert Kagan, "Time to Talk to Iran," *Washington Post*, December 5, 2007, p. A-29.

93. *Ibid.*

94. Robert Parry, "Neocons Down, Not Out," Consortiumnews.com, December 6, 2007, http://www.consortiumnews.com/2007/120507.html, accessed January 4, 2008.

95. *Ibid.*

96. Kim Sengupta, "U.S. almost opened fire on Iranian boats, Pentagon says," *Independent*, January 9, 2008, http://news.independent.co.uk/world/middle_east/article3318010.ece, accessed January 9, 2008; Robin Wright and Ann Scott Tyson, "Objects From Iranian Boats Posed No Threat, Navy Says," *Washington Post*, January 12, 2008, p. A-11.

Chapter 17

1. As Charles A. Beard, one of America's most distinguished historians, wrote: "What any particular President may do in fact depends upon his training, personality, and sympathies, upon the pressure brought to bear upon him by private interests, economic and moral, organized

and unorganized.... He brings a heritage of theories, sentiments, ideas, and attachments with him into his office." Charles A. Beard, *The Idea of National Interest: An Analytical Study in American Foreign Policy*, edited with new material by Alfred Vagts and William Beard (Chicago: Quadrangle Books, 1966), p. 304.

2. Richard Cohen, "Iraq and the 'L' Word," *Washington Post*, November 22, 2005, p. A-29.

3. Quoted in Woodward, *State of Denial*, p. 81.

4. Robert Jervis, "Understanding the Bush Doctrine," *Political Science Quarterly* 118:3 (Fall 2003), p. 379.

5. Quoted in Ron Suskind, "Faith, Certainty and the Presidency of George W. Bush," *New York Times Magazine*, October 17, 2004, online.

6. Peter Schweitzer and Rochelle Schweitzer, *Bushes*, p. 535.

7. "Woodward Shares War Secrets," *60 Minutes* (CBS), April 18, 2004, online.

8. Justin Frank, *Bush on the Couch: Inside the Mind of the President* (New York: Regan Books, 2004).

9. Gary North, "The Foreign Policy of 20 Million Would-Be Immortals," *LewRockwell.com*, July 19, 2003, http://www.lewrockwell.com/north/north188.html, accessed November 17, 2007; Stan Crock, "Bush, the Bible, and Iraq," *Business Week*, March 7, 2003, online; Mearsheimer and Walt, *Israel Lobby and U.S. Foreign Policy*, pp. 132–42.

10. David Lutz, "*Un*just-War Theory: Christian Zionism and the Road to Jerusalem," in *Neo-CONNED! Again*, p. 153.

11. *Ibid.*, p. 161.

12. Dana Milbank, "Religious Right Finds Its Center in Oval Office," *Washington Post* (December 24, 2001), p. A-2.

13. Charlie Cray, "The 10 Most Brazen War Profiteers," *AlterNet.org*, Posted September 5, 2006, http://www.alternet.org/waroniraq/41083/, accessed November 17, 2007; Nic Robertson, "Iraq contractors make billions on the front line," *CNN*, June 13, 2006, online.

14. Jeffrey St. Clair, "Sticky Fingers: The Making of Halliburton," *CounterPunch.org*, July 14, 2005, online; Byron York, "Halliburton: The Bush/Iraq Scandal that Wasn't," *National Review* Online, July 14, 2003, online.

15. Bill Press, "Making political hay out of 9/11," *CNN*, January 23, 2002, online.

16. The "red" designation comes from a recent American election illustration. During U.S. national elections, television networks display election results on a map of U.S. states – with each state assigned a color based on which party's candidate won the state. In 2000, all the major broadcast networks and all the cable news outlets began to use the same color scheme: red for Republicans and blue for Democrats.

17. Zbigniew Brzezinski, "Terrorized by 'War on Terror': How a Three-Word Mantra Has Undermined America," *Washington Post*, March 25, 2007, p. B-1.

18. "USA Today/CNN/Gallup poll results," *USA Today*, March 20, 2003, online.

19. Steve Sailer, "Which American groups back war?," *UPI*, March 20, 2003, http://www.isteve.com/2003_Which_Groups_Support_the_War.htm, accessed February 9, 2008.

20. James Webb, "Secret GOP Weapon: The Scots-Irish Vote," *Wall Street Journal*, October 19, 2004, online. Webb writes: "The GOP strategy is heavily directed toward keeping peace with this culture, which every four years is seduced by the siren song of guns, God, flag, opposition to abortion, and success in war."

21. Norman Mailer, "We went to war just to boost the white male ego," *Times*, April 29, 2003, online; Norman Mailer, "The White Man Unburdened," *New York Review of Books*, July 17, 2003, online.

22. Quoted in Scott McConnell, "America's New Nationalism," *American Conservative*, March 14, 2005, online.

23. Paul Craig Roberts, "What Became of Conservatives?," *Antiwar.com*, November 26, 2004, online.

24. Llewellyn H. Rockwell, "The Reality of Red-State Fascism," *LewRockwell.com*, December 31, 2004,, http://www.lewrockwell.com/rockwell/red-state-fascism.html, accessed November 17, 2007.

25. Sean Higgins, "Kerry, Dem Delegates Differ Over Iraq War," *Investors Business Daily*, July 26, 2004, http://biz.yahoo.com/ibd/040726/general01_1.html?printer=1, accessed August 5, 2004.

26. Alexander Cockburn, "How the Democrats Undercut John Murtha," *CounterPunch.org*, November 26 / 27, 2005, online; Justin Raimondo, "Democrats Take on Murtha," *Antiwar.com*, November 23, 2005, online; Jimmy Breslin, "Where's Hillary on Iraq?," *Newsday*, November 30, 2005, http://www.CommonDreams.org/views05/1130-35.htm, accessed November 17, 2007.

27. Robert Blecher, "'Free People Will Set the Course of History': Intellectuals, Democracy and American Empire," *Middle East Report Online*, March 2003, http://www.merip.org/mero/interventions/blecher_interv.html, accessed November 17, 2007; the media's lack of skepticism regarding Bush administration claims in the run up to war was presented by Bill Moyers, "Buying the War" (Transcript), *Bill Moyer's Journal* (PBS), April 25, 2007, online; see, also: Justin Raimondo, "The Failure of the 'Mainstream,'" *Antiwar.com*, May 7, 2007, online.

28. Tom Barry, "Liberal Hawks: Flying in Neocon Circles," *Antiwar.com*, May 22, 2004, online.

29. Anatol Lieven, "Liberal Hawk Down," *Nation*, October 25, 2004, online.

30. Thomas Friedman, "The Chant Not Heard," *New York Times*, November 30, 2003, online; Mike Whitney, "Tom Friedman, the Imperial Chronicler," *CounterPunch.org*, May 13, 2005, online; Norman Solomon, "Hooked on War: The Secret Addiction of Thomas Friedman," *CounterPunch.org*, September 6, 2007, online.

31. Lieven, "Liberal Hawk Down."

32. Thomas E. Woods, Jr., "The Progressive Peacenik Myth," *American Conservative*, August 3, 2004, online; Murray N. Rothbard, "World War I as Fulfillment: Power and the Intellectuals," *Journal of Libertarian Studies*, 9:1 (Winter 1989), pp. 81–125; Randolph Bourne, "The War and the Intellectuals," *Seven Arts*, 1917, http://www.bigeye.com/thewar.htm, accessed November 18, 2007; James J. Martin, *American Liberalism and World Politics, 1931–1941: Liberalism's Press and Spokesmen on the Road Back to War Between Mukden and Pearl Harbor* (New York: Devin-Adair Company, 1964); R. Alan Lawson, *The Failure of Independent Liberalism, 1930–1941* (New York: G. P. Putnam's Sons, 1971); Stephen J. Sniegoski, *The Intellectual Wellsprings of American World War II Interventionism* (Ph.D. dissertation, University of Maryland, 1977).

33. Tom Barry, "Liberals and Neocons: Together Again," *Antiwar.com*, February 11, 2005, online; see also: Anatol Lieven, "Liberal Hawk Down," *Nation*, October 25, 2004, online; Stephen Holmes, "The War of the Liberals," *Nation*, November 14, 2005 (posted October 26, 2005), online.

34. Richard Cohen, "The Lingo Of Vietnam," *Washington Post*, November 21, 2006, p. A-27.

35. Although leaving out the pro-Zionist connections, Mark Hand discusses the pro-war position of the DLC and the PPI in "'It's Time to Get Over It': Kerry Tells Anti-War Movement to Move On," *CounterPunch.org*, February 18, 2004, online.

36. Michael Massing, "Should Jews Be Parochial?," *American Prospect*, November 6, 2000, online.

37. Sheldon Richman, "AIPAC President Resigns," *Washington Report on the Middle East*, December/January 1992/93, online.

38. Capsule reviews of Barry Rubin, *The Transformation of Palestinian Politics: From Revolution to State-Building* (Cambridge, Mass.: Harvard University Press, 1999), Harvard University Press Reviews, http://www.hup.harvard.edu/reviews/RUBTRA_R.html, accessed December 3, 2005.

39. Wittmann explained that his initial move from left to right had been because of his support for Israel. "Gradually, though, I became disillusioned with liberalism. Like many former Jewish lefties who were becoming neo-conservatives, I thought it was a contradiction to believe in a strong Israel and a weak United States" (Marshall Wittmann, "Just a Party Pooper? No, Just Independent," *Washington Post*, September 15, 2002, p. B-2); Peter Carlson, "Quote Cuisine: He's Spooned Up Sound Bites For the Right and the Left. What Marshall Wittmann Dishes Out Is," *Washington Post*, January 4, 2006, p. C-1.

40. Mark Green with Wendy Campbell, "Exit NeoConservatives, Enter NeoLiberals," MarWen Media, June 2004, http://www.marwenmedia.com/articles_images/NeoConservatives.html, accessed November 18, 2007.

41. Mearsheimer and Walt, "The Israel Lobby," *London Review of Books* and "The Israel Lobby and U.S. Foreign Policy," Faculty Research Working Paper.

42. Eric Alterman, "AIPAC's Complaint," *Nation*, (Posted April 13, 2006) May 1, 2006, online.

43. "The Risks of War," *Forward*, April 14, 2006, online; Eric Pfeiffer, "Lieberman suggests strikes over Iran," *Washington Times*, June 11, 2007, online; Mearsheimer and Walt, *Israel Lobby and U.S. Foreign Policy*, pp. 280–305.

44. Alan Dershowitz, "Debunking the Newest – and Oldest – Jewish Conspiracy." While Dershowitz was not leading the charge for war on Iraq, he was hardly an opponent. See Tim Wilkinson, "Dershowitz and the Iraq War," *CounterPunch.org*, January 31, 2007, online.

Chapter 18

1. Brendan O'Neill, "Being antiwar isn't about the oil," *Christian Science Monitor*, January 23, 2003, online.

2. Noam Chomsky, "'Of course, it was all about Iraq's resources,'" interview conducted by Simon Mars, *Business Channel* (Dubai), December 2, 2003, http://www.ccmep.org/2003_articles/Iraq/120203_of_course_it_was_all_about_iraq.htm, accessed February 9, 2008.

3. O'Neill, "Being antiwar."

4. Pratap Chatterjee, "Halliburton Makes a Killing on Iraq War," March 20, 2003, *CorpWatch*, http://www.corpwatch.org/article.php?id=6008, accessed November 16, 2007.

5. Sam Howe Verhovek and John Hendren, "U.S. Seeking to Protect Iraqi Oil Fields," *Los Angeles Times*, March 20, 2003, online; Bill Glauber, "Oil field sabotage called halfhearted," *Chicago Tribune*, Web Edition, April 6, 2003, online.

6. Rose Brady, ed., "Rogue States: Why Washington May Ease Sanctions," *Business Week*, May 7, 2001, online.

7. Roger Burbach, "Bush Ideologues Trump Big Oil Interests in Iraq," *Alternatives*, September 30, 2003, http://www.alternatives.ca/article869.html, accessed November 16, 2007.

8. Damien Cave, "The United States of oil," *Salon*, November 19, 2001, online.

9. Anthony Sampson, "Oilmen don't want another Suez," *The Observer*, December 22, 2002, online. Anthony Sampson is the author of *The*

Seven Sisters (New York: Bantam Books, 1976), which is about oil companies and the Middle East. Also, as Dan Morgan and David B. Ottaway write: "Officials of several major firms said they were taking care to avoiding playing any role in the debate in Washington over how to proceed on Iraq. 'There's no real upside for American oil companies to take a very aggressive stance at this stage. There'll be plenty of time in the future,' said James Lucier, an oil analyst with Prudential Securities" ("In Iraqi War Scenario, Oil Is Key Issue," *Washington Post*, September 15, 2002, p. A-1). John W. Schoen wrote: "So far, U.S. oil companies have been mum on the subject of the potential spoils of war" ("Iraqi oil, American bonanza?," *MSNBC.com*, November 11, 2002, online); see also Dana Goldstein, "Iraq war not about oil, says industry insider at Brown U.," *University Wire*, February 28, 2003, via Lexis-Nexis *Academic*.

10. William D. Nordhaus, "Iraq: The Economic Consequences of War," *New York Review of Books*, December 5, 2002, online (see also his more extensive piece, "The Economic Consequences of a War with Iraq," October 29, 2002, Yale Department of Economics, http://www.econ.yale.edu/~nordhaus/iraq.pdf, accessed November 16, 2007); George L. Perry, "The War on Terrorism, the World Oil Market and the U.S. Economy," Brookings paper, http://www.brookings.edu/~/media/Files/rc/papers/2001/1024terrorism_perry/20011024.pdf, accessed November 16, 2007.

11. Quoted by Robert Bryce, "Iraq's Oil Shock," *Salon*, January 17, 2006, online.

12. Peter Carlson, "The Best-Laid Plans Go Oft Astray," *Washington Post*, January 27, 2004, p. C-1.

13. Eric Schmitt and Joel Brinkley, "State Dept. Study Foresaw Trouble Now Plaguing Iraq," *New York Times*, October 19, 2003, online; "State Department experts warned CENTCOM before Iraq war about lack of plans for post-war Iraq security," National Security Archive Electronic Briefing Book No. 163, National Security Archive, http://www.gwu.edu/~nsarchiv/NSAEBB/NSAEBB163/index.htm, accessed November 16, 2007; "Turf Wars and the Future of Iraq," *Frontline* (PBS), October 9, 2003, online; Bradley Graham, "Prewar Memo Warned of Gaps in Iraq Plans: State Dept. Officials Voiced Concerns About Post-Invasion Security, Humanitarian Aid," *Washington Post*, August 18, 2005, p. A-13; George Packer, *Assassins' Gate*, pp. 119–25.

14. Michael Isikoff and David Corn, *Hubris*, pp. 198–99; Walter Pincus, "Ex-CIA Official Faults Use of Data on Iraq," *Washington Post*, February 10, 2006, p. A-1.

15. Conrad C. Crane and W. Andrew Terrill, "Reconstructing Iraq: Insights, Challenges, and Missions for Military Forces in a Post-Conflict Scenario," Army War College, Strategic Studies Institute, February 2003. p. iv, http://www.strategicstudiesinstitute.army.mil/pdffiles/PUB182.

pdf, accessed November 16, 2007.

16. Rupert Cornwell, "Pentagon officials ignored reports on dire state of Iraq's oil industry," *Independent*, October 6, 2003, online; Jeff Gerth, "Report Offered Bleak Outlook About Iraq Oil," *New York Times*, October 5, 2003, online.

17. Charles A. Kohlhaas, "War in Iraq: 'Not a War for Oil,'" *In the National Interest*, March 5, 2003, http://www.inthenationalinterest.com/Articles/Vol2Issue9/vol2issue9kohlhaaspfv.html, accessed November 24, 2007.

18. Julian Borger, Brian Whitaker, and Vikram Dodd "Saddam's desperate offers to stave off war," *Guardian*, Nov. 7, 2003, online.

19. David Rennie, "Saddam 'offered Bush a huge oil deal to avert war,'" *Telegraph*, November 7, 2003, online; Gary Leupp, "'They Were All Non-Starters': The Thwarted Iraqi Peace Proposals," *CounterPunch.org*, November 10, 2003, online; James Risen, *State of War*, p. 123; Michael Isikoff and Mark Hosenball, "Lost Opportunity," *Newsweek*, November 5, 2003, online; Weisman, *Prince of Darkness*, pp. 184–86.

20. Julian Borger, Brian Whitaker, and Vikram Dodd "Saddam's desperate offers to stave off war," *Guardian*, Nov. 7, 2003, online.

21. Yahya Sadowski, "No war for whose oil?," *Le Monde diplomatique*, April 2003, online.

22. Quoted in Robert Dreyfus, "The Thirty-Year Itch," *Mother Jones*, March/April 2003, online.

23. Thomas E. Ricks, "Army Historian Cites Lack of Postwar Plan," *Washington Post*, December 25, 2004, p. A-1, and *Fiasco*, pp. 110.

24. Ricks, *Fiasco*, pp. 110.

25. Walter Pincus, "Memo: U.S. Lacked Full Postwar Iraq Plan," *Washington Post*, June 12, 2005, p. A-1.

26. Tenet, *Center of the Storm*, pp. 308–309.

27. Isikoff and Corn, *Hubris*, p. 200.

28. Packer, *Assassins' Gate*, p. 147.

29. Quoted in Ricks, *Fiasco*, p. 87.

30. Dave Moniz, "Monthly Costs of Iraq, Afghan Wars Approach That of Vietnam," *USA Today*, September 8, 2003, p. 1.

31. Mark Mazzetti, "Pentagon Pressed to Cut Its Budgets," *Los Angeles Times*, December 19, 2004, online; "The Pentagon's Cuts," *Washington Post*, January 10, 2005, p. A-16; Jonathan Weisman and Renae Merle, "Pentagon Scales Back Arms Plans," *Washington Post*, January 5, 2005, p. A-1.

32. "GOP Backing Out of Iraq Offensive?," Fox News, August 16, 2002, online; Todd S. Purdum and Patrick E. Tyler, "Top Republicans Break With Bush on Iraq Strategy," *New York Times*, August 16, 2002, online; Jim Lobe, "Washington goes to war over war," *Asia Times*, August 21, 2002, online.

33. Brent Scowcroft, "Don't Attack Iraq," *Wall Street Journal*, August 15, 2002, online.

34. Sidney Blumenthal, "A State of Chaos," *Guardian*, December 30, 2004, online; Peter Schweizer and Rochelle Schweizer, *Bushes*, p. 535.

35. Wilson, *Politics of Truth*, p. 297.

36. Jeffrey Bell, "Bush I vs. Bush II," *Weekly Standard*, October 13, 2003, online.

37. Michele Steinberg, "Can the Brzezinski-Wolfowitz Cabal's War Game Be Stopped?," *Executive Intelligence Review* 28.47, December 7, 2001, http://www.larouchepub.com/other/2001/2847skunks.html, accessed November 16, 2007.

38. Patrick Martin, "Growing anxiety in U.S. ruling circles over Iraq debacle," *World Socialist Web Site*, January 14, 2005, http://www.wsws.org/articles/2005/jan2005/iraq-j14.shtml, accessed November 16, 2007.

39. Zbigniew Brzezinski, "Why Unity is Essential," *Washington Post*, February 19, 2003, p. A-29.

40. "War With Iraq is Not in America's National Interest," *New York Times*, September 26, 2002, online; Daniel W. Drezner, "The realist take on Iraq," *Daniel W. Drezner*, September 25, 2002, http://www.danieldrezner.com/archives/000584.html, accessed November 16, 2007.

41. Robert Kuttner, "Neo-cons have hijacked U.S. foreign policy," *Boston Globe*, September 10, 2003, online.

42. Podhoretz, *World War IV*, p. 127. Podhoretz writes that the "most sophisticated spokesmen" of liberal internationalism included "Stanley Hoffmann of Harvard, Charles A. Kupchan of the Council on Foreign Relations, and C. John Ikenberry of Georgetown" (p. 127).

43. Podhoretz, *World War IV*, p. 132.

44. Podhoretz, *World War IV*, p. 133.

45. Howard Fineman, "The Boys Are Back in Town," *Newsweek*, November 8, 2006, online.

46. Thomas E. Ricks, "Some Top Military Brass Favor Status Quo in Iraq," *Washington Post*, July 28, 2002, p. A-1; Justin Raimondo, "Attack of the Chicken- Hawks," *Antiwar.com*, August 2, 2002, online; Doug Thompson, "Suddenly, the hawks are doves and the doves are hawks," *Capitol Hill Blue*, August 1, 2002, http://www.capitolhillblue.com/cgi-bin/artman/exec/view.cgi?archive=8&num=165, accessed November 16, 2007.

47. Mike Salinero, "Gen. Zinni Says War With Iraq Is Unwise," *Tampa Tribune*, 24 August 2002 http://www.mtholyoke.edu/acad/intrel/bush/zinni2.htm, accessed November 16, 2007; Thomas E. Ricks, "Desert Caution: Once 'Stormin' Norman,' Gen. Schwarzkopf Is Skeptical About U.S. Action in Iraq," *Washington Post*, January 28, 2003, p. C-1. Joseph P. Hoar. "Why Aren't There Enough Troops in Iraq?," *New York Times*, April 2, 2003, p. A- 21.

48. Bob Edwards (host), "Commentary: Possible Worst-Case Scenarios If War With Iraq Occurs," *Morning Edition* (NPR), March 11, 2003, online; James Webb, "Heading for Trouble: 'Do we really want to occupy Iraq for the next 30 years?,'" *Washington Post*, September 4, 2002, p. A-21; David Hackworth, "First base, first!," *WorldNetDaily.com*, November 26, 2002, online; William Raspberry, "Unasked Questions," *Washington Post*, September 30, 2002, p. A-19.

49. Ricks, *Fiasco*, p. 81.

50. *Ibid.*, p. 82.

51. *Ibid.*, p. 48.

52. Jeffrey Record, *Bounding the Global War on Terrorism,*, Strategic Studies Institute, U.S. Army War College, December 2003, p. 18, http://www.washingtonpost.com/wp-srv/nation/shoulders/report011204.pdf, accessed November 17, 2007; See, also: Thomas E. Ricks, "Study Published by Army Criticizes War on Terror's Scope," *Washington Post*, January 12, 2004, p. A-12.

53. Chuck Neubauer and Ken Silverstein, "War College Study Calls Iraq a 'Detour'," January 12, 2004, http://www.CommonDreams.org/headlines04/0112-01.htm, accessed November 17, 2007.

54. Tenet, *Center of the Storm*, p. 302.

55. John Hinderaker, "Leaking At All Costs," *Weekly Standard*, November 30, 2005, online.

56. Sarah Baxter, "Powell tried to talk Bush out of war," (London) *Sunday Times*, July 8, 2007, http://www.timesonline.co.uk/tol/news/world/us_and_americas/article2042072.ece, accessed November 17, 2007.

57. Dana Milbank, "Colonel Finally Saw Whites of Their Eyes," *Washington Post*, October 20, 2005, p. A-4; Jim Lobe, "Powell Aide Blasts Rice, Cheney-Rumsfeld 'Cabal,'" *Antiwar.com*, October 20, 2005, online.

58. Noam Chomsky interviewed by M. Junaid Alam, "On Bush, the Left, Iraq, and Israel," *Left Hook*, February 4, 2004, http://www.chomsky.info/interviews/20040204.htm, accessed November 17, 2007.

59. Virginia Tilley, *One-State Solution*, p. 113. Richard Perle, it should be noted, was not involved officially with the Office of Special Plans, nor am I aware of any evidence indicating even any unofficial involvement.

60. For a good summary of the military opposition to the neocon war agenda, see James Petras, "Iran War: American Military Versus Israel Firsters," *InformationClearingHouse.info*, November 29, 2007, http://www.informationclearinghouse.info/article18796.htm, accessed November 30, 2007.

61. See, for example: Philip H. Gordon, "The End of the Bush Revolution," *Foreign Affairs*, July/August 2006, online; Mike Allen and Romesh Ratnesar, "The End of Cowboy Diplomacy," *Time Magazine*, July 17, 2006 (Posted July 9, 2006), online.

Chapter 19

1. Margaret Giffis, "Casualties in Iraq," March 28, 2008, *Antiwar.com*, online; "Iraq Coalition Casualty Count," http://icasualties.org/oif/, accessed March 29, 2008; "The Cost of War," National Priorities Project, http://nationalpriorities.org/index.php?option=com_wrapper&Itemid=182, accessed January 19, 2008.

2. Joseph E. Stiglitz and Linda Bilmes, *The Three Trillion Dollar War: The True Cost of the Iraq Conflict* (New York: W. W. Norton & Company, 2008), pp. 3-32. This cost estimate took into account not simply direct spending on the war but also the economic value of lives lost, impact on higher oil prices, and the effect if a proportion of the money spent on the Iraq war was allocated to other causes. See also Linda Bilmes and Joseph E. Stiglitz, "The Economic Costs of the Iraq War: An Appraisal Three Years After the Beginning of the Conflict," National Bureau of Economic Research, NBER Working Papers Series, February 2006, http://www2.gsb.columbia.edu/faculty/jstiglitz/download/2006_Cost_of_War_in_Iraq_NBER.pdf, accessed January 19, 2008.

3. "USA Today/CNN/Gallup poll results," March 20, 2003, *USA Today*, online.

4. Spencer S. Hsu and Walter Pincus, "U.S. Warns of Stronger Al-Qaeda," *Washington Post*, July 12, 2007, p. A-1.

5. Record, *Dark Victory*, pp. 147-49.

6. Daniel Benjamin and Steven Simon, "Of Course Iraq Made It Worse," *Washington Post*, September 29, 2006, p. A-21; "Iraq replaces Afghanistan as terrorist 'nerve center,'" Agence France Presse, *Daily Star* (Lebanon), January 9, 2006, http://www.dailystar.com.lb/article.asp?edition_id=10&categ_id=2&article_id=21323, accessed April 6, 2008; Tom Regan, "Studies: War radicalized most foreign fighters in Iraq," *Christian Science Monitor*, July 18, 2006, online.

7. Peter Bergen and Paul Cruickshank, "Iraq 101: The Iraq Effect – The War in Iraq and Its Impact on the War on Terrorism – Pg. 1," *Mother Jones*, March 1, 2007, online.

8. Quoted in Yassin Musharbash, "Al-Qaida's next generation," *Salon*, April 16, 2007, online.

9. Bruce Riedel, "Al Qaeda Strikes Back," *Foreign Affairs*, May/June 2007, online; Spencer S. Hsu and Walter Pincus, "U.S. Warns Of Stronger Al-Qaeda," *Washington Post*, July 12, 2007, p. A-1.

10. I. Michael Abramowitz, "Intelligence Puts Rationale For War on Shakier Ground," *Washington Post*, July 18, 2007, p. A-5; Tom A. Peter, "National Intelligence Estimate: Al Qaeda stronger and a threat to U.S. homeland," *Christian Science Monitor*, July 19, 2006, online.

11. Bruce Riedel, "Al Qaeda Strikes Back," *Foreign Affairs*, May/June 2007, online.

12. Richard N. Haass, "The New Middle East," *Foreign Affairs*, November/December 2006, online.

13. Andrew J. Bacevich, "Bushed Army," *American Conservative*, June 4, 2007.

14. Karen DeYoung, "Powell Says U.S. Losing in Iraq," *Washington Post*, December 18, 2006, p. A-20.

15. "Former Pentagon chief sees damage to U.S. military," Reuters, January 25, 2006, online; Robert Burns, "Study: Army Stretched to Breaking Point," *AP*, *SFGate.com*, January 24, 2006, online.

16. Marc Kaufman, "Will We Look Like the Soviets When We Leave Iraq?," *Washington Post*, September 7, 2003, p. B-3.

17. "Analysis: How the U.S. 'lost' Latin America," BBC News, April 3, 2006, online.

18. Virginia Tilley, *One-State Solution*, p. 111.

19. Zbigniew Brzezinski, Senate Foreign Relations Committee Testimony, February 1, 2007, p. 1, http://www.senate.gov/~foreign/testimony/2007/BrzezinskiTestimony070201.pdf

20. Virginia Tilley, *One-State Solution*, p. 114.

21. Robert Dreyfuss, "Washington's Iraq Blindness," *TomPaine.com*, February 03, 2006, http://www.tompaine.com/articles/20060203/washingtons_iraq_blindness.php, accessed January 19, 2008. To counter the sectarian strife in Iraq, some Americans were proposing an even more de-centralized governing system in Iraq than that which came into being through its postinvasion constitution. On September 26, 2007, the U.S. Senate passed a non-binding amendment to a defense bill to bring about a federalized system for Iraq, which would provide more autonomy to its sectarian divisions, making de jure what was actually occurring de facto. Senator Joseph Biden claimed this approach to be a realistic alternative to outright partition. See Joseph R. Biden, Jr., and Leslie H. Gelb, "Federalism, Not Partition," *Washington Post*, October 3, 2007, p. A-23.

22. Jonathan Cook, "End of Strongmen: Do America and Israel Want the Middle East Engulfed By Civil War?," *CounterPunch.org*, December 19, 2006, online.

23. Aluf Benn, "Israel's political earthquake," *Salon*, November 22, 2005, online.

24. Seymour M. Hersh, "Plan B: As June 30th approaches, Israel looks to the Kurds," *New Yorker*, June 30, 2004, online; Laura Rozen, "Kurdistan's Covert Back-Channels," *Mother Jones*, April 11, 2007, online; "Israelis training Kurds in northern Iraq," Reuters, December 1, 2005, online.

25. William Lowther and Colin Freeman, "U.S. funds terror groups to sow chaos in Iran," *Sunday Telegraph*, February 2, 2005, online; Kim Murphy, "Iran alleges U.S. link to militant attack," *Los Angeles Times*, February 19, 2007, online; Brian Ross and Christopher Isham, "The Secret War Against Iran," *The Blotter* (a blog at *ABC-*

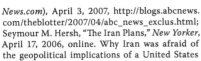

News.com), April 3, 2007, http://blogs.abcnews.com/theblotter/2007/04/abc_news_exclus.html; Seymour M. Hersh, "The Iran Plans," *New Yorker*, April 17, 2006, online. Why Iran was afraid of the geopolitical implications of a United States attack on Iraq is discussed by Parsi, *Treacherous Alliance*, pp. 240–41.

26. It should be recalled that neocons talked about "liberating" the majority Shiite Eastern Province from Saudi rule. See Frum and Perle, *End to Evil*, pp. 140–41; Max Singer, "Free the Eastern Province of Saudi Arabia," *Hudson Institute*, May 16, 2002, http://www.hudson.org/index.cfm?fuseaction=publication_details&id=1659

27. Anthony Shadid, "Across Arab World, a Widening Rift," *Washington Post*, February 12, 2007, P. A-1.

28. Claude Salhani, "Saudis' worst nightmare," *Washington Times*, December 2, 2006, online.

29. Justin Raimondo, "America's Alliance With bin Laden," *Antiwar.com*, February 26, 2007, online.

30. Seymour M. Hersh, "The Redirection," *New Yorker*, March 5, 2007 (posted February 25, 2007), online.

31. Rend Al-Rahim Francke, "Political Progress in Iraq During the Surge," Special Report No. 196, United States Institute of Peace, December 2007, http://www.usip.org/pubs/specialreports/sr196.html, accessed January 4, 2008; Marina Ottaway, Nathan J. Brown, Amr Hamzawy, Karim Sadjadpour, and Paul Salem, *The New Middle East* (Washington: Carnegie Endowment for International Peace, 2008), pp. 1, 5, online; See also: Jonathan Cook, *Israel and the Clash of Civilisations: Iraq, Iran and the Plan to Remake the Middle East* (London: Pluto Press, 2008), pp. 146-47.

32. Baruch Kimmerling, "The Pied Piper of Hamelin, or Sharon's Enigma," *Dissident Voice*, January 12, 2006, http://www.dissidentvoice.org/Jan06/Kimmerling12.htm, accessed January 19, 2008.

33. Ramzy Baroud, "Trying Times for Palestinians," *ZNet*, June 19, 2006, http://www.zmag.org/content/print_article.cfm?itemID=10453&sectionID=1, accessed January 19, 2008.

34. Avi Shlaim, "Withdrawal is a prelude to annexation," *Guardian*, June 22, 2005, online.

35. Tilley, *One-State Solution*, pp. 62–63; Fareed Taamallah, "A Thirst for West Bank Water," *Nation*, June 26, 2006 (posted June 9, 2006, "web only"), online; and Jonathan Cook, "One State or Two? Neither. The Issue is Zionism," *CounterPunch.org*, March 12, 2008, online.

36. Kathleen and Bill Christison, "'Eating Palestine for Breakfast': How Quickly They Forget the Real Sharon," *CounterPunch.org*, January 11, 2006, online.

37. Kathleen Christison, "Sharon's 92 Percent Solution: How the Misperceptions Roll On,"

CounterPunch.org, April 21, 2005, online.

38. Baruch Kimmerling, *Politicide*, p. 211.

39. Journalist Leon Hadar writes: "If anyone had to draw in 2000 an outline of a plan to ensure that Hamas would come to power, he or she would have had only to propose the same kind of policies that were advanced by the Israelis and the Americans and that helped radicalize the Palestinians and encourage them to turn to Hamas as their political saviors" ("A Perfect Geopolitical Storm Taking Shape," *Antiwar.com*, February 17, 2006, online).

40. Justin Raimondo, "Israel Crosses the Line," *Antiwar.com*, July 14, 2006, online.

41. Joshua Mitnick, "Analysts warm to Lebanon results," *Washington Times*, October 3, 2006, online.

42. Robin Wright, "For U.S. and Key Allies in Region, Mideast Morass Just Gets Deeper," *Washington Post*, June 17, 2007, p. A-16.

43. Shahak, *The Zionist Plan For the Middle East*, accessed January 19, 2008.

44. Justin Raimondo, "The Neocons' War," *Antiwar.com*, June 2, 2004, online.

45. Justin Raimondo, "Why Are We in Iraq?," *Antiwar.com*, May 28, 2007, online.

46. *Ibid.*

47. An excellent discussion of the issue of the potential "dual loyalty" of Jewish Americans is presented by Mearsheimer and Walt, *Israel Lobby and U.S. Foreign Policy*, pp. 146–50.

48. As he prepared to leave the presidency of the United States in 1796, George Washington wrote in his "Farewell Address": "So likewise, a passionate attachment of one nation for another produces a variety of evils. Sympathy for the favorite nation, facilitating the illusion of an imaginary common interest in cases where no real common interest exists, and infusing into one the enmities of the other, betrays the former into a participation in the quarrels and wars of the latter without adequate inducement or justification. It leads also to concessions to the favorite nation of privileges denied to others which is apt doubly to injure the nation making the concessions; by unnecessarily parting with what ought to have been retained, and by exciting jealousy, ill-will, and a disposition to retaliate, in the parties from whom equal privileges are withheld. And it gives to ambitious, corrupted, or deluded citizens (who devote themselves to the favorite nation), facility to betray or sacrifice the interests of their own country, without odium, sometimes even with popularity; gilding, with the appearances of a virtuous sense of obligation, a commendable deference for public opinion, or a laudable zeal for public good, the base or foolish compliances of ambition, corruption, or infatuation" ("Washington's Farewell Address 1796," The Avalon Project at Yale Law School, http://www.yale.edu/lawweb/avalon/washing.htm, accessed January 19, 2008).

49. Dorrien, *Imperial Designs*, p. 203.

50. Mearsheimer and Walt, "The Israel Lobby," *London Review of Books*, and "The Israel Lobby," Faculty Research Working Paper.

51. Hostile reviews included Lowell Ponte, "Harvard's New Protocols of the Learned Elders of Zion," *FrontPageMagazine.com*, March 23, 2006, online; Ruth R. Wisse, "Harvard attack on 'Israel lobby' is actually a targeting of American public," *Jewish World Review*, March 23, 2006, http://www.jewishworldreview.com/0306/wisse_israel_loby.php3, accessed November 18, 2007; Eliot A. Cohen, "Yes, It's Anti-Semitic," *Washington Post*, April 5, 2006, p. A-23; and Alan Dershowitz, "Debunking the Newest – and Oldest – Jewish Conspiracy." Of the more favorable reviews were Philip Weiss, "Ferment Over 'The Israel Lobby'," *Nation*, May 15, 2006 (posted April 27, 2006), online; Michael Massing, "The Storm over the Israel Lobby," *New York Review of Books*, June 8, 2006, online. Massing concludes his essay by saying, "Despite its many flaws, their essay has performed a very useful service in forcing into the open a subject that has for too long remained taboo."

52. Mearsheimer and Walt, "The Israel Lobby," *London Review of Books*, and "The Israel Lobby," Faculty Research Working Paper.

53. Ori Nirk, "Professor Says American Publisher Turned Him Down," *Forward*, March 24, 2006, online.

54. Mearsheimer and Walt, *Israel Lobby and U.S. Foreign Policy*.

55. Bill and Kathleen Christison, "Let's Stop a U.S./Israeli War on Iran," *CounterPunch.org*, December 29, 2005, online.

56. American Jewish Committee, "2002 Annual Survey of American Jewish Opinion."

57. American Jewish Committee, "2005 Annual Survey of American Jewish Opinion."

58. Leonard Fein, "Leaders to the Right, Followers to the Left," *Forward*, March 23, 2007, online.

59. "The Risks of War," *Forward*, April 14, 2006, online.

60. "The Ground Shifts," *Forward*, May 28, 2004, online.

61. George Orwell, "In Front of Your Nose," 1946, http://orwell.ru/library/articles/nose/english/e_nose, accessed January 19, 2008.

Postscript

1. "John McCain and the Neocon Resurgence," *Antiwar.com*, February 12, 2008, online; Donald Lambro, "Democrats' bickering boosts McCain," *Washington Times*, March 23, 2008, online.

2. William Kristol, "McCain's Daunting Task," *New York Times*, March 10, 2008, p. A-17. online, LexisNexis.

3. Kate Phillips, "McCain Said '100'; Opponents

Latch On," *New York Times*, March 27, 2008, online.

4. Paul Krugman, "The Right's Man," *New York Times*, March 13, 2006, p. A-21.

5. Michael D. Shear, "McCain Outlines Foreign Policy In Speech, He Vows Collaborative Approach," *Washington Post*, March 27, 2008, p. A-1.

6. "McCain warns of increasing Iranian influence," *CNN*, March 18, 2008, online.

7. "McCain in Jerusalem," editorial, *New York Sun*, March 13, 2008, online.

8. "Former POW Senator McCain Says 'U.S.-Israel Alliance is Forged in Common Values,'" *JINSA Online*, December 29, 2006, http://www.jinsa.org/articles/articles.html/function/view/categoryid/1366/documentid/3636/history/3,2359,2166,1366,3636, accessed April 12, 2008.

9. Hillel Schenker, "Will Next US Leader Proactively Seek ME Peace?," *Arab News*, May 18, 2008, online.

10. "Senator McCain Gets Support from Long Island's Jewish Business Community: Mark Broxmeyer of Fairfield Properties to Chair," US Newswire, January 31, 2008, online.

11. "A Century in Iraq, Replacing UN with 'League of Democracies,' Rogue State Rollback? A Look at John McCain's Foreign Policy Vision," Democracy Now, March 26, 2008, online.

12. John Taylor, "Caveat Emptor: Buy McCain, Get Kagan and Woolsey," Antiwar.com, April 7, 2008, online; Robert Dreyfuss, "Hothead McCain," *Nation*, March 24, 2008 (posted March 6, 2008), online; Elisabeth Bumiller and Larry Rohter, "2 Camps Trying to Influence McCain on Foreign Policy," *New York Times*, April 10, 2008, online.

13. Elisabeth Bumiller and Larry Rohter, "2 Camps Trying to Influence McCain on Foreign Policy," *New York Times*, April 10, 2008, online.

14. "Obama And McCain Debate The Troop Surge," Face the Nation, January 14, 2007, http://www.cbsnews.com/stories/2007/01/14/ftn/main2359098.shtml, accessed March 29, 2008. Paul Richter, "McCain's mixed signals on foreign policy," *Los Angeles Times*, March 16, 2008, online.

15. Paul Richter, "McCain's mixed signals on foreign policy," *Los Angeles Times*, March 16, 2008, online.

16. Michael D. Shear, McCain Outlines Foreign Policy In Speech, He Vows Collaborative Approach," *Washington Post*, March 27, 2008, p. A-1.

17. Elisabeth Bumiller and Larry Rohter, "2 Camps Trying to Influence McCain on Foreign Policy," *New York Times*, April 10, 2008, online.

18. Larry Rohter, "McCain, in Foreign Policy Talk, Turns His Back on Unilateralism," *New*

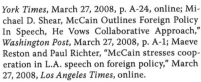
York Times, March 27, 2008, p. A-24, online; Michael D. Shear, McCain Outlines Foreign Policy In Speech, He Vows Collaborative Approach," *Washington Post*, March 27, 2008, p. A-1; Maeve Reston and Paul Richter, "McCain stresses cooperation in L.A. speech on foreign policy," March 27, 2008, *Los Angeles Times*, online.

19. Eric Margolis, "Will McCain Wield the Big Stick?," LewRockwell.com, April 1, 2008, http://www.lewrockwell.com/margolis/margolis103.html, accessed April 5, 2008.

20. "Remarks By John McCain To The Los Angeles World Affairs Council," *McCain* web site, March 26, 2008, http://www.johnmccain.com/Informing/News/Speeches/872473dd-9ccb-4ab4-9d0d-ec54f0e7a497.htm, accessed March 30, 2008; David S. Broder, "McCain's Manifesto," *Washington Post*, March 30, 2008, p. B-7; Michael D. Shear, McCain Outlines Foreign Policy In Speech, He Vows Collaborative Approach," *Washington Post*, March 27, 2008, p. A-1.

21. Michael R. Gordon and Eric Schmitt, "Attacks in Baghdad Spiked in March, U.S. Data Show," *New York Times*, April 8, 2008, online.

22. Karen DeYoung, "U.S. Has Little Influence, Few Options in Iraq's Volatile South," *Washington Post*, March 29, 2008, p. A-11; "Iraq fighting death toll nears 300." CNN, March 29, 2008, online; "Al-Sadr defies Iraq orders," *Washington Times*, March 30, 2008, pp. A-1, A-6; Ross Colving, "Analysis-Iraqi crackdown backfires, strengthens Sadrists," Reuters North American News Service, March 31, 2008, online; Phyllis Bennis, "Maliki Offensive and Bush Iraq Strategy Failing," Transnational Institute, March 31, 2008, http://www.tni.org/detail_page.phtml?act_id=18100, online; James Hider, "Nouri al-Maliki humiliated as gamble to crush Shia militias fail," Timesonline, April 1, 2008, http://www.timesonline.co.uk/tol/news/world/iraq/article3656300.ece, accessed April 1, 2008; Sudarsan Raghavan, "Between Iraqi Shiites, a Deepening Animosity," *Washington Post*, April 7, 2008, p. A-1; James Glanz and Stephen Farrell, "Crackdown on Militias Raises Stability Concerns," *New York Times*, April 8, 2008, online.

23. Kimberly Kagan, "The Second Iran-Iraq War," *Wall Street Journal* (Eastern edition), April 3, 2008, p. A-15.

24. Michael Ledeen, "The Continuing Iran-American War," *Faster, Please!: The Weblog of Michael Ledeen*, April 5, 2008, http://mt.pajamasmedia.com/xpress/michaelledeen/2008/04/05/the_continuing_iranamerican_wa.php, accessed April 12, 2008.

25. Borzou Daragahi, "Cheney disputes Iran's nuclear goals," *Los Angeles Times*, March 26, 2008, online; Kaveh L Afrasiabi, "Iran sees hope in war of words," *Asia Times*, April 2, 2008, online.

26. Greg Miller, "CIA chief asserts Iran nuclear threat," *Los Angeles Times*, March 31, 2008, online.

27. Terry Atlas, "6 Signs the U.S. May be Headed for War in Iran," March 11, 2008, *U.S. News & World Report*, online.

28. Atlas, *ibid.*; Thomas P.M. Barnett, "The Man Between War and Peace," Esquire, March 11, 2008, online.

29. Atlas, *ibid.*

30. Quoted in Paul Craig Roberts, "Iran in the Crosshairs," *CounterPunch*, March 31, 2008, online.

31. William R. Polk, "Iran: Danger and Opportunity," *Informed Consent*, March 20, 2008, http://www.juancole.com/2008/03/iran-danger-and-opportunity-polk-guest.html, accessed April 1, 2008.

32. Damien McElroy, "British fear US commander is beating the drum for Iran strikes," *Telegraph*, April 5, 2008, http://www.telegraph.co.uk/news/main.jhtml?xml=/news/2008/04/05/wiran105.xml, accessed April 5, 2008.

33. Dana Milbank, "From the GOP, the General Gets Unfriendly Fire," *Washington Post*, April 10, 2008, p. A-3.

34. By Dana Milbank, "Iraq and the Special Theory of Relativity," *Washington Post*, April 9, 2008, p. A-3; Patrick J. Buchanan, "Petraeus Points to War With Iran," Antiwar.com, April 11, 2008, online.

35. Helene Cooper, "Iran Fighting Proxy War in Iraq, U.S. Envoy Says," *New York Times*, April 12, 2008, online.

36. Peter Baker and Karen DeYoung, "Bush Backs Petraeus on Indefinite Suspension of Troop Pullout in Iraq," *Washington Post*, April 11, 2008, p. A-1.

37. Deb Riechmann, "Gates: US Troops Won't Drop to 100,000," Associated Press, *Washington Post*, April 11, 2008, online; Warren P. Strobel, "All the talk is about Iraq, but concern about Iran is mounting," McClatchy Newspapers, April 10, 2008, http://www.mcclatchydc.com/iraq/v-print/story/33306.html, accessed April 11, 2008; "Iran, al Qaeda among greatest threats to US —Bush," Reuters North American News Service, April 10, 2008, http://wiredispatch.com/news/?id=122653, accessed April 11, 2008; Robert H. Reid, "US shifts enemy in Iraq," AP News, April 10, 2008, http://wiredispatch.com/news/?id=122754, accessed April 11, 2008; Karen DeYoung "Iran Top Threat to Iraq, U.S. Says," *Washington Post*, April 12, 2008, p. A-1.

38. Hope Yen, "Hadley: Iran a Threat in Iraq," Associated Press, *Washington Post*, April 13, 2008, online. "Hadley: Iran Remains Threat in Iraq," Associated Press, *Las Vegas Sun*, April 13, 2008, online.

39. Helene Cooper, "Iran Fighting Proxy War in Iraq, U.S. Envoy Says," *New York Times*, April 12, 2008, online; Lolita C. Baldor, "Gates: Iran boosts support for militias," AP News, April 11, 2008, http://wiredispatch.com/news/?id=124266

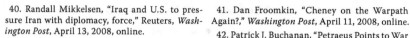
40. Randall Mikkelsen, "Iraq and U.S. to pressure Iran with diplomacy, force," Reuters, *Washington Post*, April 13, 2008, online.

41. Dan Froomkin, "Cheney on the Warpath Again?," *Washington Post*, April 11, 2008, online.

42. Patrick J. Buchanan, "Petraeus Points to War With Iran," *Antiwar.com*, April 11, 2008, online..

index

Index

CPSIA information can be obtained
at www.ICGtesting.com
Printed in the USA
BVHW030953020419
544364BV00004B/42/P

9 781932 528176